MEASUREMENT
AND ASSESSMENT
IN SCHOOLS

MEASUREMENT AND ASSESSMENT IN SCHOOLS

Second Edition

BLAINE R. WORTHEN

KARL R. WHITE

XITAO FAN

Utah State University

RICHARD R SUDWEEKS

Brigham Young University

 LONGMAN

An imprint of Addison Wesley Longman, Inc.

New York • Reading, Massachusetts • Menlo Park, California • Harlow, England
Don Mills, Ontario • Sydney • Mexico City • Madrid • Amsterdam

Acquisitions Editor: *Arthur Pomponio*
Marketing Manager: *Renée Orthals*
Project Coordination and Text Design: *York Production Services*
Cover Designer/Manager: *Nancy Danahy*
Full Service Production Manager: *Richard Ausburn*
Print Buyer: *Denise Sandler*
Electronic Page Makeup: *York Production Services*
Printer and Binder: *The Maple-Vail Book Manufacturing Group*
Cover Printer: *Coral Graphic Services, Inc.*

Library of Congress Cataloging-in-Publication Data

Measurement and assessment in the schools/Blaine R. Worthen . . . [et al.].—2nd ed.\
     p.   cm.
   Rev. ed. of: Measurement and evaluation in the schools/Blaine R. Worthen,
   Walter R. Borg, Karl R. White. c1993
     Includes bibliographical references (p.) and index.
     ISBN 0-8013-1660-X
     1. Educational tests and measurements.   2. Educational tests and measurements—
   Design and construction.   I. Worthen, Blaine R.   II. Worthen, Blaine R.
   Measurement and evaluation in the schools.
   LB3051.W65   1998
   371.26—dc21   96–8743
                                                                        CIP

Please visit our website at http://longman.awl.com

ISBN 0-8013-1660X

  345678910—MA—010099

Brief Contents

v

Detailed Contents

Interviews   338

Specifying Interview Objectives   338 ■ Developing an Interview
Schedule   338 ■ Guidelines for Constructing an Interview Schedule
and Conducting the Interview   340 ■ Pilot Testing the Interview
341 ■ Analysis of Interview Data   342

Systematic Observation   342

Observational Procedures   342 ■ Observational Objectives   343 ■
Observation Schedules   343 ■ Developing an Observation
Schedule   344 ■ Methods of Recording Observational Data   346
■ Pilot Testing the Observational System   349 ■ Training the
Observers   350

Rating Scales   350

Some Problems with Rating Scales   352 ■ Rating Errors   353 ■
Rules for Developing Rating Scales   354

CHAPTER 12   **Getting in Touch with Students' Feelings**
Measuring Attitudes and Interests   357

Measuring Affective Outcomes   358
The Influence of Attitudes on Behavior   359
Constructing Attitude Measures   361

Direct Observation of Behavior   361 ■ Measuring Beliefs and
Feelings   362 ■ Methods for Developing Attitude Measures   363 ■
Steps in Developing a Likert Scale   364 ■ Advantages and
Disadvantages of Likert Scales   372 ■ Reliability of Attitude Scales
373 ■ Validity of Attitude Scales   374

Typical Attitude Measures   375

Measures of Attitude Toward School, Teachers, and Specific School
Subjects   375 ■ Measures of Attitude Toward Curriculum   377 ■
Measures of Study Attitudes   379

Measuring Interest   380

Techniques for Measuring Interests   381 ■ Measures of Vocational
Interest   381

CHAPTER 13   **Picking the Right Yardstick**
Assigning Grades and Reporting Student Performance   385

History and Background   386
Purposes and Functions of Grading   387

Students   388 ■ Parents   390 ■ Teachers and Counselors   390 ■
Administrators   390 ■ Other Schools   391 ■ Employers   391

Preface

Measurement and evaluation play a pivotal role in today's schools. Indeed, these activities are commonplace in classrooms from nursery school to university. Determining what students have learned, what aptitude they possess for future learning, how well they are progressing toward specific educational goals, how they feel toward school, and what aspirations and interests they possess are only a few examples of the questions teachers and other educators use measurement and evaluation to answer.

To answer such questions, teachers, school administrators, psychologists, and counselors use tests, rating scales, observational records, questionnaires, and a wide array of other types of measurement instruments discussed in this book. Whatever the type of instrument chosen, the user must understand and apply sound measurement principles and practices to be certain that instrument is used correctly, rather than abused.

During the past 20 years, tests of educational achievement have increasingly come under fire because of widespread abuses in selecting, administering, and interpreting such tests. Yet public pressure for evidence that schools and teachers are effectively educating students makes it unlikely that testing efforts will be abandoned or decreased in the foreseeable future. This means that much of the responsibility for the quality of testing must be shouldered by test users, many of whom are not now being trained appropriately in educational testing procedures.

Consequently, classroom teachers, administrators, and counselors must be helped to better understand educational testing principles and practices if the quality of test use is to improve and the extent of test abuse to decline. It is no less reasonable to train educators and psychologists who work in schools to use tests effectively and efficiently than to train the surgeon in plying the scalpel deftly or the virologist in thoughtfully interpreting the world through a microscope.

To the Instructor

Numerous books discuss measurement principles, issues in testing, reliability and validity, and the selection and construction of measurement instruments, but we believe the orientation and presentation of this text offers unique advantages.

Audiences and Purposes for This Book

This book is designed as a basic text for university or college preservice courses in educational measurement or related administration, curriculum, or teacher education courses designed to teach practitioners to apply measurement tools and techniques. Our primary audience is, therefore, the same as that of other introductory measurement texts. But we also aspire to reach a second important audience that most measurement texts do not address—practicing educators (and those preparing for such roles)—who want a comprehensive but practical reference book to provide an overview of educational measurement.

This book is intended to (1) familiarize its users with basic measurement concepts, principles, and issues; (2) help readers learn to determine the quality and utility of an educational measure and to interpret correctly the results it produces; (3) provide practical guidelines for constructing and using new "home-grown" measures; and (4) provide practical guidelines for finding, selecting, and using existing measures.

Content and Orientation of This Text

Decisions about what to include in this book come largely from our experience teaching introductory measurement and evaluation courses at several universities, working in public schools, and using measurement instruments in collecting research and evaluation data for many educational studies.

Authors of other measurement texts similarly draw on their experience, consciously or unconsciously. But we have based the content also on what practicing educators view as important to know about educational measurement. First, to help us better focus the content of this text, two of us directed a study (Borg, Worthen, & Valcarce, 1986) in which 1000 classroom teachers were asked to judge the importance of a variety of measurement topics. Second, other studies dealing with teacher's measurement skills or perceptions of the importance of measurement topics were reviewed (for example, Gullickson, 1984; Green & Stager, 1985). Collectively, these studies prompted us not only to include most topics typically covered in introductory measurement texts but also to address several additional issues of current concern to educators such as "authentic" assessment approaches; national trends in achievement scores; minimum competency testing; use of tests to certify teacher competence; legal, ethical, social, and cultural issues in testing; and the use of microcomputers in classroom and school testing. Third, we have listened carefully to feedback from professors who have used the previous edition of this text. Based on their input, we dropped a chapter that dealt exclusively with technical definitions, defining all terms in this edition in the context of their use. We expanded our coverage of direct performance assessment, adding several examples of such exercises, complete with scoring rubrics, and our treatment of student portfolios is more complete. We have expanded our coverage of reliability and validity, and have updated and refined all the chapters that were retained from the prior edition. To make room for the new and expanded content in this second edition, we dropped chapters dealing with measurement of students' personal and social adjustment, and procedures for setting up schoolwide testing or evaluation programs that professors judged to be less relevant to the needs of their students.

This text also differs from other introductory measurement texts in that we have restricted its focus to *educational* measurement, treating measures that typically fall within the province of the psychologist only as they may have direct applications to education.

The book's general orientation is toward application, which has resulted in its being unashamedly practical in its approach. More than half of this volume is devoted directly to practical guidelines for using existing measures or constructing and using new measures. Checklists and step-by-step procedural guides are provided to help the beginner learn more quickly the fundamental skills involved in completing measurement tasks.

We make no pretense of covering all the interesting and potentially useful theoretical and methodological developments related to educational measurement and evaluation. We scarcely mention out-of-level testing, answer-until-correct procedures, item response theory, or dozens of other topics that measurement specialists and even some more informed practitioners are fond of. We acknowledge the usefulness and importance of such topics, but see them as less appropriate to the audiences we seek to serve. We make no apology for dealing with much that is simple. Our intent is to show how measurement principles can be applied straightforwardly to real-life situations confronted in the educator's day-to-day activities. We leave useful but more advanced concepts and techniques for the advanced graduate seminar and its accompanying text.

Space has not permitted us to treat several topics here in the depth we desired. Entire books are devoted to some of the topics that we deal with in a few pages, such as cultural biases in tests or minimum competency testing. Yet since most educators take only a single course in measurement, such critical topics should not be omitted altogether.

Finally, we have devoted more space than most introductory measurement texts to the *context* in which testing occurs. We think it more important that teachers understand why tests are criticized and what issues spark current debates about testing than that they know how to use the Spearman–Brown formula to calculate test reliability.

Presentation of Content

We have worked hard to make the content readable and useful; more specifically,

1. We use content and learning aids that employ generally acceptable presentation techniques that can be readily used by most instructors and readily understood by most students.
2. We avoid jargon, esoteric language, and sophisticated statistical and mathematical treatments in favor of clear, straightforward language, uncomplicated examples, and simple calculations. We think students can learn the essentials of educational measurement without learning to dislike the subject.
3. We reference a wide array of research studies in the expanding literature pertaining to educational measurement in order to make this book both a useful reference source and a text. Although we include mostly up-to-date sources, we do not hesitate to refer students to some of the older sources that provide valuable information.
4. We attempt to avoid both awkwardness and sexism in the use of gender pronouns by using male and female pronouns in randomly assigned chapters, rather than forcing teachers or students to be plural in all of our examples, or using the more stilted and awkward passive voice.

Teaching and Learning Aids in the Text

To simplify use for instructors and students, the book is structured as follows:

1. Each section of the book begins with a *brief orientation.*
2. Each chapter begins with a *brief overview* of the chapter content.
3. Each chapter includes a list of *specific learner objectives,* presented immediately after the overview.
4. You also will find *application problems* within most chapters. These few items and problems are designed to help students check their general understanding of the material covered in the chapter but are not intended to cover all chapter objectives. Answers to these problems appear at the end of each chapter.
5. Each chapter concludes with an *annotated list of suggested readings.*

Additional Aids for Student and Instructor

To assist the instructor, the following ancillary materials have been developed for this text:

1. An *Instructor's Manual* that includes
   - Suggestions on presentation techniques to enhance instruction
   - Additional application exercises for student assignments
   - Test items for use in assessing student knowledge and skill in relation to each chapter
2. A *Computerized Test Item Bank,* including all items from the *Instructor's Manual,* on floppy disk to facilitate instructors' efforts to create tailored tests for their classes.

Student Prerequisites

Our treatment of statistical techniques is as nontechnical as possible. We try to relate statistical techniques to the measurement context within which they are commonly associated, but avoid preoccupation with computation and formulas, which seem more appropriate for statistics courses. In our opinion, students should have at least one elementary course in statistics before taking this educational measurement course, but we have tried to make the book understandable to those who do not have a strong background in statistics.

Suggestions for Improvement

We hope that this text will meet your needs and those of your students, and we want very much to receive your comments or suggestions, since we intend to update and modify future editions to make this work as helpful as possible to those who use it.

We have included a Suggestion Sheet at the back of this book for feedback from instructors and students. Each instructor and student is asked to give feedback on at least one chapter although we would welcome comment on other chapters. The end of each chapter contains a brief set of instructions identifying (by first letter of surname) students specifically invited to make comments on that chapter. Please encourage your students to complete the Suggestion Sheet. It is designed to be torn out and mailed as a self-stamped envelope.

We would especially appreciate your comments about the entire text or as many chapters as you see fit. With your help, we hope to make the next edition even more useful to you.

Blaine R. Worthen
Karl R. White
Xitao Fan
Richard R Sudweeks

To the
Student

The main goal of this book is to help you, the student in education or the practicing educator, to become skilled and confident in using educational measurement and evaluation techniques effectively in your chosen profession.

Educational measurement is becoming ever more complex and sophisticated, which makes it a more powerful influence in educational improvement and increases the challenge of mastering the content in this field. We have tried to make the task easier by writing in clear, straightforward language, free of technical language, mathematical jargon, or formulas. So don't go into "symbol shock" when you encounter something numerical in the text. Even if you are rusty in math, our approach should help you survive without too much pain.

To help you organize the field of educational measurement and evaluation in your own mind, we include an introduction to each part of the book, and an overview and set of objectives for each chapter. The overview is designed to give you a quick overall picture of what you will learn in the chapter, whereas the objectives tell you the specific details to which you should attend. Not all objectives are of equal importance. Which are most important to you depends on your own goals—whether you are primarily interested in becoming a competent user of tests in the classroom or in making measurement a major part of your educational career.

Since many measurement concepts and techniques are difficult for the beginner to understand, we include examples to illustrate how these techniques have been applied in specific situations. Application problems are also included in appropriate chapters to help you determine whether you can apply concepts you have learned to practical problems and questions you will encounter.

Finally, we have a request to make. We very much want your specific suggestions on improving this book. It is difficult for us to use comments such as "This is a good book" or "This is a terrible book" in improving the next edition, but specific comments such as "Include more examples of how to write multiple-choice test items" or "Add a step-by-step description of how to calculate reliability for criterion-referenced measures" can be very helpful.

We would like to get your suggestions on the entire book, but *we are asking for your comments on only a single chapter.* Which chapter you comment on is your choice, but at the end of each chapter is a statement suggesting (by surname initial) which students we would invite to react to that chapter. This will assure us of getting suggestions for improving all 17 chapters. We will welcome all suggestions you can give us.

The Suggestion Sheet is printed at the back of this book and can be cut out and made into a business reply mailer.

We hope you will find this book helpful not only in completing your present academic work but in your later career as well. Good luck!

Blaine R. Worthen
Karl R. White
Xitao Fan
Richard R Sudweeks

Acknowledgments

At the outset, we wish to acknowledge the contribution made to this book by Walter R. Borg, our former colleague and co-author on the previous edition. It was his initial suggestion that we write this volume, and he participated in the development of its contents right up to the time of his unexpected death. Although the manuscript subsequently went through extensive revision, due to helpful reviews by several of our colleagues in measurement and assessment, we felt that enough of Walt endured in the final pages to warrant placing his name as originally planned, as second author of that first edition. In revising the manuscript to produce this second edition, however, the changes have been of sufficient magnitude that too little of Walt's contribution remains to justify his being accorded co-authorship. Yet he clearly belongs at the top of the list of those we acknowledge for their contributions. In his case, his contributions went far beyond this book, for he also contributed much to our enjoyment of our work environment.

We will not repeat here our appreciation to others whose contributions we acknowledged in our first edition, although we continue to be grateful for the assistance and support. We would add, however, our appreciation to Eric Gee and Michael Chen for their excellent assistance with literature searches and numerous other technical tasks, and to Sheila Jessie for her tireless and competent production of the final manuscript and myriad other tasks such as proofreading, preparing graphics, and the like. Special thanks to those who reviewed the text and provided advice: Dr. Tuerin Bratina, University of North Florida; Dr. John Badgett, Slippery Rock University; Dr. Regina Watkins, University of North Alabama; and Dr. Carol Van Zile-Tamsen, State University of West Georgia.

Finally, we would like to welcome and acknowledge the contribution of our colleagues and new co-authors, Xitao Fan and Rich Sudweeks, to this edition. They have contributed enormously to the improvements in this edition and, indeed, are responsible for most of the revision that we believe make this a significantly stronger volume than its predecessor. Both new authors bring extensive knowledge and experience in measurement and assessment to the task, and we look forward to working together on future editions of this text as well.

Blaine R. Worthen
Karl R. White

MEASUREMENT
AND ASSESSMENT
IN SCHOOLS

GETTING YOU ORIENTED

Many introductory texts in educational measurement and assessment plunge you immediately into some of the rather technical issues and content of the field: definitions, techniques, and the like. We choose rather to provide first a context for such specifics. Section I contains basic information we feel is essential to make the content that follows more understandable and meaningful. In Chapter 1 we acquaint you with educational measurement and assessment and clarify their respective roles, functions, and the various uses to which they are put in today's schools. We also summarize the historical developments and trends in measurement and assessment that have led to how they are used in today's schools. In Chapter 2 we examine several current measurement issues, including concerns about test bias, the impact of legal decisions on the use of educational measures, "right to privacy" issues, ethical considerations in using educational measures, unethical practices that pollute test score results, and the movement to use testing to certify classroom teachers.

Collectively, the information in these two chapters will help you to appreciate more fully both the contributions and challenges of measurement and assessment in our schools.

SECTION I

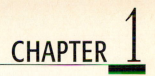

What Is Measurement, and How Did We Get Where We Are with It?

OVERVIEW

Although educational measurement is a familiar activity in today's schools, its functions and usefulness are not always well understood. To some, tests and other measures are helpful—even essential—tools for making many educational decisions such as teaching, counseling, and placing students; to others, they are merely something to be tolerated, endured, or even criticized. How you feel about measurement probably depends on how well you understand its role and potential utility in your own professional activities. Our first purpose in this chapter is to help you expand that understanding by providing a context for later, more specific, material about educational measurement.

The roles, functions, and uses of measurement did not spring full blown onto the educational scene. Each has its historical roots, and it is important to understand some of the developments and trends that have led us to where we are now. For this purpose, we also present in this chapter brief discussions of both the history of educational measurement and some of its recent developments and trends in our schools.

OBJECTIVES

Upon completing your study of this chapter, you should be able to

1. Discuss the importance of educational measurement, including its role in today's educational systems.
2. Describe various ways in which educational measures are used for making important decisions about various aspects of education.

3. Discuss the pros and cons of *objective* measurement data and *subjective* judgments in making educational decisions.

4. Describe important historical developments in measurement up to the mid-1960s, identifying the individuals, events, and forces that influenced and shaped those developments.

5. Describe major trends and developments in measurement that have occurred since the mid-1960s.

6. Discuss the importance of each development or trend you identified in Objective 5 and its implications for educational institutions.

The Role of Measurement in Education

By now, you have undoubtedly taken many educational tests and have almost certainly formed a personal opinion about their usefulness. We invite you to put your opinion aside for just a moment while we review how widely tests are used and why you are not a stranger to them.

Most people who live in a nation with a well-developed educational system are familiar with tests and examinations. School-age children and their parents in Miami, London, Winnipeg, and Seoul are all well acquainted with educational tests and concerned about test results. Further, testing is not confined to schools and universities, but plays an important role in decisions that extend from preschool to job entry, and sometimes beyond. Test results may determine who receives a scholarship or qualifies to attend a certain college, who gets hired for a decent job or receives a promotion at work. In fact, chances are that you currently attend a university or hold a job as the result, at least in part, of test scores. And you are not alone.

Despite widespread complaints and criticisms about testing, the use of tests is booming. Lasden (1985) noted two-year increases in test sales of 25 to 43 percent for companies like Science Research Associates and Psychological Services, Inc. Although we have no accurate account of how many standardized tests are administered each year, even conservative estimates are staggering. In the United States, for example, there are nearly 50 million kindergarten through high school students, most of whom take at least one standardized test each year. Since most achievement tests are multiple test batteries, and since many students actually take several such tests during the course of a year, the number of individual standardized tests administered to American students could easily approach a *quarter billion* annually. When teacher-made tests are counted, even that estimate pales. One survey of Ohio teachers (Marso, 1985) found that the typical classroom teacher gives students nearly 100 teacher-made tests during a school year. Extrapolated to teachers at large, this would mean that billions of teacher-made tests are administered annually to students in the United States alone.

In view of so much measurement in education, it is astonishing to realize that little time or resources are actually allocated to training educational practitioners or policymakers in sound methods of assessing student performance (Stiggins, 1991a).

Application Problem 1

Based on your own experience with both standardized tests and classroom tests, discuss the role of measurement in education.

Do We Need So Much Measurement?

Those who support the broad use of tests argue that tests stimulate student effort, set performance expectations, and provide feedback on accomplishments. Tests, they assert, provide relevant information on the attainment of curricular goals and the effectiveness of educational programs. Supporters question how schools could adequately assess student learning or the utility of educational programs, processes, and products intended to bring that learning about without the aid of tests. As one official in the National Institute of Education put it, "States and localities will look to test results for confirmation of whether or not their reforms— reforms with substantial costs—have succeeded" (Selden, 1985, p. 16).

Public demand for evidence that teachers and schools are effectively educating students is strong, and test scores have historically been the kind of evidence the public has asked for. It seems unlikely that this dependence on data from tests and other assessment devices will decrease in the years ahead.

States and localities are not unique in relying on tests to assess the status of educational systems. The National Commission on Excellence in Education outlined 13 general indicators of educational risk, 11 of which were based directly on educational test results.

Not everyone is happy to see tests carry as much clout as that accorded them by the National Commission. Many argue that tests do more harm than good. They point to bright students unable to evidence their learning on tests because of debilitating test anxiety, and to problems of cultural, racial, or gender bias in tests. Critics complain that tests are artificial (and rather poor) substitutes for teachers' qualitative, professional judgments about student performance.

Our own position on testing is simple. We believe that tests and other assessment instruments are essential to the educational process, *but only to the extent that they are well designed and appropriately applied by qualified persons.*

It is not hard to defend the proposition that tests and other measurement instruments are valuable tools for educators. One need only examine the wide range of important decisions that depend on test data. For example, test results are pivotal in each of the following situations:

- Assessing student attainment of particular skills or knowledge, as a basis for further instruction
- Classifying students into groups, curriculum tracks, and the like
- Selecting applicants for educational programs, jobs, or other opportunities where predicting future performance is important
- Deciding whether an individual has met some designated standard of competence
- Determining the effectiveness of particular teaching methods or curricula

Even from such an abbreviated list,[1] it should be apparent that measurement instruments are valuable tools. We find it difficult to conceive of effective teaching or learning taking place in the schools without some structured, reliable way to measure student performance.

At the same time, we recognize that naive or ill-trained users can misuse or abuse even the best tools, and that improper use of good measurement instruments is commonplace. Even worse, poorly designed measures abound. One of our goals is to help you learn how to spot poorly designed instruments so that you will avoid basing educational decisions on their possibly spurious results. Another is to provide you with the specific knowledge to use well-designed measures properly.

Subjective Judgment, Objective Testing, and Quantification

If one were to rid the earth of all tests, how would we accomplish the variety of tasks for which we now use tests and measurement data? We would rely, of course, on professional judgment. And what is so bad about professional judgment? At the risk of stating the obvious, the problem with professional judgment is that it is not always professional, and its judgments are not always sound. Educators are only human, and their judgments are colored by a variety of subtle influences, from the way a student looks to how a teacher is feeling.

Such judgments, when made without measurement data, are *subjective*—that is, personal and peculiar to that individual and likely to differ with judgments other individuals might make under the same or similar circumstances. Conversely, measurement instruments attempt to produce *objective* information—meaning that most reasonable persons who are confronted with the available measurement data would score and interpret it in the same fashion. (Of course, two persons might still make subjective judgments about the same score, leading them to different conclusions.)

The choice between subjective judgment and objective measurement should not be either/or. Personal perceptions are often insightful and may be the only way to assess certain valued educational outcomes—such as humaneness or justice—which current measures capture clumsily, if at all. Furthermore, sole reliance on measurement data is unwise, since no test score is perfectly accurate. Even shaky subjective judgments are better than scores on measures that are invalid or irrelevant to the decision at hand.

Combining objective measurement data with educators' professional judgments allows us the best of both worlds. Objective test data offer protection against the pressures, politics, and presuppositions that often result in weak, capricious judgments when subjectivity is left to carry the burden alone. And the teacher's subjective, commonsense awareness and knowledge are often vital in counterbalancing skewed or misleading test results. In our view, objective measurement data and less objective professional judgments are necessary partners in an effective educational assessment program.

---

[1]See Haladyna, Nolan, and Haas (1991) for a list of 29 uses of standardized tests.

Let us say a word about quantification, which underlies measurement and supports objectivity. *Quantification* means the assignment of numerical values to some characteristic of our interest. To many educators, some qualities seem to be unmeasurable—essentially qualitative rather than quantitative. One student seems kinder than another; Mary seems more sensitive than Bill to the feelings of others. Kindness and sensitivity are only examples of many qualities that are not easily quantified, at least not with present measures.

Other educators, however, argue that *all* important outcomes of education are measurable. To be important, the logic goes, an educational outcome must make a *difference.* If it does make a difference, then the *basis* for measurement exists (even though it may not be measurable with current tests or techniques). According to this argument, most qualities of interest to educators are, therefore, potentially quantifiable. Otherwise, they conclude, educators would despair of being able to distinguish between higher and lower "quality" on such dimensions.

We see this line of reasoning as *generally* but not absolutely true. We suggest that we will continue to rely, in the foreseeable future, on qualitative judgments on dimensions such as kindness and justice. But this does not detract from the essential importance of using quantitative measurement wherever possible. Perhaps some alternative ways suitable for your classroom or school will become clearer as we consider in the next section the various ways educational measures are used.

Application Problem 2A

Discuss the relative advantages and disadvantages of *objective* measurement and *subjective* judgment in making decisions in education.

Application Problem 2B

Describe what *quantification* means. Provide a few examples in education to illustrate the process of quantification.

Various Uses of Educational Measures

We mentioned earlier the wide range of situations in which tests are used. But who are the users of these tests? In education, almost everyone can be considered a potential test user, including

- Teachers—to determine students' progress in learning specific knowledge or skills
- Students—to ascertain if they are learning what they are being asked to learn
- Parents—to determine how well their children are doing in school

- Principals—to determine how well their students are learning
- School psychologists—to assess students' particular strengths and needs to guide prescription and treatment more effectively
- School counselors—to guide students in choosing courses of study and careers, and in making personal adjustments
- Lawmakers and policymakers—to set educational priorities and allocate resources
- Research and evaluation directors—to collect data to extend general knowledge about educational processes or help evaluate the effectiveness of particular school programs, instructional products, and the like
- News reporters—to report on the quality of schooling and other educational issues
- Lawyers—to argue for or against the appropriateness and legality of particular educational practices (perhaps even testing itself)

Although a wide range of people both in and out of education use information from educational tests, not all of them are considered "test users" in the technical sense. The *Standards for Educational and Psychological Tests* (*Standards,* American Psychological Association, American Educational Research Association, & National Council on Measurement in Education, 1974) defined a test user as ". . . one who chooses tests, interprets scores, or makes decisions based on test scores." (p. 58).[2] Based on this definition, educators are definitely "test users" because they routinely choose and use tests to make decisions about their students. To be a *competent* test user, however, requires some training in using tests and interpreting the information they produce. The authors of the 1974 *Standards* specified that "Users of educational and psychological tests in schools . . . and other places where educators and psychologists work should have had at least some formal training" (p. 58). They define competence in test use as ". . . a combination of knowledge of psychometric principles, knowledge of the problem situation in which the testing is to be done, technical skill, and some wisdom" (p. 6). Unfortunately, many test users in the educational arena lack necessary training and do not meet this definition of competence. (It is our hope that this book will provide you with the necessary knowledge and expertise so that you will not be among them.)

---

[2]The American Psychological Association (APA), the American Educational Research Association (AERA), and the National Council on Measurement in Education (NCME) have collaborated on the three successive (1966, 1974, and 1985) editions of the *Standards for Educational and Psychological Tests.* The 1966 and 1974 versions of the *Standards* (which is how we will refer to these volumes hereafter in this text, to avoid tedious referencing) listed APA as senior author, whereas the 1985 version listed AERA as senior author. There are significant differences in the 1974 and 1985 versions of the *Standards.* Although we feel the 1985 version is an important update, we still find much of use in the 1974 version. We shall designate by year whenever we refer to or quote from a particular version; "*Standards,*" with no date designation will refer to the contribution of both the 1974 and 1985 volumes together.

How do educators and relevant policymakers use tests? Again, the purposes are impressively wide ranging but can be roughly grouped into four categories based on the types of decision that will be based on the test results:[3]

- Direct instructional decisions
- Instructional management decisions
- Entry–exit decisions
- Program, administrative, and policy decisions

Direct Instructional Decisions

Observing, measuring, and drawing conclusions are ongoing activities in most class-rooms. Teachers not only test students to see what they have learned, but they also observe the learning process. Raised eyebrows, glazed eyes, and slumped posture all send signals that teachers struggle to interpret correctly. A teacher observes how children use algorithms to solve math problems in order to plan the next instructional step. Another uses a test he designed himself to diagnose the learning problems of students who seem to be having difficulty. Commercial, text-linked tests help teachers determine when it is time to move to the next unit of content. *Snapshot tests* ("Would all of you who think the answer is 'Venus' raise your hands?") provide a quick reading of how many students have internalized some bit of knowledge. Between grading periods, teachers evaluate students on everything from academic performance to manners. Indeed, measurement and evaluation are ever present in the classroom.

Let's take a closer look at four types of direct instructional decisions.

Immediate Instructional Decisions

Every teacher's day is filled with dozens of instructional dilemmas that must be resolved on the spot. Should I review this concept again, or do the students grasp it? Should I introduce exponents today, or will they understand it better after we've spent more time on multiplication? As important as those decisions are, they are more the stuff of pedagogy than measurement, since most are made without the aid of any formal assessment or measurement tools.

Grading Decisions

Here the teacher is also on familiar ground. Valid evaluation of what students have learned is impossible without some type of testing, whether it be individual interviews or a commercially prepared test. Most often, grades are based on teacher-made assessments, and grading will only be as good as the tests or other assessment devices used. Later, we will help you learn to construct and interpret your own classroom tests or alternative assessments and translate scores into grades or other performance indicators.

---

[3]In developing these categories, we have relied on Findley (1963), the *Standards* (1974, 1985), Kubiszyn & Borich (1987), Thorndike & Hagan (1977), and Anderson, Stiggins, & Gordan, (1980)—especially the latter two.

Diagnostic Decisions

Tests are probably used more often for diagnostic purposes than for any other. Teachers often base diagnostic decisions about the learning progress of students and classes on tests they have constructed themselves. Although school psychologists, special educators, and other specialists trained in the use of special standardized diagnostic measures are valuable resources, teachers face too many diagnostic decisions to rely entirely on help from others, and many small districts have few such specialists to which teachers can turn for help. It is critical, therefore, that teachers develop skill in test construction and in using alternative assessment methods where appropriate.

Instructional Planning Decisions

Teacher-made tests play an important, if sometimes indirect, role in prompting better planning. First, students' performance on classroom tests will inform the teacher about how well students have attained different instructional objectives so that more appropriate instructions can be planned. Second, developing classroom tests itself usually causes teachers to think carefully about their instructional goals and how to reach them. As Nitko (1989a) has demonstrated, tests that are integrated directly with instruction are the ideal.

Instructional Management Decisions

Instructional management decisions, which have to do with placing students in situations where they are most likely to succeed, are typically made by school administrators, psychologists, counselors, or committees, rather than by individual teachers. Such decisions fall into the two following categories.

Classification or Placement Decisions

Educators use tests as prime tools for placing individual students in particular groups, classes, or course sequences. A placement test used to sort tenth-grade students into Remedial, Standard, or Honors English is a good example. Reading readiness tests used at the beginning of first grade for grouping in reading is another. Classification and placement tests are generally broader in coverage and are used far less frequently than diagnostic tests—usually only once or twice a year. Such tests are sometimes called *prescriptive* because different scores suggest students should receive different treatments.

Standardized tests are often used for placement decisions but should never be the sole basis for grouping students or deciding what instructional program a student will follow (Airasian, 1979). Supplemental judgments of teachers and specialists are vital.

Counseling and Guidance Decisions

Tests often play a pivotal role in guiding students in their career choices or planning future educational pursuits of programs of study. Students, their parents, and guidance counselors base decisions on tests that cover broad academic areas and tell the students where they stand in relation to other students. Academic test scores should never serve as the sole criterion, however. Guidance decisions, so important to a student's future, should include interest tests, personal adjustment inventories, and other affective measures well known to most guidance counselors.

Entry–Exit Decisions

Educators depend heavily on tests to help them decide (1) who should enter particular educational institutions or programs of study and (2) who has completed the requirements to leave that program (honorably, that is). We will consider separately entry or *selection* decisions and exit or *certification* decisions.

Selection Decisions

Scores on the Scholastic Aptitude Test (SAT), the Graduate Record Examinations (GRE), and other similar tests play an important role in admissions screening at many institutions, but even test producers caution against using test scores as the sole criterion in admission decisions, proposing that prior grades, recommendations, and interviews should be used as well. But because of the ease and speed with which scores can be examined and compared, tests have become increasingly important in college admissions. Moreover, alternatives are suspect for a variety of reasons—high school grades because of differential grade inflation in different high schools; personal recommendations because of possible nonconfidentiality; and interviews because of interviewers' prejudices and the applicants' interview skills, which may have little to do with success in the programs (Ravitch, 1984).

Psychological screening tests administered by employers to job applicants are also examples of tests used in making selection decisions. Another example is found in tests used to help decide who "qualifies" for remedial programs.

It is sometimes difficult to distinguish between selection and placement, but the distinction is easier if you remember that

- In *placement,* everyone gets placed—it is only a question of in which group or track.
- In *selection,* there is a limitation on who participates—some persons will be selected and others rejected, not receiving placement in any other group or track in the relevant agency.

Measures used to help guide selection decisions are typically designed, administered, and interpreted by testing specialists.

Certification Decisions

Educators and agencies that control admission to various professions routinely *certify* whether acceptable minimum levels of skill or knowledge have been attained by students, or provide licenses that allow individuals to practice particular professions. High school diplomas, a Red Cross lifeguard certificate, and a license to practice law are all examples of credentialing decisions. A key characteristic of tests used for credentialing decisions is that the pass–fail criteria are standard for everyone taking the examination, whereas those who take a selection test like the GRE will find that different departments or colleges require different minimum scores.

As Smith and Hambleton (1990) make evident, tests used in credentialing decisions are among the most controversial and frequently challenged, no doubt because they affect individual lives so significantly. They cannot be simply filed and forgotten.

Application Problem 3

Provide several real-life examples that illustrate the distinction between using tests for *selection* and using tests for *placement*.

Program, Administrative, and Policy Decisions

These decisions do not *directly* influence individuals, but rather affect educational programs, curricula, or systems. Although information from a variety of sources enter into these decisions, many are at least partially based on information provided by various tests or measures. Three examples of such decisions follow.

Program or Curricular Decisions

Administrators often rely on testing information to answer common questions such as which of two computer-assisted writing programs is better for our school? Is our humanities curriculum producing the outcomes we desire? Unfortunately, existing measurement instruments—including standardized tests—are often unsuited for making judgments about specific local programs; therefore, new measures must be developed.

Administrative Decisions

Administrators at various levels scrutinize trends in achievement scores and other test data within the systems for which they have responsibility, and their decisions are often heavily influenced by these tests. They may ask, for example, how effective is this system in preparing students academically? Have "career ladder" merit pay increases for teachers produced better student outcomes? Administrators keep an eye on scores yielded by standardized tests and any other relevant measures to help them answer such questions.

Policy Decisions

Legislators and other policymakers look to test results for information about educational progress and problems in their jurisdiction. In fact, tests have become the single most pervasive influence in many policy decisions—often being used as the primary basis for setting national and state educational priorities and allocating funds to schools. Tests can even set implicit instructional priorities—determining the curriculum—because teachers will stress and students will strive to learn that which they know will be tested. Although test scores can inform policymakers, policy decisions should not be overly dependent on test scores, as discussed by Madaus (1985b):

> For decades, we have warned test users *never* to use a single administration of a test to make important decisions about students. I see this tradition . . . eroding in the face of policy demands. Policy makers mandate situations where test scores are used to make crucial decisions about certification and placement. . . . I was trained in more cautious times, before policy makers discovered our tests and long before the rush to litigation. However, I still believe that we should not use test scores as necessary conditions for placement, certification, promotion, or credentialing, or in merit pay schemes. Test information can play an important part in such crucial decisions, but ultimately the decisions should be made by educators. (p. 7)

We agree heartily.

A Brief History of Educational Measurement

To appreciate fully the function of educational measurement in human society, it is helpful to examine its genesis and evolution. The following discussion of developments and trends that have led us to where we are focuses on

1. early "prescientific" uses of measurement
2. development of scientific measurement techniques prior to 1920
3. important trends and developments from 1920 to 1965 that shaped today's use of educational measurement
4. recent developments and trends in educational measurement.

Early "Prescientific" Uses of Educational Measurement

Ours is not the only generation to be well acquainted with measurement and evaluation. Various means of testing human performance are sprinkled throughout recorded history. In the Bible, for example, we find (in Judges 12:4–6) the first recorded instance of a short, oral examination devised by the Gileadite armies to detect vanquished Ephraimites who attempted to escape under assumed identities. Positioning themselves at the "passages of Jordan," the Gileadites refused passage to anyone unable to pronounce the word *shibboleth* correctly, knowing that Ephraimites mispronounced it as "sibboleth." This inability to pronounce the *h* proved unfortunate for some 42,000 Ephraimites who failed to pass this single-question *final* examination and were summarily executed. Most testing, we are happy to say, has been conducted for somewhat more educational purposes.

As early as 2000 B.C., Chinese officials used civil service examinations to measure the proficiency of candidates for public office (DuBois, 1970; Rogers, 1995), and by the time of the Han dynasty (206 B.C. to A.D. 220), this had grown into an elaborate series of written essay examinations. Hu (1984) explains that success in these written essay examinations was the major route to the status and enormous wealth that came to those in high public office. But only a tiny percentage of those who took these tests passed and became eligible for public appointment. Soon all manner of clever ways were conceived to "beat the system," including cribbing, impersonation, and bribery of examiners. The state responded with preventive measures such as frisking the examinees for crib notes, patrolling during examinations, requiring proof of identity, and having examinations recopied before scoring so that bribed examiners could not recognize the handwriting of their collaborators. Some of these stratagems and counterstratagems have a familiar ring about them even today.

The ancient Greeks also used examinations as a part of the normal educational process. Socrates used oral questioning as an integral part of the teaching-learning process some four centuries before Christ. The effectiveness of this method resulted in its continued use as the primary mode of examination for many centuries. The "recitation" mode that persisted in many schools well into the 1900s is but a degenerate offspring of this early method of Socratic questioning. Of course, oral examinations have been a central part of university curricula since universities began, and remain in use even today. But by the late 1800s, oral exams were giving way to written tests that provided the first real potential for laying a scientific foundation for educational measurement.[4]

Development of Early Scientific Measurement Techniques: Pre-1920

The seeds of scientific educational measurement in the United States were sown in the last century.[5] From 1838 to 1850, Horace Mann used results of written tests to identify educational concerns in Massachusetts, simultaneously arguing persuasively for the superiority of written over oral examinations (Mann, 1845). In 1845, the Boston School Committee made the first use of printed tests for large-scale assessment of student achievement. In 1847, the testing was discontinued because no use was made of the results (Travers, 1983).

Oral tests continued to be dominant for another half century despite sporadic proposals for written examinations and objective scoring (Chadwick, 1864; White, 1886). And when written tests were used, most were essay examinations that depended on highly subjective scoring procedures.

In 1892, attention was galvanized on testing procedures by Joseph Rice, a physician turned educational reformer. In appraising American public education, Rice visited schools in 36 cities and talked with more than 1000 teachers before issuing scathing indictments of school administrators as political hacks and teachers as incompetents who blindly led innocent students in singsong drill and rote repetition. Understandably, Rice was not overly popular with many educators.

---

[4]Even though the earlier Chinese civil service examinations were *written,* they were hardly "scientific," because of the lack of objective standards and agreed-upon criteria.
[5]See Dubois (1970), Travers (1983), Haney (1984), and Rogers (1995) for more extensive treatments of the history of psychological and educational measurement.

Turning his attack on the practice of rote spelling drills, Rice organized an ambitious assessment program carried out in large school systems throughout the United States. To document his claim that school time was inefficiently used, he developed and administered specially constructed tests, under *uniform* conditions—something largely ignored before then. This was perhaps the first (although crude) use of norm-referenced comparative testing. After administering his spelling tests to some 29,000 students, he found negligible differences in students' performance from one school to another, regardless of the amount of time spent on spelling instruction. Rice used these data to support his proposals for restructuring instruction (Rice, 1897a, 1897b).

Meanwhile, several other movements were beginning to shape the future of educational measurement as calls for more scientific measurement began to mount. The first of these came from E. L. Thorndike, often termed the "father" of the educational testing movement because of his far-reaching work in both achievement and intelligence testing. His pioneer measurement textbook (Thorndike, 1904) gained support for the many standardized achievement tests and scales he and his students devised. Thorndike was enormously influential in persuading educators that it was worthwhile to employ precise measurement techniques to evaluate student learning. Largely because of Thorndike and his students, measurement technology flourished in the United States during the early twentieth century, and testing emerged as the primary means of evaluating schools. Standardized achievement tests were developed and used in a variety of subject areas, and by World War I, many large school systems had bureaus of school research working on large-scale assessments of student achievement (Madaus, Airasian, & Kellaghan, 1980).

Based on Binet's earlier development of the first successful intelligence test in France in modern sense, Terman's Stanford–Binet intelligence test, published in 1916, also had profound influence on measurement, paving the way for a barrage of individual and group mental ability tests. By 1918, individual and group tests were being developed for use in many educational and psychological decisions. Even the military accepted the notion that good decisions about individuals could be made only when objective test information was available. This belief also extended to psychologists' use of tests in screening job applicants. By the early 1900s, about 50 percent of federal jobs were awarded by civil service examinations, and tests began to appear for screening nongovernmental typists, clerical workers, and salespersons.

Meanwhile, objective testing (those depending on selected responses, such as multiple-choice items) was also getting a boost from a series of studies that found grading of written essay examinations highly arbitrary and unreliable (Meyer, 1908; Johnson, 1911; Starch, 1913). Startling variations in grades were found when the *same* persons marked the *same* paper on different occasions, or when the same paper was scored by several different teachers. Such disturbing revelations seriously undermined the credibility of subjective scoring and grading practices then in use, creating an intellectual environment in which the objective testing proposals Thorndike and others were making could take root and grow.

Application Problem 4A

In the phrase *scientific measurement techniques,* what do the authors mean by the word *scientific?*

Application Problem 4B

Based on the discussion in this chapter, what factor related to essay examination became an important catalyst for the growth of objective scoring practices?

Trends in Educational Measurement: 1920 to 1965

The 1920s saw increasingly widespread use of objective tests in public and private schools. Norm-referenced tests emerged as the new standard for measuring individual performance. In 1923, the *Stanford Achievement Tests* became the first published comprehensive achievement test battery. The New York Board of Regents examination appeared in 1927 and the Iowa tests in 1929. Commercialism in testing had come of age. Also during this period, the *Scholastic Aptitude Test* (SAT) came into existence, developed by the College Entrance Examination Board, which later became part of the Educational Testing Service. Having undergone constant revision and upgrading, the SAT is still widely used for college admission purposes.

Criticisms of the new objective tests were also launched during the 1920s by such luminaries as Walter Lippmann, the journalist, who decried psychologists' efforts to construct general tests of intelligence (Lippmann, 1922). During the 1930s, criticism continued amid growing concerns that narrowly focused tests might overemphasize particular types of content at the expense of other, more important outcomes. For example, critics of Dewey's "progressive education" philosophy maintained that students educated in those high schools would fare poorly in higher education programs when compared to students educated in conventional Carnegie-unit curricula. This controversy led to the landmark Eight Year Study, in which Ralph Tyler developed and used a wide variety of objective instruments to measure a wide range of educational outcomes in 30 high schools. The results (Smith & Tyler, 1942) showed how new objective assessment procedures could be developed to measure such important outcomes as personal adjustment, aesthetic sensitivity, critical thinking, and other higher-order mental processes.

By the mid-1930s, more than half of the states in the United States had some form of statewide testing. More and more test publishers and other commercial groups turned their attention to the production and scoring of standardized tests, including IBM's introduction of machine scoring in 1935. Buros's test compilations grew from a relatively short bibliography of 44 pages in 1934 to more than 400 pages (listing more than 4000 available tests) in 1938 (Buros, 1938). In addition, teacher-made achievement tests mushroomed, forming a basis for most school grading systems.

During the 1940s and early 1950s, earlier measurement developments were consolidated and applied. The National Council on Measurement in Education (NCME) was formed specifically to provide a forum for improving educational measurement, and in 1947 the Educational Testing Service (ETS) was established and quickly became an influential force in educational testing. Psychologists and educators joined forces in the 1950s to develop standards intended to guide both test developers and test users, an effort that would continue to the present.

Despite these developments, popular criticisms of testing continued. Such works as *The Tyranny of Testing* (Hoffmann, 1962), *They Shall Not Pass* (Black, 1962), and *The Brain Watchers* (Gross, 1962), prompted the American Psychological Association and the U.S. Congress to give serious consideration to issues of test use. Although these popular criticisms did not topple the testing industry, they did contribute to increased sensitivity about privacy rights of examinees and to later laws aimed at the protection of human subjects in research and evaluation studies.

Finally, in 1965, the *Elementary and Secondary Education Act* (ESEA) mandated evaluation studies in thousands of school districts across the United States, especially in federally supported programs for education of children from low-income families. The result was a huge influx of norm-referenced tests, chosen because of governmental support of a norm-referenced model for judging program effectiveness.

Application Problem 5

In the area of educational and psychological measurement, what document has become the most important in guiding measurement practice? What organizations were responsible for producing such a document?

Recent Developments and Trends in Educational Measurement

Since the mid-1960s, most significant developments in educational measurement have been direct or indirect responses to taxpayers' concerns about whether public education is accomplishing what they expect of it. The increasing public concern about educational accountability has caused policymakers and educators to rethink education's responsibilities and outcomes and ways of documenting them. Following are eight trends that have helped reshape educational measurement.[6]

National Assessment of Educational Progress (NAEP)

Desire to increase educational achievement has fostered student testing programs at both federal and state levels. The first of these, the National Assessment of Educational Progress (NAEP), began in 1969 with an ambitious plan to assess annu-

---

[6]Obviously, many other events and trends have influenced the field of educational measurement, but we list here only those we see as most essential to students for whom this book is intended.

ally the performance of U.S. students and young adults in ten subject areas (for example, reading, mathematics, writing, social studies) by administering exercises to a nationally representative sample at these age levels.

Concerns about potential misuses of NAEP results at first caused substantial opposition among educators, but those concerns were blunted by carefully controlled reporting that initially allowed only censuslike comparisons on such dimensions as socioeconomic status, regions of the country, gender, and the like—and resistance crumbled. Avoidance of comparisons among states, districts, and individual schools was doubtlessly one reason that NAEP gained wide acceptance among school administrators.

The general approach used by NAEP was adopted by many U.S. state departments of education in designing state assessment systems, often in response to state legislatures' mandates. Most states today conduct some type of statewide testing—often based on the NAEP design.

Within the last decade, however, NAEP's assessment plan, focus, and reporting have been modified substantially. Now known as "The Nation's Report Card," NAEP reports congressionally mandated surveys of educational achievement of American students in various curriculum areas. But far from its beginnings (when comparisons were purposefully precluded), NAEP has recently reported state by state comparisons of results of a voluntary 8th grade math assessment from 37 participating states (Mullis, Dossey, Owen, & Phillips, 1991). Such state comparisons have since been expanded to cover other subject areas and grade levels—largely because of public pressure for comparative information on school effectiveness. Such comparisons have now become a regular part of NAEP (Linn & Gronlund, 1995).

The "Accountability" Movement

Despite results reported through NAEP and state assessment programs, the 1970s saw continued skepticism about the extent to which public investments in the schools were producing desired results. Into this climate came those who proclaimed that greater "accountability" could reform education (Lessinger, 1970; Lessinger & Tyler, 1971). Not surprisingly, legislators liked the notion that school personnel should be held accountable for educating students.

Several state legislatures passed "educational accountability" laws that required each district to set educational goals, test to see how well those goals had been attained, and report results to the lawmakers. So far, so good. But excess enthusiasm caused some state legislatures to go too far, ruling that *next* year's budget for each school district would depend on how well the district's test results demonstrated it had done in attaining the objectives it had set for itself *this* year. The more success in attaining objectives, the more money next year, and vice versa. (Never mind that struggling districts might well need *more* money to succeed, not less.)

Efforts to implement such flawed legislation were met by a storm of opposition. Fortunately, this momentary flirtation with legislative insanity faded nearly as quickly as it had come upon the scene, leaving the concept of accountability (at least as defined by lawmakers) in general disrepute among most educators. But during its fleeting moment of glory, it spurred numerous efforts to match measurement instruments to local objectives. Although few legislatures today attempt to pass explicit accountability legislation, this movement left a legacy that influences countless other bits of educational legislation aimed at assuring that taxpayers' dollars are translated into acceptable levels of student achievement.

The Trend Toward Criterion-referenced Measurement

Perhaps the most important outgrowth of the accountability movement, and one of the most popularized developments in measurement during the past 20 years, is the increasing use of criterion-referenced measurement.[7] Popham and others (Popham & Husek, 1969; Popham, 1978) argued that traditional "norm-referenced tests" (NRTs) were flawed for several reasons: (1) they lacked precise instructional targets; (2) they produced mismatches between what was taught and what was tested; and (3) they purposefully omitted the very items most important to educators simply because either most examinees answered them correctly or most examinees answered them incorrectly (thus adding little to the test's ability to discriminate between high and low levels of performance). Although many thoughtful measurement experts have consistently maintained that the labels "criterion-referenced testing" (CRT) and "norm-referenced testing" (NRT) merely distinguish between different types of test score interpretations, not different types of tests, many test publishers and state education agencies began to shift away from NRTs and toward CRTs, and measurement experts (for example, Haladyna & Roid, 1983) focused attention on how CRTs should be constructed. Organizations as powerful as the National Education Association have issued resolutions supporting CRTs as a viable alternative to or replacement for standardized NRTs. More will be said about this later.

Trends in Scholastic Aptitude and Achievement Test Scores

Ever since standardized tests came into broad use, the nation has kept its collective finger on the throbbing pulse of standardized test scores—and fretted when that pulse weakened. Until the mid-1960s, test scores were generally increasing and all was well. Then in 1964, the national average score on the Scholastic Aptitude Test (SAT) slipped. A one-time fluke, most observers assumed. But the scores continued to fall every year for the next 15 years. Other tests of general aptitude showed the same unnerving downward trends between the mid-1960s and early 1980s, including the venerable *American College Test* (ACT) and the *Graduate Record Examination* (GRE).

   These remarkably consistent and alarming declines across aptitude tests were echoed by trends in achievement test scores for the same period. Waters (1981) reported that composite achievement scores for all major achievement test batteries showed pervasive downward trends beginning with fifth grade. The declines were not trivial. For example, on the *General Educational Development Test* (GED), 75 percent of the 1962 examinees passed (met minimum requirements to receive a high school equivalency credential), compared to only 60 percent of the examinees

---

[7]Criterion-referenced measurement and norm-referenced measurement (to be introduced shortly) are described more fully in later chapters.

who passed in 1979. The conclusion that the slumping average in national performance on scholastic aptitude and achievement tests reflected a national erosion of
U.S. students' ability was widespread. In one government-supported publication, it
was announced that

> This decline has been found in nearly all subjects and all regions of the country, and in
> almost all national testing programs, ranging from college entrance tests to elementary
> school achievement test batteries . . . declines tend to be more pronounced through the
> high grade levels. . . . (Anderson et al., 1980, p. 11).

Alarms were sounded. Searches were launched to uncover any plausible causes
that might have contributed to such tragic backsliding. Even presidential commis-
sions were appointed to investigate potential causes of such slippage. Some explanation of the "declining test scores phenomenon" was essential, both for valid scientific reasons and as a political form of national face-saving. Volumes of explanations
were published. Space does not permit our discussing the multiple factors—many
outside the schools' control—that could have caused declines in test scores. For excellent summaries of the many hypotheses proposed as plausible explanations of this
troubling phenomenon, readers are referred to fascinating analyses by Anderson et
al. (1980), Austin and Garbar (1982), Haney (1984), and Turnbull (1985).

We probably will never know which of the many proposed explanations actually played a part in the test score slippage, for before researchers were able to ar-
rive at any definitive conclusions, the test scores simply stopped declining. The decline ended as mysteriously as it had begun—slowing, steadying, and then
gradually turning upward for most tests somewhere between 1979 and 1982. Since
then, most national test scores made small but steady increases until the mid-
1980s, after which they have flattened or meandered in a trendless pattern.

Whatever the causes of the trends in national test scores, this much is certain:
they have had profound effects on schools. Concerns over test declines have played
a direct role in several significant educational developments:

- Educators' challenging the appropriateness of tests
- Minimum competency testing, viewed by proponents as necessary to putting
  rigor back into American education
- Increased attention to basic skills instruction in math, reading, and writing
- Litigation attacking the validity of using test scores for selection and promo-
  tion decisions

More will be said about these outcomes of the test declines in our discussion of current measurement issues in Chapter 2.

The Establishment of Minimum Competency Testing Programs

It is difficult to define "minimum competency testing" (MCT) precisely since the
term has come to be used so many different ways. We use MCT to refer to criterion-referenced, objective testing mandated by state or local governing bodies who
have decided on minimum standards of competency they will accept for key educational pass–fail decisions about individual students (or teachers).

The MCT movement was triggered at least in part by the test score declines we discussed earlier. Many educators see proposals for installing minimum competency testing programs as little more than cynical expression of continued lack of public confidence in American education. As Jaeger (1982) pointed out, "minimum competency achievement testing is primarily a political movement, not an educational movement. Such programs reflect the blind faith of state legislatures and state boards of education in their power to mandate—through law, regulation, or administrative action—some minimum level of educational success" (p. 227).

Such beliefs resulted in a legislative stampede to develop MCT programs, especially during the late 1970s. Some form of MCT program now exists or is under consideration in almost every state in the United States, mandated by either the state legislature or the state education agency. In addition, many local school districts have initiated their own MCT programs, either voluntarily or as an alternative to an otherwise required state program (Jaeger, 1989). Amid the swirling debates about whether it is wise or technically sound to use tests in this way, MCT use continues to expand. MCT has become a pervasive and controversial national phenomenon. Given the direct use of their results in making important decisions about individuals, it is not surprising that the use of MCT has been repetitively challenged in U.S. courts. We shall discuss the controversy and legal issues surrounding MCT programs in Chapter 2.

The Use of Competency Tests for Teacher Certification

The concept of testing teachers is not new. Examinations were developed to "certify" teachers for church-supported universities in medieval Europe. Several proposals have surfaced during this century endorsing the notion that teaching credentials should be awarded on the basis of test results, including the following:

- Selection of teacher education candidates on the basis of their scores on tests of intelligence, "teaching aptitude," subject matter competence, and knowledge of testing (late 1920s and early 1930s)
- Development and sale of early standardized admissions tests for teacher education programs (1920s and 1930s)
- Development and promotion of comprehensive teacher selection tests by the American Council on Education's Cooperative Test Service (1930s)—eventually resulting in development of the National Teacher Examinations (late 1930s)
- Implementation of state requirements that prospective teachers must pass competency tests to be certified or, in some cases, that experienced teachers must pass such a test for recertification (1940s to the present)

Underlying these developments were assumptions that (1) both schools and society would be well served if teacher competence could be assured; and (2) the best single assurance was having candidates for (or occupants of) teaching positions demonstrate their competence in basic literacy and "numeracy," knowledge of subject matter, and knowledge of professional principles pertinent to their practice. The move to teacher competency testing followed in the wake of reform efforts aimed at making U.S. schools more accountable, efficient, and effective. The public has shown great enthusiasm for the idea: a 1984 Gallup poll reported that 89 percent of those citizens polled favored competency testing for teachers (Martin, 1986). Many states already have implemented competency testing for teacher certification or admission to teacher education programs; several other states are in the process of doing so. In some states, even experienced teachers are required to take competency tests in order to be recertified.

These trends have not been enthusiastically viewed by many educators, and debates continue over the wisdom of such programs. Legal challenges have been made regarding the use of competency tests for recertification of experienced teachers. In Chapter 2, we will examine in greater detail the professional dialogue and legal issues surrounding the use of teacher competency testing.

Calls for Alternative, "Authentic" Performance Measures

During the past decade, the perceived urgency of educational reform has resulted in inordinate weight being given to traditional, standardized tests as indicators of the "health" of our schools. Increasing pressure on educators to "raise test scores" has resulted in high-stakes tests, where lower scores may have negative or dire consequences not only for the student, but also for their teachers and administrators. Not surprisingly, school personnel began taking pains to prepare their students well—sometimes too well—to take the high-stakes standardized tests. Soon the confidence educators could have in the results of these tests was seriously shaken.

In this context, known limitations of traditional multiple-choice tests were greatly magnified by their misuse. Those already critical of standardized tests responded by proposing use of alternative assessment devices—nontraditional measures that depended on direct, "authentic" assessment of student performance on important learning tasks. The logic of this movement is simple. Since educators are concerned about aiming their instruction so that students will perform optimally when tested, why not use as "tests" the most essential performances that we desire students to accomplish, and then "teach to the test" without apology. In short, test the actual habits and capacities that society views as essential, in the context of actual performances where those habits and capacities can be observed, rather than using tests whose items are proxies for such performances.

The results of such thinking are a variety of alternatives (to traditional tests) for assessing student learning. Long familiar assessment alternatives such as oral debates, typing tests, and writing samples mingle with less familiar alternatives such as student diaries, art portfolios, and science fairs. Much more will be said later about the potential (and some potential pitfalls) of these alternative forms of assessment. Suffice it to say here that *no* recent measurement trend has swept the field of education as quickly and aroused such sudden interest as have proposals to base student assessment more firmly on direct measures of student performance.

Application of Computers in Testing

With the rapid advances of computer technology and its infiltration into all aspects of our lives, it is not surprising to see that computers are also exerting strong influence in reshaping the educational measurement enterprise. The influence of computer technology on measurement is broad and multifaceted. For example, computers are being used as an alternative medium for test administration, for individually tailored testing (computerized adaptive testing), for more sophisticated test analysis to improve test construction, and for test score interpretation in many clinical settings and elsewhere. For educators, the most relevant computer applications in measurement are (1) using computers as an alternative medium for test administration, and (2) using computers for designing and delivering individually tailored testing. We will briefly discuss these two applications here.

Using computers for test administration. This use of computer technology is intended to replace traditional paper-and-pencil testing. Instead of a paper-and-pencil test for a student, the student takes the same test on a computer, using the computer keyboard or mouse as input devices. In other words, the computer is used as a medium for test administration, an alternative to the traditional mediums of paper and pencil.

This application of computer technology in testing offers some distinct practical advantages over traditional paper-and-pencil testing. First of all, test administration is automated and self-contained for each individual, so there is no need to have a group of students for test administration, as there is with paper-and-pencil testing. Because of this, individual students no longer have to wait for the "next" test administration to take a test; instead, they can take the test any time the testing station is open and a computer is available. All they need to do is to make appointments with the testing station when they are ready. Second, test security is enhanced because, in this situation, the test material is more securely controlled than in the case of paper-and-pencil tests. Third, students do not have to wait long for their scores; test results can be obtained immediately after the test is finished.

Although using computers as an alternative medium for test administration offers some advantages, by itself, it does not represent any breakthrough in educational measurement. A much more significant computer application is to use computer technology to design and deliver testing material tailored to individuals so that both the precision and efficiency of measurement will be significantly improved. This is the topic in our next section.

Computerized adaptive testing (CAT). In conventional tests, all students are administered the same set of items. Such fixed-length testing is inefficient for many students, especially for low- and high-ability students, because for them, many items are either too difficult (for low-ability students) or too easy (for high-ability students). In either case, these items are not useful for estimating students' ability levels and are essentially a waste of time for these students. Conversely, in a computerized adaptive test, different test items are administered to different students. The computer selects each item from a pool of items of known difficulty. The item is displayed on a computer or TV screen, and the student responds to the item either through a computer input device (keyboard or mouse) or by touching the screen at the location of the correct response. The computer records whether the response is correct or incorrect and selects the next item, based on the student's response to the previous item. If the student's response is correct, the next item selected will be more difficult; if the student's response is incorrect, the next item selected will be easier. As more items are administered, the computer calculates the student's performance on all previous items in estimating his or her mastery level and selecting the next item to be administered. As a result, the items are adapted to the level of the student. Therefore, on the whole, they will be neither too easy nor too difficult for the individual.

CAT provides several important advantages over traditional paper-and-pencil tests, or even over computer-administered tests (Hambleton, Swaminathan, & Rogers, 1991). First, CAT offers a more precise measure for each individual because the items administered to an individual are neither too easy nor too difficult, but more closely matched to the individual's ability level. Second, in CAT, high-ability students do not waste their time on very easy items, and low-ability students do not need to take very difficult items; therefore, tests can be shortened without any loss of precision. Thus, CAT offers more efficient measurement than traditional tests. In addition, CAT offers better test security: because each student is administered a different combination of items, it is much harder for the teacher to teach to the test, and the student cannot help his peers by passing on test items he remembers because most of the items administered to other students will be different. In research, it has been shown that CAT may decrease testing time by 50 percent or more, while resulting in the same or more precise measurement than conventional fixed-length tests (Linn & Gronlund, 1995; Olsen, 1989; Weiss, 1985). Some commercial tests already have CAT versions available. For example, the Educational Testing Service introduced the CAT version of the Graduate Record Examination (GRE) in 1993, and it is now widely available throughout the nation. It is anticipated that more CAT versions for commercial tests will be available in the future.

It should be noted that, on a CAT, each student's skill or ability level is measured by *which* items he answers correctly, not by *how many* items he answers correctly. In order to interpret a student's performance, the characteristics of each item (difficulty level, discrimination level, and probability of guessing the correct answer) must be known *a priori*. A large pool of test items and a sufficient number of examinees are needed for estimating the item characteristics so that CAT can be possible. For this reason, CAT is usually feasible only for large-scale testing programs, not for routine classroom measurement by classroom teachers. Furthermore, the cost for computers and software needed for CAT can also be prohibitive. With the rapid increase of computer availability, however, this will be less of a problem in the future.

Application Problem 6A

What is the trend of test scores on major standardized tests such as the SAT, ACT, and GRE between the 1960s and 1980s? What are some of the possible explanations for such a trend?

Application Problem 6B

As discussed in this chapter, what is the most powerful movement that is sweeping across the field of educational measurement now? What are the major characteristics of this movement?

SUGGESTED READINGS

Anderson, B. & Pipho, C. (1984). State-mandated testing and the fate of local control. *Phi Delta Kappan, 66*(3), 209–212.

> This article provides a brief but insightful summary of new trends involving accountability programs, criterion-referenced testing, and minimum competency testing, along with consideration of how policymakers view and use testing.

Austin, G. R. & Garbar, H. (1982). *The rise and fall of national test scores.* New York: Academic Press, Inc.

> This edited book contains a series of chapters that provide scholarly treatment of the causes and implications of national aptitude and achievement test score trends. Many common misconceptions about test score trends are corrected in this volume.

Haney, W. (1984). Testing reasoning and reasoning about testing. *Review of Educational Research,54*(4), 597–654.

> This review recounts in concise form the history of research and reasoning about mental testing and its role and influence in educational practice. Future areas of research regarding testing are also proposed.

Rogers, T. B. (1995). *The psychological testing enterprise: An introduction.* Pacific Grove, CA: Brooks/Cole Publishing Company.

> Chapter 1: Telling the Story of Testing; Chapter 3: Social Foundations of Testing. Together, these two chapters provide an interesting discussion about the nature of psychological measurement and a brief history of testing.

Selden, R. W. (1985). Measuring excellence: The dual role of testing in reforming education. *Curriculum Review, 25*(1), 14–32.

> This article provides interesting perspectives on the uses to which tests can be put to improve education, reasons for test use, problems stemming from misuse of tests, and ways test misuse can be avoided.

SUGGESTION SHEET

If your last name starts with the letter A, please complete the Suggestion Sheet at the end of the book while this chapter is still fresh in your mind.

Answers to Chapter 1 Application Problems

1. For discussion; no single answer provided.
2. a. In making decisions in education, objective measurement has an advantage over subjective judgment in that it will be less likely that the decision will be influenced by personal likes or prejudices. But objective measurement may lack the kind of insightfulness subjective judgment may offer. Also, objective measurement may be of little use for some hard-to-measure personal characteristics, such as being caring, humane, and socially appropriate.

b. In educational measurement, quantification is the process of assigning numerical values to some characteristics of our interest so that such characteristics can be described quantitatively. Many personal characteristics may not appear at first glance to be quantifiable (for example, aggressiveness), but educators and psychologists have successfully designed measurement instruments to quantify these characteristics. Educational measurement depends on quantification. If a specific characteristic is not quantifiable, then it cannot be measured, at least not in the sense of measurement as we understand it now.

3. Using tests for selection: (1) University admissions officials consider an applicant's SAT or ACT score to decide if the applicant should be admitted. (2) The U.S. Air Force administers a specific test battery to applicants for a pilot training program. Admission into the training program is partially dependent on the performance on this test battery.

Using tests for placement: (1) An ESL (English as a Second Language) program has four different levels of instruction. A new student in this ESL program is tested to see which level is the most appropriate for him or her. (2) The swimming skills of the children in a swimming program are tested so that they can be assigned to the appropriate level of training.

4. a. The word *scientific* in the phrase *scientific measurement techniques* is mainly used to indicate that the measurement process is "objective," in that testing standards have been specified and scoring criteria have been agreed upon.

b. Highly arbitrary and unreliable grading both across graders and across occasions.

5. The most important document for guiding measurement practice is the *Standards for Educational and Psychological Tests,* jointly produced by the American Educational Research Association, American Psychological Association, and the National Council on Measurement in Education.

6. a. Primarily a downward trend of these test scores, indicating a steady decline during this period. Several (not intended to be exhaustive) possible explanations are (1) demographic changes (for example, ethnic, economic, gender) in the composition of the students taking the tests; (2) less demanding high school curricula; (3) diminishing educational standards; (4) other social or family changes (too much television, less parental attention, family structure change, and so on); and (5) lower abilities of teachers.

b. Increased use of alternative forms of assessment is the most powerful movement sweeping across the field of educational measurement now. The major characteristic of this movement is calling for "authentic" or direct measurement of student performance on important learning tasks, instead of using "proxies" (for example, multiple-choice items) as in conventional testing.

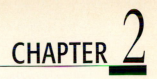

CHAPTER 2

Coming to Grips with Social, Legal, and Ethical Issues in Measurement

OVERVIEW

What has triggered the well-publicized legal battles over testing, and what have the courts decided? What impact do "truth-in-testing" laws and other related legislation have on schools? Is there substance to claims that most tests are flawed by cultural or social bias? What ethical guidelines can schools follow to be certain they are using measurement instruments properly? What impact is minimum competency testing likely to have on our educational systems? What role—if any—should competency tests play in certifying and recertifying classroom teachers? These are some of the major questions we attempt to answer in this chapter.

We have organized this chapter into six major sections dealing, respectively, with concerns about bias in educational tests, and the legal and legislative efforts to remedy perceived biases; issues in minimum competency testing; right-to-privacy issues in using educational tests; concerns about test disclosure; ethical considerations and guidelines in testing (including problems with teaching to the test); and issues in using tests for teacher certification.

OBJECTIVES

Upon completing your study of this chapter, you should be able to

1. Define "test bias," and discuss how bias can affect test results for individuals and groups.
2. Identify concerns and cautions about cultural, social, and gender bias in tests, and discuss to what extent each type of bias undermines current educational measures.

3. | Describe what impact court decisions and legislative enactments that pertain to testing in the schools have had on educational testing.

4. | Define minimum competency testing, and discuss legal and ethical issues in using such tests. List the criteria for a legally defensible minimum competency test.

5. | Discuss the impact of truth-in-testing and right-to-privacy legislation on the use of educational tests.

6. | Explain the ethical responsibilities of test users, including ethical problems associated with teaching to the test.

7. | Explain the role and utility of standards for tests and test use.

8. | Discuss unresolved issues in teacher competency testing, and identify steps necessary to resolve them.

Social and Legal Considerations Related to Test Bias

Out of all issues related to educational and psychological measurement, concern about test bias is probably the most socially sensitive and emotional. The debates about potential test bias do not end with mere intellectual jousting. As a natural outgrowth of the civil rights movement in the late 1960s and early 1970s, these disagreements about test bias have flowed over into courtrooms, legislative assemblies, and the major channels and tributaries of dialogue about the social values associated with testing.

Concern that tests be free of discrimination by reason of gender, race, color, socioeconomic status, and so on has prompted responses from professionals, such as the well-known *Standards* (APA et al., 1974; AERA et al., 1985). Those who make and use tests can no longer do so without regard to their social impact on different social subgroups, including ethnic minorities, women, and persons with disabilities. Scrutiny of testing by the legal system has become commonplace, and litigation over testing issues has proliferated to the point where it has occupied the attention of even prominent legal scholars (for example, Bersoff, 1981a, 1981b). Even the prestigious and powerful testing corporations can no longer ply their trade with impunity. What can be measured in the schoolroom is increasingly being determined by what happens in the courtroom.

In this section, we consider several aspects of educational measurement that have become the focus of legal, ethical, or social concern. We examine particularly concerns about cultural, ethnic, linguistic, socioeconomic, and gender bias in tests.

Test Bias and Discrimination Issues

Concerns about bias most often revolve around questions of whether tests discriminate against those whose cultural, linguistic, racial, economic, or social background differs from that of the majority. The possibility that many tests might have a gender bias, favoring males, has also become a concern since the 1960s.

But What Is Test Bias?

So far, we have written as if everyone understands and agrees on what test bias is. That is not the case. To prove our point, try answering the following question.

Does test bias refer to

- bias inherent in the test itself?
- bias created by inappropriate selection of a test?
- bias created by how a test is administered?
- bias in the way test results are used in making decisions?

The answer is yes to all the above. Inappropriate test construction, selection, administration, or use can all result in bias. *Many* factors might bias the scores on a test, leading to several different definitions of test bias. For purposes of this chapter, we give only the most common definition of test bias. (For more complete discussion, see Cole & Moss, 1989, and Reynolds, 1994.)

A test is biased if one group (cultural, racial, ethnic, gender, and so on) has an *unfair* advantage over others, and the unfair advantage is totally *unrelated* to what the test is designed to measure. For example, giving directions in English for a manual dexterity test might bias scores against Laotian bilingual students who are not fluent in English, resulting in erroneous conclusions that Laotians have less manual dexterity than other students. Or if the story-problem items on a mathematical placement test are loaded with words like *regatta, oarsman, opera, sonata, bassoon,* or *pirouette,* then children from wealthy families may have an unfair advantage because they may have more exposure to such vocabulary. Since the test is supposed to measure math ability, not vocabulary, we say it may be *biased in favor* of high socioeconomic children, or *biased against* middle and lower socioeconomic children. On the other hand, if this is a test designed to measure higher-level verbal skills or vocabulary, then inclusion of such vocabulary items is less likely to create test bias since vocabulary *is* what the test is designed to measure. Whoever has more exposure to such vocabulary items may be advantaged, but the advantage is *not* unfair since the advantage is directly related to what the test intends to measure.

In discussing test bias, it is extremely important to distinguish between the situation where one group has better performance as a result of higher-ability levels (for whatever reasons) in what the test is designed to measure, and the situation where one group has better performance owing to some systematic factor(s) *unrelated* to what the test is designed to measure. Test bias exists only in the latter case, not in the former. Unfortunately, such an important distinction has often been blurred in the debates concerning test bias.

In summary, any time that differences observed in test performance are caused by systematic factors *irrelevant* to what you intend to measure (for example, cultural background), and such observed differences could result in systematic unfairness toward certain groups of examinees, the possibility of test bias exists. Or stated more technically, bias is present when a test score has a different meaning or implication for one subgroup of examinees than for another, thus resulting in the interpretation of a test score being more valid for one subgroup of test takers than another (Cole & Moss, 1989; Reynolds, 1994).

Let us examine briefly each of the specific areas in which test bias is a recurring concern.

Concerns About Cultural, Ethnic, and Linguistic Test Bias

Despite significant gains during the past 30 years toward providing equal educational opportunities for all children, we obviously have a long way to go. Inequality and unfairness are pernicious specters that continue to haunt many ethnic, cultural, or linguistic minorities[1] and to penetrate school curricula, instructional materials, instruction, classroom management, school governance, and educational tests. Yet of all facets of schooling, testing is by far the most common target for those who complain of bias. Why? Probably because educational and psychological testing has become so intertwined with social and educational policies such as upward mobility, admission to higher education, or placement of individuals into special treatment programs (for example, special education programs).

The *potential* of bias against minority groups exists in *all* kinds of measurement situations—including teacher-made tests and grading, where it is more difficult to detect because of the subjectivity that is typically (though not necessarily) more prevalent. Yet standardized ability and achievement tests have borne the brunt of the criticisms alleging bias against minorities. Many studies have shown that members of some minority groups tend to score lower on standardized ability tests than members of the white majority. In some studies, the difference in average test scores has been unsettling, as Linn (1982) notes:

> a difference between average scores for white and black students of roughly one standard deviation is typical of a number of studies that have compared these two groups (e.g., Coleman et al., 1966).
>
> With differences of this magnitude it is obviously important to consider the possibility that the lower average test scores for the poor and for certain minority groups are attributable, in whole or part, to bias in the tests themselves. (p. 285)

Although this observation points out a *potential* source for score differences among some social groups, it does not eliminate the opposite possibility that the tests are not biased, and that the lower scores of some minority groups are *true* reflections of lower levels of performance. *If* the tests are not at fault, then only two other explanations seem plausible: either minorities have been deprived of some cultural and educational opportunities to develop the skills and knowledge sampled by the tests (an attempted environmental explanation), or those minorities (considered as a *group*) are inherently less able in the areas tested (an attempted genetic explanation).

This last explanation has been at the root of much controversy for several decades. Although enshrined for centuries in racial bigotry, perceptions that minorities were *by nature* inferior have never been accorded much scientific re-

---

[1] For simplicity, we will use the term *minority* hereafter to refer to those who differ from the dominant societal group in race, ethnicity, language, or culture; we recognize the overlap that frequently results because some individuals would simultaneously be classified as minorities in more than one of these areas.

spectability. Jensen (1969) reviewed findings that differences in IQ and scholastic aptitude *within white* populations were partly attributable to genetic inheritance, and he extrapolated such findings to suggest that it was reasonable to hypothesize that "genetic factors are strongly implicated in the average Negro-white intelligence difference" (p. 82).[2] The suggestion that differences in the measured IQ scores of blacks[3] and whites were the product of genetic differences created a controversy that dominated the popular and professional periodicals for quite some time. Although Jensen's thesis has been largely discounted on scientific as well as societal bases (Light & Smith, 1969; Haney, 1984), the controversy is far from dead. As Shepard (1980) observes:

> One reason that bias in mental testing is so volatile an issue is that it involves the specter of biological determinism, i.e., whether there is a large difference in intelligence (IQ) between black and white Americans which can be attributed largely to inherited differences. (p. 5)

What may have fueled the controversy most is the fact that minority students (especially African-American, Native-American, and Latin-American children) have been classified in disproportionate numbers as educable mentally retarded (EMR) students and placed in special education programs (Reschly, 1981). Many of those affected have viewed these classifications and the referral placement process as unfair, stigmatizing, and humiliating to individuals, and possibly racist. Since tests play such a pivotal role in these classifications, the possibility of test bias had led to legal challenges.

As early as 1954, of course, the landmark case of *Brown* v. *Board of Education of Topeka (1954)* established the right of minority children to equal educational opportunities, which provided the foundation for subsequent legal challenges to educational inequality. A decade passed, however, before litigation began to focus seriously on the role that testing might play in assuring all children equal access to educational opportunities. Racial minorities, objecting to their children being labeled "retarded" and being removed from regular classrooms, have taken the testers to court. Space permits us to provide only a sketchy coverage of the litigation and out-of-court settlements concerning testing in the last three decades, touching on only a few of the cases we believe to be most significant.[4]

---

[2]It should be noted that, in his early work, Jensen used the data from Cyril Burt, an infamous British researcher in the area of human intelligence. The data from Burt's research were largely discounted later by the scientific community because of the strong belief that Burt may have fabricated fraudulent data to support his position.

[3]In this section and elsewhere in this chapter, we refer to African-Americans as blacks, and to children with disabilities as handicapped children, where those terms were used in the court case or historical controversy to which we refer; elsewhere we prefer the terms *African-American* and *children with disabilities,* unless using a direct quotation.

[4]For more in-depth reviews of this topic, see Bersoff (1981a, 1981b), Lambert (1981), Menacker and Morris (1985), Childs (1990), and Kaplan and Saccuzzo (1997).

Hobson *v.* Hansen (1967)

Legal opposition to educational and psychological tests really began in 1967, in a case before the District of Columbia federal court, in which minorities questioned the constitutionality of using group IQ and achievement measures in placing children in educational tracks, since black children were overrepresented in lower-ability tracks (especially EMR classes) and white children were placed disproportionately in upper-ability tracks (especially college preparatory classes). The court prohibited the use of these tests for the purposes of grouping, holding that the tests had been standardized on mostly white, middle-class populations and therefore yielded biased results when administered to minority children.

Diana *v.* California State Board of Education (1970)

Plaintiffs on behalf of nine Latin-American students charged that the children were inappropriately placed in EMR classrooms as a result of scores on IQ tests that assumed equality of examinees' linguistic and cultural backgrounds. When these students were permitted to take the test again in their primary language, there was an average increase of 15 IQ points. This case led to an out-of-court settlement stipulating that children from non-English–speaking homes would be tested in their native language, and to subsequent out-of-court settlements specifying that IQ tests used for special education placement must be (1) normed on culturally and linguistically relevant groups, and (2) contain no culturally unfair content (see Oakland & Laosa, 1977).

Larry P. *v.* Riles (1979)

One of the two most significant legal precedents related to IQ testing comes from this celebrated California class action suit filed against the San Francisco Unified School District. Plaintiffs were parents of six black students who claimed their children had been wrongly placed in EMR classes because the standardized IQ tests used for placement were racially and culturally biased. After eight years of legal maneuvering, the court finally rendered a decision in favor of the plaintiffs. Noting that disproportionate numbers of black students were placed in EMR classes (blacks constituted about 27 percent of the total student population, but more than 60 percent of the EMR population), the court ruled that the tests used for the purpose were inappropriate and biased and banned IQ testing of black students for such placement purposes in California public schools.[5] Advocates of minority student rights rejoiced, while the state of California appealed the decision. In 1984, an appellate court upheld the court's decision.

In this famous case, the fundamental reasoning for the court decision was that there was no reason to expect performance differences between black and white students; thus since such differences occurred on the test used, the test must be bi-

---

[5]In 1992, the same judge lifted his ban on IQ testing in California schools, having concluded that such a ban was unfair to black parents who *wanted* to have their children tested for placement purposes. This effectively nullified his earlier prohibition against the use of IQ tests for placement purposes in California schools (Aiken, 1996, p. 327).

ased against black students. In other words, a difference in test scores between black and white students was accepted, without explanatory or corroborating evidence, as conclusive evidence of the existence of test bias. This reasoning is very troubling to many measurement professionals, as Lambert (1981) so aptly states:

> Psychology and psychological measurement were on trial in *Larry P.* v. *Wilson Riles.* The plaintiff and the judge chose to center attention on tests and attack them as the cause of the greater prevalence of retarded intellectual development among black children, rather than being concerned about the role of environmental factors in intellectual performance, the slow learning child's need for special educational assistance, or other remedies that would protect the rights of black children to equal educational opportunity while also insuring their rights to special education services as needed. (p. 944)

PASE (Parents in Action on Special Education) *v.* Hannon (1980)

Less than a year after the Larry P. opinion in California, a very different decision was rendered on a similar case tried before a federal district court in Illinois. In this suit, filed in 1975 on behalf of black children placed in the Chicago public school's EMR classes, the court found in favor of the state. After personally examining each test item (something the California judge did not do), the judge concluded that very few items on the tests were culturally biased and that the IQ tests did not discriminate against black children. Although the decision in this case was opposite to that of Larry P., one thing in common about these two famous cases is that the decisions were based on highly subjective and questionable rationales, and empirical research results were largely ignored in the court decisions.

Other Legal Challenges Claiming Tests Are Biased

Space does not permit our discussing all the types of lawsuits asserting that tests are biased, let alone citing examples of each. For additional examples of legal challenges to achievement, admission, placement, and licensure tests, readers are referred to Worthen, Borg, and White (1993, pp. 36–37).

So Where Does All the Litigation Leave Us?

The litigation surrounding testing bias may have clouded as much as clarified murky issues, and judicial decisions related to the issue were inconsistent. But some things are clear.

First, the court decisions have changed few minds; those who were critical of tests before the lawsuits are still largely critical, and test proponents have not been much dissuaded, even by negative rulings.

Second, test developers have become more sensitive to potential test bias, and many efforts have been made to construct unbiased measurement instruments. For example, commercial tests are now routinely standardized on *representative* norm groups, panels consisting of different ethnic backgrounds are routinely convened to scrutinize test items, and a variety of new research techniques have been developed to detect both biased items and biased tests. In this regard, the court battles have had very positive effects on test development practice.

Third, many common misunderstandings about test bias are evident in the court orders. The *assumption* of the jurists in several previously cited examples seemed to be that differences in average group performance could be taken as *prima facie* evidence of bias. Not so, as Linn and Drasgow (1987) point out. Noting that this popular view of bias confuses *measurement* of a behavior with the *cause* of that behavior, they acknowledge that differences in group performance on tests *may* indicate *potential* test bias, but they argue that it is by no means sufficient *evidence* of such bias since such differences may actually reflect a *real* difference in the ability a test attempts to measure. Factors other than test bias may be the real cause of group differences on cognitive and achievement tests.

Fourth, "the jury is still out"; court orders aside, the research evidence is far from being conclusive about the extent to which bias toward minorities is a problem in psychological and educational tests. (See Linn, 1982; Cole, 1981; and Reynolds, 1994, for insightful discussions of this research.)

Application Problem 1

In general, how did intelligence tests fare in courts? As discussed by the authors, what is the major reasoning in those court cases that ruled against intelligence or aptitude testing in schools, especially in placing students in special education classes? In your opinion, is the major reasoning behind these court cases sound? Why or why not?

Concerns About Socioeconomic Bias in Tests

Although concern about potential test bias related to ethnic, racial, and cultural minorities has occupied center stage in the test bias debate thus far, there has also been some concern about the potential of test bias against socioeconomically disadvantaged groups. But because many economically disadvantaged students are also racial or cultural minorities, it is often difficult to separate poverty from minority status in examining test scores for possible socioeconomic bias. Perhaps that is why there has been little direct litigation focusing on socioeconomic bias.

It is clear that the poor—whether of minority status or not—perform less well on achievement and intelligence tests, on the average, than do their counterparts from more affluent homes. Is it possible that lower average test scores for the poor are attributable to bias in the tests? Of course it is possible. But whether it is *true* still eludes us. In a critique of the Educational Testing Service (ETS), Nairn (1980) asserted that (1) students' SAT scores are highly correlated with family income, and (2) tests are a major instrument in preserving the socioeconomic *status quo*. In responding, the ETS (1980) (1) drew on White's (1976) data to show that family income relates no more closely to test scores of children ($r = .25$) than to grades given to those children (r = .24),[6] and (2) challenged the thinking of those who would terminate testing because tests help disclose the negative effects of unequal resources and disparate learning opportunities among children of different classes.

Care should be taken not to attribute the biases in our society to the instruments that report their cumulative effects. In many respects, our tests are only a mirror, reflecting the educational results of cultural bias, and shattering the mirror will not solve the problem.

Concerns About Gender Bias in Tests

Increased social conscience has led to a parallel increase in efforts to assure equality between the sexes in educational, vocational, and economic opportunities. As part of this effort, educational and psychological tests have been examined for possible bias against females. In 1989, for example, a federal court judge ordered New York State to stop awarding college scholarships based on SAT scores, saying the test is unfair to girls, since their SAT scores are significantly lower than males, while their grade-point averages were higher.

In general, females are found to do as well as or better than males on educational tests—perhaps because females have better performance in verbal ability or, as Waetjen (1977) suggests, because boys perform less well in stress-producing situations. Only in mathematics achievement do males seem to score higher, on the average, than females, and it is not yet entirely clear whether such differences are attributable to innate gender differences (for example, males possessing greater quantitative aptitude), or to cultural attitudes, societal expectations, and stereotypes. (For interesting discussions of this topic, see Gutbezahl, 1995; Sax, 1994; Tartre & Fennema, 1995.)

Our concern here, however, is not with innate gender differences—or even with societal attitudes and expectations. Instead, our interest lies in the question of whether cultural attitudes (or other factors) inject gender bias into educational tests. In the discussion of gender bias, many people assume that any observed differences in test performance between males and females constitute evidence of test bias. This assumption, however, makes no distinction between differential performance between the sexes resulting from *real* group differences and that caused by some *unfair* advantages one gender enjoys but which is *unrelated* to what a test is designed to measure (Linn & Gronlund, 1995, p. 493).

Application Problem 2

Provide your definition of "test bias." Give several real or hypothetical measurement examples in which test bias is most likely to be operating.

---

[6]These are correlation coefficients. A correlation coefficient statistically describes the relationship between two variables. This statistical concept will be discussed in the next chapter.

Issues in Minimum Competency Testing

We noted previously that the minimum competency test (MCT) movement has been controversial from the outset, with debate focused on the issues of test utility and fairness. Controversy has stemmed from the fact that most MCTs were proposed for use in *high-stakes* testing programs where important decisions about examinees are often based solely on their performance on such tests. Examples are awarding or denial of high school diplomas, promotion to the next grade or retention in the same grade, and the like. As can be expected with any high-stakes testing program in our schools, educators have hotly debated the advantages and disadvantages of MCTs. Interested readers are referred to Lerner (1980, 1981) and Popham (1984) for some of the pro-MCT arguments; to Pullin (1982) and Corbett and Wilson (1990) for the opposing views; to Haney, Madaus, and Lyon (1993) and Madaus (1994) for discussion of some negative consequences of MCTs; and to Brickell (1978) and Perkins (1982) for very useful overviews of arguments in favor of and against MCTs.

Standard Setting

One of the thorniest problems faced by those who initiate MCT programs is how to set the standards—that is, how to determine the acceptable minimums. If competency-testing standards are set arbitrarily, obviously students might be unfairly declared incompetent (or competent, for that matter) on the basis of factors that have little or nothing to do with their abilities. Concern that such arbitrariness be avoided has led to the development of many proposed standard-setting procedures and a voluminous research literature on the results of applying these various standard-setting methods. Coverage of this topic is beyond the scope of this book, but teachers should be aware that minimum cutoffs should not be set arbitrarily, and that considerable work has been done that can help guide them should they ever be involved in setting standards for competency tests. For those who need further information, Jaeger (1989) provides an excellent summary of prior thinking about the best way to set standards and establish defensible cutoff scores, and Webb (1995) discusses some important policy considerations related to standards and assessment decisions.

Legal Challenges to MCTs

Because most MCT programs are imposed by external bodies without any accompanying curriculum or syllabus, many school districts' curriculum and instruction are predictably not well matched with test content. As a result, many children fail, and the failure rate tends to be greater for poor and minority students (Airasian & Madaus, 1983; Haney, et al., 1993). This differential failure rate has led to a number of legal challenges to MCTs. Speaking of legal issues in competency testing, Anderson and her colleagues (Anderson et al., 1980, pp. 23–24) describe where MCT programs are most likely to "run afoul of the law":

Minimum competency testing requirements that incorporate some sanction upon students for failing to pass the tests run the greatest risk of legal challenge. These legal challenges are most likely to be raised if competency testing programs touch on any of the following issues:

- Potential for racial and linguistic discrimination
- Adequacy of advance notice and phase-in periods prior to the initial use of the test as a graduation requirement
- Psychometric validity or reliability of the tests
- Match between the instructional program and the test
- The degree to which remedial instruction may create or reinforce tracking

Failure to steer clear of these legal land mines has resulted in several lawsuits involving minimum competency testing, of which we will briefly mention only a few representative examples.

Debra P. *v.* Turlington (1981)

This case, filed initially in 1978, had its roots in Florida's 1976 legislation specifying that a functional literacy test be developed and used (along with other graduation requirements) to determine which Florida students should be awarded high school diplomas. Students would have three chances to pass the new "diploma test," which became known as the Florida Functional Literacy Test (FFLT). The first administration of the FFLT in 1977 resulted in a startling racial imbalance in its failure rate; whereas only 24 percent of the white students failed and were therefore judged functionally illiterate, 77 percent of the black students failed. By 1979, the racial imbalance was even worse (although the overall failure rates had dropped sharply), with 20 percent of Florida's black seniors and 2 percent of the state's white seniors to be denied high school diplomas. A group of black students and their parents challenged the test on grounds that it was biased and discriminatory on the basis of *race*. After six years of legal battling, focused both on the FFLT's validity and possible bias against blacks, an appeals court ruled that the test was both technically adequate and free of racial or ethnic bias, and declared that Florida had the authority to deny diplomas to students unable to pass the FFLT. This most widely publicized litigation concerning MCTs had ended with apparent victory for the proposition that the use of MCTs to deny diplomas is legally permissible, at least under certain circumstances.

Anderson *v.* Banks (1982)

Another legal test of MCTs challenged Georgia's Tattnall County School District's use of the California Achievement Test (CAT) as a proficiency exam (with students required to score at least at the 9.0 level in reading and mathematics to receive a high school diploma) on the basis that it created racially unfair diploma sanctions. After examining the test content and the district's curriculum objectives and text materials, the court found that the CAT was a fair test of the curriculum and could, as a proficiency exam, be used as a diploma requirement.

Bester *v.* Tuscaloosa City Board of Education (1984)

An Alabama school district's policy that elementary school students who fell below minimum reading levels required for their grade be retained rather than given "social promotions" triggered another challenge to MCTs. Implementation of this policy resulted in a retention rate for black students (24 percent) approximately four times that for white students (6 percent), and the plaintiffs argued that a district could not shift to a new minimum standard for reading if that shift resulted in blacks being retained more than whites. The court rejected this argument, holding that it was unreasonable to expect standards (and, by implication, minimum test scores) to remain fixed at unacceptably low levels.

Brookhart *v.* Illinois State Board of Education (1983)

This suit alleged that the Peoria school district's MCT requirement violated the constitutional rights of handicapped students. The court ruled that altering MCT content or cutoff scores to accommodate students with mental disabilities would thwart the very purpose and meaning of the diploma requirement. An appeals court did rule, however, that the schools must administer the MCTs in a manner that would minimize the impact of students' physical impairments on their test performance, making whatever modifications in test format and environment were necessary to permit physically handicapped students to demonstrate their actual knowledge.

So far, these court decisions have established general parameters concerning what MCT programs must do to avoid or survive legal challenges.

Characteristics of Legally Defensible MCTs

Recent court cases have defined the characteristics of MCT programs that are likely to withstand legal challenges. Madaus (1983) has listed the following characteristics:

1. Valid objectives describing skills that are truly basic competencies
2. A test that is a valid measure of those objectives
3. Evidence that the skills assessed are actually reflected in the curriculum and taught in the classrooms
4. Early assessment and identification of those needing remedial help
5. Provision of remedial help for all who require it
6. Sufficient advance notice and multiple opportunities to pass the competency test

Given our current societal climate, when so many disagreements end in litigation, testing programs as potentially controversial as MCT programs are likely to encounter further legal challenges. The issues surrounding MCTs will not be resolved soon. In the meantime, any educational agency contemplating using MCTs would be well advised to assure that their program meets the six criteria implicit in Madaus's list. They would also benefit from the insightful discussion of Mehrens and Popham (1992) about the legal defensibility of the high-stakes tests. Since we have not dealt here with the technical issues concerning MCTs (such as how to determine their validity) and will touch only lightly on such issues in Chapter 5, those who propose to use MCTs might wish to read Madaus's (1983) entire book or Berk's (1986) and Jaeger's (1989) excellent summaries of the status and potential of the MCT movement.

Application Problem 3

In general, how did MCTs fare in courts? What was the major issue that brought MCTs into courts? What are some major characteristics of legally defensible MCTs as discussed by the authors?

Right-to-Privacy Issues in Testing

In part to protect against invasion of privacy, governmental regulations have been established in the United States to ensure that individuals' rights—broadly understood to include not only rights to privacy, but also confidentiality and the need to obtain informed consent when such rights are waived—are protected whenever human behavior is measured.

With adults, privacy rights can be waived voluntarily through informed consent procedures; with children who are legal minors, however, the informed consent of parents (or legal guardians) to take a test is necessary if there could be any risk of psychological harm, embarrassment, or loss of privacy to the student. Routine classroom tests do not normally require such consent since they are embedded in the school curricula, and educators have traditionally been trusted to make sure that these routine tests are relevant and necessary to the educational goals being sought by the schools.

Sax (1980) makes some excellent suggestions on how not to invade students' privacy through thoughtless employment of dubious measurement devices for questionable purposes. His proposals underscore what should already be obvious to educators: students must not be exploited. Wherever measurement instruments are used for any purpose other than those of assisting students or reporting on their achievement, the purposes of using a measurement instrument must be explained thoroughly to parents, along with explanation of any potential risks, and an informed consent to test must be obtained from parents (or legal guardians).

Test Disclosure Issues in Testing

Critics feel that the testing industry and professionals who use its products are too secretive with test results, often withholding them even from examinees. Test disclosure was brought into sharp focus in the United States in 1974 with the passage of the "Buckley Amendment" (officially, the Family Education Rights and Privacy Act, or FERPA). This legislation directs those educational institutions receiving federal education funds to allow parents and eligible students access to all records pertaining directly to the student's school performance. Intended to bring student test scores and educators' interpretation of them "out of the closet," this law's impact has been limited, probably because it affects only federally funded education programs.

The concern that motivated the passage of FERPA reemerged in the form of so-called truth-in-testing proposals considered in the late 1970s in legislatures in several states, and even in the U.S. Congress. These proposals generally stemmed from a conviction that test content disclosure was a matter of simple fairness—allowing examinees to review test contents used to make important decisions about their future and permitting public scrutiny to hold the test industry accountable by ensuring that commercial tests are free of cultural, racial, or other forms of test bias.

These truth-in-testing laws, which require the disclosure of test content immediately after test administration, were eventually passed in a few states (for example, California and New York), but they met with strong resistance, both from the testing industry and from some sectors of the education profession. The major argument against test disclosure is very simple: "security" of standardized tests is important, and if you disclose items on a test, they cannot be used again in future test administration. Since producing quality test items is both time consuming and expensive, disclosure of test items and developing replacement items results in increased cost and/or decreased test quality. Not everyone accepts this rationale, however, and the debate about test disclosure continues. Interested readers are referred to Anderson et al. (1980), Bersoff (1981b), and Haney (1981, 1984) for more detailed discussion of the pros and cons of truth-in-testing.

There has been *some* apparent softening of positions on both sides, however. During the 1980s, some test publishers (for example, ETS and the College Board) moved toward liberalizing release of questions and answers on certain tests. These changes on the part of the testing industry could be viewed as bearing an olive branch to the critics. Yet the truce has been uneasy. Even amid evidence of test makers' increased awareness of test takers' feelings about test disclosure, the public clamor about this issue seems to ebb and flow. Shimberg (1990) reports that New York legislators have attempted to extend their 1980 truth-in-testing law to certification and licensing tests, even though a federal court in 1990 ruled that the state statute violated federal copyright law (Aiken, 1997, Chapter 13). So, the issue of test disclosure remains unresolved.

Ethical Considerations in Using Educational Measures

Many of the issues discussed in the previous sections are, implicitly or explicitly, *ethical* issues. Even if there were no legal constraints, the public welfare demands that all professionals who participate in the educational enterprise behave ethically in relation to all aspects of educational measurement. For most of us, potential test bias, invasion of privacy, and related issues are more ethical than legal concerns.

Testing ethics is the responsibility of two major groups: measurement professionals and test users.[7] Messick (1981) reminds his colleagues in the first group that "from the standpoint of scientific and professional responsibility in educational and psychological measurement, it seems clear that ethics, like character, begins at home" (p. 19). This sentiment has been echoed by other measurement professionals, who recognize their responsibility to protect the public's interests and have moved to ensure those interests through development and adherence to standards and principles that guide measurement practice.

Ethical Responsibilities of Measurement Professionals

Although many proposed sets of ethical guidelines and standards apply to educational measurement, and many efforts have been made to assure that measurement professionals behave ethically, the following standards seem the most directly pertinent.[8]

Standards for Educational and Psychological Tests or Testing

Earlier, we described the *Standards* produced jointly by APA, AERA, and NCME more than 20 years ago (APA, 1966) and revised twice to assure their relevance and currency (APA et al., 1974; AERA et al., 1985).[9] Long considered the bible (or at least the cardinal commandments) for test construction and use, these *Standards* were developed and approved by the three professional associations to which most measurement professionals belong. It may be overstating to say that all measurement professionals are guided by these *Standards* as they develop, refine, and critique educational measures; it is not an overstatement to say that they should be.

ETS Standards for Quality and Fairness of Testing

In 1981, the Educational Testing Service (ETS) adopted a set of standards to assure quality and fairness of their tests and testing programs. Revised later (ETS, 1987), the standards include principles, policies, and procedural guidelines of importance to test producers. Although intended primarily for use within ETS, these standards have heuristic value for any person seriously concerned with improving educational measurement through careful and ethical measurement practices.

Code of Fair Testing Practices in Education (1988)

In 1988, AERA, APA, NCME, the American Association for Counseling and Development, the Association for Measurement and Evaluation in Counseling and Development, and the American Speech-Language-Hearing Association formed a

---

[7]We recognize that these are not exclusive groups and that many measurement professionals also are "test users," but we use the latter term here to denote those who disavow special expertise in measurement.

[8]For an excellent summary of the history and development of standards and other efforts to improve tests and testing practices, see Millman and Harrington (1982).

[9]Currently, the fourth revision of the *Standards* is under way.

Joint Committee on Testing Practices whose charge was to produce this code. The purpose of the code is to clarify the obligations of professionals toward those who take educational tests used in admissions, educational diagnosis, student placement, and educational assessment. Instead of being concerned with teacher-made tests, the code is directed primarily at tests sold by commercial test publishers or used in large-scale assessment programs. The code depends on the *Standards* cited earlier, attempting to present a selected portion of those standards in a way that they can be understood by key stakeholders such as test takers and their parents and guardians.

Ethical Responsibilities of Test Users

Ethical responsibilities weigh as heavily upon the professionals who administer or interpret measurement instruments as upon those who develop and publish them. Measurement experts (for example, Sax, 1989) have outlined concerns about ethical and unethical conduct in testing. The authors of the *Standards* (APA et al., 1974; AERA et al., 1985) have developed nontechnical guidelines for test users, defining a test user as "one who chooses tests, interprets scores, or makes decisions based on test scores. (People who do *only* routine administration or scoring of tests are not included in this definition, although test users often do both.)" (APA, 1974, p. 1; emphasis added). The point that test users bear ethical responsibilities in their use of tests cannot be overemphasized. Ultimately, it is the *use* of a test that determines its appropriateness in any particular situation. No matter how good a test is, it can always be misused or abused, resulting in negative educational or social consequences.

In general, any educator who uses (or advises others in the use of) standardized tests should

1. Possess a general understanding of measurement principles.
2. Understand the limitations of tests and test interpretations.
3. Understand clearly the purposes for which a test is given and the probable consequences of scores resulting from it.
4. Be knowledgeable about the particular test used and its appropriate uses.
5. Receive (or arrange for others to receive) any training necessary to understand the test; its uses and limitations; and to administer, score, and interpret it.
6. Possess enough technical knowledge to be able to evaluate technical claims (for example, validity or reliability claims) made in the test manual.
7. Know the procedures necessary to reduce or eliminate bias in test selection, administration, and interpretation.
8. Advise examinees in advance of testing of the fact that they will be tested and of the purposes and nature of the testing.
9. Keep all standardized test materials secure at all times so as not to invalidate present or future uses of the test.
10. Provide examinees with information about correct procedures for filling out answer sheets (the *mechanics,* not the *substance* of responding).
11. Proctor and monitor examinees during testing to ensure that no academic dishonesty occurs.

12. Keep test scores confidential (except in certain circumstances that we will discuss later).

On the other hand, educators who use tests should not

1. Threaten examinees with use of test results or otherwise heighten examinees' anxiety about the test.
2. Teach the specific content of an upcoming test to future examinees.
3. Provide copies of actual test questions to examinees in advance, either in instructional materials or any other form.
4. Use standardized test questions on locally constructed tests.
5. Administer alternative forms of a test as practice for examinees scheduled to be tested with another form of the same test.
6. Deviate in *any* way from standardized procedures for administering, scoring, or interpreting a test.
7. Give extra help or any verbal or visual clues to examinees during test administration (except when clarifying a test of which the user is the author).
8. Attempt to raise examinees' scores through coercion, bribery, or competition.

Looking beyond the use of standardized tests to the broader issue of teacher competence in all forms of student assessment, a committee representing three major professional associations for teachers and measurement specialists (AFT, 1990) proposed that all teachers should be skilled in (1) choosing and developing assessment methods appropriate for instructional decisions; (2) administering, scoring, and interpreting the results of both externally produced and teacher-produced assessment methods; (3) using assessment results when making decisions about individual students, planning for teaching, and developing a curriculum; (4) communicating assessment results to students, parents, and other educators; and (5) recognizing unethical, illegal, and otherwise inappropriate assessment methods and uses of assessment information. We attempt to cover all these in this book.

Maintaining Confidentiality of Test Results

In general, it is an essential ethical canon that strict confidentiality of test scores should be maintained, and failure to do so is not only a serious ethical violation but is also illegal. In the context of measurement, *confidentiality* means that test results should not be revealed to anyone who does not have a legitimate need to know the scores. In some circumstances, however, confidentiality is not required, as in the following exceptions noted by Sax (1980):

1. If test results (for example, in a psychological examination) reveal a "clear and immediate danger" to a student or to others, other professionals or authorities may be advised of that danger.
2. If sharing a student's test scores with other professionals would be of significant help *to the student.*
3. Where test results are intended for use in making professional decisions about individuals (for example, promotion decisions) and are shared with appropriate professional personnel.
4. If a student waives the right to maintain confidentiality.

Ethical Problems Associated with Teaching to the Test

Popham (1987) popularized the term *high-stakes testing* to describe those test situations in which the results of testing (especially standardized achievement testing) were used in ways that could have severe negative consequences for *students* (for example, retention in grade, failure to graduate from high school or to gain entrance to postsecondary education), *school districts* (for example, published reports by the media that lead to ranking of districts, reductions in budget), and/or *teachers* (for example, reduced salary increments, requirements for inservice training). Based on surveys and interviews with public school teachers and administrators in all 50 states, Shepard (1990) concluded that 40 of the 50 state testing programs (or aggregation of local district test results) were in a high-stakes testing situation.

The Lake Wobegon Effect

In those situations where the results of standardized achievement testing are used to make important decisions, there is increasing concern that educators may use inappropriate strategies to raise the test scores. The controversy over such practices was fueled by a 1987 report by a West Virginia physician, John J. Cannell, that showed that the vast majority of school districts in the United States were reporting standardized achievement scores above the 50th percentile.

As anyone with a modicum of statistical training knows, it's impossible for more than half the population to be above the 50th percentile. Consequently, Cannell's observation was quickly dubbed the "Lake Wobegon" phenomenon in honor of the mythical Minnesota town immortalized by Garrison Keillor (in the "Prairie Home Companion" radio series) as a place where "All the women are strong, all the men are good-looking, and all the children are above average."

Different explanations were proposed for Cannell's Lake Wobegon phenomenon, including outdated norms and rising achievement (see, for example, Lenke & Keene, 1988; Williams, 1988). Cannell (1988, 1989) suggested that instead of these factors, the finding was best explained by inaccurate initial norms, inappropriate "teaching to the test" (or to be less diplomatic, cheating), and collusion and misrepresentation by test publishers to make schools look good and thus sell more tests.

Cannell's writing and rejoinders by others have generated a vigorous—and, in our opinion, healthy—debate over the role of standardized achievement testing in the school. That debate has highlighted the facts that (1) results from standardized achievement tests are frequently used inappropriately, and (2) some school personnel prepare students for taking tests in ways that are unethical, if not downright sleazy. Based on the currently available evidence, we do not believe that there has been any conscious effort or conspiracy on the part of publishing companies to make school districts look good for marketing purposes. Instead, we believe that the Lake Wobegon effect may be explained by a combination of the following four factors:

1. *Real gains in achievement have occurred since the time norms were calculated.* Although the gains in achievement are not nearly large enough to explain why the vast majority of school districts score above the 50th percentile, there is solid evidence that (1) achievement is improving nationally and (2) few achievement tests'

norms are kept very current. Thus the simple fact that the norms are increasingly outdated, juxtaposed with a rising achievement score trend, means that real, but relatively modest, achievement gains may be partly responsible for the dramatically better Lake Wobegon performance compared to the norms (Koretz, 1988; Lenke & Keene, 1988; Linn, Graue, & Sanders, 1990).

2. *Norms for standardized achievement tests may not be nationally representative.* Although test publishers attempt to obtain representative samples on which to calculate norms, they may not be successful for a variety of reasons. For example, Baglin (1981) showed that the reasons that determined which school districts do or do not participate in norming studies would contribute to findings similar to Cannell's report (see also Phillips & Finn, 1988; Shepard, 1990).

3. *Schools districts' efforts to match their curriculum with the test being used give those districts unfair advantages in comparisons with the norms.* A test publishing company selects schools to be in their norming sample without any consideration of how closely the curriculum in that district matches the content of the test. Thus norms are based on a sample of schools, some of which match the test objectives closely and some of which do not. When a school district selects a particular test to use, however, they may pay a great deal of attention to how well the test matches their curriculum. If efforts are made to revise a curriculum to match the test content, it should come as no surprise that their students' performance on that test may be higher than expected when compared to the norms.

4. *Inappropriate teaching to the test may yield spuriously high test scores.* Standardized test items are expected to represent the domain of instructional objectives that have been taught during the year. If the curriculum is structured so that students are given an opportunity to practice the specific items that are on the test over and over again, you would expect them to do better on the test than others who had not had an opportunity to practice those specific items. The same would be true, though to a lesser degree, with very similar items. Such dubious procedures have been referred to as "test score pollution" by Haladyna, Nolen, and Haas (1991) because they make it difficult to interpret the meaning of scores from such students in relation to the norming sample.

We believe that each of these four factors is in part responsible for Cannell's Lake Wobegon effect. Although the severity of some of these problems could be reduced by technical means (for example, more frequent norming of tests, or greater efforts to achieve nationally representative samples), teaching to the test—possibly a major contributor to the Lake Wobegon effect—is likely to remain with us as long as the results of tests are used to make important decisions.

But What's Wrong with Teaching to the Test?

There's nothing wrong with testing the same material that is being taught. In fact, it makes eminently good sense to do so. It does not make sense to give children a Spanish vocabulary test to determine how well they had mastered German vocabulary words. Such phrases as "integration of testing and instruction" (Nitko, 1989a), "instructional alignment" (Cohen & Hyman, 1991), and "measurement driven instruction" (Popham, 1987) are increasingly used to emphasize that testing and teaching should be closely related.

Although it makes good sense to test what is taught, to teach specifically the content of upcoming test items—teaching to the test or, as Linn and Gronlund (1995) call it, "teaching the test itself"—is generally regarded as unethical. In practice, it is sometimes difficult to discern precisely when legitimate efforts to ensure correspondence between what is taught and what is tested changes to inappropriate teaching to the test (that is, cheating). Not everyone agrees at what point the crossover from legitimate to illegitimate occurs. We can, however, define a number of points along that continuum and give you our recommendations.

The continuum along which we can link teaching and testing is summarized here (adapted from Haladyna et al., 1991; and Mehrens & Kaminsky, 1989), with the most legitimate linkages of teaching and testing listed first, and decreasing in legitimacy thereafter.

1. Using specific instructional objectives to guide your teaching, without knowing what objectives are covered by the particular standardized test used in your district
2. Motivating students to do their best on tests and teaching general test-taking skills (appropriate use of available time, deductive reasoning, familiarity with various testing formats, and so on)
3. Structuring the curriculum so that it corresponds to the objectives included in the standardized test used in your district
4. Teaching the specific format and objectives used in the test as a major part of the instructional activities
5. Teaching the *specific* content of an upcoming test to future examinees, but without using the actual test items
6. Under the guise of instruction, using one parallel form of a test for students to "practice," prior to administering another parallel form of the same test to students
7. Having students "practice," using the same form of the standardized test, or providing copies of actual test questions to examinees in advance, whether in instructional materials or any other form

Few would disagree with the first and second items in this list, but the third and fourth items may generate some disagreements. Probably most measurement professionals will agree that the last three items constitute inappropriate teaching to the test. Surprisingly, however, such activities are not uncommon. Gonzalez (1985) found that more than half the teachers interviewed in their study did not consider it cheating to have students practice on previous versions of the test currently used by the district. Almost a quarter thought it was acceptable for a teacher to teach students specific items from the standardized test if she happened to remember them from the last time the test was administered.

How much of an effect can teaching specific items from the test have? Quite a bit, actually. Shepard (1990) noted that for two of the most frequently used standardized achievement tests (the Stanford Achievement Test and the California Achievement Test), a third grader who scored at the median in reading, language, or mathematics would gain from two to seven percentile points by getting one additional item correct. Differences of that magnitude are likely to appear quite large when the local newspaper compares the results of two different schools.

Some people believe that the closer the alignment between what is taught and what is tested, the better the information will be about how well the students have mastered the intended content. Bright (1992) reported that many teachers held favorable views concerning aligning the curriculum with the content of standardized tests. People who take this position (for example, Cohen & Hyman, 1991; Popham, 1987; Ralph, 1994; Shaugnessy, 1994) see nothing wrong with having a one-to-one correspondence between the objectives and even the format of what is being taught and tested.

Others (for example, Linn & Gronlund, 1995; Madaus, 1985a; Mehrens & Kaminsky, 1989; Shepard, 1990) point out that in many situations, the test items are best thought of as representing a sample from a larger domain of skills, knowledge, and behaviors that are thought to be important for students to master. In these situations, close "instructional alignment" (a one-to-one correspondence of the objectives and format between what is taught and what is tested) will give a substantially inflated estimate of how well students have mastered the domain of material. To see why this is so, imagine that you are learning the Russian language. You have been informed that a list of 50 Russian vocabulary words will be the major focus of the next exam. Instead of concentrating on learning the Russian *language,* you spend a lot of time on those specific vocabulary words. The result of all this practice will likely be a high performance on the vocabulary test, which, unfortunately, does not necessarily mean you have attained good mastery of the language.

Another potential problem with such close alignment between teaching and testing is that over time, the objectives of the standardized test may begin to define what teachers are willing to spend time teaching. As Shepard (1990) pointed out, "test-curriculum alignment is a reciprocal process . . . once the test is chosen that best fits the curriculum, the practiced curriculum is adjusted further in response to the test" (p. 18). For example, Hatch and Freeman (1988) found that 67 percent of the kindergarten teachers in their sample implemented instructional practices that they thought were contrary to children's learning needs because they thought it would improve the children's scores on standardized achievement tests. Similarly, Darling and Wise (1985) found that many teachers stopped using essay tests in their classes because they had been told that the use of such tests during instruction would interfere with the students' performance on standardized multiple-choice tests.

We believe schools should provide students with broad coverage of important and meaningful content, as well as teaching them to generalize their learning to various other contexts and situations. Therefore, we believe that the objectives of any standardized test and the formats in which those objectives are measured should be viewed as a *sample* of the content in an area, not the universe of content for that area. More important, tests should not be treated as the ultimate goals of schooling. We also believe that educators should be allowed to thoughtfully establish their instructional objectives without undue concern about whether each particular objective is included on the standardized test used in their district.

Those beliefs lead us to a simple position. Even though teaching should be guided by clear instructional objectives and students should be taught general test-taking skills, it is entirely inappropriate to let teaching be substantially influenced by the objectives and item formats of a particular standardized test. It is even more inappropriate to use current or previous versions of the test as an "instructional tool."

Application Problem 4A

Provide several examples that illustrate unethical or questionable practices on the part of teachers in preparing students to take standardized achievement tests.

Application Problem 4B

Describe the Lake Wobegon effect. List all the plausible explanations you can think of for this phenomenon.

Issues in Using Tests for Teacher Certification

Tests have been used to evaluate teachers in a variety of *indirect* ways, including the unfortunate and usually unfair use of achievement test scores of students to judge teachers' ability. Here we are concerned with competency tests administered *directly* to teachers or teacher candidates as a basis for making decisions about certification or recertification.

The Impetus for Teacher Competency Testing

Sandefur (1985) contends that the movement to test teachers' competency was spawned by increased use of minimum competency testing to assess students' basic skills. As the public saw significant proportions of school students failing such tests, it seemed logical to ask how much of the blame could be traced to incompetent teaching. Soon lawmakers, responding to public opinion, were mandating that prospective teachers (and in some cases veteran teachers) be tested to assure their competency. Attitudes toward preservice testing and inservice testing for teachers are somewhat different, however. The use of competency tests for preservice certification decisions has spread quickly and is now a requirement in a majority of the United States (Jaeger, 1990). Relatively little opposition has been posed to such tests, even among teacher organizations. Not so for *re*certification tests, which have been vigorously opposed by most teachers and teacher organizations. Yet, legislators continue to ask why screening aimed at preventing those who are incompetent from entering teaching should not also be used to "weed out" the incompetent who already hold teaching positions.

Such concerns led to legislative mandates in some states (for example, Arkansas, Georgia, Texas) to test the competency of practicing educators. In a fascinating account of Texas' development and use of such a test, Shepard and Kreitzer (1987) trace the economic and political circumstances that resulted in perhaps the most widely publicized case of its type. Pressure for a "teacher test" began in 1983, when Texas' Select Committee on Public Education began conducting surveys and taking testimony relative to its charge. The committee heard numerous horror stories about the "incompetence" of some practicing teachers: "Apparently one teacher was said to have had difficulty explaining to her class why the weather was so different in Hawaii and in Alaska even though they were right next to each other (in the corner of the map)" (Shepard & Kreitzer, 1987, p. 24). Select Committee members also reported that teachers, arguing for pay raises, had sent them letters "that were peppered with bad grammar and misspelled words" (p. 24). Deeply concerned, the legislature mandated teacher testing to eliminate incompetent teachers. The result was the Texas Examination of Current Administrators and Teachers (TECAT), developed to assess minimum reading and writing skills (Shepard & Kreitzer, 1987). The TECAT was first administered to 202,000 Texas educators in 1986; the passing rate was high (96.7 percent), but 6579 teachers failed. Of those, 4704 were retested three months later, with 1199 failing this second time.

How do teachers perceive competency testing such as the TECAT? Opinions differ widely. In Texas, for example, half the teachers said that the test had done what legislators intended by getting rid of the bad teachers, while proving the majority competent. The other half complained that all teachers had been made to seem less competent by humiliation, embarrassment, and slanted media coverage that made the test seem laughably easy.

Legislative enthusiasm for testing veteran teachers seems to have crested and may now be waning. Shepard and Kreitzer (1987) reported that, when they began their study, "legislation to test practicing teachers was pending in two states and talked about in others. Today these actions are neither passed nor pending. We sense . . . that there is less enthusiasm to jump into teacher testing now than 18 months ago" (p. 31). Also, the TECAT has been ruled discriminatory by a federal agency, and its use threatens Title VII litigation (Kuehn, Stallings, & Holland, 1990). So, for those in other states, the publicity surrounding the TECAT may yet serve to cause caution in their legislative assemblies.

On the U.S. national scene, both major teacher organizations, the National Education Association (NEA) and the American Federation of Teachers (AFT), have voiced support in favor of a national test for certifying *prospective* teachers (Aiken, 1997; Shanker, 1985), but they both oppose testing of veteran teachers (Martin, 1986; Madaus & Pullin, 1987), although the AFT would soften its opposition if certain concessions were granted to teachers who failed. The National Board of Professional Teaching Standards, an organization formed for the purpose of upgrading the teaching profession, however

> has undertaken the development of systems of assessments designed for *experienced* teachers. The assessments are intended to provide accomplished teachers with an opportunity to demonstrate high levels of professional performance. Candidates who meet the Board's standards receive certification, which it is expected will be recognized and rewarded by states and districts. (Linn & Gronlund, 1995, p. 487; emphasis added)

Types of Teacher Competency Tests in Use

Teacher competency tests can take varying forms, focusing on one or more of the following clusters: (1) basic skills, (2) subject area knowledge, (3) professional knowledge and skills (pedagogical), and (4) on-the-job performance (Conklin, 1985; Linn & Gronlund, 1995). Some states use only one of these types of measures, whereas others use some combination in their assessment of teacher competency. The National Teacher Examinations (NTE) attempt to assess all but on-the-job performance. Despite the breadth of the NTE, however, the chances of serious errors in judging teaching competence by any single test or test battery are nontrivial. In addition, there exists the concern that "certification tests do not assess critical characteristics of good teachers like dedication, caring, and integrity" (Linn & Gronlund, 1995, p. 487). Because of this and other similar concerns, a multifaceted approach is considered much more promising for teacher assessment. As noted by Shulman (1987, p. 39): "The ideal teaching assessment is unlikely to take the form of a single examination for which a candidate 'sits' during a designated period, as is the case with the NTE and its state-level equivalents."

The Pros and Cons of Teacher Competency Testing

Many educationists (for example, Popham & Kirby, 1987) argue that assessment of teaching competence should not stop with *applicants* for teaching positions, but should also be required of *occupants* of such positions. And some teacher groups agree. For example, one of the strongest statements in favor of competency testing for prospective teachers originates with the AFT, America's largest teachers' union, which urges tough teacher exams coupled with high financial incentives for those who pass. Also, there is some empirical evidence that such minimum competency testing for prospective teachers improves the quality of the teaching force (for example, Tanner, 1995).

Not everyone is enamored with the idea of teacher competency tests, however. Conklin (1985) questions their use because there is no research evidence that passing such an exam is related to on-the-job success in teaching. In addition, such a requirement may further exacerbate the already acute lack of minority teachers in schools (Tanner & Pohan, 1992). The validity of teacher competency tests has also been challenged in court. Beginning in the early 1970s, a number of lawsuits charged that the NTE was being used to discriminate against minority teachers and teacher candidates.

The legal outcomes were mixed. In some (for example, *Georgia Association of Educators* v. *Nix,* 1976), the court ruled that the NTE could not be used as a criterion for awarding teaching certificates. In others (for example, *United States* v. *South Carolina,* 1977), the court dismissed the charge that state use of the NTE for teacher certification had racially discriminatory purposes. D'Costa (1993) provides both a succinct summary of the legal impact on teacher competency testing and some recommendations for legal and fair teacher competency testing.

Legal battles over the use of teacher competency tests will probably continue as long as such tests are used, and the issue of their validity remains unresolved. But experience suggests caution in basing teacher certification or recertification decisions solely on competency examinations. For those who want to pursue this topic in greater depth, we suggest reading Beckham (1986), Madaus and Pullin (1987), Shepard and Kreitzer (1987), Carlson (1990), and D'Costa (1993).

Two points can be made here, however. First, teacher competency tests can measure basic verbal and numerical ability and subject matter knowledge very adequately. Second, although they are useful in assessing whether teachers possess essential verbal and intellectual abilities, teacher competency tests are not now (and possibly never will be) of much value in measuring teaching skills.

Application Problem 5

Based on your understanding about the issues involved in teacher certification testing, what are some major social factors or concerns that have provided an environment in which teacher certification or recertification testing is urged by policymakers?

SUGGESTED READINGS

AERA, APA, & NCME. (1985). *Standards for educational and psychological testing.* Washington, DC.

This is the most recent set of standards for educational and psychological testing. This booklet describes the purpose of the *Standards* and cautions that should be exercised in applying them. The volume lists and explains (1) technical standards for test construction and evaluation; (2) standards for test use; (3) standards for particular applications in testing minorities and those with disabilities; and (4) standards for administrative procedures. The *Standards* is currently under revision at the time of this writing and may be published about the same time as this book.

Bersoff, D. N. (1981). Testing and the law. *American Psychologist, 36*(10), 1047–1056.

This article reviews court cases dealing with (1) cultural bias in educational tests, (2) the validity of employment tests, and (3) the disclosure of test materials. An excellent summary of legal interpretations of psychometric concepts.

D'Costa, A. G. (1993). The impact of courts on teacher competence testing. *Theory into Practice, 32,* 104–112.

This article provides a concise summary of the legal challenges to teacher competency testing, describing key legal provisions and examining the legal impact on testing and teacher certification. It also makes some recommendations for legal, credible, and fair teacher competency testing.

Educational Measurement: Issues and Practice (1988), 7(4).

This is a special issue devoted to Cannell's report that the vast majority of school districts in the United States have accomplished the impossible by reporting standardized achievement test scores above the median. Following the lead article by Cannell, representatives from the U.S. Department of Education and most major test publishing firms respond. The debate highlights some major issues about standardized achievement testing.

Jaeger, R. M. (1989). Certification of student competence. In R. L. Linn (ed.), *Educational Measurement* (3rd ed). London: Collier Macmillan, pp. 485–514.

This chapter contains an excellent summary of issues pertaining to the MCT movement, including (1) definitions of competency testing; (2) the breadth of efforts to use MCTs in the United States, including examples of two very different MCT programs; (3) various methods for setting standards and research evidence on their relative usefulness; (4) strategies for assuring students opportunities to learn the minimum competencies; (5) legal issues pertaining to MCTs; and (6) social and curricular consequences of competency testing.

Reynolds, C. R. (1994). Bias in testing. In R. J. Sternberg (ed.), *Encyclopedia of human intelligence.* New York: Macmillan.

This book chapter offers insightful discussion about the major issues related to test bias, especially cultural bias in testing, and the implications of this controversy in the major aspects of testing. The discussion in this chapter is concise. Nevertheless, interested readers may find the discussion very thought provoking.

SUGGESTION SHEET

If your last name starts with the letter B, please complete the Suggestion Sheet at the end of the book while this chapter is still fresh in your mind.

Answers to Chapter 2 Application Problems

In general, the application problems in this chapter deal with controversial issues, so there cannot be any standard answers. What we have provided here are tentative answers that may contain our personal bias. Our intention is not to provide prescriptive answers, but rather to stimulate and facilitate discussion. We fully realize that other answers, even some contrary to what we have provided here, may be as good as, or even better than, ours.

1. In general, intelligence tests did not fare that well in courts. In most of the court cases that ruled against intelligence or aptitude tests, the performance difference between social/cultural groups was considered sufficient evidence of test bias against minority groups. Although the performance difference between social/cultural groups may indicate *potential* test bias, other factors (for example, socioeconomic environment) may cause *real* performance differences between groups, and the test may simply function as the messenger. If this is the case, society may have a strong interest in understanding these contributing factors so that measures can be taken to correct the situation.

2. Some hypothetical examples in which test bias most likely exists.
   a. A math test contains many word problems, and the word problems require a certain level of reading proficiency. This test is administered to two groups: one group of native speakers of English who have no trouble understanding the word problems, and another group of ESL (English as Second Language)

students who are still struggling with their English language. In this situation, the math test is most likely biased against the ESL students because their performance on the math test depends not only on their math knowledge, but also, or even more important, on their English-language proficiency level. On the other hand, for the group of native speakers of English, their performance is almost solely dependent on their knowledge in math.

b. A reading test for fifth graders contains many reading paragraphs about weapons, wars, and heroic soldiers and generals. Because boys tend to be more interested in these topics in general in this culture, they may have more previous exposure to these and similar topics than girls, and consequently, they may be more familiar with the vocabulary in these reading paragraphs. If this is true, this reading test may contain some inherent bias against girls. A better reading test should contain reading paragraphs about a variety of topics so as to minimize such potential bias.

3. In general, MCTs have fared well in courts—much better than the intelligence tests we discussed previously. The major issue that caused so much litigation for MCTs is the disparity of passing rates among ethnic groups for MCTs. The most important issue for an MCT is its content validity: how well an MCT reflects school curriculum objectives. As discussed in this chapter, several characteristics are important for legally defensible MCT: valid objectives for basic competencies, such objectives are truthfully and validly reflected in the test, the skills assessed by the MCT are actually taught in the school curriculum, remedial help and multiple opportunities for those who need it for passing the MCT are provided, and so on.

4. a. Some examples of unethical practice in preparing students for standardized tests are (1) a teacher intentionally uses some actual items from the test (or items very similar to those on the test) for students to practice, and (2) a teacher uses a parallel form of the standardized test for students to practice.

b. The Lake Wobegon effect was used to describe the phenomenon that a majority of school districts reported students' performance above the national norm average. Some explanations for such a phenomenon are (1) the norms used for comparisons are outdated; (2) the norms used for comparisons are not truly nationally representative; (3) students have made real progress; and (4) under the pressure for better students' performance, many school districts have more closely aligned their school curricula with the objectives of the standardized tests.

5. Two prominent factors contributing to teacher certification or recertification testing are (1) many students were failing the minimum competency tests, and (2) the public was concerned that incompetent teaching might be partially the cause for many students' failures in minimum competency testing.

BEGINNING YOUR EXCURSION

An Overview of Basic Measurement Concepts and Principles

In this second section of our text, we attempt to accomplish three things. First, throughout this section, we provide more precise definitions of various types of measures and some of the basic concepts and principles pertaining to such measures. In Section I, we avoided dwelling on terminology, definitions, and technical concepts, but we cannot maintain that posture here. You need now to understand some of the basic concepts and principles that underlie educational measurement and assessment. If we were to consider your learning about measurement and assessment as a voyage into "strange waters" that may appear to you uncharted and possibly difficult to navigate, then we would serve you poorly if we failed to provide you with all the charts and navigational aids possible, together with a simple but solid anchor or two for when you feel yourself drifting. This section is intended to provide you with the basic navigational and survival aids you will require on your excursion. (And don't let that word "survival" scare you; you'll make it if you are just willing to keep paddling!)

Second, in Chapter 3, we help you learn to read, interpret, and understand test scores, introducing you to various types of test scores and the ways each should be interpreted. We also provide simple descriptions of some statistical concepts necessary to understanding test results.

Third, in Chapters 4 and 5, we review what makes an educational measure good or bad, trustworthy or treacherous. We outline characteristics of measures that discriminate between high and low quality measures, discussing and providing examples of a test's usefulness, validity, and reliability. We discuss how to make test results more objective and how to reduce errors in measurement. In Chapter 4 we focus on the important characteristic of reliability. In Chapter 5 we turn our attention to the vital characteristic of validity, and how it is affected by reliability. In both of these chapters we try to help you see what is necessary for an educational test to be considered really useful.

Finally, in Chapter 6, we discuss techniques for reducing errors that can readily creep into test scores if we are not vigilant in detecting and ejecting them. Dozens of extraneous factors—such as how the test is administered, or distractions in the testing environment, or students' guessing when they don't know an answer—can confound test results. Chapter 6 is intended to help you identify and be alert to such factors and enable you to take steps to reduce or eliminate their influence on tests for which you are responsible.

We know we just used a few terms that could set your alarm flags fluttering—words like "statistical concept." But don't hoist them to the masthead just yet. Give us a chance to prove that we can guide you safely across the technical and conceptual shoals where so many practitioners have shipwrecked previously. It really is not a difficult voyage, and once past it, you'll be in the deep and calm waters where you can use the tools provided in these chapters to chart your own course and sail in whatever direction you please in using educational measurement and assessment to help you ply your professional practice.

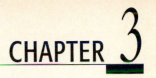

Learning to Read the Signposts

What Do Those Test Scores Really Mean?

OVERVIEW

Most of you are probably already more adept at using statistics than you think. Decisions you make every day about how far you drive your car between fill-ups, how you dress for the weather, where you invest your money, and who you think will win the World Series are all influenced and made easier by your use of statistics—conscious or not.

There are many different types of statistics, and some statistical procedures are very complex. But for virtually everything you will need as a successful educator, Ludwig Meis van der Rohe's observation that "less is more" is as applicable to statistics as to architecture. This chapter will provide you the basic tools needed to convert the raw materials of test scores and results to meaningful and useful summaries. Understanding all the techniques presented in this chapter requires only *simple arithmetic,* a hand calculator, a *willingness to try,* and an open mind. If you have not taken an introductory statistics course before, you may need to review the contents of this chapter several times. However, you will do just fine if you can count to a hundred; add, multiply, subtract, and divide; and push the square root button on a calculator.

OBJECTIVES

Upon completing your study of this chapter, you should be able to

1. Develop a frequency distribution from a set of scores, and use a frequency distribution to summarize and interpret test scores.
2. Explain the importance of a normal curve in examining human behavior.

3. Compare and contrast different measures of central tendency (mean, median, and mode), and identify situations in which different measures of central tendency would be the most appropriate.

4. Explain why the concept of standard deviation is important in interpreting test scores.

5. Understand the concept of correlation, and explain why correlations are important in interpreting measurement data.

6. Describe the pros and cons of different methods of reporting test scores (raw scores, percentiles, standardized scores, and so on), and give an example of a situation in which each method of reporting test scores would be appropriate.

7. Given a standardized test report, interpret the results for various audiences (for example, school administrators, teachers, parents, students).

Acquiring the Basic Tools of Interpretation

The French philosopher Poincaire, once said, "Science is made up of facts as a house is with stones. But a collection of facts is no more a science, than a heap of stones is a house." So it is with test scores. A test administered to a class of 100 students sometimes produces only a heap of numbers that are neither useful nor understandable. As an educator, you are responsible for making sense of that heap of numbers. Fortunately, some simple tools can help.

Organizing Measurement Data

As an example, consider a hypothetical test designed to measure students' reading comprehension. Assume that a teacher administers this 20-item reading test to 120 students and obtains the scores shown in Table 3.1.

The teacher now has a whole heap of data and a lot of questions. For example, the teacher may want to know

- What was the average score on the test?
- Are children in her class better or worse than other children of the same age?
- What percentage of her students got 80 percent or more of the questions correct?
- Which children have the highest and lowest scores on the test?

Before such questions can be easily answered, the numbers have to be organized. By looking at the information in Table 3.1, you could eventually determine that the low score was 3 and the high score was 20. Other than this, it is difficult to draw conclusions about the scores in the table. The need to interpret and use test scores is what led to organizational techniques such as those shown in Figure 3.1. Let's consider some of the advantages of each technique.

Table 3.1   List of Reading Comprehension Scores in Alphabetical Order of Students' Last Names

3	10	9	12	11	9
19	15	5	8	15	13
7	17	18	10	7	4
10	12	12	13	16	11
12	20	11	9	10	9
13	8	4	12	14	17
14	11	10	14	8	12
12	12	7	12	10	11
7	15	8	4	6	16
11	9	11	16	15	11
12	10	16	14	13	14
8	17	6	13	10	6
16	14	13	10	12	8
9	12	9	13	14	7
15	16	13	6	10	15
6	11	12	11	9	9
13	13	15	12	17	11
7	8	8	8	7	8
18	12	11	18	14	10
10	19	13	15	12	5

Frequency Distribution

The simplest organizational technique is a *frequency distribution,* such as that shown in Figure 3.1(a). To construct a frequency distribution by hand, list the possible scores *in order,* and then make a tally each time a particular score occurs. The resulting display shows the *frequency* with which scores are *distributed* across the possible range—hence the name *frequency distribution.* In situations where there are too many discrete score points to display, scores can also be grouped into score ranges, and the frequency within each score range can be tallied and displayed.

Alternatively, the information shown in Figure 3.1(a) can be represented graphically, as in Figure 3.1(b) or Figure 3.1(c). Figure 3.1(b) is a *frequency polygon* where each of the possible scores on the test is represented along the horizontal axis. For each score, the height of the dot above the horizontal baseline corresponds to the frequency with which that score occurred, and the dots are all connected by a line.

For example, two children obtained a score of 5. Hence the dot directly above the 5 on the horizontal line (representing a score of 5) is parallel with the cross-hatch corresponding to the number 2 on the vertical line. Frequency polygons are often used in computer programs to represent distributions of scores. Again, when there are too many discrete score points, a frequency polygon can be constructed for score ranges instead of individual scores.

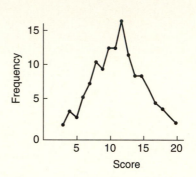

(a)
Frequency Distribution

Score	Tallies	Number of Students with Each Score
1		
2		
3	I	1
4	III	3
5	II	2
6	ℍℍ	5
7	ℍℍ II	7
8	ℍℍ ℍℍ	10
9	ℍℍ IIII	9
10	ℍℍ ℍℍ II	12
11	ℍℍ ℍℍ II	12
12	ℍℍ ℍℍ ℍℍ I	16
13	ℍℍ ℍℍ I	11
14	ℍℍ III	8
15	ℍℍ III	8
16	ℍℍ I	6
17	IIII	4
18	III	3
19	II	2
20	I	1

(b)
Frequency Polygon

(c)
Histogram or Bar Graph

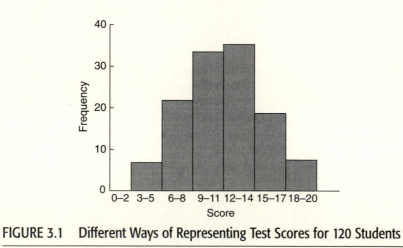

FIGURE 3.1   Different Ways of Representing Test Scores for 120 Students

Figure 3.1(c) shows another way of representing the same information as a *histogram,* or *bar graph.* In this display, values that fall within a certain range (for example, all the numbers between 6 and 8 inclusive) are shown in a bar whose height indicates the number of scores in that range. The resulting histogram, or bar graph, is particularly useful when the range of possible scores is large. In such cases, groups of scores can be combined so that the resulting graph is more readable. For example, the six scores between 3 and 5 inclusive are shown by the first bar on the left, and the 35 scores between 12 and 14 inclusive are represented by the tallest bar.

The information in Figure 3.1 shows why a picture is worth a thousand words. As sets of data become large, it grows increasingly difficult to comprehend, organize, and extract meaning from numbers without tools such as these. Generally, a frequency polygon is preferred for depicting *continuous* data (that is, data that occur along some unbroken continuum, such as test scores), and a histogram or bar graph is better for depicting noncontinuous data (for example, type of automobile—Ford, Chevrolet, Volvo, or Porsche) that cannot be ordered along a continuum. The most important consideration, however, is whether the display communicates effectively.

Application Problem 1

Listed here are 30 scores obtained on a test of biology terms for a ninth-grade science class. Construct a frequency distribution and frequency polygon for these scores.

71	75	64	71	66	70
67	68	66	69	71	67
72	66	71	67	69	69
69	70	70	68	68	68
69	68	67	68	72	68

The Normal Curve and Other Distributions

You may have already heard of the *normal curve* (often referred to as a *bell-shaped* distribution). Understanding the normal curve is fundamental to all that happens in statistics and measurement. Interestingly, many human characteristics (height, strength, ability to memorize, size of vocabulary and the like) are more or less distributed according to a normal curve.

Figure 3.2 shows a theoretical normal curve—symmetrical and shaped like a bell. Notice that it is similar to the frequency polygon you just constructed, with the numbers along the horizontal axis representing scores, and the height of the curve at any point indicating the frequency of each score. This normal curve looks a little different from the frequency polygon in Figure 3.1 because the vertical axis is omitted and the points are connected with a smooth curve instead of straight lines. Nonetheless, you can gather much of the same information by looking at a smooth curve as you can by looking at a frequency polygon. For example, from Figure 3.2, it is clear that the majority of the observations in this set of data fall between 85 and 115. The median (in this case, 100) of the distribution can be determined by identifying the point where about half the scores are above and half are below. Normal curves are used frequently in measurement to provide a general sense of score distribution.

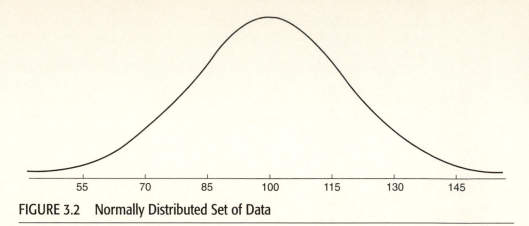

| 55 | 70 | 85 | 100 | 115 | 130 | 145 |

FIGURE 3.2   Normally Distributed Set of Data

Although many human characteristics approximate a normal curve, there are few, if any, mathematically perfect normal distributions. Because of these "departures from normality," most smooth curves you see will not look exactly like that in Figure 3.2. However, all smooth curves can be divided into two large categories: those that are approximately *symmetrical* (one half of the curve is a mirror image of the other) and those that are *asymmetrical* (one half of the curve is *not* a mirror image of the other). There are an infinite variety of curves in both categories. Figures 3.3(a) through 3.3(c) show distributions that are symmetrical though not perfectly normal. These distributions are respectively, too *peaked* (for example, the points are *scrunched* together near the middle of the distribution) or too flat, or the *tails* (for example, the part of the distribution greater than about 120 and less than about 80) are too *thick*. Unless they are too severe, such departures are relatively inconsequential for most applications.

For purposes of measurement, two departures from normality are important to understand: *bimodal* distributions and *skewed* distributions. Let us consider each.

Bimodal Distributions

To understand the term *bimodal* (which means two modes), we must define the concept of *mode*. The mode is the value within a distribution that occurs most frequently. Because frequency of occurrence is indicated by the height of the curve, the mode occurs at the highest part of the curve. Figure 3.3(d) shows a truly bimodal distribution because two distinct points are higher than all the rest (these two points, or two modes, are about 90 and 115, respectively). Although not truly bimodal, Figure 3.3(g) is often referred to as bimodal because it has two distinct "humps"—even though one is substantially lower than the other. Because most human characteristics approximate a normal distribution, you should be curious and perhaps even cautious when you encounter a bimodal distribution. Generally speaking, a bimodal distribution is more likely to occur when the number of data points included in the sample is small. Given a reasonably large sample, if you encounter a bimodal distribution, it may indicate some problems in how the variable is defined or measured, or it may simply indicate that your sample consists of two distinctively different subgroups with respect to that variable.

Examples of Symmetrical Curves

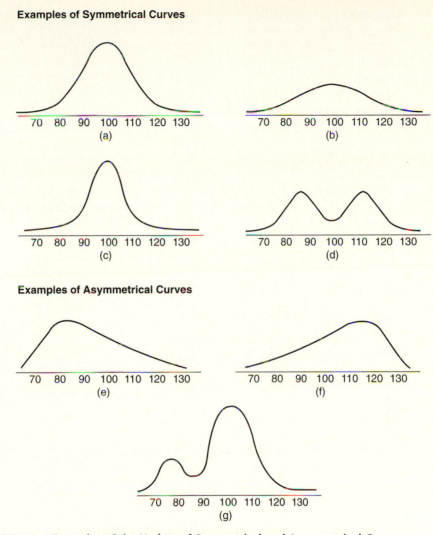

FIGURE 3.3   **Examples of the Variety of Symmetrical and Asymmetrical Curves**

Skewed Distributions

The most frequent way in which data depart from normality is when a distribution is *skewed*. A skewed distribution has the majority of the data points clustered at one end. Distributions may be *positively* skewed, for example, Figure 3.3(e), where most of the scores are bunched toward the low end with a long tail pointing toward the high/positive end, or *negatively* skewed, for example, Figure 3.3(f), where most of the scores are bunched toward the high end with a long tail pointing toward the low/negative end of the distribution.

Recognizing seriously skewed distributions is important in measurement. For example, when a distribution is positively skewed, it shows that most of the group scored poorly (the majority of the scores are bunched toward the low end of the distribution), but a few students did very well (as indicated by the much lower height of the tail pointing in the positive direction). The question to ask is, Why? It may be that most students did poorly because the test was too difficult, many of the items were confusing, the content was not taught well, or not enough time was allowed for the test. Tests that result in positively skewed distributions are said to have a *floor effect* because the majority of the scores are found to be at the *floor,* or the bottom of the distribution.

A negatively skewed distribution provides a similar warning, with most of the students bunched at the top of the distribution, and only a few students in the tail pointing in a negative direction. This is often called a *ceiling effect,* suggesting that the test may have been too easy for most of the class, or a copy of the answers may be circulating.

The shape of a distribution of test scores (for example, normal or skewed) has different implications in various testing situations. Broadly speaking, in terms of test score interpretation, two different measurement situations warrant our attention at this time: norm-referenced measurement and criterion-referenced measurement.

In *norm-referenced* measurement, we want to know where a student scores in relation to other students. In other words, norm-referenced measurement determines how a given student's test score compares with the scores of other students who took the test. The group of test scores is called the norm group. Norm-referenced measurement involves giving meaning to an individual's test score by comparing it to the scores of others taking the same test.

With *criterion-referenced* measurement, on the other hand, we are interested in how a student's test performance compares to some absolute standard without comparison to others' performance. Criterion-referenced measures are often used when a minimum level of mastery has been set that a student must attain before being allowed to proceed to the next unit of instruction. Criterion-referenced measures are typically used to determine whether students have "mastered" specific instructional content or to describe students' progress through well-defined curricula.

Norm-referenced tests that exhibit floor or ceiling effects are usually not an accurate measure of students' ability. A ceiling effect on a test suggests that some students would have done better had they not "bumped" into the ceiling. If more difficult items had been included, providing the more capable students with an opportunity to demonstrate their skills, the distribution of scores would have been more spread out because some, but not all, of them would have achieved even higher scores. With most criterion-referenced tests, however, you should expect a ceiling effect if the content has been effectively taught. The presence of a floor effect suggests that many of the test items are too difficult since the scores do not differentiate between the average and the least capable students because most of the students do poorly.

Measures of Central Tendency

Statisticians use the term *measures of central tendency* to refer to various types of averages. For most people, average connotes *being in the middle.* Because there are different ways to be in the middle, there are three commonly used measures of central tendency, each with its advantages and disadvantages under different conditions. Each measure of central tendency is an effort to describe a set of scores when we must rely on *one number* to describe a whole set of numbers. After defining and giving an example of the various measures of central tendency—the *mean*, the *median*, and the *mode*—we will help you decide which measure to use in what situation.

Definitions and Examples

Of the three measures of central tendency, the *mean* is the most frequently used. This is what most people have in mind when they refer to an "average" score. Whenever someone talks about a basketball player's scoring average or the average temperature for a particular time of year, he or she is probably referring to the mean. The mean is simply an arithmetic average: the sum of *all* the scores, divided by the *number* of scores. Because we emphasize the relevant statistical concepts, not statistical computation, throughout this book, we present the basic statistical formulas, including that for the mean, in Appendix A, rather than in the text. Interested readers should refer to Appendix A for the basic formulas involved in our discussion and some computational examples. As a simple example for the mean, consider the nine scores shown in Table 3.2. The mean of these nine scores is their sum (226) divided by the number of scores (9), which equals 25.11.

The *median* of a distribution is the value in the middle when all scores are ordered from lowest to highest, as shown in Table 3.2. It is easy to see that 25 is the score in the middle, or the median. The abbreviation most often used for median is *Mdn*. When there is an even number of scores and no one score is in the middle, the median is the arithmetic average of the two middle scores. The *mode* of a distribution is the score that occurs most frequently. The mode of this distribution is 27, since it is the only score that occurs more than once. Some distributions may have more than one mode, as explained previously in the discussion of bimodal distributions.

Comparing the Mean, Median, and Mode

Depending on the shape of distribution, the three measures of central tendency can be the same or very similar, or they can be quite different. To better understand the potential differences among these three commonly used measures, let's consider the hypothetical situation shown in Figure 3.4 for the salaries of employees in a school district.

Table 3.2   Examples of Mean, Median, and Mode

24	40	33
27	27	17
18	15	25

(a) Mean $\overline{X}$ = (24 + 27 + 18 + 40 + 27 + 15 + 33 + 17 + 25) ÷ 9 = 25.11

(b) Median (Mdn) = middle score = 25: 15 17 18 24 25 27 27 33 40

(c) Mode = most frequent score = 27: 15 17 18 24 25 27 27 33 40

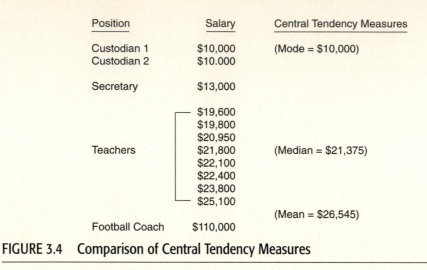

Position	Salary	Central Tendency Measures
Custodian 1	$10,000	(Mode = $10,000)
Custodian 2	$10.000	
Secretary	$13,000	
Teachers	$19,600	
	$19,800	
	$20,950	
	$21,800	(Median = $21,375)
	$22,100	
	$22,400	
	$23,800	
	$25,100	
		(Mean = $26,545)
Football Coach	$110,000	

FIGURE 3.4   Comparison of Central Tendency Measures

In this salary distribution, the mean is far from the median, which in turn, is far from the mode. Obviously, the mean is greatly influenced by one extreme value, the salary of the football coach. If you were representing the teachers union negotiating with the school district for salary increases, which central tendency measure would you prefer to use to demonstrate that the current salary level is too low? Which central tendency measure would you prefer if you were representing the school district's management and wanted to minimize salary increases? This example demonstrates a general fact: the mean can be greatly influenced by *extreme* scores, especially when you are dealing with a small group, whereas the median and mode are not.

Selecting the Most Appropriate Measure of Central Tendency

Consider the frequency polygons shown in Figure 3.5. As seen in Figure 3.5(a), when distributions are symmetrical, it makes no difference which measure of central tendency is used because all three will have the same value. It is only when distributions are positively or negatively skewed, or have several unusually extreme values, that the mean, median, and mode will be substantially different.

In general, the mean is the most stable measure of central tendency. In other words, if you were to measure the same characteristic among a group of individuals on two different occasions, the two mean scores would tend to differ less than the two medians or the two modes. Mean scores, however, are significantly influenced by extreme scores, or by *skewness,* particularly in small samples. As shown in Figure 3.5(b), a positively skewed distribution tends to pull the mean toward the positive end. A negatively skewed distribution (Figure 3.5(c)) pulls the mean toward the negative end.

Where we want to minimize the influence of extreme scores, the median provides the best indicator of central tendency. By "best" we mean that, if you have to

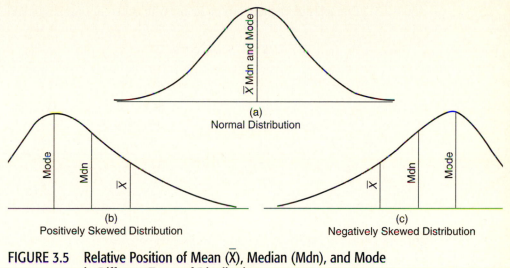

FIGURE 3.5   Relative Position of Mean ($\overline{X}$), Median (Mdn), and Mode in Different Types of Distributions

use only *one number* to describe a distribution, the median will be closer to the truth for more people. Such situations arise frequently in education, and the median should be more widely used than it is. For example, if a test is very easy, students' scores will cluster at the top of the distribution. In such cases, the median is a better indicator of average achievement than the mean.

The mode tends to be very unstable when sample size is small. Generally, where scores exist along a continuum or range, both the median and mean provide a better indication of the average.

As a final illustration of the differences among these three measures of central tendency, we repeat an anecdote given by two of our colleagues.

Five men sat together on a park bench. Two were vagrants, each with total worldly assets of 25 cents. The third was a workman whose bank account and other assets totaled $2000. The fourth man had $15,000 in various forms. The fifth was a millionaire with a net worth of $5 million. Therefore, the mode of the cash worth of the group was 25 cents. This figure describes two of the persons perfectly, but is grossly inaccurate for the other three. The median figure of $2000 does little justice to anyone except the workman. The mean, $1,003,400.10, is not very satisfactory even for the millionaire. If we *had* to choose one measure of central tendency, perhaps it would be the mode, which describes 40 % of this group accurately. But if we were told that "the modal assets of 5 persons sitting on a park bench were 25 cents," we would be likely to conclude that the total assets of the group are approximately $1.25, which is more than $5 million lower than the correct figure. Obviously, no measure of central tendency whatsoever is adequate for these "strange bench fellows," who simply do not tend centrally. (Hopkins & Stanley, 1981, pp. 32–33)

Table 3.3   Examples of Distributions of Scores with Different Degrees of Variability

		Groups		
	W	X	Y	Z
	65	50	44	30
	40	35	32	30
	30	30	30	30
	20	25	28	30
	5	20	26	30
Mean =	**32**	**32**	**32**	**30**
Median =	**30**	**30**	**30**	**30**

Obviously, even though measures of central tendency are very useful in describing most distributions, sometimes no measure of central tendency is appropriate. Often, it is best to report two or three different measures of central tendency. Or if the number of data points is small, simply report all the data.

Measures of Dispersion

Although a well-chosen measure of central tendency is informative, it generally does not tell us nearly enough about the distribution of scores. To understand why this is so, consider Table 3.3. Each of these four groups has identical median scores, and three have identical mean scores. Yet the variability of scores, that is, the difference among the scores in the various groups, is very different. Minimum and maximum scores range from 60 points in Group W to 30 points in Group X, 18 points in Group Y, and *no* difference in Group Z.

Whereas measures of central tendency provide information about a test's overall difficulty, measures of dispersion (often called measures of *variability*) provide information about differences among scores. In other words, measures of dispersion describe *distances* among scores within a group. The larger the value of a measure of dispersion, the greater the variability or heterogeneity among the scores. The three most commonly used measures of dispersion are *range, standard deviation,* and *variance.*

Range

The easiest estimate of dispersion to compute is the *range,* which is simply the difference between the highest and the lowest scores. For the scores in Table 3.3, the range for group W is 60 (65 − 5 = 60), 30 for group X, 18 for group Y, and 0 for group Z.

Although the range is easy to compute, it has one very serious deficiency: it is determined only by the two extreme scores, and it can be dramatically altered by adding or dropping just one of these extreme scores. Such instability means it can be very misleading to use the range as a basis of comparing dispersions across two or more groups.

Application Problem 2

Based on the following illustration, (a) how many people obtained a score of 37? (b) what is the range of scores shown in the distribution? (c) what is the mode of the scores in this distribution?

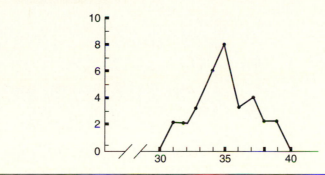

Standard Deviation and Variance

The most widely used measure of dispersion is *standard deviation*, which is symbolized by *s, SD,* or σ (the lowercase Greek letter *sigma*). A closely related measure is *variance*, which is symbolized by s^2 or σ^2. As a statistical index of dispersion among a distribution of scores, the standard deviation provides a number that indicates how far each score typically deviates from the mean. Because all scores in the group contribute to the computation of this number, the standard deviation is less influenced by extreme scores than the range. Many hand calculators have basic statistical functions and will compute the standard deviation of a set of scores. As stated before, our purpose here is to understand the meaning of standard deviation in measurement contexts, and interested readers can go to Appendix A for the statistical formulas and computational examples.

It turns out that standard deviation is essential in understanding how test scores are distributed. In every normal distribution, the standard deviation can be used to indicate the extent to which scores vary or are dispersed around the mean. By definition, for all normal curves, 34.13 percent of the scores fall in the part of the curve that is between the mean and one standard deviation from the mean. Thus, as shown in Figure 3.6, 68.26 percent of the scores in a normal distribution fall between −1.0 standard deviation and +1.0 standard deviation.

Consider some specific examples. Most IQ tests are developed to have a mean of 100 and a standard deviation of 15. Hence approximately 68 percent of the population has IQ scores between 85 and 115. The Scholastic Assessment Test (SAT, previously called the Scholastic Aptitude Test) scores (math or verbal) have a mean of approximately 500 and standard deviation of 100. Based on this information, we know that about 68 percent of those who take the SAT will score between 400 and 600, and about 16 percent will score above 600, or below 400.

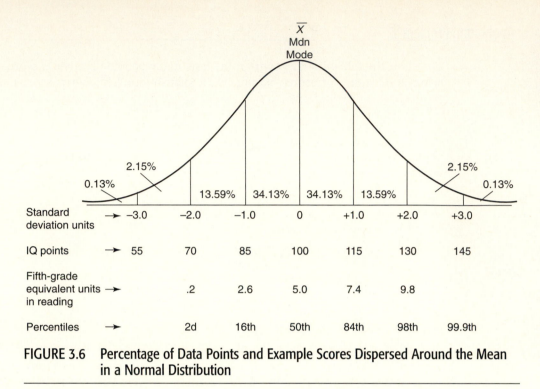

FIGURE 3.6 Percentage of Data Points and Example Scores Dispersed Around the Mean in a Normal Distribution

The concept of standard deviation vastly enhances what a few numbers can tell us about a frequency distribution. For example, knowing that the IQ score distribution is approximately normal with a standard deviation of 15 and a mean of 100, we see that a very small percentage of people will have IQ scores above 130, or below 70. This is because one standard deviation is equal to 15 points, and two standard deviations will be 30 points. Thus a score of 70 is two standard deviations below the mean, and from Figure 3.6, you can see that if IQ scores are normally distributed, only about 2.27 percent of the general population would be expected to have IQ scores less than 70. The same reasoning applies to the percentage of the general population expected to have IQ greater than 130 because the normal curve is symmetrical.

When the measurement scales used for different distributions are *comparable,* the standard deviation can be used to compare dispersion tendencies of different distributions. Since SD is an estimate of the average dispersion of scores around the mean, a distribution with a large standard deviation will contain scores that are more spread out, whereas a distribution with a small standard deviation will contain scores more closely clustered around the mean. To demonstrate, refer to Table 3.3. The standard deviation for Group W is calculated to be 20.15, whereas the standard deviation for Group Y is only 6.32. It is important to note, however, that for distributions on different measurement scales, such comparisons are *not appropriate.* For example, if you are informed that the standard deviation on SAT scores is about 100, and the standard deviation of college GPA in your university is about 1.2, obviously, it *does not* make sense to say that SAT scores are more spread out than GPA scores. As a matter of fact, such comparison is totally *inappropriate* since the two distributions are on such different metrics.

Application Problem 3

The scores of a norm-referenced standardized math test are normally distributed with a mean of 67 and a standard deviation of 6.0. Approximately what percentage of a group of 1000 examinees (assuming that the group is comparable to the norm group) would you expect to score between 67 and 73?

Application Problem 4

Horatio is enrolled in a chemistry class with 50 students. He has received the following scores on the various assignments for the first half of the year. On which test or assignment did he do the best relative to the other members of the class? On which did he do the worst?

| | Class Scores | | | | Horatio's Scores | |
	Lowest	Highest	Mean	Standard Deviation	Actual Points	Percentage Correct
Assignment 1	22	48	35	5.0	30	60
Assignment 2	8	23	14	3.0	20	80
Assignment 3	48	75	60	6.0	66	83
Midterm	56	91	70	7.0	70	70
Final	128	174	150	10.0	130	75

Hint: Assume that class scores on the assignments and exams are approximately normally distributed. Use what you have learned about standard deviation and normal curves to solve the problem.

The Correlation Coefficient: A Measure of Association

A clear understanding of the correlation coefficient can be invaluable in interpreting test scores and seeing how they relate to educational activities. Although you may use different words, you probably already use the concept of correlation frequently.

So far, we have discussed only scores within a single distribution (for example, the average salary for a group of people, or dispersion among reading test scores). Correlation describes how scores in one distribution relate to scores in another, or how one variable is related to, or associated with, another. Correlations help to answer questions like the following:

- Do people who are good at math tend to have a lower level of musical ability?
- Does student achievement tend to be lower in larger classes than in smaller classes?
- If you had good grades in high school, will you likely have good grades in college?

Definitions and Examples

Two variables are correlated if they are related or tend to "go together." For example, tall people tend to weigh more than short people. Hence we say that height and weight are correlated. Another example: some people believe that the size of an elementary school class (that is, number of students) is correlated with, or associated with, teacher job satisfaction. According to this belief, if you examined 100 elementary school classes, you would find that the most satisfied teachers tended to be those teaching the smallest classes.

Some variables are not correlated at all. If you examined the average GPA in a college math class with the number of the month in which students were born, you would probably find no association. In other words, knowing the month in which a student was born would not allow you to predict her GPA any more accurately than if you did not know it.

Our discussion will focus on the conceptual meaning of correlation coefficient, and we present the formulas and a computation example for correlation coefficient in Appendix A. Some hand calculators provide correlation coefficient if you enter the raw data. Most statistical software and spreadsheet programs also calculate correlation coefficients. We will focus on understanding and interpreting the meaning of a correlation coefficient.

A correlation coefficient has two components: *direction* and *magnitude*. With respect to direction, correlations can be either *positive* or *negative*. When high scores on one variable tend to be associated with high scores on another variable, and low scores on one variable tend to be associated with low scores on another variable, the correlation is *positive*. For example, the correlation between height and weight is positive because, in general, tall persons tend to weigh more, and short persons tend to weigh less. When high scores on one variable tend to be associated with low scores on another variable, and low scores on one variable tend to be associated with high scores on another variable, the correlation is *negative*. For example, if you find out that teachers in smaller classes tend to have higher levels of job satisfaction, and teachers in large classes tend to have lower levels of job satisfaction, the correlation between class size and teacher job satisfaction is said to be negative.

A correlation also has magnitude to indicate the *strength* of relationship. Correlation coefficients range from −1.0 to +1.0. The closer a correlation is to zero, the less two variables are related. Remember that a high correlation can be either a high negative or a high positive correlation, for example, a negative −.80 indicates the same strength of relationship between two variables as a positive +.80 even though the two correlation coefficients differ in terms of their direction. A correlation of −1.0 or +1.0 is also referred to as perfect correlation because you can perfectly predict a person's score on one variable by knowing her score on the other.

What constitutes a high, moderate, or low correlation in a measurement situation depends so much on the context that only general guidelines can be given.

High correlations are generally considered to have absolute values of .70 or higher (for example, two different forms of a well-constructed achievement test should correlate around .90 or above); moderate correlations are in the range of .40 to .70 (for example, aptitude test scores generally correlate with later grades about .50); and low correlations are less than .30 (for example, the correlation between manual dexterity and scores on a test of reading comprehension would probably be close to 0.0).

To better understand correlation coefficients, it is useful to examine what statisticians refer to as scatterplots or scattergrams. Figure 3.7 contains hypothetical

FIGURE 3.7   Hypothetical Distribution for Math Scores and Number of Days Absent for 20 Children

Name	Number of Days Absent	Score on a Math Test	Name	Number of Days Absent	Score on a Math Test
John	30	20	Artemus	18	30
Susan	23	40	Harriette	12	30
Harold	15	18	Barbara	12	43
Oliver	8	50	Collette	27	44
Nancy	23	70	William	6	90
Juan	20	46	Chad	10	66
Marie	7	78	Ellen	24	100
Hunter	30	50	Karl	12	80
Sylvia	18	80	Allyson	15	70
Brigham	25	10	Brigette	22	60

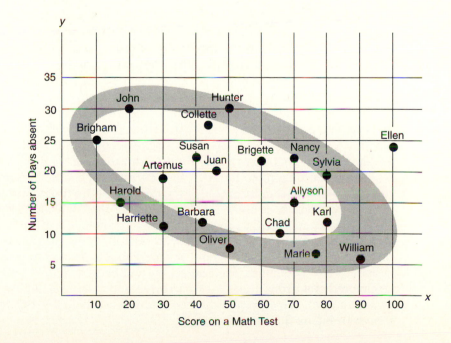

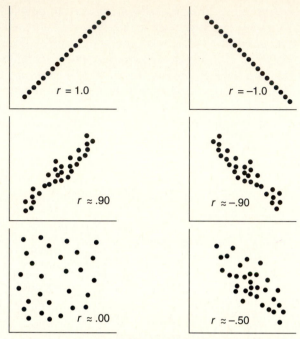

The symbol ≈ is used to indicate "approximately equal to"

FIGURE 3.8   Examples of Scatterplots Associated with Correlations of Different Magnitudes

scores on 2 variables for 20 students. In such a scatterplot, a person's position as represented by a dot is determined by the person's scores on two variables of our interest. The first score is the number of days absent during the semester, and the second score is the number of correct answers on the final math test. Is there a relationship between the test score and the number of days of absence from school? By just looking at the numbers in the top half of Figure 3.7, it is difficult to see a relationship. However, when the numbers are plotted on the scattergram in the lower part of Figure 3.7 (ignore the fact for now that part of the graph is shaded differently), it becomes clear that there is a tendency for students with fewer absences to score better on the test. The actual correlation coefficient (indicated by r) is −.33 for the 20 students. This fairly weak negative correlation indicates a tendency for people who have a *higher* rate of absenteeism to score *lower* on the math test.

As you become more familiar with correlation coefficients, you will find that you can estimate from the shape of the dots the approximate magnitude of the correlation coefficient, as shown in Figure 3.8. If the correlation is perfect (1.0 or −1.0), the scatterplot will be represented by a single line, with all dots falling directly on the line. When we have perfect relationship, knowing a person's score on one variable will tell us exactly where this person's score will be on another variable. If there is no correlation, the scatterplot will be a circle or rectangle. As the scatterplot changes from a circle to narrower and narrower ellipses (eventually becoming a line), the corresponding correlation coefficient gets larger and larger, as shown in Figure 3.8.

Table 3.4   Means, Standard Deviations, and Correlations for Different Subsets of the Data Shown in Figure 3.7

$n = 10$	$n = 19$	$n = 20$	$n = 22$
$r = -.59$	$r = -.47$	$r = -.33$	$r = +.19$
$\overline{X}_{absent} = 19.50$	$\overline{X}_{absent} = 17.53$	$\overline{X}_{absent} = 17.85$	$\overline{X}_{absent} = 18.50$
$SD_{absent} = 5.64$	$SD_{absent} = 7.60$	$SD_{absent} = 7.53$	$SD_{absent} = 10.74$
$\overline{X}_{math} = 51.60$	$\overline{X}_{math} = 51.30$	$\overline{X}_{math} = 53.75$	$\overline{X}_{math} = 53.41$
$SD_{math} = 21.56$	$SD_{math} = 23.37$	$SD_{math} = 25.22$	$SD_{absent} = 28.54$
Ten Students in the Inner Ellipse	**19 Students in the Entire Ellipse**	**All Students**	**All Students with Addition of Mike and Suzanne**

Now, refer to Figure 3.7 for a moment. A review of *all* the scores reveals a *tendency* for children who are absent more days to score lower on the test. However, there are some exceptions. Ellen, who obtained the highest score on the math test, was absent more days than anybody except for Brigham, John, Colette, and Hunter. To show how individual scores affect the magnitude of the correlation coefficient, we have calculated the correlation coefficient and means and standard deviations on each variable for several subsets of the data in Figure 3.7. This information is summarized in Table 3.4.

For the ten scores inside the narrower ellipse, the correlation coefficient is −.59. This is consistent with our previous discussion suggesting that the more closely the ellipse approximates a straight line, the higher the correlation. As the ellipse is broadened to include all students except for Ellen, the magnitude of the correlation changes to $r = -.47$.

Adding the single data point for Ellen further reduces the correlation coefficient ($r = -.33$). Since Ellen deviates from the general pattern of relationship, such an observation is generally called an *outlier*. Clearly, *outliers* can have a considerable influence on the magnitude of a correlation coefficient, especially when the data set is relatively small. To demonstrate just how serious that impact can be, consider what happens if we add just two more data points to those already shown. Assume that Mike, who has not been absent at all, scores a zero on the math test; and Suzanne, who has been absent 50 days during the semester, scores 100 on the math test. If we added these two points to the scatterplot (which were not shown on the scatterplot), the correlation would change from $r = -.33$ to $r = +.19$. Adding two such points changes the interpretation substantially. Instead of *low* scores being associated with *high* absenteeism, *high* scores would be associated (though weakly) with *high* absenteeism.

The fact that adding or deleting a few points can have such a dramatic influence highlights the need to interpret correlation coefficients very carefully when the data set is small. In almost all decisions concerning correlation coefficients, it is worthwhile to examine a scatterplot to make sure that the correlation is not being unduly influenced by one or two aberrant scores. As a data set becomes larger, however, the influence of outliers becomes smaller or negligible.

Application Problem 5

Based on a large sample of students, the correlation between hours spent on homework and scores on the semester math test is calculated to be $+.73$. Assuming there are no outliers in the data set, provide an appropriate interpretation for this correlation.

Interpreting Correlation Coefficients

Since the concept of correlation is so widely used in measurement, it is important to point out a number of cautions that you should keep in mind as you interpret correlation coefficients.

Curvilinearity.   The correlation coefficient discussed here is called a Pearson correlation coefficient, and it applies only to *linear* (resembling a straight line pattern) relationships between variables. If the relationship between two variables is not linear, but *curvilinear* (resembling a curve), a Pearson correlation coefficient obtained from such data will usually *underestimate* the actual relationship. For example, people believe that the scatterplot depicting the relation between test anxiety and performance on standardized achievement tests looks like Figure 3.9. If this were true, the correlation between the two variables would be close to $r = 0.0$, despite the clear relationship between the two variables: those with no anxiety tend to do poorly, those with moderate anxiety do best, and those with high anxiety do poorly. (We emphasize that this is a hypothetical example. The relation between anxiety and test scores is discussed in Chapter 6.) When such *curvilinear* relationships exist, it is essential to examine scatterplots of data to make sure that the presence of a curvilinear relationship is not misleading us.

FIGURE 3.9   Hypothetical Scatterplot of Scores Between Test Anxiety and Test Performance

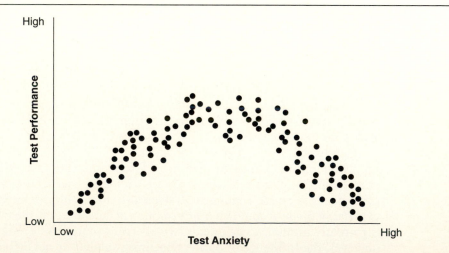

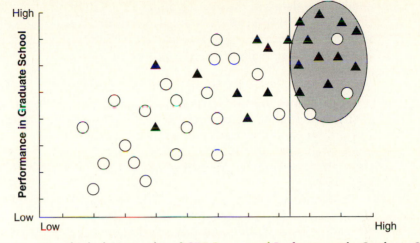

FIGURE 3.10   **Hypothetical Scatterplot of GRE Scores and Performance in Graduate School for Students Who Do Not Take the GRE (○) and Those Who Do (▲)**

Restricted Range.   Before drawing conclusions about an observed correlation between two variables, it is important to know whether data are available across the entire spectrum of possible scores for each of the variables. Where the range of scores has been reduced through selection, absenteeism, or some other factor, it is possible to have a very low observed correlation even though the two variables would be substantially correlated if the total population of scores were available. For example, Figure 3.10 illustrates hypothetical data for how a scatterplot between Graduate Record Examination (GRE) scores and performance in graduate school might look if all college students took the GRE and all went to graduate school.

A fairly strong correlation (approximately $r = .70$) exists in Figure 3.10 when these assumptions are true. However, not all college students take the GRE, and even fewer go to graduate school. Assume that the triangles in Figure 3.10 represent those students who take the GRE, whereas the circles represent those who do not. The magnitude of the correlation coefficient for that portion of the scatterplot represented by triangles is about .45. Furthermore, not all those who take the GRE actually complete graduate school. Those who do are indicated on the scatterplot by the triangles in the shaded area. The magnitude of the correlation coefficient for this group is only about .10. Are the data from the triangles in the shaded area a fair indication of how well scores on the GRE predict success in graduate school? Obviously not. Estimating the correlation between two variables in which data for one or both represent a very restricted range usually leads to an *underestimate,* sometimes, a severe underestimate, of the actual relationship.

Number of Cases.   You already know what can happen to the magnitude of the correlation coefficient when an *outlier* is introduced. (Remember Ellen and Suzanne who were frequently absent but still outscored their peers on the math test?) The smaller the data set, the greater the effect of such outliers. Consequently, correlations computed from small samples should be interpreted with caution. Especially in situations with ten or fewer cases, correlations may often be spuriously high or low, and should be treated with caution.

Magnitude of Correlation Coefficients.   There are no simple rules for deciding how large a correlation coefficient must be to be practically meaningful. Larger correlation coefficients (either positive or negative) are indicative of a stronger association between two variables. However, what is considered large in one situation may be considered small in another situation. Therefore, it is best to evaluate the magnitude of a correlation coefficient in comparison to what is typically seen in similar situations.

Let's consider some examples. The correlation between two parallel forms of the same standardized achievement or aptitude test, such as two parallel forms of the SAT, would usually have a correlation of about .90. Therefore, if you were considering the use of a new standardized achievement test that had a correlation of .70 between the two parallel forms, you should realize that although this correlation sounds high, it is much lower than what is typically observed. Alternatively, if you were studying the relationship between physical strength and abstract reasoning ability, a correlation of .30 would be considered unusually high and very rare. Several more examples may be helpful. It is not unusual for two well-constructed measures of the same academic skill to correlate about .90. Alternatively, a correlation of .65 to .75 is quite good between two affective measures such as self-concept and test anxiety. Mother–child IQs correlate about .50, IQs of identical twins raised in the same home correlate about .90, and the correlation in the general population between physical strength and IQ is about .20.

Interpretation of Test Scores

One of the most frequently encountered types of data for educational purposes comes from standardized, *norm-referenced* tests. Consequently, a wide variety of methods for reporting and interpreting such scores has been developed (stanines, normal curve equivalents, z-scores, percentiles, and so on). This section defines the various terms used to describe test scores and gives some examples to help you understand them.

Norms

Knowing that the ten-year-old girl next door is 56 inches tall provides you with a fair amount of information about her height. However, knowing that she scored 56 on her spelling test tells you almost nothing about her spelling ability. You do not know whether the words on the spelling test were easy or hard, or how well other children in the class did on the test. The major reason that "56 inches tall" is so much more meaningful than "a score of 56 on the spelling test" is that height is measured on a scale with which you have experience.

The same rules *do not* apply to most educational measures, however, because test scores are *not* usually on scales that readily allow comparisons such as measurements for height. Let us return to the spelling score of the little girl next door. If she tells her father that she got a score of 56 on the spelling test, her father will probably ask questions about how that score relates to other variables: "Out of how many?" or "How did the other children in the class do?" We tend to ask the same kinds of questions, although subconsciously, about variables such as height. If I tell you that the girl next door is 56 inches tall, you have a comparison group in mind: other children of about the same age. Thus if I go on to say that the girl is only two years old, you immediately recognize that something is wrong with either my yardstick or the girl next door. The information about the girl's height becomes meaningful when compared to the heights of other girls in similar circumstances.

In many test situations, test scores in their original form, that is, raw scores, usually lack this kind of comparability. One way to make test scores more interpretable is to create a *norm* for scores on that test. A test *norm* is simply a distribution of test scores created by administering the test to a representative, and usually large, sample of the population with whom the test will typically be used. Such a sample is called *norm group*. The distribution of scores for this group, or *norm,* typically approximates a normal curve, and this distribution is used as the criterion, or yardstick, against which the performance of other examinees can be compared. Once a test norm is created, test score interpretation becomes much easier.

In a measurement situation, if test scores are interpreted relative to the norm, it is *norm-referenced* measurement, in contrast to *criterion-referenced* measurement (Glaser, 1963). As discussed earlier, the major characteristic of norm-referenced measurement is that a person's performance on the test is compared to her peers; and whether the performance is good or poor depends on where the person stands relative to those in the norm group. In this sense, norm-referenced measurement does not inform us what Katie can or cannot do in a certain content area, but instead, it tells us whether Katie's performance is better or worse than the performance of her peers.

Criterion-referenced measurement, on the other hand, has prespecified criteria (for example, cutoff scores, criteria for mastery of the content area) against which a person's performance can be judged. So instead of telling us how Katie's performance is compared with her peers as in norm-referenced measurement, *criterion-referenced* measurement tells us what Katie can or cannot do, regardless of how her peers do on the same test. Although some authors (for example, Popham, 1990) classify tests into either norm-referenced or criterion-referenced tests, many others maintain that the distinction is *not* on tests per se, but on the way the test scores are interpreted. Many of the standardized achievement tests that are currently available can be used to compare the performance of an individual with other students (norm-referenced), or to describe exactly what skills the student has or has not mastered (criterion-referenced).

What Are the Characteristics of Good Norms?

For norm-referenced measurement, the way in which the norm is constructed is obviously very important since this is the yardstick against which all examinees who take the test will be evaluated. If something went awry with this yardstick and we did not know it, all of our comparison results would be misleading.

As discussed before, test norms are created by administering a test to a group of people whose scores are then used as a basis for comparison. Whether such norms are useful for your purposes depends on the characteristics of the people in the group. Several characteristics—relevance, representativeness, currency, and comparability—should be considered in judging the adequacy of norms.

Relevance. To whom do you want to compare your test scores? Most standardized tests provide national norms—that is, scores from a nationally representative sample of students—but some also provide norms for different subgroups, for example, boys versus girls, students who plan or do not plan to attend college. Many test scoring services also provide local norms, such as scores for all the students in your school or district who took the test. Whether the norms are relevant depends on the purpose for which you are using them.

For example, if you are counseling a student about whether to apply for admission into a prestigious university, it would be more helpful to know that her score is higher than 35 percent of those in the national norm group than it would be to know that her score is higher than 90 percent of those test takers from the local area. Such scores indicate that even though she is one of the best students in her school, she really does very poorly when compared to a national sample of students with whom she would likely be competing at the university.

Representativeness. Having norms that have been labeled in a way that sounds relevant for your purposes is not enough. You must know whether the students in that norm group are representative of a given population. For example, a norm group that consists of students in inner-city schools from Chicago, New York, and Los Angeles is clearly not representative of *all* students in the country, even if such a group is labeled a national sample. In determining representativeness, the critical issue is whether the people included in the norm sample are really representative for your purposes. Good standardized tests provide demographic information about the norming sample to help you answer this question.

Currency. How people score on a test changes over time. For example, the relative abilities of girls and boys in math has changed substantially over the past 30 years. Therefore, a math test that was normed in 1965 would not provide very useful information about the current performance of boys versus girls in your district. Outdated norms can be misleading. In such a situation, it would be best to use another test comparable in content but with current norms.

Comparability. It is often important to compare the scores from two or more tests. Norms can be very useful for this purpose, provided they are collected in approximately the same manner. Obviously, it is not very useful to know that a student scored at the 72nd percentile on Test A and the 50th percentile on Test B if the norming samples for the two tests are dramatically different. In cases where the norming procedures and samples are quite similar, you can make rough comparisons between the same types of scores obtained on different tests (for example, percentiles on math computation). Such comparisons are only approximations, and small differences should not be accorded too much importance.

Norms Are Not Standards

The term *norms* is almost always used in conjunction with "standardized" tests. But what is a standardized test? A *standardized* test is one in which test administration, scoring, and interpretation are *standardized*. In other words, (1) regardless of who administers the test, the same administration procedures as specified by the test developer are followed; (2) the same set of scoring criteria are used no matter who does the scoring; and (3) test score interpretation is based on the information and guidelines (norms) provided by the test developer.

Because the term *norms* is so frequently used in conjunction with standardized achievement tests, there is a tendency to equate the terms *norms* and *standards*. Such confusion of terms is misleading. The word *standard* denotes a level of achievement that has been established as a *goal* for all students. *Norms,* on the other hand, are descriptions of how some comparison group has performed. A standard is a description of *what ought to be,* and a norm is a description of *what is,* and the two are seldom synonymous. The fact that the average schoolchild in America watches several hours of television each day is the norm. It does not mean that watching several hours of television daily should be the standard.

Scores Yielded by Standardized Tests

The simplest type of test score is the student's raw score on the test. A raw score is one that has not yet been "cooked" in the cauldron of statistics. It is a simple tally. If the girl next door spells 56 words correctly on a spelling test of 100 words, her raw score is 56. Because raw scores are frequently not very useful for interpreting test results, a number of other types of scores have been developed.

Grade Equivalent Scores

In education, the most widely used score for reporting test results is probably the grade equivalent (GE) score. A GE of 5.0 means the student's score was comparable to the average score of students in the *norm group* at the beginning of the fifth grade. A GE score of 5.4 indicates that the student's score was comparable to the average score of students in the *norm group* in the fourth month of the fifth grade.

Although it seems logical to report that a student's score is comparable to that of the average pupil in the fourth month of fifth grade, unfortunately, a GE score can often lead to serious misinterpretations. Consider a student who is in the fourth grade, but obtains a GE score of 5.9 on a math test. Does this mean that she has mastered fifth grade math and is ready for that of sixth grade? Not necessarily. Her high GE score most probably is the result of her good mastery of math content taught up to fourth grade. Although the high GE score does mean that her math skills are well above the average fourth grader, it would be inappropriate to assume that she has learned and mastered all the math content usually taught in the fifth grade.

To understand GE scores, let's consider how they are created. First, to establish GE scores for a fourth-grade test, the test is usually administered to a group of third, fourth, and fifth graders. Suppose that the test is administered in

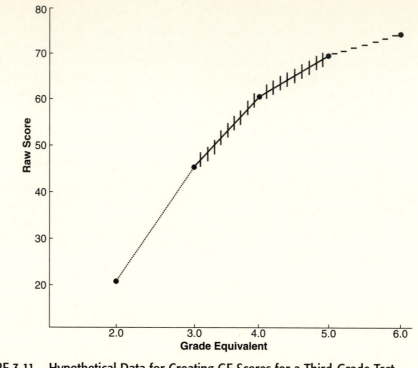

FIGURE 3.11   Hypothetical Data for Creating GE Scores for a Third-Grade Test

September and the median raw scores are 46 (for third graders), 60 (for fourth graders), and 68 (for fifth graders). These median scores are used to establish the GE scores for 3.0, 4.0, and 5.0, respectively. As shown in Figure 3.11, GE scores *between* these points are obtained by a process of *interpolation* (dividing the distance between established points into equal intervals) or *extrapolation* (extending the approximate line above and below the points for which data were obtained). Both interpolation and extrapolation result in tenuous approximations at best because both assume that there is a constant rate of growth during the year (Conklin, Burstein, & Keesling, 1979; Ramos, 1996), which may or may not be true. When GE scores are extrapolated substantially above or below the grades for which the test was designed, any attempts to interpret GE becomes very questionable.

Second, since pupils in three grades will take the test, the test must have items that cover the content areas across all three grades. So it is possible for a fourth grader to achieve a higher score than the average of fifth graders by performing extremely well on those items designed for third and fourth grades, without knowing much about the fifth-grade content. In this case, a fourth grader may have obtained a GE of 5.4, but that does not indicate that the student has learned the content area taught in fifth grade. In this sense, two students with the same GE score, especially if they are in different grades, may not be comparable in terms of the skills they have mastered.

Another characteristic of GE score is that its standard deviation becomes larger as children get older. Consequently, a child who is one standard deviation below the mean of the Comprehensive Test of Basic Skills at the beginning of first grade will have a GE score of 0.7 (only 0.3 GE units below "normal"). If that child remains at one standard deviation below the mean at the beginning of the sixth grade, she will have a GE score of 3.9 (the discrepancy has increased to 2.1 GE units!). Although it appears that the student is losing ground, she is actually maintaining exactly the same position with respect to the norm group. Standard deviations on GE scores also tend to differ among subtests of the same test. Therefore, it is difficult to say that a seventh grader who has a GE score of 6.8 on a reading test and only 6.3 on a math test is relatively better at reading than she is at math.

GE scores are often inappropriately used as a performance standard; that is, all students should obtain the respective Grade Equivalents, otherwise, there is a serious problem. People often forget that GE scores represent the average or median score for a grade, and as such, approximately half the students in the grade will be below it. The fact that half the students are "below Grade Equivalent" is not as bad as it first sounds; the statement, in fact, simply indicates that the students in the school are distributed exactly as we would expect them to be around an average score. So, if a fifth grader's performance at the beginning of the year is below a GE score of 5.0, it does not mean that her performance is particularly poor, since by design, half of fifth graders will perform below the GE score for that time of the year. Only when the deviation from the expected GE is substantially large is there any reason for alarm.

Despite the potential problems associated with using GE scores, they remain one of the most popular ways of reporting standardized achievement test results. This is probably because many teachers, administrators, and parents mistakenly believe that GE scores are easy to interpret. We recommend some caution in using GE scores. If they are used in your school and you need to explain them to parents, remember that they depend on the time of year the test is taken and are useful only for providing *a very general* indicator of whether a student is performing above, below, or about average for her grade.

Percentile

Another important and frequently used concept is that of *percentile,* also known as *percentile rank* or *percentile score.* A *percentile* conveys information about the relative position of an individual's score in a distribution, and is defined as a score in a distribution below which that percentage of examinees scored. For example, if 55 percent of examinees obtained raw scores below 78, then the raw score of 78 is at the 55th *percentile.*

In a distribution, the point below which 50 percent of the scores fall is known as the 50th percentile. In any distribution (whether it is normal, skewed, or bimodal), the 50th percentile always corresponds to the median. For a normal distribution, the 50th percentile also corresponds to the mean and the mode. If we refer to Figure 3.6, the 50th percentile of IQ scores is 100, meaning that half the persons tested will have scores over 100, and half will have scores below 100. For a normal distribution, an IQ score of 115 (see Figure 3.6) is at the 84th percentile, because 84 percent of the distribution falls below that point. An IQ of 70 is at approximately the 2nd percentile because approximately 2 percent of the group (actually 2.27 percent) have IQs lower than 70. The concept of percentile is particularly important in educational measurement because it indicates where a person stands relative to other people in the group. The major advantages of percentile scores are that they are easy to understand and applicable for almost any type of test.

The major disadvantage of percentile scores is that they divide the population of distribution of scores into unequal units, especially near the ends of a score distribution. To understand this, let's consider the following example, which appears logical at first glance, but can result in *misleading* conclusions. Between the beginning and the end of the year, Susan moves from the 50th to the 60th percentile, and Linda moves from the 89th to the 99th percentile. Since they have each gained 10 percentile points, they have made equal progress.

The problem with this statement is that, in the middle of the distribution (where Susan's score is), many persons' scores cluster together tightly, and an increase of just a few points will surpass a substantial number of persons, thus allowing a relatively large increase in her percentile score. Only a small number of persons have scores at the ends of the distribution (where Linda's score is); therefore, a substantial improvement in her score will surpass only a few persons and will result in only a small change in percentile score. This point is demonstrated in Figure 3.12 where we can see that the difference between the 50th and the 60th percentiles represents less than one-third of a standard deviation, whereas the difference between the 89th and the 99th percentiles represents almost two standard

FIGURE 3.12 Relationship Between Percentiles, *Z* Scores, and Normal Curve Equivalents (NCEs)

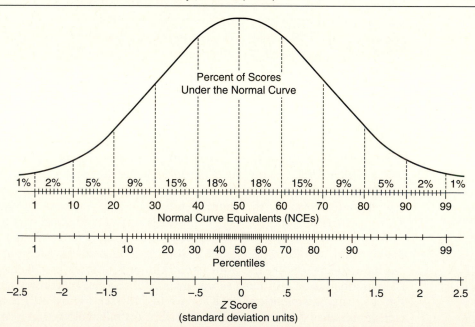

deviations. So even though Susan's progress seems to be equal to that of Linda's when expressed in percentile scores, in reality, Linda's progress is much greater than Susan's.

The preceding example clearly indicates that although percentile scores indicate the relative positions of persons as measured on a test, they are not a very good indicator of the amount of difference between scores. Because percentile scores are not measured in equal units, increases or decreases of percentile ranks for individuals can often be misleading for people who are not accustomed to interpreting percentiles. The problem of unequal units also makes it difficult to interpret the results of statistical computation based on percentile scores.

Percentile scores are also sometimes confused with percentage scores, which are often used in day-to-day testing situations in schools. A percentile score is expressed in terms of percentage of *persons,* and it is not related to the percentage of correct *items.* A percentile score of 100 does not imply a perfect raw score; neither does a percentile score of zero imply a zero raw score. In other words, a percentage correct of 55 on a test can be a percentile score of 100 (if nobody in the norm group scored more than 55 percent correct), or it can be a percentile score of zero (if everybody else in the norm group scored higher than 55 percent correct).

As long as you remember that percentile scores do not represent equal units, and that they should not be interpreted as "percent correct," they are a relatively good way of reporting test scores. They are limited by the adequacy of the norm group to which they are referenced, yet they do provide an accurate way of estimating how well students have performed with regard to that norm group. More important, they are easy to explain and understand.

Z Scores and Other Standard Scores

A *z* score tells us how many standard deviations a raw score is below or above the mean. A *negative z* score indicates that the raw score is below the mean; a *positive z* score indicates that the raw score is above the mean; and a *z* score of zero says that the raw score is equal to the mean.

A *z* score for any person on a particular test can be computed by subtracting the mean score on the test from the person's score and dividing that by the standard deviation of the test (see Appendix A for the statistical formula). For example, consider a test that has a mean of 65 and a standard deviation of 8. If Susan scored 69 on that test, she would have a *z* score of $+.50$ because $(69 - 65) \div 8 = .50$. Similarly, Jessica and Linda who scored 62 and 51 on the test would have *z* scores of $-.375$ and -1.75, respectively.

Educational tests usually have different means and different standard deviations. For this reason, original raw scores often are not very informative. For example, Tiffany has a score of 78 on the math test, and her score on the reading test is 65. Is Tiffany's performance on the math test better than her performance on the reading test, relative to her school mates? The raw scores given above do not give us this information. If we know that Tiffany's *z* score on the math test is $+1$ (a mean of 70 and a standard deviation of 8 for the math test), and that her *z* score on the reading test is 0 (a mean of 65 and a standard deviation of 10 for the reading test), we know that, relative to her school mates, Tiffany did better on the math test. This example shows that z scores ususally allow us to make performance comparisons across tests which have different means and different standard deviations. The same is true for other standardized scores discussed below.

For distributions that are approximately normal, z scores can be easily converted to percentile scores using conversion tables in most introductory statistics textbooks. A few examples will illustrate how this process works. Using Figure 3.12, you can see that a z score of zero is equal to the 50th percentile (mean). A z score of $+1.0$ is approximately equal to the 84th percentile (only about 16 percent of persons obtained z scores $+1$ or higher). A z score of -1.0 mirrors what is conveyed by a z score of $+1.0$ in the sense that it is at about the 16th percentile, and only 16 percent of people will have z scores lower than this. From Figure 3.12, it is also seen that, for practical purposes, the range between z scores -3.0 and $+3.0$ covers almost 100 percent of the distribution.

Z scores are very important because they form the basis for a number of other scores that are frequently reported. By definition, a z score distribution has a mean of 0 and a standard deviation of 1.0. A z score can be transformed to another standard score with a different mean and a different standard deviation. This is done by multiplying the z score with your desired standard deviation, and adding to the product the value of your desired mean.

$$\text{Any Standard Score} = (z \times \text{Desired SD}) + \text{Desired Mean}$$

For example, a popular standard score is a *T score* (mean of 50, and SD of 10). Any z score can be transformed to a *T* score by using the formula

$$T \text{ Score} = (z \text{ Score} \times 10) + 50$$

In the same vein, a z score on an IQ test can be converted to the commonly used IQ scale having a mean of 100 and a standard deviation of 15 by multiplying the z score by 15 and adding 100. Thus if a person obtains a z score of $+1.0$ on an IQ test, it is equal to an IQ scale score of 115. Both the z score and the new IQ score indicate that the person is one standard deviation above the mean and that the person is at the 84th percentile in the norm group.

You are probably already familiar with a number of other standard scores that are derived using similar procedures. Examples include SAT and GRE (Graduate Record Examination) scores, both of which had means of 500 and standard deviations of 100 when they were originally developed.

Normal Curve Equivalents

Some standardized test manuals also report *Normal Curve Equivalent* (NCE) scores. NCE scores were created to capitalize on the advantages of percentile scores, while avoiding (1) the disadvantages of dealing with unequal units at different points in the distribution, and (2) the confusion between percentiles and percentage correct. NCEs have a mean of 50 and a standard deviation of 21.06. As

Table 3.5   Percentage of Normal Distribution Contained in Each Stanine

Stanine	Percent of Normal Distribution
9	4
8	7
7	12
6	17
5	20
4	17
3	12
2	7
1	4

shown earlier in Figure 3.12, NCEs correspond with percentile scores at three points in the distribution: the 1st percentile, the 50th percentile, and the 99th percentile. At all points in between, NCEs have been spaced so that they are on equal interval units.

Stanines

Another popular type of standard score is the *stanine* (the word comes from a combination of "standard" and "nine"), originally developed in the U.S. Air Force. Stanines are computed by dividing a distribution into nine units, each with its own prespecified proportion of the distribution. The middle stanine straddles the median of a distribution. The proportion of a distribution falling in each stanine unit is shown in Table 3.5. The top 4 percent of the scores are assigned a stanine score of 9, the next 7 percent are assigned a stanine score of 8, and so on, until the bottom 4 percent of the scores are assigned a stanine score of 1.

The strengths of stanine scores are that they are easily computed, recorded, and manipulated. Also, since each stanine represents a band of scores, there is less likelihood that too much importance will be attached to trivial differences between two students. For example, two students who score at the 45th and 55th percentiles, respectively, on a test would both receive a stanine of 5. Although there are ten percentile points between the two students, as shown previously, a ten-percentile point difference in the middle of the distribution is a relatively small difference. The fact that both students receive the same stanine score offers some protection against overinterpreting this difference. Such protection can be a double-edged sword, however. If a difference occurs on the borderline between two stanines, it may still be very small, but may be assigned to two different stanine units.

Because stanines are frequently reported, it is good to know how they are derived and interpreted. However, since they offer relatively few advantages com-

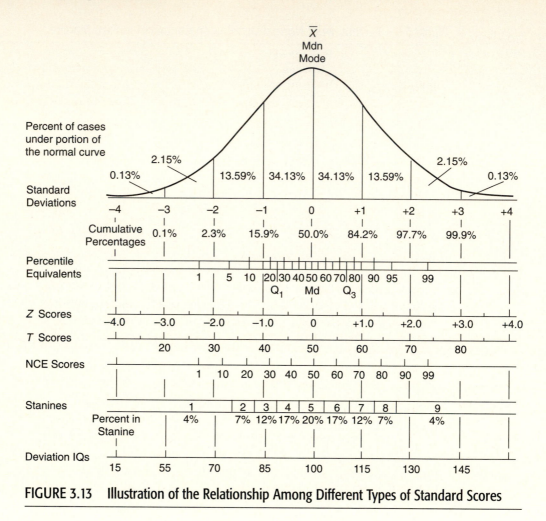

FIGURE 3.13 Illustration of the Relationship Among Different Types of Standard Scores

pared with some other standard scores, you are generally better off avoiding them and using one of the other standard scores.

Relationship Among Types of Scores

It would be nice if there were one type of score suitable for all situations in which results of standardized tests are interpreted. One reason so many different types of scores exist is that they serve different purposes and have different strengths and weaknesses. Now that you understand something about each of the specific types of scores, it is important to see how they relate to each other, as shown in Figure 3.13. Until you become familiar with the different kinds of scores, it is a good idea to keep a chart like this handy so that you can get your bearings when you encounter a score you remember having seen before, but about which you have forgotten many details.

Application Problem 6

For a large group of fifth graders tested at the beginning of the school year (assuming the score distribution is approximately normal), which one of the following is most equivalent to the percentile score of 84? Why are the other four not equivalent to the percentile score of 84?

    a. A z score of 1.0

    b. A Grade Equivalent Score of 5.0

    c. A z score of -1.0

    d. A Normal Curve Equivalent Score of 50

    e. A stanine score of 5

Reports for standardized achievement tests often report scores in a number of different forms, such as those shown in Figure 3.14 from the Comprehensive Test of Basic Skills (CTBS). This report can be used to summarize several key points discussed in this chapter.

Notice that the report provides both national percentiles and stanines that are referenced to the national norm group (a nationally representative sample of students). In addition, the report provides information about a confidence interval around the national percentile and stanine scores. This confidence interval is related to the concept of *measurement error,* which we will discuss in the next chapter. For the time being, it suffices to know that such a confidence interval helps us know how confident we can be that two scores are really different. In other words, it provides some protection against overinterpreting small differences. For example, although Language and Social Studies have national percentile scores of 53 and 58, respectively, the substantial overlap in the two confidence interval bands indicates that the difference between the two areas may not be that important. On the other hand, there is no overlap between Language and Mathematics, indicating that the difference between these two areas is more substantial.

Another score—the Objectives Performance Index—is introduced in this report. This score indicates a student's mastery or nonmastery of individual objectives under each academic area, and is an example of an increasing trend among test publishers to combine the advantages of norm-referenced and criterion-referenced tests. Information at the top of Figure 3.14 has typically been thought of as norm-referenced test information. Information on the bottom half provides some specific information about the kinds of items passed or failed—traditionally considered criterion-referenced information. Even though the number of items used to assess any one skill area is sometimes relatively small, such scores provide valuable information for instructional planning. For example, in looking at the area of Reading, we can see that this student did exceptionally well in two subareas (Basic Understanding and Analyze Text), but need some more work in two others (Evaluate & Extend Meaning and Identify Reading Strategies). This information gives the student's teacher some direction about the specific type of reading skills in which further work is needed.

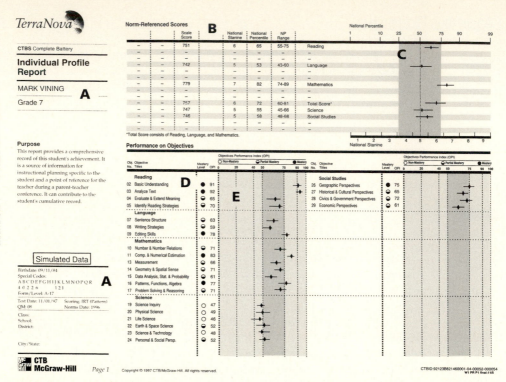

FIGURE 3.14   Example of an Individual Profile Report for the Comprehensive Tests of Basic Skills

Source: Teacher's Guide to TerraNova, 1997, CTB/McGraw-Hill, Monterey, CA. Reprinted with permission of the publisher.

Application Problem 7

The parents of the student in the report in Figure 3.14 want to know which academic area is this student's strength and which area is his weakness. Based on the report shown in Figure 3.14, what would you tell them?

Computer-generated reports of standardized achievement tests such as Figure 3.14 represent a tremendously valuable but largely untapped resource for teachers. Too often, standardized achievement testing is a district program in which teachers have little interest or involvement. Properly used, however, standardized achievement tests give teachers important instructional information. As you might guess from examining Figure 3.14, a number of different kinds of output can be requested. By becoming involved in decisions concerning the standardized achievement testing program in your district, you can help tailor the reports to make them more beneficial for you.

SUGGESTED READINGS

Angoff, W. H. (1992). Norms and scales. In M. C. Alkin (ed.). *Encyclopedia of educational research,* (6th ed., pp. 909–921). New York: Macmillan.

A more technical discussion than that contained in this chapter about the advantages and disadvantages of different types of scores. Discusses the characteristics of good norms and summarizes different techniques used for test score equating, including a brief discussion of item response theory.

Hills, J. R. (1986). *All of Hills' handy hints.* Washington, DC: National Council on Measurement in Education.

In 1983 and 1984, John R. Hills published a series of six articles in *Educational Measurement: Issues and Practice,* which provided entertaining and imaginative summaries of truths and fallacies in the interpretation of widely used test scores. The National Council on Measurement in Education assembled all six articles in this single booklet for wider distribution.

Lehman, R. S. (1995). *Statistics in the behavioral sciences: A conceptual introduction.* Pacific Grove, CA: Brooks/Cole Publishing Company.

An excellent introduction to the concepts and methods for the various descriptive statistics used in measurement and research. A very readable book with many examples and sample problems.

Tufte, E. R. (1983). *The visual display of quantitative information.* Cheshire, CT: Graphics Press.

For anyone interested in an in-depth discussion of the techniques used for displaying quantitative information such as introduced in our discussion of histograms and frequency distributions, this book is a must. Both entertaining and informative, it contains hundreds of examples of well-established and innovative ways of depicting information.

SUGGESTION SHEET

If your last name starts with the letter C, please complete the Suggestion Sheet at the end of the book while this chapter is still fresh in your mind.

Answers to Chapter 3 Application Problems

1. (No standard answer provided)
2. a. 4
   b. 8
   c. 35
3. 34 percent
4. Since the question asks how Horatio did in relation to the other class members, the key to finding the correct answer is to convert all the scores to standard deviation

units with respect to the distribution of scores in the class. Under the given assumption that the scores are approximately normally distributed, Horatio's relative standing on the five occasions may be obtained by using the standard deviation units of his scores and comparing them with a normal distribution such as that in Figure 3.6. The following are obtained:

| | Class Scores | | | Horatio's Scores | | |
	Mean	Standard Deviation	Actual Points	Percentage Correct	SD	Percentile
Assignment 1	35	5.0	30	60	−1.0	16th
Assignment 2	14	3.0	20	80	+2.0	98th
Assignment 3	60	6.0	66	83	+1.0	84th
Midterm	70	7.0	70	70	0	50th
Final	150	10.0	130	75	−2.0	2nd

It is easy to see that Horatio's relative position is the highest on the second assignment, and the lowest on the final exam (unfortunately!).

5. This correlation is *positive*. It indicates that time spent on homework and performance on the test tend to go "hand in hand"; that is, those who spent more time on homework tend to do better on the test than those who spent less time on homework. Furthermore, the correlation is *high*, indicating that this tendency is strong. Because this correlation is based on a large sample of students, it is unlikely that a few outliers might have caused such a strong correlation.

6. a. A z score of 1.0 is equivalent to the 84th percentile score.

   b. A GE of 5.0 means that the performance is comparable to the average performance of the beginning fifth graders.

   c. A z score of −1.0 is equivalent to 16th percentile.

   d. A NCE of 50 is equivalent to 50th percentile.

   e. A stanine score of 5 is approximately equal to 40th–60th percentile.

7. Based on the report in Figure 3.14, the student appears to have strength in the area of reading (mastery of two subareas and partial mastery in two others). But the student is obviously weak in the area of science (nonmastery in four subareas and partial mastery in two others), with no mastery in any of the areas under science. Similar information can be obtained by referring to the norm-referenced information expressed as national percentiles.

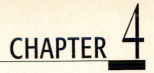

CHAPTER 4

Why Worry About Reliability?

Reliable Measures Yield Trustworthy Scores

OVERVIEW

Every test—and every other measurement instrument used in schools—has imperfections, including those you develop in your classroom, and even those developed by well-qualified experts. We hope that admission of our collective inability to produce the perfect measure will not discourage you from using these measures any more than the fact that no teacher's appraisal of a student's attitude or ability is perfectly accurate should cause you to abandon those essential tools of student assessment.

Educational measures do not need to be perfect to be useful. The critical question for any measure is whether it is good enough to be useful for our purpose. Or are its imperfections serious enough to cast doubt on the truthfulness of the story it tells about your students? This chapter and the next help you answer such questions for instruments you develop and for others you might consider using. Collectively, these two chapters provide benchmarks against which you can judge the "truthfulness," or the quality, of assessment instruments used in your schools.

In this chapter, we discuss the important concept of reliability and the issues related to it. We show why the story told by a test is not credible if that story changes with each telling. We demonstrate that an assessment instrument is not useful if it does not produce stable, consistent results. We discuss the concept of measurement error, and show how this concept is used in practice to provide a better estimate of the student's real level on the trait measured. We also describe, using simple examples, several common ways of estimating measurement reliability. Furthermore, we suggest how to interpret these reliability estimates to help you decide when a test is sufficiently reliable.

In all this, although we try to avoid statistical formulas and sophisticated psychometric concepts as much as we can without leaving you ill-prepared for the task of improving student assessment, some exposure to the basic, technical concepts and terminology is essential. So bear with us—we think you will see that the topic of reliability is not as complex as it sometimes seems, and surely not beyond the grasp of the typical classroom teacher.

OBJECTIVES

Upon completing your study of this chapter, you should be able to

1. | Explain why no measurement instrument can be considered a good measurement instrument unless it yields reliable scores.
2. | Describe the relationship of reliability to true scores and to measurement error.
3. | Distinguish conceptually between random and systematic errors of measurement.
4. | Describe different approaches for determining test reliability, and specify conditions under which each approach is appropriate.
5. | Compute a reliability coefficient for one of the five alternative approaches, and interpret reliability coefficients for all the approaches.
6. | List some major factors that may affect the reliability of a set of test scores.
7. | Estimate the reliability of scores from criterion-referenced measures.

Reliability of Educational Measures

Imagine that a high school student wishes to enter a police academy that requires candidates to be a minimum of 6 feet tall, and he asks you to measure him. Now imagine his frustration—and yours—if the only available measuring tape were made of rubber so pliable that it was impossible to pull it straight without stretching it. Your first measurement of 5 feet 6 inches is discounted, since you know you are 5 feet 9 inches and shorter than the student. Suspecting you may have stretched the tape, you relax a bit in taking a second measurement, and obtain a measurement of 5 feet 11 inches. Still concerned, you take a third measurement, dangling the tape limply, and record his height as 6 feet 1/8 inch.

Of course, no sensible person would use a rubber measuring tape. But some educational and psychological measures are rather "elastic," like the rubber rulers described here. They can yield one result on one occasion and quite a different result on another. Such instruments are unreliable, or inconsistent; and the more unreliable they are, the more untrustworthy they are. Assume that you gave your students a vocabulary test yesterday, and again today, and used the scores to rank the students' performance, on each of the two days, from highest to lowest. You notice that the rankings based on the two scores do not appear to be related to each other: some students who ranked very high on the first day receive very low rankings today. Conversely, some students who ranked quite low yesterday rank quite high today. Faced with these inconsistent results, you may wonder which of the two days' scores you should trust as providing "truthful" information about individual student's knowledge of vocabulary.

Given such discrepant results, we would say that the *reliability* of the scores obtained from the test was low, since the instrument yielded quite different results on two similar occasions. *Reliability* of measurement is defined as the degree of consistency with which the measurement provides information about examinees. In other words, a test is reliable if it measures whatever it is measuring consistently. The adage "Consistency, thou art a jewel" applies as much to measurement as to temperament. In a sense, reliability is a measure of how well a test agrees with itself—how stable and dependable it is in measuring the same thing with the same results each time.

Up to now, we have taken a bit of literary license, sometimes writing as if reliability refers to the measurement instrument itself. Not so. Technically, reliability refers to the consistency of the *results* obtained, not to the instrument itself. It is the reliability *of the test* scores obtained by using a test that is the criterion for evaluating the test use. Not surprisingly, many have adopted the shorthand of speaking of the *test's* reliability, a sin that can probably be forgiven as long as you understand this critical distinction.

Measurement Error, True Scores, and Reliability

Measurement Error

Imagine an IQ test that has been given to two people. Scott obtains a score of 108, and Christopher obtains a score of 106. Who has the higher IQ? Perhaps Christopher's *true* IQ is 115, but was feeling ill when the test was given, or was not very motivated because he was thinking about the upcoming baseball game. It may well be that Christopher's true IQ is higher than Scott's true IQ, even though on this test it appears that Scott has a slight edge.

How do we decide how accurate the results of a test really are? Think about your own testing experience and all the factors that influenced your performance on even the most "objective" tests. You can probably remember taking tests when you felt miserable, or the teacher asked the six exact questions that you did not study, or there was a big game that night and you were worried about how you would perform. On such occasions, you probably obtained a score that underestimated what you really knew.

But what about the other times? Have you ever taken a test where you just happened to make some lucky guesses? Or you studied only a third of the material, but that was the material the teacher included on the exam, and you felt that it was "your day"?

Each test score (or any measurement result) invariably consists of two major components: *true score* and *measurement error.* The *true score* is the actual ability or performance level an examinee possesses on the trait or dimension the test is designed to measure. *Measurement error* is that part of the obtained score that is contributed by factors irrelevant to what is being measured. For example, assume that you administer a math achievement test (with maximum possible score of 100) to your class, and Alfonso receives a score of 75. That is his *obtained score,* the number of points an examinee receives on a test. But is that a good measure of Alfonso's math ability? Suppose Alfonso took the same test a week later and received a score of 66. Which obtained score do you believe to be the most accurate estimate of his math ability? To answer that question, you need to know more about several factors that might have introduced error into one or both of his scores. For example, had the fact that Jim kept poking him with a pencil during the second test affected his score? Could it make a difference if Alfonso had stayed up most of the night prior to taking the second test? Might the fact that a substitute teacher who scored the second test had trouble deciphering Alfonzo's handwriting be a factor? The answer to each of these questions is "Possibly."

Unfortunately, measurement error is unavoidable, no matter how hard we try. So the question to ask is not whether our measurement has any error, but rather what is the *extent* of the measurement error in our measurement. Since we know measurement error always exists, the question becomes, "How will I ever know what Alfonso's 'true' score is—that score that would reflect his pure math ability, uncontaminated by any sources of measurement error?" You won't. We can never know a student's true score because a true score is a hypothetical value that we can never directly measure. But it is theoretically possible to get a reasonable estimate: *a person's estimated true score is the average of his obtained scores from repeated administrations of the same test under the same testing conditions,* disregarding the possible practice effect he would receive in repeatedly taking that test.

Every obtained score consists of two components: (1) the *true* score that reflects the student's ability or knowledge, and (2) an *error* component that reflects the contribution of certain irrelevant factors. We can portray this relationship as

$$\text{Obtained Score} = \text{True Score} + \text{Measurement Error}$$

It is worth pointing out that this formula does not indicate that the obtained score will always be higher than the true score. Measurement error can be either *positive* or *negative*. In the former case, the obtained score is an *overestimate* of a person's true score, whereas in the latter case, it is an *underestimate* of a person's true score. In either case, this discrepancy between the obtained and true score—measurement error—is very important in determining how much we may trust a particular test score. Knowing approximately how much measurement error exists in a particular test is crucial since the less measurement error test scores possess, the more closely obtained scores reflect the true scores.

Now you ask, "How can I determine *how much* measurement error a test score includes?" Different procedures have been developed specifically for this purpose. But before explaining different ways to estimate test score reliability, we need to say more about potential factors that can introduce measurement error into test scores, and thus lower measurement reliability.

Random Versus Systematic Error

To understand reliability, it is helpful to distinguish between two different kinds of measurement errors: *random* error and *systematic* error. Systematic measurement error occurs when, unknown to the test developer or test user, a test consistently measures something not intended. For example, suppose a test for *math* ability contains many word problems that require good *reading* skills. If such a test is administered to a group of students who happen to speak English as their second language, the test scores may contain systematic measurement error because lower scores on this test may be partially the result of inadequate *reading* skills, and reading skills is *not* something the test is designed to measure. In this situation, the obtained scores would tend to *systematically* underestimate the true scores of this group of students in math.

By definition, *random* errors are random; that is, the amount and the direction of error differs unsystematically from one measurement to another, and from one person to another. If the test mentioned in the previous paragraph was used for another group of students to whom language is not a problem, random errors would occur if the math ability levels of some students were underestimated, and others' were overestimated, and the amount of error differed in an unsystematic manner. Since the size and direction of the error differ in some unpredictable fashion from person to person, it is called *random error*.

Both random and systematic measurement error are of concern in testing situations. Random error reduces the *reliability* of test scores; thus it becomes the major topic under this chapter. Systematic measurement error reduces the *validity* of test scores, and interpretations based on such scores, thus it falls under the discussion of measurement validity, the topic of the next chapter.

The key to high measurement reliability is to reduce the influence of extraneous sources that introduce random error into the test scores. Although some of these factors may be beyond our control, we can still heighten our awareness of them and take their effects into account when interpreting test scores. Controlling all the factors that contribute measurement error to test scores may not be possible, but the more sources of random error we can eliminate, the more consistent the test results will be from one use to another. Consequently, the test scores will be more reliable.

Different Approaches for Estimating Reliability

There are four major approaches to estimating measurement reliability, and most of them depend on the concept of correlation explained in Chapter 3. These approaches may be labeled slightly differently in different texts.

Test-retest reliability. A correlation between scores from two administrations of the same test to the same students. Alternatively, such reliability estimates may be called *measure of stability, or coefficient of stability.*

Parallel form reliability. A correlation between scores of the same students on two "equivalent" forms of the same test. Some other names for this type of reliability estimate are *alternate form reliability, equivalent form reliability, measure of equivalence,* or *coefficient of equivalence.*

Internal consistency reliability. Correlation or consistency indices among items on a single test. Other names for this approach are *measures of homogeneity, measures of interitem consistency.* This approach includes

- Split-half method
- Cronbach's coefficient alpha method
- Kuder–Richardson method

Interrator reliability. A correlation between scores provided by two different scorers on the same test. *Interscorer reliability* is another name for this.

Procedures for Calculating Various Reliability Estimates

Correlation forms the basis for determining most reliability estimates. Many hand calculators have built-in statistical functions that enable you to obtain correlation coefficient for any two sets of test scores for the same individuals. Appendix A in this book provides the computation formula and an illustrative example for the Pearson Product-Moment Correlation (or Pearson r), which is used to calculate most reliability coefficients we will discuss. Any introductory statistics textbook provides instruction for computing correlation coefficient. Correlation coefficient can also be obtained through any statistical computer program, including spreadsheet programs such as Lotus 1-2-3 and Microsoft Excel. Besides, test scoring computer programs routinely provide reliability estimates also.

Besides introducing you to different approaches of estimating reliability so that you can have conceptual understanding of these approaches, for each type of reliability estimate we discuss, we also list simple, straightforward steps you would take to obtain the test scores that you will use in determining the reliability coefficient for your use of a test.

Test–Retest (Same Form) Method

This is one of the simplest ways to estimate a test's reliability, for it consists merely of giving the same test twice to the same individuals and then determining the correlation between the two sets of scores. Let us suppose, for example, that a teacher gives a group of 8 students the identical 100-item spelling test *twice* with a week interval, and obtains the following results:

	First Week	Second Week
Al	98	98
Alice	95	98
Bob	91	92
Barbara	83	87
Carl	83	85
Cathy	80	82
Dave	79	80
Donna	73	79
Mean =	85.3	87.6

By examining these scores, you can see two things.

- Overall, scores increased slightly from the first week (mean = 85.3) to the second (mean = 87.6).
- Individual student scores vary little from one week to the next; students' ranks on the first and second days are nearly identical.

We would probably all agree that this test has yielded some consistent results for this group of students. The two sets of scores are highly correlated. In fact, where a reliability coefficient of 1.00 would reflect a perfect correlation between two sets of scores, in our example, the test–retest correlation is .98, or nearly perfect.

Calculating a Test–Retest Reliability Coefficient

The step-by-step procedure for estimating test–retest reliability of a test is as follows:

1. Determine the appropriate interval between test and retest.
2. Administer the test (Time 1), and obtain Time 1 scores.
3. After the predetermined interval, administer the same test again, to the same students—that is, retest (Time 2), and obtain Time 2 scores.
4. Calculate the correlation coefficient between the two sets of scores.

The procedure for estimating test–retest reliability would be the same regardless of the time interval between the test and retest.

Issues Related to Test–Retest Reliability

Before you conclude that your spelling test is the most reliable spelling test, we need to point out some issues related to the test–retest method of estimating reliability.

Interval between two test administrations.   Test–retest reliability can be artificially inflated if a test is repeated immediately or after only a short interval. This is so because many students will recall their answers on the first test administration ("memory effect") and respond identically to many items on the second (repeating any responses to an item will raise test–retest reliability, whether or not the answer is correct). When the interval between two test administrations is too short, the test–retest reliability coefficients must be viewed with caution.

On the other hand, too long an interval between test administrations may also cause problems. Although memory may have faded sufficiently so that students cannot repeat their previous answers, new learning or other events may have occurred before the second testing. For example, suppose test–retest reliability of an English grammar test is being estimated. The longer the interval between tests, the greater the likelihood that some students' knowledge of grammar may have increased because of learning, or conversely, the greater the likelihood that some students may have forgot what they have learned about English grammar because of lack of use. If score changes from test to retest are *real* changes in the attribute measured, the reliability coefficient will be low. Thus long intervals invite unknown student growth or change; and a low reliability may be the result of such *real* change, or it may be the result of lack of consistency of the test itself, or may be a combination of both.

What is the correct time interval?   Unfortunately, there is no pat answer to this important question. Generally, the shorter the interval between test administrations, the higher the test–retest reliability tends to be. The most important consideration for the interval is to ask the question: how stable is the trait being measured? Some traits change fast, thus requiring a short interval for estimating test–retest reliability. For example, children's achievement in learning the alphabet is probably changing fast; thus to estimate the test–retest reliability of a test measuring such achievement would require a short interval, such as two consecutive days. On the other hand, intelligence is considered very stable, and test–retest intervals up to one year or more may not be unreasonable. For very unstable traits, such as mood that can fluctuate within short time interval, the test–retest method of estimating reliability may be inappropriate altogether, for this method assumes that the trait remains constant during the interval over which retesting occurs.

Potential advantages of test–retest reliability.   Assuming that an appropriate testing interval can be found, test–retest reliability does have some advantages. First, because the same test is given twice, no random error can be attributed to different items being selected for use in different forms of the test. Second, it avoids the difficult and time-consuming task of constructing alternative forms deserving of the label "parallel." Third, although it has other drawbacks, same-day testing–retesting controls random errors introduced by students' day-to-day variations. Fourth, test-retest reliability is simple to calculate. Fifth, it is appropriate for use with timed (speeded) tests. Because the test–retest reliability estimate assesses the extent to which the scores on the same test are stable across test administrations, this reliability estimate is often called the "index of stability."

Major uses of test–retest reliability.   With an appropriate interval, test–retest reliability might be used when (1) teachers are giving tests with time limits (speed tests); (2) no parallel form of the test is available or possible to construct; and (3) content is routine or familiar enough that "memorable" content will not exacerbate the problems of recall from the first test. Despite various advantages, however, test–retest reliabilities are perhaps less useful than other reliability estimates we will consider next.

Measurement error source for test–retest reliability.   Because the same test is given twice, obviously the content remains constant, and no random error can be attributed to different items used in the test. The obvious factor contributing to the inconsistency of test scores is time. In other words, test–retest reliability estimates random errors introduced by students' day-to-day variations. Because test–retest reliability estimate assesses the extent to which the scores on the same test are stable across test administrations, this reliability estimate is often called the "coefficient of stability." Whenever measurement stability across time is the concern, test–retest reliability is appropriate and should be estimated.

Application Problem 1A

You administer a *Math Anxiety Scale* at the beginning of the school year. One month later, you administer the scale again to the same group of students. Given the following data, what is the test–retest reliability coefficient of the *Math Anxiety Scale?*

	Test Score	Retest Score
Lynn	18	20
Larry	15	18
Meg	17	17
Marty	13	14
Nanci	16	18
Norman	14	12

Based on this reliability estimate, are you satisfied with the reliability of this test?

Application Problem 1B

What is/are some major consideration(s) when determining the length of interval between test administrations when the test–retest approach is used to estimate measurement reliability?

Parallel Form Method

It is often desirable to have one or more alternative, equivalent forms of the same test. Suppose a student misses his regularly scheduled examination, and the teacher is concerned that conversations with classmates about specific test items may give that student an unfair advantage if he is administered the same test. This concern is partially eliminated if an equivalent form of the test can be administered under conditions as nearly equivalent as possible.

The question, however, is whether or not the two forms are truly equivalent. To determine this, it is important to do three things: (1) analyze the content of each form to ensure that the content of each is comparable; (2) determine whether the average score obtained by the same group of students on each form is the same; and (3) examine the correlation between the two sets of test scores from the two forms. To determine the correlation, administer the two tests to the same group of students with a short interval. The short interval minimizes day-to-day variations in individuals, but memory of the first test should have little effect on student performance on the second test since the two forms would contain different (although similar) items. Interestingly, the procedure for ascertaining the equivalence of the two forms also can be used to estimate the reliability of either test. Once there are two alternate or parallel forms of a test, the correlation between scores on the two provides a basis for estimating the reliability of either test.

The critical issue in developing equivalent test forms is to have the two tests similar in content, form, and difficulty, without having them so similar that the majority of the items are the same or nearly the same (for example, 2×3 versus 3×2). Inclusion of too many identical items will result in a spuriously high correlation between the two tests, with a consequent overestimate of test reliability. Conversely, if the test items are too dissimilar, the reliability will be spuriously low. This problem underscores the difficulty of creating alternate forms that are truly equivalent. It is difficult to develop one good test, let alone two. Thus, the parallel forms of computing reliability is most often used for standardized psychological and educational achievement tests, where adequate resources make this possible.

Because of the difficulty of constructing parallel test forms, most classroom teachers will be unlikely to use this method. In situations where commercial tests are used in schools, test publishers should provide data on how nearly equivalent their "parallel" forms are, and teachers should consider such data carefully in determining when one form might appropriately be substituted for another.

Calculating a Parallel Form Reliability Coefficient

The step-by-step procedure for estimating parallel form reliability of a test is as follows, and would be the same whether the second form were administered concurrently (immediately after the first) or after a time interval:

1. Administer Form 1 of the test.
2. Administer Form 2 of the test to the same students.
3. Score both Forms 1 and 2.
4. Correlate the two sets of scores by obtaining the Pearson r, as you did earlier for the test–retest reliability coefficient.

Issues Related to Parallel Form Reliability

With or without an interval? Parallel form reliability may be calculated with or without a time interval between administrations of the two forms. When there is little or no interval between test administrations, this reliability estimate is often termed the "coefficient of equivalence," thus differentiating it from the "coefficient of stability" that results from the test–retest method. When the two parallel test forms are administered with a significant interval between them, however, it becomes a type of test–retest with parallel forms and is sometimes referred to as the "coefficient of stability *and* equivalence." The choice between these two approaches depends on what measurement error source(s) one is interested in, as discussed in the following section.

Measurement error source estimated by parallel form reliability. If two test forms are administered with minimal interval in-between, assuming that factors such as fatigue, practice effect, memory effect have negligible impact on test performance, then the obvious measurement error will be attributed to the difference in *content* of the two test forms. No two forms of a test are ever *perfectly* parallel. Test items will vary in the extent to which they measure the same objectives adequately. The more test items differ across forms, the greater the unreliability. In general, the measurement error contributed by *content* difference tends to be larger than the measurement error contributed by *time,* as in the test–retest method. For this reason, parallel form reliability estimates tend to be lower than test–retest reliability estimates. Whenever more than one form of the same test exists, we should be concerned about measurement error contributed by *content sampling,* and parallel form method is appropriate for such estimation.

In the situation where two parallel forms are administered with a substantial interval in-between (coefficient of stability and equivalence), both *content* and *time* become measurement error sources. Since such reliability estimate contains *two* major error sources rather than one, theoretically, such reliability estimate will be lower than either coefficient of stability (test–retest) or coefficient of equivalence (parallel form without interval). In this sense, this approach produces a more conservative estimate of measurement reliability by incorporating two major measurement error sources in the process.

Major uses of parallel form reliability. As the name indicates, this method is primarily used to help establish the equivalence of parallel forms. Constructing a parallel form is time consuming and difficult; therefore, this procedure may not be practical for most classroom teachers. Nevertheless, teachers should be familiar with it so as to understand and interpret parallel form reliability estimates reported for standardized achievement and psychological tests. Care must be taken in interpreting parallel form reliability coefficients since they are likely to yield lower estimates of reliability than does the test–retest method. Also, reliability for parallel forms administered at different times will tend to be lower than test–retest reliabilities, or reliabilities for parallel forms administered at the same time. Because this reliability method controls two major potential sources of error, it is likely to be a more conservative and stringent estimate of reliability.

Application Problem 2

From a pool of 300 items that test knowledge of American history, you have drawn 100 to make a classroom test. A colleague uses your 300-item pool to devise another 100-item American history test so that both of you can have alternative, equivalent forms for use at the beginning and end of your history units. You have examined the two tests and judged their content to be very much equivalent. Four of your students volunteer to take your exam and the new exam (on the same day) so that you and your colleague can examine the equivalence of the two tests. Their scores are as shown.

	Form 1 (Yours)	Form 2 (Your Colleague's)
Sandra	89	76
Sam	97	82
Tamara	93	90
Tom	89	84

Continued

Calculate the means of the students' performance on the two test forms. What would you conclude about equivalence of the forms from those means? What is the parallel form reliability coefficient for the two forms of this test? How would you interpret such a reliability estimate?

Internal Consistency Reliability

In practice, a major drawback of both test–retest and parallel form reliability is that both require two test administrations. For teacher-made tests, methods of estimating reliability that require only a single test administration are more feasible. Such methods are typically referred to as *measures of internal consistency* or *measures of homogeneity* since they are based on estimates of how well a test is correlated with itself (for example, how well two halves of a test are correlated). We shall discuss three measures of internal consistency: the split-half method, Cronbach's coefficient alpha method, and the Kuder–Richardson method for estimating reliability from a single test administration.

Split-Half Method for Estimating Reliability

In split-half procedure, the total set of items is divided into halves, and scores on the halves are correlated to obtain an estimate of the test's reliability. For this method to work, however, the test must be divided into two comparable halves that are approximations of two parallel forms (although each is only one-half the length of the total test).

When test items are sequenced in the order of their difficulty (for example, easy items first as "warm-up," difficult items later), one cannot simply divide the test into first and last halves, for obvious reasons. In this case, the odd–even split (items 1, 3, 5, 7, versus items 2, 4, 6, 8, and so on), is generally used to create two half-length tests. When using an odd–even split, it is important to keep groups of items that deal with a single problem intact since scores on such clusters of items are obviously not independent and should not be split into halves. If item difficulty is random—that is, items do *not* become increasingly difficult through the test— then the division of a test into first and last halves may be appropriate. Whatever method is used, the key is to create two halves that are comparable in both content and difficulty.

Before we discuss the split-half method further, we must take time to discuss briefly the relationship between reliability and test length.

Reliability and Test Length

Generally, assuming other things being equal (such as all the items measuring the same thing), the longer a test is, the more reliable it is. The more items there are in a test, the less likelihood there is that answering any one item differently in two test administrations will significantly reduce the reliability coefficient. Suppose a teacher administers a ten-item vocabulary test to his or her students, and splits the test into two five-item halves, scores those halves, and obtains a correlation between the scores. The resulting correlation is the reliability of each *half* of the test, rather than reliability of the test *as a whole*. Since reliability is affected by test length, the correlation between two halves in split-half approach will be an *underestimate* for the whole test. For this reason, it is necessary to make adjustment of such correlation so that it more truthfully represents the reliability of the *whole* test. The Spearman–Brown Prophecy formula is intended to correct for such underestimate when reliability is calculated on half-tests, giving an approximate estimate of what the reliability of the test would be had it not been artificially shortened into halves. According to the Spearman–Brown Prophecy formula, the reliability of the total test (R) can be estimated from the correlation of the two halves (r) as follows:[1]

$$R = \frac{2\,r}{(1 + r)} \qquad \text{(Formula 4.1)}$$

Calculating a Spilt-Half Reliability Coefficient

The step-by-step method for estimating the reliability, or internal consistency, of a test using the split-half method is as follows:

1. Determine how the test is to be divided (for example, odd–even items, which we will assume is the case for this example).
2. Add all the scores of *odd-numbered* items for each student (items 1, 3, 5, 7, and so on) to obtain that student's total score for that half of the test. Separately, add the scores of the *even-numbered* items for each student (items 2, 4, 6, 8, and so on).
3. Treat the separate totals for odd and even items as separate tests for each student, creating two scores for each student, and thus "two sets" of test scores for your class.
4. Compute a Pearson r to determine the correlation between these two "tests" (half-tests, actually), using the same procedure as outlined earlier for test–retest and alternate-form reliability.
5. Apply the Spearman–Brown Prophecy formula to correct the split-half reliability estimate, thus obtaining the reliability for the *whole* test.

Issues Related to Split-Half Reliability Estimates

Advantages and disadvantages of the split-half method. The major advantage of the split-half method is obvious in that it requires only one test administration and thus avoids any effects of practice, memory, or differential test administration or scoring, and some other practical problems. This approach, like others, also has its

---

[1]The formula presented here is only a special case of the Spearman–Brown Prophecy formula. The original purpose of the Spearman–Brown formula is to assess the impact of test length change on test reliability. Such test length change can result in either a longer or a shorter test. Furthermore, the test length change can be of any degree (one-third as short as the original, twice as long as the original, five times as long as the original, and so on). Interested readers may refer to other sources for more detailed information (for example, Crocker & Algina, 1986).

share of disadvantages. A major premise of split-half reliability is that both halves of the test are approximately parallel and equivalent. But perhaps the items actually differ enough so that the two halves cannot really be considered equivalent. Most important, split-half reliability estimates should not be used with a pure speeded test, which is defined as a test that consists of such easy items that few students miss any item they attempt, but has so many items that very few students can finish the entire test. This is in contrast to power tests, where the difficulty of items may vary from easy to very difficult, and time limits either do not exist or are sufficiently generous that most students can attempt most items. Although odd–even split sounds reasonable, theoretically, there are many different ways one can split a test into two halves. The trouble with these different ways of splitting a test is that we cannot obtain a *unique* reliability estimate; different ways of splitting a test will give us different reliability estimates.

Speed test and power test.   Tests can be categorized as being either a *speed* test or a *power* test. On a *speed test,* the test items tend to be very easy, and the interest in testing is to see *how fast* one can answer the test items. Few students will miss many of the items, but the test typically contains so many items that few can finish them all within the allotted time. Speed tests, obviously, must have strict time limits; otherwise, everyone will be able to finish all the simple test items. A *power test,* on the other hand, tends to contain more difficult test items, and performance is mainly dependent on how well one can answer the test items, not on how fast one can do so. For a pure power test, time is usually not a major consideration, and performance mainly hinges on one's knowledge level.

Split-half reliability approach, as described, is generally not appropriate for a pure speed test since such reliability estimate (for example, the correlation between two halves of odd and even items) tends to be spuriously high. Consider a speed test of very easy items, and an examinee finishes 40 out of the 50 items. For an odd–even item split of the test, the examinee will approximately have 20 items correct in each half. Similar data patterns will occur for other examinees, resulting in very high reliability between the two halves. Thus the split-half reliability gives a spuriously high estimate of test reliability. Since some classroom tests combine elements of a speed test and a power test, the split-half reliability estimate may be artificially inflated. When speed is an important element of a classroom test, it is wise for the teacher not to use the split-half approach for estimating reliability.

Measurement error source in split-half approach.   In the previous test–retest and parallel form reliability approaches, the major error sources are identified to be *time* and *content* (item sampling), respectively. Similar to parallel form reliability approach, split-half approach assesses measurement error contributed by *content* (item sampling) because score difference between two halves is most likely to be contributed by item difficulty difference, that is, content inconsistency. *Time* is not an error source in this situation since the test is taken as a whole.

Application Problem 3A

You would like to find out the internal consistency of your new social studies exam. You decide that the fastest way to do so is to score odd-numbered items versus even-numbered items. The following data results:

	Correct Responses on	
	Odd Items	Even Items
Vicki	42	43
Vern	41	43
Wendy	44	45
William	44	42

What is the correlation between scores on the odd-numbered and even-numbered items? What is the estimated reliability of your whole exam? How would you interpret such a reliability estimate?

Application Problem 3B

When the split-half method is used to estimate internal consistency reliability, why is the Spearman–Brown formula needed for adjustment?

Cronbach's Coefficient Alpha and Kuder–Richardson Formulas

One difficulty with the split-halves method of estimating reliability is that different reliability estimates would result from different ways of splitting the same test. The correlation of the odd and even items, for example, may be very different from that between the first and second halves of the test. Two other estimates, Cronbach's coefficient alpha and Kuder–Richardson Formula 20 (KR-20) provide similar internal consistency estimates but avoid the problem of deciding how a test should be split into halves. Like the split-half method, these two methods for estimating measurement reliability are determined from a single test administration. Theoretically, they provide an estimate of what the average reliability would be if *all possible ways* of splitting the test into halves were used. These estimates are obtained without actually calculating all possible split halves. Furthermore, there is no need to use the Spearman–Brown Prophecy formula to correct for shortened test length because the test is not actually split into halves for scoring.

Cronbach's Alpha Method for Estimating Reliability

Cronbach (1951) has developed an approach he terms "coefficient alpha," for estimating the homogeneity or internal consistency of the scores obtained from a single administration of a single test. Coefficient alpha can be used with all types of test items, whether test items are dichotomously scored as right or wrong (for example, most multiple-choice items), or are weighted (for example, essay type of items where partial-credit scoring is allowed). Coefficient alpha does not depend on any single correlation; rather, it conceptually depends on the average intercorrelations among all items. Without the aid of a computer program, Cronbach's coefficient alpha can be computationally tedious. Despite this, we present the formula for Cronbach's coefficient alpha and a small example here for illustration.

$$\alpha = \left(\frac{K}{K-1}\right)\left(1 - \frac{\Sigma\sigma^2_i}{\sigma^2}\right) \qquad \text{(Formula 4.2)}$$

In the formula, K represents the number of items in the test, $\Sigma\sigma^2_i$ represents the sum of variances of individual items, and σ^2 represents variance of scores on the total test. Because the computation for Cronbach's coefficient alpha by hand can be quite tedious, we present a small hypothetical example (ten persons taking a six-item test) in Appendix A to illustrate the calculation process, and if you make some effort to follow the computational process in that example, it may facilitate your understanding of the formula.

As can be seen from the small example in Appendix A, to calculate coefficient alpha by hand can be really tedious. If you have a 40-item test, you have to calculate 40 variances for all 40 items, and add up these 40-item variances. Also you have to calculate the variance of the scores on the total test. Then you can plug in the numbers into the formula. With the easy access to modern technology, it will be best to leave the calculation to computer programs.

Kuder–Richardson Formula 20 (KR-20)

As discussed earlier, coefficient alpha is suitable for estimating internal consistency reliability for all types of test items, whether the items are dichotomously scored (for example, correct/incorrect, right/wrong, or true/false), or the items are weighted with a range of possible values (for example, scores ranging from 0 to 5 for short essay questions; ratings ranging from 1 to 5 for items on an attitude scale to represent "strongly agree" to "strongly disagree," and so on). Despite its versatility, coefficient alpha was historically generalized from another formula by Kuder and Richardson (1937), which was designed to calculate internal consistency for test items that are *dichotomously* scored only. Popularly known as KR-20, the formula by Kuder and Richardson is as follows:

$$\text{KR-20} = \left(\frac{K}{K-1}\right)\left(1 - \frac{\Sigma pq}{\sigma^2}\right) \qquad \text{(Formula 4.3)}$$

where p represents the proportion of examinees who scored an item correctly, and q represents the proportion of examinees who missed the item, and as in coefficient alpha formula, σ^2 represents the variance of the total test scores. Obviously, $q = (1 - p)$. As can be seen, KR-20 looks very much like coefficient alpha formula, except that Σpq in KR-20 replaces $\Sigma\sigma^2_i$ in coefficient alpha formula (sum of item variances). It turned out that Σpq is algebraically equivalent to $\Sigma\sigma^2_i$ when the items are dichotomously scored. In other words, KR-20 is a special case of coefficient alpha, and it is suitable only for *dichotomously* scored items, whereas coefficient alpha is the general formula that can be used for *any* type of test item. We present a calculation example in Appendix A to illustrate the computational process.

In most measurement situations, there is usually no need to calculate these estimates by hand because all test scoring computer programs provide one of the two (more typically coefficient alpha) as standard output. Besides, major statistical software programs have procedures to calculate coefficient alpha. In cases when these options are not available, it is probably wise to seek some professional help rather than relying on your own hand calculation, unless the data set is very small.

Kuder–Richardson Formula 21 (KR-21)

The Kuder–Richardson Formula 20 (KR-20) has very satisfactory psychometric properties. It can be difficult to compute, however, and therefore would be useful to the typical classroom teacher only if it is provided in the output from computer analysis of test scores. Another simpler Kuder–Richardson formula is their Formula 21 (KR-21). The formula for this reliability estimate, which requires knowledge of only the number of items in a test (K), the mean, and standard deviation (SD) of the raw test scores, is

$$KR\text{-}21 = \frac{(K \times SD^2) - [Mean \times (K - Mean)]}{(K - 1) \times SD^2} \qquad \text{(Formula 4.4)}$$

Because of its simplicity, KR-21 may be useful for classroom teachers when other reliability estimates are not available. We use the data in the hypothetical example for KR-21 in Appendix A to illustrate the calculation of KR-21. From that example, we have $K = 6$, and $SD^2 = 2.49$ (variance of the total test scores). The mean of the total scores can be easily calculated to be 4.1. Using these numbers in Formula 4.4, we obtain

$$KR\text{-}21 = \frac{(6 \times 2.49) - [4.1 \times (6 - 4.1)]}{(6 - 1) \times 2.49} = 0.57$$

It is seen that KR-21 provided an underestimate of KR-20 in this example. It turns out that this is generally true.

Issues Related to Internal Consistency Measures of Reliability

Item homogeneity. Kuder–Richardson formulas and Cronbach's coefficient alpha are measures of test *internal consistency*, that is, the degree of item homogeneity. Test items are homogeneous if they measure the same underlying ability or construct. For this reason, these internal consistency measures are not appropriate for a test that contains a section for reading and another section for math because reading and math are likely to be different constructs. It is, however, appropriate to use these internal consistency measures for estimating reliability separately for each of the two sections. A review by Cortina (1993) illustrates the appropriate and inappropriate use of internal consistency reliability measures.

Speed test and missing items.   Like the split-half method, strictly speaking, all internal consistency measures of reliability are appropriate only for power tests, and may not be used with speed tests; when used on speeded tests, the resulting "estimate of reliability" would tend to be artificially inflated because of high consistency both among items attempted (speed tests tend to have simple items, thus almost all those attempted tend to be scored correctly) and among items not attempted (all treated as if scored incorrectly). Mainly for the same reason, even for a power test, if many items are not attempted (missing values), and these missing values are counted as being incorrect, internal consistency measures of reliability will tend to be inflated by the missing values. For this reason, some computer programs do not allow you to use missing values in the calculation, whereas others give you the option of either using or not using the missing values.

Measurement error source.   For internal consistency reliability measures discussed earlier, it is obvious that *time* cannot be a source of measurement error since the test is taken as a whole. The major measurement error is due to *content* and *content heterogeneity.* In other words, the more heterogeneous the items are, the lower reliability estimate will be obtained.

Major uses of internal consistency measures of reliability.   Unlike the split-half method of determining reliability from one single test administration, the Kuder–Richardson methods and Cronbach's coefficient alpha are not affected by the particular way in which the test is "split" into halves; theoretically, the estimate is the average of the correlations between *all possible* split halves, so there's no need to worry about how best to split the test. Whenever test internal consistency or item homogeneity is the concern, these internal consistency measures are appropriate. Of the three internal consistency measures we have discussed, Cronbach's coefficient alpha is the most versatile because it is appropriate for all types of test items. KR-20 is applicable only for dichotomously scored items, and in this situation, it is equivalent to Cronbach's coefficient alpha. KR-21 is an underestimate of KR-20, and it is psychometrically inferior. Since it is computationally simple, it may be used as the lower bound estimate of test internal consistency, when KR-20 or Cronbach's coefficient alpha are not available.

Application Problem 4A

Why is Cronbach's coefficient alpha considered a more general formula than Kuder–Richardson Formula 20 (KR-20) and Kuder–Richardson Formula 21 (KR-21)?

Application Problem 4B

You have two history tests. Test A is a 50-item multiple-choice test. Test B is a 30-item test that contains 15 dichotomously scored true–false items and 15 questions with multiple responses, each of which is weighted, with from 1 to 3 points for each item. Test A has a possible total score of 50; Test B has a possible total score of 60.

  a. Would KR-20 be an appropriate method for estimating the reliability of Test A? Of Test B? Why?

b. Would Cronbach's alpha be an appropriate method for estimating the reliability of Test A? Of Test B? Why?

Application Problem 4C

You have just computed scores for a 100-item, end-of-term math test that will be important in determining final math grades for your class. The mean of the test is 50, and the standard deviation is 6. What would the test's internal consistency reliability estimate be using KR-21 method? Does that estimate convince you that the test is reliable enough for your purpose?

Interrater Reliability

Test Objectivity

Different instruments may require different scoring procedures, and different scoring procedures may involve different degrees of subjectivity in the scoring process. For example, the old SAT test consisted of all multiple-choice items, and only one option was supposed to be correct for each question. In this situation, no matter who (or which machine) is scoring your test, you should get the same score. On the other hand, when you are asked to write an essay as your writing class final exam, it is easy to imagine that you may get different scores if your paper is scored by several professors. Test *objectivity* is concerned with such test scoring procedures. A test is said to be *objective* if two or more reasonable persons, given a scoring key and/or scoring criteria, would agree on how to score each item, thus agreeing on the number of points each examinee should get on a test. If such agreement is not routinely achieved, the test is said to be *subjective.*

Interrater Reliability and Its Calculation

Whenever a test is not *objective,* that is, different scorers may assign different scores to the same examinee, a legitimate question to ask is: how consistent or inconsistent is the scoring process? Interrater reliability attempts to answer this question. *Interrater reliability* estimate is easily obtained as follows:

1. Administer the test to a group of students.
2. Ask two independent scorers to score the same group of tests so that each student will get two scores on his test from the two independent scorers.
3. Calculate the correlation coefficient between the two sets of scores from the two scorers, and the correlation coefficient is the *interrater reliability coefficient.*

Use of Interrater Reliability and Its Measurement Error Source

Interrater reliability is applicable whenever test scoring procedures contain certain degrees of subjectivity. Obviously, for tests with only multiple-choice or other objective item types, interrater reliability is irrelevant. The measurement error estimated by interrater reliability is that part of measurement error contributed by the subjectivity of scoring procedures, or the inconsistency among different scorers.

Comparison of Methods for Estimating Reliability: A Summary

From the discussion presented, it is important to note that different reliability estimation procedures are designed for different purposes. These procedures differ mainly in terms of measurement error sources they are designed to assess. Because they are designed to handle different measurement errors, generally, one procedure cannot substitute for another. For example, if we are concerned about how parallel two alternate forms of a test are, the only reliability procedure that can answer the question is parallel form reliability. In the same vein, interrater reliability indicates only scorer consistency, and it tells us nothing about how consistent items are with one another. The procedures for assessing internal consistency of a test, however, are the exception, and since split-half, Kuder–Richardson formulas, and Cronbach's coefficient alpha are all designed to deal with basically the same measurement error source, they may substitute one another if other conditions permit.

Another point worthy of mention is that measurement error sources tend to be independent. This means that one type of reliability estimate tells us little or nothing about another different measurement error source. For example, if we have obtained good internal consistency reliability estimate (for example, Cronbach's coefficient alpha), we can claim only that our test has good interitem consistency, or good test homogeneity. We know very little about how test scores will fluctuate if this test is administered twice to the same students, nor do we know much about how consistent different scorers will be in scoring the test (if some items are not objective). For this reason, it is often futile to ask, "which reliability estimate should I trust?" or "which reliability estimation approach should I use for my test?" because the answer to the question depends on which potential measurement error source is of most interest to you. Also, since the different methods for estimating reliability deal with different sources of measurement error, as summarized in Figure 4.1, they are often not directly comparable. For purposes of interpretation, one cannot decide whether a particular reliability coefficient is satisfactory without knowing the method by which it was calculated.

This discussion reveals one fundamental weakness or limitation these traditional reliability procedures have: different measurement error sources can be assessed only individually, and not at the same time. To overcome this limitation, more elaborate reliability procedures have been developed that can assess the relative contribution of different measurement error sources *at the same time*. These procedures are covered under the topic of *generalizability theory*. Because understanding generalizability theory requires much more sophisticated understanding of statistics, it is a topic beyond this book. Interested readers may consult other sources on this topic (for example, Brennan, 1983; Shavelson & Webb, 1991).

To help you recall what we have said about the various methods for estimating reliability, we have summarized the most salient points in Figure 4.1.

Use and Interpretation of Reliability Estimates

Reliability coefficients discussed in this chapter theoretically range from 0 to + 1.0. The easiest way to interpret reliability coefficient is to directly interpret the reliability coefficient as the *percentage of score variance* contributed by true score (real

Comparison	Test–Retest Reliability	Parallel Form Reliability	Internal Consistency Reliability			Interrater Reliability
			Split-Half	Kuder-Richardson	Coefficient Alpha	
Primary Use	When test score stability over time is the concern	Whenever alternative forms of a test exist	When item homogeneity is the concern and test can be split into two halves	When item homogeneity within a test is the concern (for dichotomously scored items only)	When item homogeneity within a test is the concern (for any types of items)	When test-scoring procedure is not objective
Test Administration	Twice	Twice, with or without an interval in between	Once	Once	Once	Once
Sources of Measurement Error	Score variation over time	Item sampling (no interval); item sampling and variation over time (with interval)	Heterogeneity of items; item sampling	Heterogeneity of items; item sampling		Scoring inconsistency across scorers

FIGURE 4.1   Comparisons Among Six Methods of Estimating Reliability

differences among examinees) and by a measurement error source. For example, for a parallel form reliability coefficient of 0.90, the interpretation will be that 10 percent of score variance is contributed by content inconsistency across the two forms, and 90% of the score variance is due to real difference among the examinees. Readers with good statistical knowledge may notice that the correlation coefficient should be squared for the purpose of such interpretation in terms of percentage of variance, as discussed in Chapter 3. Although, in statistical sense, reliability coefficient is a correlation coefficient in many situations, psychometrically, it is different. For interpretive purposes, reliability coefficient is *directly* interpretable as percentage of variance without being squared. Interested readers may consult Crocker and Algina (1986) for technical details concerning this issue. But here are some *general* guidelines for interpreting reliability coefficients.

1. *Test scores used for decisions about an individual student require higher degree of reliability than those used for making decisions about groups of students.* When teacher-made tests are used in critical decisions about individual students (for example, passing a course), they should possess reliability coefficients of .80 or higher. By contrast, coefficients as low as .50 are acceptable if the tests are used to make decisions about groups (for example, determining when to move a class on to the next curriculum unit).

The need for higher reliability with tests used to make individual decisions is obvious if you remember that the higher the reliability, the less error associated with test scores. When averaged across all students, measurement error tends to balance out; there will be approximately as many positive errors of measurement as negative errors. Thus, across a group of scores, measurement error generally will not bias the results. For a test with low reliability, however, an individual student's observed score may be substantially higher or lower than his true score.

Although practical considerations may occasionally force teachers or others to use tests with reliability coefficients below desired limits, they can at least interpret resulting scores with great caution *and* in combination with other information if they are aware that the test results they are using are less dependable than desired.

2. *Higher reliability coefficients are essential if decisions based on test scores have important, lasting consequences that cannot be reversed or disconfirmed by other sources of information.* Some decisions about individual students have long-term, perhaps permanent, consequences. In this case, very stringent standards for reliability (coefficients of at least .90) should be set as minimums.

3. *Lower reliability coefficients are tolerable for tests used in decisions that are of less consequence, are reversible, have only temporary impact, and can be confirmed by other sources of information.* When decisions are of less importance, we can afford to be less confident in making them. In such cases, reliability coefficients need not be as high, even for decisions about individuals.

4. *Reliability coefficients for standardized achievement or aptitude tests should be around .90 or higher.* This is so for two reasons. First, since the norm groups on which standardized tests' reliabilities are calculated are usually very heterogeneous, their actual reliability in (typically) more homogeneous classes will be somewhat lower. Second, critical decisions about individual students—placement, for instance—may be made on the basis of standardized tests, and unreliable tests are an intolerable basis for such decisions.

5. *Lower reliability coefficients may be acceptable if the test is handicapped by factors or circumstances that would tend to lower its reliability, whereas higher coefficients may be judged inadequate if the test is advantaged by factors or circumstances that automatically enhance reliability.* Any limits on "acceptable" levels of reliability are necessarily arbitrary, for coefficients can be influenced by so many factors.

How to Increase the Reliability of a Test

Several conditions can directly affect the reliability coefficients resulting from methods presented in this chapter. Several of these are under the control of the teacher or the test user, and understanding how these factors work not only allows for more intelligent interpretation of reliability coefficients, but also helps users in constructing more reliable tests. Generally speaking, test reliability can be increased if one attends carefully to (1) consistency in scoring, (2) group variability (the spread of scores in the group tested), (3) the difficulty level of the test, and (4) test length.

Reliability of Scoring

Reliable scoring occurs when (1) different scorers agree with one another as they score the same test items, or (2) a single scorer assigns the same scores to the same test, if scored on different occasions. The first of these is called *interscorer reliability,* whereas the second is called *intrascorer reliability.* In both cases, the greater the agreement, the greater the reliability. Without reliability in scoring, the testing procedure is likely to be unreliable. In fact, the reliability of scoring limits test reliability since reliability of a test can be no greater than the reliability (agreement) among scorers. This is one reason objectivity has been emphasized throughout this book: objectively scored items tend to yield high interscorer agreement or reliability, and thus will increase reliability of the test scores.

For example, if interscorer reliability on an essay test is only .55, the reliability of that test can be no higher than .55 and will almost certainly be lower since other sources of error will also enter. For this reason, it is essential that scoring of essay items be made as objective as possible by developing adequate scoring systems that clearly specify points to be awarded to certain aspects of different essay responses. Increasing scorer reliability can substantially increase test reliability. Most so-called objective test items (multiple choice, true-false, matching, and completion) do not suffer from scorer unreliability.

Group Variability

In essence, reliability coefficients are statistical correlation coefficients. As we explained in the previous chapter, correlation tends to suffer whenever *restriction of range* occurs. For this reason, reliability also depends on the amount of nonextraneous variability, or true variance, of scores within the group tested. All other things being equal, the greater the variability in the scores, the higher the reliability estimate. If variability is small, and most students score at nearly the same levels, even small changes in individual scores from one testing to another can significantly shift the relative position of a student within the group. It follows logically that when scores are spread across a broader range, small changes in individual scores tend to have much less impact on a student's relative position within the group. Since reliability is higher when students remain in the same relative position from one test to another, greater variability tends to enhance reliability.

The range of scores in turn depends, to some extent, on how heterogeneous the examinees are in the trait being measured. If the group to which the test is administered has a restricted range of ability (for example, a remedial class or an honors class), reliabilities are likely to be less than if that same test were administered to a regular classroom where students tend to differ more widely in ability levels. Similarly, if tests are administered across grade levels, the group variability will be high enough that reliability estimates are likely to be substantially higher than if the same test were used at a single grade level. Similarly, the reliability of a test administered to all students in a particular grade is likely to be higher than if the same test were administered to a single class at that grade level.

If one wished to increase the reliability coefficient of a test, then it should be apparent that the test should be administered to a group with the maximum variability that is appropriate (that is, a group no more diverse than subsequent groups with which the test would normally be used). Conversely, administering tests to students with restricted ranges in ability will tend to reduce the obtained reliability coefficient, even though the actual reliability of the test has not changed.

Difficulty Level of the Test

Tests that are too easy result in clusters of scores close together at the top end of the scale. This restricted spread of scores lowers the reliability coefficient because, as noted earlier, when scores tend to cluster, even small changes in scores between tests can produce major shifts in relative positions of the examinees.

Similarly, very difficult tests cause scores to cluster at the bottom end of the scale—again lowering the reliability coefficient. Very difficult tests also encourage guessing; this introduces more random error, thus lowering reliability still further. Easy tests may be *somewhat* more reliable than difficult tests, but neither is as reliable as tests that are sufficiently moderate in difficulty to allow greater variability of scores. It follows, therefore, that one way to increase test reliability is to make sure that the difficulty level is appropriate for the students tested.

Number and Quality of Test Items

In general, the more items on a test, the higher the reliability. A longer test permits the variability of scores (group variability) to increase, thus leading to increased stability in student relative positions across test administrations. Further, longer tests provide students with a better opportunity to show their true knowledge of content, whereas shorter tests increase the probability of their attaining high (or low) scores simply because of the selection of the small number of items included in the test. A student may get lucky and guess correctly all three items on a three-item test, but he is highly unlikely to guess all items correctly on a 24-item test.

Simply lengthening the test won't guarantee higher reliability, however. If reliability is to be increased, the new items that are added must measure the same characteristic as the original items, and must be similar in quality. Adding items that are unrelated in terms of what they measure, or items that are ambiguous, vague, or otherwise poorly constructed, is likely to lower reliability even though they lengthen the test. In short, one should follow the guidelines for writing good test items presented in later chapters.

One additional caution. Since test reliability and test length generally go hand in hand, unusually high reliabilities for relatively short tests may signal that something is amiss (Wainer, 1986).

Application Problem 5A

What are some measurement situations in which lower reliability coefficients may be tolerated? Why?

Application Problem 5B

Discuss the major measurement error sources that different reliability estimation approaches attempt to capture, and why reliability estimates based on different estimation approaches are largely considered noninterchangeable.

Reliability and Standard Error of Measurement

Standard Error of Measurement

Because reliability coefficients are one essential criterion in comparing tests to determine their fallibility and are, within interpretive limits, comparable from test to test, we have devoted substantial space to helping you understand reliability coefficients. But as we have noted, the reliability coefficient is a group statistic that depends on the variability of scores in the group tested, and its utility—indeed its purpose—is to estimate the reliability of *all* scores yielded by a test (hence the common misnomer of the *reliability of a test,* rather than *the correct referent the reliability of scores produced by that test*).

If one wishes to interpret an *individual* score, however, reliability coefficients are much less directly useful than a closely related concept known as the *standard error of measurement* (SEM), which relates measurement reliability to the accuracy of our interpretation for an *individual's* score. Let's assume that we administered an IQ test to one individual 1000 times. Let's assume further that there were no memory, practice, or any other "carry-over" effects across the test administrations. Because of random measurement errors, the student obtained some high scores, some low scores, and some scores in the middle. Keep in mind that our purpose of testing is to estimate the student's "true score," or true ability level in this situation. When we put the 1000 scores together, we had a score distribution similar to the one shown in Figure 4.2. This score distribution had its mean and standard deviation. The best estimate for the student's true score is obviously the mean. The standard deviation of this distribution is often referred to as the *standard error of measurement* (SEM). SEM is extremely useful because it provides us a tool to estimate score range within which the student's true score might fall.

In practice, we can never obtain a distribution for each student like Figure 4.2. So how can we know what the standard deviation might be for individual students? It turns out that SEM can be *estimated* based on reliability estimate. If the

FIGURE 4.2   Hypothetical Distribution of Scores from 1000 Administration of the Same IQ Test to a Person

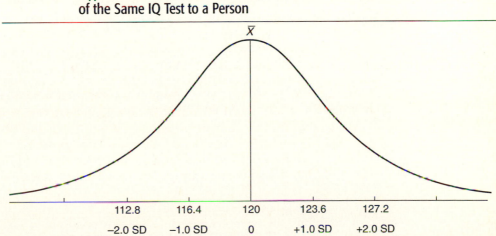

	112.8	116.4	120	123.6	127.2
	−2.0 SD	−1.0 SD	0	+1.0 SD	+2.0 SD

test were perfectly reliable, there would be no measurement error, and the results of each test administration would be perfectly consistent. Thus the standard error of measurement would be 0. When measurement error exists, as it always does, the scores for an individual through repeated testing would not be the same, and SEM would be larger than 0, as in Figure 4.2. The mathematical relationship between standard error of measurement (*SEM*), and reliability (r_{tt}), is

$$SEM = SD \times \sqrt{1 - r_{tt}} \qquad \text{(Formula 4.5)}$$

where *SD* is the standard deviation of test scores obtained from a given group. What is the practical significance of SEM? To answer this question, we need to return to the topic of normal distribution discussed in Chapter 3. Since SEM is conceptually the standard deviation of a score distribution (in this case, the score distribution for one individual), under the assumption that the distribution is approximately normal, our discussion of the normal distribution applies here. For example, if we knew that the individual's true score was 120, and SEM was 4, we could predict that if the individual were repeatedly tested for 1000 times, approximately 68 percent of his scores would fall between 116 and 124 (± 1 standard deviation), and 95 percent of his scores would fall between 112 and 128 (± 2 standard deviations).

The reality, however, is that we will never know a student's true score. What we know is only his obtained score from one test administration. So the question is reversed: given a student's obtained score, is there any way for us to predict his true score? The answer, unfortunately, is no. But before you are ready to give up on this, we do have something encouraging for you. Even if finding an individual's true score is hopeless, what we can find out is a range within which his true score is most likely to fall. This is accomplished through the use of standard error of measurement.

Return for a moment to the IQ scores obtained by Scott (108) and Christopher (106) that we mentioned at the beginning of this chapter. Which person has the higher IQ? It is easy to say that Scott's observed score is two points higher than Christopher's. But what if Christopher had a particularly bad day, or Scott made a number of lucky guesses? Now that we know about the standard error of measurement (SEM), we can estimate the range in which each true score is likely to fall. Assume that the standard deviation for the IQ test is 15 points, and the reliability is quite high (.96). The resulting standard error of measurement would be calculated to be 3. (Try this calculation by using Formula 4.5.) Since Scott and Christopher obtained scores of 108 and 106, respectively, we can estimate that (1) the chances are about 68 percent that Scott's true score falls within the range of 105 to 111, and Christopher's true score falls within the range of 103 to 109; (2) the chances are about 95 percent that Scott's true score falls within the range of 102 to 114, and Christopher's true score falls within 100 to 112. So instead of discerning the elusive true score, we calculate a score range that may contain the true score with certain degrees of probability. Because the score ranges of the two boys overlap considerably, the boys' true IQ scores are probably not very different; in fact, there is a good chance that Christopher's true IQ is higher than Scott's.

Viewed from this perspective, the concept of standard error of measurement is often more informative for individuals than the reliability coefficient (Williams & Zimmerman, 1984). This is so because the standard error of measurement combines information about the standard deviation of the test as well as the reliability of the test. Hence, you can estimate whether a particular score is likely to be in error by 1 point or by 20 points. Readers with sufficient statistical training may notice that this process is basically the same as constructing *confidence intervals* in statistical hypothesis testing. In fact, it is exactly the same.

Knowing that any observed score is made up of the true score and the error score should make you more cautious about interpreting small differences between scores as meaningful. More important, if you have information about a test's standard deviation and reliability, you can estimate how large an observed score difference should be before one can confidently conclude that the two true scores are different.

Score Bands and Profiles

Since an obtained score is only an approximation of the true score due to measurement error, in many situations, it is often better to report each student's achievement as a band or an interval along the scale of possible scores rather than as a single point. This band provides limits within which the individual's true score is most likely to be located. It also emphasizes that an obtained score is only an estimate of the student's true level of achievement. The upper limit of the band for a particular student can be determined by adding a certain number of SEMs (usually 1.5 or 2) to the person's obtained score. The lower limit can be determined by subtracting the same number of SEMs from the obtained score.

The practice of reporting and interpreting scores in terms of such bands or intervals helps to guard against the tendency to interpret small differences in the obtained scores of two students as representing true differences in their actual achievement levels. If the bands for two students overlap too much, we should assume that the observed differences are not reliable indicators of real differences, but may be caused by measurement error; the actual level of achievement for the two students may differ only minimally or not at all. This use of SEM, it turns out, is very popular in practice for reporting individuals' scores.

Many standardized tests contain several subtests. For example, an achievement test battery often provides scores for reading, math, science, and so on. Frequently, they subdivide these general areas even further. A reading subtest might include scores for word attack, vocabulary, and comprehension. The purpose of reporting these scores separately is to identify areas in which a student or group of students has particular strengths or weaknesses. This type of analysis supposedly allows instruction to be targeted where it is most needed.

Information about subscale scores in related areas is presented in a *profile*. Many standardized test publishers automatically provide a profile of subtest scores for a particular battery. Figure 4.3 illustrates an example of a profile of scores for one student on the Differential Aptitude Tests. As can be seen, the student is above average on all areas except Perceptual Speed and Accuracy. Her strongest scores are in Numerical Reasoning, followed closely by Abstract Reasoning.

Differential Aptitude Tests

FIFTH EDITION

A

INDIVIDUAL REPORT FOR

LISA J. MARTIN

GENDER   FEMALE
14 YRS 7 MOS

SCHOOL: ROSEDALE MIDDLE SCHOOL

DISTRICT: NEWTOWN

GRADE: 09
TEST DATE: 10/90
NORMS: GRADE 09 FALL
LEVEL: 1   FORM: C

DIFFERENTIAL APTITUDE TESTS		FEMALE	NATIONAL PERCENTILE BANDS	MALE	COMBND
	RS/NP	PR-S	1 5 10 20 30 40 50 60 70 80 90 95 99	PR-S	PR-S
VERBAL REASONING	34/40	81-7		84-7	83-7
NUMERICAL REASONING **B**	37/40	98-9		97-9	98-9
ABSTRACT REASONING	33/40	84-7		82-7	82-7
PERCEPTUAL SPEED & ACCURACY	48/100	39-4		53-5	47-5
MECHANICAL REASONING	50/60	96-9		80-7	89-8
SPACE RELATIONS	42/50	92-8		88-7	90-8
SPELLING	33-40	70-6		80-7	75-6
LANGUAGE USAGE	30/40	65-6		77-7	71-6
SCHOLASTIC APTITUDE (YR+NR)	71/80	95-8		95-8	95-8

FIGURE 4.3   Example of a Profile from an Aptitude Test

Source: Differential Aptitude Tests: 4th edition. Copyright © 1982 by the Psychological Corporation. Reproduced by permission.

As discussed earlier, every score contains some error. The scorebands in the profile in Figure 4.3 provide a range around each score within which the individual's true score is likely to fall. For example, on Verbal Reasoning, this student scored at the 81st percentile of girls (see the number immediately to the left of the box for that subtest). However, the score band indicates that the range that may contain the true score of the student is approximately between the 68th and the 86th percentile. Notice also that even though the observed score for Verbal Reasoning is at the 81st percentile for girls and the observed score for Abstract Reasoning is at the 84th percentile for girls, the score bands overlap substantially. Therefore, we should be cautious in concluding that this girl's ability in abstract reasoning is higher than her ability in verbal reasoning. On the other hand, we have much more confidence in concluding that her Verbal Reasoning ability is higher than her Language Usage or her Perceptual Speed and Accuracy, since the score bands overlap little or not at all. Scores that do not include these types of ranges can be easily misinterpreted (Brown, 1976, p. 199).

Obviously, a profile does not make sense unless the scores for each subtest included on the profile are on the same scale. Therefore, if you are creating a profile for a test, you must make sure that each subtest has the same mean and standard deviation. One way of doing this is to convert the scores for each subtest to percentile score or some type of standard score, for example, z score.

Profile analyses can be useful in pointing out those areas in which a particular student has the greatest need. Parents particularly like profile scores because they offer a better feeling for each child's strengths and weaknesses across the full spectrum of subjects. However, you need to be sure that parents do not overestimate the importance of small fluctuations in the profile.

Application Problem 6

You are trying to decide whether a difference between scores of 110 and 115 on your American History final is a "meaningful" difference. What measurement concept(s) discussed in this chapter is (are) most relevant to your deliberation?

The Reliability of Criterion-referenced Measures

The reliability coefficients described previously in this chapter were mainly developed for tests used in making norm-referenced interpretations. These traditional procedures may not be useful to compute the reliability of criterion-referenced measures in some situations, because the size of these coefficients is directly influenced by the amount of variation in the scores. In some criterion-referenced testing situations, there may be much less score variance (the scores are not as spread out) than scores obtained from typical norm-referenced application. In these situations, the reliability estimates discussed previously in this chapter will be less meaningful (Traub, 1994). The logic is simple. Those methods are designed for use with norm-referenced measurement and are workable only when there is at least a reasonable amount of variability in test scores. Whereas norm-referenced measures are designed to emphasize differences among individuals, criterion-referenced measures are not. Indeed, teachers might well expect all students to score relatively high on mastery tests. When teaching has been effective, variability among students' scores is not necessarily desirable, and mastery test scores could be expected to bunch together near the top of the scale. This bunching reduces variability and lowers the computed correlation coefficient. In such cases, the use of classical reliability methods with mastery tests and criterion-referenced measures may be misleading.

A variety of different procedures specifically designed for estimating the reliability of criterion-referenced measurements have been proposed. Most of these procedures are beyond the scope of this text, but some are conceptually simple and reasonably easy to compute. We will describe one of the simpler coefficients here.[2]

One use of criterion-referenced measurement is to classify examinees into categories based on their performance on a test. For instance, students in a mastery learning program are often tested at the end of each instructional unit and classified as having "mastered" or "not mastered" that particular unit. Similarly, many states require prospective lawyers, medical doctors, and teachers to be tested to determine whether they are "qualified" or "not qualified" to practice their profession.

Because of measurement error, examinees sometimes receive test scores that overestimate or underestimate their actual status. Consequently, students are sometimes misclassified. So are prospective teachers, lawyers, or other people taking a professional license or certification exam. If the test scores are very unreliable, a person who "passed" a test may be classified as "failing" if he were tested on another occasion or on another form of the test. Of course, the reverse could

---

[2]Interested readers can learn about other coefficients by studying Berk (1984).

Table 4.1   Summary Table for Analyzing the Consistency of Mastery/Nonmastery Classifications

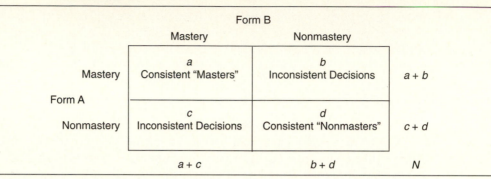

| | | Form B | | |
		Mastery	Nonmastery	
Form A	Mastery	*a* Consistent "Masters"	*b* Inconsistent Decisions	*a* + *b*
	Nonmastery	*c* Inconsistent Decisions	*d* Consistent "Nonmasters"	*c* + *d*
		a + *c*	*b* + *d*	*N*

also be true. Because of the importance of minimizing misclassification, whenever test scores are used as a basis for making classification decisions, we should be concerned about the consistency of those decisions.

Reliability of Classification Decisions

If a student takes two equivalent forms of the same test, will he be classified into the same category? Or if the student takes the same test over on another occasion, will he be classified in the same category? These questions focus on the dependability of the classification decisions. To the degree that classification decisions are consistent across alternative forms of a test or across two separate administrations of the same test, we can have confidence in the reliability of those decisions. The importance of addressing reliability issues of this type is emphasized in the 1985 edition of the *Standards for Educational and Psychological Testing* (AERA et al., 1985).

Table 4.1 provides a useful way of analyzing the consistency of classification decisions. The four cells in this table represent the four kinds of consistency or inconsistency that can occur when students are cross-classified on the basis of two test scores. The cell designated by the letter *a* represents the number of students who were categorized as "masters" on both tests. The cell labeled *d* represents the number of students who were classified as "nonmasters" on both tests. The cells labeled *b* and *c* represent the two possible types of classification errors.

To illustrate how this summary table can be used to analyze classification consistency, suppose that we had administered two alternate forms of a 10-item test to 20 students and that we wanted to determine to what degree the classifications on the two versions of the test were consistent. Assume that the standard used to distinguish between masters and nonmasters on this test has been set at 70 percent. This means that a student who earns a score that equals or exceeds 7 is classified as a master and a student whose score is 6 or less is classified as a nonmaster. Table 4.2 shows the scores earned by 20 students on each form of this test. The fourth column in this table indicates the mastery category in which each student would

Table 4.2   Raw Scores and Classification Decisions for 20 Students on 2 Different Forms of a Mastery Test

Student	Raw Score Form A	Raw Score Form B	Classification Decisions Form A	Classification Decisions Form B	Cell in Summary Table
1	7	9	Master	Master	*a*
2	5	6	Nonmaster	Nonmaster	*d*
3	10	9	Master	Master	*a*
4	7	10	Master	Master	*a*
5	7	6	Master	Nonmaster	*b*
6	6	5	Nonmaster	Nonmaster	*d*
7	9	7	Master	Master	*a*
8	8	8	Master	Master	*a*
9	5	7	Nonmaster	Master	*c*
10	6	9	Nonmaster	Master	*c*
11	7	7	Master	Master	*a*
12	7	8	Master	Master	*a*
13	5	4	Nonmaster	Nonmaster	*d*
14	6	7	Nonmaster	Master	*c*
15	10	8	Master	Master	*a*
16	9	7	Master	Master	*a*
17	8	7	Master	Master	*a*
18	8	10	Master	Master	*a*
19	9	8	Master	Master	*a*
20	5	5	Nonmaster	Nonmaster	*d*

be classified as a result of that student's score on Form A. Similarly, the fifth column lists the mastery category determined by each student's score on Form B. Inconsistent classifications occur when students who are classified as masters on Form A are subsequently classified as nonmasters on Form B and vice versa. Consistent classifications occur when students are classified either as masters or nonmasters on the basis of both tests.

The *proportion of agreement* (usually symbolized by p_A) is a single number that summarizes the consistency of mastery/nonmastery classifications (or any other dichotomous decision such as pass/fail, certified/noncertified). This statistic represents the proportion of students who are consistently classified as masters, plus the proportion who are consistently classified as nonmasters. The mathematical formula for this agreement coefficient can be expressed as follows, where *a* equals the number of persons classified as masters on both forms of the test, *d* equals the number classified as nonmasters on both forms, and *N* represents the total number of students tested (see Table 4.3).

$$P_A = \frac{a + d}{N} \qquad \text{(Formula 4.6)}$$

Table 4.3   Summary Table for Data in Table 4.2

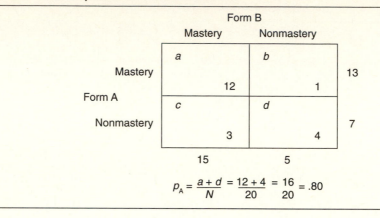

$$p_A = \frac{a+d}{N} = \frac{12+4}{20} = \frac{16}{20} = .80$$

The maximum possible value of p_A equals 1.0 (or 100 percent when multiplied by 100). This value can occur only when all the students tested were classified consistently on both forms of the test. For the data shown in Table 4.2, and summarized in Table 4.3, p_A equals .80. The meaning of this statistic is simple and direct. It simply means that 80 percent of the students were classified in the same categories on both tests. Since 80 percent were consistently classified, only 20 percent $(1 - p_A)$ were inconsistently classified.

For Those Who Want to Dig Deeper

Since p_A is likely to be inflated by some classifications that happen to be consistent just by chance, its minimum value is likely to be larger than zero. To correct for the proportion of chance agreement that is likely to occur, some measurement specialists recommend using Cohan's Kappa (coefficient κ) in lieu of p_A. However, Kappa has some serious limitations when used by itself as a chance-corrected index of agreement (Berk, 1984). If Kappa is used, it should be used *in addition* to p_A rather than in place of it (Crocker & Algina, 1986). For the sake of brevity and simplicity, we have chosen not to present and explain the formula for computing Kappa in this book. However, the formula is readily available in Crocker and Algina (1986) or Berk (1984).

Neither p_A nor Kappa is difficult to understand or compute, but each can be time consuming and laborious. Subkoviak (1988) has provided tables that can be used to obtain reasonably accurate approximations of both p_A and Kappa without all the computational time and effort.

The procedure for assessing the degree of agreement presented here requires scores from two different forms of a test. Instead of using an alternate form of the test, it is possible to administer the same test twice on a test–retest basis and then compute the proportion of agreement using the procedure presented earlier. Subkoviak (1988) has also proposed a split-half procedure for estimating decision consistency based on a single administration of a single test.

SUGGESTED READINGS

Berk, R. A. (1988). Criterion-referenced tests. In J. P. Keeves (ed.). *Educational research methodology, and measurement: An international handbook* (pp. 365–370). Oxford, England: Pergamon Press.

A brief overview of essential characteristics of criterion-referenced tests (mastery and domain-referenced), their dissimilarities to norm-referenced tests, and issues pertaining to their reliability and validity.

Berk, R. A. (1984). Selecting the index of reliability. In R. A. Berk (ed.). *A guide to criterion-referenced test construction* (pp. 231–266). Baltimore, MD: Johns Hopkins University Press.

Berk describes the various indexes that have been proposed for estimating the reliability of criterion-referenced measurements and provides guidelines for deciding which one to use in a given testing situation.

Livingston, S. A. (1988). Reliability of test results. In J. P. Keeves (ed.). *Educational research methodology, and measurement: An international handbook* (pp. 386–392). Oxford, England: Pergamon Press.

This is a nontechnical summary of the relationship between various sources of measurement error and the alternative types of reliability estimates. It includes a useful procedure for calculating interrater reliability, a topic we have not discussed directly in this chapter.

Traub, R. E. (1994). *Reliability for the social sciences: Theory and applications.* Thousand Oaks, CA: Sage Publications.

This monograph provides a comprehensive, yet concise, discussion of the topics related to measurement reliability in social sciences in general. Both norm-referenced and criterion-referenced reliability estimation procedures are discussed, and many hands-on application problems are provided. It serves as an excellent reference for both instructors and students alike.

SUGGESTION SHEET

If your last name starts with the letter D or E, please complete the Suggestion Sheet at the end of the book while this chapter is still fresh in your mind.

Answers to Chapter 4 Application Problems

1. a. If you used a hand calculator with statistical functions correctly on the data given in this application problem, you will have obtained a test–retest reliability coefficient of .82. It is difficult to decide how seriously to take this reliability estimate, which, if taken at face value, suggests the test is highly reliable. A possible concern is whether a one-month interval is sufficient so that memory does not artificially inflate the reliability estimate. Depending on how the anxiety test items are posed, memory could be a problem, but we feel one month

would typically be long enough to cease worrying much on this score. Further, math anxiety can be rather specific, being influenced by particular events (for example, a student with little math anxiety before a critical exam may feel very different two days later after learning he failed that exam). We feel that a .82 test–retest reliability reflects a test that probably is acceptably reliable for purposes proposed in this example.

   b. The major considerations concerning the length of interval are (1) sufficient length to minimize memory effect; (2) the length should not be so long that the trait under measurement is likely to have changed; (3) the stability of the trait being measured: is it reasonably stable during a given length of interval?

2. You should have obtained (1) means of Form 1 = 92, Form 2 = 83, and (2) a parallel form reliability coefficient of .30. Apparently, the content of the two forms is not as equivalent as you judged it was. Form 1 appears to be considerably easier than Form 2. The low parallel form reliability coefficient for these two forms confirms the fact that these two test forms are not really very parallel at all. Given the evidence from this coefficient and the test means, you might reexamine whatever procedure led you to conclude that the two forms contained equivalent content. Apparently, the items selected from the pool were not well selected to test parallel history knowledge.

3.   a. You should have obtained a split-half reliability coefficient (correlation between the students' responses on the odd and even items) of .22. The estimated reliability of your whole exam is .36, which you could find by applying the Spearman–Brown Prophesy formula. There is only a slight correlation between the odd and even numbered items on this test, or in other words, the test appears to possess relatively low internal consistency, which means that the items apparently are measuring different things.

   b. Because measurement reliability is related to test length. Other things being equal, a longer test is more reliable than a shorter one. In split-half approach, the correlation coefficient obtained is based on the two halves of the test, but not on the whole test. Such a correlation underestimates the true reliability of the whole test. Spearman–Brown formula is used to correct for the reduction of test length in the calculation of split-half approach so that the reliability of the whole test will be more truthfully reflected.

4.   a. Cronbach's coefficient alpha is considered to be a more general formula than both KR-20 and KR-21 because it is applicable for both dichotomously scored and weighted test items. KR-20 is applicable only for dichotomously scored items, and in this case, it is equivalent to coefficient alpha. KR-21 is an approximation of KR-20, and it produces a lower bound estimate of KR-20, but KR-21 is computationally simpler.

   b. 1. Since Test A is dichotomously scored, KR-20 can be used because it is appropriate with dichotomously scored items. Conversely, it is not appropriate for Test B since KR-20 cannot be used with weighted item scores.

     2. Cronbach's alpha would be appropriate for estimating the reliability of both Tests A and B since it can be used either with dichotomous or weighted scoring.

c. Using the KR-21 formula, the reliability is

$$\frac{(100 \times 36)\ [50 \times (100 - 50)]}{(100 - 1) \times 36} = \frac{3600 - (50 \times 50)}{99 \times 36} = \frac{3600 - 2500}{3564} = \frac{1100}{3564} = .31$$

We would suggest you avoid placing much weight on this math test in determining grades; its reliability suggests that student scores may well fluctuate on retesting, even though their ability might remain relatively constant. However, if the individual items are not reasonably similar in difficulty level, .31 may be an underestimate of the value you would obtain by using KR-20.

5. a. This question is for group discussion; refer to the relevant discussion in the chapter. Also, think of some other situations not discussed in the chapter, but in which lower measurement reliability may be tolerated.

   b. As discussed in the chapter, different procedures are designed to estimate the effect of different measurement error sources. Because the contributions of different error sources do not overlap, but are more likely to be additive or independent, estimation of one error source does not enlighten us on the effect of another error source. For this reason, reliability estimates based on different approaches (with the exception of the several approaches for internal consistency reliability) should not be considered interchangeable.

6. For this question, the most relevant concept is the standard error of measurement (SEM) because SEM provides estimation of measurement error for individual scores. By using SEM, score bands can be constructed around the two scores. If the score bands overlap too much, it indicates that the difference between the two scores could have occurred because of measurement error, and this is most probably not that "meaningful." On the other hand, if the score bands do not overlap, or overlap very little, that indicates that the difference between the two scores may not have occurred just because of measurement, and the difference may indicate true knowledge difference in the subject.

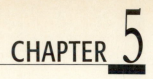

CHAPTER 5

Why Worry About Validity?

Valid Measures Permit Accurate Conclusions

OVERVIEW

In Chapter 4, we noted that every measurement instrument has imperfections, whether a teacher-made test, an interest scale administered by a school counselor, or a standardized achievement test developed by a large testing corporation. But as we noted there, tests do not have to be perfect to be useful. The critical issue for any test is *how imperfect* it is. Tests differ enormously—from excellent instruments that are directly relevant and technically sound (though still imperfect) to those that are so poorly conceived and designed that no informed test user would choose to use them.

If some tests are that bad, how do they survive? If Darwin's "survival of the fittest" theory pertained to measurement instruments, wouldn't the poor tests simply die out as better tests proved to be superior? Sometimes, but not as often as one might hope. Some horrid but hardy commercial tests survive from one decade to the next—despite evidence that they are so deeply flawed that they should be banned for school use. And many classroom or locally developed tests are never evaluated against any objective standards to see whether they are at all useful in providing the information for which they were intended.

Why are inadequate measurement instruments so often tolerated in our schools? There are two reasons. First, dependable information about quality is (unfortunately) lacking for many tests. Second, even when such information exists, many school practitioners are untrained in technical concepts and terminology necessary to understand what it means. But Chapter 4 and this chapter are intended to change all that. In them, we provide you with the tools you need to determine whether or not a test or other measurement instrument is adequate for your purposes.

Chapter 4 should have provided you with the knowledge and skills to determine whether scores yielded by any measurement instrument you use are reliable enough to fulfill your purposes. But reliability, alone, is not enough to judge any instrument to be useful, even if its reliability is very high. To use the well-worn phrase, reliability is "necessary but not sufficient" to categorize any measure as adequate, without also knowing something about the *validity* of the scores produced by that measure. Put simply, test scores must be both sufficiently reliable and valid to be useful. Although reliability allows us to ascertain whether test scores are consistent and stable, it does not tell us whether our interpretation of the scores is correct. A test may reliably (that is, consistently) yield test scores that tell the same story every time that test is used, but the story may still be false. The even greater concern is: Do those test scores accurately reflect reality? Are inferences and conclusions you draw from those scores valid—that is, do they tell the truth?

In this chapter, we explain why validity is the cornerstone of good measurement, and we describe in some detail the major approaches used to establish validity. We warn of factors that can reduce validity if you are not vigilant, and we explain how to improve validity coefficients and how to interpret them. We briefly discuss some controversies about how to measure the validity of criterion-referenced measures. Finally, we discuss at greater length how both reliability and validity determine the usability and usefulness of any educational measure.

Once again, we avoid burdening you with the more sophisticated concepts and formulas that may be of interest to the psychometrician, but we do give you a few simple and straightforward tools you can use to establish validity when you use a test or other measure. You should exit this chapter as well armed as any practitioner need be to judge the adequacy of either home-grown tests or commercial instruments.

OBJECTIVES

Upon completing your study of this chapter, you should be able to

1. | Discuss why validity is the most essential concern in every use of a measurement instrument.
2. | Differentiate among three major approaches used to collect validity evidence.
3. | Identify where and when each of these three approaches would be of primary concern.
4. | Interpret validity coefficients, describing what they mean and where they would be useful.
5. | List the major factors that decrease the validity of scores obtained from a particular instrument, and explain how to counteract them.
6. | Explain how reliability and validity relate to each other and to other psychometric characteristics in determining a test's usefulness.

Validity: The Cornerstone of Good Measurements

"How valid is it?" looms as the most important question one can ask about any educational measure. *Validity* refers to the degree to which a test measures that which it is intended to measure or, more accurately, the interpretation of test scores and inferences drawn from test scores are appropriate and adequate. Put differently, validity is concerned about the degree to which the individual differences of test scores represent true differences in the characteristic being measured, but not due to some other unintended factors. From such a definition, it should be apparent that validity is essential in educational measurement. Whatever other merits a test may have, it is useless if it does not measure what the user is intending to measure, or if our interpretation of test scores and our inferences based on the scores are wrong.

To help us understand the concept of measurement validity, let us consider a few examples. Suppose an eighth-grade math teacher administers a comprehensive final test to all eighth graders in a school in order to determine how well each student has mastered the math content areas taught during the semester. In such a situation, we typically interpret two different scores from Student A and Student B as indicating their different levels of mastery of the major math content areas: Student A with higher score has better mastery of the content areas than does Student B with lower score. Such interpretation implicitly assumes that the test items represent the major math content areas taught during the semester. If it so happens that the math teacher constructed only three test items for the test, and all of them were from the same chapter, which was covered only briefly during a two-week period, our assumption that test items represent all the major content areas might be seriously wrong. As a result, our interpretation about Students A and B is most likely incorrect, and the validity of the inferences about the two students' mastery of the math content areas is very much in doubt because the difference in scores between Students A and B may indicate only their different levels of mastery of the particular chapter covered by the items, not their mastery of all the major areas taught during the semester.

As another example, most colleges and universities require applicants to submit ACT or SAT scores for admission consideration. Why? Because it is believed that ACT or SAT scores indicate to a certain degree the applicants' potential to succeed in college or university. Based on this assumption, besides other considerations, higher scores on ACT or SAT are interpreted as indicating higher chances to succeed in college and university than lower ACT or SAT scores. Consequently, those with higher scores are more likely to be admitted. But to what degree is such interpretation of ACT or SAT scores, and the inference based on the scores, correct? Obviously, if the assumption were not correct, that is, if higher ACT or SAT scores were not related to success in college and university in any meaningful way, our interpretation of, and inference from, ACT and SAT scores would be questionable, and the measurement validity in this situation would be low.

As a final example, suppose that a psychiatrist constructed an instrument to measure her clients' suicidal tendency, with high scores indicating high probability of committing suicide in the near future (thus requiring drastic preventive measures), and low scores indicating normality. What if, in reality, high scores indicate introversion tendency and low scores indicate extroversion, instead of suicidal tendency versus nonsuicidal tendency as believed by the psychiatrist? So instead of measuring suicidal tendency, the scores on the instrument really represent extroversion/introversion tendencies. In this situation, the psychiatrist's interpretation of scores and her inferences based on the scores may be so far off the target that there would be little measurement validity in the situation.

As implied in this discussion, validity is not a property of the instrument itself. Rather, it is an indication of the extent to which the interpretation of test *results* for a particular measurement situation are appropriate for the given purpose. Therefore, validity indicates how well a test measures what it is supposed to measure for a particular use of the test, and if the scores based on the test are free from the influence of extraneous factors.

Validity is meaningful only as it pertains to the *particular* use for which the test results are intended; therefore, one should not speak of a test as "valid" or "invalid" in general; rather, test scores can be spoken of as valid or invalid with reference to the specific purpose and use for which the test was intended, and the accuracy and appropriateness of the interpretations and decisions made from the resulting scores. Scores from a particular test may be highly valid for one purpose with one population of examinees, and totally invalid if used for another purpose or with a different set of examinees.

Validity is concerned with the appropriateness of the inferences or interpretations a user draws from the test scores. The test score earned by a student provides information about that individual's performance on the set of problems or tasks that make up the test. The information provided by a student's score is used as a basis for making inferences about that student. The inferences may be about how this student's performance compares to the performance of other students, or about how this student would perform on other similar tasks or problems. In either case, there is an assumption that the scores accurately reflect the trait that the test is intended to measure, and that differences in the scores obtained by various students represent true differences in the degree to which they possess or lack that trait. However, sometimes the scores obtained from a test do not provide adequate grounds for the kinds of inferences the test user wishes to be able to make. For example, consider the following two cases.

Case 1. A six-grade teacher developed a test intended for use in assessing students' proficiency in math computation. The test consisted of ten problems similar to the following:

78	544	2097	369	95
+ 35	− 47	+ 1689	+ 57	− 83

The teacher wanted to be able to infer that students who obtained high scores on this test were proficient in math computation and that students who obtained low scores lacked this proficiency. However, none of the problems included in the test involved multiplication or division. Hence the sample of problems that made up the test was not representative of all important aspects of the task about which the user wanted to make inferences. Students who could perform successfully on these problems and would obtain high scores, but these scores would not provide sufficient evidence to warrant the conclusion that they could perform successfully on math computation problems involving multiplication and division.

Case 2. The science specialists in a State Department of Education prepared a 60-question, multiple-choice test to assess fifth graders' understanding of the basic concepts and principles in the science curriculum taught in that state. The specialists assumed that students who obtained high scores would understand the science concepts and principles better than those who obtained low scores. However, many of the questions were written at a level that required reading skills and vocabulary too advanced for many fifth graders. Since they could not understand the questions, many students earned scores that might have reflected their reading ability and did not truly reflect their knowledge and understanding of science. Thus the scores were contaminated by factors (reading skills and vocabulary) that go beyond the pure measurement of science knowledge. The meaning of the scores was distorted because they contained excess information that is irrelevant to the trait the test was intended to measure.

In both of these cases, the validity of inferences or interpretations based on the scores would be questionable.

An Integrated Concept of Validity

Since the early 1900s, textbook authors have referred to validity as if it were a characteristic of the test or the instrument from which measurements were obtained. In the last two decades, this traditional view has been replaced by the view that validity is a characteristic of the scores and the inferences and interpretations based on those scores, rather than an intrinsic property of the instrument itself. The 1985 *Standards for Educational and Psychological Testing* emphasizes this point: "The inferences regarding specific uses of a test are validated, not the test itself" (AERA et al., 1985, p. 9).

The quality of the test and the tasks that make up the test certainly have an important influence on the validity of the score-based inferences, but several other factors also influence the validity of the scores and inferences based on the scores, including (1) the nature of the group tested, (2) the conditions under which the test is administered, (3) the scoring criteria and procedures used, and (4) how the scores are used.

For example, a kindergarten readiness test may lead to highly valid inferences when used to distinguish between children who are well prepared to begin kindergarten and children who are not, but it is highly doubtful that the same test would provide any valid information if used for students entering middle school. The validity of scores from this test will vary greatly when used in the two different ways, not because the instrument has changed, but because of differences in the nature of the examinees and in the purpose for which the instrument was used. Even if this test were administered twice to the same group of young children, however, the validity of the scores would likely vary unless the test were administered under similar conditions each time, using the same scoring procedures and criteria.

The most important question that can be asked of a set of test scores is, "How valid are they for the particular purpose for which they are being used?" Posing this question is a way of asking *to what extent the scores measure what they are intended to measure, measure all of what they are intended to measure, and measure only that which they are intended to measure* (Thorndike, Cunningham, Thorndike, & Hagen, 1991). However, this multifaceted question is much easier to ask than it is to answer. Validity is not self-evident. It must be demonstrated, often empirically. As Sax (1989) so aptly stated, "Validity is not established by declaration but by evidence" (p. 292).

Establishing validity is a cumulative and ongoing process. It is not completed once and for all in a single effort. The process involves building a case that includes several different kinds of evidence. The three most commonly collected types of validity evidence are (1) content-related evidence, (2) criterion-related evidence, and (3) construct-related evidence. No one of these forms of evidence is sufficient by itself. A much stronger case is presented by accumulating evidence from each of the three categories and showing that these different types of evidence lead to a similar conclusion. Hence validity is a matter of degree; it is not a simple either-or, all-or-none question of "valid" versus "invalid." It is an attribute that exists along a continuum, from high to low, in varying degrees. Furthermore, validity is inferred or judged based on existing evidence, and it cannot be measured directly.

The traditional approach to measurement validity classifies it into three different types: (1) content validity, (2) criterion validity, and (3) construct validity. But these are not separate, independent types of validity; rather, they are different *categories of evidence* that are each cumulative. One danger of conceptualizing these three types of evidence as separate kinds of validity is the tendency to think that questions about content validity are the only validity issues that need to be considered in one measurement situation (for example, achievement testing), questions about criterion-related validity are the only important concerns in another measurement situation (for example, tests used for selection purposes), and questions about to construct validity are important only in some other situations (for example, tests used to measure psychological constructs such as creativity, anxiety, or readiness). But validity, properly conceived, is a single, unitary concept that includes each of the three categories of evidence and recognizes that each type of evidence is important when attempting to validate the meaning of inferences and interpretations based on test scores. This integrated view of validity is described in the most recent version of the *Standards for Educational and Psychological Testing* (AERA et al., 1985). However, many of these ideas had surfaced previously in the writings of several influential scholars. Currently, Messick's (1989) treatment of validity is probably the best and most comprehensive explanation of this topic.

Approaches to Establishing Validity

The process by which a test developer or test user collects evidence to support the types of inferences that are to be made from test scores is called *validation*. The goals of this process are to gather evidence that supports the particular kinds of inferences and interpretations the test was intended to serve and that discredits other plausible interpretations. In the following sections, we discuss the three types of evidence typically collected in the validation process.

Content Validation

Content validation refers to the extent to which the test's items represent the entire body of content (often called the *content universe* or *domain*) that the test is designed to measure. Although it is most commonly assessed for achievement tests or other tests of skill or knowledge, it is also possible to judge the content validity of a personality inventory, aptitude test, intelligence test, or attitude measure. The basic issue in content validation is *representativeness;* that is, how adequately do the test items represent the entire body of content that the test user intends to make inferences about? Since the responses to a test are only a sample of a student's behavior related to the domain of interest, the validity of any inferences about that student depends upon the representativeness of that sample.

In the context of content validation, the word *content* refers to *both* the subject matter topics (for example, math or reading) the test intends to cover *and* the cognitive processes that examinees are expected to apply to the subject matter. The processes to be sampled may be simple tasks such as recalling and classifying, or they may be more challenging ones such as analyzing, inferring, or applying a principle to new problem situations. The domain of interest is not merely a *subject matter* domain, therefore, but also a *behavioral* domain (Anastasi, 1988). Hence in collecting evidence of content validity, it is necessary to determine *both* what subject matter topics should be included *and* what kinds of mental operations should be elicited by the problems presented in the test, as well as what subject matter topics have been included or excluded.

Ideally, a test should *not only* sample *all* important aspects of the content domain, *but also* sample them in a *representative* fashion. No important parts of the domain should be underrepresented or excluded. Similarly, no aspects of the domain should be grossly overrepresented. Overrepresentation of one aspect of a content domain usually occurs at the expense of underrepresenting some other important aspects. For example, a high school teacher who devotes 80 percent or more of the problems in a test to assessing students' ability to recall factual information will most likely fail to adequately assess higher-order processes such as prediction, analysis, and application. In the same vein, a math computation test containing 80 percent addition and subtraction items will most likely underrepresent such important math computation skills as multiplication and division.

In practice, it is difficult to accurately determine what cognitive processes are elicited by the various problems in a test. However, any serious attempts to collect content validity evidence should include a detailed analysis of the nature of the tasks presented in the various test items and whether the items actually function as intended. A test that purportedly measures science process skills may actually assess only the students' knowledge of science vocabulary.

Linn and Gronlund (1995) emphasize the need to judge whether the problems or items in a test function as intended. As described before, a test designed for measuring knowledge in science may, in reality, be partially measuring reading skills and vocabulary instead. In some other situations, if some students are able to answer an item correctly because of a clue in another item rather than because of their knowledge or ability, then the items are malfunctioning. Similarly, if some knowledgeable students miss an item because it is vaguely worded or because it contains inappropriate vocabulary, then the item is not functioning as intended. In these cases, the cognitive task the student actually performs is not the intended task. Therefore, the validity of the scores will decrease. After all, "It is the [actual] tasks presented by the items that really define what the test measures" (Thorndike, et al., 1991, p. 126).

In summary, the two basic questions that need to be addressed in content validation are as follows:

■ To what degree does the test include a *representative* sample of all important parts of the behavioral domain?

■ To what extent is the test free from the influence of irrelevant variables that would threaten the validity of inferences based on the observed scores?

Collecting Content Validation Evidence

Content validation is especially important for achievement tests used in schools, including teacher-made tests. In situations where school curricula have specified instructional objectives, content validity it is especially pertinent since evidence reflects the extent to which the test matches or measures those objectives. Often, this is usually the primary type of validity evidence available in those situations.

Evidence of content validity is mainly a matter of judgment based on systematic analysis of relevant content areas, but this does not mean that it is a totally subjective process. Systematic procedures are available that make this process more rational and less subjective and haphazard. Collecting this evidence typically involves two major activities. First, to design a systematic plan for including items in a test so that different aspects of content and behavior domains will be adequately covered. Second, to make an informed judgment about the degree to which the subject matter covered by each item and the cognitive process that it elicits match the process and topic specified in the corresponding objective. To the extent that the items are congruent with the objectives they are intended to assess, inferences based on scores from the test will have content validity.

Tests that produce content-valid scores generally do not occur by accident. Rather, they result from careful planning and thoughtful development efforts. Evidence of content validity can be strengthened by adhering to the following steps:

1. Describe and specify as clearly as possible the domain of behaviors to be measured. For educational tests, this would typically require analysis of curriculum guidelines, courses of study, syllabi, textbooks, and other related items. This is to ensure that all relevant content areas will be covered.

2. The domain of behavior outlined in step 1 should be analyzed and subcategorized into more specific topics, subject matter areas, or clusters of instructional objectives. For example, if we were to test how well you have learned and can apply the content of this section on validity, we might decide to subdivide the

Categories of Instructional Objectives

		Knowledge	Understanding	Application
	Desired Emphasis	20%	50%	30%
"Face" Validity	10%			
Content Validation	20%			
Construct Validation	30%			
Criterion-Related Validation	40%			

FIGURE 5.1   Sample of Test Blueprint

content into the following categories: face validity, content validity, criterion-related validity, and construct validity. We also might decide that we have three categories of objectives with which we are concerned: knowledge, understanding, and application.

3. Draw up a set of test specifications that show not only the content areas or topics to be covered during the instructional processes, or objectives to be tested, but also the relative emphasis to be placed on each. Using our previous example, we could develop a set of specifications in a two-way matrix, which is shown in an uncompleted form in Figure 5.1.

4. Decide how many questions to include in the test (remembering previous discussions of reliability and test length, and also practical considerations such as examinee fatigue).

5. Determine how many items will need to be developed in each cell to make sure there is representative coverage of all content areas and categories of instructional objectives.

6. Construct or select test items appropriate for each cell.

7. Have another teacher or a content expert construct a second set of items, using the same table of specifications, or if that's infeasible, have her review your items. Reviewing similarities and differences between the two sets, or reviewing the critique, will help identify unwitting biases you might bring to the item-writing task, as well as strengthen the final set of test items that are selected.

Using steps such as these and thinking about validity *before* a test is constructed goes far toward ensuring that a school test will have a high degree of content validity. Increasing content validity *after* test items are written may involve extensive item revision or rewriting.

Although content validity is more closely related to achievement tests or other tests of skill or knowledge, it is also possible to judge the content validity of other measurement instruments, such as a personality inventory, an aptitude test, an intelligence test, or attitude measure. With these latter measures, however, establishing content validity is more difficult since these trait areas are not as clearly defined as the curriculum objectives in our schools. Also, it is not always easy to recognize whether particular test items measure personality, aptitude, or attitude.

Application Problem 1

Assume we wish to construct a 100-item test of the content and objectives outlined in Figure 5.1. How many test items would you propose for each cell?

Criterion-related Validation

Criterion-related evidence of validity refers to the extent to which one can infer from an individual's score on a test how well she will perform some other external task or activity that is supposedly measured by the test in question. This external task or activity that is to be predicted is called the *criterion*.[1] Ideally, the criterion should be some behavioral variable that is either more difficult to measure or cannot be measured at the time, such as successful on-the-job performance as an employee, or future grade-point average in college. However, performance on a different but already existing test is often used as a surrogate measure of the criterion of interest. The degree to which scores on the test being validated can predict performance on the criterion is determined by (1) administering the test being validated to a representative group of individuals for whom scores on the criterion can be obtained, and (2) then computing a correlation coefficient that statistically describes the degree to which the two sets of scores are related. The resulting correlation coefficient is called a *validity coefficient*. External criteria can be of two types: criterion measures taken at approximately the *same time* as the test is administered, or criterion measures taken *significantly later* (for example, after several months or years). Correlation with the former produces evidence of *concurrent validity;* correlation with the latter yields evidence of *predictive validity*.

Evidence of Predictive Validity

Predictive validity refers to how well a measure predicts or estimates *future* performance on some criterion other than the test itself. For example, one may wish to use a test score to predict how well the examinee will do in college or on the job—or even on a later (different) test. Predictive validity is especially important in selection and placement decisions (for example, college entrance exams or employment tests). In these situations, unless there exists criterion-related validity evidence, the decisions made based on scores on a selection test are essentially groundless.

To determine predictive validity, it is important to identify a satisfactory future criterion that can be measured successfully. Then obtaining the predictive validity coefficient is simply a matter of following the steps outlined here:

---

[1]Note that *criterion* has an entirely different meaning in this context from *criterion-referenced measurement;* do not confuse the two.

Steps	Example
1. Administer and score the test you will use for the prediction.	College Entrance Exam (CEE).
2. Wait for an appropriate time.	Allow examinees to attend two years of college.
3. Measure the external criterion on which you are attempting to predict performance.	Obtain the grade-point average (GPA) for examinees.
4. Correlate the scores on the predictor test with measurements on the external criterion.	Correlate CEE scores with examinees' GPAs.
5. Interpret the resulting validity coefficient.	Interpret the correlation of CEE and GPA scores.

A high predictive validity coefficient indicates that a test is a good predictor of the criterion because if a student scores high on the test, she also tends to score high on the criterion. A low coefficient indicates that knowing the performance on the test does not provide much insight into a student's future performance on the criterion, thus making it a poor predictor of relevant future performance.

Predictive validity is very important for standardized achievement and aptitude tests, and educators should require evidence that such tests are reasonable predictors of later outcomes before requiring students to take it. Predictive validity is seldom established for teacher-made tests, although doing so would be both feasible and informative.

Evidence of Concurrent Validity

In some situations, although it is possible to obtain measurement for the behavior domain of our interest, we may find it cumbersome to do so for some reasons. For example, an automobile company hires people to be trained to be draftsmen for designing new automobile models. Naturally, the company would want those who are good in their visual ability and who can handle mechanical relationships with relative ease, such as envision the impact one design change may have on all related parts. The company traditionally asks each individual applicant to demonstrate her mechanical ability in actual workshop settings; and make a judgment based on the applicant's actual performance. This process might be too time consuming and expensive for large groups of applicants. The company's industrial psychologist might suggest that a mechanical aptitude test be developed, and future selection can be based on performance on the test, rather than on the actual demonstration in workshop settings. Since such a test could be administered to a group, it would be efficient as a selection tool.

But before such a test is actually used to replace the hands-on demonstration in the workshop, the question has to be asked, "Does the performance on the test provide the same or similar information as that based on the traditional hands-on demonstration"? To answer this crucial question, the industrial psychologist and the company need to collect *concurrent validity* evidence in order to be sure that the two are indeed providing the same or similar information. In this situation, the hands-on demonstration is the *criterion* of our interest, and the mechanical aptitude test is the measure that needs be validated. Theoretically, these two measures can be obtained at the same time, and we simply want to use the easier one in place of the more expensive measurement. Unless *concurrent validity* evidence can be obtained, we will not be sure that the mechanical aptitude test can be used in place of the hand-on experience since the two may not provide similar information.

In many educational settings, we often encounter similar situations in which educators or psychologists are interested in validating a new test by seeing how well it correlates with an existing measure (or some other criterion) that is generally considered to be a more established and trustworthy indicator. In order to provide evidence that a new test (usually a shorter, easier or a more convenient measure) is an acceptable substitute for an established measure, evidence of concurrent validity is essential.

As another example, assume that the personnel officer of a large school district desires to screen out applicants for teacher positions who are inflexible, but finds the highly regarded "Test of Flexibility" (TOF) too expensive and time consuming because it requires individual administration. The school district may decide to fund the development of a shorter, group-administered "Flexible Attitude Scale" (FAS) instead of the more expensive TOF. Again, before FAS can be used for the purpose, it is important to demonstrate *concurrent validity* of FAS. The evidence of concurrent validity of FAS, or lack thereof, can be collected by administering both FAS and TOF to the same group of examinees at about the same time, to see if the scores from the two tests correlate highly. If they do, then FAS could be considered a valid test, based on this concurrent criterion-related evidence. Once such evidence is collected, for future applicants, only FAS needs to be administered.

The steps for determining concurrent validity are the same as those outlined previously for predictive validity, except step 2 is eliminated since the two measures are taken concurrently.

The difference between *predictive* validity and *concurrent* validity is obvious: in predictive validity, measures of the criterion are obtained later, and the predictor test is used to predict performance on the future criterion; in concurrent validity, both performance on the test being validated and that on the criterion can be obtained at the same time, and the former is usually used in place of the latter because of such factors as ease, convenience, and cost effectiveness.

Expectancy Tables to Illustrate Criterion-related Validity

Besides calculating correlation coefficient between test performance and criterion, another popular approach to present criterion-related validity evidence is to construct a table that illustrates the relationship between the scores on the predictor test and the scores on the measure of the criterion. Such a table is usually called an *expectancy table*. Table 5.1 is an example of such an expectancy table.

This expectancy table illustrates the phenomenon that those with higher scores on the Space Relations Test of DAT (Differential Aptitude Test) are more likely to receive higher grades in the watch repair course (higher percentages with higher grades), whereas those with lower grades are more likely to receive lower grades. If the number of slots in the watch repair class is smaller than the number

Table 5.1   DAT Test Scores and Percentage Receiving Various Grades

Percentiles Score on Space Relations Test	Grades Received in Watch Repair Course		
	D or E	C	A or B
76–100	None	12%	88%
51–75	None	20%	80%
26–50	20%	40%	40%
1–25	58%	30%	12%

Note: Format of table adapted from materials accompanying DAT. Used by permission.

of students wishing to take the class, and if we want to admit those with good chances to succeed in the class, one selection strategy would be to admit those with higher scores on the Space Relations Test of DAT. In essence, this situation would be the same as using ACT or SAT scores for making admission decisions in most colleges and universities. If we chose to calculate a correlation coefficient between scores on the Space Relations Test of DAT and the grades in the watch repair course, the correlation would be positive in direction and moderate to high in magnitude. One advantage of using an expectancy table to describe measurement validity is that it is intuitively easier to understand for people without statistical training than a correlation coefficient.

Validity and Reliability of the Criterion

In both predictive and concurrent validation, it is essential that the validity and reliability of the criterion be well established. A criterion will not be useful if it is unstable or invalid. Trying to predict performance on an unreliable and invalid criterion is like trying to hit a moving target that constantly changes size and shape. Whether an adolescent has a criminal record is readily determined, for instance. Similarly, a grade-point average of 3.0 is a clear target. But a concept like "success in life" is nebulous, subjective, and hard to define in a way on which everyone can agree. We cannot say whether a test is a good measure or a good predictor unless we know precisely what it is that we are measuring or predicting.

Construct Validation

Words like *assertiveness, academic self-concept,* and *anxiety* refer to abstract ideas that humans construct in their minds to help them explain observed patterns or differences in the behavior of themselves or other people. *Intelligence, self-esteem, aggressiveness,* and *motivation* are also examples of such abstractions. So are concepts like *creativity, critical thinking ability, reading comprehension, mathematical reasoning ability,* and *scholastic aptitude.* Some of these constructs come to us from scholarly disciplines such as psychology or sociology. Other examples such as *shyness, curiosity, hypocrisy,* and *procrastination* are informal constructs that are part of our ordinary language and everyday culture. Nevertheless, all these examples are constructs. A *construct* is an unobservable, postulated attribute of individuals that we create in our minds to help us explain or theorize about human behavior. Since constructs do not exist outside the human mind, they are not directly measurable.

According to Cronbach (1984), the word *construct* is a noun that is derived from the verb *to construe*. He claims that "a construct is a way of construing—organizing—what has been observed" (p. 133). Observant parents use constructs as they attempt to describe similarities or differences in the behavior of children. Teachers and other professional educators often use constructs in their attempts to account for behavioral patterns they observe in students (or one another). Sportscasters, journalists, political scientists, economists, and medical doctors all create and use constructs. In fact, thoughtful observers of human behavior in all disciplines and all walks of life develop and use constructs to explain human behavior. One can hardly read the daily newspaper, watch the TV news, or a hockey game without encountering several different examples of constructs. Some commonly used constructs are only vaguely defined, whereas others are more clear-cut.

Many different tests have been created that purport to measure different constructs used by educators. Supposedly, the Whimpleton Reading Readiness Test measures children's readiness to learn how to read, and the Syracuse Mathematics Anxiety Test provides accurate measures of students' anxiety about learning mathematics. However, just because the title of a test claims that it measures a certain construct does not mean that scores from that test are valid, dependable measures of that construct. Remember, validity is established by evidence, not by declaration. Responsible test users are skeptical of test titles and expect additional evidence that the test actually measures the construct it purports to measure, and not something else.

Construct validation is the process of collecting evidence to support the assertion that a test measures the construct claimed by the test developer. This process involves accumulating empirical data from several sources and building a logical case to support the conclusion that scores from the test *do* measure what they are supposed to measure, and that they *do not* measure other extraneous factors. Evidence of content validity and evidence of criterion-related validity are both used in this process. In that sense, content validation and criterion-related validation become part of construct validation.

For example, suppose one wanted to validate scores from a new test that supposedly measured *creativity*. Among other things, the following could be done for the purpose of collecting evidence for construct validity of the measure:

1. Systematically define the domain of tasks, abilities, attitudes, habits, or mindsets that are ascribed to *creativity*. One would then want to determine to what extent the items that make up the test are representative of all important aspects of this domain.

2. Determine how well scores from this new test are correlated with other measures and variables—to which they would be expected to be related—based on existing theories of related constructs, such as *flexibility, independence,* and *divergent thinking.* Then one could check to determine whether scores from this new measure of creativity are relatively uncorrelated with other distinctive and theoretically unrelated constructs such as *verbal intelligence.*

Logical inferences drawn from these procedures listed would be used to determine whether or not the test faithfully measures creativity rather than other constructs. Our observant readers may have noticed that step 1 described earlier is essentially the procedure used in content validation described before, and step 2 follows the procedures in criterion-related validation. This example reinforces what we said at the beginning of this chapter that validity is a unitary concept with several different categories of evidence, and that construct validation subsumes both content-related and criterion-related aspects of validity evidence.

Construct validation is a complicated process, and a variety of procedures can be used for the purpose. Here are two other procedures in construct validation:

- *Developmental changes consistent with theory.* For example, human intelligence is assumed to develop from early childhood to adulthood. If you constructed your own intelligence test, and a group of normal children at different ages took it, it is necessary that the age-related performance pattern on your intelligence test is consistent with the theoretical expectation: older kids tend to perform better than younger kids. Lack of this expected pattern will certainly put a big question mark on the construct validity of your intelligence test.

- *Group differences consistent with theory.* For example, you developed a science test to measure students' mastery of science knowledge learned during their *seventh* grade. If this test was given to both sixth graders and seventh graders at the end of the year, we would expect that the seventh graders would perform substantially better as a group than the sixth graders. In the same vein, if this test was given to the same group at the beginning of the seventh grade and again at the end the seventh grade (assuming no carry-over effect from the first test administration), we would expect that the performance at the second time would be substantially better since it is during the seventh grade that the content areas were taught. If the expected performance pattern did not materialize, we would wonder whether you were really measuring the science knowledge learned during the seventh grade at all.

The construct validation procedures discussed here are far from being exhaustive, and many others, including some sophisticated statistical methods, are available for this purpose. Furthermore, these procedures are typically used jointly in the construct validation process. Construct validity can seldom be inferred from a single empirical study, or from one logical analysis of a measure, or from one statistical index or analysis. Rather, judgment of construct validity must be based upon the accumulation of evidence indicating that the test measures the construct it is intended to measure. Construct validity differs from content validity in that the *content* to be measured in the latter (for example, Civil War history) is typically known and agreed upon, whereas the *construct* to be measured (for example, intelligence) is typically hypothesized and can be inferred only from other, observable behaviors.

In this chapter, we emphasize that validity is a unitary concept, and construct validation subsumes both content-related validity evidence and criterion-related validity evidence. In practical measurement situations, however, sometimes one type of validity evidence has more direct bearing on the situation than others. For classroom teacher-made tests, since they are directly related to instructional objectives, content-related validity evidence is obviously more relevant than criterion-related validity evidence even though the latter is still possible. For tests used for selection purposes, such as SAT or ACT, since the major reason for requiring these test scores is the belief that the performance on the tests can provide indication for applicants' future performance in college, it is essential to provide criterion-related validity evidence to support such test use. For some tests used in psychology, such as those measuring spatial ability, creativity, or numerical reasoning, since these constructs are abstract and hypothetical, construct validity evidence has more direct relevance and should be provided from different perspectives so that we can have reasonable confidence that the tests are indeed measuring what their titles claim to be measuring.

Application Problem 2

Of all aspects of validity evidence we have discussed in the chapter, which type of validity evidence is most likely to be the major concern to the high school classroom teacher attempting to develop a test of Civil War history? Which type of validity evidence is most likely to be the major concern for university admission officials who are making admission decisions based on SAT or ACT test scores? Which type of validity evidence is most likely to be the major concern for a psychologist who is attempting to develop a short version of IQ test in place of the longer but more established and widely accepted IQ test such as the Stanford–Binet test?

Face Validity

Face validity refers to the degree to which a measurement instrument appears to measure what it is intended to measure, to those who administer and/or take the test. *Face validity* is often discounted as the mere *appearance* of validity. Admittedly, matters of *appearance* are usually less important than matters of *substance,* in measurement at least. Clearly, face validity alone is not sufficient evidence that a test possesses genuine validity. Face validity is not comparable to the kinds of validity evidence we have discussed previously, and cannot replace them, for it is truly only the appearance of validity.

Although the *appearance* of validity is *less important* than true validity, it is not *unimportant.* In some cases, lack of face validity also suggests a lack of true validity. Imagine that a test were entitled, "Test of General Mathematical Reasoning Ability," but an examination revealed that *all* of its items were numerically expressed multiplication facts (for example, $3 \times 3 = 9$), and there were *no* story problems or problem-solving items of any type. Similarly, the expectations raised by a test titled "Universal Sixth-Grade Spelling Test" would be dashed when closer examination showed that it contained only lists of correctly and incorrectly spelled Latin verbs. Both of these tests could be rejected as invalid *on their face*—unless, of course, you really wanted to measure only multiplication facts or knowledge of how Latin verbs are spelled.

In other cases, an instrument might actually measure what we want to measure, but have little face validity—that is, not *appear* to measure it. So what? Isn't *what* it measures more important than what it *appears* to measure? Yes, but in our opinion (and that of Nevo, 1985, and Anastasi, 1988), in many measurement situations, low face validity can be lethal to a test for several practical reasons, and this is especially so for tests typically used in education. Those who choose tests do not always understand technical discussions of validity, and consequently, tests that appear valid are more likely to be used than those that appear invalid, regardless of their actual validity. Anastasi (1988) makes this point well.

> Face validity pertains to whether the test "looks valid" to the examinees who take it, the administrative personnel who decide on its use, and other technically untrained observers. Fundamentally, the question of face validity concerns rapport and public relations. Although common usage of the term validity in this connection may make for confusion, face validity itself is a desirable feature of tests. . . . Certainly if test content appears irrelevant, inappropriate, silly, or childish, the result will be poor cooperation, regardless of the actual validity of the test. Especially in adult testing, it is not sufficient for a test to be objectively valid. It also needs face validity to function effectively in practical situations. (p. 144)

Thus ignoring face validity can be risky in view of the many practical realities that exist in the educational setting.

Face validity alone, however, is never a sufficient criterion in choosing educational measures. Too often teachers or administrators trust titles or appearance, only to find that a test labeled a test of "creativity" turns out to be a measure of vocabulary, or verbal fluency, and nothing else. Good choices depend on thorough knowledge of genuine, objective, evidence of validity.

It should be apparent that although both content validity and face validity depend on rational processes (as opposed to empirical methods),[2] they are quite different. Where face validity requires only that the measure *appears* valid, content validity depends on a verified match between the behavioral domain of interest (in education, usually the content of the instruction) and the content coverage of the test. Face validity should never be accepted as a substitute for validity based on evidence.

Consequential Aspects of Validity

For every testing situation, there are intended outcomes. But in some situations, there may be unintended side effects and negative consequences. Related to the side effects of testing, one relatively new validity concept is known as *consequential validity* (Messick, 1988, 1993).

Previously, we defined measurement validity as the degree to which the interpretation of test scores and inferences based on such scores are adequate and appropriate, or the degree to which the test measures what it is intended to measure. *Consequential validity,* on the other hand, is concerned about the *unintended,* usually negative, consequences of testing in a particular situation. It is argued that any time a test is used, it incurs certain educational and/or social consequences, either

---

[2]It should be noted that, in professional test development, empirical methods are often used in the process of accumulating content validity evidence.

intended or unintended, or both. In order to judge measurement validity, although it is important to investigate whether the interpretation and inferences based on test scores are appropriate and adequate (traditional view of validity), it is also important to understand the unintended educational and social consequences of test use (consequential validity). For a valid measurement, not only should the interpretation of scores reflect the intended purpose of measurement, but also the use of the information from such measurement should have *constructive* consequences for the individuals and institutions involved. In this sense, measurement validity is construed to be not only an evaluation of the appropriateness of test score interpretation as in the traditional psychometric sense, but also an evaluation of the appropriateness of the use of such scores in light of educational and social values and actions.

Let's consider one example of such considerations. The multiple-choice test item format adopted by many standardized tests is often criticized to lead to more emphasis on memory and recognition in school curricula, at the expense of creative thinking, synthesis, writing, and so on. Let's assume that the test scores on these tests *truthfully* reflect students' ability or achievement. From the traditional view of measurement validity, there does not seem to be any obvious validity problem in the interpretation of such test scores since student's ability level is what we want to know, and the test score truthfully reflects that. From the perspective of consequential validity, however, the use of such measurement instruments may have some measurement validity problems since the benefits of this type of measurement may have to be weighed against the unintended negative consequences of less creative thinking, less synthesis, and less writing in curriculum caused by using such instruments. These unintended consequences are not considered in the conventional psychometric view of measurement validity (Messick, 1988).

Let's look at another *hypothetical* example of consequential validity concerns. Assume that there were a meaningful performance difference between males and females on a math achievement test, and the test scores would be used for some important decisions such as promotion or selection. In this situation, there might be negative social consequences due to the use of the math test since the promotion or selection for the lower scoring gender group members would be adversely affected. In this situation, it would be imperative to investigate whether the performance difference was due to *invalidity* of the test (for example, due to *test bias* against one gender group), or such performance difference actually reflected the reality—that is, the gender difference in math achievement were real. If we determined that the difference was not due to test bias, and the score difference reflected actual difference in the ability level between the two gender groups, we would have answered the traditional validity question adequately. The gender difference would no longer be a concern of measurement validity, but rather, a concern of social policies. Consequential validity, on the other hand, may extend to policy and social considerations: given the gender difference on the test, and the adverse impact such gender difference might have on selection or promotion, would the potential negative social consequences justify the use of the test in the situation?

Although this brief discussion of *consequential validity* is admittedly somewhat simplistic, it is obvious that this concept adds an entirely *new* dimension to the conventional measurement validity. Since this is a relatively new concept of validity, controversy still exists about its relevance as a validity concept, and about whether the social and policy considerations as represented by the concept of consequential validity will be accepted as part of the more technical definition of measurement validity (Gregory, 1996; Maguire, 1994; Popham, 1995). Interested readers may consult Shepard (1997) and Linn (1997) for some recent arguments in support of this concept, and Popham (1997) and Mehrens (1997) for arguments against the concept of consequential validity.

Factors That Can Reduce Validity

Measurement validity can be affected by many factors, most of which will be discussed in more detail in the next chapter. As test users, it is important to keep in mind that anything that introduces error into test scores will have an adverse effect on the validity of test scores. A few specific considerations are outlined next.

Interpreting—and Improving—Validity Coefficients

Content and construct validity approaches typically do not yield statistical validity coefficients, and therefore cannot be interpreted in as precise and universally understood terms as can the criterion-related validity approaches—predictive and concurrent. But even though the latter approach to validity produces validity coefficients, interpretation must be done carefully.

For Those Who Want to Dig Deeper

The following guidelines should help in interpreting validity coefficients.

1. *Predictive validity coefficients will typically be lower than concurrent validity coefficients.* This is so because the chances are higher that the former will be affected by changes in behavior of the individual during the period between the predictor test and the later criterion measure. The longer the time interval, the lower the predictive validity coefficient might be expected to be.

2. *The size of a predictive validity coefficient will be affected by the reliabilities of both the criterion and the predictor.* As for all measures, both predictors and criteria are fallible to some degree and thus subject to errors of measurement. To the extent such errors operate, the measurements of the predictor and/or criterion are unreliable, thus lowering the correlation coefficient between the two measures. When this happens, the obtained coefficient will underestimate the correlation that *would* exist between the true scores if no error were present. The implication here is that factors reducing reliability of test scores will affect the validity coefficients, too. Fortunately, this (theoretical) validity coefficient can be estimated by use of the following formula:

$$\text{Corrected Validity Coefficient} = \frac{\text{Obtained Validity Coefficient}}{\sqrt{\text{Predictor Reliability} \times \text{Criterion Reliability}}}$$

(Formula 5.1)

3. *Validity coefficients derived from scores of homogeneous groups will be lower than those from scores of heterogeneous groups.* Since the predictive or concurrent validity coefficient is statistically a correlation coefficient between scores on two measures, the effect of restricted range on correlation coefficient (see Chapter 3 for the discussion) operates to reduce the obtained validity coefficient, just as group variability affects reliability coefficients, as discussed in the previous chapter. One practical implication is that anything that lowers variability will lower validity coefficients. For example, if those who score low on a particular test of academic aptitude elect not to go to college, information on the criterion (success in college) will be available only for a more homogeneous group (those who elect to go to college), possibly leading to an incorrect inference that the test is a "poor" predictor. Popular tests required for university admission or graduate studies (for example, SAT, GRE) may suffer from such range restriction problems because of the selection process, and consequently, their validity coefficients may have been underestimated.

4. *Increasing the length of the predictor test will slightly increase predictive validity.* Added test items would need to be comparable in quality to existing test items in order for predictive validity to increase. Also, the increases in predictive validity are relatively modest, even if test length is doubled or trebled, raising questions whether this is a cost-effective or practical way to increase predictive validity.

Application Problem 3

Assume you develop a measure of mechanical aptitude and correlate it with the American Mechanical Aptitude Test (AMAT), a standardized measure, and obtain a validity coefficient of .60. Assume that the reliability of the AMAT is .90, and that the reliability of your measure is 0.85. What would the corrected concurrent validity coefficient be?

Validity of Criterion-referenced Measures

Almost all scholars in educational and psychological measurement agree that concerns about validity are just as important in the context of criterion-referenced measurement as in the context of norm-referenced measurement. However, scholars have been divided in their answers to questions about what kind of validity evidence should be gathered and what procedures should be used to collect it. On the one hand, some scholars (for example, Popham & Husek, 1969) have emphasized that validity approaches that depend upon the use of correlation coefficients are not very useful in the context of criterion-referenced measurement because of the limited variation often obtained in scores from these tests. Scholars in this camp have traditionally emphasized the need to conduct content validation studies, but they have downplayed the need for criterion-related validation and construct validation. Others (for example, Linn, 1979) have taken a different point of view. They agree that evidence of content validity is particularly important in the context of criterion-referenced measurement, but they also emphasize the importance of collecting evidence of criterion-related validity and construct validity.

The long-standing debate between these two camps has been influenced by publication of the latest version of the *Standards for Educational and Psychological Testing* (AERA et al., 1985), which refines the definition of validity to be a unitary concept and places increased emphasis on the idea that construct validity evidence encompasses both content validity and criterion-related validity. Consequently, in recent years, there has been increased emphasis on the need for collecting evidence of both criterion-related validity and construct validity in addition to evidence of content validity. Because of this view, measurement experts are increasingly taking the stance that validity of criterion-referenced interpretations is no different from any other type of interpretation.

Reliability, Validity, and the Usefulness of a Measure

Let's see now how reliability and validity interrelate and combine to determine the utility of any educational measure. Reliability is a necessary precursor to validity. One can hardly conclude that a test is measuring what it is supposed to if it measures something different every time. Conversely, scores from a test *can* be reliable without being valid, measuring the wrong thing every time, but doing so with marvelous consistency. So even though reliability is necessary, it is not sufficient. Test scores can lack validity even though they are highly reliable. In other words, they can be free from random errors of measurement, but still reflect the effects of constant (systematic) errors. In order for the testing procedure and the resulting scores to have validity, the scores must be relatively free from both random errors and constant (systematic) errors.

It is not enough for a test to be valid; it must also be usable. Tests that are too expensive, too time consuming, or too technically sophisticated for intended users to interpret may not be usable, however impressive their validity coefficients may be. Cangelosi (1982) provides a clear illustration.

> one-to-one conferencing between a trained teacher and a student is often one of the more valid means for measuring how well the student achieved a learning objective. However, if a teacher has 30 students in a class and only 5 hours a week scheduled with that class, then a more expedient (and probably less valid) means must be considered. The conferences may be rejected, not on validity grounds, but because of low usability. Expense, time, strain on students, and a myriad of other considerations affect measurements' usability. (p. 59)

A *usable* measure is not necessarily *useful,* however. An instrument that is quick, cheap, and simple to use, score, and interpret is still useless if it is not valid. A measure must be both valid *and* usable to practitioners, and both concerns must be kept in mind when such measures are designed or selected. In fact, usefulness is the ultimate criterion educators should apply in choosing or developing every

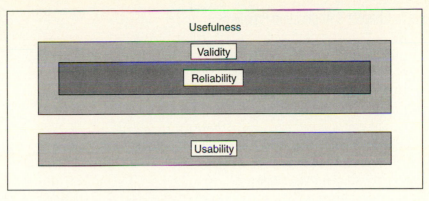

FIGURE 5.2   Components of Usefulness

Source: Reprinted with permission from Cangelosi, J. S. (1982). *Measurement and Evaluation: An Introduction for Teachers.* Dubuque, IA: W. C. Brown.

measure that will be used in our schools. The relationships among validity, usability, and usefulness are illustrated in Figure 5.2.

SUGGESTED READINGS

Messick, S. (1989). Validity. In R. L. Linn (ed.). *Educational measurement* (3rd ed., pp. 13–103). New York: American Council on Education and Macmillan Publishing Company.

Messick traces the historical evolution of the concept of validity and how various evidences of validity have been categorized. He explains the various types of validity evidence we have used in this text but goes beyond them to present a philosophically based argument that alters traditional conceptions of validity and presents validation as a unitary conception. This chapter is an excellent resource for those who wish to pursue this topic further and to stretch to assimilate exciting, new thinking in the field of measurement.

Zeller, R. A. (1988). Validity. In J. P. Keeves (ed.). *Educational research methodology, and measurement: An international handbook* (pp. 322–330). Oxford, England: Pergamon Press.

This is a very useful summary of the various approaches to test validation, including practical examples that illustrate the similarities and differences among those approaches.

SUGGESTION SHEET

If your last name starts with the letter F or G, please complete the Suggestion Sheet at the end of the book while this chapter is still fresh in your mind.

Answers to Chapter 5 Application Problems

1. Completed Test Blueprint:

Categories of Instructional Objectives

	Desired Emphasis	Knowledge 20%	Understanding 50%	Application 30%	Total Items
Face Validity	10%	2	5	3	10
Content Validation	20%	4	10	6	20
Construct Validation	30%	6	15	9	30
Criterion-Related Validation	40%	8	20	12	40
Total Items		20	50	30	100

2. In these practical testing situations, test users may be more concerned about a particular aspect of validity evidence than about others. For the classroom teacher who is developing a history test, the purpose of the test is to assess the students learning in the classroom. Obviously, the test should have adequate *content validity*. In other words, what is on the test should be what has been discussed in the history class. Without adequate content validity, the purpose of the test will not be achieved.

For university admission officials, the major purpose of using SAT or ACT scores is to predict which applicants have better potential to succeed in the university study. Because the test scores are used to predict future academic behavior in the university, it is important to show that the SAT or ACT scores have reasonable *predictive validity* for such behaviors. If no relationship exists between SAT or ACT scores with academic success in the university, it will not be meaningful to use the test scores in the admission process.

For purposes such as saving time and cost, the psychologist may be interested in developing a shorter version of the IQ test instead of using the long and established IQ test. But before such a shorter test is used in place of the longer and more established one, the important question to ask is: is this shorter test measuring the same construct as the more established one? *Concurrent validity* evidence helps answer this question. If the two measures are highly correlated, it is likely that the two are measuring the same or very similar construct.

3.

$$\frac{0.60}{\sqrt{0.90} \times \sqrt{0.85}} = \frac{0.60}{0.9486 \times 0.9219} = 0.69$$

This is the corrected concurrent validity coefficient given the reliability estimates of the two tests.

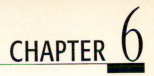

Cutting Down Test Score Pollution

Reducing the Influence of Extraneous Factors

OVERVIEW

Chapters 5 emphasized the importance of validity. Many people think of validity as a characteristic inherent within the test. However, validity is more a characteristic of how test scores are interpreted and used—it depends on factors such as how a test is administered, the purpose for which it is interpreted, the particular students with whom it is used, and the setting in which it is given. People sometimes forget that many other sources of error may render a test that is perfectly good for one purpose, quite ill-suited for another. This chapter is really a continuation of Chapter 5, and we will look more closely at some major factors that may affect the validity of test scores.

No one would use a math test to measure a student's self-concept. Other sources of error, however, are not so apparent. We will summarize some of the most frequently encountered *extraneous variables* that can affect a respondent's score on a particular test, and thereby reduce the validity of how these scores are used. Extraneous variables are those characteristics, occurrences, or behavior patterns that are *irrelevant* to what we are trying to measure, but that nevertheless affect students' scores on the test.

In the same way that industrial waste pollutes air or water, we say that extraneous variables cause test score pollution; they introduce foreign matter into what should be a pure measure of some trait, knowledge, or proficiency. In this chapter, we summarize the factors that "pollute" the meaning of test scores and suggest some procedures to minimize the effect of test score pollution. The major extraneous factors that can inappropriately influence performance on cognitive tests are summarized first. Next, the extraneous factors that can inappropriately influence performance on affective measures are outlined.

OBJECTIVES

Upon completing your study of this chapter, you should be able to

1. Explain how the validity of scores from a cognitive or affective measure can be affected by extraneous variables.

2. Describe extraneous factors that affect cognitive test scores, including test-taking skills, testwiseness, response sets, anxiety and motivation, administration factors, coaching and practice, and test bias.

3. Explain procedures and techniques that can be used to prevent or minimize the influence of extraneous variables on cognitive tests.

4. Provide definitions and examples of extraneous factors that influence the scores on affective measures, including social desirability response set, faking, problems of interpretation, self-deception or lack of insight, and acquiescence response set.

5. Explain procedures and techniques that can be used to prevent or minimize the influence of extraneous variables on affective measures.

6. Given a specific measurement situation, identify the extraneous variables most likely to affect test scores.

Extraneous Factors That Can Influence Performance on Cognitive Tests

Cognitive tests are designed to measure how well respondents have mastered specific learning outcomes or to what degree they possess certain "aptitudes." Cognitive tests are usually considered *maximum performance* measurement, in contrast to *typical performance* measurement. *Maximum performance* measurement usually involves measuring knowledge, achievement, ability, skills, job performance and so on. The purpose of maximum performance measurement is usually to determine the upper limits of an examinee's skill, knowledge, or performance on a particular task. One important characteristic of a maximum performance test is that the test is designed in such a way that responses to the test items can usually be identified as right or wrong. Some examples of maximum performance measurement are tests of academic achievement in areas such as math, history, and chemistry; scholastic aptitude tests such as SAT or ACT; assessment of job performance for auto mechanics; and tests of intellectual ability.

In contrast to cognitive tests, there exist another broad category of *affective* measures. Affective measures are usually considered *typical performance* measurement, which focuses on the affective and behavioral characteristics of people. The defining characteristic of typical performance measurement is that the responses to the measure's items normally cannot be characterized as being correct versus incorrect, nor can the performance on such an instrument be characterized as being good or poor. Instead, we focus on whether or not respondents have *truthfully* responded to the questions. Some examples of typical performance measurement are public opinion survey about some issues such as gun control and welfare, career interest inventories, and personality assessments. Although some common extraneous variables exist that tend to reduce the validity of interpretation for both cognitive and affective measurement, some unique extraneous variables or factors tend to plague affective measures only, thus making it more difficult to obtain a high degree of validity. In this first section, we discuss some major extraneous variables that affect validity of cognitive measures; in the second section of this chapter, we pay attention to those factors that may reduce measurement validity of affective measures.

Of course, validity is influenced by how well individual items are written and how well a test is constructed. Besides the quality of the test itself, some other extraneous variables can also affect scores on a test, thus reducing the validity of test use. In this section, we discuss seven such variables.

1. *Test-taking skills.* Mastery of certain skills (appropriate allocation of time, deductive reasoning and guessing strategies, and so on) allows respondents to more fully demonstrate mastery of test objectives, or true ability levels.

2. *Testwiseness.* The ability to use "clues" in the test to obtain a higher score than deserved is referred to as testwiseness. We distinguish between test-taking skills, which allow the respondent to demonstrate the full extent of her knowledge, and testwiseness, which enables a respondent to appear as if she knows more than she really does.

3. *Response sets.* Test takers exhibit certain styles or preferences in the way they respond to tests. Unless tests have been carefully constructed, these styles, referred to by Cronbach (1946) as response sets, cause people of equal ability to earn different scores.

4. *Anxiety and motivation.* Performance may be impaired by excessive anxiety or inadequate motivation.

5. *Administrative factors.* The way in which a test is administered (the extent to which cheating is tolerated, the clarity of instructions, and so on) can affect scores.

6. *Coaching and practice.* Coaching (for example, special practice drills) may affect test scores.

7. *Test bias.* The degree to which a test is biased (constructed in a way that some people have an unfair advantage over others) may cause some people to do worse or better than they deserve to based on their knowledge of the subject matter.

Test-taking Skills

Taking tests requires certain skills and behaviors generally not acquired unless specifically taught or learned through extensive practice. Unless students have acquired these basic skills, their performance is likely to be negatively affected (see, for example, Enright, 1992), and their true ability levels are likely to be underestimated by their test scores. Since tests are supposed to measure students' achievement, knowledge, or other aspects of their ability, and *not* their knowledge about *how to take a test,* test-taking skills are an extraneous variable that may potentially reduce measurement validity for some students.

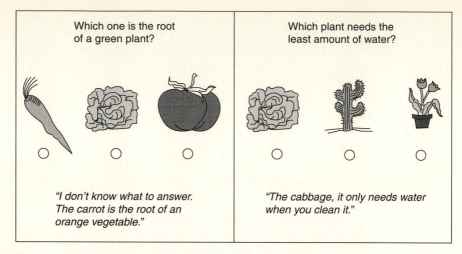

FIGURE 6.1   **Examples of Actual Standardized Test Items Where Content Has Been Mastered, But the "Best" Answer Has Been Misunderstood.**
Italicized Portion Indicates Explanations for Giving the Wrong Answer

Source: Taylor et al., 1982.

Selecting the "Best" Answer

For many tests, students are asked to select the "best" answer. If students have not been taught to think this way about test items, they may have mastered the content being tested, and still select an incorrect answer. For example, Taylor and White (1982) interviewed children who had answered standardized achievement test items incorrectly to determine *why* they had selected the wrong answer. Examples of two items, with the student's explanation in italics, are shown in Figure 6.1.

Unfortunately, a student may understand the concept and still give an incorrect answer. For example, on the right side of Figure 6.1, the respondent understood that since the cactus and flower were still growing, they would have continued need for water, whereas the cabbage head would need water only one time during washing. Someone with better test-taking skills, would have realized that even though the answer was technically correct, "cabbage" was not the desired answer.

Responding on Machine-scorable Forms

On some tests, students record their answers on machine-scorable forms, which are very different from the instructional materials with which they are familiar. When the answer format is confusing or distracting, students may miss items they would otherwise get correct. Some experts (for example, Noll, Scannel, & Craig, 1979) suggest that separate answer sheets should never be used by students below the fourth grade.

Other special skills are associated with marking machine-scorable answer sheets. For example, if the "bubble" is not filled in enough, it will not be scored by the scanning machine. Many people do not realize, however, that only one-third of the bubble needs to be darkened. Some students spend so much time carefully filling in the bubble as completely as possible, they do not have time to finish the test. Such false precision can be detrimental.

Working in Highly Structured Settings with Specialized Directions and Rules

During a test, students may be asked to respond to unusual directions given in a highly structured and often unfamiliar situation. Not surprisingly, such directions are sometimes misunderstood, and students have difficulty demonstrating what they know. Consider the following item taken from a standardized achievement test:

Read the first word, then read the words next to it. Find the word that can be added to the first word that makes ANOTHER word. Fill in the space that goes with the answer you choose.

1.   Air   land   port   road   wing
                   ◯   ◯   ◯   ◯

The correct answer, of course, is *port* to form the single word *airport*. However, a third-grade student who has never been exposed to this type of item, might have good mastery of compound words and still be confused about how to respond.

Students may also be confused by the setting in which the test is administered. For example, during testing, students are generally seated in straight rows with desks that are not touching. They frequently cannot have directions repeated, cannot obtain assistance from their teacher, and are not free to move about in the room. In some ways, standardized testing requires behavior that is exactly opposite from that for which students are usually rewarded. If students are not used to such special requirements, this reversal can be disorienting, and can interfere with performance.

Performing Under Time Limits

In most educational settings, we want students to understand exactly what is expected of them and to have adequate time to complete a task as well as they can. Some test taking is different. For example, in most standardized testing situations, directions are given only once, and there is a specified amount of time to perform the task. Students not accustomed to performing in such settings may become flustered and, as a result, may not perform well.

Following Advice to Guess

Consider the following excerpt from the instructions for a commercially available standardized achievement test:

There may be some items that you cannot do. If you are not sure of an answer, choose the answer you think is right or skip that item and go to the next one.

This instruction is advising students to guess if they do not know the right answer. Similar directions are contained in most standardized achievement tests and were a part of the procedures during the norming process. Students will substantially improve their scores if they can eliminate one or more obviously wrong answers and make their best guess from among the remaining alternatives. Appropriate guessing is a valuable test-taking skill, and the results of tests where students systematically eliminate options and "guess" appropriately are more indicative of a student's true ability. Because they are often discouraged from guessing during regular instruction, however, some students may hesitate to do so during a test.

A Test-taking Skills Summary

Taking tests in ways that demonstrate true level of mastery is a learned skill. Unless students have mastered test-taking skills, their scores will probably not be a valid indicator of what the test purports to measure. Lack of such skills can be exhibited in many ways, but in general, a student with poor test-taking skills will

- Read too quickly
- Miss important words
- Jump to conclusions
- Make random guesses
- Be confused by different answer formats
- Have difficulty adjusting to the structured setting of a test
- Not understand the concept of "best" answer

A student who has good test-taking skills has learned to

- Underline important words (where permissible)
- Analyze items systematically
- Guess (after eliminating unreasonable options)
- Pace herself during the test
- Skip difficult items and return to them if time permits
- Make sure she understands all directions

One way to reduce the influence of test-taking skills on test performance is to familiarize your students with the general requirements for taking tests prior to the time the test is administered. Some testing companies provide orientation materials specifically for this purpose, such as practice test forms with similar item types and scoring sheets, and explanation of general test-taking strategies. In classroom or school settings where locally developed tests are administered, teachers should make sure that students have adequate test-taking skills so that their performance on the test reflects what they know about the subject being tested, instead of what they know about how to take a test.

Application Problem 1

A first-year teacher comes to you for some advice about testing. It seems that she has several students who race through tests, do not appear to be carefully considering possible options to items, and then disrupt the rest of the class because they are finished early and have nothing to do. What advice would you give her?

Testwiseness

It is important to differentiate between test-taking skills and testwiseness. The concept of testwiseness has been discussed extensively for almost 50 years (see Evans, 1984; Millman, Bishop, & Ebel, 1965; and Thorndike, 1951). Millman et al. (1965, p. 707) defined testwiseness as, "a subject's capacity to utilize the characteristics and formats of the test and/or the test-taking situation to receive a high score." The testwise student will frequently

- Identify common elements between the stem and any of the options (for example, option *pasteurized* with Louis *Pasteur* in the stem).
- Recognize and use clues from grammatical construction (for example, subject–verb agreement).
- Learn the test constructor's tendency to use certain response positions more (or less) frequently (for example, a tendency for option *a* to be the correct answer on multiple-choice tests).
- In the absence of any knowledge about a multiple-choice item, select the longest option.
- Avoid options that use such absolutes as *never* and *always*.
- Use clues from one item to answer another item.

Figure 6.2 gives several examples of items in which a testwise student might be able to select the correct option even without any knowledge of the content being tested. In such cases, the testwise student will use the extraneous clues to obtain a higher score than she deserves. The importance of testwiseness is emphasized by the fact that an instrument, the *Gibb Experimental Test of Testwiseness,* has recently been developed to assess the degree of testwiseness among students (Harmon, Morse, & Morse, 1996).

The primary difference between test-taking skill and testwiseness is that the former allows the respondent to demonstrate her true level of knowledge, whereas the latter allows the respondent to take advantage of extraneous clues to obtain a score higher than she deserves. Test-taking skills increase the validity because they allow the test to more precisely measure what it is designed to measure. In contrast, testwiseness reduces validity because a student's score may reflect factors other than those the test is designed to measure (Messick, 1982). It is important to note that well-constructed tests eliminate the problems with testwiseness because unfair advantage won't exist unless inappropriate clues are present in the test. The best way to avoid testwiseness is to construct good tests.

Item	Explanation of Testwiseness Clue
The muscular system is made up of: ○ (a) bones (16.7%) ○ (b) muscles (75.0%) ○ (c) fatty tissue (4.2%) ○ (d) blood vessels (4.2%)	The words *muscular* in the stem and *muscles* in the option are obviously related.
The stretch of land between two mountains is called a: ○ (a) hill (16.7%) ○ (b) river (12.5%) ○ (c) mound (12.5%) ○ (d) valley (58.3%)	If the answer refers to land "between two mountains," then it cannot be a hill or a mound since those are similar to mountains. A river is not a stretch of land. So without knowing the word *valley*, the student can select the correct answer by a process of elimination.
The number of miles from the earth to the moon is less than: ○ (a) 225,000 (16.7%) ○ (b) 240,000 (12.5%) ○ (c) 245,000 (12.5%) ○ (d) 250,000 (58.3%)	Since the question asks for a distance that is "less than," the largest number has to be technically correct, even if it isn't what the item writer intended.

The Susan B. Anthony dollar honors:
 	
○ (a) one of our founding (29.2%)
    fathers
○ (b) a leader of the (16.7%)
    suffragette movement
○ (c) a famous baseball (16.7%)
    player
○ (d) the husband of (37.5%)
    Betsy Ross
	Susan is a woman's name, and three of the options obviously refer to men. Therefore, without even knowing what "suffragette" means, a testwise person would see that it's the only answer left.

Dwight Eisenhower: ○ (a) was a general (57.1%) during World War II ○ (b) astronaut (19.0%) ○ (c) of Russia (9.5%) ○ (d) in the United States (14.3%)	Only option (a) fits grammatically with this stem.

Note: Numbers in parentheses indicate the percentage of over 700 second- and third-grade students who selected each option in a project conducted by White et al., 1982. As can be seen, all the options are attractive choices for some students.

FIGURE 6.2 **Examples of Items That Can Be Answered Using Testwiseness Clues Even If Student Has No Knowledge of the Content**

To what degree is testwiseness a problem? The literature is not clear. Numerous researchers have claimed success in teaching testwiseness skills (for example, Bajtelsmit, 1977; McMorris, Brown, Snyder, & Pruzek, 1972; Moore, Schutz, & Baker, 1966), whereas others have been unsuccessful (for example, Board & Whitney, 1977; Dolly & Williams, 1983; Rogers & Bateson, 1991). In an extensive review of the literature on testwiseness, Scruggs, White, and Bennion (1986) concluded that training in testwiseness has little, if any, effect on achievement test scores of most students even though it has substantial effect on measures of testwiseness and some effect on reducing test anxiety.

How often are poorly constructed items a factor? Tests that are not carefully developed often have such problems (Gullickson & Ellwein, 1985; Stiggins, Conklin, & Bridgeford, 1986). However, for standardized achievement tests, it is probably not a serious problem. Although earlier studies (Metfessel & Sax, 1958) found that standardized tests contained many problems that would allow testwise respondents to use extraneous clues in raising their scores, Messick (1982) concluded in a later analysis that testwiseness was "rarely [a] demonstrable problem with professionally developed tests." The change may be due to the attention that testwiseness has received over the years.

Application Problem 2

Discuss the distinction between test-taking skills and testwiseness. Why do the two have a different impact on measurement validity?

Response Sets

Suppose you had a student who, when she did not know the correct answer, always selected the "true" option. She would do better than she deserved on tests constructed by a teacher who tended to write items that were true, and not as well as she deserved on tests written by a teacher who tended to write items that were false.

Such behaviors are referred to as *response sets,* tendencies to respond in certain consistent ways on tests. The existence of response sets has been recognized and researched for many years. Three types of response sets are most relevant to the chapter: (1) the speed versus accuracy response set, (2) the gambling response set, and (3) response sets related to item construction.

The Speed Versus Accuracy Response Set

When some people take a multiple-choice test, they work very quickly, writing down the first answer that comes to mind. Other people ponder the pros and cons of each option and move deliberately from item to item. What is the relationship between ability and the speed with which a person completes test items?

Suppose Suzanne does math problems faster than Linda. Does that mean that Suzanne knows how to do math *better* than Linda? Is Linda's slower pace attributable to less knowledge of math or to a personality factor that results in her working more deliberately? If a test is supposed to measure math ability, personality or response style factors would be irrelevant factors (extraneous variables). If these irrelevant factors affected test scores, the validity of interpretations based on these test scores would be compromised.

The relevance of this response set is mainly due to the fact that many standardized tests have time limits that prevent some students from finishing. If slowness in completing a test is caused by a lack of knowledge, then the lower score is justified; but if the slowness merely reflects a personal style, then the lower score may be an underestimate of the true ability level of the student.

As discussed in Chapter 4, tests may be classified into one of the two categories: *speed test* or *power test*. The major objective of a *speed test* is to see how fast a student can complete a certain task or activity, and as such, speed is a relevant attribute to measure. An example of a speed test is a typing test. A *power test*, on the other hand, usually focuses on knowledge or mastery of some learning objectives, and speed may be a much less or totally irrelevant factor. Although a speed component makes sense for some tests (for example, typing), most educational tests should be constructed and administered as power tests so that the vast majority of well-motivated students are able to complete them. Since most tests for classroom use are achievement tests, teachers should be sure that, wherever possible, speed of completion is not an important factor for test scores. Of course, on standardized achievement tests with prescribed time limits, the amount of time should not be changed. In such cases, you should make sure that the students understand the time limits and know how to pace themselves so that they have adequate time to complete the test.

Some research shows that speed and accuracy in completing a cognitive test do not necessarily go hand in hand. In other words, the relationship between measured ability and the rate at which tests are completed may be low for some cognitive tests (for example, Pashler, 1989; Phillips & Rabbitt, 1995; Schroeder, 1989). These findings strongly suggest that the speed is often more a function of personality rather than a reflection of knowledge and skill (Phillips & Rabbitt, 1995; Zelnilker, 1977).

The Gambling or Guessing Response Set

Some people are risk takers, others are not. In taking multiple-choice or true–false tests, some people are more willing than others to guess when they are not sure of an answer. To understand the effect of such behavior, referred to as the *gambling* response set, consider two students: Harriette, who is a gambler, and Emily, who is not. Assume that both students know the answers to exactly half the questions on a 100-item true–false test. Harriette randomly guesses on every item she does not know, whereas Emily omits them. Harriette gets 75 percent correct, and Emily gets 50 percent correct. Even though both students "know" exactly the same amount, their scores are radically different.

The gambling response set would not be a problem if everyone were equally likely to guess, but individuals may differ markedly, and these differences tend to be consistent over time (Ben-Shakhar & Sinai, 1991; Gafni & Estela, 1990; Slakter, 1969) but are unrelated to ability (Crocker & Benson, 1976). A number of scoring techniques have been developed to correct for the effects of such differences in scores. One popular correction formula is

$$S = R - \frac{W}{N - 1}$$

(Formula 6.1)

where S is the respondent's score corrected for guessing, R is the number of right responses marked by the respondent, W is the number of wrong responses, not including omitted items, N is the number of options for each item that are equally likely to be chosen if the respondent guesses blindly.

This correction formula penalizes for incorrect answers, since it assumes that the number of incorrect answers indicates the test taker's tendency to guess. The effect of applying this correction formula is demonstrated in Table 6.1. In this example, since Emily answered only the questions she knew, she did not have any incorrect answers. As a result, she did not receive any penalty for incorrect answers. Harriette made random guesses on all items she did not know (50 of them). Since the items were in true–false format, her random guesses allowed her to get approximately half of those items correct, but the other half (25 items) were incorrect answers that received penalty. After correction, the two students have the same scores.

At first glance, it seems logical that correction for guessing would improve test score validity. Research studies show, however, that the seemingly apparent advantage of correction may not exist for several reasons. First, correction formulas of this type incorrectly assumes that everyone is equally likely to guess. Second, correction formula assumes that guessing is a random process. Research studies have indicated that guessing is far from being random (Cross & Frary, 1977; Cureton, 1971). Third, the probability of obtaining a reasonably high score on a cognitive test as a result of pure guessing has been shown to be extremely small. Hopkins and Stanley (1981) showed that 68 percent of the students taking a 100-item true–false test about which they had absolutely no knowledge would score between 45 and 55, and 98 percent of the students would score between 40 and 60. Only about 1 respondent in 1000 would score 65 or higher by chance alone, and the chances of getting 75 or more of the 100 items correct is probably less than 1 in 3 million. Finally, corrected scores usually correlate highly with uncorrected scores (usually high .90s). Thus for norm-referenced measurement applications, corrections for guessing offer few advantages. For criterion-referenced applications, the corrected score for the total test may be closer to the true score, but the instructor will not know which of the objectives were achieved by guessing and which were achieved through knowledge.

Table 6.1   Scores for a Gambler and Nongambler Before and After Correction for Guessing

	Harriette the Gambler	Emily the Nongambler
True Knowledge of 100 true–false items	50	50
Scores on test where Harriette guesses for 50 items she does not know; Emily omits 50 items she does not know	75	50
Scores corrected for guessing	50 $[75 - (25 \div 1) = 50]$	50 $[50 - (0 \div 1) = 50]$

In short, not much is to be gained by the application of corrections in most cases. Because most standardized tests have constructed their norms in situations where students were encouraged to guess, students taking standardized tests should also be encouraged to guess when they are not sure of the answer. In most situations, we think this is also good advice for locally developed tests.

Application Problem 3

Imagine you have prepared a 40-item multiple-choice test with 5 options per question. Listed here are scores for three students in your class. Indicate what the "corrected" scores would be.

Student Name	No. of Correct Answers	No. of Wrong Answers	Corrected Scores
Diana	30	10	
Susan	30	5	
Vicky	30	0	

Response Sets Related to Item Construction

When unsure of correct answers, students tend to respond to test items in certain ways. If these tendencies happen to correspond or be contrary to the tendencies of the person(s) constructing the test items, obtained test scores will be higher or lower than they deserve to be. Consider several examples.

■ *The acquiescence set.* Respondents are more likely to select the option designated "true" when they are uncertain (for example, Krenz & Sax, 1987; Calsyn, 1992). If instructors include more true than false items on their tests, students with this response set will receive undeserved credit.

■ *The positional preference set.* Some early studies showed that many standardized achievement tests have fewer correct answers for the initial and final options of multiple-choice tests (Metfessel & Sax, 1958). Thus students who tend to choose options in the middle will receive undeserved credit. Later research (for example, Ace & Dawis, 1973; Jessell & Sullins, 1975) has found little, if any, effect of a positional preference set, so the problem may be more apparent than real.

■ *The option length set.* Several researchers (Dolly & Williams, 1983; Evans, 1984) have found a tendency for the longest option on multiple-choice tests to be the correct option more often than expected, and a tendency for some test takers to choose the longest option more frequently when they do not know the answer. This may no longer be a problem for well-constructed standardized tests because of the attention it has received. For tests constructed locally, the problem may still persist unless conscious efforts are made to avoid it.

All the response sets referred to here can be neutralized by good item construction. The option length set can easily be offset by inserting several long, incorrect options. The acquiescence set can be neutralized by making sure that there are an approximately equal number of true and false answers appearing in random order. The positional preference set can be counteracted by making sure that correct answers in a multiple-choice test appear in each position (for example, a, b, c, and d) approximately equally in random order.

Anxiety and Motivation

We will use *motivation* to describe students' desire to perform as best they can. *Anxiety* will be used to describe students' feelings of uneasiness, or even fear of testing situations. Motivation and anxiety can both influence test performance, and it is worthwhile to examine briefly how each operates and how they interact.

The Impact of Motivation on Test Performance

An interesting example of how motivation affects test scores appeared in *The Washington Post* (see Figure 6.3). From this article, it is clear that a test will not accurately reflect what students know unless they are motivated to do their best. Ideally, respondents will be motivated to succeed in test situations because they understand how the test score will affect them. However, motivation has been shown to differ substantially among various ethnic and socioeconomic groups (Anastasi, 1958; Huang & Waxman, 1995; Payne, 1993).

The effects of differential motivation on test performance have been examined extensively (for example, Wolf, 1995; Wolf & Smith, 1995). For example, Taylor (1981) identified 18 studies in which various rewards (money, candy, praise, and so on) were used to enhance students' motivation to do well on tests. Taylor found that highly motivated students performed substantially higher on standardized tests than poorly motivated students.

The Impact of Anxiety on Test Performance

Students who become *overly* motivated to do well on a test may become anxious. Dozens of research studies have examined the relationship between anxiety and test performance (for example, Birenbaum, 1994; Everson, 1992; Sarason, 1980; Tobias, 1984), and generally, motivation is shown to be positively related to performance, whereas anxiety is usually negatively correlated with performance (Wolf & Smith, 1995). Although some have found a moderately large negative relationship (for example, see Hill, 1984), most of this research is consistent in showing a small negative relationship between anxiety and performance on cognitive tests. The specific nature of the relationship between anxiety and test performance is still the subject of ongoing debate.

According to some, test anxiety interferes with the student's ability to recall information learned previously (Green, 1990; Hill & Wigfield, 1984; Wine, 1971; Everson, 1992). A conflicting explanation suggests that students who experience

Students Flunk Test
To Score a Point

By Katharine Macdonald
Special to The Washington Post

LOS ANGELES, April 2--You might say that the speed bumps in the parking lot at Chico High School cost $66,000. And they weren't even installed by a Defense Department contractor. In fact, it wasn't putting them in that was so expensive--it was not taking them out. That and a couple of other things. But the story is getting ahead of itself.

Chico is a small town some 90 miles north of Sacramento, where this story began more than a year ago. It was in Sacramento that the state legislature passed a package of education reforms, one of which was the California Assessment Program (CAP).

CAP is an incentive (the word "incentive" is the key) program that grants $66,000 to any state high school that annually tests 93 percent of its graduating seniors in reading, written expression, mathematics and spelling, and shows an improvement in each year's scores.

Now to Chico, and the part about incentive. It shows how smart the kids at Chico High are, even if most of them did score somewhere in the moron percentile on the CAP test.

The seniors at Chico knew about the $66,000 the school would get if they did well on the test. They also knew that if they didn't do well on the test, it would not affect their own grades or college admissions.

So, in the words of school superintendent Robert Jeffries, "They offered to negotiate."

According to principal Roger Williams, the four "ringleaders" have good academic records. This was the deal they offered: We take your test, we do well. We earn you $66,000. For our efforts we want some things. We want the speed bumps taken out of the parking lot. We want to smoke on campus. And we want a senior class trip to Santa Cruz.

What's a school to do? They said "no," of course. And then took some precautions. Before forwarding the CAP tests to the state, Chico High pulled the tests taken by the four student ringleaders. Maybe they didn't know about the leaflets the four had circulated on campus, urging all 333 seniors to fail the test.

Two weeks ago, Chico High School got the test results. It had dropped from the top third of the state's high schools to the bottom third. The overall percentile ranking had dropped from 70 percent to somewhere in the teens. In one subject category, Chico High's scores had plummeted from 73 percent to 2 percent. Suddenly, Chico High was $66,000 poorer.

Principal Williams said the four ringleaders were "reprimanded" last week after the scores were revealed but that they reacted with "indifference."

Some might think these high school seniors selfish and inflexible, with petty demands. But Kevin Turcotte, the reporter for the Chico Enterprise-Record who first reported the story, says it is not true that the students demanded the speed bumps be removed from the parking lot--just lowered.

FIGURE 6.3 An Example of How Motivation Can Affect Test Scores

high test anxiety are those with deficient study or test-taking skills (Culler & Holahan, 1980; Kirkland & Hollandsworth, 1980). In fact, Kirkland and Hollandsworth (1980, p. 438) suggest that the concept of "test anxiety" should be replaced with the phrase "ineffective test taking."

Unfortunately, research has not yet been able to pinpoint whether test anxiety depresses test scores, or whether inadequate test-taking skills result in poor performance on tests, which in turn generates high anxiety. Several experiments have been done to manipulate levels of anxiety in an effort to see how it affects test scores. Thus far, the evidence has failed to support the hypothesis that experimentally induced anxiety depresses test scores. It is clear that students who suffer high test anxiety tend to have poorer study habits and test-taking skills than other students. Unfortunately, anxiety reduction techniques seldom improve test performance. Culler and Holahan (1980, p. 18) concluded that research tended "to contradict the common stereotype of the highly anxious student who knows the subject matter but 'freezes up' at test time."

There are studies that show that test scores can be improved by changing variables that are logically related to lower levels of anxiety (for example, see Hill, 1984), but these studies do not demonstrate a causal link between test scores and feelings of anxiety. More definitive research is needed before we can know just how anxiety and test performance are related. Meanwhile, regardless of how anxiety affects test scores, we do not want to create unnecessary anxiety in our students. The fact that motivation and anxiety are closely linked, coupled with the fact that highly motivated students do better on tests, suggests that tests should be administered in such a way that students know that tests are important, and are motivated to do their best without experiencing undue anxiety.

Administrative Factors

A more complete discussion on the proper procedures for administering tests is discussed later in the book. However, it is important to mention here that there are a number of frequently encountered, but improper, test administration procedures that can pollute test scores.

Examiner Effects

A great deal of research has examined the relationship between administrator characteristics and test performance. Some people have claimed that performance on cognitive tests is maximized if the race of the examiner and race of the student are the same (for example, Abramson, 1969), but others disagree (Graziano, Varca, & Levy, 1982). It does appear that having the test administered by an examiner with whom students feel comfortable often results in higher test scores (Fuchs & Fuchs, 1986). This may be a more relevant issue for *individual* tests (for example, a test administered by an examiner to a single examinee) than for *group* tests (for example, a test administered to a group of examinees at the same time by one administrator) (Kaplan & Saccuzzo, 1997). Many intelligence tests are individual tests, and most educational tests are group tests.

In most classroom testing situations, there are many ways in which the administrator can establish rapport and make sure that students know what is expected and feel comfortable with the environment. Many other variables related to examiners have been investigated relatively infrequently. For the time being, we suggest making sure that the test is administered by someone with whom the students feel comfortable, concentrating on clarity of directions, the enthusiasm displayed, and the appropriateness of procedures used to monitor and support students during the test.

Advance Notice

Some educators argue that it is preferable to announce tests well in advance so that students will be motivated to study. They point out that unannounced quizzes and tests often increase student anxiety. It appears that students who are given unannounced quizzes are more anxious and dissatisfied with the course. Since there is no evidence that unannounced quizzes *improve* performance, it seems reasonable to provide students with as much notice about testing as possible.

Disturbances and Interruptions

Disturbances and interruptions during test taking should be minimized. This suggestion is based largely on logic since very little empirical research has been conducted to demonstrate a significant effect attributable to minor disturbances and interruptions during test taking. Nonetheless, it seems sensible to minimize disturbances and interruptions during testing.

Cheating

Unfortunately, cheating in testing appears quite widespread. In studies done several decades ago, Zastrow (1970) found a 40 percent incidence of cheating among graduate students, and Cornehlsen (1965) found that almost half of high school students felt that cheating was justified when it meant the difference between success and failure. Recent research indicates that cheating among college students is increasing rather than decreasing (McCabe & Trevino, 1996). Valid testing requires that opportunities for cheating be minimized, and that testing situations be appropriately controlled through conscientious monitoring and appropriate disciplinary action when cheating is discovered. In addition, different techniques for controlling and detecting cheating on tests have been proposed (see, for example, Aiken, 1991).

Coaching

Aptitude tests, such as the SAT (Scholastic Assessment Test, formerly known as the Scholastic Aptitude Test) or the ACT (American College Test), are used extensively by colleges and universities to help make admission decisions. There has been considerable controversy about the degree to which such test scores can be raised by *coaching*. *Coaching* means to provide intensive training or drills in test-wiseness skills or test-specific content for the purpose of raising test scores only, but minimally or not at all changing the knowledge or behavior domain underlying the performance. In contrast, *education* intends to change the behavior domain so that the performance on a specific test can be improved. If coaching can raise test scores without elevating the behavior domain, it undermines measurement validity.

As can be expected, the improvement with coaching reported in the literature is highly variable. Some studies indicated substantial improvement (Conroy, 1987; Sesnowitz, Bernhardt, & Knain, 1982; Slack & Porter, 1980;), whereas others showed more limited effect of coaching (Alderman & Powers, 1980; Donlon, 1984; Messick & Jungeblut, 1981; Pike 1978). In a review of studies of the effects of practice on aptitude tests (mostly IQ tests), Kulik, Kulik, and Bangert (1984) found gains from .25 standard deviation for a single-practice trial, up to .67 standard deviation resulting from five or six practice sessions. But substantially smaller improvement of coaching has been reported by others (for example, Messick, 1980). A more recent review on the coaching effect on the performance SAT scores indicates that coaching may have a somewhat more obvious effect on sections of SAT that are more curriculum-based such as math, and less effect on sections that are less curriculum-based such as verbal skills (Powers, 1993).

One difficulty related to this issue is that much of the research has been conducted by persons with a vested interest in the outcome—either those who have developed and who administer the aptitude tests or those who operate commercially available coaching programs. Furthermore, it is also possible that different content areas may be *differentially* susceptible to practice or coaching, thus making it difficult to draw a general conclusion about coaching effectiveness.

In studying the effect of coaching, it is important to distinguish between performance improvement limited to specific test content and performance improvement that results from broader change in the behavior domain a test intends to measure. The former is an extraneous variable reducing measurement validity, whereas the latter is not. As Payne (1982) pointed out, if coaching involves a more elaborate and broadly based educational experience through which academic skills are taught and learned, the likelihood of increasing test scores will be improved. For the time being, we believe that the summary offered by Payne (1982) in the *Encyclopedia of Educational Research* still holds.

> The crucial question here is not whether one can increase the scores, but whether the increase (1) is worth the time and financial investment, and (2) helps the student perform better in college. The response to both parts of the question is negative. Students might better spend their time being educated rather than coached. (p. 1198)

It is also important to make a distinction between coaching and training in test-taking skills. As noted earlier, some students lack test-taking skills, which results in test scores that underestimate those students' true ability. To overcome such disadvantages, many testing companies provide orientation materials for prospective test takers, including limited samples of practice tests, to reduce the effect of lack of test-taking skills so that more valid measurement can be achieved.

Another issue related to coaching is the argument that coaching may further widen the performance gap between the socioeconomically disadvantaged and privileged students since commercial coaching programs typically charge a substantial amount of money for the service. Obviously, this argument makes sense only under the assumption that coaching can substantially improve test takers' performance. The existing research, as discussed earlier, does not invite definitive conclusions about this issue.

In recent years, some school districts have begun using another type of "practice" for standardized achievement tests that may contribute to inflated and invalid test scores. Specifically, a number of commercially produced packages are now available that are ostensibly designed to teach students test-taking skills (see Mehrens & Kaminski, 1989, for a review of several of these packages). Unfortunately, the material in some of these packages is so similar to what is in the standardized achievement test for which they were designed that "it is equivalent to giving the parallel form of the test as a practice test and explaining all the answer choices to students" (Shepard, 1990, p. 19). If one wishes to draw conclusions about how much students know about a broader domain of material, based on the sample of test items, the use of such practice material is clearly inappropriate.

Test Bias

A test is biased if, "individuals from different groups who are equally able, do not have equal probabilities of success," (Anderson et al., 1980, p. 16). In Chapter 2, we briefly discussed different aspects of test bias that should be considered in the construction, administration, and interpretation of tests. Test bias is a serious issue. The existence of test bias not only compromises measurement validity, it also has serious negative social impact on those against whom the tests are biased. Because of its negative social implications, test bias has been one of the most hotly debated issues in measurement during the past few decades. Understanding test bias is important since all educators will undoubtedly encounter this issue directly or indirectly during their careers.

If a test is biased, an extraneous influence is affecting the scores of one group of respondents, but not the other. For example, if the instructions for a mathematics test include vocabulary and language that is frequently misunderstood by children from a minority cultural background, then the test is biased against those children. Such bias would be reflected in the fact that these children, regardless of their actual math ability levels, tend to receive scores that underestimate their ability levels.

Some Popular Misconceptions About Test Bias

To understand what test bias is and how to deal with the potential problem, it is important to be familiar with some major misconceptions about test bias that may hinder our efforts in understanding the issue.

Average difference between groups. A large body of empirical research indicates that, although the size of the differences vary, economically disadvantaged minority groups tend to obtain lower average scores on many different kinds of tests (both aptitude and achievement tests), than do students from higher income majority groups. Based on this fact, there are often claims that many of these tests are culturally biased against certain minority groups. It is important to note that, although group differences are causes to examine whether test bias exists, such differences are not sufficient evidence for the existence of test bias. The more important question to ask is whether such performance differences are caused by factors that are *irrelevant* to what the test is designed to measure, or whether such differences mirror the true difference among groups in what the test intends to assess. In the former case, we say that test bias exists. The latter case, however, may indicate some deficiency with the lower scoring group in what the test is measuring, which is usually meaningful for educators since we will be interested in knowing why such deficiency exists and how it can be corrected. In other words, bias exists only when *equally able* groups perform differently on a test. If two groups were indeed *not* equally able in the trait being measured, test scores should truthfully reflect the fact. For this reason, additional, preferably external, evidence is needed other than mean group difference to prove the existence of test bias. In recent years, this point has been widely misunderstood by representatives of many different groups, and often by our judicial courts, who have argued that test score differences between groups *are* sufficient to demonstrate that tests are biased and discriminatory.[1]

The basic assumption for this misconception is the belief that all groups *must* be equally able in whatever we measure. But true group differences may indeed exist for a variety of reasons, some of which we may be aware of, and some of which we may not. As a society, we have an interest in knowing where deficiencies exist so that activities can be taken to correct them. It does not help to simply blame the messenger for the news we don't want to hear.

Cultural content/stereotypes and test bias. It is often argued that many current psychological and educational tests are culturally "loaded", that is, contain certain culture-specific content or cultural stereotypes. As a result, these tests are biased *in favor of* the dominant majority group(s), and *against* other minority groups. This argument is often incorrect for two reasons. First, although cultural content of a test, especially when constrained to be too narrow or too specific, may cause a test to be biased, cultural content by itself does not *necessarily* cause bias. Consider the issue of cultural stereotyping, for example. In much traditional test material, women are often depicted in roles such as housewives, secretaries, and maids. When an abstract third-person singular pronoun is needed, *he* rather than *she* is often used. Such stereotyping may sometimes be perceived as a source of test bias against girls and women (for example, Tittle & Zytowski, 1978; Tittle, 1978).

Although such cultural stereotyping may have negative social impact, and should be avoided, there should be a clear distinction between such stereotyping and test bias—the two should not be equated. From the perspective of measurement validity, we will not know if such stereotyping has caused test bias unless the

---

[1]See the summer 1987 issue of *Educational Measurement: Issues and Practice* for a thorough discussion of both sides of this issue.

issue has been empirically investigated. If indeed such stereotyping caused girls and women to score lower on the test than when no such stereotyping exists (for example, this issue could be studied objectively using an experimental design), we can say that test bias exists because of such stereotyping. If no such evidence can be found, we cannot draw such a conclusion.

The second reason cultural content in a test does not *by itself* constitute test bias is related to the question of what should be tested, or what behavior domains should be sampled by a test. It may be true that in a society such as the United States, certain groups may be more familiar with some behavior domains than others. If this is the case, does it constitute test bias to sample these behavior domains with which cultural groups have different levels of familiarity since doing so would give an advantage to some groups but not to others?

In our view, what should be tested should be based on the relevance of the behavior domain for the purpose of measurement, but not on the consideration that a particular group may be more or less familiar with the behavior domain. If the behavior domain is valued by the society, but is less familiar to a particular cultural group, then that group has a deficiency in that area. Such deficiency should be reflected through measurement so that corrective measures can be implemented. For example, members of a subculture may not emphasize abstract reasoning because of cultural, socioeconomic, or lifestyle reasons. As a result, students of this group will usually have less exposure to and less training in abstract reasoning activities. Should such an area be sampled and measured in a test designed to assess intellectual development? The answer is probably yes if abstract reasoning is valued by the society as a whole, and if such a construct is relevant to many other behavior domains valued in the society, such as performance in various academic areas.

Test norming sample and test bias.   It is sometimes argued that many current tests have been standardized on samples consisting predominantly of subjects from the majority ethnic or cultural group. Such tests may be biased when used for some other minority groups. This question invites empirical answers. Theoretically, such test bias is potentially possible because of some factors related to item selection procedures during test development (Harrington, 1984; Jensen, 1980). Although not enough empirical research has been done to definitively answer such questions, preliminary evidence indicates that the cultural or ethnic composition of standardization samples are usually not an influential factor contributing to test bias (Fan, Willson, & Kapes, 1996; Green & Draper, 1972; Hickman & Reynolds, 1986–1987).

In the discussion of test bias, it is important to keep in mind that the evidence for test bias should be empirically based; that is, the question should be objectively studied (or as objectively as possible) rather than based on subjective declaration. Because of the seriousness of the test bias issue, a variety of procedures have been developed to detect test bias, and these procedures make it possible to systematically study this serious issue. Some of these are subjective procedures (for example, use of an experts panel to identify potentially biased content or test items), and some are empirical. Some are designed to investigate if a test is measuring different constructs for different groups, some deal with predictive bias in selection situations, and some deal with potential bias at the item level (for example, research in differential item functioning). There is a good deal of literature on test bias detection methods, but because of limited space in this book, we have simply introduced some of the major issues. Interested students, especially students with training in statistical methods, may consult Berk (1982) as a place to begin investigating these issues.

Many research studies have been conducted to investigate test bias in a variety of contexts, and there is a voluminous body of research literature. Contrary to what is often believed, as summarized by Oakland and Parmelee (1985, p. 717), "a considerable body of literature currently exists that does not substantiate a claim of cultural bias against ethnic minority children with regard to the use of well-constructed, adequately standardized intelligence and aptitude tests." Reynolds (1981) also concluded that cognitive tests "measure the same construct with equivalent accuracy for African Americans, Whites, Latin Americans, and other native-born American ethnic minorities for both genders." Additionally, based on an extensive analysis of psychometric characteristics, predictive validity, factor analyses, and item bias characteristics, Reschly (1980) could find no evidence that professionally developed standardized tests are systematically biased.

Jensen (1980) provided a summary about research related to bias in mental testing when he said

> by and large, current standardized tests of general mental ability and scholastic achievement, as well as many vocational aptitude tests, are not biased with respect to any native born, English speaking minority groups in the United States. . . . The fact that tests are not biased, however, does not guarantee that they will be used properly or wisely. Tests can be abused in the ways that they are used. Indeed it is much easier to find fault with the *uses* of tests than with the tests themselves. (p. 715)

What does this mean for locally developed tests? First, it suggests that it is possible to avoid test bias of the type that causes people of equal ability to obtain different scores. How well bias is avoided depends partially on test construction. Often, bias is another label for many of the extraneous variables discussed earlier (testwiseness, anxiety, and so on). If such extraneous variables affect members of one group more than those of another group, the test is biased. Recognizing that extraneous variables may affect members of various groups differently provides another checkpoint to consider in reviewing tests.

The intensive discussion about test bias in the past few decades, together with the prospect for legal challenges, has prompted testing companies to devote substantial resources to dealing with the problem of potential test bias. Now, when a test is being developed, and even after a test has been in use, different aspects of potential test bias are routinely investigated. It is fair to say that the issue of test bias currently receives substantially more scrutiny during every phase of test development and use than was the case several decades ago. But despite the progress that has been made, educators should continue to be vigilant about this serious issue; it is just too important to be ignored.

Application Problem 4

Discuss some measurement situations where test bias may be operating in providing one group an unfair advantage while putting another group at an unfair disadvantage. In your opinion, should group mean difference be treated as sufficient evidence for the existence of test bias? Why or why not? Provide some examples (real or hypothetical) to support your argument.

Extraneous Factors That Can Influence the Results of Affective Measures

Until now, we have focused on the extraneous variables that can pollute the interpretation of cognitive tests. Generally, when we think about assessment, we think about such cognitive tests. As discussed previously, however, there is another broad category of measurement instruments that assess social or affective variables (self-concept, friendship patterns, attitudes, values, interests, learning styles, and so on). For cognitive tests, there usually exists a correct answer to a question. However, the "correct" answers on affective measurement such as self-concept, perceptions of school climate, or vocational interest measures are whatever the respondent herself feels, perceives, or believes about a particular situation, activity, or behavior. Most affective measures are self-report measures, so information can be collected only when respondents are able and willing to share. Consequently, there tend to be a myriad of ways in which extraneous variables can affect or distort the results of such measures.

Many extraneous variables that influence scores on affective measures are similar to those we discussed in the previous section (for example, anxiety and motivation, administrative factors, or test bias) and will not be repeated here. However, several additional extraneous variables are particularly problematic for affective measures.

Social Desirability

Just as with cognitive measures, some people tend to respond on affective measures in predictable ways that are independent of the content of the question. One of the most frequently observed response sets with affective measures is referred to as the *social desirability* response set. Social desirability refers to the fact that some respondents will answer items in a way they believe would be most socially appropriate, regardless of their true feelings. Suppose you lived in a town where a task force had just completed an extensive and highly visible campaign about the dangers associated with latch-key children, and the local PTA president, who is a friend of yours, wished to interview you. Suppose you were asked to respond to the following item:

If both parents are employed, it is appropriate for them to expect their 6-year-old child to take care of herself when she comes home from school.

O	O	O	O	O
Strongly Agree				Strongly Disagree

Regardless of your true feelings, you might be tempted to answer "strongly disagree," given the social atmosphere in which the item was administered. If people give socially desirable answers, the response will be of little value because they do not represent the respondents' true feelings.

One of the earliest suggestions to counter the social desirability response set was made by Edwards (1957a), who developed a social desirability scale that could be embedded in whatever questionnaire was being used. The purpose of the scale was to assess the degree to which social desirability was affecting the respondent's answers. A number of similar scales have been proposed, a popular one being the Marlowe–Crowne Social-Desirability Scale, which has items such as the following:

I always try to practice what I preach.
I never hesitate to go out of my way to help someone in trouble.
I am always courteous, even to people who are disagreeable.

Most people tend to be somewhat inconsistent in their everyday behaviors. Consequently, if a person answers "strongly agree" to each of these and other similar items, there is a good probability that a social desirability response set is operating. The rationale behind such measures is that if those people can be identified for whom social desirability is affecting their responses, their results can be adjusted, analyzed separately, or discarded.

Another approach is to attempt to prevent the social desirability response set from occurring in the first place by using a "forced choice" item format. This requires respondents to choose between two alternatives that are designed to have equal levels of social desirability, as in this following example:

Is it better to contribute money to

_____   The United Way
_____   A college or university of your choice

Here both options are socially desirable, so the respondent must rely on what she really believes to make a choice. Forced choice items (either positive or negative) are used widely in professionally developed affective measures. Because they are more difficult to develop and interpret than other types of items, they are used less often in locally developed measures.

Another way to minimize the influence of social desirability is to assure respondents' anonymity, create a rapport with them, and convince them that the results of the questionnaire are important and will be more beneficial if responses are honest. In some cases, anonymity is difficult to achieve, but where it is possible, it appears that it can contribute substantially to reducing the social desirability response set.

Application Problem 5

The PTA president has asked you to review a questionnaire about school climate to be administered to sixth and seventh graders. You notice that students are required to provide their names and ask why. She says that she wants students' names so that she can see whether boys and girls, or sixth and seventh graders feel differently; and she thinks that students are accustomed to providing their names on tests, so this will seem familiar to them. What is your advice about whether to ask for names?

Faking

Anastasi (1988, p. 456) noted, "As long as a subject has sufficient education to enable him to answer a personality inventory . . . he probably has the ability to alter his score appreciably in the desired direction." Because affective measures do not have one correct answer, subjects can easily fake responses to achieve desired results. For example, someone who does not want to serve on a jury might try to convince the judge that she already believes that the defendant is guilty. Or a person interviewing for a job might lie about her work habits, initiative, and experience. Faking occurs. How likely it is on a particular measure depends on the perceived benefits, how easy it is to do, and the willingness of the respondent to distort the truth.

As with the social desirability response set, techniques for dealing with faking have centered on (1) detecting its presence, or (2) attempting to prevent it. A number of standardized measures, such as the Minnesota Multi-Phasic Personality Inventory and the Kuder Occupational Interests Surveys, have special subtests, often referred to as "lie scales," designed to detect the faker. In some cases, scores on the lie scale are used to adjust the obtained score. Unfortunately, adjustments based on lie scales are difficult to do and are not usually appropriate for locally developed measures.

There are alternatives, though. One is to disguise the purpose of the assessment. A questionnaire designed to investigate honesty might ask the respondent to check the number of books he or she had read from a list of alleged best-sellers. If the list contained several fictitious titles, which the respondent checked, there would be some doubt about her honesty. Such an approach is applicable only in certain very specific types of assessments. Even then, its practical and ethical problems should be carefully considered.

The most frequent approach to reducing faking is to convince the respondents that a truthful response is important and will not have negative effects for them personally. A guarantee of anonymity also helps. In situations where respondents might be motivated to lie or try to "look good," it is sometimes possible to avoid self-report measures. For example, instead of asking high school seniors how many driving citations they received during the last 12 months, it might be possible to obtain the same information from city records.

Problems of Interpretation

Many affective measures ask people to respond on a continuum like the following one:

Always Strongly Agree	Usually Agree	Sometimes Uncertain	Occasionally Disagree	Never Strongly Disagree

Unfortunately, people do not interpret such words consistently. More than 50 years ago, Simpson (1944) pointed out that when asked to interpret the word *frequently,* 25 percent said it applied to events that occurred more than 80 percent of the time, and the other 25 percent said it applied to events that occurred more than 40 percent of the time. Similar discrepancies were noted later by Sudman and Bradburn (1982). We suspect they still exist today.

Problems also exist with interpreting questions. Take the question, "Do you like school?" How much does someone have to like school to answer yes? We cannot say. A response of yes may mean, "It's the best thing in my life!" whereas another means, "Well, it's tolerable." Furthermore, one respondent may be rating recess, and another may be rating math. Better item construction reduces this problem, but it is impossible to eliminate all ambiguity with affective items.

The Acquiescence Response Set

Many items on affective measures ask for an agree–disagree response. In answering such items, some people tend to choose an "agree" response when they are uncertain. This tendency to agree with items is referred to as the *acquiescence* response set. People constructing affective measures are frequently advised to mix positively and negatively worded items to avoid the possibility that respondents will answer all items one way. Although such advice is logical, some researchers have concluded that this is not as much of a problem as has been suggested (Schriesheim & Hill, 1981). However, since it is easy to do, balancing is probably wise. It is even more important to make sure items are carefully worded and respondents are motivated to provide accurate information.

General Strategies for Reducing the Impact of Extraneous Factors

Figure 6.4 summarizes the sources of cognitive test score pollution we have discussed, and the possible remedies for each. Although there are no magic solutions, test score pollution can be minimized through careful test construction, appropriate preparation of students, and correct test administration practices. Use this checklist frequently to remind yourself of extraneous factors that can influence test scores, and to plan strategies for remediation.

FIGURE 6.4   Sources and Possible Remedies of Cognitive Test Score Pollution

Checked	Source	Possible Remedies
	Test-Taking Skills	Make sure respondents are familiar with testing format, procedures, and expectations of the test. Don't over-invest in test-taking training, however.
	Testwiseness Skills	Carefully constructed items will minimize or eliminate the effects of testwiseness skills. See specific suggestions for item construction in later chapters.
	Response Sets: *Speed vs. Accuracy*	All tests should be power tests instead of speeded tests unless speed of response is an essential characteristic of what is being measured (as in typing).
	Gambling	Instruct and encourage all respondents to answer *every* question based on their best guess. Correction formulas and complicated scoring procedures are generally not worth the effort.
	Item Construction	Double-check items to make sure that no systematic patterns of correct answers exist (e.g., more true than false, first option or longest option correct more often than chance).
	Anxiety and Motivation	Explain importance of testing information, establish rapport and comfortable testing situation, and make sure respondents know what to expect and have had experience with similar tests. Provide special attention to students with particularly high anxiety, or refer them for specialized help.
	Administration Factors	Know the test and prepare specifically for proper administration. As a test administrator, your job is to make sure students know exactly what is expected, are motivated to do their best, and have an appropriate working environment. See Chapter 9 for more detailed procedures.
	Coaching and Practice	Used primarily in conjunction with aptitude tests for secondary age students and older, coaching and practice is primarily useful for reducing anxiety and increasing self-confidence. Available evidence may not strongly support the value of intensive coaching courses for the purpose of increasing individual scores or enhancing test validity.
	Test Bias	Watch for students who, because of cultural, ethnic, or gender-based differences, may experience difficulty in understanding vocabulary/instructions, being motivated or responding to items; then make individual adjustments as necessary.

Checked	Source	Possible Remedies
	Social Desirability	Forced-choice items and embedded social desirability scales are useful for professionally developed measures, but not usually for locally developed measures. Do your best to establish rapport and communicate the importance of answering honestly. Preserve anonymity when possible.
	Faking	Forced-choice items and embedded lie scales are useful for professionally developed measures, but not usually for locally developed measures. Do your best to establish rapport and communicate the importance of answering honestly. Preserve anonymity when possible.
	Acquiescence	Although commonly considered a potential problem with self-report measures, available evidence does not support its seriousness. Balancing positively and negatively worded items is easy to do, however, and should correct any problems that do exist.
	Test-Taking Skills*	Make sure respondents are familiar with testing format, procedures, and expectations of the test. Don't over-invest in test-taking training.
	Speed vs. Accuracy*	All tests should be power tests instead of speeded tests unless speed is an essential characteristic of what is being measured.
	Anxiety and Motivation*	Explain importance of testing information, establish rapport, provide a comfortable testing situation, and make sure respondents know what to expect and have had experience with similar tests. Provide special attention and assistance to students with particularly high anxiety.
	Administration Factors*	Know the test and prepare specifically for proper administration. As a test administrator, your job is to make sure students know what is expected, are motivated to do their best, and have an appropriate working environment. See Chapter 9 for more detailed procedures.
	Test Bias*	Watch for students who, because of cultural, ethnic, or gender-based differences may experience difficulty in understanding vocabulary/ instructions, being motivated, or responding to items; then make individual adjustments as necessary.

* Although primarily a problem with cognitive tests, these sources of test score pollution can also affect results on affective tests.

FIGURE 6.5   Sources and Possible Remedies of Affective Test Score Pollution

Figure 6.5 provides a similar checklist for affective tests. As you can see, some sources of test score pollution are the same for affective or cognitive tests (see the last five sources listed in Figure 6.5).

SUGGESTED READINGS

Dobbin, J. E. (1984). *How to take a test.* Princeton, NJ: Educational Testing Service.

Published by one of the largest developers and distributors of tests in the world, this booklet is designed to help its readers take all kinds of tests with more confidence and a greater probability of success. Written primarily for high school and older students, the booklet gives advice about all aspects of test-taking from preparation, to test-taking strategies, to interpreting scores.

Jensen, A. R. (1980). *Bias in mental testing.* New York: The Free Press.

A comprehensive presentation of the evidence in support of the position that standardized tests of aptitude and achievement are not biased with respect to minority groups. Although the arguments presented herein are not accepted by all people, this book is must reading for anyone who wants to consider both sides of the arguments about bias in testing.

Messick S., & Jungeblut, A. (1981). Time and method in coaching for the SAT. *Psychological Bulletin, 89,* 191–216.

A comprehensive review of the research on the effects of coaching for the Scholastic Aptitude Test. Although available data is fragmentary and fraught with methodological problems, the authors conclude that the best available evidence suggests that coaching is of limited utility for most people.

Paulman, R. G. & Kennelly, K. J. (1984). Test anxiety and ineffective test-taking: Different names, same construct? *Journal of Educational Psychology, 76,* 279–288.

Following a brief review of the research literature on test anxiety, the authors describe a study designed to determine whether test anxiety is any different from ineffective test-taking skills. This is a readable and interesting example of how research can be used to help answer very complex questions about cognitive behavior.

Reynolds, C. R. (1994). Bias in testing. In R. J. Sternberg (ed.). *Encyclopedia of human intelligence* (pp. 175–178). New York: Macmillan.

This section in the encyclopedia provides a concise and easy-to-understand discussion about the major issues related to test bias, and the implications of this controversy in the major aspects of testing. Although somewhat short, interested readers will find this section very informative and thought provoking.

SUGGESTION SHEET

If your last name starts with the letter H or I, please complete the Suggestion Sheet at the end of the book while this chapter is still fresh in your mind.

Answers to Chapter 6 Application Problems

1. Except where prohibited on standardized tests, time limits should be established so that everyone who tries has time to complete all items. Some people tend to complete tests quickly; others are slow. This is referred to as the speed versus accuracy response set. The speed with which someone finishes the test is generally unrelated to test scores, but it is important that respondents take time to read and consider every option. If students complete the test early, they should be encouraged to review their answers and change those where they think a different answer

would be better. If there is still time, they should be monitored so that they do not disturb other students. Instruction prior to the next test for the class on how to "pace" themselves during the test may be helpful.

2. Test-taking skills refer to the degree to which the student possesses knowledge and behaviors necessary to effectively demonstrate what she knows. For example, understanding what is expected, familiarity with the format being used, ability to pace herself, and ability to eliminate obviously wrong choices and make logical guesses among the others. Testwiseness is using clues from poorly constructed tests or other strategies to get a higher score on content she really has not mastered. As discussed in the chapter, if an examinee does not have adequate test-taking skills, his performance may be hampered, and as a result, his test score is likely to underestimate real level of performance. Consequently, the test score is not as valid as it should be in describing this examinee. For this reason, having adequate test-taking skills makes it more likely to allow examinees to show what they truly know, and this will increase measurement validity. On the other hand, to be testwise is to show more than one actually knows about the subject being measured. So testwiseness, though it may increase scores, reduces the measurement validity.

3. Using the correction formula provided in the chapter, we obtain the following corrected scores:

Student Name	No. of Correct Answers	No. of Wrong Answers	Corrected Scores
Diana	30	10	27.50
Susan	30	5	28.75
Vicky	30	0	30.00

As can be seen, the rank order of the corrected score is different from the uncorrected scores because the number of items omitted by each student is substantially different. Correction formulas are usually not worth the bother unless some students omit a substantial number of items.

4. Refer to the answers to Application Problem 2 in Chapter 2 for some hypothetical examples of test bias. In our opinion, it is simplistic and naive to conclude that group mean difference should be considered sufficient evidence of test bias even though such group mean difference may indicate the existence of *potential* test bias. Other than test bias, other factors (for example, social, economical, cultural) may cause *real* performance differences between ethnic, social, cultural, or gender groups. Simply to conclude that the test is at fault whenever group differences are observed may prevent us from investigating the social, economic, or cultural factors that may have caused or contributed to the differences, and consequently, corrective measures will not be considered in policy decisions.

5. On this type of a questionnaire, there will be a tendency for students to give the answers they think teachers and administrators want to hear. Particularly if respondents are identified by name, there may be a personal benefit to giving answers that teachers want. Therefore, it makes more sense to have anonymous responses and ensure that students understand the purpose of the questionnaire and that they are convinced their concerns will be carefully considered and appropriate action taken. To see if boys and girls or sixth and seventh graders respond differently, you can include several demographic items on the questionnaire.

CONSTRUCTING NEW MEASURES

Learning to Use a Blueprint

As we suggested in Section I, there is great wisdom in using available measures—if such measures will serve your needs satisfactorily. However, sometimes existing measures just won't work. And while it is important not to waste time recreating the wheel, it is even more important not to use wheels designed for someone else's vehicle. In this section, we suggest ways of knowing when you are better off developing your own measures. We also cover ways of ensuring high quality in the measures you develop and using locally developed measures effectively to assess student performance. In addition, we provide some practical guidance for creating test items of various kinds.

Chapters 7 and 8 cover the why, when and how of building your own achievement measures, including specific steps, ways of using a test blueprint, and ways of writing various types of achievement test items— among them, multiple choice, true-false, matching, short-answer, and essay items. In addition, we discuss some alternative, less formal methods of assessing student learning.

Chapter 9 extends this topic by describing procedures for assembling and administering tests effectively. We also discuss how you can evaluate and improve your own achievement tests by use of simple item analyses procedures.

SECTION III

In Chapter 10, we turn to the increasingly popular area of performance testing. We discuss the many advantages of these alternative approaches to assessing student performance that have been proposed by critics of more traditional measurement approaches. We explore how performance measures can be used to accomplish many important ends in our schools' classrooms, and we provide specific "hands-on" examples of actual performance tests for those not yet acquainted with these useful assessment approaches. We also add several cautions to those who advocate sole use of these alternative assessment approaches while calling for abolishing all other forms of assessment. We believe such "either-or" approaches to any single form of assessment ignores the fact that each assessment approach has advantages and disadvantages that must be considered, and usually the best assessment system will depend upon both performance measures and more traditional tests, each form serving the purposes it serves best.

Chapter 11 provides practical suggestions for how to develop instruments useful in collecting descriptive information. Specifically, we discuss the uses of questionnaires, interview schedules, observation scales, and other rating scales. This chapter covers ways of constructing and using those instruments, warns of some problems you might encounter along the way, and suggests ways to resolve those problems.

Chapter 12 directs your attention to measures of attitudes and interests—indices of how students feel about school and about a multitude of other things. We include these kinds of measures in this section (rather than the following one in which other various kinds of existing measures are described), because attitude measures are often developed locally. We show how the most common type of attitude scale is developed, provide examples of some typical attitude measures, and indicate how to judge the acceptability of such instruments. Vocational and other interest measures are similarly discussed.

Chapter 13 teaches you how to translate achievement test scores into grades or other statements of student performance while maintaining both the utility and equity of your grading system. This chapter also examines several purposes of grading, and examines the pros and cons of different grading systems.

Collectively, the information in these seven chapters will help you become more comfortable and more competent in constructing and using the results of your own "home-grown" educational measures.

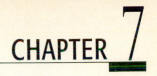
Constructing Your Own Achievement Tests

Deciding When and How To Do So

OVERVIEW

Have you ever taken a class where you thought the tests were poorly constructed, confusing, misleading, or trivial? Probably so. You may even have been responsible for constructing a few tests, and perhaps have wondered if the same criticisms could be leveled against them.

Many locally developed classroom achievement tests are poor (Stiggins & Bridgeford, 1985), but they do not have to be. The techniques and principles that result in good tests are straightforward and easy to learn. Sadly, few teachers receive sufficient instruction or practice in item writing or test construction (Gulliksen, 1986; Mehrens & Lehman, 1991) even though teachers spend substantial time constructing their own tests. Indeed, Herman and Dorr-Bremme (1982) concluded that as many as three-quarters of the assessments used in classrooms are developed by teachers. With such heavy dependence on teacher-made tests in making important day-to-day decisions about students, it is essential that teachers and other practitioners know *when* to develop their own classroom achievement measures and *how* to do so. This chapter and the next three are provided to help teachers understand the whys, when, and how of constructing local classroom achievement tests.

In this chapter, we discuss why locally developed achievement tests are so frequently used even though so many commercially marketed tests are available. We explain how commercial tests and locally developed tests can complement and enhance each other's value. The steps that should be followed in planning an achievement test are summarized, and specific guidelines and examples are given to assure that the plans will result in a high-quality test that will fulfill the purpose for which you developed it.

In Chapters 8 through 10, we turn our attention to specific steps for constructing, interpreting, and refining various types of locally constructed tests and other assessment procedures used most frequently by classroom teachers.

OBJECTIVES

Upon completing your study of this chapter, you should be able to

1. Describe situations in which it would be better to construct your own achievement test rather than using a commercially available test.

2. Explain the pros and cons of four different ways of adapting commercially available achievement tests for local needs.

3. Identify situations in which adaptations of commercially available achievement tests would be inappropriate.

4. Explain why it is important to clarify your instructional objectives before developing a test.

5. Give examples of instructional objectives that are overly narrow or broad.

6. Identify items representing different levels on a taxonomy of educational objectives.

7. Explain why most tests should include items from several different levels.

8. Demonstrate how a test blueprint can be used to guide the construction of a valid test.

Why Construct Your Own Achievement Tests?

Hundreds of standardized achievement tests are now commercially available. Constructed by teams of professional test developers to be consistent with the results of comprehensive analyses of the most widely used curricula, the items contained in the best standardized achievement tests are meticulously pilot-tested, and repeatedly revised so that only the best items are included in the final version. Computerized scoring is capable of furnishing dozens of different reports that provide information about the objectives achieved, diagnosis of the areas in which a student is having difficulty, descriptions of performance in relation to national and local norms, and various learning objectives. The variety and number of commercially available tests is almost overwhelming, and the quality and appeal of the best of these tests is excellent and getting better as a function of competition among test publishers.

You may ask, "Why do teachers ever need to develop their own achievement tests? Surely, if there are so many commercially available tests, there is probably a good one for every need, so why not let the experts develop the tests, while teachers do the teaching?" There are at least six reasons why locally developed achievement tests continue to be an extremely important part of effective teaching.

1. *Greater relevancy.* Because commercially available tests must appeal to a broad market, they focus on the objectives and content that are most frequently present in "typical" schools. Locally developed achievement tests are designed and constructed by the classroom teacher and can be tailored to the specific needs and situations in that classroom. Who knows better than the teacher the relative importance of the different concepts taught? Even the format of items in locally developed tests can be tailored to the specific classroom. At first, questions may be asked in the format used during instruction, so as not to confuse students; but later, new formats might be introduced to see how well students can generalize to other situations the information they have learned.

2. *More frequent administration.* Most commercially available achievement tests are designed to be given either at the beginning or end of the school year as a measure of students' overall achievement. They frequently require several hours or even days to administer. Because scoring and reporting options for such tests have been substantially improved over the last decade, the results can be very useful in diagnosing learning problems, providing information to students and parents, and helping administrators make decisions. However, teachers need information about student progress, weaknesses, and areas of mastery on a weekly or even daily basis—once or twice a year is not enough. Locally developed tests can provide current information on student performance as often as teachers care to create and administer them. Further, a local test can cover as much or as little of the curriculum as desired.

3. *More timely information.* The variety and quality of scoring and reporting formats in commercially available tests is one of their major strengths, but it is also one of the reasons that locally developed tests can be so valuable. Most commercial test companies require at least six weeks to provide computer-generated scoring and reporting for their tests. Teachers often need information much more quickly. For example, a teacher doesn't want to proceed to the next unit until he is sure that most of the class has mastered the information in the previous unit. Giving a quiz on Friday afternoon can provide the information he needs to plan his instruction on Monday. Furthermore, even in a relatively short quiz, he can include more items per objective than would be available on many specific topics in most standardized achievement tests.

4. *Better identification of learner needs.* Good teachers do not present material students have already mastered, or that is so far above their current level of understanding that it would be confusing. Effective instruction requires knowing whether some students can go through the material at an accelerated pace while others need to go slower. Preinstruction assessment can provide this information, but it must happen weekly or even daily to be useful. Locally developed tests can provide such information when the teacher most needs it.

5. *Greater consistency with local and state curricula.* Commercially available tests are designed to be consistent with the most frequently used curriculum objectives and goals across the country because they need to have wide appeal. But the process of developing a *good* standardized achievement test requires several years, and the curriculum in a particular school can change dramatically in the meantime. At a single meeting, the local school board may decide that the school

needs a much stronger emphasis on science than it had previously. Most commercially available achievement tests cannot respond quickly to shifts in priorities. Furthermore, since the selection of any standardized achievement test is usually a lengthy process, committees of teachers and administrators will not want to repeat the process every year just to accommodate changing priorities. Locally developed tests can be more responsive.

6. *More detailed information.* Most standardized achievement tests provide breadth of coverage, but not depth. Where a locally developed test can have half a dozen items on a single learning objective, a standardized achievement test may have only one. Additional items can provide information about what students have mastered and what they still need to learn.

Adapting Commercially Available Tests for Local Needs

Finding an appropriate test for your needs is not necessarily a decision between purchasing an existing test or developing your own. It is also possible to adapt commercially available tests to make them more appropriate for your local needs. Here, we discuss two different approaches: (1) customizing the scoring of standardized achievement tests and (2) using existing collections of test items (often called "item banks").

Customizing Standardized Achievement Test Scoring

When selecting a standardized achievement test, a committee usually tries to match the test objectives with the local curriculum objectives. No matter how carefully this is done, however, the match is never perfect. For example, assume that the test selected for the sixth grade measures beginning algebra skills. If the district does not teach beginning algebra skills until the seventh grade, students' test scores will be lower when compared to the national norms than they would have been had algebra been taught in sixth grade.

Because of this, some school districts use the information reported by the publisher to develop a customized report that indicates how well students did on only those items that measure objectives taught by the district (see Wilson and Hiscox, 1984, for a more detailed discussion of one way of doing this). The process requires a fair amount of work, but is conceptually quite simple.

1. Review test items to determine which ones measure objectives explicitly taught in your district. Be careful to look at the specific items and not just at the objectives listed by the publisher. Objectives are often stated in such broad terms that a match with the general objective does *not* ensure a match with individual items.
2. Include only the district objectives that are covered by at least three items. This ensures a more reliable estimate of how well students in the district have mastered that objective.
3. Using the publisher's scoring reports, develop a form on which you can indicate for each objective the average percentage of students who correctly answered the items that measure that objective.

4. Use the results for those objectives taught by your school to calculate the percentage correct for each objective and for each subtest. Subtest scores will be based only on those items that measure objectives that are taught within the district.

Customizing scoring procedures will generally be possible only for relatively large school districts. It can be valuable, but you should remember that such a procedure is useful only to determine how well students have mastered the objectives taught in the district. Furthermore, information on the reliability and validity of the original test may no longer be applicable because some of the items will have been dropped. Unless the test has been drastically shortened, the reliability of the test will probably be similar to the original, but the validity of using scores from the customized test for specific purposes is an unknown.

It's also important to emphasize that many people, including us, believe it is useful to know how students do on related material that has *not* been taught. As D. R. Green (1983) pointed out,

> If the students have learned fundamental skills and knowledge and understand it, they will be able to answer many questions dealing with material not directly taught. . . . Since all the specifics can never be taught . . . this development is highly desirable and tests . . . should try to assess it. This can only be done by having items that ask about content not directly taught (p. 6)

Using Previously Developed Item Banks

Over the years, a number of people have developed collections of individual test items referenced to particular instructional objectives. These item banks, which can be purchased or sometimes obtained at no charge, contain hundreds of items that teachers can use to assemble a customized test. Since the items are already written, test construction is rapid and efficient. The best item banks are carefully documented and referenced to specific learning objectives. For descriptions of item banks maintained by universities, private organizations, and state agencies, see Naccarato (1988).

Item banks should be used cautiously, however, for they will never be able to do all the things that are possible with teacher-made tests. For example, most of them have only two or three items per objective. In addition, many test bank items have never been tried out as part of an actual test, and although they look good, they may not be free from technical defects and may not be as good a match for a particular objective as items you would develop yourself. Item banks can save time and help generate new ideas if used thoughtfully. Like many shortcuts, however, they can be counterproductive if used indiscriminately.

Never Borrow Items from Standardized Tests

Although it may be tempting, *never* borrow items from commercially marketed achievement tests. Such items are protected by copyright and their unauthorized use is against the law. Furthermore, since they were designed to be used as a part of a *total* test, they may function very differently when embedded in another test. Standardized tests are not like test banks from which you can pick and choose, and should not be used in this way.

Constructing and Using Local Achievement Tests

It has been observed that "linking testing and instruction is a fundamental and enduring concern in educational practice" (Burstein, 1983, p. 99). Anyone who has spent much time in classrooms knows that testing in some form consumes a major part of every teacher's effort. This effort is justified only if testing actually contributes to effective student learning. As pointed out by Nitko (1989), the failure to appropriately link testing and teaching will often lead to situations where

1. students' motivation for learning is reduced;
2. incorrect information is given about students' learning progress and difficulties;
3. critical decisions about promotion may be made unfairly; and
4. incorrect decisions may be reached about instructional effectiveness.

Research indicates that most classroom testing involves locally developed achievement tests. In a survey of high school teachers, Salmon-Cox (1981) found that 44 percent relied primarily on their own tests in making evaluative decisions about students' achievement, 33 percent depended primarily on classroom interactions with the students, 21 percent relied primarily on homework, and only 2 percent relied primarily on standardized achievement test scores (see Kellaghan, Madaus, & Airasian, 1982; Stiggins & Bridgeford, 1985; and Yeh, 1978, for similar conclusions).

By emphasizing the importance of locally developed achievement tests, we do not mean to deemphasize the importance of standardized achievement tests. As Stiggins, Conklin, and Bridgeford (1986) point out,

Politically, [standardized testing] has given educational measurement a visible role in documenting the effectiveness of schools in our society. The coin of the realm in determining the value of schools is clearly the standardized test score. . . . [However, standardized testing] represents only a small fraction of the assessments that take place in schools and that influence the quality of schooling and student learning. Unfortunately, due to the narrow scope of measurement research, we know little about the nature, role, or quality of the preponderance of school assessment: that developed and used by teachers in the classroom. (p. 6)

In planning, developing, and applying the results of local tests, each of the eight steps shown in Figure 7.1 is important. To organize your thinking for the rest of this chapter, we also have provided brief narrative descriptions of how each step relates to the planning, development, and application process. (We show the specific steps within each of these more general processes here, but delay discussion of the specific steps for test development and application respectively, until Chapters 8 and 9.)

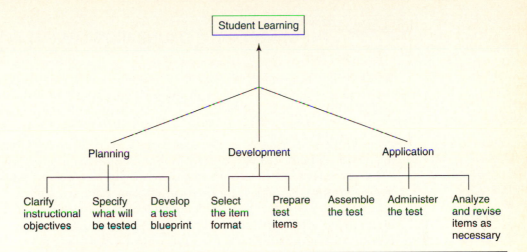

Planning Steps

Step I: Clarify instructional objectives. The most important step in developing a classroom test is to decide what you want students to learn. Include all of the objectives you think important, regardless of how difficult you may think it is to develop a test item for a particular objective. Keep in mind that broad general objectives are of little value in helping you develop test items.

Step 2: Specify what will be tested. Any given objective can be tested at many different levels. You must decide whether you are testing a student's ability to recall facts or apply principles; whether the test is being used to diagnose potential difficulties, demonstrate mastery, or motivate students; and how difficult test items should be.

Step 3: Develop a test blueprint. When a contractor builds a house, he usually follows a blueprint to make sure that he does not forget important components. Developing a test is similar. Having decided which objectives are most important and the specifics of what will be tested, you must develop a plan to guide the construction of the test so that the final product will be successful.

Development Steps

Step 1: Select the item format. Items can be written in many different forms, including true/false, multiple choice, matching, and essay. The format selected depends on your objectives and the time available for testing and scoring.

Step 2: Prepare test items. Writing test items should only happen after the preliminary decisions noted above. In addition to the content mastery, other skills are necessary to write good items.

Application Steps

Step I: Assemble the test. Just as the individual components of a house have to be assembled in specific ways if the house is to be attractive and structurally sound, test items, no matter how well they are written, need to be assembled appropriately if they are to be useful.

Step 2: Administer the test. As pointed out in Chapter 6, the way in which a test is administered can have a dramatic impact on whether it achieves its intended purpose.

Step 3: Analyze and revise items. Once the test has been given, teachers need to examine the results to make instructional decisions, and to decide whether the test needs to be revised to function more effectively.

FIGURE 7.1   Steps in Using Locally Developed Achievement Tests to Contribute to More Effective Student Learning

THE STORY OF THE DRUNKARD'S SEARCH

In his book *The Conduct of Inquiry,* Abraham Kaplan relates an anecdote which he calls the "story of the drunkard's search."* The story is about a drunkard searching under a street light at night for his house key which he had dropped some distance away. When asked why he was searching near the light instead of in the area where he had dropped the key, the drunkard replied, "It's lighter here."

Classroom teachers sometimes unwittingly rely on the kind of fallacious reasoning exhibited by the drunkard in Kaplan's story. In their attempts to assess what their students have and have not learned, teachers often focus attention on potential learning outcomes which are easily tested rather than searching for valid ways to find evidence of the degree to which their students have acquired more important outcomes that are less easily assessed. For example, a teacher who desires to assess students' problem solving skills may focus on finding out how well the students can determine whether a statement is true or false instead of assessing the students' ability to diagnose problem situations, explain the nature of the problem, and then propose a feasible solution and demonstrate that it works.

Similarly, a teacher who desires to assess students' ability to perform some complex set of skills may accept a written or verbal description of what students would do in situations of that kind rather than asking students to actually demonstrate how well they can or cannot perform the desired skill. In either case, the resulting information would be a weak substitute for what the teacher really wanted to know. However, teachers often draw conclusions about what their students have learned based on weak or insufficient evidence and then justify themselves in doing so because of the difficulty of conducting a more defensible search. They search where it's easier to see. And then, ironically, they often fail to recognize that what they found is not what they were looking for.

---

*Abraham Kaplan, *the Conduct of Inquiry,* San Francisco; Chandler Publishing, 1964, p. 11.

All three stages of the testing process—planning, development, and application—are interrelated, and each can be thought of as one leg in a three-legged stool. Together, they provide a sturdy foundation for student learning. If any one of the legs is removed, the stool collapses. For example, a teacher who ignores planning and proceeds immediately to developing test items runs the risk of omitting important instructional content from the test. Similarly, the teacher who spends a great deal of time planning and developing test items, without paying attention to the appropriate procedures for assembling and administering the test, will find that the test is not particularly useful. In the remainder of this chapter, we discuss the steps involved in test planning. Chapter 8 discusses test development, and Chapter 9 addresses the issues associated with assembling, administering, scoring, reporting, and improving your test.

Steps in Planning Achievement Tests

Each step in the planning process is essential if the test is to be successful. In the remainder of this chapter, we consider the specifics of each major step in this process.

Clarifying Instructional Objectives

What is taught in the classroom should affect what is tested. No teacher would think of asking students to define a list of German vocabulary words in an algebra class. But in many less obvious instances, the content of the test is not consistent with the content of the class.

The first step in developing an achievement test should be to systematically examine the course content and decide what is most important for students to learn. Indeed, an important fringe benefit of testing is that it helps to operationally define the instructional objectives for the class. Defining instructional objectives is easier said than done, however. One problem is achieving the appropriate level of specificity, as shown by an excellent example taken from Hopkins and Stanley (1981) and reproduced in Figure 7.2.

As indicated in the figure, it is appropriate to want a student to achieve his personal goals and fulfill his obligations to society. This objective is so broad, however, that it is almost useless in designing test items. An almost infinite number of items could be used to assess the various components of such a broad objective—and it would be very difficult to say when it had been assessed adequately. If instructional objectives are too specific, however (note the objectives at the end of the list in Figure 7.2), the teacher is likely to spend an inordinate amount of time writing instructional objectives—probably to the exclusion of some instruction.

So, how broad is *too* broad? What is the "right" degree of specificity? It is impossible to define the appropriate level of specificity for every situation. However, we suggest that instructional objectives similar to those in the middle of the list in Figure 7.2 are generally the most appropriate. Such objectives provide teachers and students with a clear set of expectations, but still provide opportu-

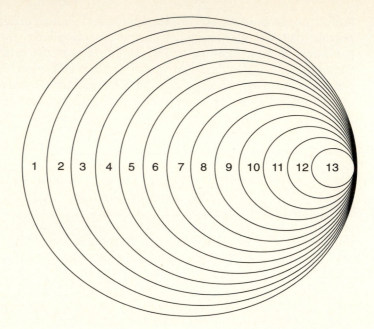

1. The student will be able to achieve personal goals and fulfill his or her obligations to society.

2. The student will be able to demonstrate functional literacy.

3. The student will be able to perform mathematical operations.

4. The student will be able to perform simple addition, subtraction, multiplication, and divisional operations.

5. The student will be able to perform simple addition operations.

6. The student will be able to add any two single-digit numbers.

7. The student will be able to add 3 and 2.

8. The student will be able to add 3 objects and 2 objects.

9. The student will be able to add 3 apples and 2 apples.

10. The student will be able to add 3 apples and 2 apples when words (not objects) are used.

11. The student will be able to add 3 apples and 2 apples when words are present in writing.

12. The student will be able to add 3 apples and 2 apples 90% of the time when the problem is posed in written form.

13. The student will be able to add 3 apples and 2 apples 90% ofthe time when the problem is phrased, "If you had 3 apples and I gave you 2 more, how many would you have?"

FIGURE 7.2   A Graphic Illustration of the Various Levels of Specificity in Objectives

nities for students to demonstrate that they can generalize or apply the skill in a broader context.

Another frequent mistake in preparing instructional objectives is to include only those easily measured by paper-and-pencil tests. This tendency leads to tests that are trivial and irrelevant, as A. Lawrence Lowell pointed out more than 70 years ago:

> The popular impression . . . is that a student whose primary object is a high grade devotes himself . . . to memorizing small, and comparatively unimportant, points in a course, and thereby makes a better showing than a classmate with . . . a larger real command of the subject. . . . As the examination questions are often made out and marked this result may, and does, occur. But if all examinations were so conducted as to be an accurate and complete measure of the education the course is intended to give, . . . then there would be no reason why the student should not work for marks, and good reason why he should. To chide a tennis player for training himself with a view to winning a match, instead of acquiring skill in the game, would be absurd because the two things are the same. . . . If marks are not an adequate measure of what the course is intended to impart, then the examination is defective. If examinations were perfect the results would command universal respect, and high grades would be a more general object of ambition. (As cited in Frederiksen, 1984, p. 193)

Of course, tests influence how students spend their time studying and how teachers spend their time teaching. Students naturally use test content to decide how they should allocate their study time. Consequently, the most easily tested instructional objectives sometimes become those on which both students and teachers focus most of their efforts.

Unfortunately, many of the most important educational objectives are difficult to teach or test. Unless such objectives are explicitly included in the planning, there is a danger that they will be excluded from testing and eventually lost as a part of instruction. This must not happen. Important instructional objectives must not be deemphasized because they are difficult to test. All important instructional objectives should be listed as the first step in developing a valid achievement test.

To clarify instructional objectives, write down what you want students to be able to do as a result of your instruction. Using the middle of the list in Figure 7.2 as a guide, select an appropriate level of specificity. Remember that if you make instructional objectives too specific, you will not have time to develop both objectives and items. If you make them too broad, you will find that they are neither very useful nor readily measurable. In either case, you will quit using them. The best criterion for whether instructional objectives are at an appropriate level of specificity is whether you find them valuable in teaching and in developing tests.

Instructional objectives should also be reconsidered periodically, for two reasons. First, instructional goals may change because of changes in administrative policy, societal shifts, or information from students' performance or parent conferences. Second, it is easier to test for how well students have achieved some instructional objectives than others. Unless you are careful, there will be a natural tendency to gradually increase the emphasis on objectives that are easy to test and exclude those that are difficult.

The value of systematically and frequently evaluating instructional objectives is supported by research. For example, Boersma (1967) found that teachers who regularly evaluated the learning objectives for their class were judged by independent experts to be better teachers.

Specifying What You Want to Test

Once you have established your instructional objectives, you must determine what type of behavior you want students to exhibit, the purpose of the test, and the difficulty of test items. We will discuss each in the following sections.

Using a Taxonomy of Educational Objectives to Select the Behaviors to Be Exhibited on a Test

Suppose you want students to learn about the election of John F. Kennedy to the presidency of the United States. What best describes what they should be able to do when the instruction is completed?

- Recognize Kennedy's name from a list of names as being a president of the United States.
- Recall Kennedy's name as being a president of the United States.
- Describe the variables and conditions that resulted in the election of Kennedy.
- Compare and contrast the attributes of Kennedy with some of his rivals, and explain why Kennedy was selected.
- Judge whether the variables and attributes that led to Kennedy's election will likely be significant factors in the next presidential election.

Each of the preceding behaviors is relevant to the election of John F. Kennedy as president, but each would require very different types of instruction and different assessment procedures. The first two require only recognition or recall of facts, whereas the last one requires the student to apply knowledge about Kennedy's circumstances and make a judgment about the probable outcome.

One of the most frequent criticisms of educational tests is that they focus too much on rote memorization and recall of facts even though everyone agrees that education should teach higher-order thinking skills such as comprehension, analysis, and evaluation. This criticism applies to professionally developed standardized tests as well as teacher-made tests.

For example, Bowman and Peng (1972) asked five experts to rate the items on the Graduate Record Examination (GRE) on whether it was primarily a measure of memory, comprehension, analytic thinking, or evaluation. The consensus was that 70 percent of the items required only memory, 15 percent measured comprehension, 12 percent required analytic thinking, and only 3 percent involved evaluation.

The predominance of memory or knowledge type items on tests is particularly unfortunate in view of research suggesting that when students have mastered items that measure higher-order skills such as analysis and evaluation, they are more likely to retain the information than if they have mastered only items that measure knowledge (Nungester & Duchastel, 1982; Gay, 1980; and Frederiksen, 1984).

Classification systems, referred to as taxonomies, have been developed for categorizing the intellectual skills or cognitive processes needed to answer test questions or other assessment tasks. The oldest, best known, and most widely used taxonomy was developed by Bloom and his colleagues and consists of the six levels shown in Table 7.1 (Bloom, Engelhart, Furst, Hill, & Krathwohl, 1956). This taxonomy has been used for more than 40 years in the United States and has been translated into at least 22 foreign languages (Lewy & Bathory, 1994; Krathwohl, 1994). Other useful taxonomies have also been suggested (see Gagne, 1985; Quellmalz, 1985; Marzano, Pickering, & McTighe, 1993) but are less widely known. For a helpful comparison of several different taxonomies, see DeLandsheere (1991).

The levels of Bloom's taxonomy are presumed to be hierarchical, with knowledge representing the lowest level of learning, and evaluation the highest. Although Bloom and his colleagues proposed six categories of cognitive functioning, it is sometimes difficult in practice to differentiate among them. For example, consider the following item adapted from Carlson (1985, p. 83):

Table 7.1   A Summary of Bloom's Taxonomy of Educational Objectives for Cognitive Domain

1.	Knowledge	Requires recall or recognition of facts, procedures, rules, or events	Most Common
2.	Comprehension	Requires reformulation, restatement, translation, or interpretation of what has been taught, or identification of relationships	
3.	Application	Requires use of information in a setting or context other than where it was learned	
4.	Analysis	Requires recognition of logical errors, comparison of components, or differentiation between components	
5.	Synthesis	Requires production of something original, solution to an unfamiliar problem, or combination of parts in an unusual way	
6.	Evaluation	Requires formation of judgments about the worth or value of ideas, products, or procedures that have a specific purpose	Least Common

Two preschool children are playing together. Child A refuses to share his toys with child B even when he is told that child B has no toys of his own. Which of the following explains the behavior of child A?

_____ Child A has not had sufficient opportunities to interact with other children.

_____ Child A has previously lent toys to the children, and they have not been returned.

_____ Child A is emotionally immature and stubborn.

_____ Child A is intellectually unable to take the role of another person.

Because the taxonomy is presumed to be hierarchical, the item obviously requires a certain level of knowledge about child development and comprehension of that knowledge. However, experts would likely disagree about the level of Bloom's taxonomy that best describes the item. A case could be made for the item being primarily one of application (using information in a context other than where it was learned), analysis (differentiation among components), or evaluation (forming judgments about value of specific procedures).

Although the taxonomy is helpful in developing items that measure different levels of learning, the difficulty in differentiating between and among some of the levels has resulted in many people recommending the use of fewer levels—perhaps dividing the taxonomy into a dichotomy, with knowledge being the lowest level and everything else (comprehension, application, analysis, synthesis, and evaluation) representing higher-order cognitive skills. Others suggest that three levels be used: (1) knowledge; (2) comprehension and application; and (3) analysis, synthesis, and evaluation. We prefer to use three levels of the taxonomy, and give the following examples of test items written at each of the three levels:

Example of an Item Measuring Factual Knowledge

The president of the United States during most of World War II was

a.   Franklin Roosevelt
b.   Harry Truman
c.   Dwight Eisenhower
d.   Woodrow Wilson
e.   Warren Harding

The answer to this item (Franklin Roosevelt) requires only recall of facts. The student does not have to interpret, translate, apply, analyze, or evaluate any information. There is nothing wrong with having some items on a test that require only knowledge. Although it is not the total aim of education, the acquisition of factual knowledge is a legitimate and necessary goal. In fact, without an adequate knowledge base, it is impossible to acquire higher-level cognitive skills. Most tests should include some knowledge-based items; otherwise, it is hard to know whether a student is having trouble with higher-level items because of an inadequate knowledge base or because of other difficulties.

Example of an Item Measuring Comprehension and Application

Here, you are given a complete sentence that you must rephrase in a way that retains the original meaning. After you have rephrased the sentence according to the directions, select the choice that contains the phrase included in your revised sentence. Your rephrased sentence must be grammatically correct and natural in phrasing and construction.[1]

Sentence: John, shy as he was of girls, still managed to marry one of the most desirable of them.
Directions: At the beginning of the sentence, substitute *John's shyness* for *John, shy*. Your rewritten sentence will contain which of the following phrases:

a. . . . him being married to . . .
b. . . . him from marrying . . .
c. . . . was himself married to . . .
d. . . . him to have married . . .

Each of the phrases in the preceding example could be used to develop a sentence, but only one of them provides a sentence that uses the phrase "John's shyness" and is still grammatically correct, natural in phrasing and construction, and retains the meaning of the original sentence. Listed next are sentences that could have been constructed using each option.

a. John's shyness with girls did not stop *him being married to* the most desirable of them.
b. John's shyness with girls did not prevent him from marrying one of the most desirable of them.
c. John's shyness with girls did not keep him single; he *was himself married* to one of the most desirable of them.
d. John's shyness with girls was not a reason for him to have married the most desirable of them.

The correct answer is option b. The other answers are either grammatically incorrect (option a) or change the meaning of the original sentence (options c and d). To get the correct answer, the student must use grammatical rules learned elsewhere and reformulate the original sentence.

---

[1]This item and the one following it are adapted from *Multiple Choice Questions: A Close Look. Educational Testing Service, 1963.*

Example of an Item Assessing Analysis and Evaluation

The shading on the following map is used to indicate

a.   population density
b.   percentage of labor force in agriculture
c.   per capita income
d.   death rate per 1000

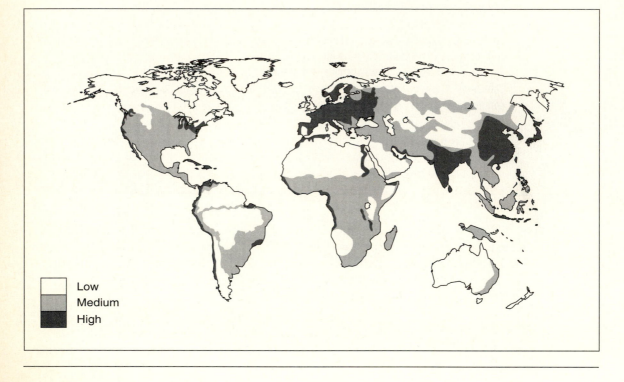

Low
Medium
High

Population density (option a) is a good choice because the darkest shading is in India, eastern China, much of Europe, the Nile Valley, and Northeastern part of the United States. Percentage of total labor force in agriculture (option b) would be an attractive alternative except for the dark shading in the northeastern United States and much of Europe. Per capita income (option c) would be an attractive choice if one looked only at the United States and Europe, but certainly would not apply to India and the Nile River area. Option (d) is not plausible because death rate per 1000 of population would probably be high in India and in China but low in the United States and Europe. Recognizing that population density is the only logical option requires analysis and synthesis of information, and then evaluation of which option fits the available information.

It is not easy to write objective test items that test higher-order thinking skills. As Green (1981) points out: "Critics of multiple choice items claim that only surface facts can be tested in this way, not deep understanding. Professional testers disagree; items probing understanding are possible, but they are certainly difficult to devise" (p. 1003). Difficulty notwithstanding, it is possible and important to include assessment tasks that require students to demonstrate their ability to reason with their knowledge and to use it productively to solve problems, exercise judgment, make rational decisions, and communicate effectively. Bloom's taxonomy and each of the others are smorgasbords from which you make pick and choose. The various taxonomies are heuristic devices (Krathwohl, 1994) designed to stimulate educators' thinking and to foster communication about the different types of intellectual skills or thinking processes that they may wish to teach and assess. None of these classification schemes is perfect, but each can be helpful if thoughtfully used. It is not necessary that you classify each of your intended learning outcomes at the "most correct" level. What is important is that you identify the various kinds of thinking skills that students should acquire in your course and that you include them in both your instruction and your assessment procedures. A taxonomy such as Bloom's or one of the others can help you remember the different types of thinking skills students should master. This reminder is useful both (1) for preparing instructional activities and materials, and (2) for assessing what has been taught. It will help ensure that you have not overlooked some important cognitive objective and will increase the likelihood that you achieve an appropriate balance between rote recall and higher-order thinking processes.

Application Problem 1

Consider the following item:
   Who was president during the most substantial escalation of U.S. military forces in the Vietnam war?

   a. Dwight Eisenhower
   b. John F. Kennedy
   c. Lyndon B. Johnson
   d. Richard Nixon

At what level is this item in Bloom's taxonomy?
Write an item that tests a higher-level cognitive skill concerning the president's involvement in the escalation of U.S. military forces in Vietnam.

Bloom's taxonomy was deliberately intended to be generic rather than subject matter specific. In other words, it was designed to describe categories of cognitive abilities that apply across many different disciplines rather than abilities that are specific to a particular subject or discipline. This is also true of the more recent taxonomies. But when you are designing a test or other assessment procedure, you will likely find it helpful to consider specific skills and abilities that are subject dependent. Consequently, you will probably find it helpful to refer to the curriculum guide or framework provided by your school district or state office of education.

With the help of federal funding, most U.S. states have recently revised or rewritten the curriculum frameworks for the various subjects taught in the public schools.

The standards booklets published in recent years by national professional organizations or consortiums are also helpful sources of ideas describing valued skills, capabilities, and dispositions in specific subjects. The standards articulated in these books provide helpful descriptions of various kinds of higher-order thinking in each of the respective disciplines as defined by professionals in that field. The standards were written for teachers to use in helping students learn important concepts, reasoning skills, and decision-making strategies. The resulting descriptions provide a helpful source of ideas to teachers who are attempting to make decisions about which skills or abilities they should focus on in planning instruction and assessments.

A list of many of the standards booklets is provided here. Your school or district office may already have copies of many of these books. If not, they can be ordered directly from the publisher at a nominal cost.

Curriculum and Evaluation Standards for School Mathematics (1989).

> Developed and published by the National Council for Teachers of Mathematics, Reston, VA.

Geography for Life: National Geography Standards (1994).

> Developed by representatives of the American Geographical Society, the Association of American Geographers, and the National Council for Geographic Education.

> Published by the National Geographic Society, Washington, DC.

Expectations of Excellence: Curriculum Standards for Social Studies (1994).

> Developed and published by the National Council for the Social Studies, Washington, DC.

What Every Young American Should Know and Be Able to Do in the Arts: National Standards for Arts Education (1994).

> Developed by the consortium of National Arts Education Associations, including the American Alliance for Theatre and Education, the Music Educators National Conference, the National Art Education Association, and the National Dance Association. Published by the Music Educators National Conference, Reston, VA.

Moving into the Future: The National Standards for Physical Education (1995).

> Developed and published by the National Association for Sport and Physical Education, Reston, VA.

National Health Education Standards: Achieving Health Literacy (1995).

> Developed by the Joint Committee on National Health Education Education Standards.

National Standards for Business Education: What America's Students Should Know and Be Able to Do (1995).

> Developed and published by the National Business Education Association, Reston, VA.

National Standards for Civics and Government (1995).

> Developed and published by the Center for Civic Education, Calabasas, CA.

There is no formula for deciding how difficult items should be. Your experience as a teacher, and your judgment about what you think students should be able to do as a result of instruction, are the best guides in deciding about item difficulty.

Sometimes you will write an item that, when used, is easier or more difficult than you anticipated. If the item is too difficult, you must consider how the instruction related to that item was delivered. Was it sufficient? Was it clear? Depending on your answer, you may need to revise the item or your future instruction.

Developing a Test Blueprint

When students complain that a test is unfair, what are they really saying? Often, they are complaining that the test's emphasis was inappropriate (for example, "We spent three weeks discussing market analysis techniques, and the test did not have a single question about that!"); or the level of cognitive skill required to answer questions was inappropriate (for example, "I thought there was more to this class than memorizing facts!"). The use of a test blueprint can help avoid such problems.

What Is a Test Blueprint?

Think for a moment about an engineer building a bridge or a contractor building a house. Without a comprehensive and detailed set of plans, it would be almost impossible to know how much concrete will be needed, whether structural reinforcing will be needed at a particular point, and whether the client will be able to afford the project. Throughout the building process, blueprints are used to make sure that everything is done in the proper order, at the right level of detail, and with the correct components. No competent contractor would ever dream of building a house without a blueprint.

As illustrated by the following scenario, constructing an achievement test is also complex.

Samuel had studied hard all semester and thought he had learned the material in his American History course. He was sick and missed the last class period before the final exam, but was not too concerned because the teacher had announced that they would only be discussing the events of the last 10 years during the last class period and only a few pages of the textbook were devoted to recent events. The night before the test, Samuel reviewed the major periods and events in American History (the Colonial Period, the westward expansion, the Civil War, the prohibition era, the Korean and Vietnam wars, and so on). Although there was a dizzying amount of information, he felt confident as he arrived at class to take the test. Imagine his feelings (frustration, anger, despair?) when he saw the following test.

American History—Final Examination

Instructions: Because you've been such a good class, I want to reward you with an easy final exam. All the questions come from our discussion last Friday, and I think you'll find them relatively easy. Good luck.

1. Who was Reagan's first secretary of state?
2. On what date was Reagan's first summit with Gorbachev?
3. During Reagan's administration, the national debt rose from $_____ to $_____ .
4. In what incident were the most American military personnel lost during Reagan's term?
5. Discuss the most important disagreements Reagan had with Congress during his two terms.

Although the preceding example is exaggerated to make a point, it is, unfortunately, grounded in the real-life experiences of many students. Such tests lack content validity because they are not a fair representation of what was taught. But there is no reason this has to happen. In the same way that a blueprint helps a contractor, a test blueprint helps teachers to be sure that (1) the content covered on the test is consistent with the content covered during instruction, and (2) the level of cognitive skill that students need to answer questions on the test is consistent with what is intended.

Table 7.2 shows a sample test blueprint that could be used for the material in Chapters 7 and 8. The left-hand column lists major content areas, whereas the top of the table is divided into three levels of cognitive skill based on Bloom's taxonomy. Not all parts of the chapter receive equal emphasis on the test, and the emphasis is not necessarily proportional to the number of pages devoted to that topic in the chapter. Instead, the number of items reflects our judgment about what is most important.

From the information in Table 7.2, you can tell that the instruction about how to write items is the most important (that category contains 65 percent of all questions and 70 percent of the questions that tap higher cognitive skills). Also, al-

Table 7.2   An Example of a Test Blueprint for a Textbook Chapter Entitled "Constructing Your Own Achievement Tests—Why, When, and How"

Content Area	Knowledge	Comprehension and Application	Synthesis & Evaluation	Total
Why construct your own achievement test?	2	2	1	5
Adapting commercially available tests for local needs	1	1		2
Clarifying objectives and developing a test blueprint	2	2	1	5
Specifying content to be tested and selecting item format	1		1	2
How to write items:				
Multiple-choice	2	4	4	10
Essay	3	4	3	10
Other	2	2	2	6
Total	13	15	12	40

though knowledge of content is obviously important (for example, every category has at least one knowledge-level item), higher-order cognitive skills are *more* important; 68 percent of the items measure higher-order skills. Finally, notice that the categories in the left-hand column resemble, but are not identical to, the topical listings for this chapter. Some topics have been combined. The test blueprint should be a flexible tool the teacher can use and adapt as necessary in making sure that the most important points are emphasized in both teaching and testing (see the differing responses of the two teachers in Table 7.3).

Table 7.3   Relative Emphasis of Two Different Teachers for the Content Taught in This Chapter

| Content Area | | *Emphasis of Teacher 1* | | |
	Knowledge	Comprehension and Application	Synthesis & Evaluation	Total
Why construct your own achievement test?	10	5	0	15
Adapting commercially available tests for local needs	5	0	0	5
Clarifying objectives and developing a test blueprint	10	5	0	15
Specifying content to be tested and selecting item format	5	0	0	5
How to write items:				
Multiple-choice	20	5	0	25
Essay	20	5	0	25
Other	5	5	0	10
Total	75	25	0	100

| Content Area | | *Emphasis of Teacher 2* | | |
	Knowledge	Comprehension and Application	Synthesis & Evaluation	Total
Why construct your own achievement test?	5	3	2	10
Adapting commercially available tests for local needs	10	5	5	20
Clarifying objectives and developing a test blueprint	2	2	0	4
Specifying content to be tested and selecting item format	2	0	3	5
How to write items:				
Multiple-choice2	2	10	10	22
Essay	2	10	10	22
Other	2	10	5	17
Total	25	40	35	100

How Is a Test Blueprint Developed?

Ideally, the development of a test blueprint begins long before the test is administered. Early development is important because the blueprint guides teaching as well as testing. The first step in developing a blueprint is to write down all the course objectives. When objectives are developed by the state or district, they may need to be modified for your particular situation, teaching style, or desired emphasis. The next step is to develop a preliminary blueprint listing course content areas down the left-hand column and the levels of Bloom's taxonomy across the top.[2]

Next, think about the proposed learning activities for the course as you decide how many items you need for each cell of the matrix. How much time will students spend in discussion groups, doing homework, doing library research and writing papers, listening to lectures, reading, going on field trips, and the like? Will these learning activities provide students with opportunities to master all the content at the cognitive level of mastery you think important? Are there activities that will contribute to learning outcomes that are not listed on your preliminary blueprint?

You may decide that in certain areas you want students only to remember facts, whereas in others, it is critical that they develop skills in analysis, synthesis, and evaluation. Some extremely important concepts may require very little time to teach, whereas other less important concepts require a great deal of time. A useful technique to ensure that each activity receives the appropriate emphasis is to assign a total of 100 points to the various cells in your matrix. Using the blueprint presented in Table 7.2, Table 7.3 shows the relative allocations for two different teachers. As you can see, Teacher 1 emphasizes acquisition of knowledge and believes that information about "Adapting commercially available tests for local needs" is much less important than does Teacher 2.

The blueprint does not indicate which teacher is correct—that depends on a myriad of factors such as local priorities, the characteristics of students, and where the course fits in the total curriculum. But the blueprint, once established, gives clear direction to what concepts should be taught and tested. The numbers in each cell of the matrix indicate the percentage of test items to be used. For example, a 50-item test written by Teacher 2 should have one item that assesses knowledge of how to write multiple-choice questions and five analysis/synthesis/evaluation items about how to write essay questions.

Particularly for older students, it is best to develop the test blueprint at the beginning of your course, and distribute it to the students so that they will understand the relative emphasis on various content and cognitive skills. This knowledge gives students a better idea about how to allocate their study time. Students who are familiar with the blueprint can also provide valuable feedback about

---

[2]We usually divide Bloom's taxonomy into three levels, as we did in Table 7.2. You may want to use six levels or use some other taxonomy. The important thing is that you use the blueprint to help you decide whether you are covering all the desired areas in teaching and testing.

whether your instruction is consistent with your testing plan. Of course, you can change your test blueprint during the course if your priorities shift, as long as you keep students informed.

SUGGESTED READINGS

Anderson, L. W. & Sosniak, L. A. (1994). *Bloom's taxonomy: A forty-year retrospective.* Ninety-third yearbook of the National Society for the Study of Education, Part II. Chicago: University of Chicago Press.

Includes 12 articles—including one written by Benjamin Bloom himself—that retrospectively evaluate Bloom's taxonomy 40 years after its development and assess its impact on curriculum, teaching, testing, and teacher education.

De Landsheere, V. (1991). Taxonomies of educational objectives. In A. Levy (ed.). *The International Encyclopedia of Curriculum* (pp. 317–327). Oxford, England: Pergamon Press.

Compares and contrasts five taxonomies in the cognitive domain and six in the psychomotor domain and describes their shortcomings and limitations. Also describes and evaluates Krathwohl's taxonomy for the affective domain. Thoughtful readers will develop an appreciation of the problems associated with developing functional classification schemes as a result of reading this article.

Gronlund, N. E. (1991). *How to write and use instructional objectives* (4th ed.). New York: Macmillan.

Describes and illustrates a practical approach to writing instructional objectives at both general and specific levels. The general level is useful for communication purposes. The specific level operationally defines the general objective in terms of behaviors that provide observable evidence of what students have and have not learned.

Nitko, A. J. (1996). *Educational assessment of students* (2nd ed.). Englewood Cliffs, NJ: Merrill.

Emphasizes that valid assessment requires careful planning. Chapters 2 and 6 provide helpful ideas for planning assessments. Chapter 2 compares Bloom's taxonomy with four other schemes for classifying targeted learning outcomes. Chapter 6 emphasizes issues that need to be considered when planning assessments and illustrates alternative ways of developing assessment plans.

Salvia, J. & Hughes, C. (1990). *Curriculum-based assessment: Testing what is taught.* New York: Macmillan.

This is an introductory book for teachers who have little, if any, experience in curriculum-based assessment. The book provides practical guidelines for assessing students' learning in classroom contexts. The first four chapters focus on issues related to planning tests and other assessment procedures.

Popham, W. J. (1990). *Modern educational measurement* (2nd ed.). Englewood Cliffs, NJ: Prentice-Hall.

The chapter on planning in most how-to-do-it books on test construction do not distinguish between the type of planning needed when developing norm-referenced measures and the planning necessary when constructing criterion-referenced measures. Popham's Chapter 9, "Specifying what a test should measure," presents practical suggestions for teachers on how to plan both kinds of measures.

Stiggins, R. J. (1994). *Student-centered classroom assessment.* Upper Saddle River, NJ: Merrill.

In Chapter 4, Stiggins emphasizes the need for teachers to clearly describe their targeted learning outcomes prior to attempting to select or construct appropriate assessment procedures. He emphasizes the need to assess a broad range of objectives, including reasoning, skilled performances, and affective categories of learning.

SUGGESTION SHEET

If your last name starts with the letter J, please complete the Suggestion Sheet at the end of the book while this chapter is still fresh in your mind.

Answer to Chapter 7 Application Problem

1. As currently written, the item is measuring the knowledge level of Bloom's taxonomy. One example, among many possibilities, of a higher-level item related to the same issues is the following:

   The most difficult aspect for President Lyndon Johnson in ordering a substantial increase in the U.S. military forces in Vietnam was the fact that
   a. He was philosophically opposed to all war.
   b. He was afraid that the backlash in voter sentiment would cost the Democrats the majority edge in Congress.
   c. He knew that escalation would require massive amounts of money that he wanted to spend on domestic programs instead.
   d. Vietnam had been an important ally in the U.S. war effort against the Japanese during World War II.

   To answer this item, the student must relate the substantial increase in the U.S. military forces to historical circumstances, and must also be able to evaluate the validity of various factors and relate those to Johnson's order to increase the number of personnel and resources committed to the Vietnam war. Although both options b and c are true, c is the best answer.

Steps in Developing Good Items for Your Achievement Tests

OVERVIEW

Classroom teachers (including college professors) spend months, if not years, of their careers developing, administering, scoring, and interpreting the results of classroom tests. Essay tests, mathematical problem-solving quizzes, and various types of teacher-made multiple-choice true–false tests are a very familiar part of schooling for teachers and students alike. Classroom testing—using locally developed tests—occupies a substantial portion of the total time teachers and students spend together, far more than the amount of time students spend taking standardized tests of all varieties. It seems safe to say that classroom tests, collectively, have far more impact on students' educational development than do all the standardized tests that they may be required to take.

If classroom tests are that important, then a crucial question is "Are they of adequate quality to fulfill the purposes for which they are used?" Unfortunately, the answer is too often no. Little has changed since Ebel reported that "The view that classroom tests . . . could be, and ought to be, much better than they often are is shared by most school teachers and college professors" (1965, p. 2).

If teachers believe classroom tests should be better than they are, then why don't they get about the business of improving them rather than lamenting their inadequacies? Don't teachers care about the quality of the assessment tools they use? Don't they care that poor student assessment can impede their students' learning? Of course they do—the occasional misanthrope aside—but caring isn't enough. As Stiggens (1991a) has pointed out, through no fault of their own, most teachers are not well prepared to plan and develop good student assessment instruments. Few universities devote enough of their teacher preparation curriculum to student assessment. The predictable result is teacher discomfort with the entire business of classroom testing.

Writing good test items and designing other useful student assessments is both an art and a science. Good classroom tests depend in part on the teacher's creativity in presenting items in ways that elicit relevant, meaningful student responses. Yet much of the task of developing good classroom tests depends more on the "science" of good item writing: mastery of the fundamentals of item writing, including principles and rules that can be readily communicated and learned. Helping you to understand such fundamentals is the purpose of this chapter. In it, we remind you of several major types of test item formats and explain their advantages and disadvantages. We provide you with guidelines and examples to help you write good test items in each format. And we provide you with ample practice to give you confidence that you can develop good classroom measures that will serve you and your students well.

OBJECTIVES

Upon completing your study of this chapter, you should be able to

1. Explain the advantages and disadvantages of the major types of item formats typically used in locally developed tests.
2. Select the most appropriate item format for testing any particular instructional objective.
3. Write high-quality test items of each of the following types: true-false, multiple choice, matching, completion, and essay.
4. Construct context-dependent item sets to assess higher-order thinking skills.
5. Use the guidelines presented in this chapter to review and identify flaws in items written by others.
6. Score responses to essay questions in a way that is objective, valid, and replicable.

Steps in Developing an Achievement Test

In Chapter 8, we discussed the three steps necessary to lay a good foundation for writing test items: (1) clarifying instructional objectives, (2) specifying what will be tested, and (3) developing a test blueprint. In this chapter, we will describe the next two major steps:

1. how to select an appropriate item format
2. how to write good test items.

Selecting an Item Format

Although there are dozens of item formats, most are some variation of the following six basic types:

■ *True-false.* A statement is presented, and the respondent decides whether it is correct (true) or incorrect (false).

- *Multiple choice.* A phrase, question, or example is presented followed by two or more options. The respondent is asked to select the option that provides the best answer or completes the phrase most accurately.

- *Matching.* Two lists are provided (names and dates, people and places, and so on). The respondent is asked to select from the first list an item that best matches each item in the other list.

- *Completion or short answer.* A statement with one or more blanks or a question is presented. The respondent is asked to supply brief information or complete the statement by providing missing information.

- *Essay.* The respondent is asked to write a paragraph or more responding to an idea or answering a question.

- *Context-dependent item sets.* Examinees are presented with data or information of some sort accompanied by a series of test items having answers that are dependent upon the information presented. Respondents are expected to use and apply their knowledge to answer the problems presented. The problems may be presented in any of the item formats mentioned previously in this list (multiple choice, essay, and so on) depending on the nature of the reasoning tasks being assessed. Hence, context-dependent items are not a distinctive item format, but simply a means of using the other types of items in the context of a problem situation that requires students to use or apply their knowledge.

Fleming and Chambers (1983) point out that teachers use short-answer questions most often in locally developed tests, use more matching items than multiple-choice or true–false items, and generally avoid the use of essay questions. Unfortunately, they also note that most items (almost 80 percent) focus primarily on acquisition of knowledge instead of comprehension and application, or analysis, synthesis, and evaluation.

The advantages and disadvantages of each type of item format are summarized in Table 8.1, based largely on information presented by Dwyer (1982).

Some people like to categorize items as "objective" (true–false, multiple choice, and matching) or "subjective" (short answer or essay items). Sometimes items are also categorized as recognition items (true–false, multiple-choice, and matching) or recall items (short answer or essay). Such distinctions have important limitations. For example, essay questions can be scored very objectively and multiple choice questions can require much more than recognition of the correct fact or name. The format selected for any particular test depends on the time available for testing and scoring, your personal preferences, and the type of information being tested.

It is important to emphasize that every type of item can be written in a way that tests higher level cognitive skills as well as recall of knowledge. But for this to happen, the person developing the test must spend time learning and practicing the skills of item writing. As Hopkins and Stanley point out (1981, p. 166), "Test construction is in one sense more of an art than a science, but this 'art form' can be dramatically improved with special instruction and systematic practice and feedback."

Table 8.1   Advantages and Disadvantages of Commonly Used Types of
Achievement Test Items

Type of Item	Advantages	Disadvantages
True-false	Many items can be administered in a relatively short time. Moderately easy to write and easily scored.	Limited primarily to testing knowledge of information. Easy to guess correctly on many items, even if material has not been mastered.
Multiple Choice	Can be used to assess broad range of content in a brief period. Skillfully written items can measure higher-order cognitive skills. Can be scored quickly.	Difficult and time consuming to write good items. Possible to assess higher-order cognitive skills, but most items assess only knowledge. Some correct answers can be guesses.
Matching	Items can be written quickly. A broad range of content can be assessed. Scoring can be done efficiently.	Higher-order cognitive skills are difficult to assess.
Short Answer Or Completion	Many can be administered in a brief amount of time. Relatively efficient to score. Moderately easy to write items.	Difficult to identify defensible criteria for correct answers. Limited to questions that can be answered or completed in very few words.
Essay	Can be used to measure higher-order cognitive skills. Easy to write questions. Difficult for respondent to get correct answer by guessing.	Time consuming to administer and score. Difficult to identify reliable criteria for scoring. Only a limited range of content can be sampled during any one testing period.

Preparing Test Items

Many entire books have been devoted to writing test items (Haladyna, 1994 & 1997; Osterlind, 1989). We make no pretense of being able to provide such detail on one topic here, given the comprehensive scope of this book. But we can—and do—provide in the remainder of this chapter a variety of aids intended to help you write high quality items of whichever format you may have selected. Of course guidelines alone are not enough. There is no substitute for practice and experience if you are to become really proficient.

Although the guidelines appear simple and straightforward, it is surprising how frequently such guidelines are ignored. As you write items, use the following suggestions as a checklist to examine each item. As you become more proficient, you will find that the guidelines tend to become second nature.

In the sections that follow, we will provide guidelines for each of the item formats we have presented. But first, we'll give some general suggestions that apply to any type of item.

General Guidelines That Apply to Several Item Formats

You will find the following nine general guidelines applicable for most items you will write:

1. *Test for important ideas, information, and skills—not trivial detail.* Sometimes it is easier to write questions about specific details (for example, What was the name of the ship on which Charles Darwin was sailing when he wrote *The Origin of Species?*). But is that really the information you want to test? Knowledge about some specific facts is important if students are to master higher-level cognitive skills. But in developing any kind of test item, teachers must continually ask themselves what knowledge, abilities, and skills are of the most worth. However, just because something requires the skills of evaluation, synthesis, and application does not mean that it is worth including on a test.

2. *Write items as simply as possible, making sure that students know exactly what information is being requested.* Irrelevant details, grammatically incorrect or logically sloppy construction, unnecessarily sophisticated vocabulary, and bias can all contribute to confusion. Often the item writers have such a clear idea of what they want to test that they does not realize how confusing an item may be for respondents. Consider the following two items, designed to determine whether the student knows when the U.S. Constitution was written:

Poor:

The United States Constitution was written in _____.

Better:

The United States Constitution was written in the year _____.

The poor example has dozens of "correct" answers (e.g. longhand, English, order to guarantee basic freedoms), most of which have nothing to do with knowing when the Constitution was written.

3. *Make items appropriate for the age and ability level of respondents.* An advantage of locally developed achievement tests is that they can be tailored to fit the skill levels of the students. Questions must be written so that the format is not a source of irrelevant distraction, vocabulary is familiar, and the task is consistent with students' ability and preparation. For example, first-grade students should not be asked to write essays regarding the four basic food groups even though they may be expected to have mastered such information. Because the writing skills of most first graders are not yet well developed, many would probably appear not to know information that they had really mastered. We are not suggesting that tests for young children should focus only on rote memorization. They should not. But you should make sure that test format and vocabulary allow students to show what they really know.

4. *Make sure that objectively scored items have only one correct or best answer.* Consider the following items:

T   F   Larger cities have higher crime rates than smaller cities.

Match the item in list A that goes best with the item in list B.

List A	**List B**
1. Dwight Eisenhower	A. President of the United States
2. Ulysses S. Grant	B. World War II General
3. Douglas McArthur	C. Civil War General

A leading cause of heart attacks is

a. Cholesterol
b. Lack of exercise
c. High blood pressure
d. Being overweight

The correct answer to each of these examples is not easily determined. It may be true that larger cities generally have higher crime rates than smaller cities, but it is relatively easy to find exceptions. The writer of the second question probably expected answers that Dwight Eisenhower was president of the United States, Douglas McArthur was a World War II general, and Ulysses S. Grant was a Civil War general. The way the item is now written, however, it would be correct to say that Dwight Eisenhower was a World War II general and that Ulysses S. Grant was a president of the United States. In the multiple choice item concerning a leading cause of heart attacks, any one of the answers could be considered correct. Even if the item had stated, *"The* leading cause of heart attacks . . . ,"* different experts might have different opinions about which answer is best.

5. *Avoid using interrelated items.* Sometimes knowing the answer to one item is necessary to answer subsequent items. This gives undue weight to the first item in a sequence. If the first item is missed, all will be missed regardless of whether the student knows the material. There are times, of course, when you will want to use the same stimulus material (for example, a paragraph of information, a graph, a picture) for a number of different questions. There is nothing wrong with this practice as long as getting the correct answer to one question is not dependent on getting the correct answer to a previous question.

6. *Avoid irrelevant clues and "give-away questions."* Test writers sometimes include unintentional clues in the items they write (for example, common elements in the stem and correct option, a tendency to use certain response positions more or less frequently, subject–verb agreement between the stem and the correct option). Although no one does this on purpose, it is surprising how frequently it happens.

7. *Avoid using direct quotations from the text.* Writing good test items is time consuming and difficult. To save time, some people use direct quotations from the text in true–false, completion, and multiple-choice items. This practice is usually inappropriate. Taken out of context, such quotations are often ambiguous or confusing. Furthermore, this practice may encourage students to focus on memorization and recognition rather than on understanding of the subject matter.

8. *Have someone else review all of your items.* It is extremely valuable to have a colleague review the items you have written. Find someone whose judgment you trust and offer to exchange item-reviewing responsibilities with them. Often, those who develop items make obvious mistakes that a less involved person will notice quickly.

9. *Avoid trick questions.* One of the surest ways to make students cynical about tests is to use trick questions that confuse trivial detail and major issues. Consider the following example.

T   F   John L. Kennedy was the youngest person to serve as president of the United States.

The item is technically false because President Kennedy's middle initial was F, not L. It is true, however, that John F. Kennedy was the youngest person to serve as president of the United States. Even if the student recognizes the incorrect middle initial, he does not know whether the initial was incorrectly typed, or whether the test developer was really concerned about the student's knowing President Kennedy's middle initial. The student should not be required to figure out the test developer's motives (or typing skills) in answering questions.

Although all the items in the preceding list are important, the point about trick questions deserves further discussion. Students often complain about trick questions, but the nature of what makes an alleged question "tricky" is not clearly defined. Roberts (1993) reports the results of a study in which he surveyed 174 college students and 41 professors using the open-ended question "What do you think a 'trick' question is?" Roberts identified seven recurring themes paraphrased here that help to identify the characteristics of trick questions as perceived by the students and faculty who responded.

1. Intention: The wording of the item reflects an intent on the part of the teacher to confuse or mislead the examinees.
2. Trivial content: The correct answer focuses on a point or idea that the examinees perceive to be insignificant.
3. Requires discriminations that are too fine: The content of the item requires examinees to make distinctions that are excessively fine compared to the less precise distinctions made during class discussion or in the textbook.
4. Item stems that include irrelevant information: The central problem or focus of the question is unnecessarily obscured by information that is completely irrelevant.

5. Several correct answers: The options are so similar and differences between them are so subtle that knowledgeable students interpret them as having more than one correct answer.
6. Opposite principle: The item focuses on assessing knowledge in a manner that is opposite to the manner in which it was presented during instruction.
7. Highly ambiguous items: The problem to be answered is so poorly defined that even knowledgeable students are unable to understand what the item calls for.

Characteristics 2, 3, and 5 in the paraphrased list of Roberts's findings seem to be a way of accusing the test developer of being "too picky." Although we agree that ambiguity is a problem, characteristics 4 and 7 in Roberts's list also appear to express concern about vagueness in the way the problem in an item is presented. Roberts's study represents an important attempt to bring clarity to our understanding of how students define tricky questions. Only the results of Phase 1 of his study are reported here; persons who have an interest in the problem of trick questions should read Roberts's study. They may also want to design and conduct research of their own. The issue of what constitutes trick questions certainly needs further research.

Much of the cynicism and distrust that students express about tests is likely to be a result of their experience with what they perceive to be trick questions. Although the idea of trick questions may be more of a stereotype than a precisely defined construct, the idea is pervasive enough that it warrants concern. Responsible teachers and testmakers should avoid the very appearance of evil in this regard. Effective test items should focus on significant ideas that are worth learning and remembering, and on meaningful distinctions that are worth making. Furthermore, they should be written in such a clear and straightforward manner that examinees who answer incorrectly do so because they did not know the correct answer rather than because of something confusing or misleading in the way the item was written. The guidelines for writing good test items as presented in this book, and other similar texts are designed to help alleviate this problem.

Guidelines for Writing True-False Items

True–false items were once the most popular form of testing. However, one rarely finds a true–false item on current standardized achievement tests. The declining use of true–false items is probably attributable to a belief that such items test only trivial information, are often ambiguous, encourage rote learning, expose students to erroneous ideas that might be accepted as truth, and are too susceptible to obtaining high scores through guessing. Although there is an element of truth in such criticisms, Frisbie and Becker (1990) claim that the criticisms of true–false items are unfounded. They conclude that properly written true–false items can be used efficiently to obtain information about students' mastery of essential knowledge and should be more widely used. One thing is clear, however, good true–false items are not easy to develop and should not be the only, or even the predominant, means of testing.

Not everyone agrees, however. After summarizing the findings of research regarding the relative effectiveness of true–false items in comparison to other commonly used item formats, Downing (1992) is more cautious about recommending the use of true–false items than Frisbie and Becker.

The format for writing true–false items is seductively simple. A statement is given, and the respondent is asked to mark whether that statement is "true" or "false." A variety of variations have been attempted, most of them designed to minimize any potential advantages of guessing. For example, some people have advocated that students be instructed to correct false items by crossing out the word or phrase that makes it false and writing in a word or phrase that makes the statement correct. Others have suggested the use of correction for chance formulas. Still others have suggested confidence scoring procedures in which the respondent indicates how confident he or she is about a particular answer, and items are weighted differentially depending on how confident the respondent is about his or her response for that item. In our opinion, these procedures add unnecessary complexity with little, if any, gain in the value of the information provided. Until more research demonstrates the superiority of such techniques, we believe that the standard, true–false item is still the best. Following are five useful guidelines for writing true–false items:

1. *Ask questions about single ideas; avoid double-barreled questions.* Consider the following true–false item.

T   F   Because of the massive amounts of financial assistance from the United States, Israel maintains one of the largest military forces in the world.

Interpreting a response to such questions is difficult because the statement has two parts. It is true that Israel maintains one of the world's largest military forces compared to its population. However, they would probably maintain a similar military force even if they did not receive financial aid from the United States. Thus, one part of the sentence is true, the other is false. A better true–false item would be the following.

T   F   The United States provides very little financial aid to Israel.

---

2. *Avoid negative wording in false statements.* Consider the following item:

T   F   The United States Constitution does not require the secretary of state to be confirmed by the Senate.

Even if someone knew that the secretary of state must be confirmed by the Senate, it is confusing to figure out whether the double negative results in a true or false answer. In most cases, it is better to be simple and direct. The proceeding statement could be better phrased as follows:

T   F   The United States Constitution requires the secretary of state to be confirmed by the Senate.

---

3. *There should be approximately the same number of true and false items, they should appear in a random order, and true items should be about the same length as false items.* If a particular teacher writes more true than false items, the testwise student would always mark true for items about which he or she was unsure. The best way to combat the negative consequences of such testwise behavior is to eliminate as many clues as possible through careful review of items and careful structuring of tests.

4. *Avoid statements that require complex construction or caveats.* Complex sentence construction and qualifications may turn items into a measure of a student's reasoning ability, vocabulary, or reading comprehension rather than a measure of content knowledge. Where complex construction or qualifiers seem necessary, it is generally better to break the item up into two or more simple items that are a direct test of the information you think is important.

5. *Avoid the use of superlatives, and such words as* all, never, *and* always. Every test item should have one, and only one, correct answer. In an effort to make true–false questions *clearly* true or *clearly* false, test writers sometimes use words such as *usually* or *generally* in conjunction with items that are true, and words such as *always, none,* or *never* in conjunction with items that are false. Testwise students quickly learn that their chances for a high score are improved if they mark items true that use words such as *usually* and *sometimes* and mark items false that use words such as *never* and *always.* Superlatives can also cause problems. Consider the following item:

T   F   Willie Mays was the greatest baseball player who ever lived.

Although some people might believe the statement to be true, others would have their own nominations for the greatest baseball player of all time. The more clear-cut the answers to true–false questions, the better those questions will generally be.

Guidelines for Writing Multiple-Choice Items

Because they are versatile, easily scored, and useful in measuring a wide variety of learning outcomes, multiple-choice items are frequently used. A multiple-choice item consists of a statement or question (which we will refer to as the *stem*) followed by a number of possible responses (which we will refer to as *options* or *alternatives*). One (or more) of the options is the correct or best response. The remaining options are distractors.

Although multiple-choice items are often criticized for measuring only recall, well-designed multiple-choice items can do much more. Consider the following two items taken from a booklet on multiple-choice questions published by Educational Testing Service (1963):

The concept of the plasma membrane as a simple sieve-like structure is inadequate to explain the

a. passage of gases involved in respiration into and out of the cell.
b. passage of simple organic molecules such as glucose into the cell.
c. failure of protein molecules to pass through the membrane.
d. inability of the cell to use starch without prior digestion.
e. ability of the cell to admit selectively some inorganic ions while excluding others.

To answer this question correctly, a student must understand how a plasma membrane functions, and he or she must evaluate and synthesize that knowledge with information about glucose, protein, starch, gases, and inorganic ions. The student who has mastered the material will realize that comparing a plasma membrane to a sieve may be adequate to explain why it allows very small molecules (such as gases and glucose) to pass through the membrane and rejects larger molecules (such as protein and starch). However, this explanation does not account for the ability of the plasma membrane to selectively admit some inorganic ions while excluding others. Thus option e is the only possible correct answer.

Directions: The sentence below has blank spaces, each blank indicating that a word has been omitted. Beneath the sentence are five lettered sets of words. You are to choose the one set of words which, when inserted in the sentence, best fits in with the meaning of the sentence as a whole.

From the first, the Islanders, despite an outward _____ , did what they could to _____ the ruthless occupying power.

a. harmony . . . assist
b. enmity . . . embarrass
c. rebellion . . . foil
d. resistance . . . destroy
e. acquiescence . . . thwart

To answer this question, the student must recall definitions of words and must also apply that knowledge in a novel setting by selecting the pair of words that creates the appropriate contrast and fits the context. Options a, b, c, and d can be eliminated because the word *despite* implies that the Islanders acted outwardly in one way while trying to do just the opposite in practice. For example, if the Islanders displayed an outward *harmony,* to *assist* the ruthless occupying power would probably create additional harmony. Similar arguments can be advanced for *enmity* and *embarrass, rebellion* and *foil, resistance* and *destroy.* Only option e implies two opposing actions.

Unfortunately, the guidelines followed by most people for writing multiple-choice items were aptly summarized by Nitko (1984), as follows: "Elder item writers pass down to novices lists of rules and suggestions which they and their item-writing forefathers have learned through the process of applied art, empirical study, and practical experience" (p. 201). In an effort to systematize these item-writing "rules and suggestions," Haladyna and Downing (1989a) recently compiled a taxonomy of multiple-choice item-writing rules "based on a consensus of 46 authoritative references representing the field of educational measurement from as early as 1935" (p. 38). In a companion article based on an analysis of 96 empirical studies, they examined the degree to which those 43 rules were supported by credible research (Haladyna & Downing, 1989b).

The results of their analyses demonstrated that many of the rules that have been "passed down by our item-writing forefathers" have not been investigated empirically. For those rules where substantial research has been done, the results are not always clear-cut, and according to Haladyna and Downing (1989b), the vast majority of rules have not been sufficiently investigated.

Until more research is completed, it seems best to rely on the wisdom of measurement experts to write effective multiple-choice items. In what follows, we have used the taxonomy suggested by Haladyna and Downing (1989a), combined with our analysis of existing research, the "wisdom of our item-writing forefathers," and our own experience to outline a list of simple, but useful, rules for writing multiple-choice items. The following nine guidelines will help you write good quality multiple choice items:

1. *Options should portray a single concept that appears plausible to students who have not mastered the material.* A multiple-choice item consists of a stem and a number of options or distractors. The purpose of a distractor is to "distract" away from the correct answer those students who have not mastered the concept being assessed. This is very different from tricking the student with trivial details or ambiguous options. In other words, options should be constructed so that they seem plausible to someone who has not correctly learned the material. Consider the following multiple-choice question:

The purpose of the Lewis and Clark expedition was to

   a.   explore and map much of the Western United States.
   b.   explore Central America to locate a site for the Panama Canal.
   c.   provide assistance to forces friendly to the United States during the Spanish American War.
   d.   survey the area that was later acquired from France as the Louisiana Purchase.

Option a is the best answer, but each of the other options are plausible for a student who has some knowledge but has not thoroughly mastered the concept. A student who remembers that the Lewis and Clark expedition had something to do with exploration and mapping might select option b or d. The term *expedition* in the stem might suggest military involvement to some students, making option c a good choice. Good options do not trick students who have mastered the concept into selecting an incorrect answer. Rather, they separate those students who have mastered the concept from those whose knowledge is limited.

Good distractors also prevent students with limited knowledge about the concept from obtaining correct answers through testwiseness. Consider the following item:

The largest city in the United States is

a. New York, New York.
b. Rigby, Idaho.
c. Gridley, California.
d. Poolesville, Maryland.

A student would have to know very little about the relative size of cities in the United States to get this answer correct. New York would be the most likely guess for an uninformed student based solely on the fact that he or she had never heard of the other three cities.

The creation of plausible distractors is one of the most difficult parts of writing good multiple-choice items, but the results are worth the time spent. The best distractors help the teacher understand what incorrect perceptions students have. Here are some suggestions to help you in creating good distractors.

- Base distractors on the most frequent errors made by students in homework assignments or class discussions related to that concept.
- Use words in the distractors that are associated with words in the stem (for example, explorer—exploration).
- Use concepts from the instructional material that have similar vocabulary or were used in the same context as the correct answer.
- Use distractors that are similar in content or form to the correct answer (for example, if the correct answer is the name of a place, have all distractors be places instead of using names of people and other facts).
- Make the distractors similar to the correct answer in terms of complexity, sentence structure, and length.

2. *Most multiple choice items should have three to five options.* Experts disagree about the ideal number of options in a multiple-choice test (see Haladyna & Downing, 1989b, for a review of this literature). Some argue that the more options you

have, the more variability the test will have and hence, the greater its reliability (Noll, Scannel, & Craig, 1979). Others argue that a three-option test discriminates just as well, is just as reliable, and is easier to construct because the test developer has to devise only two plausible distractors (Grier, 1975; Lord, 1977).

Although it is logical that tests having more options will be more discriminating and hence, more reliable, the *quality* of distractors is much more important than the *number* of distractors (Haladyna & Downing, 1989b). The important need is to create functional distractors—that is, distractors that are plausible enough to be selected by examinees who have either a partial understanding or a misunderstanding of the concept being assessed. More and more research evidence has accumulated in recent years that shows that multiple-choice items seldom include more than three useful options and that nonfunctioning distractors do not contribute significantly to the discriminating power of the test or to the reliability of the resulting scores (Cizek & O'-Day, 1994; Haladyna & Downing, 1993; Owen & Froman, 1987; Trevisan, Sax, & Michael, 1991).

3. *Words that need to be repeated in each option should be included in the stem.* Consider the following examples:

Poor:

Test reliability

a. can be improved by making items more difficult.
b. can be improved by shortening the test.
c. can be improved by changing the test from a power test to a speeded test.
d. can be improved by increasing the number of items on the test.

Better:

Test reliability can be improved by

a. using items with lower point-biserial correlations.
b. decreasing the number of items on the test.
c. changing from a power test to a speeded test.
d. increasing the number of items on the test.

---

4. *Use* none of the above *and* all of the above *sparingly.* Where absolute standards of correctness are clear (for example, in arithmetic or spelling), *none of the above* may be a plausible or even correct response. In most cases, however, *none of the above* and *all of the above* tend to be overused placeholders, not serious and plausible distractors. Such phrases are often included because the test developer had trouble thinking of one more plausible alternative.

The use of *all of the above* should generally be avoided because an examinee who can identify any two options as both being correct can readily infer that *all of the above* is the correct answer and the remaining choices can be eliminated from further consideration. On the other hand, if an examinee can identify any one option as being incorrect, then the option *all of the above* can be disregarded from further consideration.

5. *Generally, the stem of an item should present a clearly-defined, meaningful problem that can be readily understood without having to read the options.* Compare the stems in these following two versions of an item:

Poor:

The president of the United States

a.   is chosen by the electoral college.
b.   can serve a maximum of two four-year terms.
c.   must be at least 45 years of age.
d.   can be impeached only for felony offenses.

Better:

The President of the United States is chosen by the

a.   electoral college.
b.   members of the Senate.
c.   members of the House of Representatives.
d.   people directly.

In the first example, the student knows only that the problem has something to do with the president of the United States. Only by identifying the correct answer can he or she determine that the item writer wanted to test students' knowledge about the election process. The second example still tests the critical information, but it is easier for students to read and understand, and still contains plausible distractors.

6. *Avoid window dressing.* The item stem should be as precise, straightforward, and simple as possible. Some item writers provide elaborate explanations in an effort to make the item clearer. In reality, such window dressing often introduces vagueness and obscures the problem unnecessarily by increasing the amount of information the student must process to understand the question. Consider the following example:

Although many different people worked on the concept of a telephone, and several made discoveries which were key to its later development, the person who is credited with the invention of the telephone is

a.   Alexander Graham Bell.
b.   Benjamin Franklin.
c.   Guglielmo Marconi.
d.   Thomas Edison.

If the purpose of the item is to assess students' ability to distinguish between relevant and irrelevant information, then extra wording is needed and should not be considered window dressing. But in this example, the purpose is simply to determine whether the students know who is credited with having invented the telephone. Therefore, a simpler and more direct item stem would be better.

7. *Options should usually come at the end of the statement.* Although there are exceptions to this rule, items are usually easier to understand if they are phrased so that the answer is a conclusion to an incomplete statement or the answer to a question. Consider the following two examples:

Poor:

The city of _____ is the capital of California.

a. Los Angeles.
b. San Francisco.
c. Sacramento.
d. San Diego.

Better:

The capital of California is _____ .

a. Los Angeles.
b. San Francisco.
c. Sacramento.
d. San Diego.

---

8. *The correct option should be about the same length as distractors and should occur randomly.* Inexperienced item writers tend to word the correct option with more precision and make it longer than other distractors. They also tend to have the correct option appear as the first or last option more frequently. A testwise student will notice such patterns and will have an unfair advantage, even if he or she has not mastered the material.

9. *Each item should have only one correct or best answer.* This seems obvious enough, but it is one rule that is frequently violated. Consider the following example:

Choose the man who does not belong in this group.

a. Ulysses S. Grant
b. Dwight D. Eisenhower
c. Adolph Hitler
d. Charles de Gaulle

The student who recognized that Eisenhower, Hitler, and de Gaulle were all leaders of countries during World War II might select Grant. Another student who recognized that Grant, Eisenhower, and de Gaulle were all military generals might select Hitler. Thus, there are at least two different correct answers based on different interpretations of the item. The best way to identify items with ambiguous answers is to have someone else review and answer your items without having access to your scoring key. Often, they will identify a correct answer which is different from the one you have selected.

Application Problem 1

You are asked to review a test for a fellow teacher that contains the following multiple-choice question. What suggestions would you make for improvement?

Which of the following animals does not belong with the others?

a. Elephant
b. Crocodile
c. Beaver
d. Lion

Guidelines for Writing Matching Exercises

A matching exercise generally consists of two columns of information. The respondent is supposed to indicate which option in the second column best matches each item in the first column. A matching exercise is really a series of individual items. Matching exercises are most frequently used to measure knowledge of events, dates, persons, and other such matters involving simple relationships. A typical matching item looks like the following:

Directions: A number of inventions are listed on the left. The right-hand column contains names of inventors. Match each invention with the name of the person who invented it. Write the letter designating the inventor in the blank next to each invention. Each inventor's name may be used once, more than once, or not at all.

Inventions	Inventors
_____ 1. Telephone	a. Alexander Bell
_____ 2. Telegraph	b. Thomas Edison
_____ 3. Phonograph	c. Robert Fulton
_____ 4. Radio	d. Guglielmo Marconi
_____ 5. Incandescent light bulb	e. Cyrus McCormick
	f. Samuel Morse
	g. Eli Whitney

Constructing good matching exercises is relatively fast, but must be done carefully. The following six guidelines are useful in constructing good matching items:

1. *Lists to be matched should be relatively homogeneous.* When the items in each list are homogeneous, students are less likely to guess the correct answer unless they have mastered the information. For example, if the preceding exercise had also included authors and books, athletes and sports, and explorers and discoveries, a student with superficial knowledge of the content area would be able to eliminate some of the possible answers and increase the likelihood of obtaining a high score.

2. *Directions for matching exercises should specify the basis on which items should be matched, how the answers should be marked, and the number of times each option can be used.* The directions given in the previous example are a good model. Because matching exercises can be arranged in many different ways, it is very important to have explicit instructions. The most frequently omitted instruction is whether options can be matched with more than one item. Sometimes it is good to allow an option to be used more than once. In the following example, the list of items (List A) contains names of animals, and the categories in the list of options (List B) can be used multiple times.

List A		List B
_____ 1. Ostrich		A. Mammal
_____ 2. Boa Constrictor		B. Reptile
_____ 3. Elephant		C. Bird
_____ 4. Crocodile		
_____ 5. Hyena		
_____ 6. Rattlesnake		
_____ 7. Eagle		
_____ 8. Goose		

3. *Avoid matching exercises in which all items are used and each option is used once and only once.* If there are exactly the same number of options as items and each option is to be used once, the student can often get one or more answers correct by a process of elimination. A much better approach is to have several more plausible options than there are items. Look again at the matching exercise at the beginning of this section. Notice though while Cyrus McCormick and Guglielmo Marconi were famous inventors, they were not responsible for any of the inventions listed. Thus a student who knew only three of the answers could not use a process of elimination to obtain the correct fourth answer.

4. *Make sure all options are plausible.* Unfortunately, some matching items look like the following:

Directions: Listed below are the names of sports teams and famous athletes. Put the letter associated with the correct sports figure in front of the team for whom he played.

Sport Teams

_____ 1. Green Bay Packers
_____ 2. San Francisco Giants
_____ 3. Boston Celtics

Athletes

a. Bart Starr
b. Nancy Lopez
c. Willie Mays
d. Larry Bird

A student who knows only a little about professional sports and deduces that Nancy Lopez is female will know that she is not a plausible response for any of the teams listed.

5. *Matching exercises should generally be limited to no more than ten items.* With long lists of items, students have to spend a lot of time reading and organizing information before responding to the question. Such lists can be confusing and put too much emphasis on one particular content area. The best matching exercises contain only four to six items.

6. *Place all items, options, and direction, on the same page.* Tests are sometimes arranged so that students are required to flip pages back and forth to see all the options and items. This practice is unnecessarily confusing and should be avoided.

Application Problem 2

A fellow teacher asks you to review a test that contains the following matching exercise:

Directions: Match the items below.

_____ 1. The capital of the U.S. immediately following
the Revolutionary War
_____ 2. A naval hero of the Revolutionary War
_____ 3. A French military officer who assisted Washington
during the Revolutionary War
_____ 4. Site of the 1787 Constitutional Convention
_____ 5. Location of the first fighting of the Revolutionary War
_____ 6. Site of the final major battle of the Revolutionary War
_____ 7. The founder of Rhode Island
_____ 8. Settled the Colony of Jamestown
_____ 9. A traitor to the American cause during the Revolution
_____ 10. The country from whom the U.S. purchased
the Louisiana Territory

A. John Smith
B. France

C. Yorktown
D. Roger Williams
E. Philadelphia
F. Marquis de Lafayette
G. Arnold
H. New York
I. John Paul Jones

J. Lexington

What suggestions would you make for improvement?

Guidelines for Writing Completion or Short-Answer Items

Completion or short-answer items consist of a question that can be answered with a word or short phrase, or a statement having one or more omitted words, which the student is supposed to complete. For example,

---

A person nominated by the president to serve as the secretary of state must be confirmed by the _____.

The popularity of short answer or completion questions is probably tied to the ease of construction and scoring and the fact that a relatively large number of questions can be asked in a limited amount of space. The same general guidelines listed earlier for development of any achievement items also apply here. In addition, the following four guidelines will help you develop effective completion or short-answer questions:

1. *Questions should be stated in such a way that only a specific and unique word or phrase can be the correct answer.* This is probably the most difficult part of writing good completion items. Consider the following question:

The capital city of the United States is _____.

The intended answer to this question was probably Washington, D.C. But a teacher might have a difficult time defending his or her correct answer to a student who had written *large, where the president of the United States lives, pretty, in a temperate climate,* or any one of hundreds of other answers. To preclude having several appropriate answers, be aware of such possibilities as you develop items, and then have your items reviewed and answered by another teacher who is familiar with the subject matter.

2. *Omit only significant words from a statement to be completed.* Consider a completion item based on the following sentence:

The executive, legislative, and judicial branches constitute a system of checks and balances for the United States government.

The following is an example of an item that would likely to be confusing to students:

The executive, _____, and judicial _____ constitute a _____ of checks and _____ for the United States _____.

Items of this type are sometimes called "Swiss cheese items." This particular example seems to have more holes than cheese. A better question, which tests significant concepts, would be the following:

The system of checks and balances for the United States government consists of the branches of executive, _____ , and _____

3. *Completion items should contain enough information so that a person who has mastered the material can tell precisely what is being asked.* Consider the following item:

The _____ River divides the states of _____ and _____ .

Obviously, there are dozens of different correct answers to the preceding question in the manner in which it is written. If, however, the sentence were phrased as follows, the only possible answer is California.

The Colorado River divides the states of Arizona and _____ .

4. *For problems requiring numerical answers, specify the degree of precision required.* Consider the following examples.

Poor:
The size of Canada is approximately _____ .

Better:
The size of Canada (within 100,000 square miles) is _____ .

The actual area of Canada is 3,851,809 square miles. To avoid arguing about whether 6,000,000 square miles is correct, specify the required degree of accuracy.

Guidelines for Writing and Scoring Essay Questions

Essay questions are easier to construct than other kinds of test items—particularly if you want to test higher-level cognitive skills. Essay questions also provide an opportunity for the student to demonstrate his or her ability to express written thoughts clearly, concisely, and correctly—an important skill not easily measured by the other kinds of test items we have discussed. Many people also believe that students prepare more thoroughly if they think essay questions will be asked. Here are two examples of essay items.

Explain the difference between fiscal policy and monetary policy as methods of promoting national economic policy. Cite two examples of the use of each method in the history of the United States.

Compare and contrast the social conditions, prevailing political thought, and economic conditions in the North and the South just prior to the outbreak of the Civil War.

Although essay questions are used frequently and vigorously defended by many, they have also been the object of much criticism. In fact, one of the most frequently cited examples of early educational research was a study by Starch and Elliot (1912, 1913b), which showed that when different teachers were asked to independently score the same "typical examination paper" in English and history, the results ranged from nearly perfect to a very low failure. In another early study, Eells (1930) found that when a teacher scored the same paper several months apart, the results were dramatically different.

Essay questions are also criticized because it takes a relatively long time for students to respond to them, fewer instructional objectives can be addressed during the same testing time, and they are time consuming to score. Such issues have prompted a great deal of controversy about the use of essay questions and emphasize the need to write essay questions carefully and score them in ways that avoid such problems. None of these problems is significant enough, however, to preclude the use of essay tests.

In fact, although we are sure that the debate about whether or not to use essay questions will continue, we are just as sure that the essay test will continue to be widely used by teachers. Essay items appear to be simple to write, and it is this apparent simplicity that results in many of the problems noted. The following 11 guidelines will help in writing good essay items:

1. *Restrict the use of essay questions to those learning outcomes that are difficult to measure with true–false, multiple-choice, matching, or completion items.* Never use essay questions simply to measure knowledge of facts. Even though it is difficult, it is possible to select fixed response items that measure higher-level cognitive skills. In comparison, it is relatively easy to write essay questions that do this. Consider the following examples:

Poor item:

Public Law 99-457 is designed to encourage states to provide early intervention services to all children with handicaps. States who choose not to participate in P.L. 99-457 will be subject to certain sanctions from the federal government. List those sanctions.

Better item:

Public Law 99-457 is designed to encourage states to provide early intervention services to all children with handicaps. States who choose not to participate in P.L. 99-457 will be subject to certain sanctions. Identify at least three sanctions that were considered but not included in the law. Explain why you believe Congress selected the particular sanctions they did. Describe how effective you believe the sanctions will be in motivating states to participate.

The first question asks students to recall the sanctions included in the law. The second requires students not only to recall information but to present judgments about the worth or value of that information, and to predict how states will respond.

2. *Make sure that each essay question is focused sufficiently that students know exactly what is expected of them.* Sometimes essay questions are so broad and unfocused that it is difficult for students to know how to respond. Consider the following two questions:

Poor:

Discuss the migration habits of birds.

Better:

State two hypotheses about why birds migrate South in the fall. Summarize the evidence supporting each hypothesis, and defend the one you believe is most accurate.

The poorly stated question allows students too much latitude in formulating their response. The task is so broad and undefined that students will respond very differently. Some will miss the intent of the question, some will focus on one or two narrow aspects of the problem or redefine the task to fit what they know best. In fact, a testwise student may claim to have "misunderstood" the intent of the question and write a limited response based on those aspects of the question that are most familiar.

When formulating an essay question to assess students' understanding of a particular concept, the testmaker's responsibility is to define the students' task as clearly and completely as possible. Verbs such as *analyze, describe, explain, evaluate, cite examples of, justify the use of,* or *predict what would happen if,* are useful tools for defining and delimiting the task. The verb *discuss* should generally be avoided. It is too vague and nonspecific. When *discuss* is the only verb used to define the task, students can legitimately respond with vague generalizations in which they talk all around an issue without ever arriving at a specific conclusion. In addition to eliciting fluff, bluff, and other stuff, such broadly stated questions are very difficult to score reliably. If you ask vague questions, don't be surprised when you get vague, general answers.

3. *Give students guidelines on time limits and the amount of information expected.* Directions can be *too* specific and unnecessarily restrictive (for example, make your answer 300 words long). Yet, students deserve and need some guidance regarding your expectations. Suggesting that students spend *about* 10–15 minutes or write *approximately* one page establishes some useful parameters that will help them know the level of detail you expect. The best way to estimate how much time or space is needed is to write out what you believe to be an appropriate response to the question before you give the test. Remember that students will require half again as much or more time because they don't know exactly what is wanted and have not mastered the material as well as you have. Generally, you do not want essay tests to be speeded tests. Instead, you want students to have time to organize and present their thoughts concisely and logically. It is usually wise to be generous in estimating time limits.

4. *Several questions each having a relatively narrow focus are generally better than one broad question.* One of the difficulties with essay questions is achieving sufficient sampling of the domain of instructional objectives. When broad essay questions are written, this disadvantage is accentuated. A better approach is to include several, more narrowly focused essay questions that still require the student to demonstrate higher-level cognitive skills but that assess mastery of a greater number of instructional objectives.

5. *Avoid the use of optional essay items.* Generally, students' scores will be compared either directly or indirectly. Such comparisons are fair only if all students respond to the same questions. Although it may reduce students' anxiety to have optional questions, it certainly decreases the validity of using scores to make comparisons, and there is no evidence that it increases the validity of the test for other purposes.

6. *Before giving the test, develop a list of the main points that should be included in each answer and develop a scoring system.* If true–false, multiple choice, matching, and completion items have been written correctly, almost anybody who is careful can score the items. However, there is not just one correct answer to an essay question. Consequently, scoring is time consuming and difficult, and must be done carefully. To be fair and accurate it is essential to prepare a scoring key that specifies

■ the major points to be included,
■ the amount of credit to be assigned for each major point.

This scoring outline should be developed *before* the test is administered so that (1) you can make sure students have been taught what is expected in the answer, and (2) you can give students some indication of how detailed each answer needs to be.

7. *Before scoring essays, review the material students were expected to learn.* You will be much more familiar with the content being tested than will students, and in most cases, you will have enriched your knowledge with information from outside sources. Unless you are careful, you may be expecting students to use information from experiences or readings to which they have not been exposed. A quick review of course material and lectures will remind you how the course looks from their perspective and reduce the odds you will hold them accountable for material you shouldn't.

8. *Inform students how you will deal with factors that are independent from the learning outcome being measured.* Variables such as the quality of handwriting, correctness of grammar, organization, and the use of interesting examples may influence the evaluation of essay questions—whether we intend them to or not. If those variables are reflected in the learning outcomes for the course, then they should be accorded some value in the scoring system. If they are not, they must not be allowed to influence scores. In any case, students should be informed prior to the time they take the test precisely which factors will influence their scores.

9. *Score essay questions without knowing which students produced which responses.* Unfortunately, a teacher may give more credit than is deserved to an answer because he or she believes the student really has mastered the learning outcome and simply did not demonstrate it in that particular response. Even when teachers are committed to not allowing previous performance to affect their scoring, there is a powerful subconscious influence that is difficult to avoid. The best way to skirt this source of bias is not to know which students wrote which responses. If you are so familiar with students' handwriting that their identify cannot be concealed, the best you can do is to make a conscious effort to eliminate any such bias from your scoring.

10. *Score all students' responses to one item before scoring responses to another item.* Suppose you are scoring a test that contains 5 essay questions for 25 students. One of the most difficult tasks in scoring essay questions is to keep the same standards as you score each paper. An average answer often receives a higher score if it follows a poor answer than if it follows an excellent one. One way to minimize such shifting of standards is to score all the answers to the first question, shuffle the papers, and score all the answers to the second question, and so on. This way, any bias associated with the order of scoring is balanced among students. Moreover, you have to focus on only one response at a time.

11. *Questions that ask students to draw a judgment or take a position should be evaluated based on the strength of their arguments, not on whether they agree with your position.* Because essay questions are often used to test higher-order cognitive skills, students are frequently asked to evaluate information, make judgments, or defend a particular position. Some teachers have difficulty evaluating essays on the strength of the students' argument as opposed to whether the student agrees with their position. You should be aware of this potential source of bias and make sure that your scoring criteria are based on the *strength of the arguments presented.*

Creating and Using Context-dependent Item Sets

Context-dependent item sets are a versatile tool for assessing various types of cognitive learning outcomes that require more than simple recall (Haladyna, 1992; Wesman, 1971). Three examples of context-dependent item sets are shown in Figures 8.1 to 8.3. The test items in Figure 8.1 assess the ability of fourth or fifth

FIGURE 8.1   Graph Reading Test

GRAPH READING EXERCISE

Directions:
  Study the graph shown below. Then answer the following questions.

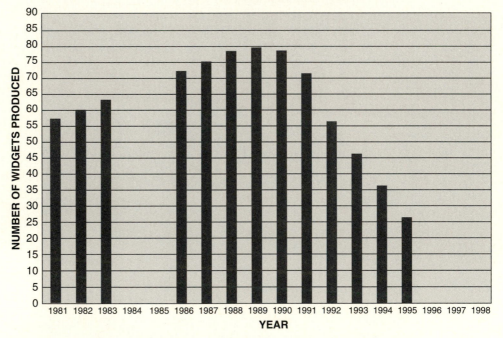

ANNUAL PRODUCTION OF WIDGETS

1. How many widgets were produced in 1986? _____

2. In which year was the largest number of widgets produced? _____

3. In which two years were the same number of widgets produced? _____

4. Which year shows the largest decrease in number of widgets produced compared to the previous year? _____

5. The records for 1984 and 1985 were lost. Based on the trend at that time, estimate the number of widgets that were produced in 1985. _____

6. Records have not yet become available for the years since 1995. If the existing trend continues, how many widgets do you estimate will be produced in 1997? _____

Box A: Questions 1–7 refer to the scenario described in this box.

A high school teacher administered a test to a group of 120 students with a maximum possible score of 50. The distribution of raw scores was unimodal and ranged from a low score of 25 to a high score of 50. The descriptive statistics for the scores are listed below:

Mean	41.10
Median	42.50
Mode	45.0
Standard deviation	5.79
25th percentile	37.5
75th percentile	45.5

The teacher later discovered that two scores were wrong. One score was incorrectly computed as 41 when it should have been 37. Another score was incorrectly recorded as 43 when it should have been 34.

Suppose that the professor replaced each of the incorrect scores with the corresponding correct score. Decide how the two replacements would likely affect each of the descriptive statistics listed below. For each statistic, choose the effect from the list at the right that would most likely occur. Each effect category may be used once, more than once, or not at all. Write the letter indicating your answers in the blanks provided.

Descriptive Statistics	Likely Effects
1. Mean	A. Decreased
2. Median	B. Increased
3. Mode	C. Not changed
4. Range	D. The effect cannot be reasonably estimated
5. Interquartile range	from the information given.
6. Standard deviation	
7. Skewness	

FIGURE 8.2   Statistics Test

---

graders to interpret information presented in a bar graph and draw simple conclusions from that information. The students are presented with an idealized graph accompanied by six short-answer questions based on information in the graph. The students are not given any verbal description of the contents of the graph other than the captions and labels presented in the graph itself. Questions 1-4 in this exercise elicit simple, literal interpretations from the graphed information. Question 5 assesses the students' ability to interpolate, and question 6 assesses their ability to extrapolate. Although each of these latter tasks is fairly simple, they both assess the students' ability to make inferences from the information given.

The exercise in Figure 8.2 was constructed for use as part of a test in an introductory statistics class. This exercise assesses students' ability to *apply* and *reason* with their knowledge of some basic concepts and principles in descriptive statistics. The problems in this exercise are presented in a matching format. To

GENETICS TEST

Directions:

In the pedigree chart shown below, the shaded symbols designate persons with attached earlobes. Answer questions 1–7 based on the information in this chart.

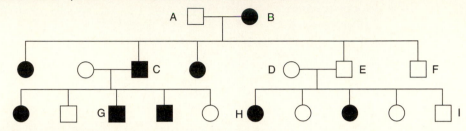

1. Evidence in this pedigree indicates that attached earlobes are--
   A. recessive
   B. dominant
   C. intermediate
   D. cannot be determined from the information provided.

2. Are attached earlobes a sex-linked gene?
   A. yes
   B. no
   C. cannot be determined from the information provided.

3. What is individual A's phenotype?
   A. attached earlobes
   B. free earlobes
   C. born without earlobes
   D. cannot be determined from the information provided.

4. What is individual D's genotype?
   A. heterozygous
   B. homozygous dominant
   C. homozygous recessive
   D. cannot be determined from the information provided.

5. If individual F marries a person who is homozygous recessive, what percent of their children will likely show attached earlobes?
   A. 100%
   B. 75%
   C. 50%
   D. 25%
   E. None

6. If individual F marries a heterozygote, what percent of their children will likely carry but not manifest the gene for attached earlobes, and what percent will probably show this trait?
   A. 100%, 100%
   B. 100%, 50%
   C. 75%, 25%
   D. 50%, 25%
   E. 25%, None
   F. None, None

7. If individual F marries a heterozygote, what percent of their free-earlobe children will be heterozygotes
   A. 100%
   B. 75%
   C. 67%
   D. 50%
   E. 33%

FIGURE 8.3   Genetics Test

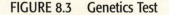

answer these problems correctly, students must carefully analyze the information described in the scenario, and then predict how the values of the seven descriptive statistics would likely change if two errors in the raw data were corrected in the manner specified.

The test items in Figure 8.3 were designed for use with students in a high school biology class who have completed a unit of instruction on genetics. This exercise assesses students' ability to apply generalizable principles they have learned rather than simply reciting rote definitions of the principles. The exercise consists of a three-generation pedigree chart accompanied by a series of multiple-choice questions. The pedigree chart displays information about the incidence of attached earlobes among the members of a fictitious family. The examinees are expected to be familiar with this type of chart and to know the various conventions that apply to interpreting such charts. For example, they are expected to know that (1) males are represented by squares and females by circles, (2) an adjacent male and female connected by a direct horizontal line represent a married couple, and (3) the children of a couple are shown in the next line directly beneath them and are connected by a vertical line to the horizontal line representing their union.

The examples in Figures 8.1, 8.2, and 8.3 illustrate common characteristics of context-dependent exercises. Each exercise consists of two parts: (1) an information display followed by (2) a series of problems that require the examinees to mentally process the information presented in the display.

If a set of items are context-dependent, then any changes in the variable elements in the display should result in changes in the correct answers to the questions. For example, the lengths of the bars and the direction of the trends displayed in the bar graph in Figure 8.1 can be varied. The same questions might be asked, but the correct answers would be different. The exercise in Figure 8.2 can be varied by changing the number, size, or location of the score corrections described in the scenario. Depending upon the corrections specified, the value of the mean or median may or may not be changed, and the same is true with the other statistics. The frequency distribution described in the existing Figure 8.2 is negatively skewed (as shown by the relative sizes of the mean, median, and mode), but this could be reversed to describe a positively skewed distribution, or it could be changed to a symmetric distribution. The same basic questions could still be used, but the correct answers would be different. Similarly, another version of the genetics test in Figure 8.3 could be created by substituting a different pedigree chart showing the incidence of attached earlobes (or some other genetic trait) among three generations of some other family. With a few minor modifications, the same basic questions used in Figure 8.3 could be used with a new chart, but the pattern of correct answers would be changed because the questions are context-dependent.

The items in a context-dependent exercise provide the examinees with a set of structured problems to be solved. The display provides the context in which these problems are situated. Together, the test items and the display provide a problem situation for the students to *think* or *reason about*. The knowledge base and thinking skills that each student brings to the task, including his or her understanding of relevant concepts and principles, provides the student with mental tools to reason with (Gregg & Leinhardt, 1994) in the framework of that situation.

The data or information in the display can be presented in various forms such as pictures; maps; charts; graphs; diagrams; cartoons; quotations; tables of numerical data; mathematical formulas; excerpts from a musical score; or excerpts from newspapers, magazines, or other reference materials. Instead of being printed on paper, the information may be presented in some other aural or visual form by other means such as a television, a projector, a tape recorder, or a poster. Or one could use actual artifacts or specimens such as rocks, plants, petri dishes, tools, and works of art.

The problems to which the student is asked to respond can be presented in any of the commonly used item formats described earlier in this chapter such as (1) short answer or completion items, (2) true-false items, (3) matching exercises, (4) multiple-choice questions, and (5) essay questions. Although some test makers prefer to limit context-dependent exercises to the use of selected-response formats (Airasian, 1996, p. 100), it is sometimes desirable to include short-answer items or essay questions. For example, if one of the purposes of a test is to assess students' ability to formulate interpretations rather than recognize correct interpretations, then constructed-response questions should be used. A single context-dependent exercise might well include items representing a combination of two or more item formats depending upon the nature of the learning outcomes being assessed.

Different Types of Context-dependent Item Sets

Scholars have distinguished between different types of context-dependent item sets (Haladyna, 1994; Wesman, 1971). The categories differ in terms of the display format used and in terms of the type of learning outcomes assessed.

Interlinear Exercises

In an interlinear exercise, students are given a writing sample that was deliberately designed to include spelling, capitalization, punctuation, grammar, or usage errors. The students' main task is to identify and correct the errors in the context of the rest of the passage.

Interlinear exercises occur in two different forms, as shown in Figure 8.4. In the constructed-response form, the student has to identify the various mistakes and then produce an acceptable way of correcting the mistake. Students respond by constructing their own answers and writing them in between the lines of the original document. Hence the label "interlinear exercise" is especially descriptive.

The selected-response form is more structured. Each error is replaced with a set of predetermined options from which the student is expected to choose an answer that is consistent with the meaning of the rest of the document. The former approach is more authentic, but this latter approach is easier and quicker to score reliably and may be more appropriate for students in the primary grades.

The two forms of interlinear exercises both focus on assessing students' ability to correct errors in context. One disadvantage of the selected-response form is that the students do not have to identify the errors; they need only to correct errors that have been identified for them. Recognizing and correcting errors in written texts are important skills, but both focus on editing rather than composing

Constructed-response Version:

Read the paragraph in the box below. Identify and correct any errors in spelling, punctuation, capitalization, grammar. Draw a line through each word that contains an error. Then write the correct word in the space above the error.

> The teachers' response suprised both Betty and I. It didn't seem to bother him. He just luaghed and smiled without loosing his cool. I felt badly because of what we done, but Betty didn't seem too worry much about it. The next day, she and myself both tried to to act like nothing had happened. but I was still scared, cause I knew he would probly talk to my dad at the Club meeting that night.

Selected-response Version:

Read the paragraph in the box below. Each time you come to a set of words in parentheses, select the best option from the choices in parentheses. Underline the word you choose from each set.

> The (teacher's/teachers') response (suprized/surprised) both Betty and (I/me). It didn't seem to bother him. He just (laughed/luaghed) and smiled without (losing/loosing) his cool. I felt (bad/badly) because of what we (did/done/had done), but Betty didn't seem (to/too/two) worry much about it. The next day, she and (I/me/myself) both tried to act like nothing had happened. (but/But) I was still scared, (cause/because) I knew that he would (probly/probably) talk to my dad at the (club/Club) meeting that night.

FIGURE 8.4   Two Different Versions of an Interlinear Exercise

skills. Hence, interlinear exercises do not provide a direct means of assessing students' ability to compose their thoughts and express them in written words and sentences.

Reading Comprehension Assessment Exercises

Many standardized achievement tests rely on this method to assess reading comprehension. This portion of the reading test typically consists of several prose passages each accompanied by a series of multiple-choice questions based on the related text. The students' task is to read each passage and then demonstrate their understanding of it by answering a series of questions about the passage. Some of the questions may assess literal comprehension of the information presented in the passage. Other questions may involve drawing inferences from the text presented.

In recent years, this approach to assessing reading comprehension has been widely criticized. Consequently, exercises of this kind are no longer used as widely as previously, and their use will likely continue to decline in the near future.

Interpretive Exercises

Interpretive exercises are designed to assess students' (1) understanding of the concepts and principles in a subject area, and (2) ability to reason with this knowledge to solve problems. Haladyna (1994) prefers to call them "problem-solving" exercises, but they might better be called interpretive exercises because they can be used to assess a broad range of reasoning (or thinking) skills such as:

1. ability to formulate and test hypotheses,
2. ability to draw warranted conclusions from data,
3. ability to recognize inferences in one's own thinking and in the thinking of others, and
4. ability to apply principles or generalizations to solve problems.

The information presented to the learner in an interpretive exercise may be in the form of words and sentences, or it could also include numerical data arranged in rows and columns. It could also be presented in the form of maps, line drawings, diagrams, photographs, or other visual displays. The bar graph in Figure 8.1 and the pedigree chart in Figure 8.3 are examples of this type of graphic display. Wesman (1971) classified pictorial or graphic forms of context-dependent exercises as a distinct category, but they are so similar to interpretive exercises in form and purpose, that we see no significant advantage in distinguishing between them.

Some teachers and prospective teachers confuse interpretive exercises with reading comprehension assessment exercises. The two may be similar in form, but they serve different purposes. Interpretive exercises are not intended to assess reading skills. To the extent that differences in the resulting scores reflect differences in the examinees' reading ability rather than differences in the ability that the exercise is intended to assess, the scores lack validity. Test makers should take specific steps to avoid creating interpretive exercises that are easier for good readers than for poor readers who are equal in terms of the ability the exercise is intended to assess.

Advantages and Disadvantages of Using Context-dependent Item Sets

The primary advantage of context-dependent item sets is that they provide a versatile means of assessing higher-level cognitive outcomes in greater depth than is often possible with single, independent items. To assess intended learning outcomes beyond the recall level generally requires that students be presented with a novel situation about which they are expected to think. To include a separate novel situation with each individual test item is not only more time consuming, but inefficient.

With concentrated effort and a little creativity, it is possible to construct context-dependent exercises that closely approximate some types of performance assessments that are discussed in the next chapter. Context-dependent exercises are generally more efficient to administer and score than performance assessments. But by their very nature, they are generally more structured than performance assessments. Consequently, they are likely to be less authentic.

The primary disadvantage of context-dependent item sets is the time and effort required to make them, and the difficulty of constructing high-quality exercises that are not unduly influenced by extraneous skills such as reading ability or general verbal ability.

Another disadvantage of using a set of items linked to a common information base is that the items within the set may be interdependent unless the test developer is careful to avoid this problem. When items are interdependent, an examinee's performance on the first or second item tends to influence his or her performance on subsequent items in the set. Consequently, a student who incorrectly answers the first item may have a higher probability of missing other items in the set. Such interlocked items have traditionally been considered undesirable from the point of view of classical test theory, but Rosenbaum (1988), Wainer and Kiely (1987), and Thissen, Steinberg, and Mooney (1989) have demonstrated that such item bundles or testlets may not be as troublesome as previously claimed. They suggest that one way to avoid this problem is to treat the items in each exercise as a set and assign a single collective score to the whole set—sort of like a multiple-point essay question—based on the student's pattern of responses. We believe that further research needs to be conducted on the consequences of using interdependent items. We also believe that context-dependent item sets can be written without including items that are interdependent.

Guidelines for Constructing Context-dependent Item Sets

The following suggestions are offered as guidelines to direct your decisions and actions in constructing a context-dependent item set. These guidelines presuppose that you have clearly defined the learning outcome you desire to assess.

1. *Select or create a novel display consisting of information that is directly relevant to the targeted learning outcome.* The information should also be novel to the students, but consistent with their curricular experience and their general reading level. The degree of novelty that is necessary and appropriate will vary depending upon the students' developmental level and their experience with the subject matter, but in any case, students should not have encountered the information in the same exact form. Otherwise, the test will function as an assessment of their ability to recognize or recall information rather than their ability to generalize or apply what they have learned to new situations.

Ideas for an appropriate display may be obtained from existing published sources such as an article, chart, picture, or map in a book, newspaper, or magazine. Reference materials such as encyclopedias, almanacs, handbooks, and atlases may be especially helpful. But materials obtained from any of these published sources generally need to be modified or revised to satisfy the purposes for using a context-dependent item set. The original source material may be too long, too detailed, or too difficult to read to serve the purpose of the test. Also, all the needed information may not be included in any single source. Consequently, you may need to combine information from various sources.

2. *Write the test items that will accompany the display.* The items in a context-dependent set should typically engage the student in mental processes that require more than just memory or recall. Instead, the item should require the student to engage in analysis, interpretation, prediction, generalization, application, or problem solving.

The problems presented must be determined by the targeted learning outcome to be assessed and must be related to the information included in the display. Consequently, this step generally must occur in conjunction with or as a part of step 1. For example, the process of constructing the graph reading exercise in Figure 8.1 was iterative. We began by making a draft version of the graph and then wrote some possible questions to accompany it. But in the process of writing these questions, we realized the need to make changes in the graph to accommodate other questions that came to mind. Then as we changed the graph we recognized the need to refine the questions we had written and also thought of some other possible questions.

When constructing context-dependent exercises, it is just as important to have test items that are free from ambiguities, extraneous clues, and other flaws as it is when writing separate, individual test items. Consequently, the guidelines for writing individual test items presented earlier in this chapter also apply when constructing context-dependent sets. The main differences that one must attend to when constructing item sets are to (1) make sure that each item in the set is clearly related to and dependent upon the information presented in the accompanying display, and (2) design an appropriate page layout that calls students' attention to the dependent relationship between each item in the set and the accompanying information.

3. *Write directions for each set of items.* Communicate to the examinees what they are expected to do. Don't assume that they will know what you expect. Use imperative sentences that are simple and direct.

4. *Develop a scoring key or rubric.* Since context-dependent item sets are usually intended to assess higher-order thinking, examinees' responses are likely to be more divergent than responses to purely factual questions. In fact, some items may have a range of acceptable answers and will require professional judgment on the part of the scorer. Hence, you need to develop an adequate answer key or set of criteria that describes the range of acceptable and unacceptable responses.

Context-dependent item sets typically have been underused by classroom teachers. Because of their versatility in assessing a broad range of higher cognitive outcomes in almost any subject area, they deserve wider use in classroom assessment. Users are limited only by their ability to articulate the learning outcomes they desire to assess and their ingenuity in creating appropriate information displays and accompanying test items that focus on the desired outcomes.

In Summary

Given all the guidelines and techniques for test development, not to mention the pros and cons of different types of test items, it is sometimes easy to forget the most important fact about testing. Namely, testing is worthwhile only if it contributes to better teaching and improved learning. To conclude this chapter, we share Frederiksen's (1984) perceptive thoughts on the powerful effect that the type of testing can have on learning.

> During World War II, . . . we conducted validity studies of the tests used in assigning recruits to naval training schools. One of our findings was that the best tests for predicting grades in gunner's mate schools were verbal and reading-comprehension tests, which didn't make much sense, in view of what gunner's mates are supposed to do . . . .
>
> Later, . . . we found that the lecture-demonstration method of teaching was used. The students studied the technical manuals, and . . . examinations [were] . . . based on the lectures and manuals. The items dealt with such topics as muzzle velocity and the function of the breech block locking bolt. Since the job for which these students were being trained was to maintain, adjust, and repair the guns aboard a warship, it seemed more reasonable to use performance tests. Accordingly, we developed a set of tests that required students to perform such tasks as . . . removing and replacing the extractor plunger on a 5/38″ antiaircraft gun. The instructors complained that the tests were too hard. They were right. Few of the students could perform the tasks, even with liberal time allowances . . . .
>
> The performance tests were nevertheless given at the end of each unit of training. . . . New students soon got word as to what the new tests were like, and they began practicing the assembly and disassembly of guns. . . . The instructors also got the point. They moved out the classroom chairs and the lecture podium and brought in more guns and gun mounts. The upshot was that students spent most of their time practicing the skills required in repairing and adjusting guns. The tests soon became too easy. The validity coefficients changed too: the verbal and reading test validities dropped, and the mechanical aptitude and mechanical knowledge tests became the best bets for predicting grades in gunner's mate school.
>
> Note that no attempt was made to change the curriculum or teacher behavior. The dramatic changes in achievement came about solely through a change in the tests. The moral is clear: It is possible to influence teaching and learning by changing the tests of achievement. (p. 201)

SUGGESTED READINGS

Coffman, W. E. (1971). *Essay examinations*. In R. L. Thorndike (ed.). *Educational measurement* (2nd ed. pp. 271–302). Washington, DC: American Council on Education.

A comprehensive review and analysis of the research supporting and opposing the use of essay test questions. Although much of the research is now dated, more recent research is generally consistent with the conclusions of this article, which remains one of the best summaries of the issues.

Carlson, S. B. (1985). *Creative classroom testing: 10 designs for assessment and instruction*. Princeton, NJ: Educational Testing Service.

Shows examples of a variety of test item types other than true–false, multiple-choice, and essay formats. The examples shown were developed by practicing teachers. Provides guidelines for developing other examples of these creative approaches.

Gronlund, N. E. (1993). *How to make achievement tests and assessments* (5th ed.). Boston: Allyn and Bacon.

A much more detailed discussion than we have had space to present of the techniques for developing achievement test items. Discusses many variations of the basic types of items. Numerous examples are included, and the measurement of higher-level cognitive outcomes is emphasized.

Haladyna, T. M. (1994). *Developing and validating multiple-choice test items.* Hillsdale, NJ: Lawrence Erlbaum Associates.

The author defines the multiple-choice item format as a comprehensive category that encompasses a number of other objectively scored types of test item formats, including matching exercises, true–false items, complex multiple-choice items, context-dependent item sets, and multiple true–false items. The book focuses on developing multiple-choice items and validating responses to multiple-choice items.

Haladyna, T. M. (1997). *Writing test items to evaluate higher order thinking.* Boston: Allyn and Bacon.

Focuses on writing test items that assess cognitive outcomes beyond the recall level. It is a practical, nontechnical paperback written for practicing teachers and prospective teachers.

SUGGESTION SHEET

If your last name starts with the letter K, please complete the Suggestion Sheet at the end of the book while this chapter is still fresh in your mind.

Answers to Chapter 8 Application Problems ■

1. The item asks which animal does not belong with the others. Unfortunately, there are a number of correct answers to this question, depending on what strategy is used to organize the information. One correct answer would be option c, using the rationale that the beaver is not indigenous to Africa as are all the others. Another correct answer would be d, using the rationale that the lion is the only animal that is not comfortable spending substantial amounts of time in the water. Another correct answer would be b, using the rationale that the crocodile is the only animal listed that is not a mammal. The item would be better if the stem were more specific, for example, "Which of the following animals is not a mammal?"

2. There are a number of problems with this matching exercise. First, even if you want to use such a heterogeneous group of items, the directions could be made much clearer. More appropriate directions would read something like the following:

Directions: Two columns of information are listed below. Place the letter corresponding to the appropriate person or place from the list on the right in front of the number that matches from the list on the left. Each person or place can be used only once.

Of course, the exercise is more heterogeneous than we would recommend for a single matching exercise. Four of the options are names of cities, one is a country, four are names of persons, and one is a plural noun. There are also several clues that would enable a student to get some credit even if he or she had not mastered the material. For example, only one item calls for the name of a country and there is only one country listed in the options. Only four items need to be matched with the names of persons. Without too much difficulty, the student can make some pretty good guesses at these items. For example, item 3 is probably a French name. Of the four possible names (d, f, g, and i), only Marquis de Lafayette sounds French. Item 3 is a "give-away" because most people associate Benedict Arnold with being a traitor even if they've never studied American History. Thus, the student has a 50/50 chance on the remaining two names. Item 8 is the only item that calls for a plural ("they"), and so option a is another giveaway. If you look carefully, you can see a number of other clues a testwise student could use to get a good score on this item without having mastered the material.

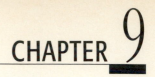

The Process of Becoming an Expert Tester

Assembly, Administration, and Analysis

OVERVIEW

We have never met a perfect tester. In fact, there are very few expert testers, but the secret to becoming better is twofold. First, remember that testing consists of more than writing technically correct items. Second, use your experience and the information available from past tests to improve your skills as a test developer and administrator.

This chapter summarizes a process and teaches you the skills you will need to improve your ability as an educational tester. Having mastered the skills of writing technically correct items (Chapters 7 and 8), you are now ready to master the skills that separate the professionals from the also-rans.

The purpose of testing is to produce accurate information about students' knowledge, skills, and attitudes. But even the best items can yield misleading or inaccurate information if the test is inappropriately assembled or administered. By analyzing the results of items you write, you can continually improve their quality. This chapter describes a cyclical process (consisting of assembly, administration, analysis), which can be used to substantially improve the quality and usefulness of information produced by tests.

OBJECTIVES

Upon completing your study of this chapter, you should be able to

1. Describe the advantages in and procedures for maintaining a file of test items.
2. Summarize the issues that should be considered in reviewing test items.

3. Explain how individual items should be arranged and formatted for a test.
4. Describe the key elements of good test directions.
5. Explain how to make testing a positive and productive experience for students.
6. Explain the pros and cons of different scoring techniques.
7. Explain how to discuss test results with students.
8. Explain the benefits and dangers of using item analysis procedures.
9. Demonstrate an item analysis procedure that can be used with teacher-made, norm-referenced tests.
10. Demonstrate an item analysis procedure that can be used with teacher-made criterion-referenced tests.

Assembling the Test

Most tests you give will be ones you have written. If you think about tests like Christmas presents, commercially available tests come preassembled, but teacher-made tests have to be assembled before they are given. Unfortunately, like the exhausted parent on Christmas eve trying to assemble the bicycle from "easy-to-read" instructions, teachers often leave test assembly to the last minute when they are exhausted and not likely to do their best work.

The process of assembling a good test can be broken into four steps.

- Collecting or developing test items
- Reviewing test items
- Formatting the test
- Preparing directions for the test

If you purchase a standardized test, these steps have already been completed. But for tests you develop, you will have to do all these steps yourself.

Collecting Test Items

Some teachers write test items a few hours before administering the test. The dangers (as well as the unnecessary stress) of this approach are obvious. A better procedure is to regularly develop item cards such as the one shown in Figure 9.1. Such cards can be written as you prepare lesson plans or at the end of each teaching session. By developing items as you teach each day, it is easier to create items for those aspects of instruction that you consider most important.

A collection of such cards is referred to as a *test item file.* Such a file gives greater flexibility and will lead to more effective tests. For example, you will always teach more material than you can include in a test. If you have already prepared items for all of your lesson concepts, you can select a representative sample, or items to emphasize particular concepts. A pool of items also allows you to develop

COURSE _History_   UNIT _Revolutionary War_

OBJECTIVE

ITEM

Who was the most influential in convincing the French to assist the Americans during the Revolutionary War with England?

- a) George Washington
- b) Marquis de Lafayette
- *c) Benjamin Franklin
- d) Benedict Arnold
- e) Count de Rochambeau

Date of last revison: _November 1991_

FIGURE 9.1   Example of Test Item Card

parallel forms of a test so that you can give students practice or makeup tests. Practice tests give students an opportunity to become familiar with the test-taking format you use so that their test performance will show what they know, instead of how well they have mastered the format and procedures.

A test item file also increases test security because you will have many more items than will be administered on any single test. Thus you can use different items each time, making it impossible for students to cheat by obtaining a copy of a previous test. A test item file also contributes to the development of technically adequate items. If you have a pool of items from which to choose, you can afford to discard or rework items that exhibit weaknesses based on analyses of prior use.

Finally, an item file can help to focus your teaching. Usually you will want to be teaching content that can be measured by a test item. Having a test item file provides a convenient way of double checking the importance of material included in your lesson plans. If there are not items in your test file for the information being taught, you should usually either create items, or reevaluate the amount of time spent teaching that concept. Obviously, there are some important concepts for which it is difficult, if not impossible, to create a test item. But the majority of information covered should be testable as well as teachable.

Instead of maintaining a card file of test items, a teacher may wish to store test items in a computer file. Developments in microcomputer technology have made it possible to facilitate the process of writing test items, creating test item files, and generating tests from these files (Baker 1989; Ward & Murray-Ward, 1994). An indexed collection of test items stored in a computer file is called an item bank. One of the main advantages of having an item bank is that equivalent forms of a test can be generated from the items in the bank. Some teachers use traditional word processors and database management software to create item banks and generate tests (Vockell & Fiore, 1993), but several software companies now manufacture software packages that are specially designed for this purpose. In addition to allowing the user to store and retrieve individual test items, a good item banking program allows the user to write new items and to produce tests in a ready-to-administer form. Some authors refer to such programs as test generators (Roid, 1989; Vockell & Fiore, 1993).

Baker (1989) as well as Ward and Murray-Ward (1994) describe different kinds of information that should be included in an item bank. At a minimum, this information should include (1) the text of each individual test item with any accompanying graphics, (2) coded descriptive information that can be used to classify and access individual items by variables such as subject, item format, and objective, and (3) statistical information discussed later in this chapter about the item's previous use and performance such as its difficulty index, discrimination index, frequency of use, and the date of its last use.

Test generators are generally designed to treat each individual test item as distinct pieces of information that can be stored and retrieved as single units. Consequently, a common limitation of these programs is that they are not designed to handle a series or cluster of items that function as a set. Hence they typically do not accommodate either context-dependent item sets or matching exercises.

Teachers who are proficient at using a word processor may be disappointed with existing test generators because of their inflexibility and limited word processing capabilities. Such teachers may be better advised to use their word processor to create a series of text files, each consisting of test items related to a particular instructional unit. This process will make it easier for users to enter and revise individual items, but they will have to cut and paste from different files each time they create a test. Although this may seem cumbersome, some teachers may be willing to make this tradeoff in order to gain greater efficiency in entering and editing items, greater flexibility in the kinds of items permitted, and more options in designing the output layout.

A microcomputer equipped with item-banking software can be a helpful means of expediting the process of creating and maintaining a test item file and using it to generate tests, but prospective users should not assume that the computer will solve all the problems associated with the job of creating and maintaining a set of high-quality test items. Potential buyers should carefully compare the capabilities and limitations of several competing programs before selecting one. They should also realize that the main responsibility for quality assurance rests on the user. The quality of the resulting tests depends upon the quality of the items that make up the file and the choices the user makes when instructing the test generator how to select items from the file. Test generators are just as susceptible to the "garbage in, garbage out" phenomenon as any other computer application.

Also, teachers who use computers to create and store test item files should take adequate security precautions to prevent unauthorized access to their test files. At a minimum, these precautions should include steps to prevent students from gaining unauthorized access to the items or the answer key, and to prevent them from altering their scores on completed tests.

Reviewing Test Items

One major advantage of a test item file (whether you keep it on index cards or in a computer) is that you will have time to review and refine items prior to each use. You can even have other people review the items to see whether the test results are likely to provide useful information. No matter how carefully items have been written, some will inevitably have weaknesses. For example, there may be verbal clues to the correct answer in the item stem. An item may be too difficult or may contain distractors that are implausible. Sometimes, a second correct answer will mistakenly be included in a multiple-choice item. Your test-writing skills will improve substantially if you set items aside for a few days after writing them, and then review them from the vantage point of the test taker.

As you review items, remember that each should provide information about how well students have mastered the content you are teaching. The following questions may help in refining the items you have written:

1. *Is the item format appropriate for what you want to test?* The item should require students to exhibit the type of behavior you wanted them to learn. For example, identifying the correct definition among a group of possible alternatives is very different from providing the correct definition when no alternatives are presented. In the former case, a multiple-choice item would be appropriate, but in the latter, a short-answer format would be better.

2. *Is the intent of the item clear and unambiguous?* Whether a student answers an item correctly should always be a function of how well he or she has mastered the content, not whether he or she understands the question. For example, items should have no awkward sentence construction, "double-barreled" questions, inappropriate vocabulary, or ambiguous intent. Reviewing items some time after writing them will help you to identify problems you may have missed as the item was written.

3. *Is the item straightforward and concise?* Some item writers include extra material in the introduction of an item, as if to justify the content being tested, or perhaps in an effort to make the item more interesting. Such information may distract students from what is being tested and give an advantage to better readers. In most cases, items should be as concise as possible. Information not contributing directly to the skill being tested should be eliminated.

4. *Is the item written at the appropriate level of difficulty?* The difficulty level for criterion-referenced or mastery tests should be very different from that for norm-referenced tests. In a mastery test, you want to know whether all students have mastered the minimum competencies. If instruction has been successful, you would expect all students to get most items correct. For a norm-referenced test, you want items that will "spread out" the members of the class, creating a continuum where there is a direct relationship between how well students have mastered the material and how many items they answer correctly. Ideally, with a norm-referenced test, about 50 percent of the class would answer most items correctly.

5. *Does the item have a "best" answer?* Items that test students' knowledge of factual material should have unambiguous correct answers (for example, 11 + 14 always equals 25). Items that ask students to provide the *best* answer or make the *most appropriate* interpretation can be problematic unless the distractors are carefully worded.

6. *Is the item free from bias?* All items should be written in language that is acceptable, nonoffensive, and equally understandable to different groups of people. Stereotypes (for example, men consistently in executive roles, minorities in subservient roles, or women in homemaking roles) should be avoided.

7. *Is the item free from irrelevant clues?* Some items contain clues that allow a person to get the correct answer without having mastered the content. Such technical errors are often apparent only after an item has been set aside for a while.

Until now, the review process has focused on individual items. Even if you had perfect individual items, however, combining them into a test can create problems unless you pay attention to the following issues:

1. *Is the group of items representative of the course content?* Although it is usually impossible, because of time, to test all the material you have taught, make sure that items included on the test are *representative* of the material covered. In a course on American history, for instance, you would not want all the items to be based on the post–World War II era. Referencing items to course objectives, or to a test blueprint during the assembly process, helps to assess representativeness.

2. *Do the items adequately cover the material taught?* Coverage goes beyond representativeness by asking whether items provide the information necessary to make desired interpretations. For example, consider a test on American history that contains one true–false item from each of the following periods:

Prior to and including the Revolutionary War
Between the Revolutionary War and the Civil War
Between the Civil War and World War I
After World War I

Such a test could be said to be representative of American history in that each period is equally represented by items. Nonetheless, it probably does not provide enough information about any single period to allow meaningful interpretations. Although the number of items needed to make such interpretations will vary depending on the purpose of the course and the age of students, adequate coverage of each period will usually require more than a single item.

3. *Is the group of items free from unnecessary overlap and duplication?* Unnecessary duplication occurs when you have a number of items testing the same objective, but no items testing other equally important objectives.

4. *Are items independent?* Sometimes the stem of one item provides an unnecessary clue to the answer of another. Other times, items are written so that the correct answer can be known only if previous items have been answered correctly. In most cases, items should be independent. However, individual items within a context-dependent set are not always independent of each other. Consequently, some educational measurement specialists recommend that the items within each set be scored as a set instead of as individual items (Rosenbaum, 1988).

5. *Is the time required to answer the items appropriate?* Balancing the need for greater coverage or more in-depth information with appropriate expectations for students' endurance and concentration is always difficult. You are in the best position to estimate your students' attention span and the length of time they can work at full capacity. Gauge the length of the test for the attention span of the lower third of the class rather than for the best students. In this way, students' ability to remain on task is less likely to play a role in their performance.

Application Problem 1

Assume you are a seventh-grade biology teacher. A friend who is teaching seventh-grade biology in another school asks you to review her midterm examination because she knows you have been teaching this class. Describe briefly the issues you would consider in reviewing her test.

Formatting the Test

Imagine you have all the components necessary to assemble a computer laid out on the table in front of you. Even though each component has been engineered to exact specifications, you couldn't produce a functioning computer by putting all the components into a bag and rattling them around for a while. Similarly, items haphazardly tossed together will not produce a coherent or effective test. Having developed, reviewed, and fine-tuned test items, it is important to assemble them correctly. The following guidelines will help:

1. *Items with similar formats should be grouped together.* A test will be more understandable if all the true–false items are grouped together, all the matching items are grouped together, and so on. Grouping items that use a similar format has several advantages. First, fewer sets of directions are required. Second, students can answer more items in the same amount of time because they do not have to continually "switch mental gears." Third, scoring—particularly handscoring—is facilitated. And, fourth, there is less chance that students will be confused by alternating formats.

2. *Proceed from the easiest to the most difficult items.* How frustrating it must be for a student who is already apprehensive to discover he or she is unable to answer the first five questions. Many measurement experts believe that putting a few items that everyone can answer at the beginning of the test gives students confidence and allows them to better demonstrate what they really know (Sax & Cromak, 1966; Towne & Merrill, 1975). Although the position is logical, the empirical evidence is inconclusive (Hambleton & Traub, 1974; Klosner & Gellman, 1973). Nevertheless, in the absence of contrary evidence, it is probably best to arrange items from easiest to hardest.

3. *Make the test as readable as possible.* Tests that are neatly typed with clear illustrations and uncrowded spacing seem less threatening and difficult. Be sure that each item is distinct from the others. Diagrams or drawings should be accurately portrayed and placed above the stem of the item so that students do not lose track of what is being asked. Keep the stem of the item and the options on the same page so that students do not miss information or have to flip back and forth to answer questions. When matching exercises or context-dependent item sets are used, all the items in a set should be kept on the same page.

4. *Avoid predictable response patterns.* Answers should not follow a predictable pattern: for example, TFTFTF, or CDBACDBA. Rather, answers should be arranged in an unpredictable or random pattern. That way, students will not waste time trying to figure out the pattern, but will focus on answering the questions.

Preparing Directions for the Test

The teacher who spends a lot of time carefully developing test items and assembling them into a representative test only to throw directions together at the last minute is like the expedition leader who carefully assembles his or her equipment, engages in weeks of physical conditioning, and then sets off without a map.

Clear, concise, understandable test directions are essential if a test is to accomplish its purpose. It is particularly important that the directions be understood by *all* students taking the test—especially those who have difficulty reading or using standard English. It is often worthwhile to read directions aloud to the students while they follow along. Directions should always be written, even if given orally, because written directions provide a source of information for students to refer to during the test. Test directions should explain what the student is to do, how to do it, where to record the answers, and how the information will be used. The following guidelines can assist you in preparing test directions:

1. *Provide a specific set of directions for each different type of item format.* Although general directions are useful, each group of items with a similar format should have directions explaining how answers are to be recorded, what to do about guessing, and how many points each item is worth.

2. *Explain the basis for scoring.* Directions should indicate whether partial credit will be given; whether points will be subtracted for lack of neatness, grammatical errors, or spelling mistakes; and whether students are expected to show their work.

3. *Specify the amount of available time.* In addition to noting how much time students have for the entire test, indicate the approximate time expected for each section so that students can pace themselves. Such guidelines also help students know how much detail is expected. It is usually better to provide too much time than to make time limits so restrictive that some cannot finish.

4. *In addition to providing written directions, make sure* every *student understands what is expected.* Because you want to know how well students have mastered the content being tested, instead of how well they can understand the directions, it is important to make sure they understand what is expected. Written directions should be sufficiently detailed so that a student can understand exactly what is expected without having it discussed orally. However, for those students who have difficulty processing written information, it is important to discuss the test directions.

It is often useful to try out your directions with other teachers or with pupils of about the same age and ability level as your own before an actual test. Having others read through the directions and explain which parts are unclear or confusing can save substantial time during the test administration. A particularly useful technique is to ask reviewers to explain in their own words what they think is required on the test. Figure 9.2 provides you with a checklist that will assist you in assembling a good test.

TEST ASSEMBLY CHECKLIST

____ 1. Are items clear, concise, and free from jargon or unnecessarily difficult vocabulary?

____ 2. Do items avoid sexual or racial bias?

____ 3. Has someone else reviewed the items?

____ 4. Has the answer key been checked?

____ 5. Are items grouped according to type or format?

____ 6. Are items arranged from easiest to most difficult?

____ 7. Are items appropriately spaced?

____ 8. Are items stems, options, and support material (e.g., diagrams) appropriately arranged?

____ 9. Is the answer sequence random?

____ 10. Are items representative of the material taught?

____ 11. Can the test be completed in a reasonable time?

____ 12. Have directions been checked for clarity?

____ 13. Has someone else proofread the final copy for errors?

____ 14. Is a space provided for students to write their names?

FIGURE 9.2   A Checklist to Use in Assembling Items into a Useful Test

Application Problem 2

The following directions are for a true–false test in a fifth-grade social studies class.

Directions: Listed below are 30 questions. For each question, circle whether you think the answer is True (T) or False (F).

What else should be included?

Administering the Test

Although there are some differences, the general principles of test administration apply both to commercially available and teacher-made tests. Whether the test is a norm-referenced, criterion-referenced, applied performance, or a weekly quiz, certain principles will make results more valid and usable (not to mention the fact that proper test administration will reduce students' anxiety).

It is important to remember that all classroom activities, including testing, should be *positive experiences* that result in *productive outcomes*. Students should leave the test feeling good about themselves and the work they have accomplished. Furthermore, the test should produce valid information about how well students have mastered the goals of instruction, and it should contribute to more effective future instruction.

All tests should give students a fair opportunity to demonstrate their mastery of whatever is being measured. Therefore, the test taking environment should be structured so that factors other than students' mastery of learning outcomes are minimized. If we are giving a chemistry test, we want the students' scores to reflect their knowledge of chemistry, not their test-taking ability, mood, or ability to ignore distracting influences during testing.

Test taking will be a positive and productive experience for both students and teachers if we create a situation in which (1) students have mastered appropriate test-taking skills, (2) students are motivated to try their best, and (3) appropriate test administration procedures are used. Here are some guidelines to help you in creating such an environment.

1. *Be positive!* Threatening students with tests if they misbehave, or with negative consequences if they fail a test, will convince them that tests are punishments rather than educational tools. Testing is already a traumatic experience for some students. Teachers can reduce the anxiety associated with testing by approaching it as a normal, important part of the educational experience and by demonstrating throughout the year that test results *will* be used to improve instruction. It is also important to convince students that they will be valued regardless of their test scores.

2. *Make sure the physical space is appropriate.* Tests should be administered in a physical setting that is familiar, and comfortable, whether it is an end-of-year standardized achievement test or a regularly scheduled Wednesday quiz. A simple way to reduce unnecessary distractions is to close the classroom door and hang a sign on the outside that says, DO NOT DISTURB—TESTING. Check the seating arrangement. Students should not feel tempted to look at others' papers or be distracted every time someone needs to sharpen a pencil or leave the room. Having an aide assist with testing is highly desirable. Because most standardized achievement tests use aides during norming, you should particularly try to use an aide during standardized achievement testing.

3. *Motivate students to do their best.* Balance your efforts at reducing test anxiety with communicating a need for students to do their best. Research has demonstrated that highly motivated students do substantially better on standardized achievement and aptitude tests than similar, unmotivated students (Taylor & White, 1982). One of the most effective ways to reduce anxiety and increase motivation is to honestly convey to students the valuable contribution that testing makes to improving the teaching and learning process. Students who understand the reasons for testing are likely to do much better.

Avoid making statements that suggest that test results do not matter or that testing is unimportant. Imagine how students will respond if the teacher announces a test by saying,

I know you would rather be doing other things today and so would I. Unfortunately, the school board is requiring us to take this stupid test. You probably won't know a lot of the answers, and I don't really care how you do because I don't use the results anyway. But I will get in trouble if I don't give you the test, so let's just get through it as best we can.

4. *Know the test.* If you have developed the test yourself, you will already be familiar with the content and format. With standardized achievement tests, however, becoming familiar with the test requires extra effort. One of the best ways to become familiar with a test is to take it yourself. Admittedly, this is time consuming, but you're likely to find it time well spent. Afterwards, you'll have a much better idea how results can be useful in teaching, and you will understand how students might become confused or frustrated by various items.

5. *Make sure students understand what they are to do.* Standardized achievement tests often require students to do things that are outside their regular routine. Without careful preparation, such tests may measure students' test-taking skills rather than their knowledge of content or skill in applying that knowledge. For example, standardized achievement tests require students to answer questions in formats that may be unfamiliar, to understand vocabulary that they may not have heard before, and to work more independently than usual. Since these expectations are not a part of most day-to-day classroom environments, some students may have difficulty demonstrating their knowledge of the content being tested. Consider the results of a study conducted by White and Carcelli (1982). Second-grade students were tested on exactly the same arithmetic items presented in eight different formats from popular standardized achievement tests. As Figure 9.3 shows, students' scores ranged from 26 percent correct to 81 percent correct.

Similar examples abound. The best way to make sure students understand what they are to do is to administer a *practice test* that is similar in format and content to the actual test. Almost all widely used standardized achievement tests provide practice tests and base their norms on test administrations that gave practice tests. Such practice tests tend to reduce students' anxiety by giving them a chance to become familiar with format and procedures. Students who are less anxious are in a better position to demonstrate what they really know—thus increasing the value of test results.

Your responsibility to make sure students understand what is being asked of them does not end with the practice test. During test administration, you may clarify directions as long as such clarification is not expressly prohibited by the standardized instructions. Most directions for standardized achievement tests allow students to ask questions after the directions have been given. However, most students are reluctant to pose questions. An alert teacher will watch for students who seem confused and make sure they understand what is expected before commencing the test.

6. *Equalize advantages.* Some students are better test takers than others. Do what you can to equalize test-taking skills. For example, you might instruct students when it is best to guess at answers they don't know, and remind them about the general test-taking strategies such as checking answers if they finish early, and skipping over difficult items and coming back to them later. Never give hints to stu-

TYPE OF FORMAT		RESULTS Percentage Correct on 12 Items
FORMAT #1	Wide Range Achievement Test Level I "Jack had six marbles. He found two more. How many did he have?" Oral response	43%
FORMAT #2	Stanford Achievement Test Level II Form A "Read the problem to yourself and then mark under your answer." 11 6 5 N $2 + \square = 8$ O O O O	39%
FORMAT #3	Stanford Achievement Test 2 26 8 5 N $+6$ O O O O	74%
FORMAT #4	SRA Achievement series Level C Form 1 "Work the problem, then fill in the space in front of the right answer." 2 8 4 26 12 $+6$ O O O O	81%
FORMAT #5	Iowa Test of Basic Skills Level 7 Form 7 "What is two added to six? What is two plus six? Mark your answer in the row with the bird." 7 8 10 N 🖐 O O O O	78%
FORMAT #6	Iowa Test of Basic Skills $6 + 2 =$ 12 8 9 N O O O O	67%
FORMAT #7	Key Math "These are addition problems. You may use a pencil if you wish." 6 $+2$	72%
FORMAT #8	Key Math "Tell me about the number that goes in the box" $6 + \square = 8$	26%

FIGURE 9.3 Percentage Correct for 12 Arithmetic Items Answered by Students Using Different Formats

Source: White and Carcelli, 1982.

dents about the correct answers. Make sure all students understand rules about time limits, marking answer sheets, and clarifying directions. Keep the amount of time between breaks appropriate for those students with less endurance or shorter attention spans. A general guideline for the maximum amount of testing between breaks is given here.

Grade	Amount of Testing Time
K–3	30 minutes
4–6	60 minutes
7–12	90 minutes

7. *Monitor the test administration.* Most of us have seen teachers who pass out tests and then grade papers or read while students work. The fact that the tests have been distributed does not mean that the teacher can take a break. Indeed, this is one of the most important times if the students are to be able to demonstrate what they really know. The teacher is responsible for minimizing distractions, preventing cheating, and keeping students on task. Circulating about the room and establishing eye-to-eye contact or prompting a student whose attention is beginning to wander are ways of keeping students on task.

Cheating is more of a problem. Thirty years ago, DeCecco (1968, p. 640), noted,

> Failure to prevent cheating may have serious deleterious effects on student achievement: 1) when cheating occurs with impunity, honest achievement goes unrecognized or punished and reduces student motivation to achieve; 2) there is no way to assess validly or reliably what the student has or has not learned; and, 3) ingenuity in devising ways to cheat becomes more important than attainment of the instructional objectives.

The same is true today. Recognized problems with cheating have led to such countermeasures as alternative seating arrangements or parallel testing forms, but research has shown that such techniques are not particularly effective (Houston, 1976). What's more, they're often impractical. Where there is good student–teacher rapport, and students are convinced that tests are helpful rather than punishing, cheating is less of a problem. An alert teacher who carefully monitors test administration with the intent of helping students do their best seems to be the best deterrent to cheating.

8. *Documenting threats to test validity.* No amount of preparation can totally remove the influence of unexpected events that impact on the validity of a particular test for a specific student. If Rachael is not feeling well the day of a test, it doesn't matter that she has good test-taking skills, feels positive about tests in general, and is motivated to do her best. She still won't perform well. Such threats to test validity are less a problem for interpreting the results of locally developed tests since they are given more frequently, and substandard performance on any single test will be balanced by more typical performance on others. Because standardized achievement tests are given infrequently, however, you should be particularly alert for incidents that may explain a lower than deserved score for a particular student.

Student Name					Comments
John Albania		X			
Frank Savage					
Harriet Rosenbaum					
Tom Braddock			X		typical lack of attention, needs help before next test.
Liza Melmed					
Gary Barnett				X	
Chuck Harris			X		
Chris Henkle					
Nadine Olson			X		
Marcia Golonca					
Katie Smith					
Monica Thomas	X				not sure she knew what was expected on matching exercise.
Cheryl Nilson					
Reed Rowland	X	X	X	?	didn't appear to feel well, may have been copying from Mark.
Mark Argstrom					
Brad Illich					
Marcia Gonzales			X		left unusually early, which is not like her.
Carl Englestrom					
Harold Nordica					
Sophia Zimmerman		X			
Vicky Roskle		X			

April 18, 1992 (Date of Test)   SAT-Word Attack (Name of Test)

FIGURE 9.4   Example of a Completed "Teacher Index to Valid Test Performance" for a Standardized Achievement Test

Although you will usually not have the luxury of readministering a standardized achievement test for students who do poorly, it is important to note factors that may have contributed to their subpar performance. Such information can help you interpret test results and make better instructional decisions. One way of doing this is by using the *Teacher Index to Valid Test Performance* (Taylor et al., 1982). An example of what this index might look like when completed for a typical third-grade class during standardized achievement testing is shown in Figure 9.4.

Standards for Test Administration

Problems caused by poor test administration have prompted a number of organizations to develop standards and guidelines to govern testing. One particularly clear set of standards was developed by the American Psychological Association (1985). Standards from that document that are most relevant for testing in schools are given here.

Standard 15.1	In typical applications, test administrators should follow carefully the standardized procedures for administration and scoring specified by the test publisher. Specifications regarding instructions to test takers, time limits, the form of item presentation or response, and test materials or equipment should be strictly observed.
Standard 15.2	The testing environment should be one of reasonable comfort and with minimal distractions. Testing materials should be readable and understandable.
Standard 15.3	Reasonable efforts should be made to assure the validity of test scores by eliminating opportunities for test takers to attain scores by fraudulent means.
Standard 15.4	In school situations not involving admissions . . . , any modification of standard test administration procedures or scoring should be described in the testing reports with appropriate cautions regarding the possible effects of such modifications on validity.
Standard 15.7	Test users should protect the security of test materials. (AERA et al., pp. 83–84)

Another important test administration issue is the competence of those who administer the tests. Some tests should be administered only by those who have had extensive training and experience in using those precise instruments, whereas other tests can be administered with basic instructions and limited orientation. Although there are exceptions, the degree of competence generally required to administer various types of tests is outlined as follows:

Type of Test	Necessary Qualifications
Projective tests (e.g., Rorschach) Personality tests Individual intelligence tests (e.g., WISC-R)	Extensive training and experience in administering these instruments, and in the underlying psychometric theory
Aptitude tests Interest and inventory tests Attitude tests Teacher-made tests	Knowledge of the principles of testing, including some acquaintance with its technical and statistical aspects
Standardized achievement tests	Orientation to the testing procedures and familiarity with content of the test manual

We do not hold with the prevalent view that classroom teachers are not competent to use educational tests (although we do agree that some test administrations require special competence, as noted earlier). The words of McCall (1936) echo to us from a half a century ago.

Many years ago, certain specialists sought to secure a monopoly of the privilege of using standard tests by trying to persuade educators to regard the tests as possessing certain mystic properties. A few of us with Promethean tendencies set about taking these sacred cows away from the gods and giving them to mortals. Can teachers be entrusted with tests? If not, then teachers ought not to be trusted with 90% of their present functions. We now entrust them with the far more difficult task of teaching reading, creating concepts, and building ideals. Let us not strain at a gnat when we have swallowed fifty elephants (p. 3).

We share McCall's viewpoint. Teachers can and should be taught to use tests well.

Scoring Tests

When students hand in their tests, their work is done, but yours is just beginning. How will you score the tests? There are many different techniques, each offering advantages and disadvantages. The "best" technique depends on the type of test, the ages and abilities of the students, and the resources available. During your own experience taking tests, you were probably exposed to most scoring techniques, but did not pay much attention since you were more concerned about your score than the process used to produce it. To get an idea of the issues you are facing now, try your hand at the following quiz. Mark each item with a T or F.

1. Separate answer sheets are always preferred for objective tests because they provide a more accurate measure of what the student really knows.
2. By weighting items differentially, you can substantially improve the precision and validity of a test.
3. Computerized scoring services should not be trusted because of the errors made by optical scanning equipment.
4. Before submitting tests to a publisher's scoring service, you should not make or erase any marks on the separate answer sheet that accompanies the test.
5. Once tests have been corrected and handed back, it is acceptable to give credit for an alternative answer.
6. It is always inappropriate to consider factors other than the content being tested (neatness, spelling, grammar, and so on).
7. Discussing specific items on the tests with students too soon after the test has been completed often results in unnecessary anxiety and frustration.

Scoring a test is not just a matter of marking answers and adding up numbers. Issues such as those in the preceding quiz (incidentally, all the answers except number 5 are false) emphasize the need to be informed about different approaches to scoring. We will focus on objective tests since they constitute the majority of the tests you will be administering and scoring.[1] With objective tests, you have two basic choices: hand scoring and machine scoring.

Hand Scoring

Because scoring objective tests is essentially a clerical task, many educators do not devote as much attention to it as they should. Unfortunately, there are many opportunities to make mistakes. For example, Phillips and Weathers (1958) found

---

[1] In Chapter 8, we discussed ways to improve the scoring of essay tests.

mistakes in almost 30 percent of approximately 5000 Stanford Achievement Tests scored by teachers as a part of their regular administration. Goodwin (1966) found similar results when the tests were scored by clerks.

A number of techniques have been developed to increase the efficiency and reduce the errors in scoring tests. One is to prepare an answer key on a strip of paper that you can lay over the student's paper alongside the answers. This enables you to score rapidly. But rather than just marking the incorrect responses, it's a good idea to mark every item—perhaps by using a ÷ for correct answers, and an x for incorrect answers.

Another method is to use a stencil the same size as the response sheet with holes punched out to note the location of the correct answers. This stencil, often referred to as a *scoring template,* can be laid over the top of the student's test form, and a mark made in each hole where no student answer is present. Before using such a key, you should scan the answer sheets to identify any questions for which more than one alternative was selected.

If separate answer sheets are used, students must be familiar with the format and process necessary to complete them. Always administer a practice test using the same type of answer sheet. Research suggests that separate answer sheets should not be used with children at the second grade or under (Cashen & Ramseyer, 1969; Ramseyer & Cashen, 1971; Gaffney & Mcguire, 1971); older children, however, can use them quite successfully.

Before giving the test, develop an answer key even if you wrote the questions yourself. This may sound obvious, yet many people have been embarrassed by skipping this step, then discovering that some questions had multiple correct answers.

If you hand score tests, you will likely be doing the scoring yourself. However, if you have clerical assistants, remember that they will probably not be as motivated as you, and consequently may not be as careful. Make sure that clerical assistants have been thoroughly trained and have had an opportunity to score practice tests before doing the actual tests. You should also have about 10 percent of the tests rescored during each scoring session to check error rates. If you discover that an unacceptable number of errors are being made, you should rescore all the tests. Having scorers initial each test is useful since they are more likely to be careful if they know that mistakes can be traced to them.

Although a great deal has been written about weighting test items differentially, there is no evidence that this results in more reliable scores (for example, Echternacht, 1976; Hakstian & Kansup, 1975; Raffeld, 1975). Differential weighting does make scoring more complex and introduces more opportunity for error.

Should students be given credit for partial knowledge of test content? This is a difficult question. One way of giving partial credit is to have students indicate how confident they are of each response. But although this method has received a great deal of interest among psychometricians, there is little evidence to suggest that it makes scores more reliable or valid. Furthermore, it introduces another variable of complexity, which can result in other errors. Our advice at present is that weighting systems and confidence-scoring procedures are not worth the extra effort.

There is nothing wrong with having such variables as neatness, spelling, grammar, or completeness of computations considered in scoring. However, it is essential to inform students well before the test if such variables are to be included in the score.

Machine Scoring

Given proper preparations, machine scoring can be very efficient and accurate. Although machine scoring (a combination of an optical scanner and a computer) is most common for commercially available tests, many larger school systems have test-scoring machines for locally developed tests as well. The general guidelines are the same.

First, make sure that students are familiar with the format and the procedures for providing answers. This is especially critical if a separate answer sheet is used. Give a practice test prior to the actual test so that there won't be unnecessary anxiety or confusion. Second, after students have finished the test, check the answer sheets to make sure they have been filled out completely. Darken any answers that have been filled in too lightly (otherwise, the optical scanning machine may miss them), and erase any stray marks or marginal notes the student has made. If such marks are not erased, the optical scanner may count them as intended responses. When multiple answers are marked where a single answer was requested, they will generally be marked incorrect but check to see how your program does it.

Discussing Test Results with Students

Think about your own experience taking tests. When you did well, you felt the test was fair, and felt good about yourself and the teacher. What about those times when you didn't do so well? You were probably frustrated and may have thought that the test was unfair. Those feelings emphasize the need, clearly supported by research, for discussing test results with students (Anderson, Kulhavy, & Andre, 1971; Wexley & Thornton, 1972). Such discussion, often referred to as debriefing, not only gives them an opportunity to "let off steam," but often results in substantially improved test items and a valuable learning experience for them.

Here are a few guidelines about handling such a debriefing. First, debrief as soon after testing as feasible when impressions are still fresh. You will occasionally discover items that are subject to misinterpretation. Discuss such discoveries before handing tests back to students. Let students know that you are receptive to ideas about improving the test. But remember that students are more likely to listen if they do not yet have tests in their hands and are not thinking about their grades.

After you have returned the tests, listen to students' reactions. The purpose of such discussion is to improve the tests and help students learn. As they raise issues about specific items, let them know that you will not be changing any scores until you have considered those issues. Ask them to write brief notes about any items they would like reconsidered. Remember that students are likely to be more emotionally involved in their grades than you are. Throughout these discussions, be as nondefensive as possible. Remember that attacks on the unfairness of a test are not necessarily attacks on you personally.

If you do decide to make changes, make sure students know such changes will apply to all students, not just those who raised objections. Also, ask students to double check the arithmetic to make sure there are no clerical errors. Although students' feedback about the test can be useful, remember that the items they dislike the most are not necessarily bad. Student feedback should, therefore, be considered in conjunction with the results of analyses discussed in the next section.

Another important reason for discussing the test is to discover misconceptions students have about the content you have been teaching. Discussion after testing can help clarify instructional objectives and suggest how misunderstandings arose. Armed with such insights, you may find better ways to present the content.

Analyzing Test Items

Students will always remind you when you discuss test results that there is no such thing as a perfect test. Frank Baker summarized it well in the *Encyclopedia of Educational Research* (1982) when he said,

> But even when [the best techniques of item writing] are employed by a skilled item writer, the resulting items are an enigma. It is not possible to evaluate an item as "good," or "bad" by inspection alone. The content covered may be appropriate, the distracters plausible, and the vocabulary at the level of the target population of the examinees, yet the item may be "bad" in some sense. (p. 959)

Sounds hopeless, doesn't it? If bad items creep in like air pollution and higher taxes, what can a teacher do? Some teachers conclude that the "bad items" are the ones about which students complain the loudest. Not necessarily. This section provides some simple but powerful tools to assist you in improving the quality of test items. The tools we describe here are based on classical test theory and have been used by test developers for more than 50 years.[2] Unfortunately, they are not used

---

[2]Most professional test developers now use item analysis techniques based on item response theory (also referred to as latent trait theory). Although most psychometricians agree that item response theory offers significant advantages to classical test theory (Crocker & Algina, 1986; Hambleton, 1989; Yen, 1992), it has not been as widely used by classroom teachers because of its computational complexity and the requirement of large sample sizes for analyses. With the wider availability of computers and appropriate software, item response theory has gained popularity. However, for most classroom applications, using item response theory is like using a helicopter instead of a step ladder to climb up on your roof. Either one will get the job done, but the helicopter requires a much greater investment of time, money, and training. For most classroom applications, item analysis techniques based on classical test theory are more than adequate and will lead to the same conclusion with dramatically smaller investments. Suen (1990, Chapter 7) provides an easy-to-read introduction to the basic ideas of item response theory. In addition, Hambleton and Jones (1993), Loyd (1988), and McKinley (1989) are also helpful introductions to the basic concepts and applications. For a more extensive treatment of the issues and applications see Hambleton, Swaminathan, and Rogers (1991).

as frequently as they should be by classroom teachers. In the remainder of this chapter, we describe some simple step-by-step procedures for doing item analyses with norm-referenced and criterion-referenced tests.

Overview of Item Analysis Procedures

Before getting into specifics, let's look at the forest instead of the individual trees. The use of item analysis procedures with a norm-referenced test assumes that individuals possess knowledge or ability (for example, spelling ability, knowledge of history, musical aptitude) to varying degrees. Given a group of test items representative of that knowledge or skill, we expect people with more skill to do better on individual items than those with less skill. Thus there should be a positive correlation between success on any given item and total test score. Items that are negatively correlated with the total test score are viewed with suspicion. For example, if students who do well on the remainder of the test consistently miss a particular item, we should question whether that item is measuring something different, is miskeyed, is ambiguous, or is misleading.

Item analysis procedures provide a systematic method to examine items and determine whether students are answering them in suspicious ways. Item analysis results should never be the final word. Instead, item analyses provide clues for use in conjunction with the teacher's professional judgment by answering such questions as

- What percentage of people pass or fail a particular item?
- Were some options selected more or less frequently than expected?
- Were there items for which high scorers did poorly, or low scorers did well?
- Were there items that appear to be generally misunderstood, responded to randomly, or miskeyed?

In other words, item analyses tell you whether individual items functioned as you intended. Item analyses also offer the following fringe benefits:

- *Better class discussions of test results.* Although group discussion of test results can be an effective instructional technique, you do not want to spend time discussing items that most students already understand. The results of item analyses can help you focus on those concepts that students find difficult.
- *Better focus for reviews and remediation.* Item analysis will help you identify areas requiring review and remediation. For example, you may discover that a substantial part of the class doesn't understand subtraction items that require borrowing.
- *Assist in becoming a better teacher.* The results of item analysis help reveal which teaching strategies were most effective, allowing you to emphasize them in the future. You can also identify curriculum areas that are consistently too simple or too difficult to learn given current teaching techniques.
- *Improve test development skills.* Examining item analysis results will make you a better test constructor. You will become increasingly sensitive to such nagging problems as ambiguity, ineffective distracters, and poor wording. You will also learn to construct items that assess application and interpretation as well as knowledge.

The benefits of item analysis have been documented by research. For example, Blessum (1969), in a study with university faculty, concluded that the use of item analyses "resulted in an improvement, not only in the quality and fairness of each individual examination, but also in the technical and educational quality of successive tests" (p. 5). Given the substantial benefits associated with consistent use of item analysis data, more teachers should make the practice a part of their teaching repertoire.

A Step-by-Step Item Analysis Procedure for Classroom Use

Whether you are using a computer program or doing it by hand, the basic concepts of item analysis are the same. Because not all teachers have access to a computer item analysis program, we will describe a technique that is simple enough to be used without a computer, but accurate and complete enough to yield useful information. If you have a computer item analysis program, the rationale and principles summarized here can be applied just as well to the results of that program.

Let's assume we have an American history class of 32 students. We are analyzing a 50-item test on the Revolutionary War. To gather the information we need, we will be comparing the results of the ten highest-scoring students with those of the ten lowest-scoring students. Why do we select the ten highest- and lowest-scoring students? Kelley (1939) claimed that item analyses would be most accurate if based on the top and bottom 27 percent of the class; Henrysson (1971) recommended the upper and lower 33 percent; and D'Agostino and Cureton (1975) recommended the upper and lower 21 percent. For most applications, it doesn't matter whether you use 21, 25, 27, or 33 percent. Using the top and bottom ten students (25 percent to 40 percent of typical classrooms) makes the arithmetic easier and has minimal impact on results. We will also give you the general formula so that you can use the procedure with larger groups, but if you are doing item analyses for much larger groups of students (say, 150 or more), you may wish to use one of the many available computer programs.

A simple but accurate item analysis can be accomplished using steps we will illustrate with one of the multiple-choice items from our hypothetical American history test on the Revolutionary War. The same procedure is applicable for any item format (true-false, multiple choice, matching, or short-answer completion) for which there is a right and a wrong answer.

Assume you have just given the test to the 32 pupils in your class. You will conduct your item analysis using the steps listed here and then discussed in detail in what follows.

1. After scoring the papers, rank order them from highest to lowest scores.
2. Put the ten papers with the highest scores in one pile, and the ten papers with the lowest scores in another. Set aside the remaining papers since they will not be used in the analysis.

Number of students in high
and low scoring groups who
selected each option (n = 10
per group)

1. Who was the most influential in convincing the French to assist the Americans during the Revolutionary War with England?

High Scorers	Low Scorers	
0	1	(a) George Washington
1	4	(b) Marquis de Lafayette
8	2	* (c) Benjamin Franklin
0	0	(d) Benedict Arnold
1	3	(e) Count de Rochambeau

FIGURE 9.5   Item Analysis Results for One Item on an American History Test

3. For each test item, count the number of students in the high-scoring group who selected each alternative. Do the same for the students in the low-scoring group, and record this information as shown in Figure 9.5.
4. Compute the *difficulty level* (the percentage of the 20 students you are using in the analysis who got the item correct) of each item.
5. Compute the *discrimination index* (how well each option distinguishes between high scores and low scores) of each option.
6. Evaluate the *efficiency* of each of the options.

Let's discuss exactly how to do each of these steps. The first three consist of collecting and tabulating data necessary for the analyses. Clerical help can do this tabulation as long as you supervise it closely to ensure accuracy. As Figure 9.5 shows, none of the students in the high-scoring group selected George Washington as the correct answer, and only one of the students in the low-scoring group did so. The correct answer (Benjamin Franklin) was selected by eight students in the high-scoring group, and by only two students in the low-scoring group. Students in the low-scoring group opted most frequently for the French names (Marquis de Lafayette and Count de Rochambeau). Nobody selected Benedict Arnold.

The information in Figure 9.5 should begin to give you a feeling for the value of item analysis. About half the class got the item correct (10 of the 20 students included in the analysis), with most of the students in the high-scoring group getting the right answer, and most of the students in the low-scoring group selecting one of the incorrect options. Although this is the way you would expect it to be, think how important it would be to identify items where this was not so. If most students in the high-scoring group selected incorrect options, you would question whether the item was functioning as intended. That is exactly the purpose of item analysis—to reveal items to which students are responding in suspicious ways. Steps 4, 5, and 6 of the item analysis procedure provide a systematic way of identifying suspicious items. Let's discuss those steps now.

Computing Item Difficulty Level

The *difficulty level* of an item is the percentage of students who respond correctly to it. In cases where the calculation is based on 10 students in the high-scoring group and 10 students in the low-scoring group,[3] this will be the sum total of correct answers in the high- and low-scoring groups divided by 20. In our example, this translates to 8 plus 2 divided by 20, or 50 percent.

Most items in norm-referenced tests should have levels of difficulty in the 20 percent to 80 percent range so that scores will be spread out along a continuum of content mastery. If almost no one or almost everyone answers an item correctly, very little information is gained to spread students along this imaginary continuum. (Note that this rank ordering is very different from the purpose of criterion-referenced tests.) In our example, 50 percent of the class answered the item correctly. This assumes, of course, that the 12 students in the middle of the class scored about the same as students in the upper and lower groups. You could get a somewhat more precise estimate of the difficulty level for each item by including in your calculation the answers of this middle group, but experience has demonstrated that the small gain in precision rarely justifies the extra work.

Using 10 students from the upper and lower groups (wherever that is a reasonably close approximation of 25 percent of the total class) greatly simplifies your calculations. You should generally be able to compute the percentage in your head. Add together the number of students in the upper and lower groups who got the item correct ($8 + 2 = 10$), divide by 2 ($10 \div 2 = 5$), move the decimal one space to the right (50), and add a percentage sign (50%). You will soon be able to rapidly calculate the difficulty level of each item just by looking at the tabulated data. The item difficulty in our example is 50 percent, which is ideal. Ideal difficulty level, however, does not necessarily imply an ideal item.

Computing the Discrimination Index

The *discrimination index* of each item tells how well that item distinguishes between students who did well on the total test and those who did poorly. The discrimination index is computed by subtracting the number of students who got the item right in the low-scoring group from the number of students who got the item right in the high-scoring group, and dividing the answer by the size of each group. For the illustrative item in Figure 9.5, the discrimination index is $(8 - 2) \div 10 = .60$.

The index of discrimination can range from -1.0 to $+1.0$. Hopkins and Stanley (1981, p. 276) suggest the following guidelines for interpreting the index of discrimination:

---

[3]If you are doing an item analysis for a much larger class, we suggest taking the upper and lower 25 percent of the class and using the same approach. The formula would then be the number of students who got the item right in the high scoring 25 percent, plus the number of students who got the item right in the low scoring 25 percent, divided by the number of students in the high-scoring group plus the number of students in the low-scoring group. For example, if you have 60 students in your class, 25 percent of 60 is 15. The formula would be the number of the high-scoring 15 who got the item right plus the number of the low-scoring 15 who got the item right divided by 30.

Index of Discrimination	Item Evaluation
.40 and up	Very good item
.30 to .39	Good item
.20 to .29	Reasonably good item
.10 to .19	Marginal item, usually subject to improvement
Below .10	Poor item, to be rejected or revised

A positive index of discrimination suggests that getting that particular item right correlates positively with higher total test scores. A negative index of discrimination suggests that students who get that item right generally score lower on the test than students who get the item wrong. Assuming that each item is measuring a part of the content covered by the total test, it is worrisome if success on an individual item is not positively correlated with success on the total test.

If you base your item analysis on ten students in the upper and lower groups, the index of discrimination can be computed very quickly. Subtract the number in the lower group who got the item right from the number in the higher group who got it right (in our example: $8 - 2 = 6$), move the decimal point one space to the left (.6), and add a zero (.60). The same formula would apply when more than ten students are used in the higher- and lower-scoring groups, but could not be worked out as quickly. Teachers are more likely to use item analysis procedures if they are simple. Hence we recommend using the highest- and lowest-scoring 10 students for any class of 25 to 40 students.

A more precise way of conveying information about an item is to compute the discrimination index for each option. Instead of saying that the discrimination index for the item in Figure 9.5 was $+.60$, we would say that Option A has an index of $-.10$, Option B an index of $-.30$, Option C an index of $+.60$, Option D an index of .00, and Option E an index of $-.20$. Based on these results, we see that the item performs exactly as we would hope. The correct answer has a high positive discrimination index, and all the incorrect answers, or distractors, have discrimination indices that are negative or zero. The option with the largest negative index is also the option most frequently selected by low scorers in relation to high scorers. This suggests a misconception on the part of some students that should be addressed during instruction.

Evaluating the Effectiveness of Distractors

In good multiple-choice or matching tests, students are given a number of alternatives from which to choose. A good test offers distractors to the correct answer that are plausible, but incorrect. If you want a multiple-choice item that has five options, but no one selects two of the five options, you really have a three-option instead of a five-option item. Distractors should be worded so that you not only know which students are missing which items, but so that you can make a good guess as to why. In the illustrative item in Figure 9.5, George Washington and Benedict Arnold were probably included as options because they were prominent figures in the American Revolution. The Marquis de Lafayette and Count de Rochambeau were probably included because they were Frenchmen associated with the Revolution and the item stem mentions France.

Evaluating the effectiveness of distractors requires noting how many students in the high- and low-scoring groups selected each option. In tests taken by relatively large groups of students, the best items will be those where *each* option is selected by at least a few students. Low-scoring students should select incorrect options more frequently. In our example, it *might* be possible to improve the item by replacing the Benedict Arnold option. However, one must be cautious about doing this based on only one test administration. One advantage of collecting systematic item analysis data for several test administrations is that decisions about refinement can be based on larger groups of students. For more information about conducting distracter analyses, see Oosterhof (1994, pp. 199–202).

Recording Item Analysis Data

Earlier, we suggested that you create a test item file on cards or on a computer, and pointed out how such a file could be used to substantially improve test effectiveness. Each time you use an item from your file, you should conduct an item analysis and record the results in your file with that item. If you are using file cards, a convenient place to record the results is on the reverse side of the test item card, as shown in Figure 9.6. (Note that the information shown in Figure 9.6 would be on the back of the card shown in Figure 9.1.) As Figure 9.6 shows, the results of item analyses taken over time can provide important insights into item quality. First, we see that this particular item functions fairly consistently across years. Second, minor problems that appear to be present in one year (the fact that Benedict Arnold wasn't chosen at all in 1995) disappear in subsequent years. This is not an uncommon occurrence and suggests that we should not be too hasty about making major changes based on single test administrations. Particularly with small sample sizes (for example, 25 to 40 students), sampling fluctuation is expected. Therefore, minor problems in an otherwise good item are probably best overlooked until a second administration.

FIGURE 9.6   Example of How to Record Results of Item Analyses on Reverse Side of Cards in Test Item File

Date Used	Number of Students Tested	Group	A	B	C*	D	E	Omit	Difficulty Level	Discrimination Index
1/21/95	27	Upper 10	0	1	8	0	1	0	.50	.60
		Lower 10	1	4	2	0	3	0		
1/19/96	31	Upper 10	1	0	6	0	3	0	.45	.30
		Lower 10	2	3	3	1	1	0		
1/22/97	29	Upper 10	1	0	8	0	1	0	.60	.40
		Lower 10	1	1	4	2	2	0		
		Upper 10								
		Lower 10								
		Upper 10								
		Lower 10								
		Upper 10								
		Lower 10								

(Header above options: ITEM ANALYSIS DATA — Response to Each Option)

Using Item Analysis for Revision and Improvement

The primary purpose for doing item analyses is to improve the way a specific item functions. The results of item analyses should be used as a guide, not as criteria to follow blindly. In conjunction with your experience and professional judgment, item analyses can be invaluable in enhancing the information provided by items. Consider the five items shown in Figure 9.7, in which the clerk who scored the test computed and wrote the difficulty level and the index of discrimination for each option in the left-hand margin of a copy of the test.

Item 17 has a difficulty level of .95. Ten students out of ten in the high-scoring group and nine out of ten in the low-scoring group answered it correctly. If the test were being used for norm-referenced purposes, this item would not be particularly useful to retain. It may be that all the students knew the answer prior to the instruction (in which case, we can hope the teacher did not spend too much instructional time on this objective), or perhaps the distracters were too easy. If you were convinced that students did not know the information prior to the instructional unit, you could attempt to revise the item by using other distracters (for example, Canada, France, Spain, and Holland might be good distracters since all were involved in colonizing North America).

The final decision about whether to revise an item or simply drop it depends on the purpose of the test, the teacher's assessment of students' knowledge at the beginning of the unit, and the amount of instructional time that is devoted to the concept. The results of item analysis suggest the need for a closer look, but they should not be followed slavishly or replace the teacher's judgment. For example, if the item analysis indicates that 1, 2, or 3 of the items in a 40-item test are quite easy, the teacher might consciously decide to leave them in the test at the beginning so that all students have a few easy items at the start. It takes very little extra time and gives all students a positive start.

In item 18, we see a different problem. High-scoring students chose Options B (industrialized states versus agricultural states) and C (states with large populations versus states with small populations) with about the same frequency. This suggests some ambiguity about the answer, or the way the information was presented. In reality, experts would have a very difficult time agreeing on whether B or C was the better answer. The difficulty level of the item is also borderline. Together, these results suggest that the item should probably be revised. One revision would be to change Option B to read, "Cotton-producing states versus tobacco-producing states." This might attract students who remembered vaguely that the dispute had something to do with agriculture, but did not clearly understand that the dispute was between agricultural and manufacturing states rather than two types of agricultural states. The goal of distracters is to attract those students who have misconceptions or limited understanding, not to seduce students into selecting "tricky" answers.

Item 19 is one we have already seen. It has close to ideal difficulty level, a very good discrimination index, and all the options except D function very well. We could replace Option D with something more attractive. However, given the small sample size, differences in frequency of selection for Options A and D may easily be a chance occurrence. Even when the item statistics are nearly perfect, as here,

AMERICAN HISTORY MIDTERM (continued)

Difficulty Level	High vs. Low Group Scores	Discrimination Index	
	10 - 9	+.10	**17.** In the American Revolutionary War, the thirteen colonies were fighting against:
	0 - 0	0	* (a) England
.95	0 - 1	−.10	(b) Argentina
	0 - 0	0	(c) Kenya
(too easy)	0 - 0	0	(d) Finland
			(e) Japan
	0 - 3	−.20	**18.** During the Constitutional Convention of 1787, there were major disagreements between:
			(a) Those wanting to reunite with England versus those wanting to remain independent
	5 - 1	+.40	(b) Industrialized states versus agricultural states
.20	4 - 0	+.40	* (c) States with large populations versus those with small populations
	0 - 3	−.30	(d) Rich states versus poor states
(ambiguous)	1 - 3	−.20	(e) Northern states versus southern states
	0 - 1	−.10	**19.** Who was the most influential in convincing the French to assist the Americans during the Revolutionary War with England?
	1 - 4	−.30	(a) George Washington
.50	8 - 2	+.60	(b) Marquis de Lafayette
	0 - 0	.00	* (c) Benjamin Franklin
(good item)	1 - 3	−.20	(d) Benedict Arnold
			(e) Count de Rochambeau
	3 - 1	+.20	**20.** In what way did the American Revolution affect economic conditions of Europe?
			(a) Economic conditions in Europe were depressed as a result of the expenses associated with the war
	1 - 2	−.10	* (b) European countries were less able to use their respective colonies primarily for economic gains
.15	2 - 2	.00	(c) Economic chaos resulted because European peasants wanted the same freedoms gained by American colonials
(too difficult, random	2 - 2	.00	(d) European monarchs drastically cut taxes to avoid domestic unrest
response)	2 - 3	−.10	(e) The American Revolution fueled economic expansion in most European countries.
	1 - 3	−.20	**21.** Which of the following was the most important contributor to starting the Revolutionary War?
	1 - 0	+.10	(a) Taxes paid by the colonies to England were extremely high
			(b) England eliminated all of the local legislatures and assemblies in the colonies
	0 - 1	−.10	(c) The British were not providing the colonies with sufficient military protection
.25	7 - 2	+.50	(d) The colonies were upset about what they perceived to be taxation without representation
(good item, but mis-keyed)	1 - 4	−.30	* (e) The British tried to impose the Church of England as the official state religion for the colonies.

FIGURE 9.7   Illustration of How Item Analyses Results Can Be Used for Revising and Improving Items

it is not necessarily a perfect item. Only the teacher can decide whether an item is testing content that is relevant and important. However, item statistics provide a context in which to make such a decision and point out where unexpected factors are affecting the way it functions.

Item 20 obviously has problems. Not only is the difficulty lower than we like (.15), but the discrimination index for the correct answer is negative, and the responses to distractors appear to be almost random (about the same number of people in both the high- and the low-scoring groups chose each of the distracters). This suggests that the item is too difficult, the content was not adequately covered, or the differences between right and wrong options are so subtle that students cannot differentiate. Again, the teacher must decide whether the objective measured by the item is important enough to justify revision. If so, substantial revision is necessary. The options appear to be clearly worded and logically distinct, which suggests that the problem may have been with the instruction.

The item analysis results for item 21 indicate an embarrassing, but not infrequent, problem. Option E was keyed as correct. If this were true, the item would have a difficulty level of .25 and a discrimination index of −.30 for the correct answer. Such item statistics suggest that it ought to be dropped or substantially revised. However, on closer examination, it becomes apparent that the item was miskeyed. Option D is really the correct answer. If the item were keyed correctly, it would be nearly perfect based on item statistics. The difficulty level is .45, and the discrimination index is +.50. Although a miskeyed item is an embarrassing mistake, it is easily corrected.

In summary, the items shown in Figure 9.7 demonstrate how item analysis data can be used to identify items that are too easy, too difficult, ambiguous, or miskeyed. Remember, however, that *item analysis statistics provide only guidance and should never replace teacher judgment.*

Cautions About Interpreting the Results of Item Analyses

The results of item analyses can provide important insights, but criteria for labeling items good or bad should not be rigid. *There is no substitute for teacher judgment.* Following are some cautions to keep in mind as you interpret item analysis data:

1. *A good index of discrimination does not necessarily indicate a valid item.* The sine qua non of testing is that the test is measuring what it is expected to measure. In interpreting item discrimination statistics, we implicitly use the total test as a criterion to validate each individual item. This is not a bad assumption where content is relatively homogeneous (for example, the ability to add two-digit numbers). However, where the content is heterogeneous, item discrimination indices may be low because a person is able to master one part of the content but not another. If your test content is quite heterogeneous, you should expect that discrimination indices will be somewhat lower.

2. *Low indices of discrimination do not necessarily indicate defective items.* When the index of discrimination is low, check the item for ambiguity, inadvertent clues, inappropriate level of difficulty, and other technical defects. If none are found, and you believe that the item is measuring an important concept, it should probably be retained. Remember that difficulty level also contributes to the index of discrimination. Items at the 50 percent difficulty level have maximum potential of discrimination. As we move away from this optimum difficulty level (as items become

easier or more difficult), the maximum index of discrimination goes down. For example, Hopkins and Stanley (1981) point out that the maximum discrimination index for an item that is at a .10 or .90 level of difficulty is only .20. At times, you will want to retain items in the test that are relatively easy or difficult because they measure content you believe is important.

3. *Sampling fluctuation is not uncommon in item analysis data from small samples.* The results of item analysis data are so concrete that it is easy to be misled into believing that they represent "real truth." Our discussions about sampling error in Chapter 4 should make you cautious about accepting such statistics too literally. The results of item analyses for the same test will vary from one group to another, depending on total class performance, the students' educational background, and the instructional techniques used. When statistics are based on ten students in each group, the answers of two or three can have a dramatic effect on results. The smaller the number of students in an analysis, the greater the potential for sampling error (Pyrczak, 1973). Thus, for most classroom applications, item analysis results should only be used for guidance.

Application Problem 3

An item analysis of a 9th grade American History test given to a class of 30 students yields the information shown below for one multiple-choice item. The numbers in the three columns at the left indicate indicate the number of students in the high, middle, and low scoring groups who selected each option. The high and low groups each included 10 students. Fourteen of the 30 students who took the test answered the item correctly. Compute the difficulty index for this item and the discrimination index for each option. Based on the resulting statistics, explain what suggestions you would give for improving this item.

			During the Civil War, Congress enacted the first national draft law. Which political party supported the draft?
High Group	Middle Group	Low Group	
6	5	3	*a. Republications
4	5	7	b. Democrats
0	0	0	c. Secessionists
0	0	0	d. Whigs
0	0	0	e. Abolitionists

Item Analysis Procedures with Criterion-referenced Tests

Criterion-referenced tests (also referred to as mastery tests) and norm-referenced tests serve different purposes. Since criterion-referenced tests are designed to indicate how well students have mastered prespecified objectives—instead of where their scores fall on a continuum of mastery—the interpretation of item analysis data for criterion-referenced tests is quite different. The process of tabulating results is similar, but the data are used in different ways. As we shall see, indices of discrimination and difficulty are less meaningful, but an analysis of item scores and selected options still provides useful information.

Item Difficulty

With norm-referenced tests, the ideal difficulty level is .50. With criterion-referenced tests, the ideal difficulty depends on the teacher's expectations. If it is a learning outcome that you expect *all* students to achieve, then the ideal difficulty level would be 1.0.[4] When you cover objectives you do not expect all students to master, the ideal difficulty might be .50 to .70.

For criterion-referenced tests, items are not revised to achieve a level of difficulty that will maximize the potential for discrimination. The standard formula for item difficulty referred to earlier can be computed for criterion-referenced items, but should not be interpreted in the same way. Most criterion-referenced items have very high levels of difficulty (.80 or higher) if the instruction has been effective.

Index of Discrimination

Discriminating between high and low achievers is also not the goal for criterion-referenced tests. Some of the best criterion-referenced items will have zero indices of discrimination (for example, if all students in the class answered an item correctly). For norm-referenced tests, such items would probably be eliminated or revised because they do not provide information useful in ranking students along a continuum of mastery. On criterion-referenced tests, such items provide evidence that instructional objectives have been achieved.

Effectiveness of Distracters

Although you expect a higher percentage of students to answer a criterion-referenced item correctly, the quality of distracters is still important. Distracters should still let you know which misconceptions are causing students to answer incorrectly. Examining the frequency with which each distracter is selected can help you understand where confusion exists and what parts of instruction need emphasis.

Analysis of Criterion-referenced Items

If a criterion-referenced test is used as both a pre- and a posttest, it is useful to portray the results in a format similar to that shown in Figure 9.8, which shows the results for ten students for the first four items of a criterion-referenced test. The key question in evaluating a criterion-referenced test is, "To what extent do the

---

[4]Remember that the term *difficulty level* means exactly the opposite of what you might expect. An item with a difficulty level of .80 is answered correctly by 80 percent of the respondents. Some writers have suggested that the term be changed to *item ease,* (see Gronlund, 1985, p. 247), but the suggestion, although logical, has not gained broad acceptance.

Student	Pre	Post	Pre	Post	Pre	Post	Pre	Post
Harold S.	−	+	+	+	+	−	−	−
Suzanne R.	−	+	−	+	+	+	−	+
Manuel G.	−	+	+	+	−	−	+	−
Eliza K.	−	+	+	+	+	−	−	−
Tom B.	+	+	+	+	+	+	−	+
Karl A.	−	+	+	+	−	−	−	−
Linda H.	−	+	+	−	+	−	+	−
Allyson W.	−	−	+	+	+	−	−	−
Lewis A.	−	+	−	+	+	+	−	−
Matt T.	−	−	+	+	+	−	−	−
Percentage Correct	10%	80%	80%	90%	80%	30%	20%	20%
Sensitivity to Instructional Effects	.70		.10		−.50		.00	

FIGURE 9.8   Portraying the Results of Criterion-referenced Tests

test items measure the effects of instruction?" Indicating whether students got an item incorrect (represented by a minus) or correct (represented by a plus) yields a useful visual representation.

For example, item 1 is a very good test item for a criterion-referenced test. Only one person got the item correct prior to instruction, and eight out of ten got it correct after instruction. This indicates that the instruction was effective and that the item was able to measure its impact.

Item 2 was either too easy for both the pre- and posttest or the instruction was misdirected. About the same number of students (the majority of the class) got the item correct before and after instruction.

Item 3 indicates a relatively rare situation in which many more students got the item correct prior to instruction than following instruction. Such a situation could be caused by a badly written or confusing item, or if instruction was so poor that it confused students.

Item 4 either is too difficult or is based on content not covered by instruction since a small number of students scored correctly before and after instruction. This response might also occur if the item were acceptable but the instruction was poor.

As with norm-referenced tests, item analyses of criterion-referenced tests requires professional judgment. Specific response patterns may reflect characteristics of the item or of the instruction. In most cases, both item and instructional characteristics interact to produce the results, and teachers are best qualified to interpret data for their particular situations.

In interpreting the results of criterion-referenced tests, a measure of *sensitivity to instructional effects* is sometimes used (Haladyna & Roid, 1981). This index is a good way of summarizing the kind of information shown in Figure 9.8. Sensitivity to instructional effects (indicated by *S*) is obtained by subtracting the number of pupils who got the item right *before instruction* from the number who got the number right *after instruction* and dividing the result by the total number of pupils who tried it both times. For example, in item 1, eight students got the item right after instruction, and one student got it right before instruction. Ten students tried it both times; therefore,

$$S = (8 - 1) \div 10 = .70$$

The index of sensitivity to instructional effects for the other items in Figure 9.8 is computed in the same way. As can be seen, S is interpreted much like the discrimination index in that larger numbers indicate better items. Based on that criterion, the best item in Figure 9.8 is item 1. Analysis of the other items suggests either poor item construction or ineffective instruction.

Keeping a record of how items on criterion-referenced tests function is just as important as keeping records of items on norm-referenced tests. The same record-keeping system stored on the backs of index cards or in a computer file can be used. The information recorded in that file should be reviewed periodically, especially right after each test administration, to help you improve instruction and test development skills.

SUGGESTED READINGS

Clemens, W. V. (1971). Test administration. In R. L. Thorndike, (ed.). *Educational measurement* (2nd ed., pp. 188–201), Washington, DC: American Council on Education.

An excellent discussion of the issues to be considered as a part of test administration procedures. Issues are discussed from the perspective of the test author, the administrator, and the examinee. Many specific suggestions are given for improving test administrations.

Crocker, L. (1992). Item analysis. In M.C. Alkin (ed.). *Encyclopedia of educational research* (6th ed., pp. 652–657). New York: Macmillan.

Focuses on traditional approaches to item analysis, but briefly discusses recent developments, including item response theory, differential item functioning, and new technology. Claims that traditional item statistics have become easier for most teachers to obtain and use because of the pervasiveness of personal computers.

Haladyna, T. M. (1994). *Developing and validating multiple-choice test items.* Hillsdale, NJ: Lawrence Erlbaum. (See Chapter 8, "Analyzing item responses," pp. 143–159.)

Describes procedures for analyzing item response patterns as a basis for evaluating and improving test items. Discusses the use of traditional item analysis statistics plus instructional sensitivity indexes, distracter analysis, and other recently developed ways of analyzing item performance, including information from polytomous scoring models.

Voeckel, E. L. & Fiore, D. J. (1993, July/August). Electronic test generators: What current programs can do for teachers. *Clearing House, 65,* 356–362.

The authors suggest eight desirable features that test-generating software should possess. They evaluate 11 commercially marketed test generators in terms of these criteria and identify the common shortcomings of such products. They also describe how traditional word processors and database programs can be used to construct item banks and generate tests.

Ward, A. W. & Murray-Ward, M. (1994). Guidelines for the development of item banks. *Educational Measurement: Issues and Practice, 13*(1), 34–39.

Describes the functions and uses of test item banks. Includes step-by-step procedures for constructing an item bank, sources of additional information about item-banking software, and a list of issues that potential users need to consider when selecting an item-banking program.

SUGGESTION SHEET

If your last name starts with the letter L, please complete the Suggestion Sheet at the end of the book while this chapter is still fresh in your mind.

Answers to Chapter 9 Application Problems

1. Whether or not the items on the test require students to exhibit the type of behavior that the teacher had in mind can be decided only by the person who is teaching the class. However, as a biology teacher yourself, you should be able to provide valuable opinions about whether what is being asked is clear and unambiguous, and whether each item has a single correct answer. You could indicate any items that are too wordy, and items that, based on your experience, appear to be too difficult or too easy. You could identify items you think contain bias or that have irrelevant clues to the correct answer. You cannot provide a definitive judgment about whether the items are representative of all the material covered in the course or whether adequate coverage of the most important concepts is provided since your friend may teach the course somewhat differently than you do, but you can certainly make suggestions in each of those areas for your friend to think about as she finalizes the test.

2. The directions are good as far as they go, but more information is needed. It would be good to note that each item is worth 1 point, that students will have 15 minutes to complete the test, and that if they are not sure of the correct answer they should make their best guess and continue on to other items and then come back if they have time. Rather than just writing the directions at the top of the sheet, it would be useful to read the directions aloud with the students and make sure that they all understand exactly what they are supposed to do. By the fifth grade, students will probably be familiar with true–false tests, but you may have some students in your class who have recently immigrated to the United States or who might have other difficulties so that it would be worth spending time with them individually to make sure they know what is expected.

3. Difficulty level for the item is .47, and the discrimination index for the item is .30. If you want to compute discrimination indices for each option, it would be .30 for Option A, −.30 for Option B, and 0.0 for Options C, D, and E. Based on this in-

formation, it appears that the item is quite successful in discriminating between high scorers and low scorers, but little is gained by having a five-option question instead of just a two-option question since no one chose options C, D, and E. This may be because students realize that only two major political parties (Republicans and Democrats) were active at the time. If the intent of including an item like this is to learn more about how well students understood the politics surrounding the national draft law, you may want to reword the question. As it is now worded, they may be answering based on their knowledge that there were only two major political parties at the time without knowing much about the national draft law.

Note that the information about the performance of the middle group is used when computing the difficulty index, but is not used when computing the discrimination indexes. The discrimination index for each option compares the performance of the high-scoring and low-scoring groups on that particular option.

CHAPTER 10

To Use or Not to Use Alternative Assessment?

OVERVIEW

Few current movements have caught the attention of educators as quickly as the move toward more direct assessment of student performance. Efforts to develop useful alternatives to traditional testing modes have proliferated during the past several years (Baron & Wolf, 1996; Darling-Hammond, Ancess, & Falk, 1995; Kane & Mitchell, 1996). More and more state and national associations of professional educators are sponsoring symposia or special conferences to consider alternative ways to assess student performance. And not to be left behind, some state legislatures have enacted laws that mandate use of direct assessment of student performance as the means of determining how well individual schools, districts, and their statewide education systems are performing (Guskey, 1994). In short, alternative assessment's rising tide has overflowed most of education's shoreline, and schools are increasingly being flooded with calls for more direct assessment of student performance.

Despite the surge of interest in alternative assessment, criticisms of this movement by those who favor more traditional means of assessment create a strong undertow. Differences between proponents and opponents have sparked vigorous debates (for example, Wiggins, 1991; Cizek 1991a, 1991b), resulting in cross-currents that leave many educators feeling rudderless as they attempt to direct their school on the optimal assessment course.

In this chapter, we propose to (1) explain what alternative assessment is, (2) show how it differs from more traditional forms, (3) outline clearly our position concerning alternative forms of assessment, (4) identify some major issues that educators must resolve if alternative assessment is to reach its full potential in our schools, (5) suggest some criteria schools may use to determine how quickly to expand their use of and dependence on nontraditional methods of assessment, and (6) describe how portfolio assessment might be useful in your school or classroom.

OBJECTIVES

Upon completing your study of this chapter, you should be able to

1.	Identify the main characteristics that distinguish between alternative assessment and more traditional forms of educational assessment.
2.	Identify five factors that have led many educators to view alternative assessment as a promising means of improving student assessment.
3.	Discuss the relative merits and potential utility of recently proposed "authentic assessment," "performance assessment," and alternative methods of assessing learning outcomes.
4.	List the main steps involved in constructing a performance assessment exercise.
5.	Explain how you might use portfolio assessment appropriately in your classroom.
6.	Describe 12 critical issues that need to be resolved if alternative assessment is to be successful.
7.	Evaluate the readiness of a school with which you are associated to begin using alternative assessment to evaluate students' achievement.

What is Alternative Assessment?

Several labels have been used to describe alternatives to traditional, norm-referenced, achievement tests, with the most common being *direct assessment, authentic assessment, performance assessment,* and the more generic *alternative assessment,* which we shall use hereafter.[1] Although these various descriptors reflect subtle distinctions in emphasis, the several types of assessment all reflect three central commonalities. First, they are all viewed as *alternatives* to traditional selected-answer (multiple-choice or true–false) achievement tests. Second, they all refer to *direct* examination of student *performance* on significant tasks relevant to life outside of school. Third, they are all based on a different view of learning and competence that assumes that knowledge is a function of the context in which it is learned and used (Brown, Collins, & Duguid, 1989; Raven, 1992; Resnick & Resnick, 1992). Since the advocates of alternative assessment have a different view of what it means *to know, to understand, and to act competently,* they require different forms of evidence that students have learned.

---

[1]Many authors place the now familiar label of *portfolio assessment* in this list, but that title refers more accurately to one of several ways that alternative assessment data can be recorded and reviewed, and thus is less a descriptor of this general type of assessment than it is of one of its *tools,* which we will describe later in this chapter.

Proponents of alternative assessment prefer it to more traditional assessment that relies on indirect, "proxy" tasks (usually test items). Sampling tiny snippets of student behavior, they point out, does not provide insight into how students would perform on truly "worthy" intellectual tasks. Conversely, they argue that student learning can be better assessed by examining and judging a student's actual (or simulated) performance on significant, relevant tasks. "Authentic" tasks involve more than recall of atomistic fragments of information. Instead, they are integrated, holistic tasks that are valued in the world outside of school (Newmann & Archbald, 1992; Wiggins, 1992, 1993).

Leinhardt (1992, p. 24) suggests that a task can be authentic in either of two different ways: "A task can be authentic because it is part of the world outside of school (for example, a grocery store), or because it is part of the culture of a particular discipline (such as mathematics or chemistry)." Hence, authentic tasks can also refer to the kinds of activities performed by skilled individuals proficient in their particular discipline. According to this second view, it is not enough for students to learn science concepts that have some transfer value to solving real-world problems, we may also want them to learn how to think as scientists think. Similarly, in a history class, we may want students to learn how to reason as historians reason. From this point of view, knowledge is assumed to be generative. Hence knowledgeable students should possess inquiry skills and/or learning skills that enable them to produce or generate new knowledge by formulating questions or hypotheses and conducting relevant investigations focused on those issues.

Most proponents of alternative assessment also emphasize the need for a close alignment between what is taught and what is assessed (McTighe, 1997; Wiggins, 1989). Although Wolf and Reardon (1996) do not use the word *alignment,* they emphasize this idea.

> Far too much of the current discussion about changes in assessment focuses on the single shift from multiple choice to open-ended items. Another shift which is at least as critical is the change from curriculum-independent to curriculum-embedded assessment. In many school settings the abundant lack of connection between what children work on and what they are tested on promotes a keen indifference to investing in the assessment. It feels disembodied, students sense being unprepared, and there are few, if any, learning-related consequences for doing well. It is not unusual for students to make random patterns of dots on their answer sheets and for teachers to ignore the results (except where they bring shame and anger). We clearly need a system of assessment that is curriculum-dependent. Such assessments reconnect effort, teaching, assessment, and results (p. 19).

Alternative assessment, then, is a loosely defined, umbrella term that covers a broad range of approaches to assessing what students know and can do. Like many other authors, Khattri and Sweet (1996) use the terms *alternative assessment* and *performance assessment* as if they are interchangeable. They provide the following descriptive definition of performance assessment: "Performance assessment refers to a type of assessment that requires students to actually perform, demonstrate, construct, [or] develop a product or a solution under defined conditions and standards" (Khattri & Sweet, 1996, p. 3).

Khattri and Sweet (1996) also provide two other useful tools for understanding the notion of performance assessment. They include (1) a description of the common characteristics shared by performance assessments, and (2) a classification system for identifying various subcategories of performance assessments. Their description of the shared characteristics is as follows: "All performance assessments require students to structure the assessment task, apply information, construct responses, and in many cases, explain the process by which they arrived at the answers" (Khattri & Sweet, 1996, p. 5).

In their classification scheme, Khattri and Sweet (1996) identified five different varieties of performance assessments.

1. *Portfolios* that consist of collections of a student's work and developmental products, which may include drafts of assignments.
2. *On-demand tasks* or *events* that require students to construct responses—either writing or experiments—to a prompt or to a problem within a short period to time.
3. *Projects* that last longer than on-demand tasks, and are usually undertaken by students on a given topic and used to demonstrate their mastery of that topic.
4. *Demonstrations* that take the form of student presentations or project work.
5. *Teachers' observations* that gauge student classroom performance, usually designed for young children, and primarily used for diagnostic purposes (Khattri & Sweet, 1996, p. 5)

The idea of directly observing and assessing students' performance is not new. Teachers have kept anecdotal "running records" and folders of student work long before such records have been both legitimized and refined by recent attention to better ways to use portfolios of student work to assess student learning. Samples of student products or performances have long been the basis for teachers' evaluation of student outcomes in areas as diverse as music, drama, debate, art, shorthand, creative writing, and physical education. Many teacher-made tests present students with important, "real-life" tasks that they must perform correctly to receive passing scores. Creative teachers have had students engage in self-assessment and peer assessment. In short, our nation's classrooms have been quietly awash in such performance-based assessment for decades.

Then why has performance assessment become so much more popular in recent years? Why the urgent appeals that direct assessment replace norm-referenced achievement tests, minimum competency tests, and other indirect assessments? Why propose performance assessments as the basis for judging not only how well individual students are performing, but also how well schools, districts, and states are fulfilling their educational mission? The answer lies in several forces that have flowed, in succession, through education's tangled tributaries in the past two decades. We will not expound on these forces here. Instead, let us merely identify the various factors that have collectively sparked the increasing interest in alternative assessment.

1. *Demands for accountability in our schools.* Loss of public confidence in public schools led to a spate of new "educational accountability" laws requiring educators to provide external evidence of student achievement.

2. *Use of test scores to make high-stakes decisions.* Both minimum competency tests and standardized achievement tests were used to make "high-stakes" decisions; not only were student promotion and graduation decisions based on such test scores, but the test scores have been increasingly used in unanticipated ways that have far-reaching consequences for individual teachers, schools, and school districts.

3. *Negative consequences of high-stakes testing programs.* The pressures that accompanied high-stakes testing resulted more often in other, less beneficial practices and outcomes including measurement-driven instruction, the sometimes innocent but nonetheless insidious practice of teaching to the test, or the more pernicious problem of outright test cheating, where teachers coached students on actual test items.

4. *Increasing criticisms of standardized tests.* As scores on such tests began to be used for increasingly crucial decisions, the tests' limitations loomed larger.

5. *Changing views of aptitude, learning, and knowledge.* During the last 40 years, the narrow, restrictive views of student aptitude that were so prevalent previously have been replaced with broader, more democratic views of intelligence and potential for learning (Gardner, 1992; Shepard, 1992; Wolf, Bixby, Glenn, & Gardner 1991; Wolf & Reardon, 1996). At the same time, the emergence of the cognitive sciences and the notion of constructivism have led to new views of what constitutes knowledge and how learning occurs. Consequently, many people are no longer as willing to accept responses to true–false or multiple-choice questions as evidence of meaningful learning and substantive achievement (Glaser & Silver, 1994; Khattri & Sweet, 1996; Resnick & Resnick, 1992, 1996; U.S. Congress, Office of Technology Assessment, 1992).

This unscrolling of forces across the past four decades has set the stage for increased hopes that alternative assessment will prove helpful in improving student assessment—and classroom instruction. Yet sharp differences still divide advocates and opponents of such assessment methods. Although consideration of all the potential benefits and drawbacks of alternative assessment is beyond the scope of this chapter, several critical issues must be discussed, for they will prove pivotal in tilting the balance either in favor of alternative assessment or against it. Before addressing these issues, our position concerning alternative assessment should be made clear.

Our Position Concerning Alternative Assessment

In our view, alternative assessment holds great promise. It has the potential of enriching and expanding the very nature of the information assessments provide. It should be the very backbone of assessment procedures within individual classrooms. Because content of high-stakes tests is unlikely to be ignored by educators, including more worthy and relevant assessment tasks on such tests should spur educators to develop more appropriate instructional emphases. Indeed, education's ultimate goals should be directly represented in the complex performances selected as the alternative assessment tasks. These tasks should provide *direct* measurement of *real* performance on important tasks. Whenever it is feasible to use valid, representative, direct assessment tasks, they are preferable to indirect measurement where inferences about student learning depend on performance on surrogate indicators. At the end of this chapter, we discuss briefly some issues facing authentic assessment that, if not addressed thoughtfully, could sap this exciting assessment approach of many of its potential advantages. Before addressing such issues, however, we need to first give concrete examples to make sure we have communicated clearly what we mean when we use the term *performance assessment*.

Performance Assessment

Many valued skills that teachers want their students to learn cannot be directly assessed using objectively scored, paper-and-pencil tests. A few examples of such skills include the ability to

- Compose a letter
- Prepare an employment résumé
- Prepare and present a speech
- Play a musical instrument
- Use a word processor
- Use a microscope
- Design and conduct an experiment
- Write a report

The current emphasis on teaching thinking in the classroom has been accompanied by the realization that classroom assessment practices should focus more on assessing the thought processes that students' employ. Since thinking is an act, and since this act often creates a product of some kind, performance assessment can be used as a means of evaluating students' cognitive functioning in various subject matters if the teacher is creative enough to formulate challenging tasks that engage the students in thinking and allow their thought processes to be observed or tracked carefully as they respond to the task. More and more classroom teachers are beginning to use performance assessment to assess the reasoning students employ in their attempts to interpret their experience; formulate and test hypotheses; draw conclusions; solve problems; and evaluate objects, events, and policies that they encounter. Therefore, two common purposes for using performance assessment in classrooms today are (1) to evaluate students' proficiency in performing complex tasks that have relevance and utility in the world outside of school, and (2) to assess students' thinking skills in various subjects such as mathematics, science, language arts, and social studies.

Performance assessments occur in numerous forms and varieties. Some focus on tasks that are relatively simple; others are much more complex. Some are short and brief; others are more structured and more time consuming to prepare, administer, and score. Some require very little—if any—equipment or materials; others require the use of specialized materials or equipment that are not readily available in typical school classrooms. Three examples are described in this section. None of these examples is presented as being the ideal, but together they illustrate some of the more commonly used approaches to performance assessment exercises.

Example 1: Constructing Series and Parallel Circuits

This sample exercise provides a direct, hands-on assessment of students' understanding of the difference between series and parallel circuits. Each student is supplied with four 1.5 volt D-cell flashlight batteries, four bulbs, a set of precut wires, and the necessary battery holders and bulb holders.[2] The exercise includes three tasks.

1. Construct four specified circuits.
2. Explain the reasons for the observed differences in the brightness of the bulbs in the respective circuits in terms of differences in voltage, resistance, and current.
3. Predict what will happen if additional bulbs or batteries are added to the various circuits.

The four circuits to be constructed include the following:

1. A circuit with two bulbs connected in series, powered by one battery
2. A circuit with two bulbs connected in parallel, powered by one battery
3. A circuit with one bulb lighted by two batteries connected in series
4. A circuit with one bulb lighted by two batteries connected in parallel

The directions for performing the various tasks are shown in Figure 10.1. First, the students are asked to build two circuits in which each includes two bulbs and a single battery. In one circuit, the bulbs should be wired in series, and in the other they should be connected in parallel. After constructing the two circuits, the students are asked to predict how the brightness of the bulbs in each circuit would be affected if an additional bulb were added to that circuit. The students are also asked to write an explanation giving reasons for the observed differences in the brightness of the bulbs in the two circuits.

Then, the students dismantle the circuits they have constructed and perform the next task. This time they are asked to construct two circuits with each containing two batteries and a single bulb. In one circuit the batteries should be arranged in series, and in the other circuit they should be arranged in parallel. After constructing these last two circuits, the students are again asked to write an explanation of the observed differences in the brightness of the bulbs and to predict how the bulb brightness would be affected if one more battery were added in each circuit.

This exercise is safe and students generally report that they find it challenging and enjoyable. It provides a direct assessment of students' ability to demonstrate differences in series and parallel circuit configurations, and their ability to explain the reasons for the resulting differences in circuit behavior. One disadvantage is the amount of equipment needed. Four batteries, four bulbs, four battery holders, four bulb holders, and at least seven precut wires are required for each student who takes the test at a given time. Several students can take the test simultaneously if sufficient equipment is available. Another disadvantage is the amount of time re-

---

[2]These materials can be obtained from suppliers such as Delta Education in Nashua, NH; Carolina Biological Supply in Burlington, NC; or Pasco Scientific in Roseville, CA.

Name_____   Date_____

Electrical Circuits Assessment

How to Proceed

1. Using batteries, bulbs, and wires provided, create two circuits. Each circuit should contain two light bulbs and a single battery. In one circuit, arrange two bulbs in series. In the other circuit, arrange the bulbs in parallel.

2. After you have completed making both circuits, draw each of them in the space provided. Draw wires connecting the battery and bulbs so that the drawings accurately depict the circuits you made.

Two Bulbs in Series	Two Bulbs in Parallel

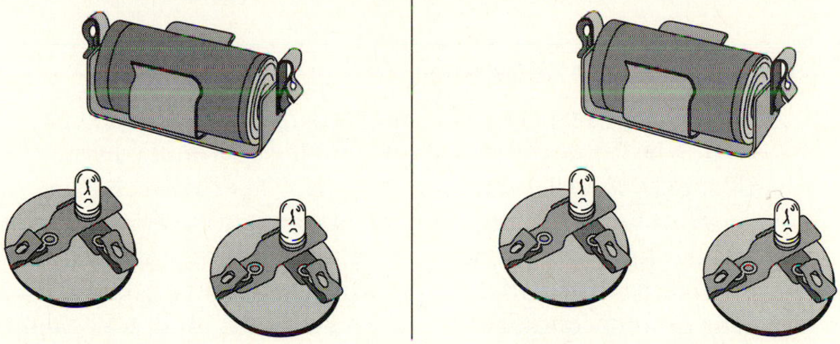

3. Show your circuits and drawings to your teacher. Ask the teacher to verify whether your drawings accurately represent the circuits you have constructed.

4. Write a brief essay comparing the two circuits you constructed. What evidence, if any, indicates that the current in the two circuits is different? How is the current in each circuit influenced by the arrangement of the bulbs and wires? Why? Explain the differences in current in terms of the voltage and resistance in each circuit.

FIGURE 10.1   Directions and Recording Sheet for Electrical Circuits Assessment

quired to complete this activity. Proficient students can usually construct all four circuits and answer all the questions in less than 20 minutes, but students with misconceptions or partial knowledge usually take more time and sometimes become frustrated when they think they have performed correctly but are unable to get the circuits to function.

Two simulated versions of this performance assessment have been constructed. Both have the advantage that they do not require actual batteries, bulbs, and wires. Martineau (1997) developed a computer simulation of the circuit construction exercise. The computer is programmed to display pictorial representations of the batteries and bulbs on the computer screen. The examinee selects a simulated wire and then uses the mouse to point and click where the wires are to be connected. When the student constructs a circuit correctly, the bulbs light up. The computer is programmed to store a pictorial record of the wiring configuration each student constructs. Students are asked to answer the same questions as in the hands-on assessment, but they write their responses on an accompanying answer sheet rather than on the computer.

Sudweeks and Clay (1995) developed a paper-and-pencil version of the circuit construction test in the form of two context-dependent item sets (see Chapter 8). Instead of using actual batteries, bulbs, and wires, the participants were given incomplete drawings of the four circuits, each displaying pictorial representations of the batteries, bulbs, and bulb holders, but without any wires. The task posed to the students was to complete the circuits by drawing lines on their paper to represent the wires needed to create the designated series and parallel wiring configurations. Instead of observing which circuit produced brighter bulbs, students were simply asked to predict which circuit would produce brighter bulbs. They were also asked to answer explanation and prediction questions similar to those in the hands-on, circuit construction exercise.

Example 2: Balancing a Checking Account

The ability to manage a checking account is a skill that has practical utility in today's world. Individuals who are proficient in performing this task can save themselves time and money as well as reducing the risk of personal embarrassment that accompanies an overdrawn account. Many people now use computer software to accomplish this task, but knowing how to do it without a computer is still a relevant and useful skill.

Figures 10.2 through 10.6 display the components of a performance assessment exercise designed to assess students' ability to balance an account owner's personal record of his or her checking account with the monthly statement of account activity provided by the bank. Copies of the following materials are provided to each student as part of this exercise:

- Instructions to students (see Figure 10.2)
- Two sample pages from a simulated checkbook register (see Figure 10.3)
- Four photocopied pages showing copies of simulated cancelled checks and deposit slips processed by the bank that month (see example of one in Figure 10.4)

FIGURE 10.2   Instructions Given to Students in the Checking Account Balancing Exercise

Objective:
This exercise is designed to assess your ability to balance a checking account by reconciling the monthly statement provided by the bank with the account owner's personal record of account activity.

Materials Provided:
1. Monthly account statement issued by the Bank of the Northern Redwoods.
2. Cancelled checks and deposit slips processed by the bank.
3. A copy of corresponding pages from the account owner's checkbook register.

Directions:
1. Balance the checking account using the documents provided and a hand calculator. Identify and correct any errors that need to be resolved.
2. Write a brief paragraph expressing your judgment as to whether or not the account is balanced. Cite specific evidence to justify your conclusion and describe any discrepancies which have not been resolved.

CODE OR NUMBER	DATE	DESCRIPTION OF TRANSACTION	PAYMENT/DEBIT OR FEE (−)	T	DEPOSIT OR CREDIT (+)	BALANCE FORWARD	
						485	50
654	2/18	To Car Doctor				Pay't or Dep. 95	79
		For Carburator Repair				Bal. 389	71
ATM	2/21	To First Security Bank				Pay't or Dep. 50	00
		For Cash for Emily				Bal. 339	71
SVC	2/21	To				Pay't or Dep.	50
		For				Bal. 339	21
655		To Mayfair Market				Pay't or Dep. 38	12
		For Groceries				Bal. 301	09
656	2/27	To Alpha Beta				Pay't or Dep. 27	63
		For Groceries				Bal. 273	46
657	2/28	To Lower Fortiss Golf Course				Pay't or Dep. 141	67
		For				Bal. 131	79
EFT	3/1	To Deposit			321	44	Pay't or Dep.
		For				Bal. 453	23
658	3/1	To American Cancer Society				Pay't or Dep. 50	00
		For Donation				Bal. 403	23
659	3/3	To Lazy Oaks Trailer Park				Pay't or Dep. 55	00
		For				Bal. 358	23
660	3/5	To Alpha Beta				Pay't or Dep. 21	12
		For Groceries				Bal. 337	11
ATM	3/3	To BNR				Pay't or Dep. 40	00
		For				Bal. 297	11
661	3/7	To Texaco				Pay't or Dep. 15	00
		For				Bal. 282	11
662	3/9	To Merchants Bank				Pay't or Dep. 68	00
		For Visa Payment				Bal. 214	11
663	3/11	To Francine Waller				Pay't or Dep. 25	00
		For Manicure				Bal. 189	11

← Balanced to HERE 3/2/98

FIGURE 10.3   Checkbook Register

- A simulated monthly statement from the bank (see Figure 10.5)
- Reverse side of the simulated bank statement (see Figure 10.6)

Figure 10.2 displays the written instructions provided to each student. This page includes a short description of the purpose of the assessment, a list of the materials provided to each examinee, and brief directions. Note that the directions encourage students to use a hand calculator. The sample pages from the simulated checkbook register are shown in Figure 10.3. The record of account activity in this register includes two omissions: a computation error and a recording error. The omissions refer to one check written against the account that was not recorded in

CODE OR NUMBER	DATE	DESCRIPTION OF TRANSACTION	PAYMENT/DEBIT OR FEE (–)	T	DEPOSIT OR CREDIT (+)	BALANCE FORWARD	
664	3/12	To Alpha Beta / For Groceries				Pay't or Dep. 23 46 / Bal. 165 65	
ATM	3/12	To BNR / For				Pay't or Dep. 20 00 / Bal. 145 65	
EFT	3/15	To Deposit / For			408 71	Pay't or Dep. / Bal. 554 36	
665	3/16	To AVON / For				Pay't or Dep. 31 53 / Bal. 522 83	
666	3/19	To Alpha Beta / For Groceries				Pay't or Dep. 17 18 / Bal. 505 65	
667	3/23	To Pacific Bell / For Telephone				Pay't or Dep. 47 83 / Bal. 457 82	
668	3/25	To Cal Power / For Electricity				Pay't or Dep. 52 05 / Bal. 405 77	
ATM	3/21	To First Security Bank / For				Pay't or Dep. 220 00 / Bal. 185 77	
SVC	3/21	To / For				Pay't or Dep. 50 / Bal. 185 27	
ATM	3/24	To FSB / For Emily's Cash				Pay't or Dep. 100 00 / Bal. 85 27	
SVC	3/24	To / For				Pay't or Dep. 50 / Bal. 84 77	
		To / For				Pay't or Dep. / Bal.	
		To / For				Pay't or Dep. / Bal.	
		To / For				Pay't or Dep. / Bal.	

FIGURE 10.3   Continued

the register, and one automatic teller withdrawal that was not recorded. The other two errors include a subtraction error in computing the account balance after writing one of the checks, and a transposition error committed in recording the amount for one of the checks listed in the register.

Figure 10.4 displays an example of one of the four pages of showing canceled checks and processed deposit slips. One side of the simulated bank statement is shown in Figure 10.5. This statement shows the beginning and ending balances in the account for that month plus a list of all transactions processed by the bank during that month. Figure 10.6 shows the reverse side of the simulated bank statement. It contains a blank copy of a typical form supplied by banks to assist the ac-

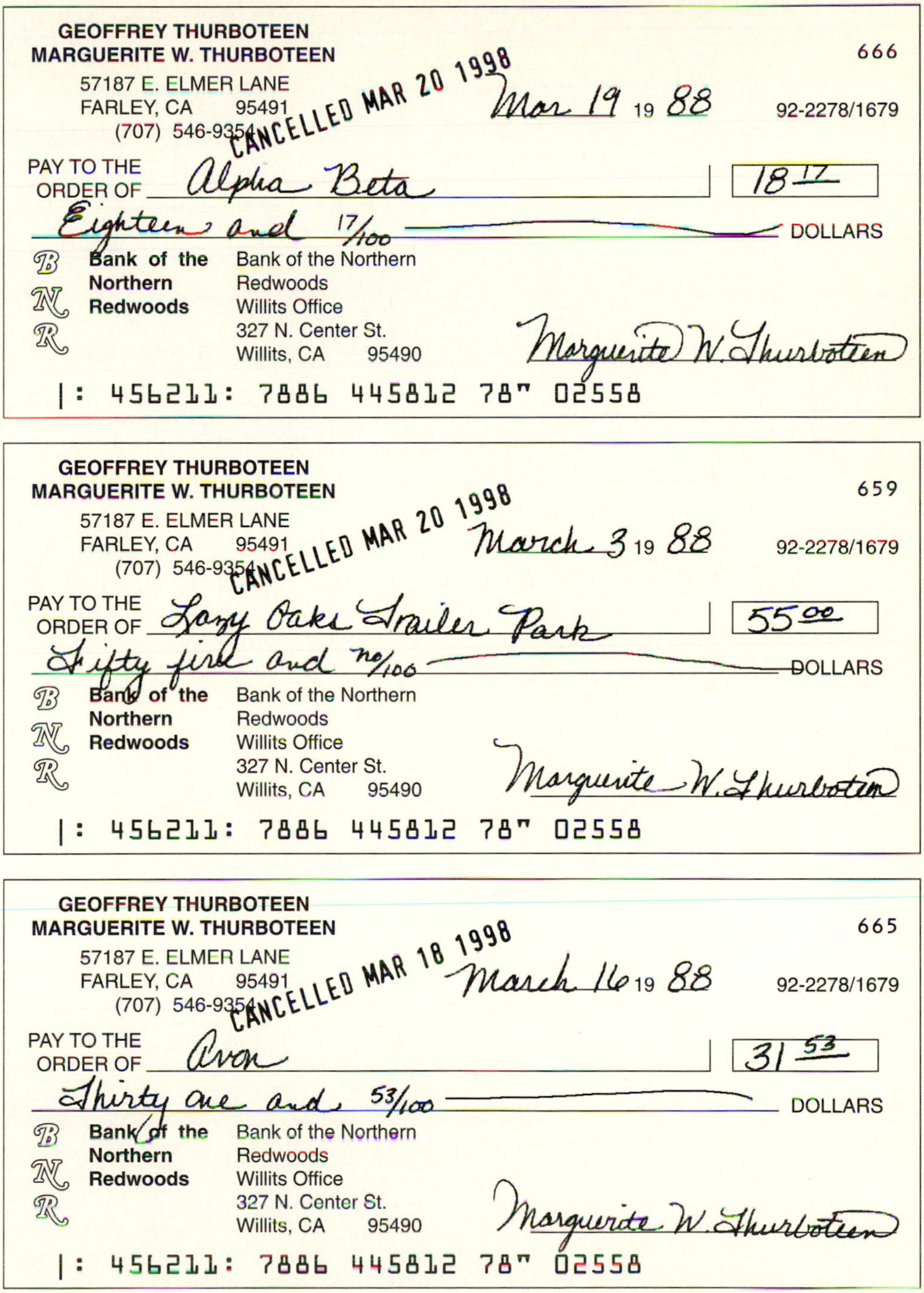

FIGURE 10.4   Simulated Canceled Checks and Deposit Slips Processed by Bank

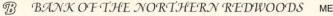

BANK OF THE NORTHERN REDWOODS   MEMBER FDIC

Willits Office
327 N. Center St.
Willits, CA   95490   (707) 667-9832

GEOFFREY THURBOTEEN
MARGUERITE THURBOTEEN
57187 E. ELMER LANE
FARLEY, CA
                    95491

IMPORTANT -PLEASE NOTIFY US OF ANY CHANGE OF ADDRESS
INTEREST RATE OF 5.25%

Account Type	
STUDENT - CHECKING	
Account No.	Page
23-13887	1
Statement Period	
2/27/88 - 3/24/88	

Balance	Credits	Debits	Interest	Service Charge	Present Balance
301.09	780.15	906.58	0.00	1.50	173.16

DATE	ACCOUNT ACTIVITY	DEPOSITS	WITHDRAWALS/ CHECKS	BALANCE
02/27/88	Previous Balance			301.09
03/01/88	EFT- Cal Pwr Paychk	321.44		622.53
	Chk- 656		27.63	594.90
03/03/88	ATM- BNR Farley Ofc		40.00	554.90
	ATM- Plus system- ZFNB Utah		50.00	504.90
	SVC- Plus Access		.50	504.40
03/05/88	Chk- 657		141.67	362.73
03/07/88	Chk- 660		21.12	341.61
03/12/88	ATM- BNR Frisco Ofc		20.00	321.61
03/15/88	EFT- Cal Pwr Paychk	408.71		730.32
	Chk- 662		68.00	662.32
	Chk- 663		25.00	637.32
	Chk- 664		23.46	613.86
03/18/88	Chk- 661		15.00	598.86
	Chk- 665		31.53	567.33
03/20/88	Chk- 659		55.00	512.33
	Chk- 666		18.17	494.16
03/21/88	Dep- BNR Farley Ofc	50.00		544.16
	ATM- Plus system- FSB Utah		220.00	324.16
	SVC- Plus Access		.50	323.66
03/24/88	Chk- 658		50.00	273.66
	ATM- Plus system- FSB Utah		100.00	173.66
	SVC- Plus Access		.50	173.16
	Interest- 5.25% ($1000.00+)	0.00		173.16

=+

Has your car lost its last battle with
road salt and grime?

Check out our auto loans!
Now just 14.1% on a 72-month loan!
Call your loan department today!

FOR YOUR CONVENIENCE AN ACCOUNT RECONCILIATION FORM IS PROVIDED ON THE BACK OF YOUR STATEMENT.
PLEASE RECONCILE YOUR ACCOUNT MONTHLY.

FIGURE 10.5   Simulated Monthly Bank Statement

CHECKS OUTSTANDING	
CHECK NUMBER	AMOUNT
TOTAL CHECKS OUTSTANDING (TRANSFER TO LINE 9)	

RECONCILING YOUR CHECKBOOK BALANCE TO YOUR STATEMENT BALANCE

1. SORT CHECKS INTO CHECK NUMBER ORDER.

2. IN CHECK NUMBER ORDER CHECK OFF EACH CHECK THAT HAS BEEN CHARGED TO YOUR ACCOUNT DURING THE STATEMENT PERIOD IN YOUR CHECKBOOK REGISTER. CHECKS WRITTEN AND NOT CHARGED TO YOUR ACCOUNT ARE LISTED AT THE LEFT AS OUTSTANDING CHECKS.

3. FOLLOW THE INSTRUCTION BELOW IN LINES 1 THROUGH 10.

CHECKBOOK		
1. LIST YOUR CHECKBOOK BALANCE		
2. ADD ANY DEPOSITS OR OTHER CREDITS LISTED ON THE FRONT OF THIS STATEMENT WHICH YOU HAVE NOT RECORDED IN YOUR CHECKBOOK SUCH AS PAYROLL CREDITS OR OTHER DIRECT ELECTRONIC DEPOSITS.		
3. SUBTOTAL		
4. SUBTRACT ANY CHARGE LISTED ON THE FRONT OF THIS STATEMENT WHICH YOU HAVE NOT RECORDED, SUCH AS SERVICE CHARGES, AUTOMATIC TRANSFERS, ELECTRONIC TRANSACTIONS AND OTHER MISCELLANEOUS CHARGES.		
5.		

STATEMENT		
6. LIST YOUR CURRENT STATEMENT BALANCE.		
7. ADD DEPOSITS MADE BUT NOT YET SHOWN ON THIS STATEMENT.		
8. SUBTOTAL		
9. SUBTRACT TOTAL OF CHECKS OUTSTANDING.		
10. ADJUSTED STATEMENT BALANCE		

THESE TWO BALANCES SHOULD AGREE

FIGURE 10.6   Job Aid From Reverse Side of Bank Statement

count holder in making a list of outstanding checks not yet processed by the bank and a list of deposits made that had not yet been recorded in the checkbook register. The back side of the bank statement includes a two-column algorithm typically provided by banks for knowledgeable persons to use in reconciling differences in the monthly statement and checkbook register.

This exercise illustrates the use of simulation in performance assessment. It also demonstrates that performance assessments can sometimes be administered in the form of paper-and-pencil exercises. The information in the bank statement, the checkbook register, and the cancelled checks and deposit slips provide the situational context in which a series of problems are embedded. The problems include (1) account transactions that were processed by the bank, but not recorded in the checkbook register, and (2) computational and recording errors. The students' task is to identify the errors, correct them, and reconcile the balance in the checkbook register with the balance shown on the monthly statement. The supplied materials provide an element of realism to the task, but the authenticity of the task is determined more by the number and types of errors that need to be identified and resolved than by the appearance of the materials. Additional realism might be built into this exercise by training another student to play the role of a partner or spouse who becomes angry at the examinee for failing to record all the transactions in the checkbook register, or for committing the recording or transposition errors. However, including such a partner would complicate the exercise unnecessarily and would most likely be irrelevant to the purpose for administering this assessment unless the examiner wanted to assess the student's ability to resolve problems in interpersonal relationships.

The use of this exercise presumes that students have previously been taught how to use a checking account and how to reconcile the account each month. Proficient students can successfully complete the task in about 24 minutes. However, less proficient individuals often need 35 minutes or more. The test can be administered simultaneously to many students in the same room. Two products should be generated by each examinee: (1) a written reconciliation sheet recorded on the supplied algorithm form or on a piece of blank paper, and (2) a written conclusion indicating whether the account is balanced, and what unresolved discrepancies, if any, exist. Proficient students should be able to identify the errors, resolve them, and then conclude that the account is balanced. However, there are numerous alternative procedures that are acceptable ways of arriving at this conclusion. The procedures used by a student to reach his or her decision should be evident from the completed reconciliation sheet. Hence, it is not necessary for the teacher or examiner to observe all the students' activities as they complete the exercise. Although it was designed to be administered to individual students, each performing separately, this exercise can be administered to students working together in pairs. The disadvantage of allowing students to work together is that the results do not provide an unambiguous assessment of each student's ability to complete the task individually.

One advantage of this exercise is the fidelity of the tasks to real life. Another advantage is that it directly assesses practical know-how that is valued in the world outside of school. One disadvantage is the limited number of transactions and the limited sample of errors built into the exercise. the exercise could be extended to include more transactions and other types of typical errors, but making these changes increases the time required to complete the exercise and the costs of the materials. For classroom assessment purposes, the tasks presented are probably adequate. Another disadvantage of the exercise in its present form is that the printed materials are generally not reusable since the students typically mark up the various materials in the process of completing their work. Consequently, some teachers may find that the reproduction costs exceed their budget. Nevertheless, this exercise is a reasonably efficient means of finding out which students can and which students cannot successfully balance a checking account.

Example 3: Grouping and Counting Objects by 2s

One procedure sometimes used to assess children's ability to count by 2s is to give each child a pencil with a blank piece of paper. Ask each child to write the numeral 2 on the paper and then continue by listing the sequence of even numbers that follows by writing 4, 6, 8, 10, 12, and so on in a list. This is basically a memory task. However, writing or reciting the series of even numbers 2, 4, 6, 8, 10, and so on is not the same as counting the number of objects in a set by 2s. In other words, students who are proficient at reciting a string of even numbers in sequence may not be as proficient in grouping objects into subsets of two and skip counting by 2 until the total number of objects in the whole set has been determined.

A more direct assessment of a child's ability to group and count objects by an interval of two is to present the child with a zip-lock bag containing a set of pennies (or beans, or plastic counters) with the directions shown on the index card in Figure 10.7. These directions should be read to the child. Then the teacher or some other qualified person should observe the child's actions in performing the grouping and counting tasks, and rate the child's performance using a predetermined set of relevant criteria.

The objects to be grouped and counted need not be pennies. In fact, it may be better to use objects other than coins. The type of object used is not the most important issue although it is important to use objects that are discrete from one another, relatively uniform in shape and size, but small enough in size that the child can readily rearrange them in groups.

What is important is that the nature of the task be clearly communicated to each child, and that the teacher-observer be very familiar with the task and the scoring criteria. A suggested rubric for scoring children's performance of this task is displayed in Figure 10.8.

This exercise is designed to be administered individually to one child at a time because it is necessary to have a knowledgeable person observe the processes used by each child in performing the grouping and counting tasks. A teacher who desires to administer this exercise simultaneously to several students would be well advised to prepare a zip-lock bag of counters for each student in advance, and to vary the number in each bag. However, the teacher would also be well advised to

FIGURE 10.7   Directions to Be Read to Children in the Counting by 2s Exercise

> Find out how many pennies are in this bag. Take the pennies out and arrange them in groups so that you can count by 2's. Show me how you do it, by counting out loud and pointing to the pennies as you count them.

4 points	Groups the counters correctly. Counts correctly by consistently incrementing by 2. Does not omit any groups. Counts each group once and only once. Counts aloud at a consistent pace without undue hesitation or verbal awkwardness.
3 points	Groups and counts correctly without assistance, but counts in a hesitant or halting manner.
2 points	Groups the objects correctly, but counts the groups incorrectly by making one or more of the following mistakes. – Fails to count one or more groups, or counts some groups more than once. – Uses inconsistent increments [e.g., "2, 4, 7, 9, 10, 12, 13 . . ."].
1 point	Obtains an incorrect count, because the objects were grouped incorrectly. OR, performs both tasks correctly but only with assistance.
0 points	Fails to complete both tasks.

FIGURE 10.8   Scoring Rubric for Assessing Children's Ability to Group and Count Objects by 2s

recruit additional persons to assist in observing and rating the children's grouping and counting behavior. These volunteers could be parents, older students from another class, student teachers, or other individuals qualified to assist.

The number of counters used should match the developmental level of the children. Several variations or extensions of this exercise can easily be created for use with more advanced children. For instance, the exercise can be varied to assess children's ability to count by intervals other than 2, such as grouping and counting by 5s or by 4s. Four minor changes are needed to vary the interval used: (1) increase the number of counters provided in the set, (2) revise the instructions to specify the new interval, (3) modify the scoring rubric to include the new interval, and (4) make certain that the observer-rater is adequately trained in observing and rating students' use of this new interval.

It is not necessary to restrict the total number of counters to an even multiple of the counting interval. In fact, the teacher may wish to deliberately use an odd number when having the students count by 2s, or a number not evenly divisible by 5 when using this interval. This makes the exercise somewhat more difficult, but it permits the teacher to find out if the students know how to revert to counting by 1s when they reach a final set that is incomplete. This variation may make the task more realistic because in the real world outside of school, when a person needs to group and count by 2s (or some other interval), it is not uncommon to find situations where the total number of objects is not evenly divisible by the interval used.

How to Create Performance Assessment Exercises

Before deciding to use performance assessment in a given situation, potential users should identify the costs and consider the tradeoffs involved. It is important to distinguish between intended learning outcomes that warrant the extra time, effort, and resources needed to assess performance and those that can be validly assessed by some other, more efficient mode of assessment. Performance assessment should be reserved for instructional objectives that involve the use of complex cognitive skills that are more validly assessed by direct observation of performance than by less direct means.

The step-by-step procedure for constructing a performance assessment exercise presented here is designed for teachers who wish to develop such an exercise for use in their own classrooms:

1. Define the performance that you desire to assess.
2. Create the performance tasks or exercises.
3. Define the criteria and rating guidelines.

Defining the Performance That You Desire to Assess

Begin by defining and describing as clearly as possible the nature of the skill or performance that you intend to assess and the focus of the assessment. A clearly stated description should specify the following:

1. The set of skills, proficiencies, and behaviors that skillful performers are likely to use.
2. The subject matter domains that successful performers are likely to draw from in making decisions about what to do, how to do it, and why it should be done.
3. The relevant criteria that should be used to judge the quality of a student's performance.
4. Whether the assessment will focus on observing and judging the process students use, the products they create, or both process and products.

Although it is important during this early stage to identify each of the main criteria proposed for use, it is not necessary that the criteria be fully articulated at this point. Each criterion represents a describable characteristic that provides a defensible basis for determining how well a student has performed. Criteria are ideas about what is good that people use to distinguish between varying levels of good performance and less desirable performance. Hence they are values that people appeal to when they (1) make judgments about quality, or (2) attempt to justify or defend a judgment they have made. It is not necessary to develop explicitly defined scoring rubrics or rating scales during this first step, but it is important to describe the main criteria well enough that one can decide what will count as evidence in making decisions about varying levels of quality performance.

Knowing what skills and proficiencies are involved and what kind of evidence is most relevant provides a basis for making an informed decision about whether to focus on the process, the product, or both. To the extent that it is important to judge how well the student followed a prescribed procedure, the assessment needs to focus on the process used by individual students. To the degree that two or more alternative procedures are equally acceptable, and to the extent that the result is more important than the means of arriving at it, the assessment should focus on the product of the student's effort rather than the process used.

Creating the Performance Tasks or Exercises

The next step is to create tasks or exercises that elicit behaviors that display the degree to which students possess or lack proficiency in using the skills, knowledge, and thinking processes you desire to assess. Make certain that each task closely matches the targeted learning outcome you plan to assess. Also, check to see that each task provides a means of directly observing and assessing students' proficiency level. Be careful to avoid tasks that require irrelevant skills or prior knowledge that is not directly related to the skills and abilities you intend to assess.

One of the most important parts of creating performance tasks or exercises involves writing the instructions that will be given to the students. It is important to communicate to the student what you expect him or her to do. When students are not told enough information, they are left to infer what is expected of them, and their performance may underrepresent what they can do and would have done if they had known more about what the teacher expected. On the other hand, the teacher should avoid providing unnecessary information that overly structures the task or provides unnecessary prompts.

Part of the process of developing performance assessment exercises involves obtaining or creating appropriate stimulus displays that need to be provided as part of the testing situation. The generic term *stimulus displays* refers to the materials, equipment, tools, or other objects provided for the students to use or manipulate as they respond. These objects might include information, reference materials, or job aids that persons would typically have access to and use in performing the task in real life. For example, the pennies or counters used in the grouping and counting by 2s exercise and the batteries, bulbs, wires, battery holders, and bulb holders in the circuit construction exercise are all stimulus displays. The incomplete circuit drawings that the students are expected to complete are also stimulus displays. So are the checkbook register, the bank statement, the blank reconciliation algorithm, and the canceled checks and deposit slips provided for students' use in the checkbook balancing exercise.

Another important part of creating performance assessment exercises involves deciding how many tasks the students should be asked to perform. The research previously cited clearly shows that performance on one task is generally not a good predictor of how students will perform on other apparently similar tasks. A teacher can generally obtain a better estimate of a student's ability by observing and rating his or her performance on several similar tasks. For this reason, the circuit assessment example includes two main tasks. In the first task, the students are asked to construct two circuits, each including one battery and two bulbs: one circuit in which the bulbs are arranged in series, and another circuit in which the bulbs are to be arranged in parallel. Then in the second task, the students are asked to construct two circuits, each including two batteries with a single bulb: one in which the batteries are arranged in series, and another in which the batteries are to be connected in parallel. Similarly, the checkbook balancing exercise intentionally includes several errors that students need to identify and correct.

Adding tasks generally improves the dependability of the scores obtained from a performance assessment, but each additional task also increases the time and expense involved in administering and scoring the exercise. Since this added time and expense reduces the feasibility and usability of the exercise, a teacher must check to see that the benefits accrued from the added tasks clearly outweigh the extra time and other resource costs.

Defining the Criteria and Rating Guidelines

Some teachers become so preoccupied with developing challenging and meaningful assessment tasks that they ignore the need to specify procedures and criteria for rating the students' performance. Any attempt to use performance assessment exercises without judging the individual student's performance is not really assessment. The resulting experiences may be very beneficial in helping students learn, but they are not assessment. The very nature of performance assessment requires judgment. Until a student's performance has been rated or judged, it has not been assessed.

The most difficult part of developing a performance assessment exercise usually involves articulating a set of relevant criteria and operationally defining these criteria in the form of a useful scoring rubric. A rubric is a set of well-defined rules that describes varying degrees of quality ranging from very poor performance to exceptionally good performance. One reason that developing a rubric is an arduous task is that it involves defining what is "good" and trying to distinguish between what is exceptionally good from what is fairly good, mediocre, and unacceptable. Most of us are not accustomed to needing to make such fine distinctions.

One of the best ways to prepare for the difficult task of developing scoring guidelines is to observe numerous examples of the targeted process or product. A veteran teacher may have already observed a broad range of examples of the target performance, including students who performed very well and others who performed poorly. A teacher who has had less exposure to examples of the particular performance in question needs to get more experience. Ideally, this experience should include exposure to a broad range of quality, including numerous examples at varying levels of proficiency. For example, in order to develop a scoring rubric for the circuit assessment task, the authors watched dozens of students attempt to complete this task. They also examined the circuit drawings completed by more than 100 students. As a result of this experience, they became much more aware of the different mistakes that students could make and their creativity in constructing various types of flawed circuits.

After becoming very familiar with the range of quality that can be expected, the teacher should classify the examples observed into tentative categories that represent varying levels of proficiency. One way to do this is to sort the examples into three categories: (1) those that represent very good performance, (2) those that represent performance that is clearly unacceptable, and (3) the borderline cases that are not clearly acceptable or unacceptable. If a large proportion of the examples observed are classified into one of these three categories, it may be helpful to further subdivide that category into two or more subcategories. Once the examples have been adequately classified into categories, the teacher should compare the members within each category and contrast them with the other categories in an attempt to answer the following two questions:

- What characteristics do the members of each category have in common?
- What characteristics distinguish between the various categories?

The next step is to articulate the criteria by generating written descriptive statements that define the characteristics that distinguish between the various categories. The resulting statements should then be organized into a rating scale (see Chapter 12) or a rubric. Pate, Homestead, and McGinnis (1993) offered the following definition of a rubric: "A rubric is a scaled set of criteria that clearly defines for the student and teacher what a range of acceptable and unacceptable performance looks like. The criteria provide descriptions of each level of performance in terms of what students are able to do and assign values to these levels."

The tentative rubric should then be tested or checked. Try it out by using it to assess several new examples of students' performance, including processes or products that are likely to represent high-quality performance and other examples that are likely to represent very poor performance. How feasible is the proposed rubric? Does it help you know what to look for and how to interpret what you see? What important characteristics, if any, have been overlooked or not adequately defined? In what ways, if any, does the rubric need to be revised or clarified?

We recommend that the teacher also ask a colleague who is informed about the subject matter content to review the proposed rubric carefully. Ask her to review the clarity of the written statements. Ask whether she believes the criteria you have proposed are defensible. Ask if she is aware of any other criteria that you have overlooked, but should have included. Ask if she thinks you have overemphasized any aspects of the performance that may not be as important as your rubric suggests. After completing the tryout and review process, the teacher should make whatever changes, additions, deletions, or clarifications are needed.

There may be a temptation to skip this tryout and review process or to go through the motions without seriously questioning the adequacy of the proposed rubric. Shortcutting either process is almost always a mistake. We have constructed rubrics and rating scales for a wide variety of performance assessments. Without exception, when we have submitted the proposed rubric to a series of serious tryouts and when we have obtained a careful review from at least one informed colleague, the result has been well worth the effort, and we have ended up with a better rubric that is easier to use and defend.

Performance assessments are ultimately based on the judgment of the person doing the rating. Consequently, it is essential to have well-defined, defensible criteria and to have a rater who has a thorough understanding of the criteria and how to apply them. Stiggins (1991b) has offered a useful standard for judging the clarity of criteria. Paraphrased, Stiggins's standard states that a teacher has developed clearly defined criteria when she can articulate to a student who performed poorly the specific reasons why the student's performance was judged to be inadequate and what the student needs to do differently to succeed.

But what constitutes "defensible" criteria? Quellmalz (1991) has provided a provocative and insightful discussion of the issues related to this question. Furthermore, she attempted to answer the question by proposing six desirable characteristics that all criteria used in performance assessment ought to possess. Her six desirable characteristics are criteria for criteria; that is, they are generic criteria that teachers can use to assess their own proposed criteria. Quellmalz's six desirable characteristics are listed here. Each characteristic is accompanied by a paraphrased definition of its meaning.

According to Quellmalz, criteria used to assess examinees' performance should possess the following characteristics:

1. *Significance:* Criteria used to assess performance should focus on knowledge and strategies known to characterize skilled performance.
2. *Fidelity:* Criteria used in a performance assessment should be as similar as possible to the criteria used to assess performance under typical real-world situations.
3. *Generalizability:* Criteria should apply to a class or set of similar tasks rather than to one particular task.
4. *Developmental appropriateness:* Criteria should describe a reasonable range of developmental levels or milestones that correspond to the range of achievement among the intended examinees.
5. *Accessibility:* Criteria should be defined clearly enough that students, parents, and other lay persons can understand them.
6. *Utility:* Criteria should be useful to students in helping them understand the strengths and weaknesses of their performance and how they need to improve.

In the next section, we focus on another form of performance assessment that involves displays of representative samples of students' work to demonstrate what they can do. Although the focus is changed somewhat, much of what we have learned about clarifying criteria and articulating defensible rubrics also applies to the process of rating students' portfolios.

Potential Uses of Portfolio Assessment in Your School[3]

Portfolios are not new. They have been used by artists, architects, models, writers, and similar professionals for many years to provide a sample of their work that will demonstrate their skills and achievements. For example, an artist's portfolio would include samples of the artist's work that reveal the depth and breadth of the artist's experiences. Similarly, portfolios have long been used by teachers to document students' accomplishments in art, writing, vocational education, and the like.

What *is* new is that more and more schools are beginning to use portfolios as the primary means of assessing student outcomes in areas typically dominated by traditional paper-and-pencil tests. This increased and altered use of portfolio assessment has entered the educational arena in response to the demands for alternative assessment strategies, especially in light of the criticisms of traditional testing discussed in the preceding section. Before discussing uses of portfolios, however, it may be useful to define just what they are.

---

[3]Appreciation is expressed to Vanessa D. Moss for sharing insights into portfolio assessment gained not only from reviewing literature on the topic but also, and more important, from extensive experience in using portfolios to assess students' learning. Many of the ideas presented in this section also draw on the writings of Vavrus (1990) and, to a lesser extent, on those of Valencia (1990).

What Is a Portfolio?

Portfolios, coming from the word *port,* which means "carry," and *folio* which means "paper," have also been called "school literary folders" (Jongsma, 1989), "authenticity measures" (Valencia, 1990), and "collaborative assessment" (Valencia, 1990). The term *collaborative assessment* refers to the fact that well-conducted portfolio assessment can strengthen the relationship between student and teacher as they become partners in learning. The involvement of students in actively assessing their progress by reviewing and analyzing the performances documented in their portfolios is one of the greatest potential strengths of this method.

Arter and Spandel (1992) define a portfolio as "a purposeful collection of student work that tells the story of the student's effort, progress, or achievement in (a) given area(s)" (1992, p. 36). Arter and Spandel further specify that "this collection must include student participation in selection of portfolio content; the guidelines for selection; the criteria for judging merit; and evidence of student self-reflection" (1992, p. 36).

What Does a Portfolio Look Like?

Unlike some common misconceptions, a portfolio is not merely some expandable, flexible file stuffed full of miscellaneous art sketches or snippets of writing. Those who view portfolios as merely containers full of aggregated stuff either have never seen a portfolio or, at best, have seen only poor examples. As Vavrus points out, "it is what's in the container, rather than the container itself, that becomes a student's portfolio" (1990, p. 48). Yet, unfortunately, some educators seem more preoccupied with the container than with what to put in it. Valencia (1990) has covered the essential concerns about the portfolio's physical dimension in saying that it must be larger and more elaborate than a report card, yet smaller and more ordered than a storage trunk filled with accumulated artifacts. Whether it is a large expandable file folder or a segmented chest with styrofoam-lined compartments depends on whether the student's products are displayed on paper or sculpted in clay.

Vavrus (1990) has insightfully noted that the more important physical aspect of a portfolio is how the documents used to record students progress are actually arranged. Portfolios may be structured so that documents are ordered chronologically, by subject area, or by type or style of product. A portfolio could be focused entirely on a student's writing, for example, or it could be divided into sections, each containing the student's work in a different content area. Whatever the organizing scheme, the student should have a say in how the contents of the portfolio are arranged. Having students participate in the critical thinking that determines how the portfolio will be organized is one of the important reasons for using portfolios (Jongsma, 1989).

In addition, Vavrus points out, each good portfolio also contains a less obvious but not less important conceptual structure, which reflects the teacher's (and perhaps the student's) underlying goals for student learning. We will say more about this later in discussing the philosophy underlying use of portfolios.

What Should a Portfolio Contain?

This question cannot be answered well here, for even the appropriate candidates for inclusion—let alone inappropriate items—are nearly as diverse as are the combinations of content and intent that lead to portfolios being kept. The range of what to include is almost limitless. The key is to provide a variety of types of indicators of learning so that teachers, parents, students, and administrators can build a complete picture of the student's development.

The content of a portfolio should contain whatever documentation is necessary to show changes and growth over time in the student's understandings, skills, and achievements. Examples of what might be placed in portfolios include, but are not limited to, the following:

1. Samples of the student work selected by the teacher, student, teacher and student, or parent(s) in areas such as
   a. Writing assignments (essays, stories, book reports, research papers, and so on) that reflect student progress in writing
   b. Worksheets showing samples of complex math computations or calculations involved in solving increasingly complex story problems
   c. Science lab reports, including description of how findings were reached and interpreted
   d. Works of art produced by the student
   e. Photographs of items constructed by the student
   f. Audiotapes of student reading, singing, playing a musical instrument, or performing a role in a dramatic production
   g. Audiotapes of the student talking about pictures in a book
   h. List of books read by the student
2. Reflective critiques of the various samples of the student's work written by the student
3. Progress notes submitted by the teacher and student as they collaboratively review the student's growth
4. Teachers' observational notes
5. Notes from parent–teacher conferences

The first two categories listed—samples of the student work and reflective critiques written by the student—are the essential parts of a portfolio. The other three items are options that may or may not be included. The critiques should provide evidence of evaluative thinking on the part of the student in light of relevant criteria. They should identify specific strengths and weaknesses of each work sample as viewed by the student. The critique may also include statements from the student describing what she learned from the experience of producing the work and indications of what she would change if she were to attempt to improve upon the current version of the product.

The examples of student work listed here are only a few of the items you might find useful to include in student portfolios. Rather than producing a long "laundry list" of likely ingredients in a portfolio, it may be more useful to provide you with several guidelines for how to decide what to include. Of course, the exact nature of the portfolio will vary depending on the student and the curriculum goals, making it difficult for us to prescribe what you should include in any particular portfolio. However, the following guidelines should prove helpful.

First, Vavrus has suggested several questions that can serve as a useful checklist for determining what goes into a portfolio. Before determining what to include ask yourself the following questions:

- Who is the intended audience for the portfolios? Parents? Administrators? Other teachers?
- What will this audience want to know about student learning?
- Will the selected documents or artifacts show aspects of student growth that test scores don't capture? Or, will they corroborate evidence that test scores already suggest about student performance?
- What kinds of evidence will best show student progress toward your identified learning goals?
- Will the portfolio contain best work only or a progressive record of student growth or both?
- Will the portfolio include more than the finished pieces—for example, ideas, sketches, and revisions? (1990, p. 50)

Second, make certain that portfolios are not merely collections of each week's graded paper, tossed into the portfolio rather than into school or home wastebaskets. The process of determining what to include should be selective to be sure that the items selected reflect well the progress of the student in relation to what you and the student have agreed will serve as the benchmarks for measuring growth in knowledge or skill or both.

Third, periodically review with the student and parents the contents of the portfolio to determine if they are serving their purpose. Do they clearly portray how the student is doing? Are they helpful to you and the student in identifying both progress and areas in need of further work? If the answer to either of these questions is negative, adjust what you are putting into the portfolio until you can answer those questions affirmatively.

Fourth, use your key curriculum and instructional goals to guide your selection of the contents of each portfolio.

Fifth, have the student review the portfolio at regular intervals, focusing her attention on specific items or themes that run through the items, tracing either chronological or thematic growth. The student's written reflections about what the portfolio's contents show about his or her growth can also become useful records to include for later review.

Sixth, do not select the contents of the portfolio from a single source, even if that source is the most obvious—the student. In addition to the student's products or descriptions of processes used, your own anecdotal records of the student's activities or behavior are important, as are observations of parents and other children (carefully selected to exclude any that would be inappropriate, of course). Information shared during parent–teacher conferences can be especially helpful.

Seventh, you may find it especially helpful to include a table of contents or a "summary form" in each portfolio to facilitate review and synthesis of the information it contains.

Where Should Portfolios Be Kept?

The answer to this question obviously depends on the size of the portfolios and the amount and location of available storage space. One general guideline to follow, however, is that portfolios should be placed in a spot in the classroom that is easily accessible to students as well as teachers. According to Valencia, "Unlike the secretive grade book or the untouchable permanent records stored in the office, these are working folders. There location must invite students and teachers to contribute to them on an ongoing basis and to reflect on their contents to plan the next learning steps" (1990, p. 339).

In addition to being accessible to both students and teachers, portfolios should be accessible to parents. Parents are encouraged not only to access materials from the portfolio but also to add items or to advise the student on what should be placed in the portfolio.

Of course, a student's portfolio should not be accessible to other students unless she approves such access. All students should be taught to respect one another's portfolio privacy, even while being encouraged to share items in their portfolio with other students as they desire.

Now that we have described what portfolios are, what they look like, what they should contain, and where they should be kept, you might ask why one would choose to use an assessment tool that is obviously as time consuming as the portfolio. The question can be answered only in the context of a full understanding of the purposes and philosophy that undergirds and overarches the use of portfolios.

What Philosophy and Purposes Underlie Portfolio Assessment?

At the core of portfolio assessment is the recognition that instruction and assessment should be closely intertwined. Those who use portfolios are not concerned with the time they consume, for they recognize that portfolios are as much an instructional tool as they are an assessment device. Perhaps Valencia says it best:

> Portfolios represent a philosophy that demands that we view assessment as an integral part of our instruction, providing a process for teacher and student to use to guide learning. It is an expanded definition of assessment in situations before, during and after instruction. It is a philosophy that honors both the process and the products of learning as well as the active participation of the teacher and the students in their own evaluation and growth (1990, p. 340)

Valencia also underscores the fact that portfolios are continuous, ongoing, ever-changing instruments in which revisions are made frequently as teachers become more aware of student needs. Therefore, a central feature of portfolio assessment is that both the process and the outcomes (products) of learning are continually evaluated. Thus, "When we are positioned to observe and collect information continuously, we send a message to student, parents, and administrators that learning is never completed; instead, it is always evolving, growing and changing" (Valencia, 1990, p. 338). This type of assessment tool is intended to "capture the authentic, continuous, multidimensional, interactive requirement of sound assessment" (Valencia, 1990, p. 339).

The use of portfolios also is an attempt to help students take greater responsibility for their own learning. Wiggins has urged that "Teachers need to rethink their relationships with students and consider their roles as coaches or enablers of student performance. . . . The whole point is to put the student in a self-disciplined, self-regulating, self-assessing position. Portfolios can help in this process" (Wiggins, 1990, p. 51). Viewed in this manner, assessment is not only a process that is within the teacher's control but also one that can be partially directed by the student, thus helping her identify how well she has learned and what she needs to learn next.

This process is facilitated by having students study their portfolios at various times during the year. When studying, students should ask themselves the following questions:

- What do I like most about this work?
- What was important to me when I wrote it?
- If I revised this, what would I change?
- How has my writing changed since I wrote this?
- How is it like other pieces of my work? Is it my best sample? (Vavrus, 1990, p. 52)

As students reflect on such questions, it is important that frequent student–teacher discussions be held to review portfolio contents and to help guide students if they have difficulty in answering the questions. At least four or five sessions should be held with each student, and monthly sessions—or even more often, if possible—would be better. During such discussions, the teachers can discern how students are accomplishing learning tasks rather than simply viewing end products such as those produced by most traditional approaches to assessment. This is especially important in subjects in which the process is as important as the product, such as writing.

To summarize, portfolios can serve a variety of both instructional and assessment purposes. Specifically, portfolio assessment can serve as

- An instructionally linked way to assess student performance
- A method for portraying a broad view of a student's achievements across a broad range of content
- A way to document adequately a student's growth in a particular content area
- A mechanism to enable students to identify their own strengths and weaknesses
- A method for encouraging students to participate in and take more responsibility for their own learning
- A valuable source of information for parents and administrators

Does Portfolio Assessment Have Any Significant Weaknesses?

Portfolios obviously have numerous strengths, and nearly everything we have written so far points to inherent advantages that can be gained from their proper use. But are there any significant drawbacks in using portfolio assessment? Of course.

Everything has some drawbacks, and portfolio assessment is no different. Even though we think it well worth your serious consideration if you are not already using portfolio assessment, there are several drawbacks we should mention.

First, portfolios obviously require an additional investment of time by already overextended teachers. This problem is not trivial and should not be overlooked or downplayed. The research conducted by Wolfe and Miller (1997) led them to conclude that the most troublesome barrier to the use of portfolios is the amount of time required. This includes the in-class time required for students to prepare their portfolios and the amount of out-of-class time required to review and evaluate them. School systems that are serious about using portfolios need to find ways to help teachers solve this problem. Although we agree with Wiggins (1990) that it may be possible to free up and redistribute some portion of teachers' total time, it seems unlikely that there will be major changes in the way teachers are currently spending their time (unless there are a lot more teachers than we think who are counting milk money and engaging in other tasks that are instructionally peripheral or irrelevant). There does not seem to be an easy answer for where to find the additional time to allow teachers to engage in the more labor-intensive portfolio assessment process. Perhaps the best answer is to leave it to each teacher, hoping that the vision of the potential advantages of this technique motivates her to identify other less important activities that can be jettisoned or streamlined to make room to use portfolio assessment in at least some subject areas.

Second, the work samples included in a particular student's portfolio may not be representative of what that student actually knows and can do (Arter & Spandel, 1992). This question of representativeness is especially important because parents and other interested stakeholders tend to assume that the examples are typical of what the student can do. To the extent that this assumption is not true, the portfolio may lead parents and other interested individuals to either overestimate or underestimate the student's ability level. In either case, the resulting interpretation would be a distortion of the student's abilities and achievements.

Third, Valencia (1990) has pointed out that, ironically, one of the greatest strengths of the portfolio approach—its flexibility—could well lead to its greatest flaw. This flexibility could lead to unreliability, inconsistency, and inequity in classrooms, schools, and districts (Valencia, 1990). But the difficult task of finding appropriate ways to standardize portfolio-based student assessments still resists solution. Without some acceptable standard, it will be difficult for the schools in Maine to know how to interpret (or relate to their own placement standards) the Portfolio Assessment Summary that accompanies a newly arrived student from Virginia. As Valencia notes, the development of a common instructional goal throughout the school and district could reflect consistency into the portfolio approach, and the use of the nearly continuous measurement could add reliability and consistency to individual students' total scores or grades in an area. Yet the more one moves toward standardization, the more one risks losing the rich individualization that is one of the major reasons for opting for portfolio assessment in the first place. How to solve this conundrum is one of the daunting issues that still confronts portfolio assessment.

A closely related challenge is that of deciding how portfolios should be scored or evaluated. The teachers surveyed by Wolfe and Miller (1997) reported that problems associated with scoring was the second most troublesome barrier impeding the use of portfolios. So far, very little useful information about this topic exists in the literature about portfolios. In essence, the whole concept of a portfolio lies in trying to get away from using a single score to determine a student's grade. Most evaluation of portfolios is subjective and qualitative, which does not necessarily mean *bad,* but which seldom means *good.*

Vavrus has suggested, "The key to scoring a portfolio is in setting standards relative to your goals for student learning ahead of time. Portfolios can be evaluated in terms of standards of excellence or on growth demonstrated within an individual portfolio, rather than on comparisons made among different students work" (1990, p. 53). Good advice, but not very well operationalized. As with most writers, Vavrus developed this section the least. Beyond general hints, little helpful counsel is provided on just how to evaluate portfolios. Unfortunately, we have no sudden wisdom in this area either. Just how to score and evaluate portfolios so as to retain their individuality while permitting adequate standardization is a puzzle that awaits solution, a solution that we hope will come from the combined efforts and cooperation of assessment specialists, teachers, and other educational practitioners.

Finally, portfolios may prove too unwieldy to serve well as a means of providing information needed for educational accountability at district, state, or national levels. For example, a recent report stated that "portfolios may be useful for teachers to gauge students' writing abilities, but a new Education Department study indicated they may prove unwieldy for national assessment" (Report on Education Research, 1992a, p. 1). The difficulties encountered by assessment specialists in using portfolios in this national assessment are likely to be found at state and district levels as well.

Steps to Take in Using Portfolio Assessment

The limitations just discussed do not suggest to us that portfolios should be abandoned but rather that their limitations should be honestly acknowledged even as we use them for the benefits they can provide. Vavrus (1990) has provided a simple but useful set of steps for using portfolios. In the remainder of this section, we offer adapted excerpts of her very straightforward but powerful suggestions. We will not expand at length on each point but will offer only simple examples since much of the activity that would be carried out under several steps has been suggested earlier in this section.

Step 1. *Deciding What the Portfolio Should Look Like.* This step would include (1) deciding on the physical aspects of the portfolio, including both the container and the structure or organization of its contents, and (2) deciding on the conceptual structure—that is , the learning goals and their linkage to instructional activities and assessment tasks.

Step 2. *Deciding What Goes into the Portfolio.* Here we refer you to our prior section on this topic, including Vavrus's guidelines. What is essential is that you select the student's portfolio samples from the variety of daily and weekly learning activities and assessment tasks that are a part of your ongoing instruction–assessment cycle. And be sure to add those "reflective records" in which students review and appraise their earlier efforts and progress.

Step 3. *Deciding How and When to Select Portfolio Samples.* Will your selection follow natural instructional cycles, such as end of unit, semester, or year? Who will select the contents? The teacher? The student? Or, and of course this is the preferable answer, both, working collaboratively? Answers to these questions may seem trivial, but failure to reflect on them early often results in a portfolio that is merely a hodgepodge. Even when it comes to items you select directly for inclusion, you need to establish some system of dating and providing explanatory captions to help you later remember the sequence of activities and products you selected and why they were chosen instead of other items. An error as simple as forgetting to date your own observations about a student that you file in his or her portfolio will rob those observations of much of their usefulness later on.

Step 4. *Deciding How to Evaluate Portfolios.* Although admittedly a difficult task, this step is still essential. Vavrus suggests you must set some standards, perhaps developing a scale that lists a progression of performance standards a student might be expected to attain over time. Sometimes it is useful to consult other teachers nearby who are using portfolios or even to contact schools featured in national media as deeply involved in portfolio assessment to learn how they are scoring and evaluating their portfolios. Although their systems are not likely to have resolved all the challenges we discussed earlier, they are likely to be far more advanced than your pioneer efforts would be without their greater experience to guide you.

Step 5. *Deciding How to Pass Portfolios On.* What do you do with a portfolio at year's end? Send it home with the student or pass it on to the student's next teacher? Perhaps the answer should be yes, for both possibilities have merit. Parents can benefit from careful review of the student's year-end portfolio. But ideally that portfolio should find its way to the student's next teacher. Perhaps a careful selection can be made of key information to be retained for use by future teachers, and the remainder sent home with the student, thus also paring down the accumulating bulk of a multiple-year portfolio to a manageable size. Photocopying portfolio contents or printing duplicate copies if the product is on a computer disk is a way to have the best of both worlds. However you choose to decide this issue, it is an essential step if any portfolio is to have its optimal impact.

As stated previously, we believe that performance assessment holds great promise as a means of improving what is taught in the schools and how it is assessed. However, this high potential can be realized only to the extent to which the following 12 issues are successfully resolved.

Critical Issues Facing Alternative Assessment[4]

Each of the following 12 issues is a challenge that must be met before alternative assessment can reach its full potential. Of course, alternative assessment will continue, in the various forms listed previously, whether or not the following issues

---

[4]This section draws heavily on an article by one of the authors published in the *Phi Delta Kappan* (Worthen, 1993a).

are addressed. Yet use of these nontraditional methods is unlikely to play the pivotal role in education that alternative assessment's advocates propose for it unless these 12 issues can be resolved.

Conceptual Clarity

As yet, there is too little coherence to the concepts and language being used in both written and oral discourse about alternative assessment, performance assessment, authentic assessment, direct assessment, and practical testing (Ruiz-Primo & Shavelson, 1996). Authors of various descriptors for these types of assessments have not carefully tacked down their definitional edges or delineated clearly what belongs to a particular label and what does not. For clear communication to occur, especially in technical and scientific endeavors, it is important to use language in which each concept is invariably described by the same term, and each term refers to only one phenomenon (Neurath, Carnap, & Morris, 1955). Until this occurs, the entire alternative assessment movement risks becoming trapped in thickets of tangled terminology and conceptual clutter and confusion. Those who recall how interest in the "discovery" method of teaching surged through the schools in the 1960s will remember how quickly it slowed to a trickle in the 1970s when it became clear that one teacher's "guided discovery" method was identical to the "expository" method of another, while closely resembling the "independent discovery" method of a third, and so on. This promising field of instructional inquiry sank and was soon submerged in semantic swamps that no one had bothered to drain. If alternative assessment is to survive the decade and develop into a potent force for educational improvement, then its advocates must take time to clarify its concepts and terminology. It cannot continue to be, as one friendly critic put it, a movement whose only definition is that "it is everything that a multiple-choice test is not."[5]

Mechanisms for Self-Criticism

No reform movement should be without those who are as skeptical of their own efforts as they are of the efforts they seek to change or displace. Yet such internal self-criticism has been scarce among proponents of alternative assessment. Ironically, the future of alternative assessment could be threatened by its very popularity. As voices of caution are drowned by the clamor for more rapid adoption of alternative assessment methods, advocates of those methods could easily forget that self-criticism is the only road to continuing improvement of any movement and, indeed, is essential if that movement is to make a lasting contribution.

Fortunately, some of alternative assessment's most articulate advocates have recognized this problem and urged that it be addressed:

---

[5]From comments made by Joan Herman in a speech delivered to the Consortium on Expanded Assessment (sponsored by ASCD), San Diego, November 5, 1991.

If the current interest in alternatives to standardized testing is to be anything but this decade's flurry, we have to be as tough-minded in designing new options as we are in critiquing available testing. Unless we analyze the workings of these alternatives and design them carefully, we may end up with a different, but perhaps no less blunt, set of assessment instruments. (Linn, 1990)

As with any form of assessment, the familiar, difficult, and nasty issues of efficiency, equity, and evidence persist. Whereas there is considerable criticism of the approaches taken by standardized tests, as yet we have no such critical tradition for new modes of assessment. And we cannot be without one. (Wolf et al. 1991, p. 60)

A few other scholars (for example, Baker, 1994; Bateson, 1994; Linn, 1993; Resnick & Resnick, 1996; Ruiz-Primo & Shavelson, 1996; Wiggins, 1993; Wiley & Haertel, 1996) have helped to foster a spirit of reflective questioning and constructive criticism among advocates of alternative assessment. Since education is being flooded with an outpouring of enthusiasm and euphoria for assessment alternatives, there is an urgent need for more of this reflective questioning. If not channeled and filtered by careful and constructive self-criticism, this outpouring is as likely to wreak havoc with assessment as it is to improve it.

Training Educators in Using Alternative Forms of Assessment

The very nature of alternative assessment (and one of its major strengths) pivots on the close linkages of assessment with instruction (McTighe, 1997). Thus the classroom teacher is the gatekeeper of effective alternative assessment; indeed, it would be hard to imagine a successful large-scale performance assessment taking place without teacher cooperation. To be feasible, large-scale alternative assessment would require teachers to help administer and score measures. Further, optimal performance assessments should be developed at least partly by the teachers from whose curricula the instructional targets are drawn.

Of course, performance assessment's heavy dependence on teachers would require that they be competent to perform high-quality alternative assessments. To a much greater degree than in traditional assessment, the quality of alternative assessments will be directly affected by how well teachers are prepared in relevant assessment knowledge skills.

Good alternative assessment obviously requires a somewhat different set of assessment competencies than what is needed in traditional multiple-choice testing. But *different from* does not mean *less than*. Scoring rubrics and criteria necessary for several types of performance measures will prove as challenging for most teachers as have grade equivalent scores. Staff development programs to provide practitioners with confidence and competence to function effectively in all relevant areas of assessment is essential if the full potential of alternative assessment is to be realized. Guskey (1994) emphasized that attempts to implement authentic assessment without providing teachers with extensive and sustained training in how to use this approach are likely to fail. The research reported by Aschbacher (1994) and Shepard et al. (1996) also demonstrates the importance of providing teachers with needed training in effective use of alternative assessment.

Shavelson and his colleagues (1994) developed an inservice education program for classroom teachers designed to help them understand the nature of different performance assessments and scoring systems, how to judge the quality and usefulness of different assessments, and how to use them in their classrooms. Their experience in implementing this staff development program provides reason for concern as reflected in the following quote:

> After implementing the program more than 10 times, we learned that many teachers think of performance assessments as anything that asks students to manipulate materials (the hands-on part of the assessment). Not surprisingly, the characteristics of the task demands, the response formats, and the scoring system are not considered in judging the quality of the assessments (the mind-on or -off part of the assessment). (Ruiz-Primo & Shavelson, 1996, p. 1059)

Technical Quality and Truthfulness

Although several scholars have proposed lists of technical specifications and criteria that should be used to judge the quality of alternative forms of assessment (Baker, O'Neil, & Linn, 1993; Dunbar, Koretz, & Hoover, 1991; Linn, Baker, & Dunbar, 1991; Linn & Baker, 1996; Messick, 1994, 1995b), there is as yet no clear consensus in the field. Some assessment specialists would redefine or replace common conceptions of validity or reliability with alternative touchstones of acceptability (for example, Moss, 1992, 1994; Wiggins, 1991), whereas others argue that alternative assessment will not be useful if its measures are not held to the same high standards of reliability and validity education has demanded of existing paper and pencil assessments (for example, Cizek, 1991a).

The issue is not simple. Thorny technical questions abound. Can one generalize satisfactorily from specific performance assessment tasks to the broader domain of achievement needs? When students evidence that they can complete a specific hands-on science project is that evidence that they can "do science," do science projects of that type, or only that they can do that particular science project? Is performance task-dependent or generalizable from task to task? If task-dependent, how many tasks must students perform before one can generalize to meaningful levels of competence that transcend the specific task? At first glance, these may seem like technical questions that only researchers should worry about, but Oosterhof (1996) explains why classroom teachers must worry about them too. As he points out, "a teacher usually has no choice but to generalize. A teacher can observe only a small fraction of potential student performances and realistically must generalize beyond what is observed" (Oosterhof, 1996, p. 46). Oosterhof explains the problem further and identifies a significant issue that teachers need to address if they are to make defensible decisions about individual students.

> When a teacher formally or informally assesses students, the teacher observes only a small fraction of what might be observed. For instance, a written test incorporates only a portion of items that could be included in the test. A performance assessment typically asks a student to complete just one task out of many that the student might have been asked to perform. A typical portfolio includes only a fraction of the material that

potentially could be included. Within informal assessments, a teacher casually observes a given student for only a fraction of the time that the student might have been observed. Likewise, when a teacher spontaneously asks questions during instruction, these questions represent but a small number of those the teacher might have asked.

The fact that assessment involves only a small sample of potential observations raises a very important question. *Would the conclusions a teacher draws based on what was observed be different if what was not observed were included?* If what a teacher observed does not generalize to what was not observed, the conclusions are useful, at best, only within the narrow context of the observation (p. 45; emphasis added).

One of the major problems associated with performance assessment is that students often obtain inconsistent scores on similar tasks selected from the same domain. Consequently, a student's score on one task generally does not provide an adequate basis for predicting how that student will perform on other similar tasks in the same domain. A number of researchers have reported findings supporting this conclusion (Dunbar, Koretz, & Hoover, 1991; Gao, Shavelson, & Baxter, 1994; Shavelson, Baxter, & Gao, 1993; van der Vleuten & Swanson 1990). Interested readers who want to learn more about this problem should study the articles by Linn (1993), Linn and Burton (1994), and Brennan and Johnson (1995). Some reasons for the inconsistency in students' performance across tasks that appear to be similar may be that students' performance on a particular task depends on their prior knowledge of the domain, the way the directions are worded, the context in which the problem is presented, and the nature of the subject-matter content embedded in the task. Further research needs to be conducted to better understand the nature of this problem and the factors that contribute to it.

The crux of the issue is whether or not the alternative assessment movement will be able to evidence that its assessments are able to reflect accurately a student's true ability in significant areas of behavior relevant to adult life. Whether called reliability, validity, or something else, some evidence that the technical quality of the assessment yields a truthful portrayal of student abilities is essential. To succeed, alternative assessment must show that its tasks and measures genuinely reflect authentic assessment (not merely authentic-*looking* assessment). Otherwise, the promise it holds for helping improve teaching and learning will be unfulfilled.

Standardization of Assessment Judgments

Some proponents of alternative assessment are excited by its potential to allow flexible, diverse assessment, tailored to the individual student. Wolf and her colleagues (1991) have argued persuasively that scoring rubrics for performance assessments, portfolios, and exhibitions often assume erroneously that all students progress from novice to expert along the same unidimensional scale. They note that "as we move to different modes of assessment, the contest between idealized, universal descriptions of progress and differentiated but potentially divisive rubrics will be fierce" (p. 63). They make a convincing case that insistence on uniform standards would make a mockery of the important and time-honored role that educators' clinical judgments and diversity of opinions has played. Yet others are quick to note that insistence on such diversity, however ideal, could easily undermine the alternative assessment movement by rendering its results too variable to support comparisons that governing boards, legislators, and the public are demanding as part of educational accountability (Wiggins, 1991, 1997). It would be rather optimistic, if not naive, to assume that the clamor for accountability would be stilled simply by informing school patrons and key decision makers that alternative assessment is not intended to support such comparisons. Maeroff (1991) addressed this issue in his analysis of the alternative assessment effort in Rhode Island.

> Furthermore, there must be standardization of some sort, as Rhode Island hopes to achieve. Otherwise, there is no way to put the findings of an assessment in context. . . . And the work doesn't stop with declaring, for example, that students will submit portfolios. What should be in the portfolios? What should students be asked about the contents of their portfolios? How can some element of standardization be lent to the process so that one student's portfolio may be compared with another's? Putting less emphasis on comparisons is fine, but at some point a child and his parents have a right to know whether the child's progress is reasonable for his or her age and experience. (pp. 275–276)

Resolving how to standardize criteria and performance levels sufficiently to support necessary comparisons without causing them to lose the power and richness of assessment tailored to the student's needs and achievements is a key issue to the future of this movement, especially if alternative assessments are to be used to support high-stakes decisions.

Ability to Assess Complex Thinking Skills

One of the key reasons for promoting alternative assessment is the conviction that such assessments can measure complex, higher-order abilities that are difficult, if not impossible, to assess with traditional measures (for example, Bracey, 1989). Although there are examples of well-developed multiple-choice tests that *do* assess high-order thinking skills (HOTS) and even have HOTS subscales (for example, the *Metropolitan Achievement Test,* 6th ed.), even supporters of standardized multiple-choice tests are unlikely to argue that measuring HOTS is a particular strength of such measures. Yet that is widely thought to be the signature of alternative assessment, and analyses of research data and surveys of professional educators' opinions concerning the utility of direct assessment versus objective tests (for example, Suhor, 1985) seem to bear this out.

But do alternative modes of assessment *necessarily* require the use of more complex cognitive processes by students? Can we be assured that we are measuring reasoning ability, problem-solving skills, or other HOTS just because we use some form of performance assessment? Obviously not. As Linn and his colleagues (1991) remind us: "The construction of an open-ended proof of a theorem in geometry can be a cognitively complex task or simply the display of a memorized sequence of responses to a particular problem, depending on the novelty of the task and the prior experience of the learner" (p. 19).

Very few research studies have empirically examined the assumption that performance assessments engage students in higher-order thinking. However, Baxter and her colleagues conducted two studies focused on this issue (Baxter, Glaser, &

Raghaven, 1993; Baxter, Elder, & Glaser, 1995). The results of the second study provide evidence in support of the claim that performance assessments assess higher-order thinking skills, but the results of the first study are not so supportive. Ruiz-Primo and Shavelson (1996) interpreted the findings of the first Baxter et al. study as follows:

> Their [Baxter, Glaser, & Raghaven, 1994] findings suggested that performance assessments may not necessarily lead to higher-order thinking. Characteristics of the assessment task hold the key. Tasks that provided procedural instructions to students may not allow them to show what they know and can do. Also, scoring systems that were inconsistent with the characteristics of the task, and did not reflect students' meaningful use of knowledge and problem-solving procedures, tended not to capture higher-order thinking. In one of the tasks analyzed, for example, the authors concluded that even though the task of exploring the maplecopter was rich in providing students opportunities to engage in higher-order thinking, the scoring system failed to capture the essence of proficient students' performances. The scoring system ignores the scientific validity of the way students manipulate the variables; it considers only the number of variables used by students.
>
> Even though performance assessments intend to measure higher-order thinking processes, poorly designed assessments do not guarantee that such thinking processes occur. More research linking performance assessment scores with students' cognitive processes is needed before we can be sure that performance assessments measure higher-order thinking.
>
> If performance assessment tasks are to measure higher-order thinking, the assessment should permit students to demonstrate what they know and can do, rather than direct their performances. *Assessment structure* (i.e., task and response format structure) then becomes an important issue in the design of performance assessments. (Ruiz-Primo & Shavelson, 1996, p. 1055)

If alternative assessment is to develop its full potential for assessing HOTS, great care must be taken to select and present assessment tasks in ways that require students to use—and show—complex thinking skills in their response rather than simply *assuming* they are using such skills because they are responding to a hands-on task. Similar care must be expended in developing and validating scoring systems that adequately account for differences in the nature of the thinking processes employed by the students.

Acceptability to Education's Stakeholders

The earlier discussion of standardization of assessment judgments hinted at a critical issue to the future of alternative assessment, and that is the extent to which this movement proves acceptable to education's key stakeholders—legislators, school boards, parents, teachers, students, and associations of professional educators, to name only a few (we say more in a later section about how to judge key stakeholders' readiness for alternative assessment). Some schools may have stakeholders who readily accept the importance and usefulness of alternative assessment, whereas other schools may confront outright public rejection of any non-traditional forms of student assessment because their accountability-oriented stakeholders perceive that these forms will not provide them with readily manageable information. Most boards of education can, with little orientation, interpret test scores intelligently, whereas they will likely find it more difficult (though by no means impossible) to deal with summaries of student performance on other indices such as portfolios. Useful as many of these methods are for describing student performance in meaningful ways to the teacher and perhaps to individual parents, most of these assessment methods are more difficult to summarize across individuals, making it difficult to use them for reporting learning outcomes for entire classes, schools, districts, or state systems. Yet, beyond the individual parent, these are precisely the levels at which educational administrators, policymakers, legislators, the lay public—and even many teachers—feel the greatest need for information. Public demand for evidence that teachers and schools are effectively educating students is increasing, and test scores are typically the kind of evidence the public finds most credible. Until and unless the public ceases to demand such assessment-driven accountability, proponents of alternative assessment must grapple with this simplistic view of educational reform and find ways to convince stakeholders that alternative assessment can play a pivotal role in improving teaching and learning that far transcends its inability to generate simple snapshot data for decision makers.

A related key to the future of alternative assessment is the ability of its advocates to guide it along the narrow path that winds between the swamps of "underselling" and the pitfalls of "overpromising." It will take patience to persist on that pathway when the publics and many educators clamor for immediate solutions to critical problems in our schools. Some leading proponents of performance assessment have suggested privately that it will take a decade before these forms of assessment are sufficiently developed and tested to allow widespread dependence on them to support educational decisions. Given the recent trends seen in mandating of performance assessment by many legislative bodies and funding agencies, alternative assessment is unlikely to have a decade in which to mature before being judged on its ability to solve some of education's thorniest problems.

In their eagerness to eradicate traditional modes of testing, advocates of alternative assessment sometimes downplay the significance of the political factors described in the two previous paragraphs. By so doing, they jeopardize the success of the assessment reforms they are attempting to implement. The rise and fall of the short-lived California Learning Assessment System (CLAS) is a case in point. CLAS was an ambitious attempt to mandate alternative assessment on a statewide basis in place of the existing California Assessment Program (CAP). However, the new program became very controversial and failed after its first year of implementation because of organized opposition from various groups of constituents, including parents, the California Teachers Association, the California School Boards Association, conservative religious groups, and the governor (Honig, Alexander, & Wolf, 1996). Many parents, teachers, and religious groups expressed concerns that CLAS was unnecessarily intrusive and violated their privacy. Others were concerned that the program failed to provide information about students' achievement of basic skills. In their analysis of California's failure, Kirst and Mazzeo (1996) identified three categories of factors that contributed to the program's failure.

These include (1) the tension between political concerns and technical factors (for example, sampling issues and concerns about the reliability and accuracy of the resulting scores), (2) the lack of consensus among key stakeholders regarding the goals and priorities of the project (for example, should the assessments focus on providing accurate scores for each student or accurate estimates of achievement aggregated by school or district?), and (3) antipathy toward the state government.

The failure of California's attempt to mandate high-stakes alternative assessments on a statewide basis and similar controversies at the local school level (for example, the Littleton, Colorado, 1993 school board election described in Rothman, 1995) illustrate the political nature of attempts to reform assessment in the schools. These experiences also emphasize the importance of involving the various stakeholder groups in making decisions and working with constituents to build a sense of ownership for a proposed innovative assessment program.

Of course, there are also legal issues involved in high-stakes testing. "The higher the stakes, the more there is concern for individual fairness and the more likely there is to be a legal challenge to the testing requirement" (Phillips, 1994, p. 709). Bond (1995) and Madaus (1994) call attention to issues of bias and fairness that need to be considered. Phillips (1993) discusses potential legal challenges that high-stakes performance assessments are likely to face. She emphasizes the need for performance assessments to satisfy basic psychometric concerns (for example, validity, content sampling, scorer reliability, and freedom from bias) to be defensible in court. Since we live in a litigious society, policymakers and others advocating greater use of performance assessment can ill afford to overlook these concerns.

It is critical that thoughtful proponents of nontraditional assessment help education's stakeholders to see alternative assessment's *potential,* while adjusting and refining their expectations to align them with what is appropriate for a promising but still young movement. Wherever possible, promises to (and expectations of) stakeholders should be tempered to provide time to develop, pilot, and modify nontraditional forms of assessment before launching alternative assessment as the flagship of educational reform. Even then, as Cizek reminds us, it would seem wise to remember that "Performance assessment does have potential to make a positive contribution to reform efforts by providing unique information about student ability . . . [but] It should not be promoted . . . as *the* cure for what ails us" (1991a, p. 153).

Appropriateness for High-Stakes Assessment

It is too early to be certain about the appropriateness of alternative assessment in high-stakes environments, but it is not too early to recognize this as a pivotal issue because of three unknowns about alternative assessment that raise questions about their usefulness in this context. First, does alternative assessment provide sufficient standardization to defend high-stakes decisions based on such measures? Second, will alternative assessment result in ethnic minorities scoring better than on traditional measures, or more poorly, as now appears quite possible? (for example, see Darling-Hammond, 1991). Third, will the inevitable legal challenges aimed at high-stakes decisions based on alternative assessment be more difficult to defend because the validity of such measures may be less certain to psychometricians and thus less convincing to the courts? Until questions such as these are answered, it is unclear whether or not alternative assessments can simultaneously serve well the dual needs of assessment for instructional purposes and accountability purposes.

Brewer (1992), who has been involved in Vermont's vanguard development of alternative assessments in the schools, sees this issue clearly.

> the friends of performance assessment must understand that the tilt of the field has changed. Until now, performance assessment has been winning without having had to perform as a vehicle of assessment in an accountability system, and while performance assessment is not a "star wars" technology, as some have likened it, even its friends have been asking probing questions . . . .
>
> Before the stakes grew it was possible to slough off the tough questions relating to consequences, equity, or reliability by pointing out that performance assessment was good because we were assessing real writing or real mathematics: This kind of assessment would lead to better instruction. This is no longer enough. We all need to agree that there are legitimate questions to be resolved as we proceed. . . . Nationally the questions are tougher and so is the environment for studying the results. In a different climate we could do evaluation work, improve approaches, let a hundred flowers bloom, picking the best where we found them. That luxury is gone. . . . When performance assessment moved into the high-stakes arena we lost our "license to fail." (p. 28)

Yet, not all alternative assessments are proposed for use in high-stake settings. And not all alternative assessments are subjected to the scrutiny received by those that are high-stakes—and thus high-profile—assessments. For those who still have the luxury, there is wisdom and prudence in developing and testing alternative assessment approaches and measures in *low-stakes settings* where they can serve needs for better classroom assessment. Thus we would learn more about how to select worthy and representative tasks, how to set criterion levels and standardize scoring enough but not too much, how the assessment results could be used in improving instruction and stimulating reform, how to provide professional development to enable educators to use nontraditional assessment effectively, and how to obtain and maintain stakeholders' permission for its use. With that foundation, the effort to consider the use of alternative assessment in high-stakes settings would seem more likely to succeed.

Feasibility

One of the most frequently debated issues is whether or not alternative assessment is feasible for large-scale efforts to assess student performance. Legislators, state boards of education, and local school boards are always concerned about costs. And authentic assessments are expensive (Hardy, 1996; U.S. Congress, Office of Technology Assessment, 1992). No one, whether proponent or opponent of nontraditional assessment, would claim that its measures are as inexpensive, efficient, or as quick as scantron scoring of multiple-choice tests' bubble answer sheets. Obviously, scoring of students' constructed responses to performance assessment tasks costs enormously more by the time such responses (for example, writing samples or art portfolios) are scored. The labor intensity of scoring and appraisers' observation of performance over extended periods are primarily responsible for the relatively high costs for performance assessments. The key question is whether legislators and school board members will view the benefits as justifying the added cost. Monk (1996) provides the best discussion of the issues and problems involved in attempting to estimate the costs associated with performance assessment.

Cost should not be the only criterion, however, as supporters of alternative assessment are quick to point out. The more important criterion should be cost-benefit. Does alternative assessment produce sufficiently greater benefits to justify its increased costs? Are there benefits that are so intertwined with teaching and learning that it is naive to think they can be separated out by traditional cost–benefit analyses? No definitive answers can be given to such questions until considerably more research has addressed these issues. In the meantime, it seems reasonable to suggest that no assessment method will ever be rated high on its cost benefit if it is unaffordable in the first place, as many assessment specialists contend (for example, Popham, 1991).

Numerous suggestions have been offered for how to make alternative assessment more feasible beyond the individual classroom. Perhaps the most common is the use of sampling, where both the students and items (tasks) to be assessed are selected by precise scientific methods. The result might be a system where only a limited number of schools in a district or state would be sampled, within them only a small proportion of the students would be selected, and each student in the sample would receive only a sample of the assessment tasks. Obviously, such a system would be far less costly to operate and, therefore, would be much more feasible.

For this strategy to succeed, however, school boards and legislatures would need to be convinced to test less and to be satisfied with very different reports on student performance—reports based on much more in-depth assessment of the performance of far fewer students, possibly at far fewer grade levels. Only additional time and experience will tell whether or not such a sampling approach will make alternative assessment affordable beyond the classroom and, if so, whether such a sampling approach is acceptable to educators and key educational policymakers.

A second proposal aimed at making the use of alternative assessment more feasible does so by restricting its scope to classroom or possibly school level but, in doing so, creates another issue concerning "continuity" of assessment.

Continuity and Integration Across Educational Systems

If it is doubtful whether one assessment can, or should, be used to satisfy both instructional and accountability purposes, then why not use two separate assessments? And if traditional tests can more efficiently and inexpensively collect assessment data from large groups of students, then why not use them in appraising and reporting on student performance at national, state, district, and possibly school levels? Similarly, if alternative assessment is linked closely to teaching and learning, and is more feasible when closely integrated with the classroom curriculum, then why not use such assessment methods within the classroom? Why not use two "parallel" systems rather than forcing either to be used in an environment to which it is ill suited? Such questions have led some schools or districts to propose a two-layer assessment system, where the first layer consists of performance assessment used to enrich classroom assessment, and the second depends on standardized, multiple-choice tests used to assess the performance level of larger groups of students, reporting on average achievement levels for the state, the district, or possibly the school.

Although such an approach may appear to be a case of simultaneous cake-having and cake-eating, it poses some difficulty. Such a two-pronged system could easily become rather schizophrenic, with classroom (and possibly school) assessment dependent on intensive sampling of performance assessment and school district or state levels using standardized test programs. This may well create a dualistic view of student attainment, however, with standardized test data continuing to be as irrelevant to most classroom decisions as before, and the potential richness of alternative assessment data not extending beyond the local level to enhance the information available to those who make high-stakes decisions. In some ways, this would formalize the presently disjointed situation where classroom teachers use their own methods of assessing students' learning (most often some type of performance testing), whereas high-stakes decisions would continue to be based on multiple-choice instruments not designed to assess student performance directly. Not many commentators argue that this disjointed approach to educational assessment is optimal. Thus for the alternative assessment movement to be completely successful, it must find a way to link assessment for accountability more effectively to assessment for individual student diagnosis and prescription.

Utilization of Technology

The role that technology will play in alternative assessment is still largely unresolved. Although only technology enthusiasts are optimistic about technology's ability to resolve complex educational problems single-handedly, it would seem that better use of technology should be particularly helpful in solving some of the major challenges to alternative assessment discussed earlier. For example, use of computers would seem an obvious way to simplify labor-intensive techniques and make them feasible. Kurland's (1991) "Text Browser" is a promising effort to use a network system to support highly individualized instruction and assessment, including portfolio management and scoring. Computerized adaptive testing is viewed by some (for example, McBride, 1985) as so advantageous that such tests will eclipse most paper-and-pencil tests within this decade. And videotapes and audiotapes, already the core of some alternative assessment efforts, will doubtlessly become more practicable as those technologies advance.

One caution, however. Advancement of technology will not automatically lead to its use in improving alternative assessment. In commenting on the impact of computer technology on large-scale assessment programs, Haney and Madaus (1989) note that "At present, the major impact of computer technology on testing has been in the creation of more efficient multiple-choice tests rather than in the exploitation of computer technology to create real alternatives to standardized multiple-choice tests" (1989, p. 686). How to harness technology to make alternative assessment less labor intensive and, therefore, more feasible, is an important issue that will impact directly on the future of this assessment movement.

Avoidance of Assessment Monopolies

There is little sense in "recreating the wheel" by having every school attempting to develop all of its own performance assessment tools. As far back as 1975, the U.S. Office of Education had funded assessment and evaluation specialists in establishing a national clearinghouse for applied performance measures (Sanders & Sachse, 1975). Though funding for this program was later discontinued, this excursion into cataloging and exchanging fugitive performance measures was a valuable resource for schools and other agencies that wished to use performance tests but lacked the time and/or the expertise to develop their own. Resurrection of this approach today could provide an even more important service, in view of today's greater popularization of such measures.

There is also wisdom in drawing on existing expertise to develop high-quality performance assessments, such as some already produced by American College Testing and the Psychological Corporation (for example, the battery of performance assessments contained in the College Outcome Measures Project). But there is also an element of risk if well-financed testing companies are allowed to become the primary source of alternative assessment instruments. Sole dependence upon measures developed in isolation from local curricula would clearly undermine one of alternative assessment's greatest strengths, namely, the integration of instruction and assessment. Although testing companies can and should provide well-developed, "common-denominator" performance assessments that would serve some assessment needs in the school, thoughtful and energetic efforts will be needed to develop locally relevant assessment alternatives as the core of any alternative assessment effort. Failure to do so would result in testing companies' current monopoly on standardized multiple-choice tests being extended to a monopoly on standardized alternative assessments. Much thought is needed about how to capitalize on the considerable assessment expertise of existing testing corporations without abandoning to them responsibility for that which would better be served by local development of assessment measures.

Until the Issues Are Resolved

In the meantime, until the issues discussed here are resolved, what stance should educators take? In our view, schools should be quick to capitalize on alternative assessment, whenever appropriate, for it seems most clear that it offers much at the local level. District, state, and national assessment efforts should follow NAEP's lead in using performance assessment tasks whenever feasible, especially in low-stakes settings that are more permissive of experimentation. Educators should help to shape the future direction of alternative assessment by gaining experience using this approach, and finding out what approaches work well and which ones lead to difficulties. Finally, although we are optimistic that performance assessment can and will lead to improved assessment practice, we believe that educators should be as slow to accept claims that alternative assessment is the panacea for all education's ills as they are to believe critics who portray alternative assessments' pimples as terminal acne.

Such open-minded "neutrality" will not be easy, especially in a field where decisions about new approaches are more likely to be based on the zeal or passion of their supporters or critics than on any solid empirical base. In the meantime, what criteria should be used to determine when (or whether) your school should move to expand its use of such measures? The next section attempts to answer that question.

Criteria for Determining Your School's Readiness for Expanding the Use of Alternative Assessment[6]

Assuming that you are convinced that you want to expand the use of alternative assessment in your school, how can you determine if you are ready to do so? How well prepared is your school to expand its use of this form of assessment, which requires teachers, administrators, students, and patrons to alter their views of student assessment and perform their various assessment roles rather differently?

Figure 10.9 is a presentation and brief discussion of a simple "self-check" profile of ten considerations that your school may wish to contemplate carefully before embarking on any new alternative assessment effort. The following expansion of this profile is intended to help you identify the areas where your school is already well prepared, as well as areas that could threaten your efforts before they are well underway. (Obviously, this profile may be less directly useful to schools already far along in their efforts to implement new modes of student assessment.)

1. *Desire for Better Assessment Information.* Change seldom is spawned by contentment. If your school staff is satisfied that the information from current assessment activities is yielding all the information they need, then there would seem to be little reason to abandon present assessment efforts in favor of others that are less familiar. But be certain your present student assessment methods are really adequate. Do they provide you with a solid, defensible basis for deciding which students should be targeted for special help or challenged by placement in programs for the gifted and talented? Do your teachers have good diagnostic information about specific learning problems of each student? Does present student assessment information provide a good road map for day-to-day instructional decisions? Does it provide a foundation for decisions about the school curriculum? Answers to such questions should serve as a good barometer of your school's contentment with your present assessment system.

2. *Indications of Negative Side-Effects.* The negative impact of high-stakes testing on our schools has already been discussed at some length in Chapter 2, and need not be repeated here. But if high-stakes testing has permeated your school and left a residue of such side-effects in any of your student assessment efforts, it would surely signal a need to contemplate alternatives.

---

[6]This section is taken from an article by one of the authors published in the *Phi Delta Kappan* (Worthen, 1993b).

Directions: Check whether your school is high, medium, or low on each dimension listed below (each dimension is discussed briefly later in this chapter).

		High	Med.	Low
1.	Desire for better classroom and/or school assessment information than now exists			
2.	Indications that current classroom/school assessment is creating negative side effects			
3.	Openness of staff to new educational innovations			
4.	Conceptual clarity about alternative assessment			
5.	Staff "literacy" in relevant assessment concepts			
6.	Clarity about desired student outcomes			
7.	School emphasis/priority on content and curricula difficult to measure by traditional tests			
8.	Existence of some good examples of local (in-class or in-school) alternative assessments to build on			
9.	Willingness of staff to be constructively self-critical			
10.	Patrons' and policy makers' openness to new forms of assessment more linked to instruction than to accountability			
	SUMMARY			

FIGURE 10.9   A Profile of Considerations in Determining a School's Readiness for Expanded Use of Alternative Assessment

3. *Staff Openness to New Innovations.* It is not difficult to get innovative, forward-looking teachers and administrators to entertain new approaches to their jobs. Educators who keep themselves on the cutting edge are probably already well aware of alternative assessment and may even be experimenting with it. But the more critical issue is how your school's faculty and administrators would be rated on any "innovativeness" scale you may devise. If your administrators or key influence leaders on your faculty are resistant to new ideas, you may find promoting new modes of assessment an uphill struggle. If faced with such reactions, then before you try to immerse your school in alternative assessment activities, you would be well advised to use staff development, teacher mentoring, or other means to help spread the vision of how alternative assessment could enhance student assessment.

4. *Conceptual Clarity About Alternative Assessment.* This was one of the 12 issues we discussed previously, and we will not repeat that discussion here. But it is important that your school's staff members have clear ideas about what alternative assessment is and is not, how it differs from traditional modes, and how those differences impact on educational practice. They also should be able to articulate these differences and the potential advantages of proposed assessment innovations to patrons without too much tangled terminology.

5. *Staff Assessment "Literacy".* Stiggins (1991a) has reported that few educational practitioners are well informed about even the basics of student assessment, largely because university education programs are flawed. Good alternative assessment obviously requires a somewhat different set of assessment competencies than that needed in traditional objective testing. But *different from* does not mean *less than.* It will hardly be progress if a school switches from struggling with standardized tests to floundering with portfolio assessment. If competence in areas relevant to alternative assessment is insufficient to support such efforts, expanding the staff's assessment capability through staff development may be a necessary precursor to revamping your student assessment program.

6. *Clarity About Desired Student Outcomes.* Fuzzy targets are the bane of any assessment specialist. They are particularly problematic for those who propose to use alternative forms of assessment. The signature of most such methods is that the assessment task *is* the desired student outcome. This means that a school must have a clear idea of what they want students to be able to do, *specifically,* as a result of their schooling, before they can develop or select assessment tasks that will reflect those desired student outcomes. If higher-order thinking skills are something your school hopes to develop in your students, for example, those skills need to be carefully identified and linked to assessment tasks. Otherwise, students may be assumed to be using complex thinking skills just because they are responding to an apparently complex task. The more clear your school is about desired student outcomes, the more probable it is that alternative assessment will prove useful.

7. *Content or Curricula Ill-Suited to Traditional Tests.* If, heaven forbid, your school curriculum consists primarily of "drill them till you kill them" approaches to subject matter, then objective testing can probably track your students' achievement without difficulty. (This statement should not be misconstrued as meaning that objective testing is more *suitable* to assessing the results of drill and practice pedagogy than assessing other more valued educational outcomes, but only that it is *sufficient* to such a task.) The assessment challenges increase, however, with many types of curricula or instructional approaches that focus more on holistic performances than on those that can appropriately be subdivided into more atomistic components. A curriculum that emphasized the whole language approach and artistic visual expression could lead naturally to alternative assessment methods such as direct (holistic or analytical) writing assessment and judging student art portfolios. The more your school or classroom curriculum lends itself to—or perhaps requires—assessment by nontraditional techniques, the more important it is for your school to add such methods to your school's assessment arsenal.

However, teachers and school administrators need to understand that performance assessment comes with some strings attached. The use of performance assessment presupposes that students have received instruction focused on helping them (1) acquire an understanding of the important concepts and principles associated with the topic, and (2) develop proficiency in using and applying this understanding. Functional competence is practical, operative know-how. It is manifest by being able to perform a given task efficiently, confidently, and in compliance with publicly accepted criteria. Pupils taught by teachers who define teaching as stuffing students with information are not likely to perform competently on performance assessments. Students need opportunities to practice applying their knowledge with tasks and situations that are closely aligned with the assessment tasks and situations. This does not mean that the same tasks and situations that were used in instruction must be used for assessment purposes. But it does mean that the instructional tasks and situations should be reasonably parallel with the assessment tasks and situations.

The notion that practice makes perfect is only partially correct. Without guidance, students are prone to practice inappropriate responses and to develop bad habits. Corrective feedback from a teacher or coach is a means of helping a student identify what he or she is doing well and what improvements need to be implemented. This guided practice reduces the likelihood that students will develop inappropriate habits. Without knowledge of the strengths and weaknesses of their performance, students are unlikely to modify their performance in hopes of improving it. With this knowledge, they can become active participants in helping to improve their own performance.

Another important advantage of having explicitly defined criteria is that the characteristics of desirable performance can be directly taught to the students. Then individual students can begin to function as their own coach or instructor. Students then become less dependent upon the instructor and better equipped to judge their own performance and to make informed decisions about what they are doing well and how they need to do to improve. Once students have learned the criteria, they can help each other learn.

Performance assessment implies the use of performance-oriented instruction. Otherwise, teachers who use performance assessment are setting themselves up to fail. The recently published research by Shepard et al. (1996) provides a sobering reminder that replacing traditional forms of assessment with performance assessment does not necessarily lead to improvements in student learning. Even the best tools, used poorly, are unlikely to produce masterpieces, either in art or in education.

8. *School Examples of Alternative Assessment.* It would be difficult to find a school bereft of instances of direct performance assessment, such as oral reading assessment or typing tests. The challenges faced by most teachers or schools come, however, when they attempt to devise direct performance measures to assess student learning in areas usually assessed by traditional tests—areas such as reading vocabulary and comprehension, math computation, or math problem-solving ability. It is helpful in times of transition if there are already a few local instances where new approaches have been implemented successfully, or at least tried, as long as the effort was enlightening. There is something deeply comforting about having someone nearby who "has been there" and can demonstrate new methods to neophytes or critique their embryonic efforts. The closer to home your school can find those who have implemented such alternative assessment efforts successfully (especially if *in* your school, district, or state), the better prepared you are to launch such assessment on a broader scale.

9. *Staff Willingness to Critique Their Assessment Methods.* This criterion is not aimed at *present* assessment methods, which were the focus of the first two points on this profile. Rather, it concerns the willingness of your school staff to be constructively self-critical of their efforts to implement better assessment alternatives

(or supplements since adopting alternatives does not require your school to drop appropriate use of traditional paper-and-pencil tests). As we argued earlier, it is important that those who launch new alternative assessment efforts must be careful that they do not allow the popularity of such methods to lessen the scrutiny to which they are subjected.

10. *Patrons' and Policymakers' Openness to New Forms of Assessment.* Although increasing numbers of state legislatures and school boards are mandating use of alternative assessment, many policymakers and patrons continue to favor easily summarized test scores. Indeed, parents and politicians who are obsessed with notions of educational accountability are often unwilling to support any assessment approach unless it yields results that can be easily summarized into a numeric index that reflects the "success" of the school(s). Moreover, the drift of our culture is toward competitiveness and away from cooperation, and this is nowhere more evident than in our schools, even putting athletics and other school-sponsored competition aside. Count the patrons of your school who would be as thrilled with the statement that "Your child is the most nurturing and cooperative learner in her class" as with the declaration that "Your child received the highest scores in her class in math and language arts." Garrison Keillor's Lake Wobegone whimsy about a setting where "all the kids are above average" reflects a culture where "average" is no longer an acceptable label to most, yet where few seem willing to contemplate alternatives that would not allow comparisons among students or schools.

Of course, some schools do find their publics tolerant of noncomparative assessment methods, and many parents are enthralled by assessments that provide them with a rich array of their child's performances rather than a few test scores. And some alternative assessments provide a basis for comparing student attainments, if desired. But the critical question is whether your schools' patrons and policymakers have a fanatical fixation on achievement scales and scores that invite direct comparisons among students. If so, they may become apoplectic in attempting to determine how to rank students on the basis of their portfolios. It may be hard to convince parents who push to know their child's relative rank in a kindergarten class to throw their support behind an assessment system in which ranking is both less easy and less relevant.

As you contemplate launching an alternative assessment effort for your classroom or school, it will be useful to reflect on the preferences of your publics. If they tilt toward simple numerical indicators of what students have learned, then you may have a selling job to do before you can proceed very far. To garner the support of your policymakers and patrons, you must be able to convince them that alternative assessment can play a vital role in improving and reporting student learning sufficient to offset its inability to generate simple status snapshots.

Caveat Emptor

If you use this profile, a few "let the buyer beware" cautions should be kept in mind. First, the ten considerations are not exhaustive, and you may have others you wish to add. Second, with minor rewording, and slight refocusing of points 3, 7, and 10, the profile could serve as well for assessing your school's readiness to expand or revise a traditional assessment system based on paper-and-pencil tests, or shift to a different system of the same form. Third, no scoring mechanism has been suggested for fear it would be simplistic. Obviously, one could assign a score of 3 to each "high," 2 to each "medium," and so on, to produce a summary "readiness score" that could vary from 10 (low readiness) to 30 (high readiness). It seems more useful, however, to view this profile as a heuristic device to stimulate you to reflect on which of these, or other, considerations are likely to help or hinder your efforts to implement or expand alternative assessment efforts in your classroom or school.

SUGGESTED READINGS

Arter, J. A. & Spandel, V. (1992). Using portfolios of student work in instruction and assessment. *Educational Measurement: Issues and Practice, 11*(1), 36–44.

This instructional module is designed to clarify readers' understanding of portfolio assessment and help potential users make informed, thoughtful decisions in their attempts to design a portfolio assessment system. The authors caution readers about potential pitfalls and offer suggestions for improving the use of portfolios.

Baron, J. B. & Wolf, D. P. (eds.) (1996). *Performance-based student assessment: Challenges and possibilities.* Ninety-fifth yearbook of the National Society for the Study of Education, Part I. Chicago: University of Chicago Press.

Includes 14 essays describing the underlying tenets and assumptions of performance assessment, technical issues, and challenges that need to be resolved; the experiences of various states and school districts that have used alternative assessments; and future possibilities.

Brown, J. H. & Shavelson, R. J. (1996). *Assessing hands-on science: A teacher's guide to performance assessment.* Thousand Oaks, CA: Corwin Press.

This book is written specifically for science teachers, but anyone who wants to learn more about performance assessment will find it interesting and helpful. The eight chapters include examples of performance assessments in science plus practical guidelines for teachers in any subject to use in constructing and using their own performance assessments. The authors emphasize four important characteristics of high quality performance assessments. These qualities include reliability, validity, utility, and practicality.

Darling-Hammond, L., Ancess, J. & Falk, D. (1995). *Authentic assessment in action: Studies of schools and students at work.* New York: Teachers College Press.

Reports case studies of five schools (three high schools and two elementary schools) that had made schoolwide attempts to implement authentic, performance-based assessment. The case studies are each based upon classroom observations and interviews with staff, students, and parents. The researchers focused on six main issues: (1) How the schools' assessment strategies work; (2) how the assessment strategies were developed and introduced; (3) what problems were encountered in attempting to use the strategies; (4) how the assessments affected instruction; (5) what changes in classroom activities and student activities occurred as a result; and (6) what effects the assessments had on student learning.

Guskey, T. R. (ed.) (1994). *High stakes performance assessment: Perspectives on Kentucky's educational reform.* Thousand Oaks, CA: Corwin Press.

Describes the experience of Kentucky educators and policymakers as they attempted to implement a high-stakes assessment in response to the Kentucky Educational Reform Act of 1990. The assessment program included portfolios, "performance events," and "transitional tests." The authors describe how this ambitious assessment program influenced educational practice, and the problems that result when performance-based assessments are used in a high-stakes context.

Kane, M. B. & Mitchell, R. (eds.) (1996). *Implementing performance assessment: Promises, problems, and challenges.* Mahwah, NJ: Lawrence Erlbaum.

Includes ten essays written by various scholars on the promises, problems, and challenges of performance assessment. Treats topics that are central in the debates about the value and usefulness of performance assessment, including technical issues (reliability, validity, and generalizability), cost and feasibility issues, implementation problems, and policy questions.

Rothman, R. (1995). *Measuring up: Standards, assessment, and school reform.* San Francisco: Jossey-Bass.

Examines the shift in thinking about testing by describing how this change occurred and what the new approaches look like. Provides a general overview written to lay persons from the perspective of a journalist. Describes problems that states and school districts have encountered in their attempts to implement assessment reforms.

Wiggins, G. P. (1993). *Assessing student performance: Exploring the purpose and limits of testing.* San Francisco: Jossey-Bass.

This book is an attempt to critically examine traditional testing practices in American schools and to suggest alternatives. It is based on the assumption that American education is "in the grip of too many unthinking and harmful habits related to testing of all kinds at all levels in education" (p. xii). The author's recommendations for improving assessment practice are based on two postulates: (1) student assessment should improve performance, rather than just monitor it, and (2) testing should be only a small part of assessment.

SUGGESTION SHEET

If your last name starts with the letter M, please complete the Suggestion Sheet at the end of the book while this chapter is still fresh in your mind.

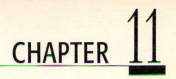

Constructing and Using Descriptive Measures

Questionnaires, Interviews, Observations, and Rating Scales

OVERVIEW

Many questions related to education call for descriptive information that cannot be collected by existing tests. In this chapter, we discuss four methods of collecting descriptive information: questionnaires, interviews, observations, and rating scales. Questionnaires are a relatively low-cost method for collecting specific information such as years of teaching experience and teacher–child ratios. Interviews are useful for collecting more complex and sensitive information such as teachers' perceptions about school climate and parents' ideas about school discipline. Interviews permit clarifications by the interviewee and probing for more detailed answers by the interviewer, whereas questionnaires do not.

Direct systematic observations in various educational settings can provide valuable information about variables such as students' involvement in school work and effective teaching methods. Finally, we discuss rating scales since these measures are widely employed in education. We will examine some of the problems in using rating scales, and make some suggestions about developing and using these measures more effectively.

OBJECTIVES

Upon completing your study of this chapter, you should be able to

1. Briefly describe three methods of gathering descriptive data, and list at least one advantage of each.
2. Explain how open-form questionnaire items can be used to develop closed-form items.

3. | Describe two situations in which open-form questionnaire items would provide more useful data than closed-form items.

4. | Describe rules you should follow in constructing questionnaire items.

5. | Briefly describe procedures for analyzing questionnaires.

6. | Define and discuss the use of structured, semistructured, and unstructured interviews.

7. | Describe guidelines for constructing an interview schedule and conducting interviews.

8. | Discuss some of the questions that can be answered by pilot testing the interview schedule and procedures.

9. | Describe the advantage of using systematic observation to study the classroom.

10. | Describe four methods of recording observational data, and give an example of an appropriate educational question for each method.

11. | Discuss some of the issues to be considered when pilot testing an observational schedule and procedure.

12. | Briefly describe the steps necessary to train observers.

13. | Explain some of the problems and errors often encountered when using rating scales.

14. | List various ways that rating scales are commonly used in education today.

15. | List rules that should be observed in developing rating scales.

Collecting Descriptive Data

Educators often need to collect descriptive data for the following types of activities:

- Surveys in which information is collected about various aspects of a school system, such as administrative procedures, curriculum, and the experience of teachers
- School census conducted to predict future enrollment and related educational needs
- Parent–teacher interviews to gather data about student problems
- Questionnaires to gather information from students about extracurricular activities
- Observation of teachers who have been especially successful in teaching reading to bilingual children
- Interviews with students about the causes of low morale in the school

The tools most often used to collect descriptive information are questionnaires, interviews, observations, and rating scales. All these techniques must be carefully planned and controlled so that the data will be *standardized, objective,* and *quantifiable.* Obtaining standardized information requires that the same procedures be used to collect the same data from all individuals. Furthermore, it is desirable to use procedures that are as objective as circumstances permit. Finally, descriptive information about individuals is usually combined so that averages, frequencies, and other descriptive statistics may be used to interpret the data. However, the data must be quantifiable (convertible to a numerical format) if these tools are to be employed.

Questionnaires, interviews, rating scales, and observations are often used to collect information about attitudes, and behavior patterns, that the individual may be reluctant to divulge. It is much easier to collect accurate descriptive data on relatively less personal variables, such as years of teaching experience and students' extracurricular activities, than on highly personal variables, such as teacher morale and students' use of drugs. Collecting sensitive data is difficult and requires considerable training and experience. In some cases, it can stir up a hornet's nest of controversy in the community. For this reason, you should carefully lay the groundwork in the school and community before collecting data on controversial topics. For other affective variables, such as study attitudes, we recommend the use of existing affective measures such as those discussed in Chapter 12 whenever possible. However, a teacher who is interested in collecting descriptive data that is unique to the local situation often cannot find relevant measures. In such instances, the techniques described in this chapter should prove helpful.

Questionnaires

Questionnaires are frequently used to collect information about current educational issues. Following are a few recent questionnaire studies that can provide insight into the variety of problems addressed using this method.

Griffith, J. (1996). Relation of parental involvement, empowerment, and school traits to student academic performance. *Journal of Educational Research, 90,* 33–41.

Luckner, J. L. (1991). Mainstreaming hearing-impaired students: Perceptions of regular educators. *Language, Speech, and Hearing Services in Schools, 22,* 302–307.

McNeal, R. B., Jr. (1995). Extracurricular activities and high school dropouts. *Sociology of Education, 68,* 62–81.

Winnans, C. & Brown, D. S. (1992). Some factors affecting elementary teachers' use of the computer. *Computers and Education, 18,* 301–309.

Young, J. H. (1993). Collaborative curriculum development: Is it happening at the local school level? *Journal of Curriculum and Supervision, 8,* 239–254.

In most cases, questionnaires are aimed at collecting very specific descriptive data; thus it is rarely possible to use a questionnaire developed in earlier research. Usually, it is better to develop your own questionnaire, tailored to the local situation.

Framing Questionnaire Objectives

To develop a questionnaire, start with a broad objective such as "To determine the vocational goals of tenth grade students in the Riverside School District." Then, translate this broad objective into multiple specific objectives, each of which might become the basis for a question. The wording of each question depends on the interests of the questionnaire designer. For example, a committee developing a vocational counseling program might ask

- What persons have substantially influenced the student's vocational choice?
- How committed are students to their vocational choices?
- How accurate are students' perceptions of the academic preparation needed to achieve their vocational goals?
- How realistic are students' vocational goals given other information—such as grades in relevant subjects, aptitude test scores, and vocational interest test scores?

Many other specific questions might be relevant to a survey of student vocational goals. It is usually best to start with more questions than you will eventually need and evaluate each possible question to determine which ones will yield the most useful data.

Constructing Questionnaire Items

The next step is to write prototype questionnaire items to obtain information about each objective. Constructing questionnaire items is not as simple as it may appear, and as a result, many questionnaires in education are poorly written. Poorly written items usually produce incomplete, inaccurate, or biased responses, resulting in data that may be useless or, even worse, may lead to erroneous conclusions and bad decisions.

Questionnaires are best for gathering concrete data such as the number of different schools a student has attended, his or her place of birth, or the names and ages of his or her siblings. However, questionnaires can also be used to collect more abstract information, such as a student's educational plans, parents' perceptions of school discipline, or teachers' evaluations of faculty meetings. As the information sought becomes more abstract, respondents must make more inferences and judgments, and the task of constructing good questionnaire items becomes more difficult.

Several books covering the construction of questionnaire items in depth (see Suggested Readings) are well worth consulting if you plan to construct a questionnaire that deals with complex issues. However, if your informational needs are straightforward, the following rules will get you started.

Rule 1. *Relate items to objectives.* It is easy to get "carried away" when writing questionnaire items, adding questions that are interesting but are not relevant to the purpose of your study. Before you decide to include a proposed question, you should be able to specify how the information obtained from that question is related to your objectives, and how the results will be quantified and analyzed.

Rule 2. *Avoid double-barreled questions.* Items that include two questions masquerading as one produce uninterpretable results. Notice the following example:

Do you assign homework and give tests?

a. Yes

b. No

Suppose that a teacher responds by marking No. Should you interpret that response as indicating that the teacher does not assign homework, does not give tests, or does not do either? This ambiguity can be avoided by using two separate questions each focused on a single issue. Questions containing the conjunctions *or* or *and* should be checked to determine whether they consist of two questions with only one answer expected.

Rule 3. *Use closed-form items.* In most cases, you should construct closed-form (for example, multiple-choice) items rather than open-form (for example, essay) items. Closed-form items require less time and effort on the part of the respondent and are much easier for the investigator to quantify and analyze. As the time and effort required to answer your questions increases, more people will refuse to answer.

Although closed-form questions are usually preferable, there are some situations where open-form items should be used—when you cannot anticipate the range of possible answers, for instance. Suppose your school was planning to start an English program for bilingual students and you wanted to learn what specific kinds of English instruction parents favored. If you were unable to predict their responses, you could start by asking a small group of parents a series of essay questions. Their responses could be categorized and the results used to frame plausible closed-form alternatives for use in the revised questionnaire.

Open-form items are useful when you suspect that closed-form items may limit or cue the kinds of responses obtained. For example, in the closed-form question developed in Application Problem 1, some of the alternatives could suggest a classroom management technique that a teacher had not considered. In this case, a teacher might check this alternative even though he would never have thought of it if he had not been cued by the closed-form item.

Application Problem 1

This is a class problem.

1. Each class member should respond to the following open-form item: "Suppose you are teaching in a seventh-grade classroom. John Bogus, the class clown, makes several silly remarks each period that disrupt the class. Briefly describe how you would stop this behavior." The objective of this item is to learn what strategies teachers use to deal with disruptive behavior in their classrooms.
2. Collect the responses from each person, and classify the responses into categories containing similar suggestions.
3. For each category, write a single brief description.
4. Construct a closed-form item using the brief descriptions as response options.

Open-form questions at the end of a questionnaire also allow respondents to provide any additional information that they believe is pertinent but that was not elicited by your closed-form items. The final item might be, "If we have forgotten to ask something or if you have any additional comments, please provide that information here."

Rule 4. *Include an "other" choice.* When writing closed-form questionnaire items where some unexpected responses might occur, it is useful to include an "other" choice for respondents to write answers that do not fit any of the alternatives. By providing the "other" choice, you may elicit new ideas or unconventional approaches that would not otherwise be obtained.

Rule 5. Rule 5. *Strive for clarity.* It is important that questions have the same meaning for all respondents. The clarity of items can be increased by observing the following guidelines:

- Use short, simple sentences. Long complex questions are more difficult to understand and often lead to misinterpretations.

- Avoid vague words such as *several, many, most,* and *usually.* These words have no precise meaning and will be interpreted differently by different respondents (Belson, 1981).

- Avoid negative items; some respondents overlook the negative word, thus giving answers that are actually opposite their real opinion.

- Avoid using technical terms, jargon, acronyms, and abbreviations, or be sure to explain them. Use the simplest language that clearly conveys your meaning to the target audience.

Rule 6. *Avoid biased or leading questions.* Respondents who are given hints may tend to give the answer you are seeking. Also, emotional or value-laden words can bias responses. A question such as, "Do you support segregating students by ability?" is likely to receive a large number of negative responses because of the word *segregating,* which arouses negative feelings in many people. In contrast, "Should students be grouped by ability so that instruction can be matched to individual students' needs?" is biased in the opposite direction since it includes the concept of meeting individual student needs—a popular idea among educators.

Another way in which closed-form items are sometimes biased is demonstrated by the following item:

How important is it for the public schools to teach basic American values to elementary pupils?

a. This is the *most important* thing that is taught.
b. It is *extremely important* to teach these values.
c. These values are *very important.*
d. These values are *more important* than most other subjects.
e. These values are *less important* than the basic skills.

Notice that four of the five choices are positive. Such an item increases the probability that respondents will select one of the favorable choices.

Leading questions also tend to slant responses in one direction or another. For example, compare the following items:

- In view of the many persons killed each year by handguns, do you believe owning these guns should be illegal?
- Since the police in many areas are unable to protect citizens from violent crime, should law-abiding citizens be permitted to own handguns for self-protection as guaranteed by the Constitution?

Both these items attempt to lead the respondent. To learn what people really believe, write items in neutral terms and avoid value-laden language.

Application Problem 2

1. Write a closed-form item that is biased in favor of teaching evolution in the public schools.
2. Write a closed-form item that is biased against teaching evolution in the public schools.
3. Write a closed-form item that is neutral on the question of teaching evolution in the public schools.

Frame all three items so that they can be answered *yes, undecided, or no.*

Questionnaire Format

When an individual receives a questionnaire, he or she must decide whether or not to complete it. The appearance of the questionnaire contributes to that decision. Therefore, you should give considerable attention to your questionnaire's appearance and format.

The following guidelines for questionnaire format based on the research of Berdie and Anderson (1974) and Heberlein and Baumgartner (1978) should be considered carefully:

1. Make the questionnaire attractive. Consider using colored ink or colored paper.
2. Organize and lay out questions so that it is as easy to complete as possible.
3. Number the items and pages.
4. Put the name and address of the person to whom the form should be returned at the beginning and end of the questionnaire even if a self-addressed envelope is included.
5. Include brief, clear instructions, printed in bold type.
6. Use examples before any items that might be confusing.
7. Organize the questionnaire in some logical sequence. For example, group together related items or those that use the same response options.
8. Begin with a few interesting, nonthreatening items, and do not put important items at the end of a long questionnaire.
9. If questions of a sensitive or potentially threatening nature are asked, make the response anonymous if possible.
10. Avoid using the words *questionnaire* or *checklist.* Many persons are prejudiced against these words.

11. Include enough information for items to be meaningful to the respondent. Items that are interesting and clearly relevant to the study will increase response rate.

12. Longer questionnaires tend to reduce response rate, so the questionnaire should be as short as you can make it and still cover the objectives of the study.

Pilot Testing the Questionnaire

Always pilot test your questionnaire to increase clarity and correct other deficiencies before sending it out to respondents. To pilot test, administer the questionnaire to a small sample of individuals similar to the group you plan to survey. For example, if you wanted to survey all parents of fifth-grade pupils in your school, you could pilot test your questionnaire with 20 to 30 parents of fifth-grade pupils from another school that serves a similar neighborhood. You may also find it helpful to administer the questionnaire to a few students individually. Ask each student to read the questions out loud and to think out loud as he or she responds. Then listen carefully. This will help you identify questions that are difficult for the students to understand, and it will give you insight into the thinking processes elicited by the questions. Another useful approach is to administer the pilot questionnaire as an interview to identify items that are not clear.

Once results from the pilot test have been collected, carefully check responses to each item for indications that respondents did not understand or did not have the information necessary to answer. Read all comments and suggestions for improvement. Finally, tabulate the results using the same procedures you plan to employ with the final version. At this point, you should ask whether the questionnaire produced the information you needed. Based on the information you have collected, revise the questionnaire.

Analysis of Questionnaire Data

Very simple analysis procedures are sufficient for most questionnaires. In this section, we describe basic analysis strategies for different types of questionnaire items.

Analysis of Closed-Form Items

To analyze closed-form items such as multiple choice, the simplest approach is to tally the number of respondents selecting each option for a given item, then convert these frequencies into percentages, which can be reported in a table.[1] If answers to items are on a logical continuum, it is useful to compute mean or median scores for single items, clusters of related items, or all items on the questionnaire. For example, given a multiple-choice item dealing with use of punishment, a nu-

---

[1]Statistical techniques referred to in this section are usually covered in the first course in statistics. We will not deal with statistical computation here, but suggest you consult an introductory statistics text when you want to employ any of the statistical techniques mentioned.

Table 11.1   Responses to a Questionnaire Item Arranged for Analysis

Respondent Groups	Multiple Choices*				
	a	b	c	d	e
Teachers ($n = 30$)	16%	27%	37%	12%	8%
Parents ($n = 554$)	5%	15%	25%	40%	15%
Students ($n = 397$)	39%	31%	15%	8%	7%

*Table entries give the percentage of persons in each group who chose each alternative.

merical value could be assigned to each answer based on the severity of the punishment advocated by that choice. For categorical variables, that is, those where the different responses to a multiple-choice item have no quantitative meaning, analysis is usually limited to simple frequency counts. For example, consider an item asking the individual to check the choice that indicates his or her racial or ethnic origin. Although these various choices could be assigned numbers, the numbers would have no quantitative meaning. Thus it would be meaningless to combine the responses of all respondents to this item and compute a mean or a median.

When a questionnaire is administered to respondents from different populations—such as parents, teachers, and students, comparisons are often made between the responses of the different groups. For example, suppose you administered a questionnaire to gather information on the fairness of graduation requirements at your school. You would probably want to analyze parent, student, and teacher responses separately. One way of depicting the data to make interpretation easier is shown in Table 11.1. Each entry in Table 11.1 indicates the number of individuals in a particular respondent group who selected a given option of a multiple-choice item. Thus 16 percent of teachers, 5 percent of parents, and 39 percent of students selected option a of the multiple-choice item. By inspecting Table 11.1, you can see that teachers, parents, and students responded differently to this item. Most teachers selected option c, most parents preferred d, and most students preferred a.

Analysis of Open-Form Items

The principal problem in analyzing responses to open-form items is to meaningfully categorize responses and assign numerical values to the categories of responses. Suppose you employ an essay item that asks students to describe the study methods used in preparing for a science test. The first step is to scan the responses and set up categories into which most of the responses can be classified. These categories might be nominal, in which a number is arbitrarily assigned to each particular study strategy. Or the categories might have quantitative significance; that is, you might rate each response on a scale of one to five, indicating the overall effectiveness of the study methods cited. Having set up a system to categorize responses, you could then assign numerical values to each type of response. Then you would need to read all responses again and categorize them according to your system.

Categorizing student responses is a time-consuming task, especially if a questionnaire has been administered to a large number of persons. Unless you classify open-form responses into categories, however, it is virtually impossible to draw any overall conclusions from the data. Once you have categorized responses, you can conduct the same types of analyses you might perform with closed-form items.

Interviews

Interviews are frequently more effective than questionnaires for gathering data about sensitive and complex questions. An interviewer can probe for details and clarifications, and thereby gain insights that rarely emerge from a questionnaire. For example, if you used a questionnaire to determine why students were dropping out of high school, most dropouts would likely give brief, socially acceptable responses. A skillful interviewer would be more likely to discover each individual's *real* reasons for dropping out—and would thus emerge with far more useful information.

However, interviews are not without problems. For example, interviews are much more costly than questionnaires because large amounts of time must be devoted to training interviewers and conducting interviews. Also, interviews are generally much less objective than questionnaires. Interviewers must decide what questions to ask and what responses to record. Not all interviewers will make the same decisions about such things, and thus the data tend to be somewhat subjective. An interviewer may, for example, record information that supports his or her preconceived notions while failing to record information that contradicts them.

Specifying Interview Objectives

The process for defining objectives is essentially the same for an interview as for a questionnaire. The first step is to specify a broad objective that can then be translated into specific questions. Since interviews often explore more complex educational questions than questionnaires, it may be more difficult to frame your objectives in precise terms. However, it is better to aim for as much precision as the broad objective of your interview permits.

Developing an Interview Schedule

An interview guide helps to increase objectivity and focus the interview on the designated issues. Figure 11.1 illustrates a brief interview schedule designed to obtain parents' perceptions of teacher contributions during parent–teacher conferences. The specific objectives of this interview are to obtain information on the following questions:

- Did teachers provide appropriate information on students' academic progress?
- Did the teachers provide appropriate information on students' social adjustment?

Fill in before parent arrives: Parent's name _____

Student's name _____ Date of Int. _____ Date of P-T conf _____

Opening Remarks (**Do not read this.** Instead memorize and rehearse until you are at ease. You need not use the exact words but should cover all underlined concepts.)

"Come in Mrs. _____ and take a seat. We want to **thank you** for volunteering to share your ideas with us. As you know, we are interviewing parents who were here for **parent-teacher conferences** last week. The purpose of the interview is to find out how we can **make our parent-teacher conferences more useful to parents.** Since you had conferences with several of your child's teachers, we want your **overall impressions. You need not name individual teachers** in your comments. Your comments will be kept **strictly confidential.** We plan to combine all parents' comments and focus our inservice training program on the areas that need improvement."

---

1. Shall we get started? First, did teachers give you specific information on **(student's name)** academic progress? Were there things you wanted to know that teachers didn't cover?* (Probe as necessary)

2. Did the teachers tell you how _____ was getting along with other students? (Probe as necessary)

3. (Ask only if academic or social problems were discussed) Did the teachers suggest things you could do to help _____ with these academic or social adjustment problems? (Probe as necessary)

4. Did teachers ask for your suggestions on how to work with _____ in the classroom? (Probe as necessary)

5. What suggestions can you give us that would make the conferences more useful to you? (Probe as necessary)

*After each question, space would be provided to write down parents' answers. On this sample, space for answers has been omitted.

FIGURE 11.1   Sample Interview Schedule

- Did teachers suggest what parents could do to enhance students' academic progress or social adjustment?
- Did teachers ask for parents' suggestions?
- What suggestions did parents have for making conferences more useful?

The typical interview guide contains space for the name of the respondent and other demographic data such as sex and age. Questions based on the specific interview objectives are then listed, each with space for the individual's response to be recorded. Probing or clarification questions are often included as well. Based on the level of structure provided in the interview schedule, interviews can be classified into three categories.

Unstructured Interviews

In an *unstructured interview,* the interviewer is guided only by the broad objective of the interview. There is usually no interview schedule, and the interviewer follows whatever line of questioning he or she feels will accomplish the interview's goal. This approach is widely used in such areas as clinical psychology, where it is often difficult to establish specific objectives or anticipate the most useful questions. Unstructured interviews are also useful when educators are confronted with a new or ill-defined problem. An open structure leaves the interviewer free to follow leads and look for patterns that are difficult to anticipate. Keep in mind that results from unstructured interviews are hard to summarize if different questions are asked in each interview.

Fully Structured Interviews

Fully *structured interviews* maximize objectivity by allowing the interviewer very little latitude. Such interviews consist primarily of closed-form items. The interviewer asks each question exactly as written on the interview schedule and records the response. Few, if any, probing or follow-up questions are asked. If follow-up questions are included, they tend to be tightly structured. The same rules discussed for questionnaire items apply to constructing a fully structured interview schedule. In fact, the fully structured interview is much like a questionnaire administered orally. However, a higher percentage of respondents cooperate in interview studies than in questionnaire studies. It is difficult, for instance, to skip over certain items when the interviewer is asking questions and recording responses. Fully structured interviews are not widely used in education, however, because similar information can often be collected by questionnaire at a much lower cost.

Semistructured Interviews

For most educational information gathering, the *semistructured interview* is most useful. In this form, the interview schedule lists questions that relate to all the specific objectives identified by the investigator. Most questions for such interviews are open-form, which greatly reduces the chances of leading respondents. The schedule often includes supplementary questions that may be asked if an individual's initial response is inadequate or incomplete. Some degree of branching is often provided so that if the respondent gives an answer that fits into category A, the interviewer asks follow-up question X. A category B answer is followed by question Y, and so on. The *semistructured* interview provides much of the flexibility of the unstructured approach while achieving more objectivity and consistency that make responses easier to quantify and analyze.

Guidelines for Constructing an Interview Schedule and Conducting the Interview

Most rules for constructing questionnaire items also apply to constructing interview schedules. However, since most questionnaire items are closed-form and some interview items are open-form, the following rules are also appropriate:

1. Prepare an introduction the interviewer can use to open the interview—for example, a greeting, description of the broad objective of the interview, information on how interview results will be used, and assurances that the respondents' remarks will be kept confidential.
2. Keep the number of questions to a minimum. The more you ask of the respondent, the harder it is to maintain rapport and motivation.
3. Do whatever you can to maintain a neutral interview. Never hint, by your remarks, facial expression, tone of voice, or other cues what response you want.
4. Always treat respondents respectfully.
5. Design the interview schedule so that it is easy to complete and results are easy to collate and analyze.
6. Keep in mind that open-form questions accompanied by an introduction to the topic usually produce more information and more accurate information than short closed-form questions (Bradburn, Sudman, et al., 1981).
7. Structure the guide so that the writing demands on the interviewer are not excessive.
8. Train the interviewers. The amount of training and practice needed by each interviewer is determined by the experience of the interviewers, the complexity of the procedures, and the sensitivity of questions asked. The best way to determine when the training is sufficient is to observe the interviewer at intervals during training until he or she reaches an acceptable level of performance.
9. Pilot test the interview. This is by far the most important step in developing both the interview procedure and the interview guide.

Pilot Testing the Interview

Because interviews are somewhat subjective, it is important to try out both the procedures and the schedule before starting to collect information. The first step in pilot testing is to select a small group of individuals who are similar to those who will later be interviewed. Usually 10 to 20 interviews are necessary to try out procedures and make necessary revisions. In conducting the pilot test, you should consider the following questions:

- Are there any words in the interview schedule your subjects do not understand?
- Are any other communication problems evident? For example, if the interviewer and subjects come from different socioeconomic or ethnic backgrounds, they may have difficulty understanding each other.
- Does the interview schedule allow responses to be recorded quickly and with minimal effort?
- How long does it take to conduct the interview? Can sufficient time be scheduled?
- Do the questions produce the information you need? Are there any questions respondents cannot answer? Are there any questions you don't need?
- Were respondents motivated to cooperate with the interviewer? If not, what steps can be taken to increase their motivation?
- Does the interviewer's opening statement adequately describe the purpose of the interview? Does it put respondents at ease?

In addition to improving the interview schedule and procedures, the pilot test gives the interviewer a chance to practice and improve his technique. If you plan to train interviewers, you should observe them and offer feedback on their performance. Tape-recorded training and pilot test interviews may help identify flaws in the interview schedule or procedures that would otherwise go overlooked. By listening to the tape, an interviewer can take a more objective view of his handling of the questions, often noticing strengths and weaknesses that were less obvious to him while he was interviewing.

Analysis of Interview Data

For interviews with open-form questions, the first steps in preparing data for analysis are to define categories of responses for each item, assign numerical values to different response levels, and score the interview schedule. Tentative response categories are usually set up during the pilot test. Because some new responses will likely occur during the regular interviews, these categories will usually need to be revised as the interviews proceed. Once all responses have been read and assigned numerical values, the analysis itself can employ the same statistical procedures used to analyze questionnaire data.

Systematic Observation

Direct, systematic observation of teacher or student behavior is one of the most effective tools for improving teaching. In recent years, educators and educational researchers have become increasingly aware of the advantages of direct, systematic observation in the classroom. In a recent study by McKellar (1986), observers recorded 13 specific peer tutor behaviors and 7 specific tutee behaviors. Each behavior was correlated with performance on a test of the material being learned to determine which behaviors were related to better achievement. The most frequent tutor behavior (more than 60 percent of the time) was reading information to the tutee from the study guide. There was virtually *no relationship* between this behavior and achievement. Alternatively, elaborating on the information being learned and rephrasing it in the tutor's own words were both closely related to achievement, although they occurred less frequently.

Findings such as these have clear relevance for the teacher who wants to use peer tutors. It is unlikely such information could have been gathered using questionnaires or interviews. Although direct systematic observation can be time consuming and expensive, it often yields valuable information that is impossible to collect in any other way.

Observational Procedures

Good observational procedures have the following characteristics:

- They involve direct observation of participants in educational settings and the simultaneous collection of the desired information.
- Specific objectives are identified to be achieved by the observation.

- The behavior to be observed is defined in operational terms.
- A structured format is used to record the relevant behavior.
- The observation focuses on specific observable behavior instead of general or abstract characteristics. For example, a number of teachers' questions asked can be directly observed, but motivation or enthusiasm cannot be observed directly and must be inferred from the behavior that is observed.
- Observers are trained so that they can reliably identify and record the targeted behavior.

Observational Objectives

The process of developing objectives for an observational study is essentially the same as for a questionnaire or interview. A broad goal is stated, then translated into a set of specific objectives or questions upon which the observations will focus. However, the kinds of objectives that can best be achieved by observation are different from those best achieved by self-report techniques. Observation is best to use when we are interested in what people actually do (their *observable* behavior) instead of ideas, interests, and perceptions.

Observation Schedules

Many observation schedules already exist. Some, like Flanders's system (1970), have been used in literally hundreds of observational studies, and much is known about them. Most, however, have not been used widely and cannot be considered standardized in the sense that most published achievement test batteries are standardized. Sources of information about these schedules are listed in the Suggested Readings for this chapter.

There are several advantages to using an available observation schedule instead of developing your own. The main advantage is that you will save a great deal of work. Also, if your needs are met by a schedule that has been extensively tested, it is likely to be technically superior to a schedule you might develop.

To help you understand the nature of such systems, look at the Flanders ten-category system of interaction analysis in Table 11.2, and read the category descriptions. Although this system is quite old, it has been used frequently and is a good example of a well-developed system. Seven of the categories used by Flanders are used to classify teacher talk, two are used to classify pupil talk, and the last category is used to record short periods of silence or confusion. The observer uses tally marks for each three-second interval to indicate who is speaking and what category is applicable.

The main problem with using existing observation schedules is finding one that measures the specific behavior in which you are interested. For example, if you were interested in the specific *kinds of praise* used by teachers, the Flanders ten-category system would not be appropriate since all praise, regardless of type, is recorded in category 2.

Table 11.2   Flanders's Interaction Analysis Categories (FIAC)

Teacher Talk	Response	1.	***Accepts feeling.*** Accepts and clarifies an attitude or the feeling tone of a pupil in a nonthreatening manner. Feelings may be positive or negative. Predicting and recalling feelings are included.
		2.	***Praises or encourages.*** Praises or encourages pupil action or behavior. Jokes that release tension, but not at the expense of another individual; nodding head, or saying "Um hm?" or "Go on" are included.
		3.	***Accepts or uses ideas of pupils.*** Clarifying, building, or developing ideas suggested by a pupil. Teacher extensions of pupil ideas are included, but as the teacher brings more of his own ideas into play, shift to category 5.
	Initiation	4.	***Asks questions.*** Asking a question about content or procedure, based on teacher ideas, with the intent that a pupil will answer.
		5.	***Lecturing.*** Giving facts or opinions about content or procedures; expressing his own ideas, giving his own explanation, or citing an authority other than a pupil.
		6.	***Giving directions.*** Directions, commands, or orders to which a pupil is expected to comply.
		7.	***Criticizing or justifying authority.*** Statements intended to change pupil behavior from nonacceptable to acceptable pattern; bawling someone out; stating why the teacher is doing what he is doing; extreme self-reference.
Pupil Talk	Response	8.	***Pupil talk—response.*** Talk by pupils in response to teacher. Teacher initiates the contact or solicits pupil statement or structures the situation. Freedom to express own ideas is limited.
	Initiation	9.	***Pupil talk—initiation.*** Talk by pupils which they initiate. Expressing own ideas; initiating a new topic; freedom to develop opinions and a line of thought, like asking thoughtful questions; going beyond the existing structure.
Silence		10.	***Silence or confusion.*** Pauses, short period of silence, and periods of confusion in which communication cannot be understood by the observer.

Source: Flanders, N. A., *Analyzing Teacher Behavior* (p. 34). Copyright 1970, Addison-Wesley Publishing.

Developing an Observation Schedule

Suppose you wanted to determine how much time students in your class were "on task" with their school work. First, you would decide what kind of observable student behavior would indicate that the student was on task, and what behavior would indicate he was off task.

One of the authors recently conducted observations in this area using the schedule in Figure 11.2. Study it for a minute before proceeding. Before starting, the observer enters his name, the date, the teacher's name, and the time at the top

_____   _____   _____   AM   PM _____
Observer   Date   Teacher

___ ___ ___ ___   _____ ____ ____ _____ ___ ___

                                                                              Totals

1. Lesson content: _____   I I I I I I I I I I I I I I I I I I I I I I I I I   _____
   _____   O O O O O O O O O O O O O O O O O O O O O O O O O   _____
   Pupil _____ Instruction Type _____   M M M M M M M M M M M M M M M M M M M M M M M M M   _____
                                           S S S S S S S S S S S S S S S S S S S S S S S S S   _____

2. Lesson content: _____   I I I I I I I I I I I I I I I I I I I I I I I I I   _____
   _____   O O O O O O O O O O O O O O O O O O O O O O O O O   _____
   Pupil _____ Instruction Type _____   M M M M M M M M M M M M M M M M M M M M M M M M M   _____
                                           S S S S S S S S S S S S S S S S S S S S S S S S S   _____

3. Lesson content: _____   I I I I I I I I I I I I I I I I I I I I I I I I I   _____
   _____   O O O O O O O O O O O O O O O O O O O O O O O O O   _____
   Pupil _____ Instruction Type _____   M M M M M M M M M M M M M M M M M M M M M M M M M   _____
                                           S S S S S S S S S S S S S S S S S S S S S S S S S   _____

4. Lesson content: _____   I I I I I I I I I I I I I I I I I I I I I I I I I   _____
   _____   O O O O O O O O O O O O O O O O O O O O O O O O O   _____
   Pupil _____ Instruction Type _____   M M M M M M M M M M M M M M M M M M M M M M M M M   _____
                                           S S S S S S S S S S S S S S S S S S S S S S S S S   _____

5. Lesson content: _____   I I I I I I I I I I I I I I I I I I I I I I I I I   _____
   _____   O O O O O O O O O O O O O O O O O O O O O O O O O   _____
   Pupil _____ Instruction Type _____   M M M M M M M M M M M M M M M M M M M M M M M M M   _____
                                           S S S S S S S S S S S S S S S S S S S S S S S S S   _____

6. Lesson content: _____   I I I I I I I I I I I I I I I I I I I I I I I I I   _____
   _____   O O O O O O O O O O O O O O O O O O O O O O O O O O   _____
   Pupil _____ Instruction Type _____   M M M M M M M M M M M M M M M M M M M M M M M M M   _____
                                           S S S S S S S S S S S S S S S S S S S S S S S S S   _____

7. Lesson content: _____   I I I I I I I I I I I I I I I I I I I I I I I I I   _____
   _____   O O O O O O O O O O O O O O O O O O O O O O O O O O   _____
   Pupil _____ Instruction Type _____   M M M M M M M M M M M M M M M M M M M M M M M M M   _____
                                           S S S S S S S S S S S S S S S S S S S S S S S S S   _____

8. Lesson content: _____   I I I I I I I I I I I I I I I I I I I I I I I I I   _____
   _____   O O O O O O O O O O O O O O O O O O O O O O O O O O   _____
   Pupil _____ Instruction Type _____   M M M M M M M M M M M M M M M M M M M M M M M M M   _____
                                           S S S S S S S S S S S S S S S S S S S S S S S S S   _____

9. Lesson content: _____   I I I I I I I I I I I I I I I I I I I I I I I I I   _____
   _____   O O O O O O O O O O O O O O O O O O O O O O O O O O   _____
   Pupil _____ Instruction Type _____   M M M M M M M M M M M M M M M M M M M M M M M M M   _____
                                           S S S S S S S S S S S S S S S S S S S S S S S S S   _____

10. Lesson content: _____   I I I I I I I I I I I I I I I I I I I I I I I I I   _____
    _____   O O O O O O O O O O O O O O O O O O O O O O O O O O   _____
    Pupil _____ Instruction Type _____   M M M M M M M M M M M M M M M M M M M M M M M M M   _____
                                            S S S S S S S S S S S S S S S S S S S S S S S S S   _____

1. Large-group
2. Small-group recitation
3. Individual help or tutoring

4. Seatwork—teacher circulates
5. Seatwork—teacher attends
6. Seatwork—teacher does not attend

7. Noninstructional
   activity
8. Lecture

FIGURE 11.2   Classroom Management Observation Schedule

of the form. He then enters the content of the lesson, the pupil's name, and the type of instruction. The eight types of instruction are listed at the bottom of the form. He observes the first pupil for two minutes and records what the pupil is doing every five seconds. Only four categories of pupil behavior are recorded: involved in class work (*I*), off task (*O*), mildly disruptive (*M*), and seriously disruptive (*S*).

If the pupil is off task during the majority of the first five seconds, the observer puts a slash through the first *O*; if involved for the majority of the next five seconds, the observer puts a slash through the second *I*; and so on. The observer records the pupil's behavior 24 times during 2 minutes, making a slash through one of the four symbols (*I, O, M, S*) for every 5 seconds. He then observes the next pupil for two minutes. Changes in lesson content and type of instruction are made in left-hand columns as they occur. The behavior of 10 pupils can be recorded on this form during a 20-minute period.

Using such a system, we could get objective answers to important questions like the following:

- During the total school day, for what percentage of time is the average student involved in class work?
- Which students are off task more than 50 percent of the time?
- What is the average percentage of time that students are involved in their class work for different content areas?
- What type of instruction results in the highest level of pupil involvement?

Methods of Recording Observational Data

There are a number of different methods for recording observation data: (1) duration recording, (2) frequency-count recording, (3) interval recording, and (4) continuous recording. Let's consider each.

Duration Recording

In duration recording, the observer watches for one or more specific behaviors and records the amount of time that each behavior occurs. For example, suppose you are interested in the amount of time that teachers in your school talk during instruction. Since time devoted to teacher talk reduces opportunity for student participation, this kind of observational data could be very useful in letting teachers know whether their behavior during class discussions facilitates student performance.

In using duration recording to collect such data, the observer could use a stopwatch to record the number of seconds consumed by each teacher remark. Then, the total discussion time would be recorded. The time used by the teacher could then be summed and divided by the total discussion time to determine the percent of discussion time the teacher was talking.

Duration recording can be used to observe more than one behavior, provided the behaviors being observed will not occur simultaneously. For example, teacher talk in the preceding example could be divided into several categories: (1) questions, (2) responses to student remarks or questions, (3) content remark not in response to a student, (4) classroom management remarks, and (5) other teacher remarks.

| Teacher | Observer | Subject Being Taught | Date |

a. Starting time: _____ _____ _____
                      hr.   min.   sec.
b. Ending time: _____ _____ _____
                      hr.   min.   sec.

c. Each time the teacher makes a praise remark, cross out a number in the appropriate category:

1. General praise—academic: Total: _____

    1 2 3 4 5 6 7 8 9 10 11 12 13 14 15 16 17 18 19 20 21 22 23 24 25

2. Specific praise—academic: Total: _____

    1 2 3 4 5 6 7 8 9 10 11 12 13 14 15 16 17 18 19 20 21 22 23 24 25

3. General praise—nonacademic: Total: _____

    1 2 3 4 5 6 7 8 9 10 11 12 13 14 15 16 17 18 19 20 21 22 23 24 25

4. Specific praise—nonacademic: Total: _____

    1 2 3 4 5 6 7 8 9 10 11 12 13 14 15 16 17 18 19 20 21 22 23 24 25

d. Total discussion time in minutes: _____

e. Praise per minute: General praise—academic $\dfrac{c1}{d}$ = _____

                           Specific praise—academic $\dfrac{c2}{d}$ = _____

                           General praise—nonacademic $\dfrac{c3}{d}$ = _____

                           Specific praise—nonacademic $\dfrac{c4}{d}$ = _____

         Total praise per minute: $\dfrac{c1 + c2 + c3 + c4}{d}$

FIGURE 11.3   Sample Observation Schedule for Frequency-Count Recording

Frequency-Count Recording

In this method, the specific behaviors to be observed are listed on the observation schedule, and the observer enters a tally mark each time one of the target behaviors occurs. For example, suppose you want to determine the amount of praise used by each teacher in your school. Since most praise statements are very short, recording their frequency might be more useful than recording their duration. An observation schedule such as that in Figure 11.3 could be used to record frequencies of different kinds of praise.

The difficulty of making frequency-count recordings of observed behavior depends on the number of behaviors being observed, the frequency with which each occurs, and the ease with which behaviors can be classified. When most of the behaviors to be observed are easy to classify and occur at a low frequency, observers can be trained to reliably identify and tally 20 or more different behaviors during a single observation. When more than one target behavior can occur at the same time, frequency-count recording is more reliable than duration recording.

Interval Recording

Using this method, the observer checks the target subject at regular intervals and records his behavior during that interval. In the observation schedule described earlier (see Figure 11.2), the observation interval was five seconds. The observer had a portable tape recorder that beeped in his or her ear every five seconds. At each beep, the observer recorded the behavior of the student being observed. Every two minutes, a longer beep redirected his attention to the next student. Thus during a period of 2 minutes, a student was observed 24 times for 5 seconds each.

Continuous Observation

In this method, the observer attempts to record all relevant behavior of the subject during the period of observation. This method is used most often when the investigator does not know what specific behaviors are relevant to his objective. For example, suppose you want to identify teaching techniques that relate to higher student achievement in algebra. You have identified ten algebra teachers in your school district whose students consistently make the highest scores on standardized achievement tests. You could use continuous observation to identify what methods these teachers are using. In this case, the observer would attempt to record all teacher behavior that seemed to relate to effective teaching of algebra. After the observations were completed, the observer would try to identify patterns of behavior (specific teaching methods) that might account for the higher student achievement.

Continuous observation is more difficult than other procedures for recording observational data, and should be used only when other methods cannot be applied. Because the observer cannot usually record everything that happens, he must constantly make decisions and choices. This tends to make the method highly subjective.

Level of Inference

In developing an observation schedule, it is important to remember the level of inference required of the observer. It is much easier for the observer to accurately record the number of times a teacher smiles than it is to rate the amount of "warmth" the teacher displays in interactions with students. A *low inference* behavior is one where the observer does not have to use much judgment to interpret what is observed. To rate a teacher on warmth, the observer must use his own judgment. What is "warm" to one observer may seem neutral or even negative to another. Thus exhibiting warmth is a *high inference* behavior.

High inference variables such as warmth, dedication to teaching, creative imagination, or enthusiasm are much more difficult for the observer to evaluate than are low inference behaviors such as use of praise, giving specific examples, or using pictures to illustrate points in a lesson. The frequency and/or duration of low inference behavior is usually recorded as it occurs. For high inference categories, the observer usually rates the subject on a quality scale at the end of the observation period. Low inference behavior deals with specific events; high inference ratings usually deal with overall impressions.

Admittedly, many important educational questions can be explored only by attempting to evaluate high inference data. But conclusions based on such data should be drawn with extreme care. There are many advantages to making direct observations of low inference behavior, and this approach should be employed whenever possible.

Developing Operational Definitions

The most difficult task involved in making an observation schedule is developing operational definitions of each behavior to be observed. To produce reliable information, the observer must be able to recognize each behavior when it occurs and discriminate between the target behavior and similar, but different, behaviors. The best way to develop clear operational definitions is to write a tentative definition and then use it in conducting a few hours of observation.

As the observation progresses, you will usually see some relevant behaviors that cannot be classified by your tentative definition. You should record such behaviors, and then revise your definition so that each of these behaviors can be classified. During this preliminary observation, you should also note examples and nonexamples of each behavior included in your schedule. These should be added to the operational definitions since they help to clarify exactly what the definition means.

Pilot Testing the Observational System

Once you are satisfied with your operational definitions, you should pilot test the observational system. This pilot test provides an additional check of the operational definitions and gives you an opportunity to check the procedural details and analysis strategies for the study.

The following questions should be considered during the pilot test:

- Do any newly observed behaviors require further revision or elaboration of the operational definitions?
- How much observation time is needed to obtain a stable indication of the behaviors you are observing? Obtaining a stable measure of low frequency behaviors (for example, number of serious student discipline problems) requires a longer time than measuring a high frequency behavior.
- Can the data be recorded quickly and easily onto the observation schedule? Is the format easy to follow? Is enough space provided? Can the data be combined easily to obtain desired totals and subtotals?
- How do the subjects respond to the observation? If they are distracted by the observation, they are less likely to behave naturally, and your results will be biased. One approach to reduce such problems is to spend several hours in the observational setting before beginning to collect data. Another strategy is to place yourself where you can easily see the subjects but they cannot easily see you.

- Can the observer keep up with what is going on? Is he being asked to observe more behavioral categories than is feasible?
- Can behaviors be observed reliably? This can be checked by having two observers independently observe the same subjects during the same time period and compare the results.

Training the Observers

The first step in training observers is to have them study the operational definitions of the behaviors they are to observe, and to become familiar with the schedule they will use. To classify an observed behavior quickly and accurately, the observers must be *very familiar* with these materials. It is usually advisable to test the observers after they have studied the definitions and schedule to assure they have mastered this material before proceeding.

It is often a good idea to show the observers brief videotapes that illustrate the behaviors they will observe. For example, if you wanted observers to note teachers' listening behaviors during class discussions, you might use a videotape illustrating such behavior—with some variations so that observers learn what to look for and how to recognize it. Have the trainees observe the tape and record the behaviors on the observation schedule. Then replay the tape, stopping whenever a target behavior occurs. Check how each observer classified the behavior, and explain what the correct classification should have been and why.

Repeat this procedure until the observers agree on their classifications. If fairly simple behaviors are being studied, observer agreement as high as 95 percent can be reached quite rapidly. For more complex behaviors, you may decide to be satisfied with a lower rate of agreement. Take time to discuss questions that may arise, since further clarification of the definitions and improvements in the observational schedule can only enhance the reliability of your results.

If observations are to be done for an extended period, observers should be given refresher training sessions at two-week intervals. During these sessions, they can discuss any difficulties they have encountered classifying target behaviors. They should also observe another videotape to recheck interobserver agreement. If refresher sessions are not held, observers gradually (and usually subconsciously) change the definitions they are using to identify the target behaviors. This is called *observer drift,* and if left uncorrected, it progressively undermines reliability.

Rating Scales

Ratings are a pervasive part of our culture. Job applicants are rated to help determine who should be hired. Employees are rated to determine who should be promoted or receive a raise. Applicants for admission to colleges, universities, and other specialized schools are rated to determine who will be admitted and who will receive a scholarship. Banks and other lending agencies rely on credit ratings to identify potential borrowers who are likely to default on repaying a loan. Dancers, debaters, public speakers, musicians, swimmers, and gymnasts who engage in competition are rated as a means of judging the quality of their performance. Students are rated by their teachers, and teachers are rated by their principals and by parents. In some high schools and in most colleges, teachers are rated by their students. Schools are rated by journalists, realtors, parents, and politicians. Hotels, restaurants, and consumer products are also rated.

The act of rating is a human process that involves estimating the degree to which some person or object possesses some describable trait or characteristic. The ratings may be *quantitative* (for example, estimates or frequency or amount) or *qualitative* (for example, estimates of what kind? or how good?). In any case, the rating process generally requires the rater to make a judgment of some kind, and it is subjective by its very nature.

A *rating scale* is a tool or device designed to assist raters and to improve the quality of the ratings they produce. A rating scale typically consists of an ordered set of points or categories arranged along a continuum. Each point or category represents varying degrees or levels of the characteristic being rated. Three different examples are shown in Figure 11.4. Each of these scales was designed to assess how effectively teachers use verbal reinforcement to help students learn.

Rating scales are designed to help raters by (1) focusing their attention on specific features or attributes of the person, object, or process being assessed; (2) providing a common frame of reference for making comparisons and for interpreting what they observe; and (3) providing a convenient form on which to record their ratings. However, the rater is the real instrument or measuring device, not the rating scale (Remmers, 1963, p. 329).

FIGURE 11.4 Rating Scale Formats

a. Rate the teacher's use of verbal student reinforcement on the following scale (circle one):

Excellent   Good   Average   Weak   Poor

b. Rate the teacher's use of verbal student reinforcement by placing an X at the point on the following scale that best reflects your rating:

Excellent   Good   Average   Weak   Poor

c. Rate the teacher's use of verbal student reinforcement by checking the most appropriate level on the following scale:

_____1. Excellent—The teacher makes reinforcement remarks for most of the correct student actions or responses. Undesirable student behavior is never reinforced by teacher attention.

_____2. Average—The teacher makes reinforcement remarks for some of the correct student actions or responses. Undesirable student behavior is occasionally reinforced by teacher attention.

_____3. Poor—The teacher almost never makes reinforcement remarks. Attention is often given to undesirable student behavior.

Rating scales are widely used in education from kindergarten to graduate school. They are also widely used in business, industry, and the military as well as in clinical settings. Wolf (1994) claims that rating scales are probably "the second-most widely used measurement procedure, exceeded only by teacher-made achievement tests" (p. 4923). Such scales are used to rate concrete observable variables such as neatness and punctuality, as well as complex abstract traits such as integrity or creativity. These scales may be used to describe or assess behaviors and other characteristics of persons of any age, but they are particularly useful for describing and documenting the behavior of young children (Piacentini, 1993). Generally, teachers will want to create their own rating scales tailored to serve their specific purposes, but counselors, psychologists, special educators, or other clinicians desiring to make diagnostic decisions about individual students may find it helpful to purchase a published, commercially available rating scale with normative information. For a review of some commonly used published rating scales designed for use with young children, see Witt, Heffer, and Pfeiffer (1990).

Although rating scales have been widely used in schools for many decades, they have become even more important and more widely used in recent years as a result of the growing popularity of the authentic assessment movement. Authentic assessment in its various forms emphasizes the need for students to demonstrate their ability to perform complex tasks in realistic settings and for their performance to observed and judged holistically. Hence the need for well-defined rating scales is greater than ever before.

Some Problems with Rating Scales

Perhaps the most common format for rating scales is a five-point scale, such as shown in Figure 11.4(a). This figure asks the rater to make a qualitative judgement ("how good") rather than a quantitative judgement ("how much" or "how often"). Unfortunately, it is impossible to determine exactly what qualitative terms such as *excellent* mean to the raters. If several raters are involved, there are probably different standards being used to decide what rating to give each individual. If each subject is rated by several raters, a composite rating may be obtained by summing the numerical values assigned across raters and then computing an average.

A common error in constructing rating scales is to use too many levels. For rating low inference behavior that is easily observed, as many as seven levels may be used successfully. However, for high inference traits, most raters cannot reliably discriminate among more than three levels. When in doubt, use fewer levels rather than more.

When a scale such as that in Figure 11.4(a) is used, some raters may decide that some individuals are really *between* two points on the scale. To deal with this problem, a format such as that shown in Figure 11.4(b) may be used. The use of this graphic format permits the rater to place a mark at any point along the continuum represented by the horizontal line. Then a transparent overlay with five divisions is placed over the rating by the scorer to assign a numerical value to the rating. Or the distance from one end of the line can be measured and recorded to provide a continuous score, but this creates an illusion of precision in rating that does not exist.

As a rule, more accurate ratings will be obtained by supplying definitions for each level, as illustrated in Figure 11.4(c). However, the rater may be unable to accurately apply these definitions unless he uses the rating scale along with observations of the teacher. Notice in Figure 11.4(c) that the words *most, some,* and *almost never* are used at the three levels. These words are, of course, just as ambiguous as *excellent, average,* and *poor.* If we substituted *more than half* for *most,* the definition would be a bit more precise. But without making a *systematic* observation of the teacher, it is unlikely that the rater would recall whether the teacher used reinforcement more or less than half of the time. On the other hand, if a systematic observation were made, the observer could actually count the teacher's reinforcing remarks, and the rating scale would be unnecessary.

Other problems arise when we attempt to collect accurate data with rating scales. Persons are often asked to rate other individuals on characteristics that they have had little or no opportunity to observe. For example, principals have been asked to evaluate teachers on such characteristics as integrity, dedication to teaching, and love of children. Principals rarely see teachers in situations where a characteristic like integrity can be observed. Unfortunately, rating scales often deal with traits that cannot be observed directly. In such cases, it is left up to the rater to decide what they mean. In addition, raters are often not motivated to give the ratings the time and thought needed. If the rater regards the evaluation as a disagreeable chore to be gotten out of the way as quickly as possible, the results may be meaningless or even misleading.

One dilemma often encountered in obtaining ratings is that the persons who are best qualified to make the ratings are often unwilling to do so because of friendship, emotional attachments, or identification with the person being rated. The ideal rater would usually be someone who had observed the individual a great deal but who had no strong feelings—positive or negative—about the individual. Such people are usually not available. So, the typical rater is likely to be someone who has observed the individuals being rated but whose observations are distorted by an unknown combination of likes and dislikes.

Another potential problem is likely to occur when the rating task presupposes that the rater accurately remembers some previous situation or series of events such as how the person being rated behaved in past situations. The retrospection of the person doing the evaluation, based upon an unknown amount of contact over an extended period, is likely to be biased in a number of ways. For example, recent behavior is usually more easily recalled and may be given disproportionate weight. Like other humans, raters tend to remember unusual behavior better than ordinary behavior. Despite such problems, however, rating scales, anecdotal records, and behavioral checklists continue to be used widely.

Rating Errors

As a result of the problems involved in using rating scales, the following errors are often made by raters:

- *Error of central tendency.* If a rater is unsure of the correct rating for a given individual, or if he or she has limited information on which to base the ratings, he or she is likely to rate near the center of the scale.

■ *Error of leniency.* Some raters rate nearly everyone near the top of the scale. This usually reflects a reluctance to give anyone a "bad" rating. The error of leniency, like the error of central tendency, may also indicate an effort to avoid making the unpleasant decisions that are a part of many rating procedures.

■ *Halo effect.* This error occurs when the rater allows his or her general opinion of the person or object being evaluated (either positive or negative) to influence his or her ratings of other unrelated characteristics. For example, a school principal who correctly rated Mrs. Brown to be a poor teacher in terms of classroom management skills may mistakenly rate her low in terms of how well she works with students in setting individual progress goals. Conversely, the same principal may mistakenly rate Mrs. Green very highly in terms of how she works with students in setting individual progress goals because the principal knows that she is a strict disciplinarian. Whenever, a rater allows his or her preconceived views about one characteristic to influence his or her views about some other unrelated characteristic of the person or object being evaluated, the resulting erroneous judgment is an example of halo effect. This error is more pervasive and more difficult to correct than the other types of rating errors. For a thorough discussion of problems associated with halo error, see the literature review by Cooper, 1981.

Rules for Developing Rating Scales

Here are some guidelines to help you develop better rating scales.

1. Whenever possible, focus on specific observable behaviors of the person or specific observable features of the product rather than on vaguely defined traits or characteristics.
2. Always define the characteristics being rated as precisely as you can and give examples.
3. Only ask raters to provide information about variables they have had an opportunity to observe.
4. Whenever possible, provide a description for each level of the trait to be rated rather than relying on a single qualitative term such as *excellent, good,* or *unsatisfactory.*
5. Try to communicate the importance of the rating to the raters so that they will be motivated to do a careful job.
6. If possible, have the ratings done under supervision. This allows you to explain their purpose, answer questions, and motivate raters to do their best.
7. Use as few rating levels as necessary to collect the data you need. It is rarely advisable to use more than five.

SUGGESTED READINGS

Aiken, L. R. (1996). *Rating scales and checklists.* New York: John Wiley.

Provides a comprehensive treatment of rating scales and checklists, including how to design, construct, administer, score, and analyze data obtained from them. The book comes with a DOS-formatted computer disk that contains dozens of programs dealing with the construction, analysis, and applications of rating scales and checklists.

Bakeman, R. & Gottman, J. M. (1986). *Observing interaction: An introduction to sequential analysis.* New York: Cambridge University Press.

The authors' main theme is that the collection of sequential data in observational studies permits educators to study many questions that cannot be studied with typical methods of observation. Most of the topics in the book, such as developing a coding scheme, recording behavioral sequences, and assessing observer agreement, are relevant to any study that employs systematic observation. A good source for students or teachers who plan to conduct an observational study.

Cox, J. B. (1996). *Your opinion, please!: How to build the best questionnaires in the field of education.* Thousand Oaks, CA: Sage Publications.

This is a useful resource for educators who want further guidance about how to construct and use questionnaires. Presents practical guidelines for writing questions and directions, validating the instrument, classifying respondents into meaningful categories, analyzing the data, and reporting the results.

Evertson, C. M. & Green, J. L. (1986). Observation as inquiry and method. In M. C. Wittrock (ed.). *Handbook of research on teaching* (3rd ed.). New York: Macmillan.

This excellent chapter is recommended to anyone considering an observational study. After a brief historical orientation, the authors explore the observation process. Four broad systems of recording observational data are then discussed in detail. The authors are especially skillful in using tables to summarize and figures to illustrate important processes. A very extensive reference list is included.

Foddy, W. (1993). *Constructing questions for interviews and questionnaires.* Cambridge, England: Cambridge University Press.

Focuses on how to formulate effective questions for use in interviews and questionnaires. Provides guidelines both for writing question stems and for phrasing the response categories. Written for anyone who uses questions in social research.

Oppenheim, A. N. (1992). *Questionnaire design, interviewing and attitude measurement* (2nd ed.). London: Pinter Publishers. [Distributed in the United States by St. Martin's Press, New York.]

This is an expanded, updated edition intended to be a comprehensive, college-level textbook on questionnaire design and use. Presents practical guidance intended to help novices in the field avoid common pitfalls. Includes chapters on research design, sampling, data processing, and statistical analysis as well as several chapters on questionnaire planning, question wording, and interviewing.

Simon, A. & Boyer, E. G. (1974). *Mirrors for behavior III: An anthology of observation instruments.* Wyncote, PA: Communications Materials Center.

The original anthology was published in 1967 in 6 volumes and covers 26 observation instruments. Volumes 7 through 14, published in 1970, cover 53 additional instruments. Two supplemental volumes to the 1970 edition covered an additional 12 observation systems. This 1974 anthology provides an extensive coverage of instruments related to education. Brief abstracts are provided that help the teacher or administrator locate instruments that may meet his or her needs. These are followed by a more detailed treatment of each system, which briefly describes the system on eight dimensions and also defines the categories of behavior observed.

Tolar, A. (ed.) (1985). *Effective interviewing.* Springfield, IL: Charles Thomas.

Each chapter discusses a different type of interview. Most of the types described can be employed in education such as the behavioral interview, the oral history interview, and the research interview. Should be checked by students planning an interview study.

Wolf, R. M. (1994). Rating scales. In T. Husen and T. N. Postlethwaite (eds.). *The international encyclopedia of education* (2nd ed., pp. 4923–4930). Oxford, England: Pergamon Press.

Provides a comprehensive overview of the issues related to the use of rating scales. Describes four different types of rating scales, various ways of developing scale anchors, alternative ways of assigning scale values, how to determine the number of categories to use, procedures for minimizing rating errors, how to train raters, and ways of assessing the reliability of the ratings.

SUGGESTION SHEET

If your last name starts with the letter N, please complete the Suggestion Sheet at the end of the book while this chapter is still fresh in your mind.

Answers to Chapter 11 Application Problems

1. Many multiple-choice items could be developed for this objective. The following is an example of one such item:

   Suppose you are teaching in a seventh-grade classroom. John Bogus, the class clown, makes several silly remarks each period that disrupt the class. Which of the following strategies would you use to stop this behavior?

   a. Talk with him after school, and explain why he must stop.

   b. Send him to the principal's office.

   c. Set up an agreement with him that gives him a reward for each 15 minutes that he does not disturb the class.

   d. Make him stand out in the hall for five minutes each time he disrupts the class.

   e. Sharply tell him to be quiet each time he makes a silly remark.

   f. Other (briefly describe):

2. Many different answers could be correct for this problem. The following is one example:

   1. Since evolution is a proven scientific fact, do you favor teaching this important concept in the public schools?

   2. Since the theory of evolution is in total conflict with creation as described in the Holy Bible, do you oppose teaching this theory in the public schools?

   3. Should the theory of evolution be taught in the public schools?

CHAPTER 12

Getting in Touch With Students' Feelings

Measuring Attitudes and Interests

OVERVIEW

In this chapter, we examine the measurement of two related constructs—attitudes and interests—both of which have an important impact on education. In our first section, we briefly discuss why formal measurement of attitudes, interests, and other affective variables is not common in our schools. In the second section, we introduce the measurement of attitudes, beginning by considering what attitudes are and how they influence our lives. We divide attitudes into the three separate components of belief, feeling, and behavior, and examine how each is related to the measurement of attitudes. In our third section, we show how teachers and other educators can construct tailored attitude scales for their own use in the classroom or in research or evaluation studies. In the fourth section, we describe several commercially available attitude measures that are of possible interest to teachers and discuss the validity and reliability of such measures. Finally, we briefly examine the measurement of *interests,* which typically reflect activities that persons like or dislike. We narrow the broad area to focus on students' academic and vocational interests, and briefly describe a few widely used instruments designed to assess such interests.

OBJECTIVES

Upon completing your study of this chapter, you should be able to

1. Define *attitude* and identify five common characteristics of attitudes.
2. Describe how attitudes influence the way people deal with problems and adjust to their environment.

3. Explain why most attitude measures focus on beliefs and feelings rather than on behavior.

4. Describe the steps you would take to develop (a) a Likert attitude scale, and (b) a "semantic differential" scale for use in your classroom.

5. List and briefly describe at least one commercially available attitude measure appropriate for measuring each of the following: (a) attitude toward school, (b) attitude toward curriculum, and (c) attitude toward study methods and habits.

6. Describe methods that can be used to estimate the reliability of an attitude scale, and explain why attitude scales usually have lower reliability than standardized achievement tests.

7. Define interests and distinguish between interests and attitudes.

8. List and briefly describe one measure of academic interest and one measure of vocational interest.

Measuring Affective Outcomes

Most tests employed in the schools, such as achievement tests, diagnostic tests, and scholastic aptitude measures, are cognitive. In contrast to cognitive tests, which measure some form of knowledge, many tests measure noncognitive variables such as attitudes, interests, and values.

Many public school objectives are concerned with affective outcomes, such as social relationships, achievement motivation, and attitudes toward school; and there appears to be an increasing emphasis by researchers upon noncognitive objectives. However, although teachers often notice developing interests and attitudes among their students, their perceptions are almost entirely subjective. Few schools make any systematic effort to collect evidence of student growth in the achievement of affective objectives. One reason for this is that affective objectives are somewhat more difficult to measure than cognitive outcomes. Also, although there are many affective measures available, they tend to be less valid and reliable than cognitive measures.

Another problem with the measurement of affective objectives is that they are often stated in such abstract and general terms that it is difficult to decide specifically what outcomes should be measured to determine the degree to which the objective has been achieved. To illustrate this point, Krathwohl and his associates cite a typical affective objective: *The student should become interested in good books.* This objective can be interpreted in several ways.

- The student should be able to distinguish between good books and not-so-good books.
- The student should want to know more about what makes a book good.
- The student should read an increasing number of books that experts classify as good.
- The student should express a desire to read more good books.
- The student should purchase good books for his personal library (Krathwohl, et al. 1964, p. 22).

Each of these interpretations would suggest a different measure, making the process complex and difficult. Finally, schools tend not to measure affective objectives because they do so little to promote their achievement. Although individual educators may aspire and strive to create positive attitudes in students, a review of curriculum guides reveals few specific strategies for achieving such outcomes. Despite the absence of good measurement strategies, however, affective outcomes are often just as important as cognitive outcomes. In this chapter, we will discuss two important affective variables, attitudes and interests, and learn how they can be measured.

The Influence of Attitudes on Behavior

Personality theorists believe that attitudes perform a number of functions for the individual. First, attitudes tend to simplify (indeed, *over*simplify) many of the problems that people encounter in their environment. An individual with a given attitude tends to react toward the attitude object in terms of it being either good or bad. It is much easier to react to all members of a minority group as being bad than it is to consider and analyze all the individuals in the group and recognize that each one is different.

Many psychologists believe that attitudes are related to the maintenance of a favorable self-concept. Attitudes such as the feeling that we are members of a group that is better than other groups tend to bolster the individual's self-esteem.

Attitudes also help individuals find acceptance within their environment. We frequently choose people for friends who have attitudes similar to our own, and therefore their attitudes gain them acceptance with us. Our friends also tend to support and encourage us to maintain our attitudes. Thus, in effect, such groups tend to reward their members with social acceptance, and a feeling of belonging. Such reinforcement generally fosters consistency between attitudes and behavior. For example, assume an Alaskan fisherman has a negative attitude toward Japanese fishermen who ply the Alaskan waters. If this attitude is prevalent in his community, if it has resulted in abusive behaviors such as cutting the nets of their Japanese "competitors," and if his friends praise him for joining in this behavior, then his behavior will likely become consistent with his attitude. But if federal marshals come to Alaska and start arresting persons who abuse Japanese fishermen, his behavior may quickly change even though his attitude may persist.

So far we have talked as if we all share a common understanding of what attitudes are. Such is not the case. Moreover, we cannot measure anything effectively unless we know what it is. And in the case of attitudes, a good definition is a bit tricky to pin down.

What sort of evidence leads us to say "John has a poor attitude toward school"? Is it what John says? What he does? How he appears to us? Since we cannot measure something we cannot define, psychologists have tried hard to capture this elusive concept. As a result, there are now nearly as many definitions of the term attitude as there are scientists who have studied it. Our definition, which draws from several sources (for example, Allport, 1935; Triandis, 1971; Anderson, 1994, Eagly

& Chaiken, 1992), is as follows: an attitude is an enduring system of evaluative *beliefs* and *feelings* about an *object, situation,* or *institution* that influences an individual to respond positively or negatively toward that object, situation, or institution.

Attitudes are directed toward some target object. For example, the target could be oneself, other people (peers, parents, teachers, authority figures, members of the opposite sex, strangers), institutions (city government, school, business corporations, church), or some specified issue (merit pay for teachers), practice (corporal punishment), or policy (a school's policy on truancy or tardiness).

In addition to involving feelings and focusing on a target object, attitudes have three other common characteristics according to Anderson (1994).

1. *Direction.* The feelings associated with an attitude tend to be positive or negative, but may also be neutral. A student may have positive feelings toward studying history, but negative feelings toward studying mathematics. Similarly, another student may have positive feelings about homework, but negative feelings about a particular assignment.

2. *Intensity.* The feelings associated with attitudes vary in intensity. Two students may both have positive attitudes toward school, but one student's positive feelings may be very positive, whereas the other student's feeling may be only slightly positive. Similarly, one individual may have very positive feelings toward studying mathematics, whereas his or her feelings toward studying history may still be positive but considerably less intense.

3. *Consistency.* A person who has positive attitudes toward competitive athletics will likely display these positive feelings in various settings or situations. In other words, attitudes are more general than temporary emotional reactions that are manifest in one situation, but not in other similar situations.

Triandis (1971) claimed that attitudes have a cognitive component, an affective component, and a behavioral component. By *cognitive component* he means that the individual has certain concepts (*ideas* or *beliefs*) about the attitude object. These concepts may or may not be supported by any factual information, but they nevertheless represent the beliefs of the individual. For example, a person who has a negative attitude toward lawyers may believe that they are deceptive and untrustworthy. Such beliefs may have little or no factual basis, but still form an important component of the individual's attitude. Attitudes also typically involve *feelings* about the attitude object; there is an emotional or affective component that is separate from the cognitive component. An individual who has strong feelings for or against an attitude object will frequently continue to display such feelings even if his or her beliefs about it are shown to be false.

The third component of attitude, which Triandis calls "predisposition to action," suggests that the individual's attitude influences his or her *behavior* toward the attitude object. For example, the *beliefs* and *feelings* of racial bigots are what prompt their unacceptable *behavior* toward racial minorities.

To summarize,

- Cognitive component → beliefs about the attitude object
- Affective component → feelings about the attitude object
- Behavioral component → behavior toward the attitude object

To illustrate these three components, consider a child who has a negative attitude toward school. The cognitive component of her attitude would be reflected in her belief that school is a waste of time. The affective component could involve feelings of resentment toward the teacher and the school administration for forcing her to waste her time by attending school. And the behavioral component could be reflected in her refusing to do homework, truancy, defying the teacher, and displaying acts of aggression against students, teachers, and school property.

Many, if not most, current attitude theorists and researchers question the tripartite view that attitudes include a cognitive and behavioral component in addition to a feeling component (For a summary, see the reviews by Tesser & Shaffer, 1990, pp. 480–482; and Olson & Zanna, 1993, pp. 119–120.) Instead, current theorists prefer a unidimensional definition that emphasizes the central role of evaluative feelings. However, even though they reject the view that all attitudes have affective, cognitive, and behavioral components, these modern theorists acknowledge that attitudes are influenced by affective, cognitive, and behavioral antecedents (Zanna & Rempel, 1988) and that they can result in affective, cognitive, or behavioral consequences (Eagly & Chaiken 1992; Fazio, 1989; Greenwald, 1989).

Constructing Attitude Measures

Classroom teachers and other educators will often find it very useful to measure attitudes. After all, one societal function of education is to help students develop healthy attitudes, and measuring changes in attitude across time is necessary to determine the extent to which that is occurring. Also, you may find it easier to motivate and challenge students to do their best if attitude measurement has helped you identify those whose negative attitudes are impeding their progress in school or in personal or social development. In addition, it is frequently useful to know how students' attitudes toward particular subjects, activities, or teachers affect their academic achievement so that strategies can be implemented to ameliorate the negative effects of such attitudes.

Frequently, you can find an existing attitude measure that will suit your needs, for there are many in the sources discussed later in Chapter 14 (and we will describe and discuss several such measures later in this chapter). But often you will find that no existing measure really fits the bill. In such cases, you may wish to develop your own instrument to use with students or others whose attitudes are important for you to understand. Before discussing some particular techniques for developing attitude scales, however, it is important that we present some general considerations you need to keep in mind.

Direct Observation of Behavior

Many psychologists would regard the behavioral component of attitude to be the most important. Yet some attitude research has shown that looking only at behavior may not give us an accurate estimate of an individual's attitude, since how he will behave depends to a great extent on the setting in which his behavior occurs.

For example, if you observed a sixth grader being persistently belligerent toward teachers who give him directions, you may well conclude he has a negative attitude toward adult authority figures. But if you had occasion to observe him enthusiastically following the directions of his scoutmaster or angelically conforming to the requests of a Sunday school teacher, you may realize that his schoolroom behavior may reflect something other than a generalized negative attitude toward adult authority. Therefore, although an individual's behavior may tell us a great deal about his attitude toward a particular attitude object, observing a few samples of behavior may not give us a very accurate estimate of his general beliefs and feelings about it. If we want to estimate his overall attitude toward a given group or class of individuals very accurately, it would probably be necessary to observe his behavior over a fairly long period and in a variety of different situations. This would give us a broader representative sampling of his behavior, but such extended observation of behavior quickly becomes an expensive and time-consuming way to measure attitudes. In fact, nearly endless observation would be needed to become fully confident about an individual's attitudes.

If direct observations are conducted in an unobtrusive or nonreactive fashion, the subject may not even know that he is being observed. And even if the subject does know, he may have little or no knowledge of what kind of information the observer is collecting. This reduces the chances that the subject will "fake" a response by answering a verbal or written question in what he perceives as a "societally acceptable" way. Advantageous as this is, it is usually more than offset by the prohibitive time and cost needed to observe an individual's behavior long enough and in a wide enough variety of settings to estimate his attitude accurately. Consequently, most attitude measures involve efforts to determine beliefs and feelings rather than using direct observations of behavior.

Measuring Beliefs and Feelings

Because behavioral observations are time consuming and expensive, the usual procedure for measuring attitudes focuses on the cognitive and affective components rather than on the behavioral component. For example, instead of observing students' behavior toward an attitude object, we ask them specific questions about it and infer their attitudes from their answers. This approach, which typically uses questionnaires wherein respondents are asked to respond to attitude scales, is much easier and less expensive than making direct observations of behavior. In many instances, this is the only feasible way to collect attitude data that would be too costly to obtain otherwise. Another important advantage of this approach is that it can elicit information about a person's private feelings and beliefs that would not be accessible by any other means.

Written attitude scales have three limitations, however, that are shared with any other measurement techniques that collect *self-report* information. First, we are assuming that our respondents know what their attitudes are, which requires more self-awareness than some people possess. Second, we must assume that they are willing to reveal their attitudes on the questionnaire or to the interviewer, something that requires a high degree of honesty and personal security. Third, we assume that they remember prior events accurately. These assumptions may not be true.

When using attitude scales, we must keep in mind that such measures generally contain items or questions that are highly reactive. When we ask a *reactive* question, the respondent can determine a question's purpose from reading it and can structure his response to fit the impression he wants to make. This problem (which is an example of the second limitation listed) can be largely offset by allowing individuals to respond anonymously to written attitude scales whenever there is reason to believe they may be sufficiently threatened by the questions to allow dishonesty and deception to creep into their responses. Thus use of written attitude scales is perhaps the most widely used—and most useful—means educators have for assessing attitudes of students and other important groups.

Methods for Developing Attitude Measures

There are a number of different methods of developing instruments to measure the beliefs and feelings of individuals concerning a given attitude object. Before describing any particular method, it may be useful to ask why we need formalized, written instruments to ascertain what attitudes are held by certain individuals or groups. Why not just ask people how they feel about the attitude object? The answer lies partly in our earlier discussion of how individuals may not always reveal their true feelings when confronted with a question or situation, especially where they cannot respond anonymously. And anonymity is obviously sacrificed when questions are posed directly—and in person—to the respondent. Even if the respondent is permitted to answer anonymously in writing, it is difficult to know how to interpret or aggregate narrative descriptions of one's attitudes. Variations in language facility and the frames of reference of the respondents make it extremely difficult to summarize or score such "attitude essays" without injecting the scorer's personal attitudes and biases. This does not mean that narrative descriptions of attitudes are useless, but only that they are not objective, and earlier we underscored the importance of objectivity if our measures are to provide us with information that can be interpreted and judged by scientific standards. In short, objective information about attitudes will not be obtained simply by asking individuals how they feel or what they believe about a certain entity. Instead, it is preferable to use either appropriate, commercially available, objective measures or objectively tailored measures you can develop yourself using methods described hereafter.

Methods That Use Adjectives

One objective method of measuring attitudes involves presenting individuals with a series of scales anchored at the end by evaluative, bipolar adjectives, and asking them to mark each scale according to how they feel about one single attitude object. For example, attitudes toward "mathematics" could be measured by having students mark for each scale in Figure 12.1 the position that best reflected their true feelings. Each response would be weighted, with the midpoint of each scale neutral, and responses summed across scales to produce a total "attitude score." Such scales, termed "semantic differential scales" or "bipolar adjective scales," are versatile and appealing because of their apparent simplicity. They are frequently

MATHEMATICS

important	(+2)	(+1)	(0)	(−1)	(−2)	unimportant
very sad	(−2)	(−1)	(0)	(+1)	(+2)	very happy
interesting	(+2)	(+1)	(0)	(−1)	(−2)	boring
good	(+2)	(+1)	(0)	(−1)	(−2)	bad
ugly	(−2)	(−1)	(0)	(+1)	(+2)	beautiful
relaxed	(+2)	(+1)	(0)	(−1)	(−2)	tense
useful	(+2)	(+1)	(0)	(−1)	(−2)	useless
hard	(−2)	(−1)	(0)	(+1)	(+2)	easy

FIGURE 12.1   Example of a Semantic Differential Assessing Attitudes Towards Mathematics

criticized, however, on grounds that the scales depend on unwarranted assumptions about (1) true bipolarity of the paired adjectives, and (2) integrity of the midpoint as truly neutral. Although resolution of the debate is beyond the scope of this book, we believe this method is potentially useful for practicing educators. We bypass further attention to it here, however, in order to devote more space to methods for constructing a Likert scale, which we see as the most useful attitude measure for the classroom. Those who wish to learn more about how to construct and use semantic differential scales to assess attitudes will find helpful guidance in Anderson (1981) and Mueller (1986). For a more complete explanation of this technique, consult Osgood et al. (1957).

Methods That Use Statements

The most common objective method of measuring attitudes is to provide individuals with a series of statements and ask them to react to each statement in the list by marking some graduated scale according to their actual feelings about the content of the statement. The three most frequently used scales are Likert scales, Guttman scales, and Thurstone scales (each of which is named after its originator). Of the three, only Likert scales will be discussed in this text, for the other two are much more difficult to construct and use.[1]

Steps in Developing a Likert Scale

Well over a half century ago, Likert (1932) proposed a relatively simple way to measure attitudes that has come to be called both the Summated Rating Scale and, not surprisingly, the Likert scale. By far the most widely used type of attitude scale, the Likert scale consists of a series of written statements that all relate to attitudes toward a single object (for example, "my teacher"). A response scale is provided for each statement, and each respondent is asked to indicate on the scale the extent to which they

---

[1]Students interested in learning more about constructing and using different kinds of attitude scales, including Guttman and Thurstone scales, should consult the suggested readings at the end of this chapter.

endorse the statement. Typically, the scale response options reflect varying degrees of agreement, from "strongly agree" to "strongly disagree." A typical statement and response scale used to measure attitudes toward "my teacher" would be

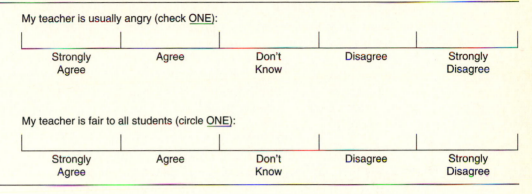

My teacher is usually angry (check <u>ONE</u>):

| Strongly Agree | Agree | Don't Know | Disagree | Strongly Disagree |

My teacher is fair to all students (circle <u>ONE</u>):

| Strongly Agree | Agree | Don't Know | Disagree | Strongly Disagree |

This approach to measuring attitudes does not require that an actual, visual scale be drawn. For example, a "scale" depending only on words would serve as well.

The two preceding illustrations reflect two types of statements that appear on Likert scales. The first is an unfavorable statement, whose endorsement (agreement with the statement) indicates a *negative* attitude toward the attitude object (my teacher, in this case). The second is a favorable statement, whose endorsement indicates a *positive* attitude. A well-developed Likert scale should contain approximately the same number of favorable and unfavorable statements.

Likert's original scales contained five response options ranging from "strongly agree" to "strongly disagree." Subsequently, a great variety of modified Likert scales have appeared (sometimes referred to as "Likert-type" scales). These scales have included two-point or three-point scales (for example, agree—disagree, or agree—undecided—disagree) typically intended for younger or less well-educated respondents thought to be incapable of making finer discriminations. Scales with up to seven response options are commonly used with older or better educated respondents. More response options—up to a reasonable limit of perhaps seven options—permits finer discriminations and increases scale reliability (for reasons we will discuss shortly). A typical seven-option scale would be

| Agree Strongly | Agree Moderately | Agree Slightly | Uncertain | Disagree Slightly | Disagree Moderately | Disagree Strongly |

Various labels can be used for the middle option, including "don't know," "not sure," "uncertain," "undecided," "?," and many more. The choice seems to be a matter of preference.

Some researchers prefer to use an even number of response options (for example, four or six options) out of concern that respondents may tend to use the neutral middle option to avoid making a real choice. Thus respondents are "forced" to choose between options that reflect varying degrees of positive or negative attitudes toward the object. A six-point scale, for example, could be identical to the seven-point scale just described, with the middle option omitted. However, excluding the middle option and forcing everyone to select one of the other choices assumes that all the respondents have a preformed, clearly defined position on the issue at hand. Often, this is a tenuous assumption. Persons who are either uninformed about or uninterested in the matter may well have neutral feelings on the subject. If they are not given an opportunity to mark the neutral category, they will either leave the item blank or select a response that doesn't really represent their attitude. Both of these responses are undesirable. The former increases the omission rate, which creates a problem for the researcher when attempting to compute a summary score for that individual. (For more information about how to deal with omits, see Anderson, 1994, p. 388.) The latter decreases the validity of the summary scores.

Also, the format of the scale can vary widely, including those shown earlier where a check mark is placed on the scale (above the selected option) and those where the words denoting the selected option are circled. Another frequently used format has respondents circle numerals that form the scale. The numerals may all be labeled, as in Example A, or only the ends of the scales may be anchored, as in Example B (which is a very common scale that departs somewhat more from Likert's approach and has some resemblance to individual semantic differential scales). These scales have the advantage of direct scoring without having to translate the responses into quantitative form.

Example A

My teacher is polite when speaking to the class. (Circle *one*)

Strongly Agree	Agree	Undecided	Disagree	Strongly Disagree
1	2	3	4	5

Example B

My teacher makes my school days unpleasant (Circle *one*)

Strongly Strongly Disagree						Agree
1	2	3	4	5	6	7

Perhaps the most commonly used scale, however, is the original five-point scale, presented in a format where the side choices are abbreviated response options. This has the advantage of allowing the respondent to have each response option on the scale itself while still being a parsimonious and convenient format. Example C shows such a scale.

Example C

Circle the *one* option for each statement below that best describes your agreement or disagreement with each statement.

1. My teacher treats some students better than others.

Strongly Agree	Agree	Undecided	Disagree	Strongly Disagree
SA	A	U	D	SD

2. My teacher makes it fun to learn.

SA	A	U	D	SD

The sequence of the response options (that is, which end is labeled with "strongly agree") is arbitrary, just so the assignment of scores to responses is done in a way that establishes whether high or low scores connote positive or negative attitudes (as we will discuss shortly).

Against this backdrop of a general introduction to Likert scales, we can now describe the steps necessary to develop a Likert scale for use in your classroom or school.

Step 1: Identifying Diverse Beliefs and Feelings About the Attitude Object

Prior to actually putting pen to paper, you may want to examine three other sources of relevant statements that express a variety of both favorable and unfavorable *beliefs* and *feelings* about the attitude object. The first is to peruse collections of attitude instruments (see the sources outlined in Chapter 14) to identify existing instruments that have been developed to assess attitudes toward the same or a similar attitude object. You may find one that suits your needs well, but more often you will find several that are close to the target but none that hit the bullseye. In such cases, you may find some "attitude statements" that you can use as a heuristic to help you generate your own original ideas.

The second source is to listen to oral statements or browse through written opinions (for example, articles, books, or even newspaper "letters to the editor") of those who hold strong views (either favorable or unfavorable) toward the attitude object. For example, toward teacher professionalism, you might find useful statements scattered through written statements on the topic from teachers' professional associations, in books or journal articles on the topic (including those critical of education), or in the papers' editorial pages when teacher strikes or other relevant controversial issues are newsworthy. You also might get some very useful statements from sitting in at open PTA meetings, school faculty meetings, and the like.

The third way to generate relevant statements is to ask your target group (for example, your students) to write about the attitude object (for example, how I feel about working on computers). Good statements for your attitude scale can often be found in the resulting essays.

Step 2: Writing Statements for Your Scale

Drawing on the sources listed in step 1, you now need to compose statements that reflect different degrees of acceptance or rejection of the attitude object. To do this, your statements will need to range from very favorable to very unfavorable, and should be written in a form that permits the respondent to agree or disagree with the statement.

The best suggestions we have found for writing statements for inclusion on attitude scales are from Edwards's (1957b) classic list, is as follows:

a. Avoid statements that refer to the past rather than the present.
b. Avoid statements that are factual or capable of being interpreted as factual.
c. Avoid statements that may be interpreted in more than one way.
d. Avoid statements that are irrelevant to the psychological object under consideration.
e. Avoid statements that are likely to be endorsed by almost everyone or almost no one.
f. Select statements that are believed to cover the entire range of the affective scale of interest.
g. Keep the language of the statements simple, clear, and direct.
h. Statements should be short, rarely exceeding 20 words.
i. Each statement should contain only one complete thought.
j. Statements containing universals such as *all, always, none,* and *never* often introduce ambiguity and should be avoided.
k. Words such as *only, just, merely,* and others of a similar nature should be used with care and moderation in writing statements.
l. Whenever possible, statements should be in the form of simple sentences rather than in the form of compound or complex sentences.
m. Avoid the use of words that may not be understood by those who are to be given the scale.
n. Avoid the use of double negatives (pp. 13–14).

Step 3: Classifying the Statements to Identify Those That Are Most Clearly Favorable and Most Clearly Unfavorable

In writing the statements for your scale, you know which ones you intended to be favorable or unfavorable, but there is no guarantee that your target audience will interpret them the same way. Therefore, it is useful to obtain the opinions of a sample of respondents drawn from your target group, to act as "judges." These individuals can be presented with a list of all the statements you have written, in a form that allows them to record their rating of each statement as favorable, unfavorable, or neither. Or you could add very favorable and very unfavorable to their rating, using a form like the one shown here.

Do You Think This Statement Is (check one)

Statement	Very Favorable	Favorable	Neither Favorable nor Unfavorable	Unfavorable	Very Unfavorable
1. Politicians are corrupt.					
2. The world is better off because of politicians.					

Whether you use a three- or five-point rating, it is important to have a neutral, "neither" category. Any statements that are classified as neutral by many of your judges should be eliminated. The best statements for the first version of your scale will usually be those that are classified by most of your judges as belonging in one of the outer "bipolar" extreme categories. Once you have selected the statements, you are ready to develop an initial pilot version of your attitude scale.

Step 4: Developing a Pilot Version of Your Attitude Scale

Make up a prototype scale in which the selected positive and negative statements are placed in a random order, with each statement followed by a five-point Likert scale (or whatever adaptation you prefer) on which the respondents can indicate their level of agreement with the statement. The prototype scale should contain an approximately equal number of positive and negative statements. You usually need at least twice as many items on the prototype as you want in the final form of the scale since many will be found to be unsatisfactory when the prototype is tried out.

Appropriate directions must be added at this point, telling respondents how to mark the response options so as to show their feeling about each statement. Respondents should also be told that there are no right or wrong answers. The purpose of the scale can also be stated if the explanation does not result in bias by causing some attitudes to seem more "socially desirable" than others.

Step 5: Administering and Scoring the Pilot Version of the Scale

Administer the prototype form to a sample of respondents who are drawn from the population that you wish to study. For example, a Likert scale intended for use with all high school freshmen in the school district would be administered to a sample of 50 to 100 freshmen. If you are developing a scale for use only in your own classroom, you should try it out in one or two classes taught by colleagues. Compute the score of each person in the tryout sample using the following weighting system. For positively worded items (those favorable to the attitude object), assign a score of 1 for "strongly disagree," 2 for "disagree," 3 for "undecided," 4 for "agree," and 5 for "strongly agree." For negative items, (those unfavorable to the attitude object), items are scored in reverse (a score of 1 for "strongly agree" and 5 for "strongly disagree"). On a Likert scale, the person's total score equals the

Humane Attitude Toward Pets Scale

Reflects positive or negative attitude	Statements	Strongly Agree	Agree	Undecided	Disagree	Strongly Disagree
(+)	1. People should choose only pets that can adapt well to a human environment.	SA (5)	A (4)	U (3)	D (2)	(SD) (1)
(+)	2. I would be willing to confront a neighbor who was mistreating his or her pet.	SA (5)	A (4)	U (3)	D (2)	(SD) (1)
(−)	3. It is better to abandon a pet than to bring it to an animal shelter to be killed.	SA (1)	(A) (2)	U (3)	D (4)	SD (5)
(−)	4. Pet cats can usually take care of themselves when a family goes on vacation.	(SA) (1)	A (2)	U (3)	D (4)	SD (5)
(+)	5. I approve of using spaying or neutering if such operations are necessary to control pet overpopulation.	SA (5)	A (4)	U (3)	D (2)	(SD) (1)
(−)	6. If I couldn't take my dog with me on vacation, it would be kinder to let it run loose than to leave it in a boarding kennel.	SA (1)	(A) (2)	U (3)	D (4)	SD (5)

FIGURE 12.2   Example of Scoring Prototype Attitude Scale Items

sum of the numeral weights of the individual responses that he circles or checks (which is why Likert scales are sometimes referred to as summated scales). Figure 12.2 illustrates how a respondent's completed prototype scale items would be scored (the numerical scoring key weights and the labeling of items as positive or negative would not appear on the actual prototype).

The responses marked on Figure 12.2 would be scored by adding up the respective numerical weights $(1 + 1 + 2 + 1 + 1 + 2 = 8)$ and dividing by the number of items (6) to obtain a *mean attitude* score $(8 \div 6 = 1.33)$. Since a 3 on this scale would be regarded as reflecting a neutral attitude, scores below 3 would be considered negative, and scores above 3 would be considered positive. Our respondent's score of 1.33 on issues related to pet care reflects an attitude that is sufficiently negative that it would be of real concern to the Humane Society.

Two cautions. First, it should be apparent that mislabeling positive or negative statements or inadvertent reversals in the numerical weights would yield confusing or spurious results. Of course, one could arbitrarily define low numerical values as indicative of positive attitudes and higher values as reflective of negative attitudes. But the usual convention is to construct your scale so that positive attitudes are shown by higher scores and negative values by lower scores.

Second, many persons choose to use the *total* score (the undivided sum, which is 8 in Figure 12.2) rather than averaging to obtain a mean attitude score. Generally, there is no problem with that approach if one is working only with scores on that one scale (and they are the easiest score to use in revising your scale, as we will describe shortly). Total attitude scores cannot be compared across scales, obviously, since they depend on the number of items in the scale. However, readers should note that use of the total score to describe a student's location along the underlying attitudinal continuum assumes that the student responded to all the items in the scale. Students who omit items will necessarily have lower scores. If a student fails to respond to an item, the average score computed by dividing that individual's total score by the number of items to which the student responded will provide a more valid estimate of the student's attitude.

Step 6: Deleting Items That Perform Poorly

Even though you had judges help you rate the statements that went into your prototype scale, those statements will not all work equally well. You can usually spot the poorer items by the following very simple "item analysis technique." First, place your respondents' completed prototype attitude measures in order, by total score. Select those papers with the highest total scores (the highest 25 or 30 percent would be a good sample), and then choose the same number of papers with the lowest total scores.

Second, compute the average numerical score attained *on each item* by those in your high-scoring respondents and by those in your low-scoring group. The items that discriminate the best would be those with the greatest difference between these mean scores for the two groups. For example, the maximum discrimination between the upper and lower groups would be obtained if all the persons in the upper (positive) group strongly agreed with the statement given in the item, and all the persons in the lower (negative) group strongly disagreed with that statement.

Third, select half of the total number of items you want in your scale from positive items that most clearly differentiate between the individuals obtaining the highest and the lowest total scores, and an equal number of discriminating negative items.

A more precise way to decide which items should be eliminated is to compute an item-total correlation coefficient for each item in the scale. For each item, this coefficient summarizes the degree to which the students' response to that item is correlated with their total score for the whole scale.[2] If your goal is to create a scale with some predetermined number of k items (for example, $k = 8$), then you should retain the eight items with the highest correlation coefficients and delete all other items. An alternative approach is to delete any statement whose correlation with the total score is less than .40 (Spector, 1992). The use of either of these procedures will tend to produce a scale having a high degree of internal consistency. This internal consistency is a desirable property that we shall later discuss more fully in connection with estimating the reliability of attitude scales. Do not skip the item analysis step because until it is carried out, you have no way of knowing which items most clearly differentiate between individuals with different attitudes.

---

[2]The most preferred way to compute this correlation coefficient for each item is to correlate the students' response to that particular item with their total score on the remaining items in the scale. Spector calls the resulting correlation the "item-remainder coefficient" (Spector, 1992, p. 30). Some authors refer to it as the item-adjusted total correlation.

Step 7: Revising Scale into Final Form

Once you have selected the items that best differentiate between individuals with different attitudes toward the attitude object, put them into the final form of your attitude scale. When deciding on the order of items, here are a few practical suggestions.

- The first statement (and possibly the second) should not be so controversial as to risk offending the respondent.
- Controversial statements should not be lumped all together in the scale.
- General statements should precede more specific statements on the same topic.
- Statements should be sequenced so that there is a logical flow between and within topics, if such logic (or its absence) would be evident.
- Insofar as possible after the preceding suggestions have been followed, randomly mix the positive and negative items. If all the positive items are listed first, followed by all the negative items, there is a danger that individuals will develop a *response set*.[3] By placing the items in random order, it is impossible for respondents to predict whether the next item will be positive or negative, and therefore they must read the item in order to decide what level of agreement to indicate.

Advantages and Disadvantages of Likert Scales

Some of the most important advantages and disadvantages of Likert scales are as follows:

Advantages

- It is easy to construct (relative to other attitude scales).
- It is easily administered.
- Scoring is easy and objective, whether manual template or computer is used.
- It can be adapted to measure most any attitude.
- It allows collection of attitude data that may be infeasible to collect any other way.
- It results in reliable measurement of attitude if scales are constructed properly.
- It can be used to measure both intensity and direction of attitude.

Disadvantages

- It depends on respondents' honesty and/or security in revealing true feelings.
- Although it is easier to construct than other attitude scales, a good Likert scale still involves a considerable amount of effort.
- The difficulty in disguising the purpose of the scale often allows respondents to "fake" by giving only responses they consider to be socially acceptable.

---

[3]The notion of a response set—the tendency to mark the same level of disagreement or agreement for all items without thoughtfully considering the content of each individual item—was discussed in Chapter 6.

■ The different response patterns can produce the same total or mean score (for example, a person who marked a neutral 3 on each item would receive the same mean or total score as another person who marked 1 on half the items and 5 on the other half, but the blasé feelings of the first scarcely resembles the strong but inconsistent sentiments of the other).

Application Problem 1

Based on what you have learned about Likert scales so far, identify all errors or weaknesses you can find in the following attitude scale:

Attitude Toward Educational Measurement Text

1. After sex education, this is the most fascinating subject I've studied.	SA	A	U	D	SD
2. Hanging is too good for the guys who wrote this book.	SA	A	U	D	SD
3. There are many things in this book that are worth knowing.	SA	A	U	D	SD
4. This book is far better than most texts used in education courses.	SA	A	U	D	SD
5. I've learned many things about tests that will help me succeed as a teacher.	SA	A	U	D	SD
6. Educational measurement should definitely be included in the teacher education program.	SA	A	U	D	SD
7. College preparation is important.	SA	A	U	D	SD
8. The language in this book never obfuscates the point being made, and the examples seldom are not useful to illustrate the point either.	SA	A	U	D	SD
9. This book was relevant.	SA	A	U	D	SD
10. I would rather see the authors go on welfare than have them write.	SA	A	U	D	SD

Reliability of Attitude Scales

Several of the methods for calculating reliability described in Chapter 4 can be used to estimate the reliability of scores obtained from attitude measures. When only a single form of the attitude measure is available, internal consistency (as estimated by the split-half method or Cronbach's Alpha) is usually used. For those few commercially published attitude measures for which more than one form has been developed, alternative form reliability, which produces a coefficient of equivalence, is often used. Since most attitudes are fairly stable over time, the test-retest method that yields a coefficient of stability is also appropriate.

The reliability coefficients obtained for attitude scales are typically lower than those obtained for cognitive measures such as achievement tests. This is partially because reliability is determined to a large extent by length of the measure, and the average attitude scale has fewer items than the average achievement test. Also, affective measures in general deal with more complex and less well-understood constructs than cognitive measures, and this probably contributes to their lower reliability. However, the most commonly used commercial Likert scales often have reliability coefficients above .80 and occasionally report reliabilities above .90. According to Anderson (1988), internal consistency estimates for well-developed attitude scales of 20 items can approach .90, and similarly high-reliability estimates are found for stability coefficients over periods as long as five weeks.

If your purpose in using an attitude scale is to obtain an overall estimate of the attitudes of students in your classroom, reliabilities of .70 or higher would be sufficient. However, if you wish to use the scale results to help give you insights into the attitudes of individual students, you should select attitude scales with high reliabilities, and as a rule, you should not use scales with reliability coefficients below .85 for individual diagnosis or interpretation.

As with other measures, reliability and length (that is, number of items) are positively correlated. This is true not only of the number of statements involved in the scale, but also of the number of response options for each statement. For example, using seven-point response options increases the number of total response opportunities respondents have, which is analogous to increasing the number of dichotomously scored items on a typical achievement test. The resultant increase in reliability should be apparent (if not, refer to our discussion of this point in Chapter 4). Similarly, using only a three-point response option depresses the reliability estimate for the scale. Of course, it would make little sense to use nine-point response options (or more) if respondents could no longer discriminate meaningfully among points on the scale; sacrificing validity in an effort to increase reliability would be a poor tradeoff.

Validity of Attitude Scales

The validity of attitude scales is difficult to establish. Some attitude scale developers attempt to establish content validity by having "experts" independently inspect the scale items and report their judgments on the validity of each item. If such judgments are consistent across raters, you may conclude that this provides some evidence of content validity.

Concurrent validity is perhaps the most widely reported type of validity evidence for attitude scales. This is determined by computing correlation coefficients between scores on the measure being validated and a criterion measure obtained from the same subjects at about the same time. For example, an attitude scale that purports to measure student attitudes toward teachers could be validated by observing the frequency of positive and negative behavior of different students toward their teacher and then correlating their attitude scale scores with a composite score representing their classroom behavior toward the teacher.

As a rule, concurrent validity coefficients of this sort range between .20 and .50. Higher levels cannot be expected for two reasons. First, validity coefficients are lowered because of the fact that neither the scale score nor the criterion score is perfectly reliable. Second, many of the criterion measures used in computing concurrent validity only measure a small part of the individual's overall attitude toward the attitude object. You will recall that construct validity is concerned with the degree to which a measure is related to or based upon a theory or theoretical construct. Few developers of attitude scales address the question of construct validity (Gardner, 1975). When construct validity issues are addressed by attitude scale developers, expert opinion is usually used to judge the degree to which the scale is based upon its underlying theoretical construct.

Typical Attitude Measures

We have taken a rather close look at attitudes and attitude scale construction because virtually all public school teachers and administrators are convinced that obtaining good student attitudes toward learning is one of the schools most important educational objectives. This is supported by research that typically finds significant positive relationships between scales measuring attitudes toward school subjects and cognitive measures such as achievement tests (Steinkamp & Maehr, 1983). A number of attitude scales are available that measure various aspects of students' attitudes toward school, teachers and peers, specific school subjects, vocational attitudes, and study attitudes and habits. Other attitudinal areas are also important in the school environment. These include racial attitudes, alienation, achievement motivation, and level of aspiration. Such measures can give you insight into your students' attitudes, which in turn can help you improve the classroom learning environment.

Let us now look briefly at a few examples of commercially published attitude measures that are readily available. But first, we should note that such measures are not very plentiful. However, a great many attitude measures have been developed for research projects or are available from the Educational Testing Service (ETS) test collection. Fifteen ETS bibliographies deal with attitudes toward school or with attitudes of interest to educators. In the test collection bibliography entitled "Attitudes Toward School and School Adjustment, Grades 7-12 and Above," more than 140 attitude measures are listed. All measures listed in the test collection bibliographies are available from the developer, the publisher, or from ETS. If you are interested in using attitude scales in your classroom, it is advisable to purchase copies of the test collection bibliographies that are most closely related to your interests.[4]

Measures of Attitude Toward School, Teachers, and Specific School Subjects

We will limit our discussion to two commonly used attitude measures.

---

[4]A list of available bibliographies is given in Chapter 14.

FIGURE 12.3   Sample Item from the Attitude Towards School Questionnaire

The Attitude to School Questionnaire (ASQ)

The ASQ is a 15-item scale designed to measure school-related attitudes of children in kindergarten through second grade (Strickland, 1970). On this test, children view a cartoon depicting a school situation while a narration is read to them. The children are asked to express their feelings about the situation by circling a happy, neutral, or unhappy face (this is a variation of Likert scaling often used with young children). There are two forms of the test—one for girls, and one for boys. Each test item is printed on colored paper. Five different colors are used so that the teacher can see at a glance if children are responding to the correct pictures during the test. A typical item from this test is shown on Figure 12.3. As the child looks at the picture, the test administrator says, "Now look at the blue page. It is time for school to begin. Show how you feel about this. Circle the face like your face."

Factor analysis based on various revisions of this measure has revealed three factors: school, school work, and school personnel.[5] The current version of the ASQ was developed based on these factor analyses. Correlations among the three ASQ factors range from .44 to .67 (Strickland, Hoepfner, & Klein, 1976). It has been suggested that these relatively high intercorrelations indicate that attitude toward school is a unidimensional trait for young children. Thus the ASQ is designed to produce only one score that indicates the child's overall attitude toward school. Percentile norms for boys and girls based on about 10,000 cases per grade level are provided in the test manual.[6] Reliability data were computed for approximately 10,000 children at kindergarten, first grade, and second grade. The internal consistency reliabilities were .81 for kindergarten, .78 for first grade, and .76 for second grade.

---

[5]Factor analysis is a statistical procedure that determines which test items are related, the degree of the relationships, and the probable construct (factor) that is being measured by each set of items.

[6]This test may be obtained from Monitor, P.O. Box 2337, Hollywood, CA, 90028.

The Quality of School Life Scale (QSL)

The QSL contains 27 items in true–false, multiple-choice, and Likert scale format, and provides scores on three subscales. The "Satisfaction With School" subscale is concerned with students' general reactions to school. The "Commitment to Classwork" subscale deals with students' reactions to classwork. The "Reactions to Teachers" subscale examines responses to instruction and personal interactions with teachers. You will notice that the three subscales on this measure correspond closely with the factors that emerged in the factor analysis of the Attitude to School Questionnaire (ASQ).

This scale may be group-administered within a time frame of about 20 minutes. The authors indicate that most students in grades four through 12 can read and interpret the items without difficulty. They provide information on the characteristics of the norming group by grade level and show comparisons of the sample with U.S. populations. Therefore, it is possible for users to compare the students in their local school districts with those tested in the norming group. Such comparison is important if users are to know the degree to which the norms are relevant to local populations.

Reliability coefficients for this scale are reported as ranging from .86 to .89 (Epstein & McPartland, 1976). Estimates of concurrent validity were obtained by comparing QSL scores to scores on a large number of criterion measures concerned with school activities, school evaluations, family experiences, personality measures, and student aspirations. Information on concurrent and construct validity are both provided in the test manual.

In summary, the QSL is somewhat more rigorously developed than most school attitude scales and deserves careful consideration for use in local schools.[7]

Measures of Attitudes Toward Curriculum

A number of attitude scales focus on specific subject areas. In Chapter 14, for instance, there are separate ETS bibliographies for attitudes toward mathematics and attitudes toward reading. These are by far the best source for these measures.

Here are brief descriptions of two attitude scales in this area.

The ME Scales

This set of very brief scales is intended for use in the elementary grades. The primary version provides scores for attitudes toward school, reading, math, physical education, art, and music. The intermediate version covers the same subjects plus social studies and science. Each scale is based on the students' responses to five items. For each item, the child responds on a three-point rating scale consisting of drawings of a happy, neutral, and sad face. The child circles the face that best represents his or her response to the item. For example, to assess a student's attitude toward mathematics, the following scale item is used:

---

[7]Readers who are interested in learning more about this scale and about research on the quality of school life should see Epstein (1981).

What face do you wear . . .
    When it is time for math?
    During math time?
    When math is over?
    When you are doing something in math?
    If you never had to go to math again?

Responses are scaled 0, 1, and 2 for each of the five items, giving a score range from 0 to 10 on each scale. Reliability coefficients for each of the scales range from .61 to .89. The lower reliabilities were obtained for the school and the reading scales. Omitting the school and reading scales, the median reliability is .84, which is very good for scales containing only five items. A factor analysis of the scales indicates that the items in each scale fit under the construct for that scale. This provides some evidence of construct validity.[8]

Survey of School Attitudes (SSA)

This measure is designed to appraise students' attitudes toward four major curricular areas: reading and language arts, mathematics, science, and social studies. The primary level of the instrument is designed for use in grades one through three and the intermediate level for students in grades four through eight. Two comparable forms of the measure (A and B) are available at each level. The format of the scales at the two levels is very similar. At each level, the students respond to each drawing by marking one of the three faces. At the primary level, the administrator reads the text that accompanies each picture. For example, for picture 7 (Figure 12.4), the administrator says, "Here you see a boy looking at the stars. Fill in the face to tell if you like to learn about the stars." Reliability coefficients are reported in the test manual for two measures of internal consistency: the split-half and coefficient alpha. Split-half reliabilities for the primary level range from .80 to .91. Reliabilities for the intermediate form are at .80 or higher for all grade levels for which data have been collected (Hogan, 1975). Alpha reliabilities are very similar although they tend to average two or three points lower. Reliability coefficients at this level are good for estimating overall class attitudes and are satisfactory for individual diagnosis, when the instruments are valid and used in conjunction with other evidence.

Some evidence of construct validity, based upon factor analyses, is presented in the manual.

The SSA appears to be a carefully developed measure that can give the teacher useful information about a student's attitude toward the four subject areas covered.

---

[8]See Haladyna, T., & Thomas, G. (1979a, 1979b) for more information on these scales. A copy of the ME scale and manual may be obtained by writing Dr. Tom Haladyna, Arizona State University—West, 2636 West Montebello, Phoenix AZ 85017.

7. Studying about the stars

LIKE

Not Sure or
Don't Care

DISLIKE

FIGURE 12.4   Sample Item from the Survey of School Attitudes

Measures of Study Attitudes

A number of self-report inventories can be used to give the teacher or counselor insight into student performance. Many of these instruments deal with both study methods and study attitudes and typically provide subscores for each of these areas. They can be used by teachers for several purposes, such as (1) identifying students with poor study habits or attitudes, (2) helping diagnose the problems of students having academic difficulties, and (3) providing a basis for helping such students improve their study habits and attitudes. We will briefly describe two measures of this type that have been widely used in the public schools over a number of years.

Survey of Study Habits and Attitudes (SSHA)

Two very similar forms of this measure are available, one for use with college freshmen and the other for use at grades 7 through 12. The SSHA has been widely used not only in the public schools but also in research. We will limit our description to the secondary school measure (Form H).

This instrument, which contains 100 items, takes the form of a modified Likert scale. Scores are provided on four basic scales: *delay avoidance* (student promptness in completing academic assignments); *work methods* (efficient work and study procedures); *teacher approval* (attitudes toward teachers); and *educational acceptance* (perceptions of educational objectives and practices). A "study habits" score is obtained by combining the first two of these subscores, and a "study attitude" score is obtained by combining the remaining two subscores. An overall score, "study orientation," is the sum of all four subscores.

The test manual reports test–retest reliability above .90 for the four subscales of Form H and .95 for the SSHA total score. Several concurrent validity coefficients are reported in the test manual, with an overall average of .49. Norms are provided for each of the four basic scales plus subscale combinations.

This test is easy to administer and score. Most students complete it in less than 35 minutes. It may be scored by hand or by using optically scanned answer sheets.

The SSHA is a carefully developed measure with high reliability and satisfactory validity that can be useful to teachers in identifying students with poor study habits or study attitudes and diagnosing their specific deficiencies.

Study Attitudes and Methods Survey (SAMS)

This instrument is a modified Likert scale that can be administered to high school students in 50 to 55 minutes. Factor analysis has yielded six dimensions for which scores may be obtained: academic interest, academic drive, study methods, study anxiety, manipulation, and alienation toward authority (Michael, Michael & Zimmerman, 1980). These subscores are somewhat different from those obtained on the SSHA. Both high school and college norms are provided for each of these six dimensions. Split-half reliability coefficients for the six subscales range from .83 to .90. Some limited evidence related to construct, predictive, and concurrent validity is presented in the test manual. Correlations between high school grades and the various SAMS scales are generally low. When SAMS scales were correlated with biology grades, coefficients ranged from .05 to .33.

This measure reports lower reliabilities and less validity evidence than the SSHA. Generally, validity is higher for the first three scales (academic interest, academic drive, and study methods) than for the three remaining scales (anxiety, manipulation, and alienation). SAMS scales would be useful in situations where the teacher is particularly interested in some of the subscores that are not available on the SSHA.

Measuring Interest

Interests appear to be closely related to attitudes. You will recall that attitudes have three dimensions: belief, feeling, and behavior. Based upon these dimensions, individuals *accept* or *reject* the attitude object. Interests seem to involve the same three dimensions. Based on their beliefs and feelings about a class of activities, individuals engage to a greater or lesser degree in these activities. Although attitudes lead to *acceptance* or *rejection* of the attitude object, interests lead the individual to *like, be indifferent to,* or *dislike* engagement in a set of activities. For example, a high school student who is *interested* in aviation may read books on that subject, take private pilot lessons, build model airplanes, aspire to a career related to aviation, and engage in other activities related to this area of interest. This student would also reveal a positive attitude toward aviation if he were administered an attitude scale on this subject.

At best, distinctions among the family of affective constructs that include attitudes and interests is not clear enough for us to reliably distinguish among them in all cases. We need a better understanding of how interests develop and change, and how they differ from attitudes and values (Davis, 1980). However, in spite of our limited understanding of the nature of interests, they can be measured reliably, and information from interest inventories can be very useful in helping teachers to understand their students and assist students in making better educational and occupational decisions.

Techniques for Measuring Interests

Interests can be measured by the same methods that are used to measure attitudes. Observation of behavior related to the interest being studied, interviews, and ratings by persons who know the person in question have all been used to measure interests. However, most research on interests and virtually all the interest measures available have employed the self-report questionnaire.

The research on interests was concerned with the development of valid measures of vocational interests. One outcome of this emphasis on applied research has been several carefully developed and validated vocational interest measures that are extensively used in the public schools as aids in vocational counseling.

There are also a few measures that are concerned with students' educational or academic interests, and these can be of use to teachers and counselors in helping students choose classes and other school activities in harmony with their interests. For example, more than 50 measures of academic interest are listed in the ETS *Test Collection Bibliography*. Most measure interest in different curriculum categories at the secondary or college level. Many include subscores dealing with both academic interests and academic attitudes, again illustrating the rather fuzzy line differentiating these constructs. A few attempt to measure the school-related interests of elementary students. These measures have not undergone the extensive validity studies conducted on the best vocational interest inventories, however, and they sometimes appear nearly indistinguishable from them. Therefore, we will limit our focus to inventories of vocational interests relevant to school.

Measures of Vocational Interest[9]

Several excellent measures have emerged that are now extensively used in vocational counseling, primarily at the secondary level. Here we describe very briefly some of the measures that have resulted from the important work by Strong and Kuder and their associates.

Strong–Campbell Interest Inventory (SCII)

The SCII is the latest revision of the Strong Vocational Interest Blank, which was first published in 1927. This measure has been widely used in vocational counseling at the high school level—and counselors often share students' scores with teachers. As with most vocational interest measures, the SCII compares the students' interests with the interests of persons who are successfully employed in a wide variety of occupations.

This measure can be scored for 264 different scales, including 6 general occupational themes such as "realistic," "artistic," and "social"; 23 basic interest scales in such areas as "agricultural," "mechanical activities," and "social service"; 207 specific occupational scales such as "art teacher," "dental assistant," and "secretary"; 2 special scales designed to measure introversion-extroversion and degree of

---

[9]For an overview of occupational measures, see Grisafe (1979).

comfort in an academic environment; and 26 administrative indices that help identify invalid or unusual profiles. This instrument has probably undergone as much careful research and development as any other educational measure.

Test–retest reliability over a two-week period is .90 or higher for most of the SCII scales, indicating a highly reliable measure. The median test–retest reliability of the occupational scales over a three-year period is .87, demonstrating the stability of these interests over time.

Many studies of the concurrent and predictive validity of this measure have been conducted. Most of the occupational scales discriminate effectively between persons in different occupations and are reasonably accurate in predicting an individual's later occupational choice.

The Kuder Interest Inventories

The first of these inventories was published in 1939, and it has undergone several revisions. Currently, two measures are in general use.

The Kuder Occupational Interest Survey Form DD (Revised).   This instrument compares student interests with those of satisfied workers in 126 specific occupational groups. It is widely used for occupational counseling in high schools. Median test–retest reliability is about .90 over a two-week period, and .82 over a three-year period. Predictive validity studies have shown more than half of sampled examinees to later be in occupations suggested by interpretations of their inventories.

Kuder E General Interest Survey.   This measure, which can be used for students in grades 6 to 12, covers 10 vocational areas such as outdoor, mechanical, and artistic. These are somewhat similar to the general occupational themes covered in the SCII. Median test-retest reliability coefficients (over a 6-week interval) are about .82 for grades 6 through 8 and .87 for grades 9 through 12. Internal consistency coefficients (KR-20) are similar to the test–retest reliabilities.

SUGGESTED READINGS

Anderson, L. W. (1994). Attitudes, measurement of. In T. Husen & T. N. Postlethwaite (eds.), *The international encyclopedia of education* (2nd ed., pp. 380–390). Oxford, England: Pergamon Press.

This brief, encyclopedic article provides an excellent, up-to-date overview of attitude measurement, including a discussion of (1) the definitions of attitude, (2) factors that influence attitude change, (3) similarities and differences in the scaling methods commonly used to obtain self-report measures of attitudes, (4) procedures for determining the technical adequacies of attitude scales, and (5) other procedures for measuring attitudes that do not depend upon self-report data.

Eagly, A. H. & Chaiken, S. (1993). *The psychology of attitudes.* Ft. Worth, TX: Harcourt Brace Jovanovich.

Provides a comprehensive review of theory and research on the psychology of attitudes. Although much of the book focuses on attitude change processes, it also includes important chapters on the definitions of attitude, the structure of attitudes, the measurement of attitudes, and the relationships between attitudes and behavior. This book is extraordinary in its scope, thoroughness, depth of coverage, and balanced treatment of issues in the study of attitudes, but it is not an easy book to read.

Harmon, L. W. (1992). Interest measurement. In M. C. Alkin (ed.). *Encyclopedia of educational research* (6th ed., pp. 636–642). New York: Macmillan.

Presents a brief overview of interest measurement. Explains how interest inventories work, describes the relationship between interest measurement and theory, discusses current issues in interest measurement, and suggests guidelines for selecting an inventory

Mueller, D. J. (1986). *Measuring social attitudes.* New York: Teachers College Press.

Each of the major methods of attitude scale construction is discussed. Steps are clearly described, and examples are given. Procedures for determining reliability and validity are described. Methods of attitude measurement are briefly discussed. This is a very useful handbook that covers the essentials in slightly more than 100 pages.

Renninger, K. A., Hidi, S., & Krapp, A. (eds.) (1992). *The role of interest in learning and development.* Hillsdale, NJ: Lawrence Erlbaum.

Includes 17 chapters by a variety of authors that focus on the role of interest as a bridge between cognitive and affective variables that influence learning and development. Documents the rejuvenation taking place in the scientific study of "interest" and "interestingness."

Schiefele, U. (1991). Interest, learning, and motivation. *Educational Psychologist, 26,* 299–323.

Contends that interest is an important construct that warrants greater attention on the part of educational practitioners and researchers. Identifies six characteristics of this construct that distinguish it from motivation. Distinguishes between different forms of interest and discusses the findings of research investigating the consequences of interest on several different aspects of learning. Proposes a model of causal relations between interest and other variables that influence the learning process. Offers suggestions for future research.

Spector, P. E. (1992). *Summated rating scale construction: An introduction.* Newbury Park, CA: Sage Publications.

This 72-page paperback was written to provide practical guidelines to individuals who want to learn how to construct Likert scales and other types of summated ratings to measure attitudes. It includes chapters about defining the attitudinal construct you intend to measure, planning an appropriate scale, conducting item analyses, conducting validity and reliability studies, and establishing norms. The book is easy to read.

Snow, R. E., Corno, L., & Jackson, D., III (1996). Individual differences in affective and conative functions. In D. C. Berliner & R. C. Calfee (eds.). *Handbook of educational psychology* (pp. 243–310). New York: Macmillan.

This chapter reviews research on affective and conative differences in relation to research on learning, teaching, instruction, and educational development. The authors describe a "provisional taxonomy of person differences" and attempt to show how affective variables (attitudes, values, characteristic moods, and temperament traits), conative variables (interests, motivation, and volition), and cognitive factors (beliefs, knowledge, skills, and abilities) are interrelated.

SUGGESTION SHEET

If your last name starts with the letter O, please complete the Suggestion Sheet at the end of the book while this chapter is still fresh in your mind.

Answers to Chapter 12 Application Problem

1. You should have identified at least the following errors on weaknesses:

    1. The attitude object ("educational measurement text") is ambiguous. Did you assume it was this text? From the information given, there is no way to tell.

    2. No instructions are given. Do you circle *one* response for each statement, cross out all the options you don't like, or just what do you do?

    3. No response option key is provided. Did you assume "SA" meant "strongly agree" rather than "somewhat appropriate"?

    4. The first item is likely to offend many respondents (in fact, we think it's in poor taste), and the second one is nearly as bad. Never put sensitive or offensive statements at the beginning, or you may receive an incomplete response.

    5. Statements 1, 5, 6, and 7 do not really pertain to the text, which is supposedly the object of this attitude scale, but rather (except for 7) to the topic of educational measurement. Statement 7 has strayed completely off the target.

    6. The number of positive statements (8) far outnumbers the negative statements (only 2 and 10). Does that imbalance hint that we might have (unconsciously, of course) biased the statements a bit?

    7. Statement 8 violates good practice in several ways: (1) the statement is overly long, complex, and ambiguous; (2) it contains a double-barreled thought, being really two statements smashed together; (3) it includes a double negative; (4) the use of *never* is a no-no; and (5) the unnecessary use of *obfuscate* obfuscates the statement.

    8. The past tense in item 9 is troubling. Even if the book was relevant, is it now? And to whom and for what is it relevant? Ambiguity strikes again.

    And there are probably other sins in our example that we didn't notice. Maybe hanging is too good for the guys who wrote this book.

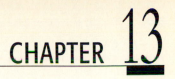

Picking the Right Yardstick

Assigning Grades and Reporting Student Performance

OVERVIEW

Grades are ubiquitous at all levels of education from preschool through the university, but the appropriate use of grades is not as straightforward and simple as many people assume. As Scriven (1970) noted, "Like so many other everyday practices, grading has often seemed too humble to merit the attention of high-powered test and measurement people. My feeling is that it is far more important and in more need of help than anything else they work on" (p. 14). Scriven is not alone in thinking that grading practices need a lot of work. In fact, many people have advocated that grades be abolished altogether.

This chapter describes how grades contribute to effective educational practices. After a historical overview of grading practices, the purposes and functions of grading are described. Next, the pros and cons of various types of grading systems and some of the most frequent problems with grades are discussed. Finally, we provide guidelines for using grades effectively and fairly.

OBJECTIVES

Upon completing your study of this chapter, you should be able to

1. Explain the purposes for which grades are typically used.
2. Identify other sources of information that should be used to supplement grades.
3. Describe the way grading has changed throughout this century.
4. Give examples of how grades can be appropriately used by students, parents, teachers, and counselors, administrators, other schools, and employers.

5. | Compare and contrast different types of grading systems.

6. | Discuss why alternatives for traditional grading are not more widely used.

7. | Summarize the most frequent objections to grades, and indicate which objections have the most merit.

8. | Explain how well grades can be used to predict future success.

9. | Describe how to develop an effective grading system.

10. | Explain why parent conferences should be an important part of any grading system.

11. | Summarize the variables that contribute to effective parent conferences.

History and Background

Grades of some type have always been used to report students' performance. The importance of grades is underscored by the fact that references to grades have become an important part of how we describe activities in many other areas of our lives. Without realizing that they are borrowing from education, people refer to such things as Grade-A eggs and Triple A Bonds. When the U.S. secretary of education described the current status of education as deserving a B– everybody knew exactly what he meant. Or did they? At least on a general level, people know that a B– is a long way from excellence and somewhat above mediocrity. But using a B- to describe something as complex as the American educational system leaves a lot unsaid.

Which brings us face to face with both the advantages and disadvantages of grades. Grades are a way of summarizing complex information about a student's performance in a particular area. Reducing that information to a single number or letter makes it more manageable, comparable, and recordable. But the resulting advantages are achieved at some cost. Because they are summative and general in nature, grades can never tell the whole story. Critics have argued that grading is not only unreliable and superficial, but also misleading, demotivating, and harmful (for example, Kohn, 1993, 1994; Wallace & Graves, 1995).

Some people believe that grading is an inevitable part of education (Geisinger, 1982), some see it as valuable (for example, Moynihan, 1971), and others see it as damaging for students and uninformative for parents (for example, Glasser, 1969). Almost everyone agrees that grading is a difficult and time-consuming process. By the end of a given year, most school teachers will have spent several hundred hours grading and collecting the information necessary to determine grades. As noted by Hopkins and Stanley,

> Converting scores and performance into grades, is at best a rather arbitrary process, which is further complicated by public relations problems in reporting to parents. Frequently, these difficulties produce double-talking teachers and confused students and parents. (1981, p. 320)

So much time and effort has been spent debating the pros and cons of various grading systems, one would think that substantial progress would have been made over the last several decades. However, the issues being debated in the 1920s and

1930s are still being debated today. Let's look briefly at how grading practices have evolved over the years.

Prior to the early 1900s, teachers had total authority for judging a student's performance, and in most cases, parents respected that authority and had little interest in being kept informed. At about the turn of the century, objective tests began gaining popularity. The desire to be more objective in all aspects of education led to the development of systematic grading systems. According to Cureton (1971), the most frequently used grading system assigned each student a percentage between 0 and 100 to indicate the percentage of the material that the student had learned. After this system became well established, studies by Johnson (1911) and Starch and Elliot (1912, 1913a & 1913b) demonstrated the subjectivity and arbitrariness of such grading even in areas such as arithmetic. Findings such as these led to the first published proposals for the abolition of grading (Dadourian, 1925), and such suggestions are still made periodically (for example, Kohn, 1993, 1994).

In the 1930s and early 1940s, most educational institutions switched from percentage grades to letter grades. This shift was accompanied by the development of the so-called progressive education movement with its emphasis on the need for freedom and democracy in the classroom and the child's need for support and encouragement. Widespread support for this progressive philosophy spurred criticism of the competition associated with grading and a growing belief that grades encourage students to pursue overly narrow objectives.

By the 1950s, the progressive education movement had begun to wane, and people were arguing that grading needed to be more consistent with educational objectives (Smith & Dobbin, 1960). By the 1960s and early 1970s, concern over the quality of education led to increased emphasis on "basic education," and there were renewed calls for more formal evaluations of student progress and more rigorous standards for attainment. Concerns about the rigor associated with grading became even more pronounced in the 1980s and 1990s as a function of the educational accountability movement, minimum competency testing, and grade inflation.

The history of grading is like a roller coaster riding the rails of prevailing educational trends. At one point, grades are seen as a threat to personal freedom and individuality. Then, before we have come to terms with that perspective, we're swept along by demands for increased rigor and accountability. It is easy to point out problems with grading practices. Yet, many people continue to believe that grading is an essential part of education (Linn & Gronlund, 1995). Many of the arguments we hear today are not new; but, amid the furor, it is easy to lose sight of the purposes for grading. Before discussing different types of grading systems, therefore, let's clarify exactly what grades are supposed to accomplish.

Purposes and Functions of Grading

The primary purpose of grades is to condense a large amount of information into a concise summary, uncluttered by detail. To communicate information concisely and efficiently to a variety of audiences who will use that information for different purposes, grades must be limited in scope. Other methods are available for giving a more detailed and comprehensive description of a student's perfor-mance in any particular area. Take a hypothetical biology student, for example. As Feldmesser (1971) points out, grades were never designed to indicate to that student

> that his lab work was weak while his grasp of abstract concepts was strong, that he was high on understanding of cell-structure but low on understanding of ecological relation-ships and middling on understanding of reproductive systems. He [needs] to know what it all adds up to—whether, all things considered, he did "well" or "poorly" . . . (pp. 2–3)

By emphasizing that grades serve a limited purpose, we are not suggesting that other forms of information and feedback (for example, test scores, written com-ments on tests and papers, verbal discussions with teachers and other students) are not valuable. However, grades cannot serve all those purposes. When we recognize the limited, but valuable purpose grades are designed to meet, many of the criti-cisms are less compelling.

Whenever we summarize information about a student's academic performance into a single letter or number, important detail is necessarily ignored. (For exam-ple, did the student receive a low grade because of a lack of effort, lack of progress, or limited aptitude? Did the student's poor grade in math result from poor perfor-mance in *all* aspects of math, or was it due to dismal performance in decimals and average performance in fractions and story problems? The purpose of a grade is to communicate general performance, not to detail how or why that particular judg-ment was made.

Grades are used to communicate important information to a number of diverse audiences, each of whom uses that information for different purposes. These au-diences include

- Students
- Parents
- Teachers and counselors
- Administrators
- Other schools
- Employers

Let's consider the ways in which grades are used by each of these audiences.

Students

Research and common sense suggests that knowledge of past performance will im-prove subsequent learning. The type of information students need to enhance learning can be divided into short-term and long-term needs. In the short term, stu-dents need answers to questions like these:

> Why did I get a B instead of an A on this composition?
> Should I spend my time this weekend studying fractions or decimals?
> Of the 15 objectives in this chapter, which ones have I mastered?

In the long term, students need answers to questions like these:

> Should I sign up for Algebra I or Intermediate Math next year?
> How does my reading ability compare to other students' in the class?
> What are my chances of being admitted to law school?

Helping students make decisions in both areas is important. Grades are most useful, however, for making long-term decisions because they cannot reflect the level of detail needed for short-term decisions. Such detailed information should be given in daily feedback via verbal reports, written comments on tests and papers, and class interactions.

Many educators believe that appropriate grading can motivate students to perform better, but some scholars claim that grades function as extrinsic rewards that reduce students' intrinsic motivation to learn (Butler & Nissan, 1986; Kohn, 1994). Clark (1969) found that graduate students performed better in situations where they competed for grades. However, Moeller and Reschke (1993) found no difference in the achievement level of students who were graded on the basis of the correctness and completeness of their work and a control group who were not graded. Covington (1992) contended that grading was detrimental to motivation. Mac Iver and Reuman (1994) found that traditional grading and student recognition practices were at least partly responsible for low levels of student effort in school. Research on this question has not resolved the debate, but it has yielded insight into the complexity of the issues involved (see Chapter 6 in Milton, Pollio, & Eison, 1986. See also Natriello, 1987, 1996; Mac Iver, Reuman, & Main, 1996; and Sansone & Morgan, 1992). However, psychologists now know that both achievement motivation and academic performance are influenced by other factors such as students' self-efficacy (their beliefs about their own ability to perform successfully) and their beliefs about what knowledge is and how learning occurs (McCown, Driscoll, & Roop, 1996).

Whatever you believe about the role of grades in motivating students, it is important to remember that motivational techniques affect students differently. Some students are motivated most by supportive encouragement, others through mild chastisement, and others through fear of negative consequences. Thus any motivational benefit associated with grades will be different depending on the student.

Some people argue that grades do not help prepare students for life (for example, Warren, 1971) because after they finish school, they will seldom be judged by their performance on written tests, homework assignments, or term papers. However, the kinds of judgments made in life are quite similar to the overall judgments made in assigning grades. For instance, overall judgments are used to decide whether someone receives a salary increase, continues on the job, or is promoted.

Regardless of how grades are used, it is vital that they be as accurate as possible. Unfortunately, according to LaBenne and Greene (1969), some teachers knowingly give some students better grades than they deserve because the teachers feel sorry for them or think they have done their best. Even though this is done with the best intentions, students cannot benefit from inaccurate feedback.

Parents

The grades written on a report card are often the only information many parents receive about their child's academic performance. Although this information can be useful, it is not sufficient if we want parents to be active participants in their children's education. A good reporting program for parents supplements grades with regular written information, parent conferences, summaries of standardized achievement test scores, and telephone calls or notes to suggest how parents can support the school program.

If they understand the purpose of grades, and if grades are supplemented with other information, parents can become effective partners in the educational process. Grades alone, however, will not be enough. Knowing that a child has received a C in reading will not be as helpful as knowing the specific problems she is having, and receiving some suggestions about how reading can be supported at home.

Teachers and Counselors

Grading has two types of benefits for teachers and counselors. First, in determining the grade and analyzing information from many different sources, a teacher must set priorities, evaluate patterns and exceptions, and compare students' performance to her own expectations. This summarization process often gives the teacher new insights into students' learning styles and needs, or reveals alternative instructional strategies she might not have considered. Second, previous grades provide a foundation for teachers to collect additional information that can guide instructional decisions for that student. It is important to emphasize that grades are only a beginning and should lead to consideration of such information as diagnostic test scores, observations of the child's interaction with other students, homework, and discussions with parents.

Administrators

Administrators often use grades in making decisions about promotion, awarding academic honors, selecting students for participation in extracurricular activities, awarding scholarships, or determining the value of a particular program. Depending on how they are used, grades can yield very good information for administrative decisions, or they can be totally inappropriate. For example, if Ms. Sampson knows that the success of her new American History course will be judged solely by comparing this year's students' grades with last year's students' grades, she might allow that knowledge to influence her grading practices. If so, grades would be a very poor measure of success.

Are grades a good source of information for administrative decisions? That depends on the decision. For example, done appropriately, grades can be quite useful in determining students' eligibility for extracurricular activities or in awarding academic honors (for example, deciding who will be listed on the school's honor roll). Although grades provide a broad-based indicator of a student's academic performance, they are clearly subject to somewhat subjective criteria. They are not a good measure, therefore, in cases where very detailed information is required, or where the people assigning grades are in a position to benefit or be damaged by the outcome of the decision.

Other Schools

High school grades are frequently used in deciding which students should be admitted to a particular college; similarly, undergraduate grades are used in decisions about admission to graduate school. Jencks and Riesman (1968) argue that such a practice is discriminatory because students who do not perform well in high school, are denied the opportunity for further education, which is the only way they can improve their performance. Alternatively, Glazer (1970) contends that grades provide an objective measure by which students from minority backgrounds can demonstrate their ability to succeed in college. Even though this argument remains unresolved, it is generally recognized that earlier grades are one of the best predictors of later grades (Lavin, 1965; Willingham, 1974; and Geisinger, 1982). This emphasizes the importance of assigning grades accurately since they may be used later to make important decisions.

Employers

Grades are sometimes considered by employers in making hiring decisions. Warren (1971) points out that prestigious law firms routinely hire only those students who graduate near the top of their classes. Employers may use such information without understanding the process by which grades are assigned or the limited information grades provide. Indeed, there is substantial evidence that college grades have very little relationship to occupational success (Hoyt, 1970; O'Leary, 1980). This is not surprising when we recognize that grades are a very general indicator of academic mastery, whereas success on the job consists of many attributes besides technical skill (such as personality, motivation, willingness to work hard, and just plain luck).[1]

Types of Grading Systems

One of the earliest documented grading systems is described by Kunder and Porwoll (1977). A report card issued in 1851 for a student at the Tuscarora Academy in Pennsylvania read as follows: "Behaviour tolerably good; tolerably studious; in Arithmetic, 2; in English Grammar, 2; in Algebra, 3; in all other exercises respectable. Recited 445 [Bible] verses, and lost but little time by absence." More than a century later, report cards in a neighboring district in Pennsylvania had become

---

[1]For a brief discussion of the vagaries of using students' cumulative grade-point average as a predictor variable, and the problems associated with using the correlation coefficient in studies that attempt to determine how well college grades predict subsequent success in the workaday world or in graduate school, see Milton, Pollio, and Eison (1986).

substantially more complex, as shown in Figure 13.1. Notice how this report card provides information separately for academic achievement, effort, and social development. Also note how a four-point grading system is used instead of the more traditional five-point system. As we continue, you will see that there are an almost infinite number of ways in which grades can be reported.

All grading systems can be classified with respect to two variables: (1) the type of comparison used in assigning grades, and (2) the type of symbol used to represent that grade. In what follows, we will explore the most frequently used types of grading systems to familiarize you with various options. In most cases, classroom teachers decide what type of comparison to use, and the school or institution decides on the symbol to be used for reporting. Thus it is possible that the type of comparison would differ from teacher to teacher in the same school even though grades are reported using the same symbol.

Type of Comparison Used in Assigning Grades

All grading systems consider how well a particular student has done in comparison to some standard. The five most frequently used standards are

- Other students
- Absolute standards
- Aptitude
- Effort
- Improvement

Let's look at each of these standards next.

Using Other Students as a Basis of Comparison

A teacher who *grades on the curve* relies on a predetermined notion about how student performance should be distributed among the members of a population. The teacher assumes that only a small percentage of students in a group can excel, that a small percentage must fail, and that the majority will be spread out in between these two extreme categories. Some prespecified percentage of the class will be assigned As, a certain percentage will be given Bs, and so on. Consequently, the grade assigned to any given student depends on how his or her classmates perform as well as the student's own performance.

Grading on the curve was suggested more than 75 years ago by Meyer (1908), and became popular during the 1920s and 1930s. Although teachers who grade on the curve vary somewhat in the quotas they use for each of the A, B, C, D, and F categories, the different approaches all involve the idea that the distribution of grades assigned to a group of students should be approximately similar to the distribution of the normal curve developed by the German mathematician Carl Friedrich Gauss. According to Cureton (1971), the most common method uses 1.5 standard deviations or more above the mean for As (about 7 percent), .5 to 1.5 standard deviations above the mean for Bs (about 24 percent), .5 standard deviation above the mean to .5 standard deviation below the mean for Cs (about 38 per-

JUNIATA VALLEY SCHOOLS
(Alexandria, Pennsylvania)   Team _____

Student _____

Year in School: K 1 2 3 4 5 6 7

SUBJECT DEVELOPMENT

Marking Key: A = Excellent; B = Good; C = Fair
D = Having Difficulty

Reading	Instructional Level				
	Gains Skills Needed to Read				
	Learns and Uses Sounds				
	Reads Well Orally				
	Understands What Is Read				
	Shows Interest and Makes Effort				
Language	Communicates Well Orally				
	Communicates Well in Writing				
	Shows Interest and Makes Effort				
Spelling	Spells Correctly in Written Work				
	Masters Assigned Lists				
	Shows Interest and Makes Effort				
Handwriting	Prints Legibly (manuscript)				
	Writes Legibly (cursive)				
	Shows Interest and Makes Effort				
Mathematics	Understands Number Concepts				
	Masters Number Facts and Skills				
	Solves Word Problems				
	Shows Interest and Makes Effort				
Social Studies	Understands Main Ideas				
	Shows Interest and Makes Effort				
Science	Understands Main Ideas				
	Shows Interest and Makes Effort				
Music	Learns Concepts and Skills				
	Shows Interest and Makes Effort				
Art	Learns Concepts and Skills				
	Shows Interest and Makes Effort				

Phys. Ed.	Learns Concepts and Skills				
	Shows Interest and Makes Effort				
Library	Learns Concepts and Skills				
	Shows Interest and Checks Out Books				
DAYS ABSENT					

Unmarked spaces indicate that these items are not applicable at this time.

SUBJECT DEVELOPMENT

Marking Key: S = Satisfactory   N = Needs Improvement

Works Neatly			
Works Quietly			
Finishes Work on Time			
Follows Directions			
Listens Well			
Obeys Cheerfully			
Works and Plays Well with Others			
Tries to be Courteous			
Tries to keep the School Clean and Attractive			

TEACHER COMMENTS

_____

_____

_____

_____

_____

_____

_____

FIGURE 13.1   Example of a Report Card

cent), .5 standard deviation below the mean to 1.5 standard deviations below the mean for Ds (about 24 percent), and more than 1.5 standard deviations below the mean for Fs (about 7 percent).

In most classroom applications, grading on a curve should not be used because the type of grade a student receives depends more on the other students in the class than on how well a particular student has mastered the objectives of the course. Furthermore, the process is prescriptive and Proscrustean rather than descriptive because the obtained distribution of students' scores is forced to fit an *a priori* notion of how students ought to perform. If it is used at all, grading on the curve should be used only where the class is relatively large and it is not unreasonable to assume that the students represent the full range of ability on whatever subject is being graded. There are many instances where this assumption is not met. For example, Hopkins (1998) describes how, to help their husbands succeed in college, wives of World War II veterans enrolled in courses in which their husbands were enrolled and did little or no work. The wives received the predetermined number of Fs and Ds, assuring their husbands a grade of C or better. Wallace and Graves (1995) present further arguments of why educators should not grade on the curve.

Comparison to an Absolute Standard

This method of grading, sometimes referred to as *mastery grading,* compares the performance of each student to the material the instructor wants mastered, using a percentage grade. According to this system, a grade of 87 percent indicates that the student has mastered 87 percent of the material. Percentage grades are not as precise as they may appear at first. For example, a person may score 90 percent on a test either because the test is very easy or because he or she has mastered the material. Given the same content, a teacher might construct an easy test on which students scored 95 percent, or a more difficult test on which the class average was only 60 percent.

The so-called absolute standard is also based indirectly on an implicit comparison of present students with previous students. In other words, the standard is established based on the teacher's perception about what previous children have been able to master when taught the same content. Unfortunately, this fact is often ignored when people argue that "children should be measured against performance standards, not against each other." Grading compared to an absolute standard is particularly difficult to use in subject areas that are not well defined (for example, the development of critical thinking skills) and easier in well-defined areas (for example, mastery of spelling words).

Achievement Compared to Aptitude

Some educators believe that grades should be based on a comparison of performance to aptitude. Given the same level of achievement, a student with relatively low aptitude would receive a better grade than a student with greater aptitude. Although this approach is logically appealing, it must be considered in light of how difficult it is to measure aptitude. Our best measures of aptitude are relatively crude approximations and are possible only using standardized aptitude tests that are not routinely administered in many places. Further, this approach assumes that aptitude is unchanging, which is probably untrue. Finally, Thorndike (1969) demonstrated that teachers often overestimate or underestimate how well students should do based on aptitude scores. Interestingly, Geisinger and Rabinowitz (1979) found that relatively few university faculty members assigned grades based on aptitude, but Geisinger, Wilson, and Naumann (1980), and Terwilliger (1966) found, respectively, that a substantial number of community college faculty and more than 50 percent of high school teachers employed this method. In most cases, this approach to assigning grades is potentially misleading.

Improvement as a Basis for Comparison

Some teachers assign grades according to how much improvement a student demonstrates. A student who begins a class knowing very little in the subject area but learns a moderate amount would get a better grade than a student who begins a class knowing almost everything and learns only a little. Students in such classes usually learn quickly that they need only to "play dumb" at the beginning of the course in order to receive a high grade. In addition, most people interpret grades as an indication of proficiency. If grades are used as an indicator of improvement, it is extremely important to make that clear to people who use the grades. Improvement is certainly important, but where grades are designed to serve as an overall indicator of students' level of academic mastery, degree of improvement is irrelevant.

Using Effort as the Basis for Grades

Some educators argue that those students who try the hardest should receive the best grades. Grades assigned in this way no longer describe the degree to which the student has mastered the material. Instead, they provide information about how hard the student tries. Although information about effort may be very useful, it is important to keep the information presented by grades as clear-cut as possible. Some schools have solved this problem by assigning one grade for academic achievement and a separate grade for effort. Such grades must be reported separately and their meaning made clear. When grades become a hodge-podge of different variables such as achievement and effort, their meaning becomes confounded. For example, it is not clear whether a low grade signifies a lack of effort, a lack of achievement, or both.

Contract Grading

Another approach, referred to as *contract grading,* uses an absolute standard, but the standard varies from student to student (Hassencahl, 1979). In the tradition of legal contracts, the grade desired by the student, the learning goals that will be demonstrated, and the procedures for measuring goal attainment are specified. There is mutual agreement about the "contract," and if the student completes her part of the contract, she receives the grade specified. Although there is evidence that learning contracts can be an effective pedagogical tool (Christen, 1976), others argue that because the *quantity* of work is easier to describe than the *quality,* the work often deteriorates (Kirschenbaum, Simon, & Napier, 1971). This type of

Table 13.1 Percentage of U.S. School Districts Using Different Grading Systems by Grade Level

Type of Grading System Used	Grade Level				
	K	1–3	4–6	7–9	10–12
Letter grades (A, B, C, D, F)	15%	55%	79%	82%	80%
Percentage grading	5%	16%	21%	27%	29%
Number grades	2%	4%	4%	7%	9%
Pass–fail grading	3%	2%	2%	7%	13%
Credit–no credit grading	1%	2%	2%	10%	17%
Satisfactory–unsatisfactory grading	51%	36%	17%	8%	7%
Anecdotal comments	53%	44%	39%	26%	24%
Rating scale	20%	19%	9%	2%	2%
Item checklists	41%	21%	15%	5%	5%
Other	3%	2%	2%	1%	1%

Note: The total percentage in each column exceeds 100 because many of the school districts surveyed used more than one grading system.

Source: Adapted from Robinson, G. E. & Craver, J. M. (1989). *Assessing and grading student achievement.* Arlington, VA: Educational Research Service.

grading encourages individualized learning, but it is questionable whether it provides a more accurate measure of that learning. Because it is individualized, it definitely provides a different type of information than do traditional grades (a fact that should be made clear to reporting audiences). Consequently, it must be viewed cautiously as a replacement for grades.

Type of Symbol Used

Individual teachers usually decide what kind of comparison will be used to assign grades, but the school or institution usually decides what symbol will be used in reporting grades. The two most common grading systems, letter grades and percentage grades, have been supplemented in recent years by pass–fail grades, narrative reports, and parent conferences. Educational Research Service (Robinson & Craver, 1989) has reported the frequency with which different types of grading symbols are used, based on a nationwide survey of school districts (see Table 13.1).

Letter grades (for example, A, B, C, D, and F) and percentage grades account for more than 70 percent of the grading in the elementary schools (except in kindergarten), and more than 90 percent of the grading in secondary schools. Satisfactory–unsatisfactory grades are the most commonly used grades in kindergarten. Similar results have been reported in previous nationwide surveys (for example, Kunder & Porwoll, 1977).

Letter Grades

The most widely used grading system is based on letters that portray a student's position on a scale ranging from excellent to failing performance, as shown in Table 13.2. The exact percentages and descriptive statements associated with each

Table 13.2   Example of Percentage Grades Typically Associated with Different Letter Grades

Letter Grade	Numbered Grade	Typical Percentage Grade	Typical Description
A	4.0	90–100	Excellent
B	3.0	80–89	Above average
C	2.0	70–79	Average
D	1.0	60–69	Below average
F	0	Below 60	Failing

letter grade vary from teacher to teacher and school to school. In most cases, a grade of F indicates failing performance. Other letters may also take on special significance. For instance, an A may be used to select students for the honor role, or Ds may indicate passing performance that does not count toward graduation. The ease with which tests, homework assignments, class presentations, and written papers can be scored on a numerical basis and then converted to a letter grade with roughly similar meaning probably accounts for the widespread use of such a system.

Many teachers or schools add pluses and minuses to the letters to further discriminate among students. Letter grades are also frequently converted to a *grade-point average (GPA)*. To compute a GPA, the numerical value associated with the grade in each course is multiplied by the number of credit hours assigned to that course. These products are then summed over all courses taken, and the sum is divided by the total number of credit hours.

Percentage Grading

Up until the early 1920s, *percentage grading* was the most popular system for reporting students' achievement (Smith & Dobbin, 1960). In this system, each student is assigned a number between 0 and 100, with the number supposedly reflecting the percentage of material the student has mastered. Concern over the accuracy with which teachers could differentiate between small increments on the scale led to its decline in the 1920s and 1930s.

Pass–Fail Grading

In the early 1960s, many colleges and some high schools introduced a *pass–fail* option for grading. The following rationale was offered:

- Since grades are unimportant outside the academic world, it is inappropriate to emphasize them in school.
- Concern about getting good grades prevents students from taking courses from which they would benefit.
- Pressure to get high grades interferes with learning for the sake of learning and encourages cheating and poor study habits, such as cramming just before a test.

Although there is some merit to each of these concerns, most schools have not found pass–fail grading to be a viable solution. For example, Gold et al. (1971) found that student achievement declines when pass–fail grading is used, and Rossman (1970) reported that graduate and professional schools were less likely to accept applicants who had numerous pass–fail courses. Ebel (1979) suggests that pass–fail grading reduces motivation and leaves students with an incomplete or inaccurate record of their achievement.

> Most of us want to be valued as persons. Most of us don't particularly want to be evaluated, but we can't enjoy the first without enduring the second. The weakness of a pass–fail grading is that by doing a poor job of evaluating, it keeps us from doing a good one of valuing. (p. 244)

Parent Conferences

Recognizing that one of the primary purposes of grades is to communicate information to parents, many schools supplement grades with systematic parent conferences. As a substitute for grading, parent conferences are not very effective, but as a way of supplementing the limited information contained in grades and enlisting the support of parents in their children's education, parent conferences can be extremely valuable.

Parent conferences provide two-way communication between parents and teachers. Instead of just receiving a general summary of how their child is doing, parents can ask questions about the school's programs, tell the teacher about the child's out-of-school activities that may help in planning instruction, and learn about activities they can provide at home to improve the child's educational achievement. Such conferences also provide a good opportunity to clarify and interpret the student's most recent standardized test scores, which are sometimes difficult for parents to understand. The disadvantage of parent conferences is that they take a great deal of time and skill on the part of the teacher, and many parents are unwilling or unable to participate.

The effectiveness of parent conferences is enhanced if a structured guide, such as that shown in Figure 13.2, is used. Such a guide helps ensure that important topics are not missed, and documents what occurs during the conference. Completing the form during the conference and giving a copy to the parents is also an effective way of involving the parents in their child's education. Written documentation of past conferences can also help the teacher prepare for future meetings.

Narrative Reports

Some people advocate the use of narrative reports as an alternative to symbols used in traditional grading (Bellanca & Kirschenbaum, 1976; Burba, 1976). A narrative report can provide a qualitative description of a student's accomplishments, learning style, and strengths and weaknesses, and can also offer suggestions for improvement. Like a letter of recommendation, the narrative should include information about *how* the student learns as well as *how much* she has learned.

PARENT CONFERENCE GUIDE

_____   _____   _____   _____
(Student)   (Parent)   (Teacher)   (Date)

ACADEMIC ACHIEVEMENT
Discuss: ___ past performance (class participation, homework, overall grades)
            ___ recent standardized test scores
            ___ future plans

Reading: _____
English _____
Handwriting _____
Social Studies _____
Math _____
Science _____
Music _____
Art _____
Physical Education _____

PERSONAL GROWTH
Discuss: ___ level of functioning
            ___ suggestions for school or home effort

Respects rights of others _____
Attitude towards school _____
Works up to potential _____
Follows directions _____
Tries hard _____
Uses time well _____
Gets along with others _____

HEALTH
Discuss: ___ any concerns or problems

Vision/Hearing _____
Health Habits (grooming, eating, etc.) _____
General Health _____
Attendance _____

SUGGESTIONS AND ACTION PLANS FOR SCHOOL OR HOME

_____
_____
_____
_____

FIGURE 13.2   Example of Form To be Used as Guide and Reporting Mechanism for Parent Conferences

Although word processing technology makes such an alternative to grading more feasible, narrative reporting of each student's performance is still a very large undertaking for teachers. Furthermore, even if such reports were more understandable for parents, it is doubtful they could be used effectively by administrators and admissions offices because of the amount of paperwork that would be generated. Finally, according to Geisinger (1982), narratives have a tendency to focus on students' personalities rather than their mastery of academic material. Consequently, narrative reports have limited appeal as an alternative to traditional grading practices. If the logistics of generating such reports can be dealt with successfully, however, narrative reports can be a useful supplement to grades, particularly for parents.

Objections to Grades

Grades have often been attacked, and there have been frequent suggestions that they should be abolished. In fact, it has been said that a grade is an inadequate report of a biased and inaccurate judgment of the extent to which a student has attained an undefined level of mastery of an unknown proportion of unspecified material.

Calls for the elimination of grading usually cite some combination of the following seven issues.

1. *The fact that grades are not comparable from school to school, or even from instructor to instructor, means they are inaccurate.* There is some truth to this statement. Carter (1952) found that boys tended to receive lower grades than girls of equal achievement. Hadley (1954) found that teachers gave higher marks to students they liked than to students of equal achievement whom they liked less. Baird and Feister (1972) found that the average grade at most colleges was the same whether the average student at the college was scoring at the 95th percentile or the 5th percentile of ability. Palmer (1962) noted that some instructors used grades as rewards or punishments, independent of how well students were mastering learning outcomes. These findings demonstrate that grades can be misused. The solution is not to abolish grades, but to teach people to use them more appropriately. After all, unless we abolish *all* forms of student evaluation, these same problems would continue.

2. *Grades cause feelings of anxiety and failure among less able students.* Glasser (1969) states "The school practice that most produces failure in students is grading" (p. 59). Such reasoning is like saying that we increase the national debt by measuring and reporting it. It is unfortunate that some students do not succeed in school, but there is no evidence that they would perform any better if their performance were not measured and reported. Most people are aware of failure, even when it's not explicitly reported. Any first grader knows which reading group she is in, and whether or not she is one of the better readers in the group. Obviously, it is possible to inappropriately ridicule and draw attention to someone's failure, but grading per se is not the cause of such inappropriate behavior.

3. *The assignment of grades leads to a reliance on extrinsic motivation and excess competitiveness.* Although frequently claimed, there is little evidence that this is true. In fact, Gold et al. (1971) found that achievement and learning actually declined when students took courses on a pass–fail basis. Similarly, Vasta and Sarmiento (1979) found that when liberal grading practices are implemented, achievement declines. As Ebel (1965, p. 440) points out, "There is nothing wrong with encouraging students to work for high marks, if the marks are valid measures of achievement."

4. *Grades encourage students to cheat.* This is like saying that money is bad because it encourages people to steal. If we eliminated all forms of evaluation, students might be less tempted to cheat, but it is also probable that they would learn less. Also, it is doubtful that students would be less likely to cheat with any other form of evaluation than they are with grades.

5. *Grades are an ineffective way of communicating among teachers, students, and parents.* If grades are the only means of communication, this objection is certainly true. However, nothing about grades suggests that they should be used to the exclusion of other forms of communication. As a concise overall indicator of students' performance, grades are remarkably effective. However, any reporting system based on a single technique will be less effective than one based on several complementary methods.

6. *Grades fail to measure some of the most important educational objectives.* Sometimes grades are used only to communicate information about the attainment of cognitive objectives, but nothing says that grades could not be used in a similar way to report students' performance in affective areas. It is clear that some teachers do not use grades appropriately, and fail to report students' performance on important educational outcomes. This failing is not a problem of grading itself, but of the evaluation procedures selected by the teacher. The solution, therefore, is not to abolish grading, but to improve the process by which we identify activities and outcomes to be evaluated.

7. *Because of grade inflation, the information contained in grades is no longer meaningful.* Since the 1960s widespread grade inflation has occurred in the United States, both in public schools and in colleges and universities (Levine, 1987; Sabot & Wakeman-Linn, 1991). Between the mid-1960s and the early 1970s, GPAs based on a four-point letter grade system increased an average of about half a letter grade even though there was no apparent increase in students' achievement. The most probable causes of grade inflation include (1) changes in grading policies, including the more frequent use of pass–fail grades (Geisinger, 1979); (2) a shift from norm-referenced grading to individualized, noncomparative policies (Geisinger, 1980); (3) increased use of student ratings in teacher evaluation procedures, accompanied by the desire of faculty to receive high student ratings (Zangenehzadeh, 1988); and (4) competition for a declining student population (Longstreth, 1979). Some have suggested that grade inflation has reduced the value of grades because (1) grades are no longer an incentive, (2) academic honors have less meaning, and (3) grades are less useful for making admissions decisions. However, Warren (1979) found no basis for these complaints. Although it is clear that grade inflation has occurred, some believe that the inflationary period is over (for example, Summerville, Ridley, and Maris, 1990). The inflation that has already occurred has undoubtedly skewed the distributions in a somewhat more negative direction. However, there is still enough variation in grades to distinguish between good and poor students, so fears about grades having become meaningless are unfounded.

Most objections about grading arise because of inappropriate evaluation procedures, or a failure to recognize that grades are not intended to provide a detailed, comprehensive, individualized report of students' progress. Although any grading system is imperfect, some method of evaluating and reporting student performance is desired by virtually all teachers, parents, and administrators. As one part of the reporting mechanism, grades have endured the test of time. Until a better alternative is found, we should continue to use grades as effectively as possible.

Application Problem 1

A teacher in your school believes that assigning end-of-quarter grades encourages cheating, and interferes with the love of learning that students should be developing. She claims that good teachers do not need to use grades to motivate students, and advocates changing all courses to a pass–fail system. Imagine you are the school principal. How would you respond?

How Well Do Grades Predict Future Success?

Many people believe that grades are valuable because they predict future performance. Yet we have just pointed out that different teachers might assign different grades to the same students; grades are often contaminated by personality and stylistic differences; different teachers use different standards of comparison; and average grades have tended to drift upward over the last several years. Given all these problems, is it possible that grades *can* be effective predictors of future performance?

In a word, yes. Although the criticisms are valid to some degree, they are not as serious as many people assume. For example, Fricke (1975) and Werts, Linn, and Joreskog (1978) found that grades were remarkably consistent over the four years of college; and Hicklin (1962) found a correlation of .73 between grades received by students at grades 9 and 12. Grades correlate in the .70 range with student scores on standardized achievement tests (Nell, 1963), and a number of studies (for example, Lavin, 1965; Richards & Lutz, 1968) have found that high school grades are even better predictors of college grades than are standardized achievement and aptitude tests.

All this suggests that even though they are frequently maligned, and are sometimes used inappropriately, grades *are* good predictors of future success. Too frequently grades have been used as a convenient scapegoat for the ills of education. But remembering the limited purposes they are designed to serve and the difficulty people have had in suggesting a feasible alternative, grades are a remarkably useful tool that should not be eliminated.

Guidelines for Assigning Grades

Grades provide a concise summary of student performance. By definition, any kind of summary leaves out some important information, and grades are no exception. Almost always, therefore, grades should be supplemented with other information.

For example, if a new reading teacher is designing a reading program for Loretta, she might first look at Loretta's grades from the previous year, but she should not stop at this point. The fact that Loretta received a C– in reading indicates that she was experiencing some difficulties, but further information using standardized tests, diagnostic tests, observation, and perhaps discussions with Loretta's previous teacher should all be used to design an appropriate reading program. Previous grades provide a useful starting point, but they cannot tell the whole story.

Similarly, if Ms. Barclay wants to know why her daughter, Kirsten, does not enjoy school, she should not look to the grades on Kirsten's report card for a complete answer. The fact that Kirsten's grades have slipped from a B+ average the previous year to mostly Cs and Ds during the current year may well have prompted Ms. Barclay's concern. But a review of Kirsten's grades will not reveal whether her negative attitude is causing a decline in performance, or whether the decline itself is causing her to view school negatively. A parent–teacher conference, a visit to the school, discussions with other parents, and perhaps a discussion with Kirsten should all be used in trying to understand the shift in Kirsten's attitude and grades.

The value of grades is not that they are perfect for any single information need, but rather that they provide useful information for so many different situations and audiences. Like the proverbial jackknife, grades are useful in a great many different situations—although probably not ideal for any one. Therefore, grades are best used in combination with other sources of information such as

- Results from standardized achievement and aptitude tests
- Written reports (including periodic newsletters, notes on homework, or notes written to individual parents)
- Diagnostic tests
- Parent conferences

Because we have previously discussed standardized achievement, aptitude, and diagnostic tests, we will not repeat that information here. With regard to written evaluations, there are an almost infinite number of ways to provide useful information to parents, administrators, and other teachers. Some parents may need a personal letter, admissions officers frequently want letters of recommendation in addition to transcripts of grades, and employers may want the results of applied performance tests. All are part of an effective reporting system. Our focus in this chapter, however, is primarily on grades. Additionally, because we think parent conferences are an essential part of explaining a student's performance, we will also give some suggestions about holding effective parent conferences.

Developing and Reporting Grades

Developing and operating an effective grading system requires substantial time and effort. In most cases, it is best to develop the general framework for grading at the district or institutional level to avoid unnecessary duplication of effort. However, no system will be entirely appropriate for every school in the district, or even for every classroom in a school. Individual teachers or schools should be able to modify and adapt any grading system to their specific needs. The following suggestions should help:

1. *Those who need information from grades (teachers, administrators, parents, students and the like) should have a voice in designing the system.* It is unfortunate when a grading system is imposed from the top down so that those who consume the information have little say in how it is structured. A committee approach in which major audiences help design a grading system that is responsive to their needs is more effective, and heightens the probability that information from the system will be used. Student input is particularly important for older students since feedback to them is one of the primary purposes of grading.

2. *A grading or reporting system should be consistent with the purposes it is designed to serve.* If all consumers of grades understand the limited information grades provide, they can design other types of information to supplement grades. Clearly, in a district that viewed grades as the primary means of communicating with parents, a system would be structured differently than in a district that wanted grades primarily to serve the informational needs of students.

3. *A single grade should not mix information about academic performance with information about other areas of concern such as citizenship, effort, improvement, work habits, and attitude.* Grades can be used effectively for reporting different types of information if separate (and usually somewhat different) systems are used to report academic achievement and performance in areas such as work habits or attitude. Grades in academic areas should be a pure measure of academic achievement with separate grades or marks being given for performance in other areas.

4. *The objectives most important to the school should be addressed by grades.* Time limitations and other practical constraints make it impossible to use grades for measuring performance in all areas of interest. It is important to prioritize educational objectives and make sure that top-priority objectives are addressed first. As a part of the grading system, the committee should consider what type of performance or behavior will serve as sufficient, observable indicators that important objectives have been achieved.

5. *Grading systems must achieve a balance between detail and practicality.* All audiences want information that is as comprehensive as possible. The need for detail must, however, be weighed against the amount of time available to collect information and prepare understandable reports for pupils, parents, employers, and school personnel. The need to maintain an archive of reports in school records should also be considered.

6. *Information on which grading is based should be collected as systematically, accurately, and objectively as possible.* When grades are assigned on the basis of irrelevant or trivial achievements, or when they are contaminated by personality or other unrelated factors, they lose their meaning. The highest grades must go to those students who best master the relevant educational objectives.

7. *If percentage grades are used, they must be interpreted cautiously.* Unless a percentage grade is based upon a sample of problems or tasks that is representative of a well-defined, clearly delimited domain of tasks or problems, it provides an inadequate basis for generalizing about the student's mastery of a subject matter domain. Teacher-made classroom tests typically include a variety of tasks or problems that vary in difficulty and assess a range of different objectives from one or more broadly defined units such as the Civil War and Reconstruction Period (U.S.

History); the Endocrine System (Human Biology); or Work, Power, and Energy (Physics). Percentage scores from such broad, vaguely defined domains can be appropriately used as a basis for making decisions about students' relative standing in a group (norm-referenced decisions), but they usually provide an inadequate basis for making inferences about what proportion of the subject matter content the students have mastered (criterion-referenced decisions).

Frary, Cross, and Weber (1993) raised this concern after surveying the testing practices of more than 500 secondary teachers in Virginia. Many of the teachers they surveyed reported that they constructed typical norm-referenced, classroom tests, including a range of problems and tasks of widely varying levels of difficulty selected from broad, vaguely defined content domains. Many of these teachers later reported that they preferred to report the results as percentage scores and use these percentages as a basis for concluding how well their students had mastered the domain. Jumping to conclusions in this manner tends to overestimate the students' knowledge and abilities. This use of percentage grades would be much better served if the percentages were obtained from criterion-referenced tests consisting of a larger sample of problems or tasks from narrower, more clearly defined, homogenous domains.

8. *The grading system should provide ample opportunity for parent conferences and discussion.* The importance of parent conferences cannot be overemphasized. Although grades provide useful information, they should be a starting point for discussions that can substantially enhance the parent–school partnership by helping both sides discover the reasons behind the grades.

9. *Student–teacher interaction should be a normal part of grading.* Opportunities for students and teachers to discuss the meaning of grades, the way in which grades are assigned, and steps the student can take to improve grades should be a normal part of the grading process. Too often, such discussions are undertaken in the spirit of protest, and then only as a last resort, when a student feels that she has been graded unfairly. When students are angry and teachers defensive, the probability of a reasonable or useful discussion is minimal.

10. *The weight associated with different components should be consistent with their perceived importance.* Grades combine information about students' performance on tests, homework, everyday class work, and so on. This means teachers have a great deal of flexibility in combining information to derive a final grade indicating overall mastery of course objectives. Generally, it is better to have homework play a relatively minor role in the summary because it is usually an opportunity for students to practice skills rather than an opportunity to demonstrate mastery. Other kinds of information (for example, tests, demonstrations, observable in-class performance) should be weighted in proportion to how important you think they are in demonstrating mastery.

11. *Where possible, the basis for comparison should be the same within a given school.* Grades can be assigned by comparing a student's performance to that of other students in the class, to some absolute standard, or to each individual's potential (as defined by that individual's aptitude, effort, or improvement). In most cases, some combination of comparison to peers and an absolute standard is best. It is generally better if each teacher within a given school uses approximately the same basis of comparison so as to avoid confusion among students as they move from class to class.

12. *The criteria and process for assigning grades should be clear to all stakeholders.* Because grades are a summary of so much information, it is often useful to attach to the grade report a brief summary of the procedures and criteria so that different audiences will understand exactly how the grades were determined. Students themselves need to know in advance how grades will be computed so that they can allocate their efforts accordingly. Nothing is more frustrating to students than to be graded differently from what they expected.

The preceding suggestions can reduce, but never eliminate, all the problems—many of which can result from imperfect implementation. Nonetheless, it is illogical to conclude that because grading systems are not perfect, they should be abandoned. As Moynihan (1971, p. 4) observes,

> One of the achievements of democracy . . . is the system of grading and sorting individuals so that young persons of talent born to modest or lowly circumstances can be recognized for their worth. (Similarly, it provides a means for young persons of social status to demonstrate that they have inherited brains as well as money, as it were.) I have not the least doubt that this system is crude, that it is often cruel, and that it measures only a limited number of things. Yet it measures valid things, by and large. To do away with such systems of accreditation may seem like an egalitarian act, but in fact it would be just the opposite. We would be back to a world in which social connections and privilege count for much more than any of us, I believe, would like.

Suggestions for Holding Effective Parent Conferences

Parent conferences are not a good substitute for grades, but they are an essential supplement to grading. Whenever possible, parent conferences should be used to explain how the student is performing in school and to enlist the parents' support in helping their child learn most effectively. Unfortunately, much useful information lies buried in school cabinets where parents never see it. Parent conferences provide an opportunity and an excuse for retrieving this information and discussing it in ways that can benefit students, parents, and teachers.

Some educators avoid presenting much of the available data on child performance because they believe parents will misinterpret the information, or they mistakenly believe that education is the domain of professional educators, and parents have only a minor role to play. Although it is true that information must be presented carefully and skillfully, following adequate preparation, there is no reason to presume that parents are incapable of understanding well-presented information, or that conferences will not be beneficial. The following guidelines for effective parent conferences are based on suggestions made by Hopkins (1998) and Linn and Gronlund (1995).

Do's of Parent Conferences

1. Review the student's school records prior to the conference, and organize the information you want to present to the parents.
2. Collect samples of the student's work that are indicative of her typical performance.

3. Use a structured outline such as the one shown in Figure 13.2 to guide the discussion and record information.
4. Hold the conference in a comfortable, informal setting in which you will not be interrupted.
5. Use language that will be understandable to parents without talking down to them.
6. Treat parents as equal partners in the home–school relationship. Be willing to listen, and encourage two-way communication.
7. Be honest, but fair, about describing the student's strengths.
8. Describe areas needing improvement in a positive and tactful manner.
9. Accept appropriate responsibility for any problems the student is having.
10. Work with the parents to identify solutions, but be cautious about giving advice related to parenting or home activities.
11. Conclude the conference with a summary of the discussion, and check to see if the parents agree with your summary.
12. Use a checklist to give parents a copy of the written summary to take home.

Don'ts of Parent Conferences

1. Don't argue with parents or blame them for problems the child is having in school.
2. Don't compare their child with other students.
3. Don't make derogatory remarks about other students, teachers, administrators, or school practices.
4. Don't interrupt the parents.
5. Don't betray confidences.
6. Don't do all the talking.
7. Don't ask parents questions that might be embarrassing.
8. Don't make excuses for any mistakes you may have made.

Conducting effective parent conferences requires practice, sensitivity, and a willingness to keep trying. It is unrealistic to expect your first parent conference to be completely successful. By following these guidelines, however, and being committed to the concept of using parent conferences to enhance the partnership between home and schools, you can become much more effective, and students will be the major beneficiaries.

Application Problem 2

Imagine that a friend comes to you with a concern about the parent conferences required in the spring each year. She complains that, as a teacher, she finds the conferences time consuming and unenjoyable, that parents frequently get upset with her when their child is performing below average, and that most parents do not understand much of the information that is presented. She wants to enlist your support in asking the principal to discontinue the practice of required parent conferences. How would you respond?

Suggested readings

Carey, L. M. (1994). *Measuring and evaluating school learning* (2nd ed.). Boston: Allyn and Bacon.

Chapter 14 presents practical suggestions for creating a gradebook as a means of keeping a documented record of students' performance and progress. Since grades will not accurately reflect students' progress and achievement unless they are based upon accurate information, it is essential that teachers have a functional, organized system for recording and retrieving information about the performance of individual students.

Frisbie, D. A. & Waltman, K. K. (1992). Developing a personal grading plan. *Educational Measurement: Issues and Practice, 11* (3), 35–42.

Lists the main value questions that teachers need to consider in formulating their own grading philosophy and then outlines the procedural questions teachers need to resolve in order to develop a plan for grading the achievement status of their students. Concludes by analyzing the strengths and weaknesses of several common methods of assigning grades.

Guskey, T. R. (ed.) (1996). *Communicating student learning.* Washington, DC: Association for Supervision and Curriculum Development.

Presents a series of articles written to teachers about using grade reporting systems to improve communication with students and their parents. Includes articles about the effects of cooperative learning on grading practices, problems that need to be resolved when grading gifted students or students with learning disabilities, honesty and fairness in grading, the use of modern technology in reporting student progress, and others.

Natriello, G. (1992). Marking systems. In M. C. Alkin (ed.). *Encyclopedia of educational research* (6th ed., pp. 772–776). New York: Macmillan.

Describes the various purposes that scholastic grades are intended to serve, the problems associated with establishing appropriate criteria and standards, procedures for collecting evidence of achievement, factors involved in appraising students' level of achievement, and alternative procedures for communicating the results to stakeholders.

Terwilliger, J. S. (1989). Classroom standard setting and grading practices. *Educational Measurement: Issues and Practice, 8*(2), 15–19.

Recommends a flexible, practical grading process that uses both criterion-referenced and norm-referenced approaches. Course objectives are divided into two categories: one that focuses on basic skills and knowledge, and another that focuses on higher-level cognitive outcomes. Students' achievement in each category is assessed separately.

Waltman, K. K. & Frisbie, D. A. (1994). Parents' understanding of their children's report card grades. *Applied Measurement in Education, 7,* 223–240.

Reports the results of a survey of 285 parents of 4th-grade students in a sample of 16 Iowa schools. The results show that parents generally did not understand the meanings that teachers intended to be communicated by the grades they had assigned. The researchers conclude that the typical report card cannot carry enough information to ensure clear communication. Hence they recommend that report cards need to be transformed.

Wiggins, G. (1994). Toward better report cards. *Educational Leadership, 52* (2), 28–37.

Presents Wiggins's analysis of the deficiencies of traditional report cards and his thoughtful recommendations for correcting these problems. Note the conceptual distinctions he proposes between *progress* and *growth,* between *grades* and *scores,* and between *degree of difficulty* and *quality of performance* as a means of clarifying our thinking about assessment and how student achievement is described and reported.

SUGGESTION SHEET

If your last name starts with the letter P or Q, please complete the Suggestion Sheet at the end of the book while this chapter is still fresh in your mind.

Answers to Chapter 13 Application Problems

1. Before responding to the teacher, talk a few minutes about why she feels the way she does, and what kind of experience she has had with alternative grading systems. If she is concerned about grades not being useful, she probably has had some negative experiences with grades. Depending on how she responds, you would want to include at least the following points in your discussion:

   1. Although there is evidence that grading systems are sometimes implemented inappropriately, students do need some feedback about how well they are learning the intended material. A pass–fail system provides some information about that, but probably not enough.

   2. Many other people besides students depend on information contained in grades (parents, other teachers, administrators, future employers, other schools, and so on). Any kind of alternative to grades would have to consider their needs as well as the students'.

   3. Research data suggest that students do not try as hard, or learn as much, in situations where a pass–fail system is used as an alternative to traditional grading.

   4. The negative side effects she has noticed about grading may be real, and it is important to find ways to resolve those problems, even if a traditional grading system is continued.

   5. It may be useful to appoint a committee to review the entire grading and reporting system. As someone who has strong feelings about grading, she might play an important role as a member of that committee.

2. At least the following points should be included in your response to the friend who wants to enlist your support in discontinuing parent conferences:

    1. Even though she has not felt very successful with previous parent conferences, many people find them to be very useful. Consequently, she may want to consider some alternative approaches to parent conferences before asking that they be eliminated.

    2. Although it is clearly time consuming, some advance preparation in terms of reviewing the student's file, assembling samples of the student's work, and listing specific issues she would like to discuss with each parent may help to make the conference more productive.

    3. Reviewing the list of Do's and Don'ts contained in this chapter may provide some hints about improving the conference. It may even be useful to have a teacher who feels that conferences are beneficial to sit in one as an observer.

    4. The use of a structured guide to summarize the results of the conference, along with specific activities that both parties have agreed to do, would be useful.

    5. Parent conferences are effective only if true two-way communication occurs. It may be useful to collect some approximate data on how successful she has been in getting parents to talk in the conference. If she is doing most of the talking herself, it may explain why parents do not seem to enjoy the conferences.

    6. Emphasize that since grades provide very limited information about a student's achievement, parent conferences and other means of communication are absolutely essential in helping parents understand what is happening in the school.

USING EXISTING MEASURES

A Shopper's Guide to the Measurement Supermarket

The old adage about saving your energy by not reinventing the wheel is as relevant in measurement as anywhere. Educational measures abound; yet far too often educators labor to create their own tests and measures, only to find in some undiscovered test repository measurement "wheels" that would suit their purposes just as well, or perhaps even better.

In the preceding section we provided guidelines for designing your own measures when appropriate ones do not exist. In this section, we acquaint you with the veritable supermarket of tests and measures that are readily accessible to you. We also show you how to "browse around" to locate those measures that best fit your needs. We urge you, whenever you are faced with a situation that requires measurement, to look first at what is already on the shelves.

In Chapter 14 we discuss some of the more common criticisms of educational tests, examine whether those criticisms are legitimate, and look at how cautions against misuse of tests can reduce or solve many—if not all—of the concerns posed by test critics. We use that discussion as a springboard for telling you where to locate available instruments and how to choose intelligently among them.

SECTION IV

Chapter 15 presents information on *standardized achievement tests and batteries,* including a discussion of how they are developed and how you can estimate their content validity. We also present, as examples, one comprehensive test battery so that you will see what information you can typically obtain from such a test battery.

Chapter 16 defines *aptitude tests* and explains how they are used and what makes them valuable. This chapter covers the classification of aptitude tests, benefits of proper use, and potential dangers of improper use.

Chapter 17 covers the issues of using tests for diagnostic purposes as well as using tests for some special student populations. For diagnostic tests, we discuss the elements necessary to integrate such tests into systems that support diagnosis, prescription, and instruction. Examples of some diagnostic measures are included in this discussion. For special student populations, we discuss the legal considerations for assessment of some special populations, different types of special needs and related assessment issues, and some example assessment measures for different types of special populations.

Collectively, the information in these four chapters will help you to shop wisely in the educational measures marketplace and avoid the costly experience of creating tests no better than—and often not as good as—those already on the shelves.

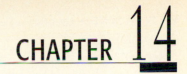

CHAPTER 14

Understanding the Criticisms of Published Tests and Selecting the Best Measures for Use in Your Schools

OVERVIEW

Published tests can provide information and insights to help solve many classroom problems. How does the performance of our students in eighth-grade math compare with that of the national norm? Is the low performance of John and Mark in math due to their low level of aptitude in math or due to their low motivation? What is at the root of Scott's reading difficulties? Does the class need more work in basic reading skills? These and similar questions can be better answered when good test information is added to the teacher's observations and experience.

The educational testing enterprise in general, and the practice of standardized testing in particular, have had their share of criticism. But how valid are the criticisms of educational testing? Is it true that standardized tests are unsuitable for measuring classroom learning? Is local control of education threatened by standardized testing programs? Do standardized aptitude and achievement tests categorize and label students in ways that cause damage to individuals? Are such tests racially, culturally, and socially biased? To what extent do tests invade the privacy of students or their families? Do widely used educational tests measure only superficial student knowledge and behaviors, often penalizing bright, creative students? Do such criticisms of tests result from flaws in the tests themselves or from instances where the tests are misused? What defenses can be mounted for tests in general and for standardized tests in particular? Can criticisms be blunted by developing better tests or changing the ways tests are used? Does research show standardized tests to have beneficial or harmful effects on our schools? Before we plunge into the task of selecting appropriate published measures (many of which are standardized tests) to solve our educational problems, we need to consider carefully the criticisms and cautions concerning educational tests, especially those concerning standardized tests.

Using a published measure to help solve an educational problem requires five steps: (1) define the problems, (2) identify the major variables related to the problems, (3) locate published measures of these variables, (4) evaluate and select the most appropriate measures, and (5) administer the selected measures. The step-by-step sequence provided in this chapter should help you locate measures that can be used to help solve your educational problems.

We have organized this chapter into four sections, dealing, respectively, with (1) major criticisms of educational testing, (2) analysis of the validity of these criticisms, (3) steps in locating published measures, and (4) evaluating and selecting published measures to be used in educational settings.

OBJECTIVES

Upon completing your study of this chapter, you should be able to

1. List at least 10 common criticisms of educational tests and the types of tests toward which each criticism is directed.

2. List five major rebuttals of these criticisms; explain whether you find the criticisms or the rebuttals more compelling.

3. List at least 10 common misuses of educational and psychological measures that contribute to criticisms of testing. For each, discuss how such misuse can be avoided.

4. Explain why results from educational measures should not be used as the only source of information to solve educational problems.

5. Given an educational problem, prepare a specific problem statement, identify the major variables related to these causes, and locate relevant measures.

6. Describe the *Mental Measurements Yearbook* and the *ETS Test Collection Bibliographies,* and explain how each is used to locate tests.

7. Given an educational problem, describe the steps in conducting a manual search to locate appropriate available tests.

8. Using the Test Evaluation Form, locate and evaluate a test related to your area of interest.

9. Describe the major issues in administering published measures.

Criticisms and Cautions Concerning Educational Tests

In our overview of historical trends, we described briefly several waves of criticism that have washed across educational testing (and test makers) during the past 30 years. We now turn our attention to a more thorough examination of *why* educational tests have so frequently come under fire.

Common Criticisms of Standardized Tests

Norm-referenced, criterion-referenced, and minimum competency tests can all be standardized, but norm-referenced tests are by far the most common type of standardized test. Not coincidentally, most test criticism has been leveled at standardized, norm-referenced tests. But other types of testing receive their measure of invective also. Criterion-referenced tests are criticized not so much for what they are as for what they may lead to, such as arbitrary establishment of cutoff scores. Minimum competency tests have been not only targets of criticism but also of lawsuits. In this chapter, we focus primarily on eleven historically pervasive and thematic criticisms of standardized, norm-referenced achievement and aptitude tests we have drawn from the mass of literature produced by testing critics. Later, we will add a new twist or two to this list as we discuss some recently emerging criticisms of standardized tests.

1. *Standardized achievement tests do not promote student learning.* Critics charge that standardized achievement tests provide little direct support for the "real stuff" of education, namely, what goes on in the classroom. They do nothing, critics contend, to enhance the teaching–learning process, provide diagnostic help to the teacher, or provide students the immediate feedback so essential to their learning.

2. *Standardized achievement and aptitude tests are poor predictors of individual student performance.* Critics of testing argue that although some tests may accurately predict future performances of *groups,* they are often inaccurate predictors of individual performance. Examples such as "Einstein flunked sixth-grade math tests" are cited, showing where test scores earned by particular students were uncorrelated with later achievements in school or career.

3. *The content of standardized achievement tests is often mismatched with the content emphasized in a school's curriculum and classrooms.* Because standardized tests are intended for broad use, they make no pretense of fitting precisely and equally well the specific content being taught to third graders in Salt Lake City's public schools and their counterparts at the Tickapoo School downstate. That mismatch, which can result in discrepancies between what is being taught and what is being tested, provided much of the impetus for the criterion-referenced testing movement.

4. *Standardized tests are unsuitable for evaluating school programs or curricula.* If standardized tests do not reflect the goals or content of a particular curriculum, program, or instructional innovation, there would seem little point in using such test results as the basis for judging its success. Yet this is exactly what often occurs, to the distress of critics of standardized measures.

5. *Standardized tests dictate or restrict what is taught in ways that violate the principle of local control of education.* The claim that standardized tests dominate school curricula and result in teaching to the test are familiar allegations, and can be leveled at any standardized test that has serious consequences for the schools in which it is used. It may seem inconsistent to claim that standardized tests are mismatched with what is taught in the schools (see criticism 4) and also to complain that the tests "drive the curriculum" in many school systems, but those two allegations are not necessarily at odds. The first criticism is directed at the notion that schools ought to be free to vary in what they teach. The second merely acknowl-

edges the flip side of the coin: that *any* case in which the tests intrude into decisions about what is taught is unfortunate, for local schools have then partly lost their freedom to determine educational priorities.

6. *Standardized achievement and aptitude tests categorize and label students in ways that cause damage to individuals.* One of the most serious allegations against standardized tests is that their use frequently results in irreversible harm to students who are permanently categorized by test scores that follow them unrelentingly thereafter. Call it classifying, pigeonholing, labeling, or what you will; the result is the same, critics argue, as individual children are subjected to demeaning and insulting placement into categories. The issue is really twofold: (1) the fact that tests are not infallible (and that students can and do change) can result in tragic misclassifications of individual students; and (2) even when tests *are* accurate, categorization of students into groups that carry a stigma or negative connotation may cause more harm than any gain that could possibly come from such classification.

7. *Standardized achievement and aptitude measures are racially, culturally, and socially biased.* Critics claim that most published tests favor economically and socially advantaged children over their counterparts from lower socioeconomic families. Ethnic and cultural minority group members and women note that many tests have a disproportionately negative impact on their chances for equal opportunities in education and employment. (Because of the societal importance of these claims, we discussed them at greater length in Chapter 2 and Chapter 6.)

8. *Standardized tests often penalize bright, creative students.* By their very nature, critics suggest, standardized tests discourage creative and imaginative thinking. The emphasis on one "right" answer is wrong, they say, for it promotes simple choices rather than fostering reflective thought. As Shepard (1991) has thoughtfully observed, children may well conclude that their job is to get the correct answer that resides in the head of the test makers, even if they have to guess to do it.

9. *Test anxiety accompanying standardized achievement and aptitude testing interferes with student performance and distorts the test results.* Many educators are concerned that standardized testing creates so much anxiety for students that they "choke" and perform far below their true ability. Teachers tell of top students who excel in typical classroom quizzes but freeze when confronted with the formality of the Iowa Test of Basic Skills or the urgency of the state's test for determining promotion or graduation.

10. *Standardized achievement and aptitude tests measure only limited and superficial student knowledge and behaviors.* Critics censure tests for measuring only a narrow spectrum of the student abilities on which educators need information—and for failing to measure many of the most important human characteristics, like justice, humaneness, or love. Some critics (for example, Frederiksen, 1984; Nickell, 1993) have argued that multiple-choice tests seldom measure the more complex cognitive abilities, but the economy and efficiency of such tests have increased their popularity in schools, at the expense of measures better suited to assess higher-level mental processes.

11. *Standardized achievement tests do not promote quality or foster accountability in our schools.* Advocates of other types of testing (or even no testing at all) argue that standardized measures have very limited value for holding teachers, schools, or

school systems accountable. If teachers' salaries are to consume large portions of the public purse, the argument goes, then teachers must be accountable for demonstrating what those expenditures have produced. Even properly used, however, standardized norm-referenced tests do not yield this information—thus failing to accomplish what many feel should be the primary function of testing programs.

Critiquing the Criticisms of Testing

Are the criticisms of standardized testing we have listed all deserved? No. But that does not mean that we can afford to ignore them. As one of the foremost measurement experts in America has reminded us,

> Criticism of tests and testing practices is desirable. Tests obviously play an important part in the lives of many people. The tests, and more importantly, the uses that are made of them, deserve close scrutiny. Furthermore, criticism from within and from outside the profession has led to long-needed positive changes in testing practices, and more can be expected. (Linn, 1982, p. 279)

We agree. Moreover, there is legitimacy, in our opinion, to some of the concerns we have reported. Yet, many allegations aimed at standardized testing themselves deserve critique. Even thoughtful criticisms frequently turn out, upon further examination, to be overstated, unfair, or just plain wrong, as the following points indicate:

- The concern that standardized tests do not reflect school curriculum is less an indictment of the tests than of those who chose inappropriate tests to begin with.
- The charge that standardized tests can damage students through labeling or mislabeling is more correctly a condemnation of those who use the tests unintelligently and/or unprofessionally.
- The claim that standardized tests measure trivial information or require only low-level mental processes appears exaggerated at best since close examination of actual tests shows that large proportions of test items measure more complex mental process (see, for example, Rudman, 1977).

Although these preceding comments do not attempt to refute the eleven criticisms listed in the previous section, perhaps they serve to demonstrate that not *all* criticisms of standardized testing are unassailable. Let's look next at five reasons why the salvos of criticism fired by the antitest movement during the past quarter century have not convinced us to join in the chorus of those who call for all standardized tests to be abolished.

Standardized Tests Are Strongly Supported by Many Practitioners, Parents, and Policymakers

Standardized testing has a strong contingent of supporters as well as an enthusiastic group of detractors. Predictably, many measurement experts support such tests although many censure "measurement malpractice" and offer specific suggestions for improving testing efforts. But beyond the measurement community, many educational practitioners have registered strong support for testing programs. The debate is no longer between the "practitioner critics" and the conglomerate "testing industry" (including testing specialists), but rather between practitioners, parents, and policymakers who advocate testing and practitioners, parents, and policymakers who oppose it. For example, analysis of the positions of professional associations a decade ago showed that some groups of school principals and some teachers' associations had taken a strong stance against standardized tests, whereas other teachers' and principals' associations had spoken out just as strongly in their favor (*Educational Measurement,* 1982). Recently, it appears that more professional associations are urging policymakers to slow down and rethink their use of such tests as indicators of school success or failure, but educational practitioners are still seriously divided on this issue.

And what of parents and policymakers? In a Gallup poll, some 81 percent of U.S. parents described standardized tests as very useful (Learner, 1981). Policymakers seem to find these tests equally favorable. Darling-Hammond and Lieberman (1992) note that support for using standardized testing to improve education is increasing rapidly, especially at the federal level, where a national test is being devised for use in periodic pulse-taking to determine the health of the nation's educational system.

These examples should suffice to show that both testing supporters and critics exist in almost all groups, including teachers, principals, professors, parents, policymakers, and self-appointed school watchers.

More Research Needs to Be Conducted Investigating the Criticisms of Testing

We simply do not have a solid research foundation on which to base many of our claims—or counterclaims, for that matter—concerning standardized testing. We are left in that somewhat tenuous position where one person's opinion is just as good as another's. Almost two decades ago, Airasian summed up the situation nicely:

> The rhetoric, and that is what it largely is, that produces claims and counterclaims about the uses and misuses of standardized tests has taken on a life of its own. Battle lines have been drawn and for many participants in the controversy there is no middle ground of uncertainty; if you're not for their position on testing you must be against it. In articulating their positions, both proponents and opponents of standardized testing have been guilty of distorting the historical development of testing and of failing to recognize that *there is precious little empirical evidence to support claims of test use or misuse.* (1979, p. 2; emphasis added)

Since then, substantially more research on the influence of standardized testing on educational practice has been reported. In Arizona, a state that had mandated annual use of standardized tests with all students in grades 2 through 11, surveys of school practitioners showed that the testing was having a dramatic impact on district curriculum (Haladyna et al., 1989, 1991). The common criticism that standardized tests "drive the curriculum" was confirmed, at least in Arizona, where the testing tail was clearly wagging the educational dog. Surveys of Arizona teachers also showed that pressure on educators to produce high test scores was resulting in a variety of doubtful practices teachers were using to achieve high scores. Although many teachers engaged in teaching to the test or other ethically dubious methods to "prepare" their students for the test, others used blatantly dishonest techniques such as teaching the students the actual test items in advance or dismissing low-achieving students on testing day (Haas et al., 1989; Nolen, et al., 1989).[1] Similarly, based on teacher interviews and classroom observations in 2 elementary schools over a 15-month period, Smith (1991a, 1991b) reported that teachers determine to do whatever is necessary to avoid low scores and that standardized testing programs *can* in fact narrow curricular offerings, reduce time available for instruction, and focus instruction on basic skills to the exclusion of more complex cognitive processes. Smith summarized her findings as follows:

> Whatever the actual consequences of test results might be, teachers act according to their beliefs that low test scores contribute to negative evaluations of their efforts on the part of the public and school administrators and lead to decreased teacher autonomy and teaching methods. For teachers, the stakes are high, and they react by doing what is necessary to prepare children to take the external tests (Smith, 1991b, p. 525)

Two important points should be made here. First, these and other similar studies (summarized nicely by Haladyna et al., 1991) show that the negative effects of standardized testing on classroom practice occur when the test scores are perceived by educators as having important consequences, such as linking educators' continued employment or salary advances to students' test performance. In short, high-stakes use of standardized test scores seems to interfere with good curriculum and instruction. (Note that it is the misuse of tests, not the tests themselves, that cause these problems. Performance assessments would most likely cause the same effects if they were misused in this manner.)

Second, this research on the effects of standardized testing is relevant only to two of the common criticisms we have listed; on the remaining criticisms, the jury is still out. Much more empirical investigation would be necessary before we will know unequivocally how much credence to give to each of the common criticisms of standardized testing.

Many Criticisms of Standardized Testing Assume Teachers and Other Test Users Are Naive and Credulous

In the dark scenarios developed by critics, promulgation of testing is the ploy by which greedy testing corporations extract excessive profits from schools, leaving them with precious little to show for their investment except disillusioned administrators, distressed teachers, and damaged students. The common theme of most such scenarios is that school practitioners are gullible and readily plucked by crafty charlatans whose hunger for profits prompts them to peddle measures that are at best unhelpful and, at worst, misleading and harmful. Airasian (1979) says it well:

---

[1]This topic is discussed in greater detail in Chapter 2 in a section on "Ethical Problems Associated with Teaching to the Test."

the mass of teachers and school administrators are often portrayed as lambs, innocently and uncritically accepting standardized test results as the most valid piece of evidence available about a child and, on the basis of that evidence, wreaking havoc—and worse—on pupils, their school experiences and future lives. In reality, teachers are neither as naive nor as blind to limitations of standardized tests as many commentators who purport to speak for teachers would have us believe. (p. 5)

We agree. Those who operate our schools are not as credulous and naive as they are sometimes cynically portrayed to be. Indeed, we take vicarious offense at the insult to teachers and administrators implicit in many criticisms of test use in the schools.

Standardized Tests Are Not Perfect, but Neither Are the Currently Available Alternatives

All but the most rabid advocate of testing would concur that no test is perfect and that, taken as a whole, educational and psychological measurement is still (and may always be) an imperfect science. Why, then, promote imperfect measures? Because so far the alternatives have been just as fallible. Ravitch (1984) offers this insightful comment:

> In education, tests have grown more important to the extent that other measures have been discarded or discredited. Although it is easy to forget the past, we should recall that the tests helped to replace an era in which many institutions of higher education made their selections with due regard to the student's race, religion, class, and family connections . . . .
>
> So long as there are educational institutions where there are more applicants than places, there must be an objective way to decide who gets in ... [and] no other objective means has been discovered to take the place of ability testing. (1984, p. 23)

The authors of the 1974 *Standards* also cautioned that the call to abolish tests seems futile because

> it requires a corresponding but unlikely moratorium on decisions. Employers will continue to make employment decisions with or without standardized tests. Colleges and universities will still select students, some elementary pupils will still be recommended for special education, and boards of education will continue to evaluate the success of specific programs. If those responsible for making decisions do not use standardized assessment techniques, they will use less dependable methods of assessment. (APA, 1974, pp. 2–3)

Although we oppose misuse of standardized tests, we generally support the correct use of such measures and will do so until more adequate alternatives emerge. (In Chapter 10, we discussed efforts to develop such alternatives.) In the meantime, existing measures must be improved and used properly—which brings us to the final reason that criticisms of testing have failed to erode our (qualified) confidence in the value of traditional educational tests.

Most Criticisms of Standardized Tests Are Really Not Criticisms of the Tests but Rather of Their Misuse or Abuse

On their own, tests are incapable of harming students. It is the way in which test results can be misused that is potentially harmful. Yet critics of standardized testing seldom focus on test *misuse,* preferring to target the instruments themselves, as if they were the real culprits (see, for example, Neill & Medina, 1989). Such behavior is rather like condemning hammers because they have on occasion been used to commit mayhem. Or blaming the hemlock for Socrates' fate.

In short, it is nonsense to blame all testing problems on tests—no matter how poorly constructed—while absolving users of all responsibility. Not that bad tests should be condoned, of course. But eliminating test misuse would go far toward eliminating the criticisms currently directed against educational testing.

Standardized tests can be misused or abused in countless ways. We list next only a dozen of the more common misuses we have observed, which, incidentally, can occur with other types of testing as well.

1. *Using the wrong tests.* Schools often devise new instructional goals and curriculum plans, only to find their success being judged by tests that do not reflect those goals or plans but that are imposed nonetheless by some higher administrative level (for example, district or state). Faced with such absurdity, two courses of action are open to teachers and local administrators: (1) persuade higher levels of administration to select new standardized achievement or minimum competency measures that better match the local curriculum content and goals, or (2) supplement those tests with measures selected (or constructed) specifically to measure what the school is attempting to accomplish. Trying to measure goal attainment with tests insensitive to those goals is, as our colleague Jim Popham puts it, like trying to measure mileage with a tablespoon—it is simply the wrong measure.

It is also "using the wrong tests" when schools employ tests for purposes for which they were never intended. Few would chasten the scalpel (or the neurosurgeon who wields it) just because it proves useless to the carpenter in driving nails. More subtle but equally absurd mismatches of purpose and instrument abound in educational testing. Misuse of tests would be largely eliminated if every test administered were carefully linked with the decision at hand.

2. *Assuming test scores are infallible.* Every test score contains possible error; a student's *observed* score is rarely identical to that student's *true* score (the score he would have obtained had there been no distractions during testing, no fatigue or illness, no "lucky guesses," and no other factors that either helped or hindered that score). Measurement experts can calculate (using techniques we described in Chapter 4) the probability of an individual's *true* score being within a certain number of score points of the *obtained* score. Yet many educators ignore measurement error and use test scores as if they were highly precise measures.

Assume, for example, that a school sets a cutoff score of 100 on a math placement test, admitting students who score 100 or higher and rejecting those who score 99. Yet such a test likely contains sufficient "measurement error" that a difference of two points on *obtained* scores reflects no real difference between the *true* scores of the admitted and rejected students. Forgetting that test scores all contain *some* error can result in serious abuses of tests, and of those who take them.

3. *Using a single test score to make an important decision.* Given the possibility of error that exists for every test score, how wise is it to allow crucial decisions for individuals (or programs) to hinge on the single administration of a test? What about the basketball player who hits a miserable 15 percent of his shots in his first varsity game? Bench him for the season, right? Not if you have seen him hit 70

percent of his field goal attempts in practice and also learn he was informed of his grandfather's death just before game time. A single test score is too suspect—in the absence of supporting evidence of some type—to serve as the sole criterion for any crucial decision.

4. *Failing to supplement test scores with other information.* This misuse overlaps with the prior misuse, but adds a slightly different point. Supporting evidence for a *single* test score could be *another* test score (on the same or a corollary test), or it could be information from sources other than tests. For example, what about the student who can quote Chaucer and Shakespeare at ease in class, but when faced with a test is so terrified he or she cannot recall who said, "To be or not to be?" Doesn't the teacher's knowledge of the student's ability count for anything? In our judgment, it should. Though our individual perceptions as teachers and administrators may be subjective, they are not irrelevant. Though we would seldom trust them alone, because they *are* subjective (and therefore potentially biased), our private observations and practical awareness of students' abilities are essential supplements to more objective test scores.

5. *Setting arbitrary minimums for performance on tests.* When minimum test scores are established as critical hurdles for selection and admissions, as dividing lines for placing students in special or regular education programs, or as the determining factor in awarding diplomas or certificates, then several issues become acute. Test validity, always important, becomes crucial; and the minimum standard itself must be carefully scrutinized. Is there any empirical evidence that the minimum standard is set correctly, that those who score higher than the cutoff can be predicted to do better in subsequent academic or career pursuits? Or has the standard been set through some arbitrary or capricious process? Setting and enforcing arbitrary minimum test scores to make critical decisions is potentially one of the most damaging misuses of educational tests.

6. *Assuming tests measure all the content, skills, or behaviors of interest.* Every test is limited in the behaviors it elicits and the material it covers. Seldom is it feasible—because of limited testing time, student fatigue on long tests, and other such factors—to measure all that is of interest, or to test more than a sample of the relevant content, skills, or traits the test is designed to assess. Sometimes students do well on a test just because they happen to have read the *particular* chapters or studied the *particular* content sampled by that test. Given another test, with a different sampling of content from the same book, the students might fare less well. When educators ignore the fact that test scores reflect only *samples* of behavior, they risk misleading conclusions about the individuals or groups being tested. The use of performance assessments does not solve this problem because they too represent only a sample of a student's behavior, and estimates of a student's ability are still just as likely to vary from one sample to another (Brennan & Johnson, 1995; Gao, Shavelson, & Baxter, 1994; Linn & Burton, 1994).

7. *Accepting uncritically all claims made by test authors and publishers.* Blind faith in any test can have unfortunate consequences. Most test authors and publishers are enthusiastic about their products, and some are downright zealous. Excessive zeal can lead to "overpromising" what the test can measure and how well it measures it. A so-called creativity test may really measure only verbal fluency. A math "achieve-

ment" test administered in English to a group of Inuit Eskimo children (for whom English is a second language) may test understanding of English much more than understanding of math. It is essential that the *user* check publisher's claims about technical qualities of a test or its usefulness for particular purposes.

8. *Interpreting test scores inappropriately.* There are many ways to interpret test scores inaccurately or inappropriately. For example, many educators fail to realize that the score *per se* tells us nothing about *why* an individual obtained that score. Or a student's test *score* may erroneously be accepted as a qualitative evaluation of performance rather than as a mere numeric indicator that lacks meaning in the absence of some qualitative criterion defining what constitutes "good" or "bad" performance. Still, another common interpretive error is failing to consider the appropriateness of norms before using them to draw inferences about individual or group performance.

Misinterpretation of test scores is far too pervasive a problem in our schools, and what makes this particular misuse especially harmful is not only its frequency but also the fact that such errors often go unnoticed. Once collected, test data may take on a life of their own, telling a story that turns out to be more fiction than fact.

9. *Using test scores to draw inappropriate comparisons among individuals or schools.* Unprofessional or careless comparisons of achievement test results can foster unhealthy competition among classmates, siblings, or even schools because of ready-made bases for comparisons, such as grade-level achievement. Such misuses of tests can harm the schools and children involved, and also create a backlash toward the tests that might better have been directed toward their misuse.

10. *Allowing tests to drive the curriculum.* If tests drive the curriculum, dictate subject matter content, and even curtail creative teaching, who is responsible? The test makers or marketers? The test users? Or the tests?

Isn't the conspicuously correct answer the *users?* In every instance, some individual or group has selected the tests and decided how to use the scores. If a test unduly influences what goes on in a school's curriculum, then someone has allowed it to override priorities that educators and the school board have established. When tests drive curricula, it is the flawed *use* of the tests that should be critiqued rather than the tests. Whereas using standardized tests to make high-stakes decisions results in a variety of negative influences on the quality of classroom instruction (see Haladyna et al., 1991; Nolen et al., 1989; Smith, 1991a), the tests would have no such detrimental influence if used properly.

11. *Using poor tests.* Why employ a poorly constructed or unreliable test if a better one is at hand? Tests can be flawed in a multitude of ways, from measuring the wrong content or skills (but doing it well), to measuring the correct content or skills (but doing it poorly). Some err in both directions. Every effort should be made to obtain or construct the best possible measures, and one of our primary purposes in this book is to help you in this effort.

12. *Using tests unprofessionally.* Whether in medicine, dentistry, psychology, or education, professionals are expected to use the tools of their trade ethically and effectively. When educational tests are used in misleading or harmful ways, inadequate training of educators in test selection and use is often at fault. When test scores are used to label children in harmful ways, the fault generally lies with those

who affix the labels—not with the test. When test scores are not kept confidential, it is the fault of the person who violated the confidence, not the test maker. Incompetent or unethical use of tests results in serious misuses that scar the image not only of testing but of education as a profession.

In Summary

There are clear misuses of standardized (and other) tests, and these account for much of the criticism aimed at educational testing. Not all criticisms of tests can be deflected, however, by claiming that they merely reflect test misuse. There are also apparent weaknesses in many specific measures, based in part on the fact that we have yet a good deal to learn about measurement. We know enough already, however, to state unequivocally that no test score will ever be unequivocal. Uncertainty and error will always be with us, and no test of learning, mental ability, or other characteristics can ever be presumed absolutely precise in its measurements. The professional judgments of teachers and other educators will continue to be essential in sound educational decision making. Correctly used, tests produce for any educational enterprise a solid base of vital information that supplements the teacher's observation and professional judgment. Incorrectly used, they simply produce errors and problems. Unfortunately, misuse is likely to continue until society and the education profession provide resources sufficient to develop greater "assessment literacy" among our nation's educators.[2]

But important as traditional tests are, they are not the only potentially useful approach to assessing student outcomes.

Steps in Locating Appropriate Educational Measures

Normally, a teacher follows six steps in using educational measures to solve problems or answer educational questions.

1. Define the problem or question in specific terms.
2. Identify the major variables relating to the problem.
3. Locate measures of these variables.
4. Evaluate the measures and select those that seem most appropriate.
5. Administer these measures to the students.
6. Interpret the results and plan a course of action based on the information gathered.

Read the first five steps again, and remember them so that you can fit each into the larger context as you read. The last step will be discussed in later chapters.

Defining the Problem

Thousands of measures can help shed light on educational problems you want to address. Before you can select those most relevant to the problem, you must define the problem in precise terms. It is often helpful to put it in the form of a question,

---

[2]The lack of assessment literacy was demonstrated by Stiggins (1991a).

stating it and restating it until it is clear and specific. The usual school problem contains two or three concepts. Here are a few typical questions that educational measures can help the teacher answer.

- Four students are failing my beginning algebra class. Why?
- I never see Scott playing with other children in the class. Why?
- My fifth-grade students' arithmetic achievement test scores were well below the district average. In what specific areas do they need remedial work?
- Bill, a tenth grader, seems to try hard, but his progress in all academic subjects is well below average. What is his level of scholastic aptitude? How does it compare with his achievement level?

Valuable information relevant to each of these questions can be gathered by using appropriate published measures. Published measures can offer information that will provide better insight or simplify decisions related to virtually any educational problem. They should rarely be the sole basis of decision making, but their additional information should be combined with other perceptions and experience to *improve* decision making.

Identifying Major Variables of the Problem

Once you have stated the problem in specific terms, you're ready to identify possible variables that can and should be measured to determine their significance to the problem. A *variable* is a characteristic or kind of performance that a test measures. Music aptitude, test anxiety, mathematics achievement, vocational interest, intelligence, typing speed, and reading comprehension are a few of the many variables measured by educational and psychological tests. They are called "variables" because student performance or test scores *vary* from person to person.

Let's consider the first example of a problem cited earlier: why are the four students failing algebra? Here are several possible causes among the many that exist.

1. Their foundation in arithmetic is weak.
2. They have poor study habits.
3. They have negative attitudes about algebra, mathematics, the teacher, or school in general.

The variables you could measure to get more information include arithmetic achievement, study habits or study methods, and school-related attitudes—especially attitudes toward mathematics.

Determining What Tests Are Available to Measure These Variables

The three possible variables related to the problem in algebra listed previously could be explored by locating appropriate tests of the identified variables, administering them to the four students, and interpreting the results. Knowledge of arithmetic could be measured by an arithmetic achievement or diagnostic test. Several tests are available in this area. Similarly, there are measures of student attitude or study habits that can provide insight into these variables. However, the process of locating potentially useful measures, selecting those that are most appropriate for your specific problem, and interpreting the results requires information and experience. (Remember that even after appropriate measures are found, it is very important to supplement by interviewing the failing students or observing their behavior during class.)

Locating Relevant Measures

A variety of printed sources list educational measures. Some reference books are devoted entirely to listing and reviewing available measures. Publishers also distribute catalogs describing available tests. Different sources are likely to list different kinds of tests. Thus a single search will usually not uncover all potentially useful measures. Nevertheless, to keep things simple, we have decided to give you a simple step-by-step strategy that will usually be sufficient for locating measures relevant to most of the educational problems and questions you are likely to encounter.

The easiest procedures and those most likely to locate the tests you need are described first. You should not stop with the first test you find that seems to be appropriate. Instead, plan to identify at least two or three alternative tests for *each* variable to be measured. Then evaluate these tests to select the best measures for your specific problem. If you are dealing with a major educational problem or have an important decision to make, one that involves testing a large number of students, for instance, you may choose to complete the entire sequence so as to locate most of the available relevant measures.

Step 1: Checking the Most Recent Edition of *The Mental Measurements Yearbook (MMY)*

The Mental Measurements Yearbook (*MMY*), published by the Buros Institute of Mental Measurements at the University of Nebraska at Lincoln, is a comprehensive information source about published educational and psychological tests. The series has been published at irregular intervals over the past 50 years. The most recent volume of *MMY* is the *Twelfth Mental Measurements Yearbook* (Conoley & Impara, 1995). Most university libraries contain the entire set of *Mental Measurements Yearbooks*. Because each new volume of *MMY* covers tests published or revised since the publication of the previous volume of *MMY*, each *MMY* volume is designed to supplement previous *MMY* volumes. For information on older tests, it is often necessary to check the earlier *MMY*s. For each test included in *MMY*, the following information is usually included: (1) descriptive information of the test, (2) reviews of the test written specifically for *MMY*, (3) review excerpts about the test from other sources (for example, professional journals), and (4) bibliographies for the test. The test reviews in *MMY* are usually written by qualified experts in the relevant areas, and as such, these critical reviews are very useful in helping a teacher identify the strengths and weaknesses of the measures reviewed. Besides the highly informative test reviews, the *MMY* includes basic practical information crucial for test selection, such as the age or grade for which the test is appropriate, the variables measured, the administration time, the cost, and the name of the publisher.

In the *Tests and Reviews* section of *MMY*, tests are listed in alphabetical order by title and numbered consecutively. These numbers are called the entry numbers and are used instead of page numbers in the various indices. To locate tests in a particular subject area, refer to the *Classified Subject Index* of *MMY*. Here you will find tests classified under a number of broad categories: Achievement, Personality, Foreign Languages, Intelligence, and so on. Under each category are the titles and entry numbers of tests available in that area of interest. After locating tests in this *Index*, note the entry numbers, check each number in the *Tests and Reviews* section of the book, and read the reviews to decide which test seems best for your needs.

A *Score Index* lists (in alphabetical order) all the variables for which scores can be obtained for all tests included in the *MMY*. If you are looking for arithmetic measures, you will find some entry numbers after the word *arithmetic* in the *Score Index*. Each of these numbers identifies a test that yields a score for arithmetic. You can look up each number in the *Tests and Reviews* section and scan the information to see whether the test is appropriate. If none appears suitable, you can check the *Score Index* of the previous *MMY*, which lists some additional measures for arithmetic published earlier. Measures included in the *Score Index* can be quite broad (like *arithmetic*) or rather narrow (like *misplaced modifiers*).

Many of the tests you locate will measure not only the variable in which you are most interested, but also several others. Some of these additional variables may also be useful in addressing your problem or question. If not, the time devoted to measuring them would be wasted, so look for a test or subtest that measures *only* the variables that are relevant to the problem you are addressing, or a test divided into subtests so that you can administer only the subtests you need.

In addition to the *Classified Subject Index* and the *Score Index*, the following indices are sometimes useful:

Index of Acronyms—gives the full title and entry number of tests, many of which are commonly referred to in the literature by their acronyms rather than their full titles (for example, CAT for California Achievement Tests).

Index of Titles—gives the entry number if you know the title of the test. Also indicates whether the test is new (N) or revised (R). If revised, check earlier *Yearbooks* for information on earlier versions.

Index of Names—lists names of all test authors, reviewers, and authors of cited references. This is useful if you know the test author's name but not the test title.

Publishers Directory and Index—gives the names and addresses of the publishers of all tests included in the *Yearbook*. You can write to publishers for their catalogs or for additional information on tests you are considering.

When reviewing test information in the *MMY*, check for answers to the following questions, and record the data for each test on the Preliminary Screening section of the Test Evaluation Form shown in Figure 14.1.

- Does the test purport to measure the variable you want to test?
- Is the test appropriate for the age or grade level of students you want to test?
- Can the test be administered given the time and help you have available? (Be sure to note whether the test is administered to individuals or groups, and whether special training is needed for test administrators.)

TEST NAME_____ PUBLISHER/SOURCE _____

VARIABLES MEASURED: _____

PART I: Preliminary Screening: Generally, a test which does not meet any one of the following criteria should be eliminated.

1. Measures the variables needed to address your problem.	Yes	No
2. Publisher claims test is appropriate for students to be tested and the purposes needed.	Yes	No
3. Test can be administered in the time and with the resources available.	Yes	No
4. Cost of using the test is within available budget (this includes scoring costs if scoring must be done by publisher).	Yes	No
5. Reading level is satisfactory for your students.	Yes	No

PART II: Test Evaluation: Read all of the administration instructions, read each item, and mark your answers. As you take the test, write down potential problems. If the test can be hand-scored, go through the entire scoring process and grade your answers. Then answer the following items.

1. Appropriate Content: Rate whether the test items match the content you want to measure (1 [low] to 5 [high]).

2. Format: Rate the format, organization, and appearance of the test from 1 (poor) to 5 (excellent).

3. Ease of Administration: Rate the administration procedures for the test from 1 (different/complex) to 5 (easy/straightforward).

4. Scoring: Rate whether the instructions for scoring are logical and understandable (1 [poor] to 5 [excellent]).

5. Interpretability: Rate whether the test yields information which is specific and relevant to your needs (1 [poor] to 5 [excellent]).

6. Reliability: Rate whether the evidence concerning test reliability is sufficient for your purposes and is supported by specific evidence (1 [poor] to 5 [excellent]).

7. Validity: Rate whether there is evidence that the results of the test will be valid for the students and purposes for which you will be using it (1 [poor] to 10 [excellent]).

8. Norms: If normative comparisons are needed, rate whether appropriate norms are provided for students similar to yours (1 [norms absent or inadequate] to 5 [excellent norms]).

TOTAL POINTS
Add up all of the points in Part II for each test evaluated. Tests with the most points are preferred, assuming all answers to Part I were affirmative.

FIGURE 14.1 Test Evaluation Form

- Is the cost within your budget for the number of students you want to test?
- Is the reading level satisfactory for your students? (The test catalog and the test itself must usually be checked for this information.)

Figure 14.2 is a test description from the *Twelfth Mental Measurements Yearbook* showing where answers to most of the preceding questions may be found. In most cases, the *MMY*s are the only test reference books you will need to consult for commercially published measures. They describe more published measures than other test reference books and usually provide more information about them. Unfortu-

[127]

Early School Assessment.

Purpose: Designed to measure prereading and mathematics skills.

Population: End of prekindergarten to middle of kindergarten, middle of kindergarten to beginning of grade 1.

Publication Date: 1990.

Acronym: ESA.

Scores, 7: Prereading (Language, Visual [also used in Mathematics total], Auditory, Memory, Total), Mathematics Concepts and Operations (Visual [also used in Prereading total], Total).

Administration: Group.

Levels, 2: 1, 2.

Price Data: Price data available from publisher for test materials including: complete testing kit including 35 machine- or hand-scorable test booklets (select level), 35 practice books, scoring key, class record sheet for hand scoring, and examiner's manual (81 pages, select level); 35 parent conference forms (select level); teacher's guide (51 pages, select level); preliminary norms book; preliminary technical bulletin; test organizer; scoring service available from publisher.

Time: 229 (Level 2) to 239 (Level 1) minutes over 8 sessions.

Authors: CTB MacMillan/McGraw-Hill.

Publisher: CTB MacMillan/McGraw-Hill.

FIGURE 14.2 Test Description from the *Twelfth MMY*

---

nately, they cover only commercially published tests. Because revisions are infrequent, *MMY* in printed form may become increasingly out of date as the time passes since the publication of the most recent *MMY*. Fortunately, Buros Institute of Mental Measurements also provides an online service, with the computer database updated *monthly*. The online database can be accessed through Bibliographic Retrieval Services (BRS), and it provides the most current information about published tests. For access to BRS, consult your university librarians.

Step 2: Checking ETS Test Collection Bibliographies

If you fail to locate the measures you need in the *MMYs*, the next step is to search the *Test Collection Bibliographies* published by the Educational Testing Service (ETS). A current list of the major areas covered in the Test Collection Bibliographies is shown here, with several examples given in each area. The ETS collection constitutes, by far, the most comprehensive compilation available, including information on more than 14,000 tests.

Achievement

> Fine Arts and Foreign Language
> Language Arts
> Mathematics
> Other School Subjects
> Reading
> Science
> Social Studies
> Miscellaneous Achievement Tests

Aptitude

> Creativity
> Intelligence
> Memory
> Reasoning

Attitudes and Interests

> Academic interest
> Attitudes toward mathematics
> Racial Attitudes

Personality

> Depression
> Leadership
> Projective measures
> Self-concept

Sensory Motor

> Auditory skIlls
> Sensory-motor abilities
> Visual Perception

Special Populations

> American Indians
> Mentally retarded
> Spanish speakers

Vocational/Occupational

> Business skills
> Professional occupations
> Vocational interests

Miscellaneous

> Classroom Interaction
> Environments
> Piagetian Measures
> Social Skills

The *Test Collection,* which covers both published and unpublished tests, is frequently updated, thus overcoming the main limitation of the printed *MMYs.* However, they provide much less information than the *MMY*—usually including simply the name of the test, author, date the test was published, age or grade levels for which the test is appropriate, name and address of the publisher or developer, and a brief description of the variables the test is designed to measure. For experimental measures having no commercial publisher, the author is frequently listed as the publisher. Many such measures, which are not available from commercial publishers, can be obtained from ETS on microfiche, which may be purchased for individual measures or in sets of 50. Since many universities have purchased these sets, you should check with the reference librarians of universities in your area before purchasing them yourself.

To use the *Test Collection Bibliographies* to locate a measure, do the following:

1. Check the list of *Test Collection Bibliographies,* and decide which are most likely to list tests measuring the variables of your interest.
2. See if the *Test Collection Bibliographies* you need are available in any of the reference libraries in your vicinity. University departments of psychology and testing–counseling centers may also have these on file. If they are not locally available, order the bibliographies you need from ETS Test Collection, Educational Testing Service, Princeton, NJ 08541-0001.
3. Read the selected bibliographies, and identify measures that fit your needs. Fill out Part 1 (Preliminary Screening) of the Test Evaluation Form (Figure 14.1) for any measures that appear to meet your needs.
4. Obtain single copies of the measures you have identified from ETS or the test publishers.

If you have located the instruments you need, you are ready to evaluate the measures and make your final selection—and you can skip the following Steps 3 and 4. If not, you should check the other sources of test information as described in Steps 3 and 4.

Step 3: Checking Some Other Sources

Another very useful information source of available tests is *Tests* (Sweetland & Keyser, 1991), which is a description of thousands of available tests in psychology, education, and business. Although *Tests* does not provide evaluations of an instrument, it does provide a brief description of the instrument and some basic information about its purpose, cost, scoring, publisher, and so on, thus serving as a good guide for locating tests. The same authors put out *Test Critiques* (Keyser & Sweetland, 1984–1994), a publication series that contains critiques of individual tests contributed by measurement specialists, including description of a test, practical applications of the test, technical information about the test, and so on. Special efforts are made to make the test critiques understandable to readers with little training or experience in measurement. *Test Critiques* is another useful information source besides *MMY,* which provides critical reviews of available tests.

Step 4: Searching the Test Catalog File

Most commercial test publishers have catalogs describing the measures they offer. Frequent users of educational tests, such as counselors and psychologists, usually maintain a file of current test catalogs. If you want to use commercially published tests and cannot locate the measures you need in the *MMYs*, or the *ETS Test Collection Bibliographies,* contact the testing center, department of psychology, or library at your university to see if such a test catalog file is available.

The main advantage of the publishers' catalogs over the *Mental Measurement Yearbooks* and the *ETS Bibliographies* is that they are more current and are usually supplied to educators and psychologists free of charge. However, the *Test Collection Bibliographies* are nearly as current as publishers' catalogs and list both commercially published and unpublished measures.

Application Problem 1

Check the *Twelfth MMY* and locate *two* group-administered instruments that you can use to measure sixth grade students' self-esteem.

Evaluating and Selecting Measures

Having located several measures that appear appropriate, you must now decide which is best for your specific needs. You have already begun this process in one sense, having carried out a preliminary screening. For the remaining measures, you should enter descriptive information at the top of the Test Evaluation Form and check the five items under "Preliminary Screening." One form should be prepared for each measure you plan to evaluate (see Figure 14.1). Besides the first five items under "Preliminary Screening," information about the following major aspects of test and test use need to be carefully studied before any decisions can be made.

Test Validity

The most important characteristic of any test is its validity. When evaluating a test, keep in mind for what purpose the test is intended to be used, and which aspect of validity evidence is the most relevant for that purpose. For example, for content-related tests such as achievement measures, content validity evidence is usually considered the most important. For tests usually used to estimate a criterion variable or to predict future performance as in a selection situation (for example, aptitude tests), criterion-related validity evidence is usually considered most important.

The most useful source of information on the validity of published tests (except for content validity, which requires a match between test content and local curriculum content) is the *MMY* and *Test Critiques,* provided the measure you are evaluating is reviewed in those sources. These critical reviews are useful and insightful, and should be read very carefully. If the test you are considering is not reviewed in *MMYs* or *Test Critiques*, the test manual is often a useful source—although this manual is usually written by the test author, and may be somewhat overly optimistic about the technical quality of the test.

Test validity can often be difficult to establish. As a result, many tests wind up being used even though there is little or no evidence to demonstrate that they are valid. Absence of *evidence* does not mean that a test is invalid. It may mean that the necessary research has not been done to determine how valid it is. Thus although it is best to select tests for which validity has been demonstrated, one must sometimes use tests supported by very little evidence of validity if they appear to be the best available.

Test reviews can be very useful in helping you evaluate data on validity. They are usually written by experts in the field, whose judgments are likely to be more sophisticated than those of an untrained critic. Reviews also discuss reliability and point out problems or difficulties in interpretation, administration, or scoring.

Test Reliability

In contrast to validity, test reliability is relatively easy to determine. Reliability coefficients are reported in most test reference books and the test manual itself. If reliability data are not reported in the test manual, it may be assumed that it is low because it is an easy matter to compute some form of reliability. It is desirable to have reports of reliability based on different estimation methods, such as test-retest, parallel form (if parallel forms exist), and internal consistency. It is desirable to have reports of reliability estimates from several different studies because such information helps you estimate the range over which reliability coefficients may occur. Also, multiple studies increase the likelihood that students in one study will be similar to the students you plan to test—thus giving you a basis for predicting the approximate reliability level *you* can expect.

Keep in mind that tests with low reliability have large measurement errors and are thus of little value for diagnosis or assessment of individual students. Different kinds of tests differ in their typical reliability levels. For example, good standardized achievement tests usually have reliability coefficients ranging from .88 to .95. On the other hand, some of the best self-report personality inventories have reliabilities as low as .60.

Normative Data

Normative data provides a basis for comparing the performance of your students with that of the samples of students who were tested in developing the test norms. Although an increasing number of criterion-referenced tests are becoming available, most commercially published tests are "norm-referenced" and provide tables of norms to simplify test score interpretation.

In evaluating normative data, you should consider how appropriate the norms are for your students and for the specific question you are trying to answer. You may also be interested in norms obtained from samples of important national populations, such as "all fifth-grade students in U.S. public elementary schools." For such samples to be truly representative of a national population, they must include students from different geographical areas, different socioeconomic levels, and different kinds of communities (rural, small city, large city). In addition to the composition of the norm group, the size of the sample should be considered. Other things being equal, the larger the norm sample, the more accurately it represents the population from which it was selected. Refer to Chapter 3 for more detailed discussion about some major issues related to test norms

Administration and Scoring

When evaluating a test, carefully review the procedures described in the test manual for administering and scoring. The administration instructions should be clear and detailed. For many measures, these procedures include

Instruction on how to prepare for giving the test
Materials needed
Verbatim instructions on what to say
Suggestions for responding to student questions

Scoring instructions usually include instructions or procedures for

Checking answer sheets for omissions and errors
Using the key (if the test is to be hand scored)
Dealing with unclear answers
Arriving at a raw score
Converting the raw score to some form of standard score, such as grade equivalent score, percentile score, or T score

In reviewing the administration and scoring instructions, consider carefully the level of objectivity. *Objectivity* is the degree to which the administration and scoring are independent of the persons doing these tasks. When the instructions are incomplete or unclear, or when inferences must be drawn or judgments made about the administration or scoring, then the procedures become less objective and the chance of error increases.

Some measures require special training for proper administration and scoring. Information on this training is usually given in the test manual, and may also be discussed in test reviews. If test administration or scoring requires training that you have not had and cannot readily obtain, you should look for another measure that you are qualified to administer, score, and interpret. Specific information on the *interpretation* of test scores should also be given in the test manual. These interpretation instructions are also discussed in test reviews.

Read interpretation instructions *very carefully* when evaluating a test. Are they clear and specific? Do they deal with those aspects of your problem or question that you want to explore? Does interpretation require special training or qualifications that you do not have and cannot readily obtain?

Many test manuals also report information on reading level. This is also discussed in many critical reviews. A good way to determine whether the reading level is acceptable for your students is to review the test and, if in doubt, administer it to a few students who are similar to those you plan to test. If the reading level is too high, you may very well be measuring reading skills instead of the variable you want to measure. This is ample justification for rejecting a test, even if it appears to meet your needs in other respects. Alternatively, if your students are likely to have trouble with only a few words, and if an alternative measure is not available, you may choose to explain those words before administering the test. Remember, however, that such a procedure will probably change some students' scores and place in doubt the degree to which the test norms can be applied.

Clarity of Test Content

Clarity is best evaluated by studying the test itself, and it can usually be considered at the same time you appraise the reading level. Here are some questions to ask in judging clarity.

- Is the test organized in such a way that students can move easily from question to question, and section to section?
- Are the questions written in clear, simple language, avoiding trick questions and complex sentences?
- Are language and illustrations modern, timely, and recognizably familiar?
- Is it clear what each question is asking for and precisely how students should respond?

You can learn a great deal about any test by administering it to yourself. Even if you are teaching first grade, the process of placing yourself in the role of a child and trying to see the test as he or she might see it will give you some valuable insights.

Cost of the Test

One important test selection criterion often not considered is that of cost. The overall cost of testing should be carefully estimated to make sure that it fits the school budget. Anderson et al. (1980) identify four categories of costs that compose the actual cost of testing: (1) test developmental costs, (2) test administration cost, (3) test scoring costs, and (4) costs of interpreting and disseminating test scores.

Test developmental costs include things such as

- Time required to determine the purpose of testing and the type of test needed
- Time to locate and review available tests
- Costs of purchasing test materials (booklets, answer sheets, manuals, and so on)
- Costs involved in developing tests (for example, item writing, test validation)

Test administration costs include time to

- Plan the test administration
- Train test administrators
- Coordinate distribution of materials

- Administer the test
- Collect test results

Test scoring costs include

- Time required to develop scoring procedures
- Time to train judges
- Time required to score items
- Costs associated with computer scoring or optical scanning

Costs of interpreting and disseminating test scores involve such activities as

- Organizing and interpreting test scores
- Disseminating scores to decision makers

Application Problem 2

Compare the *two* instruments located in Application Problem 1 in terms of (1) validity, (2) reliability, (3) normative data, if any, and (4) cost of the test (you will need to read both the test description and the professional reviews for this purpose). Based on this comparison, which test should you use if you were to assess your students' self-esteem?

Administration of Published Tests

After a test is selected for local use, the important aspect of using such a published test in schools is to follow strictly the administration procedures specified in the test manual, especially when the test scores will be interpreted normatively, that is, when the normative data of the test will be used in the interpretation of local school test results. Because the test norm was obtained under certain uniform test administration conditions as specified in the test manual, any deviation from the test administration procedures as specified in the test manual may potentially reduce the validity of score interpretation in local schools to an uncertain degree.

In our daily classroom testing where tests are developed locally, such as one developed by the teacher of the eighth-grade math class, it is not unusual for the teacher to decide on the time limit of testing, or to explain a few words that may be confusing for some students, or to give some slow students a few extra minutes to finish the test, or to clarify some concepts during testing as the teacher sees fit, or to adjust scoring criteria a little bit after the results have been obtained, and so on. How about administering published tests? Do these and other seemingly innocuous practices matter? The answer is definitely Yes. It can never be overemphasized that it is absolutely crucial to follow the test administration, test scoring, and interpretation procedures verbatim when using published tests. Failure to do this tends to reduce the validity of test results to an unknown degree, making it very difficult or impossible to meaningfully interpret the test results from local administrations.

This point may not be well understood by many school administrators or teachers because many of these questionable practices do indeed seem to be so harmless. The major reason for adhering to the specified test administration procedures has been hinted or discussed in previous chapters (for example, Chapters 3 and 6): if test administration procedures are not followed strictly, the published norms (in norm-referenced testing) or mastery of objectives (in criterion-referenced testing) are probably less valid, or even no longer valid, for local interpretation since it is unknown how the norm sample would have performed under these altered conditions.

Out of many aspects of good test administration practice, which have been discussed in several previous chapters, the following should draw our close attention:

1. Make sure that students have adequate test-taking skills, that is, that students understand what they are required to do.
2. Motivate students to give their best performance (in a maximum performance measurement situation) or to provide their honest responses to questions (in a typical performance measurement situation).
3. Provide the test administration instructions as provided by the test publisher or author.
4. Strictly implement the testing time limit by accurately keeping the time.
5. At the end of the time limit, collect test materials promptly, and make sure all materials are collected from each examinee.
6. If any unexpected events occur during the testing session, record the events for later reference in score interpretation.

When using published tests, it is important to guard against any questionable or unethical practices. Chapter 6 has provided discussions about these issues.

SUGGESTED READINGS

Keyser, D. J., & Sweetland, R. C. (1984–1994). *Test critiques* (Vols. 1–10). Austin, TX: Pro-Ed.

This ten-volume work dating from 1984 to 1994 contains critiques of tests selected by specialists in the given areas, and therefore the more widely used measures are usually reviewed. Each review includes five sections: a detailed description of the measure; a Practical Application/Uses section, which provides information on administration, scoring, and interpretation; a section on Technical Aspects, which is concerned primarily with reliability and validity; an overall Critique, which is very useful in helping the potential user evaluate the test; and a brief list of References dealing with the measure and related topics. Additional volumes are published periodically. In using these volumes, the best approach is to check the most recent volume, which will contain cumulative indexes covering all volumes. These volumes, along with the *Mental Measurements Yearbooks,* are the best sources of evaluation information on available tests. The main advantage of *Test Critiques* is the thoroughness of the information provided for each measure.

Sweetland, R. C. & Keyser, D. J. (1991). *Tests—A comprehensive reference for assessments in psychology, education, and business* (3rd ed.). Austin, TX: Pro-Ed.

This reference provides information on thousands of tests. Information on each test includes a description, statement of purpose, administration time, grade range, scoring information, cost, and publisher. Tests are listed under three major headings: Psychology, Education, and Business and Industry. Each of these sections is in turn divided into several specific subsections. For example, subsections under Education include Academic Subjects, Achievement and Aptitude, Intelligence, Reading, Special Education, and so on.

SUGGESTION SHEET

If your last name starts with the letter R or S, please complete the Suggestion Sheet at the end of the book while this chapter is still fresh in your mind.

Answers to Chapter 14 Application Problems

1. If you scanned the Score Index of the *Twelfth MMY,* you found that five instruments are listed under *self-esteem* (78, 82, 190, 377, and 385). A closer look at the five measures reveals that both 78 and 377 are appropriate for measuring self-esteem of sixth-grade students.

2. No standard answer is provided for this application problem.

CHAPTER 15

What Have My Students Learned?

An Introduction to Standardized Achievement Measures

OVERVIEW

Bettering students' academic achievement is generally considered the primary goal of the public schools. Achievement is usually measured by a test such as a teacher-made test, a curriculum-embedded test, or a standardized achievement test. Although all different types of tests can provide important information, this chapter focuses on standardized achievement tests. Because of their widespread use in the public schools, standardized achievement tests must be well understood by teachers. The chapter describes how standardized achievement tests are developed, summarizes how they are used, and illustrates a simple process for estimating content validity. It also describes a few important standardized achievement test batteries, with one of them, the Comprehensive Test of Basic Skills, described in some detail as an example.

OBJECTIVES

Upon completing your study of this chapter, you should be able to

1. Describe the characteristics of the typical standardized achievement test.
2. Briefly describe the major kinds of achievement measures used in schools.
3. Summarize the process for developing a standardized achievement test.
4. Explain why when selecting a standardized achievement test for local use, a local school or district should determine the content validity of the standardized test.
5. Describe the steps a teacher would take in estimating the content validity of a standardized achievement test for the curriculum taught in his or her class.

6. Describe some of the ways that teachers, administrators, and counselors can use standardized achievement test information.

7. Briefly describe the limitations that must be considered in interpreting standardized achievement test scores.

8. State in your own words the steps a teacher should follow to gain an understanding of a standardized achievement test battery.

Types of Achievement Measures

Parents and teachers generally agree that enhancing students' achievement in such subjects as mathematics, reading, and science is the schools' primary function. Several types of educational tests have been developed to measure how well schools are teaching such academic subjects. The most frequently used tests for measuring academic achievement or progress include

- teacher-made tests
- curriculum-embedded measures
- standardized achievement test batteries

Although teacher-made tests and curriculum-embedded measures are described briefly in this chapter, the main emphasis is on standardized achievement test batteries. Throughout the chapter, we have selected some typical standardized measures as examples. However, their inclusion does not mean that they are *superior* to others. Before discussing standardized achievement tests, let's discuss the other types of achievement measures briefly.

Teacher-made Achievement Measures

Whether students are in the primary grades or studying for advanced degrees, most of the achievement measures they encounter are developed by their instructors. These measures can range from being very poor to excellent in quality, and the usefulness of these measures depends directly on how well these measures are constructed. A good teacher-made measure is often more useful than the standardized achievement measures available from publishers. Teachers who develop superior tests are skillful workers of test items, who use a variety of procedures to continually improve test quality. With the wide availability of microcomputers and word processors, it is becoming increasingly easy for teachers to develop a file of high-quality test items.

The area where appropriately developed teacher-made tests are most often superior to standardized achievement measures is *content validity*. In this context, content validity is the degree to which the items of a test adequately cover the content areas that have been taught. Classroom teachers know best what they have taught their students, and are in a position to develop a test that is more appropriate in terms of content validity than any standardized achievement measure is likely to do. Because teacher-made achievement measures can play a very important role in measuring students' progress, each teacher should be familiar with the skills needed to develop, evaluate, and interpret his or her own measures.

Curriculum-Embedded Achievement Measures

Many of the curriculum materials available to today's schools include measures to monitor student progress, plan instruction, and assign grades. Curriculum-embedded tests are often made up for each unit of work so as to provide the teacher with frequent checks of students' progress. Such measures are typically criterion-referenced and measure whether a student has mastered the program's specific objectives.

Standardized Achievement Test Batteries

Standardized achievement test batteries have several characteristics that distinguish them from teacher-made tests and other achievement measures. The term *standardized* refers to standard or uniform conditions or procedures in three areas: (1) administration conditions, such as instructions, time limits, and materials; (2) scoring procedures; and (3) interpretation of test scores based on the criteria provided by the test publisher. The goal of standardization is for each student to be exposed to the same testing situation so as to minimize errors and to provide comparable information. Those who administer such measures must study the procedures carefully and motivate the students to make a maximum effort because many important decisions will be influenced by these test scores. Research suggests that low motivation and careless test administration can significantly lower students' scores (Taylor & White, 1982).

Prior to being distributed for use in the schools, most standardized achievement tests are administered to large samples of students in different geographical areas to determine the distribution of scores obtained by students at different grade levels. These data, as discussed in Chapter 3, are called "norms," and norms are provided to test users to facilitate the comparison of local students' performance with that of the norming sample. Many of these tests are also criterion-referenced because they provide data on students' mastery of specific objectives, based on the criteria established by the test developers. Most standardized achievement measures available today also provide lists of objectives, individual student profiles, class record sheets, school district summaries, and guides for interpreting the test data.

Selecting a Standardized Achievement Battery

The use or the choice of standardized achievement tests in schools is often beyond the control of classroom teachers since it is mandated at the state level by either the legislature or the state education department, or the decision is made at the school district level. Despite this, educators in general should understand the importance of and process for selecting an appropriate standardized achievement battery to be used in local schools.

The most important consideration in selecting a standardized achievement test for local use is the content validity of a test. In other words, the first question to ask is: "To what extent do the objectives of the standardized achievement test under consideration match local curriculum?" Let's consider some of the factors that are particularly relevant in the selection of standardized achievement measures. First, during the preliminary screening, be sure that subtests are available in all major achievement areas you want to assess because not all standardized achievement test batteries cover the same subject areas at the same grade levels. Also check the availability of alternate forms in case you want to give alternate forms in alternate years. Carefully review any evidence of the comparability of alternate forms. Assuming that alternate forms of a test produce closely comparable scores—when in fact they may not—can lead to serious misinterpretations.

Second, test validity, especially content validity is important for achievement measures. Review what the test manual says about content validity, but don't accept that evidence as sufficient. Test publishers usually establish content validity by studying a collection of curriculum guides, state courses of study, and popular textbooks, then developing test items that measure a sample of the content areas most frequently found in these sources. This approach aims at producing a test that is *reasonably well suited* to the curricula of most local schools. However, because local schools may emphasize different content areas, the objectives on a given standardized test may not be relevant to a particular situation. Therefore, it is also important to compare the test content with the content in your curriculum. Although all major test publishers use a similar approach, the objectives measured from test to test can differ considerably. Even in mathematics, where the curriculum tends to be most uniform, there are striking differences in the topics covered by different standardized tests (Freeman, Kuhs, Knappen, & Porter, 1979; also Floden, Porter, Schmidt & Freeman, 1978).

Test reliability for most standardized achievement batteries is high, usually above .90 for each test in the battery. However, many of the tests will also provide several subtest scores. For example, the mathematics test in the *Stanford Achievement Test Battery* contains three subtests: Concepts of Number, Math Computation, and Math Applications. If you plan to use scores from the subtests to evaluate your students' performance, also check the reliability of these subtests. If subtest reliabilities are below the .80 to .90 range, scores for these subtests should be used cautiously in interpreting an individual student's performance.

Comparisons between norms and local students' performance are commonly used to estimate students' progress. Therefore, carefully review the characteristics of the norm groups and compare them with the characteristics of your own students to determine how valid such a comparison might be.

A Simplified Content Analysis

The only way to establish the content validity of a given standardized achievement test *for your school* is to conduct a content analysis of the objectives covered in *both* the local curriculum and the standardized test. The following steps describe a process for determining how well a standardized test fits your local curriculum. Figure 15.1 gives hypothetical results of such an analysis for a short subtest on geography.

Step 1. Analyze the curriculum for each subject and grade level, and list the broad content objectives in column 1, and the specific objectives related to each broad objective in column 2. For example, a broad objective in your sixth-grade mathematics curriculum could be "The student completes multiplication problems with one-, two-, and three-digit numbers." A related, more specific objective could

Geography	6	18	Natl. Ach. Battery	Int.	A
Subject or Content Area	Grade Level	N Test Items	Standardized Test Name	Level	Form

A. Specific objectives not covered by any item: <u>3 of 8</u> = <u>37%</u>
B. Test items not related to any curriculum objective: <u>7 of 18</u> = <u>39%</u>
C. Curriculum Materials: <u>20 pages in "Our World"</u>

Column 1	Column 2	Column 3	Column 4	Column 5		Column 6	
Broad Instructional Objectives or Content Areas	Specific Content Objectives or Concepts Covered in Local Curriculum	Items Related to this Objective	Items not Related to any Object; This Grade	Curriculum N	%	Test Emphasis N	%
Geography	1. Understand longitude and latitude	1,8	(4, 5, 6, 12, 13, 14, 16)	11	5	2	11
	2. Locate points on map and give their long. and lat.	9, 10, 11		19	9	3	17
	3. Give examples of natural resources	7, 15		42	20	2	11
	4. Understand compass directions	2, 3		10	5	2	11
	5. Enter names of nations on a map of Western Hemisphere	0		28	14	0	0
	6. Identify sun, moon, and planets on solar system map	0		31	5	0	0
	7. Relate raw materials in a region to industry	17, 18		40	19	2	11
	8. Identify continents and oceans on a world map	0		26	13	0	0
		Total = 11 Items	Total = 7 Items				

FIGURE 15.1   Hypothetical Content Validity Analysis of a Standardized Achievement Measure Using the Content Analysis Form

be "The student will correctly multiply a two-digit number by a two-digit number for 80 percent of the given problems." The example in Figure 15.1 shows in column 2 the eight specific content objectives for geography from the district's curriculum guide.

Step 2. Read each test item and enter the item numbers of those items related to each specific objective in column 3. In our example, test items 1 and 8 from the NAC social science geography subtest are related to the first curriculum objective. If an item does not fit *any* of the specific objectives for your grade level, or covers content areas not taught, enter the item number in column 4. Remember that since a given level of the achievement test will contain items related to more than one grade level, items in column 4 may fit specific objectives in higher or lower grades. Thus it is desirable for teachers at all grade levels to work cooperatively in conducting the content analysis. In our example, 7 of the 18 items from the geography subtest do not relate to any of the 6th-grade objectives in the district's curriculum guide.

Step 3. Add the number of specific objectives listed in column 2. Then add the number of objectives for which no items are listed (column 3). Divide the number of objectives not tested by the total number of objectives, and multiply by 100 to estimate the percentage of your curriculum *not* covered on the test. Enter the result in space A near the top of the form. In the example, three of the eight geography objectives (or 37.5 percent) were not tested. Since a given level of the test will often be designed for more than one grade level, and since students at a given grade level differ in achievement level, a satisfactory test must include items for more than one grade. However, the approach described here will still provide a good estimate of how well a test fits your school's curriculum for your grade level.

Step 4. Add the number of items on the test that do not relate to any objective at your grade level (column 4). Divide this sum by the total number of test items in the subtest. Multiply by 100 to determine the percentage of the test that is not relevant to the curriculum taught at your grade level, and enter the result in space B at the top left of the form. In our example, 7 of the 18 subtest items (or 39 percent) measured concepts not covered in the district curriculum.

Step 5. The results of steps 3 and 4 will give you a reasonable basis for estimating the content validity of different standardized achievement measures for your local curriculum, and for comparing the content validity of two or more tests.

Step 6. Estimate the emphasis given to each specific objective or concept in the curriculum. You might base this estimate on the amount of class time devoted to the objective, the number of pages in the text relating to the objective, or any other reasonable measure of emphasis. In our example, the textbook contains 207 pages on geography. The number of pages related to each of the eight specific objectives is entered, and the percentage of pages relating to each objective is entered into column 5. Another approach that can be used for this step is to rate the curriculum emphasis of each objective high (H), moderate (M), or low (L), and enter your estimates in column 5.

Step 7. Test emphasis can also be classified as high, moderate, or low, depending on the number of items listed for each objective in column 3. Compare the test emphasis, based on your estimate in column 6, to the curriculum emphasis, estimated in column 5. The closer these match, the more appropriate the test is for your curriculum. In our example, we have used another method by entering the number of test items related to each objective in column 6 and converting this to a percentage of the total 18 items on the geography subtest.

Even this simplified procedure to determine content validity requires considerable time. However, it is time well spent, and it does provide a way of estimating the content validity of each test the district is considering. It is probably best accomplished by a committee of teachers.

Probably none of the tests that are analyzed will provide a *fully* satisfactory match with the local curriculum. However, content validity can be increased by custom scoring, which omits test items not related to local instructional objectives.[1] The district may also supplement the standardized test items with locally developed items designed to measure local objectives not covered by the standardized test. This is a useful compromise solution, but it does require substantial extra work. You must also remember that the national norms for the standardized test should not be used once the test content has been changed in any fashion.

Application Problem 1

Using the Content Analysis Form, select one broad instructional objective for a subject and grade level you teach. You may use an objective from a district curriculum guide or may develop one from a section of a textbook you use. Enter the broad objective into column 1 of the Content Analysis Form. Next write the specific objectives that relate to your broad objective into column 2 of the CAF.

Select a standardized test appropriate for your grade and subject area.[2] Read each test item in the section related to your subject area, and decide if it is related to one of the specific objectives in column 2. Record the following information: total test items in your subject area, number of specific objectives covered by at least one test item, number of specific objectives not covered by any test items, and number of test items not related to any of your objectives. Based on the information you've compiled, decide how well the test content fits the curriculum content for this broad objective.

Application Problem 2

There are different aspects of test validity evidence, such as content validity, criterion-related validity, and construct validity, as discussed in Chapter 5. When selecting a standardized achievement test to assess students' learning, what aspect(s) of validity evidence is(are) the most immediate concern(s) for educators? Why?

Development Process for a Standardized Achievement Test

To better understand how information from standardized achievement tests should be used, it is helpful to understand the basic process used to develop standardized achievement measures. Previous chapters have already alerted you to the complexity of constructing a test. The process employed in developing standardized achievement measures is considerably more elaborate than that employed in

---

[1]Some test publishers provide custom scoring through which schools may specify which items to score, based on the content of the local curriculum.

[2]There are several ways you can obtain a standardized test for this application problem: (1) see if a nearby university maintains a test file from which you can borrow; (2) borrow a test copy from a local school district; (3) purchase a specimen set of an appropriate test from a test publisher.

preparing teacher-made tests. Educational Testing Service (ETS) reports that developing an entirely new test requires about two years (Educational Testing Service, 1983). During that time, the following major steps are taken.[3]

Step 1. *Define the test characteristics and objectives.* First, the test developers must ask some important questions:

- Why will the test be given, and how will the results be used?
- Who will take the test?
- What specific content should be assessed?
- What kinds of questions should be included in the test?
- How long should it be?
- How difficult should it be?

Advisory committees are often used to consider these questions. A committee for a standardized achievement test would likely include experts in the test content areas, experienced teachers who teach the subject, and representatives from the test company staff.

Developing sound, relevant objectives is critical and demands careful, thorough examination of local curricula. For example, in developing objectives for the *Comprehensive Test of Basic Skills* (CTBS), which we will discuss later in the chapter, the developers examined current curriculum guides from state departments of education and large school districts throughout the country, and analyzed the content of recently published textbook series and instructional programs (CTB/McGraw-Hill, 1997).

Step 2. *Write the test item.* Once test objectives and specifications have been clearly defined, test questions can be written. First-draft questions are typically prepared by teachers and subject matter experts. They are then revised and improved by item writing specialists, without whose help many test items are likely to have serious deficiencies. Since many items are rejected, it is usually necessary to write two to three times as many items as will be required on the final form of the test. When the format and content of an item are judged satisfactory, the readability and difficulty level of the vocabulary is checked to assure appropriateness for the intended test takers.

Step 3. *Assemble the prototype.* Once all test items have been written, a prototype test is assembled and administered to small samples of students similar to those for whom the test is intended and the results analyzed. Item analysis procedures (similar to those discussed in Chapter 9) are used to determine if items are ambiguous or incorrect, or need revision.

Step 4. *Administer the tryout edition.* Following the initial prototype administration, a larger tryout sample of students at the appropriate grade levels in private and public schools is selected. This sample typically comprises several hundred students. Teachers who administer the "tryout edition" are asked to make suggestions concerning content, instructions, time limits, and illustrations. Their feedback is considered together with data from an additional item analysis in determining how

---

[3]These seven steps are a composite of those listed by several leading text publishers and are indicative of current practice in the field.

the test should be revised. After this tryout, more sophisticated analysis procedures are typically used to check the quality of test items, including such characteristics as item difficulty, item discrimination, item ambiguity, and item bias against certain subgroups of the intended population. These analysis results will be used for further revision.

Step 5. *Conduct sensitivity reviews.* During the initial development of test items, item writers follow guidelines designed to eliminate language that reflects racial, sexual, or other forms of stereotypes and potential bias. Editors, test development committees, or panels also review the items for possible stereotypes and bias both before and after the tryout. Items are also reviewed by specially trained persons, including professional educators who represent various racial and ethnic groups, to identify and eliminate biased material.

Step 6. *Revise the test.* Based on evidence gathered from the tryout edition, necessary revisions are made to ensure that items appearing on the final form are relevant to the subject matter, are representative of the content to be tested, and are appropriate in difficulty. The revised test is again reviewed by content specialists, test specialists, and outside experts. Each reviewer answers all questions independently and prepares a list of correct answers.

Step 7. *Develop normative data.* Most standardized achievement tests now in use are norm-referenced. To establish test norms, the test publishers administer the revised measure, called the standardization edition, to a large national sample of students at the appropriate grade levels. Data from this large national testing are then used to develop tables of norms.

Application Problem 3

Select a small unit of work, such as a textbook chapter, on a subject you expect to teach. Follow steps 1, 2, and 3 for developing an achievement test for that unit. For step 4 (tryout), administer the test to a colleague or, if you are teaching, to a small sample of your students. For step 5, you can ask a colleague of yours to review your items for possible social and cultural stereotypes and bias. Then revise the test as described in step 6.

Some Widely Used Standardized Achievement Tests

We will now have a look at a few widely used standardized achievement tests. We will also examine one typical such test in some depth to help you understand what these measures contain and how they can be helpful. Let us again emphasize that our use of various measures as examples is not meant to be an endorsement of the measures themselves.

California Achievement Test

The *California Achievement Test,* or CAT (from CTB/McGraw-Hill), is designed to cover basic skill areas for grades K through 12. The content areas or test objectives for each grade level covered by CAT were determined through a comprehensive analysis of curricula of school districts sampled nationally. In the analysis, those skills and concepts identified as being central to each grade were selected to be measurement objectives. Although the areas measured vary from grade to grade, CAT has subtests measuring achievement in common areas, such as spelling, reading vocabulary, language, mathematics, and study skills. Additional subtests are available for different grades.

As a standardized achievement test, CAT provides norm-referenced scores for performance comparison with the national norm sample. As a broadly defined achievement test, CAT also provides *criterion-referenced* scores in relation to the objectives the test attempts to measure, to indicate the degree to which a student has mastered the set of objectives ("mastery," "partial mastery," or "nonmastery"). As is typical of standardized achievement tests, extensive empirical data exist to attest to the psychometric quality of CAT, such as reliability and validity.

Iowa Tests of Basic Skills (ITBS)

Published by the Riverside Publishing Company, the ITBS is a multilevel test battery for grades K through nine that has been a major player among standardized achievement tests for at least half a century. Similar to CAT, achievement in content areas such as reading, spelling, vocabulary, language, math, and study and reference skills is assessed although subtests vary from grade to grade (Hieronymous & Hoover, 1985). Supplemental subtests are available for such areas as Social Studies and Science. ITBS undergoes revision and restandardization every few years. As an achievement test series, content validity of ITBS was based on analysis of representative school curricula, and on the collaboration of both curriculum experts and testing specialists. One potentially very useful feature of ITBS is that it was concurrently normed with the Cognitive Abilities Test (CogAt), a group-administered aptitude test that we will discuss in the following chapter. Such concurrent norming provides a potentially useful tool for identifying students who are not performing on the achievement test to their potential as indicated by their performance on aptitude test.

Similar to CAT, ITBS provides both norm-referenced test scores and criterion-referenced score interpretations for the skills and content areas covered by the test (skill analysis). These skill analyses help to identify individual student's strengths and weaknesses so that instruction can be tailored specifically to each student's needs. The available data indicate that the psychometric quality of ITBS is good, and expert reviews have been overwhelmingly positive (Raju, 1992; Willson, 1989).

Metropolitan Achievement Tests (MAT)

Again, this is one of the veteran standardized achievement tests in the educational arena published by the Psychological Corporation. The purpose of MAT is to measure students' achievement in the major skill and content areas of the school curricula. Similar to ITBS, MAT also has the concurrent norming feature with an aptitude test, the *Otis–Lennon School Ability Test* (OLSAT), which we will discuss in the following chapter about aptitude testing. Owing to this concurrent norming feature, if a student shows a meaningful discrepancy between her achievement and aptitude performances (for example, substantially lower achievement than aptitude test score), such discrepancy will be treated as an indication that the student may not be performing to his or her full potential. Consequently, such information may be used to help identify factors that prevent the student from doing better in learning.

Designed for K through 12, MAT consists of three components: Survey Battery, Diagnostic Batteries, and Writing. The Survey Battery yields *norm-referenced* scores for most traditional curricula areas such as reading (vocabulary, word recognition, reading comprehension), mathematics (concepts, problem solving, computation), language (spelling, grammar), science, social studies (geography, history, economics, political science). The Diagnostic Battery provides *criterion-referenced* information for fundamental skills in three basic areas: reading, mathematics, and language skills, with each of the three areas finely defined. The psychometric quality of MAT is good although some reviewers have indicated that it would be desirable to have more criterion-related validity evidence (for example, Nitko, 1989b; Rogers, 1989).

Stanford Achievement Test Series

Published by the Psychological Corporation, the *Stanford Achievement Series* consist of three test batteries designed for different age groups ranging from kindergarten to first year college level. The best known of the series is the *Stanford Achievement Test* (SAchT) for grades one through nine. The Stanford Achievement Test was concurrently normed with both the Metropolitan Achievement Test (MAT) and the *Otis–Lennon School Ability Test* (OLSAT), a group intelligence test that we will discuss later in the book. Because of the feature of concurrent norming, scores on SAchT are readily comparable to scores from MAT. Also, like MAT, the concurrent norming with the group intelligence test OLSAT makes it possible to identify students who show a substantial discrepancy between achievement and aptitude. Such information is often believed to be helpful for educators in identifying potential learning problems.

SAchT assesses achievement in a variety of basic areas: word-study skills, reading comprehension, vocabulary, listening comprehension, spelling, language, concepts of number, mathematics computation, mathematics applications, social science, and science. Like other similar standardized achievement tests, the content areas of SAchT were carefully designed to reflect important areas in typical school curricula. The psychometric properties of SAchT are satisfactory although some reviewers indicate that more validity evidence (criterion-related and construct validity evidence) may be needed (Brown, 1992; Stoker, 1992).

Tests of General Educational Development (GED)

The *Tests of General Educational Development* (GED) is another widely used achievement test battery. Developed by the American Council on Education, this test battery is not intended for students in schools; instead, it is generally used for *adults* who did not finish high school, but who desire a high school equivalency certification. GED allows individuals who did not finish high school to demonstrate their equivalency of high school education so that they can further their educational, vocational, or professional objectives. The GED is widely used. For example, in 1982, about 800,000 were administered GED nationwide, and more than half earned their high school equivalency (Walsh & Betz, 1995). More than 10 million adults have earned GED credentials in the past 25 years (*USA TODAY,* 1996).

Because GED is designed for people who have been out of high school for some years, its content emphasizes concepts and generalizations, rather than specific details, of those important areas of educational competency and knowledge comparable to high school education. Consisting of multiple-choice items (except some items in the writing skills section that require written responses), GED assesses five broad areas: writing skills, social studies, science, reading skills, and mathematics.

In general, GED has good psychometric properties in terms of both reliability and validity evidence. There is some evidence that the GED standards for high school equivalency are more stringent than those used in typical high schools. Whitney, Malizio, and Patience (1985) showed that about 30 percent of high school graduates would have failed to reach the level of high school equivalency had they taken GED.

The Comprehensive Tests of Basic Skills (CTBS)

To have a better understanding of the features of typical standardized achievement tests, we now examine CTBS in some depth. The most recent CTBS is part of the *TerraNova Assessment Series* published by CTB/McGraw-Hill. CTBS itself, however, consists of a series of tests designed for different assessment purposes: CTBS Survey, CTBS Complete Battery, and CTBS Basic Battery. Table 15.1 describes the components of CTBS, levels available for different grades, and supplemental tests within each test of the battery.

The major difference between CTBS Survey and CTBS Complete Battery is that the CTBS Survey has fewer test items, requires less time to administer, and is used primarily to provide *norm-referenced* achievement scores. The CTBS Survey is appropriate when shorter test administration time is strongly desired. On the other hand, the CTBS Complete Battery includes all CTBS Survey test items, plus some additional test items. As a result of the additional items, the CTBS Complete Battery provides more measurement precision for each. In addition to norm-referenced performance information, the CTBS Complete Battery provides a full array of *criterion-referenced* achievement scores in the form of *objective mastery scores* called *Objective Performance Index* (OPI). These objective mastery scores for each instructional objective provide educators with additional tools for diagnosis of the strengths and weaknesses of individuals and groups of students. These criterion-referenced scores can also be used to establish or adjust instructional priorities.

The CTBS Basic Battery contains only the Reading/Language Arts and Mathematics tests of the CTBS Complete Battery version. As such, it provides the same norm-referenced and criterion-referenced performance information as the CTBS Complete Battery for Reading/Language Arts and Mathematics, but it does not have the tests for the Science and Social Studies areas.

Table 15.1 CTBS Components, Levels, and Availability for Different Grades

Grade	K	1	2	3	4	5	6	7	8	9	10	11/12
CTBS Level	10	11	12	13	14	15	16	17	18	19	20	21/22
CTBS Survey												
Reading/Language Arts			✓	✓	✓	✓	✓	✓	✓	✓	✓	✓
Mathematics			✓	✓	✓	✓	✓	✓	✓	✓	✓	✓
Science			✓	✓	✓	✓	✓	✓	✓	✓	✓	✓
Social Studies			✓	✓	✓	✓	✓	✓	✓	✓	✓	✓
Survey Plus Supplemental Tests												
Word Analysis			✓	✓								
Vocabulary			✓	✓	✓	✓	✓	✓	✓	✓	✓	✓
Language Mechanics			✓	✓	✓	✓	✓	✓	✓	✓	✓	✓
Spelling			✓	✓	✓	✓	✓	✓	✓	✓	✓	✓
Mathematics Computation			✓	✓	✓	✓	✓	✓	✓	✓	✓	✓
CTBS Complete Battery												
Reading/Language Arts	✓	✓	✓	✓	✓	✓	✓	✓	✓	✓	✓	✓
Mathematics	✓	✓	✓	✓	✓	✓	✓	✓	✓	✓	✓	✓
Science			✓	✓	✓	✓	✓	✓	✓	✓	✓	✓
Social Studies			✓	✓	✓	✓	✓	✓	✓	✓	✓	✓
Complete Battery Supplemental Tests												
Word Analysis		✓	✓	✓								
Vocabulary		✓	✓	✓	✓	✓	✓	✓	✓	✓	✓	✓
Language Mechanics			✓	✓	✓	✓	✓	✓	✓	✓	✓	✓
Spelling			✓	✓	✓	✓	✓	✓	✓	✓	✓	✓
Mathematics Computation		✓	✓	✓	✓	✓	✓	✓	✓	✓	✓	✓
CTBS Basic Battery												
Reading/Language Arts			✓	✓	✓	✓	✓	✓	✓	✓	✓	✓
Mathematics			✓	✓	✓	✓	✓	✓	✓	✓	✓	✓
Basic Battery Supplemental Tests												
Word Analysis			✓	✓	✓	✓	✓	✓	✓	✓	✓	✓
Vocabulary			✓	✓	✓	✓	✓	✓	✓	✓	✓	✓
Language Mechanics				✓	✓	✓	✓	✓	✓	✓	✓	✓
Spelling				✓	✓	✓	✓	✓	✓	✓	✓	✓
Mathematics Computation			✓	✓	✓	✓	✓	✓	✓	✓	✓	✓

The supplemental tests for the CTBS Survey, the CTBS Complete Battery, and the CTBS Basic Battery are designed to provide additional performance information that is more focused on some basic areas related to reading and mathematics. The supplemental tests for the CTBS Complete Battery and the CTBS Basic Battery are the same. But the supplemental tests for the CTBS Survey contain fewer items for each instructional objective than those for the CTBS Complete Battery and the CTBS Basic Battery, and they are used primarily for providing norm-referenced information.

Table 15.2   CTBS Levels and Target Grades

CTBS Level	10	11	12	13	14	15	16	17	18	19	20	21/22
Target Grade	k.6	1.6	2.0	2.6	3.6	4.6	5.6	6.6	7.6	8.6	9.6	10.6
		|	|	|	|	|	|	|	|	|	|	|
	1.6	2.6	3.2	4.2	5.2	6.2	7.2	8.2	9.2	10.2	11.2	12.9

Although the CTBS is available in 12 levels (Level 10 to Level 21/22) that cover grades K.0 to 12.9, and each level is primarily associated with one grade level, the adjacent test levels overlap in terms of the grades they cover. The CTBS levels and the grades they cover are shown in Table 15.2. As can be seen, both the level and variability of student achievement increase as we move into the higher grades. Thus although Level 10 (the first level) covers only 1.0 grade (K.6 to K1.6), Level 21/22 (the last level) covers 2.3 grades (10.6 to 12.9).

Since various CTBS levels overlap each other, a teacher may not be sure which level is most appropriate for his or her class. For example, students at the end of fourth grade could be tested either with Level 14 (grades 3.6 to 5.2) or Level 15 (grades 4.6 to 6.2). For a highly heterogeneous fifth-grade class, the weakest students may best fit Level 12 (2.0 to 3.2), whereas the strongest students might need Level 17 (6.6 to 8.2). To help teachers select the most appropriate test level for a student, CTBS provides optional locator tests that are quick to administer and score and that greatly reduce the chances of using a wrong level of test for a student.

Functional Level Testing

Usually, in school testing, all students at a given grade level are administered the same level of the standardized achievement battery. Although this approach, referred to as "on-level" testing, is satisfactory for most children, an on-level test that is administered to a group of students will usually be too easy for some and too difficult for others. A test that is too easy will not adequately test the upper levels of the student's achievement since the student is likely to know more than the test allows him or her to demonstrate. On the other hand, if a test is too difficult, it will not reveal what lower-level skills he or she has developed.

Such problems have encouraged many schools to use functional level achievement testing. Although functional level testing provides a more accurate picture of what each student can do, it also requires that the school determine the level at which each child will be tested. In most cases, "locator tests" are used for this purpose, but teachers' judgments and the results of prior achievement tests are also considered at some schools.

Functional level testing has been shown to have many advantages, such as allowing all students to experience some success in the testing situation, reducing boredom for high achieving students and frustration and discouragement for low-achieving students, and avoiding unreliable extreme scores (Haynes & Cole, 1982). In practice, functional level testing also poses some additional challenges, such as increased testing time for determining individual students' expected performance levels, and some difficulty in explaining the results from different tests so that test takers understand that they are being treated fairly (Wheeler, 1995).

Learning to Use the CTBS

If your school purchases a new standardized achievement test, you should plan to devote several hours to studying the test, the objectives, the kinds of scores, and the various computer-generated record sheets available from the publisher. On the following pages, we will use some examples from the CTBS to help you understand the steps involved in getting to know any of the standardized achievement batteries now being used in the schools.

Step 1. *Get an overview of the content and organization of the test.* The *Teacher's Guide to TerraNova* provides a good and very readable overview of the test battery, including procedures used for test development, content areas measured, and interpretation of test results. The teacher should give particular attention to the content areas measured by the test levels that are most likely to be used in her classroom. For example, in the area of reading, items measuring the objective *visual recognition* are included only at Level 10 (K.6 to K1.6), whereas the objective *capitalization* is covered at Levels 10, 11, and 12. Thus although all levels of the CTBS contain a reading test, the specific objectives measured may be quite different.

Step 2. *Study the test objectives.* The developers of most standardized achievement measures relate test items to a set of objectives based on their analysis of textbooks and other curriculum materials. Although it is important for a teacher to review these objectives to see how well they match what she is teaching, doing so can be problematic. If a test claims to measure hundreds of specific objectives, can teachers hope to sensibly and systematically interpret test results? Alternatively, if objectives are too broad, how can teachers know what specific content is tested or whether the test measures achievement in the same areas covered in the local curriculum? To solve this problem, test developers often write two or three levels of objectives, attempting a compromise between breadth and specificity—and usually achieving reasonable success.

Items on the CTBS are related to 52 content objectives in the areas of reading, language, mathematics, science, and social studies. Each objective is further broken down into several smaller subskill areas. An objective is measured only at certain levels of the test. For example, Objective 1, *Oral Comprehension,* is measured only at Levels 10 and 11. However, Objective 11, *Computation and Numerical,* is measured at all levels, 10 through 21/22. The teacher should note which objectives and subskill areas are measured by the CTBS subtests to be used in her classroom, and should compare those objectives and subskill areas to what is included in the local curriculum. Local objectives are often described in district or state curriculum guides or in the teacher's own curriculum-planning materials.

If you were to examine the 52 objectives for the CTBS, you would notice that these objectives are usually somewhat broad in definition. It is often necessary to focus on the subskills under each objective to gain an understanding of what are being measured. When objectives or even subskills are too general, the best recourse is to examine the text items themselves. This leads us to the next step.

Step 3. *Review the test booklet.* The *Teacher's Guide to TerraNova* gives the information needed to relate specific test items at each level of the test to each of the subskills under each of the objectives. For example, if a teacher's class were to be tested with the Form A of Level 13 of the CTBS, she could consult Appendix B of the *Teacher's Guide to TerraNova* to identify the 12 test items designed to measure Objective 11 in the CTBS Complete Test Battery, and to identify 9 items to measure the same objective in the CTBS Survey. Reviewing the actual items is the *most important step* a teacher can take in ensuring that the test will provide useful information for students in his or her classroom.

Step 4. *Learn to interpret test results.* Skillful test interpretation requires a basic understanding of the measurement process itself. Test developers often publish material that briefly describes measurement terms and concepts helpful in understanding a particular test. For example, Part 6 of the *Teacher's Guide to TerraNova* includes a description of the kinds of test scores available for the CTBS as well as a description of the various computer-generated report forms that organize and summarize the test data for both individuals and classes.

Step 5. *Use the test results in the classroom.* Standardized achievement test results can be used in a variety of ways: for identifying individual and class strengths and weaknesses with regard to national norms and specific test objectives, grouping students for certain instructional activities, planning instruction, monitoring individual and class progress, and evaluating the success of instructional methods.

CTBS Report Forms

A knowledge of report forms available for particular standardized achievement tests is important in helping you to use the test results effectively. We will continue to use the CTBS as an example of the kinds of report forms typically available.

Class Record Sheet (CRS).   This form is the basic report provided by CTB/McGraw-Hill's scoring service. One example of CRS is presented in Figure 15.2. Understanding this report, or similar ones from other standardized achievement tests, is essential for educators to effectively use the results of this type of test.

CRS provides performance information for a group of individual students, as well as performance information for the group as a whole. Note that the example in Figure 15.3 contains four different kinds of scores for each component of the test battery (Reading/Language Arts, Math, Science, and Social Studies). In addition, a Total Score consisting only of Reading/Language and Mathematics is provided. A school or district can request up to six different kinds of scores from a total of nine: number correct scores, scale scores, grade equivalents, normal curve equivalents, national percentiles, local percentiles, national stanines, local stanines, and anticipated achievement scores. Although each of these scores provides useful information, a school district might want only one or two of them.

Using the information in Figure 15.2, let's interpret the data available for Stephen Arnold. This student has national percentile scores of 57 and 41 for Read-

TerraNova

CTBS Survey

Class Record Sheet

Class: JONES   **A**

Grade 6

B

Purpose

This report provides a permanent record of test results for students in a class, or some other specified group, and summary data. The results may be used to evaluate individual and group achievement compared to the nation, determine overall performance, and identify areas of strength and need.

Simulated Data

No. of Students: 26

A

Form/Level: A-16

Test Date: 04/01/97   Scoring: IRT (Pattern)
QM: 29   Norms Date: 1996

Class:
School:
District:

City/State:

Students	Scores	Reading		Lang.		Math		Total Score*	Science	Social Studies		
Abby, Karen **D**	NP	68	–	36	–	67	–	59	71	41	–	–
Birthdate: 2/26/85	NS	6	–	4	–	6	–	5	6	5	–	–
Special Codes:	NCE	60	–	42	–	60	–	56	62	45	–	–
ABCDEFGHIJKLMNOPQRST.	SS	758	–	723	–	758	–	748	763	734	–	–
............12122221.												
Form: A Level: 16												
Arnold, Stephen A	NP	57	–	41	–	91	–	45	56	33	–	–
Birthdate: 6/21/85	NS	5	–	5	–	8	–	5	5	4	–	–
Special Codes:	NCE	53	–	45	–	82	–	47	54	39	–	–
ABCDEFGHIJKLMNOPQRST.	SS	743	–	728	–	797	–	735	749	721	–	–
............12122222.												
Form: A Level: 16												
Ruiz, Alejandro J	NP	55	–	18	–	70	–	49	42	37	–	–
Birthdate: 8/22/85	NS	5	–	3	–	6	–	5	5	4	–	–
Special Codes:	NCE	53	–	31	–	61	–	49	46	43	–	–
ABCDEFGHIJKLMNOPQRST.	SS	741	–	699	–	765	–	736	734	729	–	–
............12222221.												
Form: A Level: 16												
Chong, Louisa A	NP	89	–	71	–	75	–	79	56	62	–	–
Birthdate: 8/07/85	NS	7	–	6	–	6	–	7	5	6	–	–
Special Codes:	NCE	77	–	60	–	64	–	67	53	56	–	–
ABCDEFGHIJKLMNOPQRST.	SS	786	–	758	–	766	–	767	749	756	–	–
............22222222.												
Form: A Level: 16												
Class Summary **E**	MDNP	60.0	–	37.2	–	68.2	–	52.0	60.3	49.2	–	–
Form/Level: A–16	MNS	6.0	–	4.5	–	6.8	–	5.3	6.0	5.2	–	–
	MNCE	55.0	–	43.8	–	60.4	–	51.8	55.1	49.8	–	–
	MSS	750	–	724	–	759	–	742	752	743	–	–
Number of Students		26	–	26	–	23	–	23	25	26	–	–

C

Individual Scores

NP: NATIONAL PERCENTILE
NS: NATIONAL STANINE
NCE: NORMAL CURVE EQUIVALENT
SS: SCALE SCORE

Group (Summary) Scores

MDNP: MEDIAN NATIONAL PERCENTILE
MNS: MEAN NATIONAL STANINE
MNCE: MEAN NORMAL CURVE EQUIVALENT
MSS: MEAN SCALE SCORE

* TOTAL SCORE consists of Reading, Language, and Mathematics.

CTB McGraw-Hill   Page 1   CTBID:92123B821460001-04-00052-000054   W1 CRS P1 final:10/18

FIGURE 15.2   Class Record Sheet

Source: Teacher's guide to TerraNova, 1997. CTB/McGraw-Hill, Monterey, CA. Reprinted with permission of the publisher.

ing and Language, respectively, indicating that his performance in these two areas are close to the national median (percentile score of 50). Stephen's percentile score on the Math test, however, is 91, much above the national median, and his score in Social Studies (33) is substantially below the national median. The information in this report indicates that Stephen's performance is quite uneven across the five academic areas measured, with excellent performance in Math, average performance in Reading, Language, and Science, and below average performance in Social Studies.

The group means (Class Summary) given near the bottom of the record sheet show that although the class as a whole is slightly above the national norms in some areas (60th percentile for Reading, 68th for Math, and 60th for Science), the class as a whole is quite weak in Language Arts (37th percentile), and scores at about the national average in Social Studies (49th percentile). These comparisons with the national norms provide good information for educators to understand what the strong and weak areas are for the individual and the group of students.

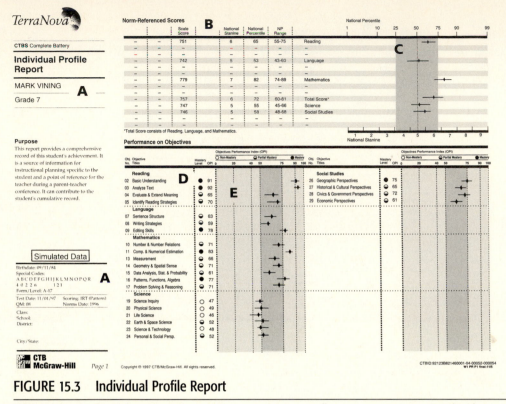

FIGURE 15.3   Individual Profile Report

Source: Teacher's guide to TerraNova, 1997. CTB/McGraw-Hill, Monterey, CA. Reprinted with permission of the publisher.

Individual Profile Report (IPR).   IPR provides comprehensive and very detailed information about an individual student's achievement in the various areas assessed in CTBS. The detailed information in IPR can help educators in education planning. An example IPR is shown in Figure 15.3.

The IPR provides both test scores (up to six types of scores can be selected) and score bands for the score of National Percentile (these are confidence intervals with one standard error of measurement above and below the score). The confidence interval around each percentile score helps to remind the teacher that test scores are only performance estimates, and a student's true score may differ to some extent from the obtained score. Two score bands that do not overlap indicate that the performance difference between the two areas of interest is probably real, whereas two score bands that overlap substantially indicate that the difference between the two may well be the result of measurement error. For example, again for Mark Vining in the IPR in Figure 15.3, the difference between his Mathematics and Language performances is most probably real since there is no overlap between the two. But the performance difference between Social Studies (58th percentile) and Language (53rd percentile) is much less certain, because such a small difference can easily be the result of measurement error.

Note that the top of this form summarizes an individual student's performance on the major components of the test battery, such as Reading, Language Arts, Math, Science, and Social Studies. These scores give a quick overview of a student's general achievement, but are of somewhat limited value for diagnosis. The lower half of IPR provides more detailed information on the specific objectives assessed under each major component of the test battery. The Objectives Performance Index (OPI) also provides criterion-referenced information in the form of mastery/nonmastery of the objectives (shaded, half-shaded, and white circles). The OPI ranges from zero to 100, and it is the estimated number of items that would be correctly answered by a student if the student were presented with 100 items of similar difficulty covering the same area. The information on these specific objectives under each major component of the test battery is often very helpful for instructional planning. For example, consider Mark Vining in Figure 15.3. His performance in Reading is uneven across the objectives, with excellent performance in the areas of Basic Understanding and Analyze Text (mastery scores of 91 and 92, respectively), but he has weaker performance in the areas of Evaluate & Extend Meaning and Identify Reading Strategies (partial mastery scores of 65 and 70). Of course, his performance in Science is the worst, with nonmastery for most of the areas.

Home Report (HR)

This form (Figure 15.4) provides easy-to-understand information about an individual student's performance for parents. The height of each bar indicates the performance level in terms of the national percentile—that is, a student's performance is compared with the national norm. The shaded region represents average performance, the region above that represents above-average performance, and below the shaded area represents below-average performance. The reason that the region for average performance looks wide is that measurement error has been taken into consideration. It is obvious that Mary Brown has the best performance in Math (above average), whereas her scores in other areas are close to the national averages. The report can be used to identify areas of strength and weakness for the student.

Objectives Performance Report (OPR)

The Objectives Performance Report (OPR) in Figure 15.5 provides an analysis of the strengths and weaknesses for both a group of students and for individuals with regard to the objectives assessed under each major component of the CTBS battery. Mastery, partial mastery, or nonmastery is indicated by shaded, half-shaded, or white circles. The information in this report can be used for two purposes. First, by comparing the local average Objective Performance Index (OPI) with the national average OPI, instructional priorities can be established for the group as a whole. In the example in Figure 15.5, the difference between the local and national OPIs is small across different areas. This indicates that performance of this group of students matches well with the national norm group. If local average OPIs in

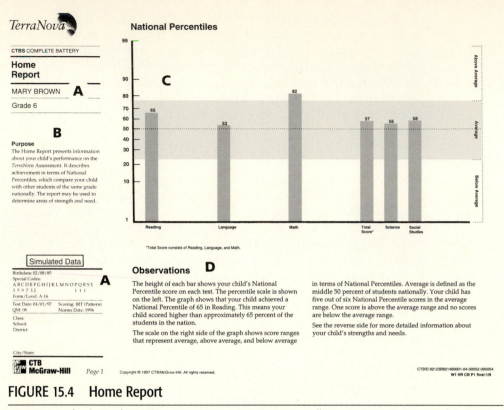

FIGURE 15.4 Home Report

Source: Teacher's guide to TerraNova, 1997. CTB/McGraw-Hill, Monterey, CA. Reprinted with permission of the publisher.

some areas were substantially lower than national average OPIs, it should alert local school educators about possible deficiencies in the local school curriculum in relation to the national average.

In addition to this norm-referenced interpretation, the OPI provides criterion-referenced performance information. Even if the local OPIs are comparable to the national OPIs, this does not mean everything is fine because comparability does not mean mastery. For example, the local OPI is comparable to the national OPI in both Basic Understanding (Reading, 72 vs. 70) and Geometry & Spatial Sense (Mathematics, 45 vs. 43). But the former indicates mastery (well, almost!), whereas the latter indicates partial or nonmastery. If local educators view Geometry & Spatial Sense as an important objective, this will be an area where more instructional emphasis may be needed.

In addition to the group comparison discussed earlier, individual students' strengths and weaknesses are easily identified from this report. For example, we see that Daniel Kaz has mastered almost all the instructional objectives assessed by the CTBS battery, whereas whereas Julian James has deficiencies in almost all the objectives.

In summary, standardized achievement tests typically provide different computer-generated forms to aid educators in their interpretation of scores. The ones dis-

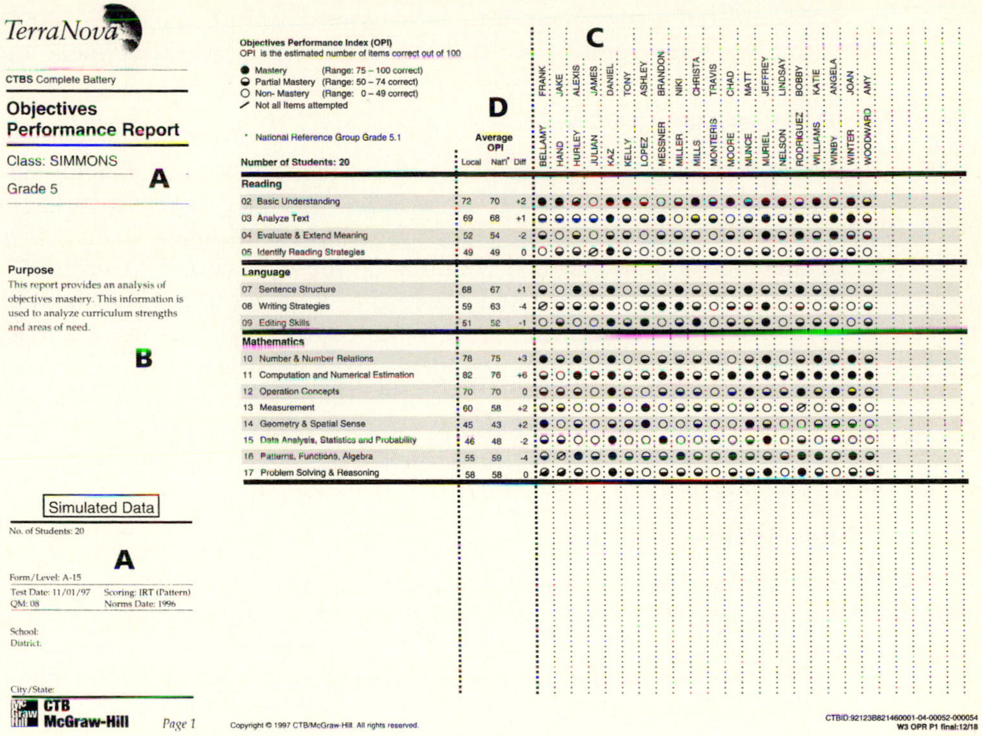

FIGURE 15.5   Objectives Performance Report

Source: Teacher's guide to TerraNova, 1997. CTB/McGraw-Hill, Monterey, CA. Reprinted with permission of the publisher.

cussed here for the CTBS are very similar to what can be expected from other standardized achievement tests. Most testing companies also provide customized score reporting or provide only those reports requested by the school. Thus knowing what reports are useful in a particular school testing situation can often save money.

Application Problem 4

Examine Figure 15.2 and answer the following questions:

a. Which area appears to be the weakest for Alejandro Ruiz? Why?

b. Which student had the largest difference between the performance in Reading and the performance in Science?

c. If the teacher wants to give instructional priority to one of the five areas (Reading, Language, Mathematics, Science, and Social Studies) during the new semester, which area should receive the first priority? Why?

Cautions in Interpreting Standardized Achievement Test Data

Standardized achievement tests have certain limitations an educator must keep in mind when interpreting scores. Let us consider a few of the most important.

Chance Scores

Since virtually all standardized achievement measures employ multiple-choice items, the student is likely to get a certain number correct by guessing. For example, the Reading Comprehension subtest of the *Stanford Achievement Test* (Intermediate 2, Grades 5.5–7.9) contains 60 multiple-choice (4 options) items. Theoretically, a student who could not read a single word of English would still obtain a raw score of 15 on this subtest by randomly marking answers to all sixty items. A raw score of 15 equals a grade equivalent of 2.8. An uninformed fifth-grade teacher might interpret this as meaning that a child receiving this score could read as well as the average child at grade 2.8, which in the case of our non-English speaking student, would clearly be untrue.

Base Scores

Standardized achievement tests also have base scores below which a person cannot score. The base grade equivalent score of the aforementioned Reading Comprehension subtest is 1.0. This means a student who does nothing except turn in a blank answer sheet with her name on it will receive a score that some might interpret as evidence that he or she reads as well as the average child at Grade 1.0 level.

Time Limitations

Nearly all achievement measures have time limits for each subtest. The time allowed is usually sufficient for most students. However, a very slow student could receive spuriously low scores on timed tests because she does not finish. Culyer (1982) reports a case in which a student answered correctly 28 of the 30 items he attempted on a 60-item subtest, giving him a grade equivalent score of 7.2. On the following day, he was given enough time to complete the test. His grade equivalent score increased from 7.2 to 10.0. This score was far more indicative of his actual achievement level.

In interpreting achievement test scores, the teacher should be alert to the scores obtained by students who work slower. Although the time limits given should be followed in order to use the test norms, the teacher may want to follow the procedure described by Culyer to gain additional insight into a particular student's achievement level.

Inadequate Content Validity

A good estimate of a test's content validity requires a careful comparison between local curriculum content and test content. If there is not time to do the type of content analysis described earlier in the chapter, the teacher can make a rough estimate of content validity by reading each test item and checking those that are covered in the curriculum. For some standardized achievement batteries, the teacher can obtain detailed item-by-item reports on the performance of her class. The teacher who knows which and how many items in each subtest fit the local curriculum is in a better position to correctly interpret test reports and student test scores.

The Need for Flexibility

The typical standardized achievement measure is designed to measure student achievement over several grade levels: for example, the first three years of elementary school or the middle school years. Since students at any grade level can be expected to vary widely in their achievement, the standardized achievement tests for use at the junior high school level must measure not only the concepts taught at that level, but also concepts typically learned at the elementary and senior high levels. To complicate the matter, the range of student achievement becomes larger as students advance through the grades, and standard achievement tests must be designed to accommodate this increase. For example, the CTBS discussed previously has 10 to 12 overlapping levels, covering achievement from the beginning of kindergarten to the end of grade 12. Early levels have an achievement range of about one grade, whereas levels aimed at the end of secondary school cover more than two grades.

Because a standardized achievement test covers a wide range of achievement, as well as several different subject areas, the number of specific concepts tested in each area is limited. Therefore, standardized achievement test scores, although providing an overall picture of student achievement, may not provide enough information about the specific strengths and weaknesses of the individual student.

Using Educational Achievement Data

Various types of standardized achievement tests provide information that can assist teachers, school administrators, and counselors in making a wide range of decisions, as listed here. Note that our list is merely intended to be an aid to help you organize your ideas about standardized achievement tests. This list is not intended to be exhaustive, nor does the list represent any kind of rigid classification. Following the list, we will discuss each use of standard achievement data in more detail.

Teacher uses
- Evaluating student performance
- Diagnosing student learning difficulties
- Organizing student learning groups
- Evaluating instructional methods
- Developing individualized education programs
- Planning instruction

Administrative uses

- Evaluation of student learning outcomes
- Evaluation of program and curriculum
- Teacher evaluation
- Identification of educationally deprived children, and selection of students for special classes or activities
- Classification of students for purposes of funding or to provide special instruction
- Provision of information to local, state, or federal agencies

Counseling uses

- Educational counseling
- Vocational counseling

Teacher Uses of Achievement Data

Teachers use tests for many different purposes. Among the most frequent are evaluation of student performance, diagnosis of student learning difficulties, formation of student learning groups, evaluation of instructional methods and strategies, and development of individualized education programs. Let us discuss each of these next.

Evaluation of Student Performance

Many instructional decisions made by teachers can be aided by the objective results of standardized achievement measures. Such information can be used to help assess students' learning needs, set priorities among curriculum objectives, and evaluate the results of instruction.

Standardized test batteries usually provide the teacher with an overview of each student's performance. For example, a careful study of the previously discussed Class Record Sheet for the Comprehensive Test of Basic Skills in Figure 15.2 shows a great deal of information about the class as a whole and about each child in the class. Such information is a rich source that the teacher can use to assess student performance.

Diagnosis of Student Learning Difficulties

Normative data on standardized achievement batteries can identify subject areas in which individual students and the class as a whole are not performing up to local or national norms. An individual's achievement is also often related to a set of objectives so that the teacher can estimate the degree to which each objective has been mastered. Both kinds of information can be useful in helping to diagnose specific learning problems and plan remedial instruction.

One caution is warranted when information is used in such a fashion. If the objectives of interest are too specific, and consequently, only very few items are actually used on the test for each objective, the test score information on these specific objectives should be used with caution. As discussed in Chapter 4, fewer items usually result in lower measurement reliability. For example, performance on five items that measure addition skills would generally not provide conclusive evidence about whether a student had mastered an objective relating to addition. Thus, although the overall percentile score a student obtains on a standardized achievement battery will usually be highly reliable, the student's score on a *specific content objective,* such as "Reduce a common fraction to its simplest form," will be less reliable because it will usually be based on just a few items.

Formation of Student Learning Groups

Elementary schools often divide the class into a number of subgroups, each comprising students who are roughly comparable in their achievement relating to a given subject.[4] Many achievement measures provide information to assist teachers in setting up such instructional groups. For example, the Objective Performance Report available for the CTBS discussed previously (Figure 15.6) lists students who failed to master each instructional objective covered by the test. Teachers could use this information to organize student groups for related clusters of objectives.

Evaluation of Instructional Methods and Strategies

Not all instructional approaches are equally effective for all teachers or students. To find the most effective teaching approaches for a given situation, teachers must constantly evaluate new approaches. Standardized achievement scores can help a teacher appraise the effectiveness of whatever approach he or she is using. For example, a simulated United Nations General Assembly session might stimulate a great deal of student interest in current events. However, if an achievement test with objectives related to civics shows little mastery of the concepts the session was designed to teach, the teacher must consider carefully whether the simulation was worth the time, even if students enjoyed it. Teachers who use a variety of different forms of feedback to evaluate and improve their instructional methods are likely to become more effective than those who merely follow hunches.

Development of Individualized Education Programs

Most children with disabilities are now placed in regular classrooms for at least part of the school day. By law, the school is required to prepare an *Individualized Education Program* (IEP) for each child with a disability that includes, among other things, the following components:

- A statement of the child's present levels of educational performance
- A statement of annual goals, including short-term instructional objectives
- Appropriate objective criteria and evaluation procedures and schedules for determining, on at least an annual basis, whether the short-term instructional objectives are being achieved (Education of the Handicapped Act, 1977)

---

[4]Although this approach is widely used, some researchers have questioned the value of the approach in general, as well as the wisdom of using standardized test results to group students (Culyer, 1982).

Standardized achievement measures can be valuable in meeting several of the aforementioned requirements. For example, standardized achievement measures can be used to estimate a child's present level of educational performance and to determine whether instructional objectives are being achieved. Such measures, *when combined with other information,* are also useful in preparing annual goals and short-term instructional objectives.

Administrative Uses of Achievement Data

Just as teachers use tests for many different purposes, so do administrators. The most frequent ways in which administrators use test results are discussed here.

Evaluation of Student Learning

Teachers are generally most interested in the achievement of individual students in their classes, whereas school administrators are more interested in the overall pattern of achievement in the school, district, or state. The standardized achievement test battery is often used for appraising the overall progress of students and comparing this progress with students in other schools, districts, or states. Such comparisons can be misleading because there may be differences in curriculum from school to school that make a given achievement test more or less appropriate for one school than for another. In spite of this limitation, standardized achievement tests are often used as an overall measure of the quality of education.

Program and Curriculum Evaluation

Closely related to the overall evaluation of student learning is the use of standardized achievement measures to evaluate various curriculum areas. If a district's students score above the national norms in mathematics, science, and language arts, and below the national norms in social studies, school administrators should probably take a careful look at the social studies curriculum. A low district score in one subject area, however, may mean that the test is a poor match for the district's curriculum in that area, and a good match in the other areas. Thus the school administrator may wish to conduct a content analysis of the local curriculum and the achievement test being used to determine the degree to which the measure covered the content being taught.

If significant differences are found between local curriculum content and the standardized achievement test content, several things can be done. First, local curriculum content can be reassessed for appropriateness. If it is determined that local curriculum content is less appropriate than what is covered by the standardized measure, an adjustment can be made in the local curriculum. If, on the other hand, the local curriculum is judged to be appropriate, two other approaches may be considered to increase content validity of the standardized measure: (1) developing a supplementary achievement test designed to measure local objectives not covered by the standardized achievement test; and (2) using only those items on the standardized achievement test that fit local objectives, then computing an adjusted score. The latter approach, described by Wilson and Hiscox (1984), is gaining popularity in a number of areas.

Never assume that a standardized achievement test is valid for local curriculum evaluation until you have compared its content with local objectives. Why this is important is shown in a study by Jolly and Gramenz (1984) who found that, for a given district, the proportion of standardized achievement test items that matched local grade level mathematics objectives ranged from a low of 58 percent at grade six to a high of 66 percent at grade four. In other words, a *third* or more of the local objectives may not have been measured.

Teacher Evaluation

Teacher evaluation takes many forms. In recent years, many educators have advocated the use of standard achievement measures to evaluate teachers' effectiveness. If the main goal of the school is to educate students, they argue, then the standardized achievement battery is perhaps the most accurate measure of a teacher's success. The teacher whose students make the greatest achievement gain during the school year may reasonably be regarded as the most "effective" teacher.

The problem with this argument is that a great many factors influence student achievement—many of which have nothing whatever to do with the performance of the teacher. For example, students with a higher scholastic aptitude tend to achieve more in any environment, regardless of how effective the teacher is. Other factors, such as students' self-concept, motivation, and socioeconomic status are also related to academic achievement. It is easy to see how these variables can confuse the issue. Of course, results from standardized achievement tests may be used as a part of a teacher evaluation system. But any fair system of teacher evaluation based on student achievement must take all these other variables into account. Designing teacher evaluation that is fair and accurate is a challenge with which education continues to wrestle.

Placement of Students

Standardized achievement measures are used, in conjunction with other measures such as scholastic aptitude test scores and teachers' judgment, as a basis for many placement decisions in public schools. Many schools employ some form of ability grouping to ensure that pupils in a given classroom are similar in ability or other important factors. For example, in assigning students to different sections of ninth-grade algebra, educators might review students' eighth-grade achievement test scores in arithmetic, and then create three sections: those performing about on grade level, those requiring special help, and those ready for an extra challenge.

Classification of Students

State and federal laws often require the use of standardized test scores in conjunction with other assessment data for identifying and classifying children with disabilities. The first step in the classification process is usually administration of a screening test to alert school personnel of the *possible* existence of a disability. If a potential problem is suspected, more explicit diagnosis is made by a team of persons from different disciplines, including at least one teacher (Wilson, 1980). Typically, for the purpose of identifying students who may need special education, performance on standardized achievement measures plays an important role. The amount of information that standardized achievement measures can provide for this purpose, however, depends on the match between the curriculum and the standardized test. This is clearly illustrated in a study by Jenkins and Pany (1978) in which children were evaluated who had mastered all words in a given reading program. They found large discrepancies between the grade placement scores children obtained on different standardized tests. The deficiencies illustrated by this study occur because tests differ in their content validity for various reading programs. Therefore, it is vital to use achievement measures that have *high content validity* for the *local curriculum* if the scores are to be valid for making classification decisions.

Many administrators assume that standardized test scores are more valid than teacher judgment. This assumption is often incorrect. When an achievement test score conflicts with other evidence, further information should be collected before making a decision.

Provision of Information

School districts are often asked to supply standardized achievement test information to local agencies (for example, the school board or PTA), state agencies (for example, legislature or department of education), and various federal agencies. Besides these agencies, the public tends to be immensely interested in this kind of information. Publishers of current standardized achievement measures can provide virtually any summary information that may be required by the schools.

Counseling Uses of Achievement Data

Results of tests are also used in counseling students regarding educational and vocational decisions, as summarized in the next two sections.

Educational Counseling

A student's achievement test scores are often useful in personal educational planning. Research has shown that the past achievement in a given subject area is usually the best predictor of a student's future performance in that same area. However, such predictions are not infallible. In most cases, a student should not be denied the right to take a given course purely on the basis of past achievement, but should be warned that she may have difficulty.

Vocational Counseling

Various standardized measures—such as scholastic aptitude tests, vocational interest tests, measures of specific aptitudes, and standardized achievement test batteries—play an important role in appraising a student's potential for a given vocation. Research has revealed much about the academic demands of various occupations. Such information can be very valuable to a student in matching her own aptitudes with those of successful individuals in the vocation she is considering. Additionally, a number of standardized tests can assist students in deciding how closely their interests are aligned with the typical activities in various occupations. By providing students with systematic information on both aptitudes and interests as it relates to vocational choice, the probability of the student making an appropriate decision is increased.

Suggested readings

Carey, L. M. (1994). *Measuring and evaluating school learning* (2nd ed.). Boston, MA: Allyn and Bacon.

This book provides very detailed instruction and gives exercises for hands-on experience about developing achievement tests for school and classroom use. It contains many examples about all aspects of school assessment. It covers not only objective tests (for example, multiple choice, matching), but also alternative assessment (for example, essay, product development, active performance).

Mehrens, W. A. (1984). National tests and local curriculum: Match or mismatch? *Educational Measurement: Issues and Practices, 3*(3), 9–15.

The author reviews some basic facts about standardized achievement tests, and discusses the amount of mismatch between standard tests and local curriculum and the implications of this mismatch. A good introduction to the topic of content validity written in clear, simple language.

Mehrens, W. A., & Lehmann, I. J. (1991). *Using standardized tests in education* (4th ed.). New York: Holt, Rinehart & Winston.

The authors describe types of standardized tests and their use in the schools. One chapter focuses on use of all major standardized achievement tests in education and on the various uses of achievement test results.

Millman, J. & Greene, J. (1989). The specialization and development of tests of achievement and ability. In R. L. Linn (ed.). *Educational measurement* (3rd ed., pp. 335–366). New York: Macmillan Publishing Company.

This chapter was written for the professional test developer, but it contains some interesting information for teachers about how standardized achievement tests should be developed. The content is much more technical than the material in the text. It proposes guidelines for specification of objectives, item writing, test assembly, and norming.

Peterson, N. S., Kolen, M. J., & Hoover, H. D. (1989). Scaling, norming, and equating. In R. L. Linn (ed.). *Educational measurement* (3rd ed., pp. 221–262). New York: Macmillan Publishing Company.

Comparing results from two or more different standardized achievement tests is not as simple as it might appear at first. This chapter provides a comprehensive, but somewhat technical, summary of the essential considerations in making such comparisons.

Suggestion sheet

If your last name starts with the letter T or U, please complete the Suggestion Sheet at the end of the book while this chapter is still fresh in your mind.

Answers to Chapter 15 Application Problems

1. No example answer to this exercise can be given because of the individual nature of the application problem.

2. Evidence of content validity is usually the most immediate concern for educators. If a standardized achievement test is used to assess students' learning, it is obvious that unless the standardized test is a reasonable match with the school curriculum in terms of the content areas covered, the test will be of little use in assessing students' learning that can be achieved by using the test. In addition to content validity, criterion-related and construct validity are important, but they are meaningful only after content validity has been established.

3. Because the results to this exercise will depend on the chapter chosen, no example answer can be given. However, whatever chapter is chosen, it is important to pay close attention to the match between what the test covers and what is actually taught.

4. a. Language appears to be the weakest area for him because his score in Language is only at the 18th percentile, whereas his scores in other areas are substantially higher.

   b. Louisa Chong has the largest performance discrepancy between Reading (89th percentile) and Science (56th percentile). Such a large discrepancy indicates that the difference is most likely significant, and very unlikely to be the result of measurement error.

   c. Language is the area that should probably be the first priority. This is because, as a group, the class is at about the 37th percentile nationally in the area of Language, whereas it ranks either above the national average or close to it in the other four areas. The low performance in the area of Language indicates that more curricula emphasis is probably needed in this area.

CHAPTER 16

Assessing Your Students' Potential

A Look at Aptitude and Readiness Measures

OVERVIEW

Every experienced teacher or parent knows that different children learn at different rates and are capable of mastering different materials. To predict how well and in what ways students will learn, educators use many different kinds of information—they listen to parents' reports, observe the child in the classroom, and consider the child's past performance in similar areas. In addition, they may use *aptitude* tests to predict how well a student will perform in a particular area.

Some people think only of intelligence or IQ tests, when they think of aptitude tests; and it is true that intelligence tests are one form of aptitude test. But aptitude is much broader than what is measured by intelligence tests. Different types of aptitude tests are used to predict how well a person will do in a particular course, vocation, or profession, or whether he or she is ready to begin school.

This chapter will help you understand what aptitude tests are, how they are used, and what makes an aptitude test effective. We will give you a classification system for organizing information about aptitude tests. We will also discuss how the proper use of aptitude tests can assist you in being an effective teacher or school administrator, and point out the dangers associated with the inappropriate use of aptitude tests.

OBJECTIVES

Upon completing your study of this chapter, you should be able to

1. Compare and contrast aptitude and achievement tests.
2. Give examples of various types of aptitude tests.

3. Give examples of appropriate ways to use aptitude measures.

4. Describe the purpose and utility of culture-fair (sometimes referred to as culture-free) aptitude tests.

5. Summarize the factors to consider in judging the appropriateness of an aptitude test for a given purpose.

6. Explain how genetic and environmental factors contribute to measures of intelligence.

7. Summarize the pros and cons of using individual and group administered aptitude tests.

8. Describe the rationale for multiple aptitude batteries.

9. Explain how school readiness tests can be used to improve instruction.

The Use of Aptitude Tests

By predicting future performance, aptitude test results allow us to select students most likely to succeed, identify those needing help, or make our instruction more effective. If you knew that the students enrolled in your algebra course were the 15 brightest students in the school, you would approach the design and delivery of instruction differently than if they were the 15 slowest learners in the school. This example raises some major issues.

- Is aptitude the same as intelligence?
- How many different kinds of aptitude tests are there?
- What can you learn about someone from scores on an aptitude test?
- What are the characteristics of a good aptitude test?
- How useful are aptitude tests with students from cultural minority groups?

Let us look at these issues now.

What Is Aptitude?

An *aptitude* is a *natural* or *acquired* ability that is necessary or facilitative for a particular purpose or activity. No matter what the area—riding a bicycle, communicating effectively with other people, doing algebra, riding horses, understanding how mechanical engines operate—some people have more aptitude than others. In other words, they learn it faster or do it better. Consequently, aptitude predicts how well a person will do some activity to a certain degree.

How an aptitude is measured depends on what is being predicted. A measure useful for measuring bicycle riding aptitude would probably not be useful for measuring aptitude to solve word puzzles. If you wanted to know the aptitude of a particular student for learning the major subjects typically taught in school, you might give a test that was designed to measure the child's ability to do such things as perceive stimuli accurately, recognize and recall what had been perceived, think logically, abstract general principles from specific information, generalize knowledge from one situation to another, and identify relationships. Such abilities might be measured on a series of tasks in which the child was asked to detect similarities and differences, recall words and numbers, solve analogy problems, classify information, and recognize absurdities. Because such tasks are related to what we expect students to learn in school, but are not subsequently influenced by the child's previous school experiences, her score on such a test would provide valuable information about how well and how quickly she would learn the material typically presented in school.

Alternatively, if you wanted to know about a child's aptitude for learning algebra, you would need a test more closely related to algebra than to general learning. Such a test might include some questions about her ability to think logically and recognize relationships, but it would also measure her ability to to do tasks similar to what she had been taught in previous math classes. If you wanted to measure a person's aptitude for clerical work, you might devise a series of tasks that are similar to the work she would actually be doing on the job—tasks that would measure attention to detail, ability to identify errors or inconsistencies, and skills in processing data. In short, the nature of the aptitude test will vary greatly depending on what is being predicted.

There is no such thing as an aptitude measure that indicates a person's general capacity to do any cognitive, physical, creative, or social activity. Although a person who has high aptitude in one area is more likely to have higher than average aptitude in another area, there is no way to measure general aptitude in the same way that we measure height or distance.

A difficulty with virtually all measures of aptitude is that they are imperfect predictors of whatever task is of interest. Not surprisingly, the more specific and closely related a measure is to the task being predicted, the more accurate the prediction tends to be. It is also important to recognize that any aptitude measure provides us with information about a student's aptitude *at a particular point in time.* That aptitude may change later as a result of maturation, learning, or experience.

To assist in understanding the many different kinds of aptitude measures, Sax (1980) proposed a framework in which aptitude tests are organized along a continuum ranging from global to specific, as shown in Figure 16.1. Global measures, such as the *Stanford–Binet Intelligence Scale,* are moderately good predictors of many different activities, whereas more specific measures, such as the *Minnesota Clerical Test,* are predictive only in a very narrow area. Tests at one end of the continuum are not necessarily any better than tests at the other, but are designed for different purposes. For example, a professional aptitude test such as the *Medical College Admissions Test* (MCAT) focuses on the specific aptitudes predictive of success in medical school, whereas a general aptitude test such as the *Stanford–Binet Intelligence Scale* includes items predictive of more general intellectual functioning. Consequently, the Medical College Admissions Test is more highly correlated with success in medical school, but it is not as good a predictor for general intellectual ability because of the way it was designed.

What Are Aptitude Tests Used For?

Using aptitude tests appropriately means using the right test for the right purpose. Let's consider some of the purposes for which aptitude tests are used most frequently.

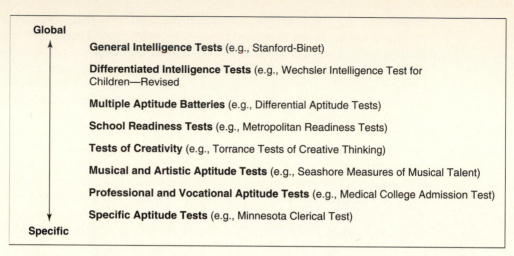

FIGURE 16.1 Arrangement of Various Types of Aptitude Tests Along a Continuum of Global to Specific

Source: Adapted from Sax, 1980.

Selecting Students for Special Programs

Often a school will have a special program for which it has more applicants than openings. In such cases, participation in the program may be limited to students who are most likely to succeed. No aptitude test can correctly identify all those who will succeed. But a good aptitude test can substantially increase the likelihood that the most appropriate candidates will be identified.

For example, consider Table 16.1, which shows the scores received by 111 students enrolled in a watch repair training school who took the *Differential Aptitude Tests* at the beginning of the school term and were graded on their performance at the end. There is a strong relationship between scores on the Space Relation subtest at the beginning and grades in the watch repair training school at the conclusion of the training. In fact, 88 percent of those scoring above the 76th percentile on the Space Relations test got an A or a B in the course. Similarly, 88 percent of

Table 16.1 Percentage of 111 Students Receiving Various Grades as a Function of Scores on the DAT Space Relations Test

Score in Percentiles on Space Relations Test	*Grades Received in Watch Repair Course*		
	D or E	**C**	**A or B**
76–100	None	12%	88%
51–75	None	20%	80%
26–50	20%	40%	40%
1–25	58%	30%	12%

Note: Format of table adapted from materials accompanying DAT. Used by permission.

those scoring below the 25th percentile got a C or lower in the course (30 percent + 58 percent). If the school had limited openings, it would be more efficient to admit only those who did well on the Space Relations subtest of the *Differential Aptitude Tests*. However, some mistakes would be made. For example, 12 percent of those who scored *below* the 25th percentile, obtained an A or a B in the course. For the total group of 111 students, the aptitude test scores led to good, but (as is always the case) not perfect, predictions.

Obviously, there are some ethical considerations in using a less than perfect test to select people who will be granted some educational opportunity. Our point here is not to argue whether such decisions *should* be made, but simply to indicate the ways in which aptitude tests *are* frequently used.

Aptitude tests are also used frequently to select children for gifted and talented programs. Since most classroom instruction is geared toward the needs of children with average ability, gifted children sometimes go unchallenged. As noted by Lyon (1974),

> Prevented from moving ahead by the rigidity of normal school procedures, . . . the gifted youngster typically takes one of three tacks: (1) he drifts into a state of lethargy and complete apathy; (2) he conceals his ability, anxious not to embarrass others or draw their ridicule by superior performance; or, (3) not understanding his frustration, he becomes a discipline problem. (p. 65)

Appropriate aptitude tests can be very useful in identifying such gifted children, who may then be placed in accelerated or advanced programs.

Because even the best aptitude tests are imperfect, such measures should be used in conjunction with other information about students' motivation, past performance, and attitude. Always remember that some students who score poorly on a given aptitude test will still be successful, and some students who score well will do poorly. Thus aptitude tests should be used to supplement—but not to replace—sound professional judgment.

Identification of Children Needing Remediation

Many children experience difficulty in school. Unless difficulties are identified and remediated early, a child can become frustrated, and the problem usually becomes worse. Over the past three decades, many special education and compensatory education programs have been developed to help students who need extra support to succeed. It is not always easy, however, to identify which children need special help. Children with severe disabilities are easy to identify, but many children without identified disabilities are also performing marginally. The sooner such children can be identified, the better their chance for success. Although federal law prohibits the placement of children in special education programs based solely on aptitude tests, such tests can help make correct decisions. Because aptitude tests are not perfect predictors, the law requires that placement decisions be based on multidisciplinary evaluations, scores on aptitude tests, observations by teachers, information from parents, and consideration of the child's past performance. Aptitude tests are sometimes particularly useful, however, because they can help identify whether a student's achievement is consistent with her potential.

Tailoring Instruction for Individual Students

Given any task, students progress at different rates and achieve different levels of mastery. An important question is whether students are achieving to their full potential. You would be appropriately concerned if you had a student who scored high on a test of general school aptitude, but was performing poorly in reading. You would want to check whether the student was experiencing health problems, having difficulty at home, felt unmotivated for some reason, or simply not responding to the instructional methods you are using. Without the aptitude test results, though, you might never get around to asking these important questions.

It is very important to make a distinction between what is measured on achievement tests and what is measured on aptitude tests. Achievement tests assess very specific types of instructional objectives such as the ability to spell certain words. How well a student does on an achievement test depends on how well she has mastered these specific instructional objectives. By contrast, aptitude tests are designed to measure abilities that do not directly depend on the particular instruction to which the student has been exposed. By comparing aptitude and achievement test scores, it is possible to know whether a student is performing at about the level you would expect. If she is performing much lower than expected, alternative instructional techniques may be needed, or other problems may be interfering with her performance.

Unfortunately, aptitude tests can also be used inappropriately in this context. If a student scores low on an aptitude test, it would be a terrible mistake for a teacher to conclude that since the student obviously lacked the potential to learn, it would be a waste of time to even *try* to help him. Even though some teachers occasionally use aptitude test scores in such an inappropriate way, we should not blame the tests. As noted by Mehrens and Lehman (1991),

> The teachers in inner city schools who do not try their hardest because of preconceived ideas that their students cannot learn have not obtained their ideas of student deficiency primarily from aptitude tests scores. Such factors as the parents' educational level, socioeconomic status, race, and occupation, all contribute to teachers' opinions concerning a child's aptitude. (p. 337)
>
> *Aptitude tests can help teachers develop realistic expectations for their students.* While we do not condone—in fact we condemn—teachers who develop fatalistic attitudes toward the learning abilities of their students, we do not think aptitude tests should be made the scapegoat. (pp. 337–338)

Organizing Instructional Groups

Many educators believe that instruction can be more effective if students of similar ability levels are grouped together. Although we are not arguing for or against this practice,[1] aptitude tests can be a useful aid in deciding which children should be placed in which group. Some people who oppose ability grouping blame the al-

---

[1]Indeed, many other educators are vehemently opposed to this practice. See, for example, Esposito (1973).

leged problems of such practices on the use of aptitude tests, and have argued that the tests are unfair to some subgroups and consequently should be ignored in making decisions about ability grouping. Though the pros and cons of ability grouping can be legitimately debated, it is inappropriate to blame the use of aptitude tests for the perceived problems with this instructional approach. In fact, research has shown that the use of aptitude tests has provided beneficial opportunities to children from low socioeconomic groups that would not have existed had more subjective criteria been used as the basis for grouping (Findley & Bryan, 1971).

Of course, decisions about the organization of instructional groups, made with the help of aptitude test scores, should not be viewed as permanent. The whole point of instructional groupings is to provide children an opportunity to learn more efficiently. If instructional grouping is used to achieve this goal, it will be necessary to periodically restructure instructional groupings.

Counseling Students About Educational and Vocational Plans

Many different aptitude tests are used in counseling students about vocational and educational options. It is logical that someone who is considering a career in mechanical engineering will probably be more successful if she scores high on aptitude measures of space relations and mechanical reasoning, whereas someone who wants a job as a secretary should possibly reconsider if she scores poorly in clerical speed, spelling, and language usage.

Aptitude test scores can be useful in predicting success in specific occupations (for example, law enforcement, computer programming). This is often done by comparing the aptitude test scores of people considering such an occupation with the scores of successful people in those same occupations, or the scores of those who successfully complete training courses for various jobs, professions, or vocations. Again though, it is important to consider scores from such aptitude tests in conjunction with other information.

Aptitude test scores should be used carefully in counseling. To see why, consider the data reported by Hopkins, Stanley, and Hopkins (1990, p. 369; see Figure 16.5 in this chapter) where they noted that the average IQ of accountants, teachers, and lawyers was approximately 120, whereas the average IQ of welders, plumbers, and auto mechanics was about 105. Does this mean that anyone who has an IQ lower than 120 should not consider becoming an accountant or lawyer? Of course not. Even though the average IQ of accountants and lawyers was 15 to 20 points higher than that of welders, plumbers, and auto mechanics, approximately 20 percent of the welders, plumbers, and auto mechanics had IQs that were higher than those of about 25 percent of the accountants and lawyers. Thus although aptitude scores can offer useful guidelines, we should not let them make decisions for us.

When aptitude tests are used to counsel students for vocational choices, it is much more useful to use tests designed to measure specific aptitudes than to use global aptitude measures, such as the *Stanford–Binet Intelligence Scale* or *Wechsler Adult Intelligence Scale*. Because global aptitude measures are less directly related to the specific requirements of different professions and vocations, they tend to be less predictive of success in different vocational areas.

Comparing Achievement and Aptitude Tests

Achievement tests measure what has been learned; aptitude tests predict the ability to learn; and intelligence tests measure general cognitive ability, which is one specific form of aptitude. Although the foregoing distinctions appear straightforward and simple, confusion arises because the three types of measures are interrelated. To some degree, all of them are a measure of what has been learned, and all of them can be used to make predictions about a student's ability to learn. They differ in the kinds of learning measured and the kinds of predictions each facilitates.

Achievement Tests

If you want to know how well a student has mastered the specific content presented in school, you should use an achievement test. Some achievement tests (particularly locally developed tests) are very course specific. Others (for example, the *Stanford Achievement Test*) are measures of general educational development that provide information about a student's knowledge across a range of courses and learning experiences. Because achievement tests are designed as measures of what a student has learned, there should be consistency between what has been taught and what is being tested. In other words, you would not expect a student to get an item correct unless she had been given relevant instruction.

Even though achievement tests are primarily designed to describe what a student has already learned, they are also useful predictors. A student's performance in the first semester of social studies is usually a good predictor of how well she will perform in the second semester of social studies. However, the scope of such prediction is usually quite narrow. Success in a specific area is a good predictor of success in that same area, but is generally not as good a predictor of success in other school-related areas. For example, even though first-semester success in social studies may be quite a good predictor of second-semester success in social studies, it is generally not as good a predictor of second-semester success in math.

So far, so good. But, some comprehensive achievement test batteries such as the *Stanford Achievement Test* predict future learning in a variety of school subjects almost as well as the best aptitude tests (Merwin & Gardner, 1962).

Aptitude Tests

Even though achievement tests are designed primarily as measures of what students have learned, if comprehensive achievement tests are such good predictors of future achievement, why do we need aptitude tests? Next, we will summarize several reasons why aptitude tests are useful in addition to achievement tests.

■ *Aptitude tests are relatively quick and economical to administer.* Whereas comprehensive achievement tests require as much as 10 to 12 hours to administer, most aptitude tests can be given in less than an hour.

Summary of the Differences Between Achievement and Aptitude Tests

It should be clear by now that achievement and aptitude tests have many similarities, but they also have important differences. In general, aptitude tests measure broader skills such as verbal and numerical problem solving, abstract reasoning, and classification skills, whereas achievement tests are tied more closely to specific school subjects and instruction. Further, achievement tests generally focus on recent learning that has occurred at school, whereas aptitude tests measure learning that has occurred over an extended period—much of it outside of school. In addition, aptitude tests are designed to predict future learning, whereas achievement tests are designed to describe current knowledge. Achievement tests are often good predictors of achievement within a narrowly focused range of related skill areas, but aptitude tests can often predict future learning across a wide range of skills or subjects. Both types of tests serve an important function in designing effective educational programs.

Characteristics of Good Aptitude Tests

The characteristics of a good aptitude test resemble those of most other tests used in education. They must demonstrate appropriate reliability and validity given their intended purpose and the students with whom they will be used. Since aptitude tests are most often used to predict some type of future performance in a variety of situations (for example, performance in college and in graduate school, job performance, or performance as a pilot), the most important evidence of validity for an aptitude test is the evidence of *predictive validity*. It is particularly important that aptitude tests differentiate between people who are likely to be successful in a specific area and those who are not. Further, the test must be feasible to administer given the constraints that are present. In many cases, the test must have appropriate norms that can be used in making selection, placement, or counseling decisions.

Because aptitude tests are frequently used to make important decisions about individuals, it is important that you adopt a "show me" attitude in judging the quality of the test that you are considering to use, such as its reliability, validity, and norms. As noted by Salvia and Ysseldyke (1988),

> Do not expect test authors to admit in the manuals that the test was poorly normed because there was no money to pay testers or that the test had inadequate reliability because they didn't develop enough test items. Test authors put the best possible face on their tests, as might be expected. You simply cannot accept the claims made by test authors and their colleagues who write the technical manuals. If you accepted them at their word, they would only have to say that they had a "good, reliable, valid, and well normed test." Test authors must *demonstrate* that their tests are reliable, valid, and well normed . . . demand numbers; do not settle for statements as to the test's [appropriateness]. Make the authors show you the proof. (pp. 549–550)

Different Types of Aptitude Tests

There are many types of aptitude tests. This section should help you understand some prominent issues related to aptitude tests and help you identify appropriate tests for your specific needs.

Intelligence Tests

Almost everybody has an opinion of what intelligence tests measure. Unfortunately, many of these opinions are incorrect. So before we move to specific examples, it is important to clarify some key concepts about intelligence tests.

What Do Intelligence Tests Measure?

People have been trying to measure intelligence systematically since the later part of the 19th century. Francis Galton, an English biologist, was one of the first to try. Encouraged by the work of his cousin, Charles Darwin, regarding the natural variation within species, Galton believed that intellectual ability could be measured using various tests of sensory discrimination and reaction time. Building on the work of Galton, James McKeen Cattell (1890) first used the term *mental test*. His test consisted of a variety of tasks requiring muscular strength, speed of movement, sensitivity to pain, reaction time, and sensory discrimination. Although Galton and Cattell found that such characteristics could be measured accurately, they were disappointed that measures of such characteristics were not consistent with other observations about mental ability.

Binet and Simon (1905) in France used a very different and more successful approach. Binet believed that characteristics such as memory, attention, and comprehension were more directly related to mental ability than the types of variables proposed by Galton and Cattell. Using this approach, Binet developed a scale consisting of 30 tasks requiring higher mental processes, and used this scale to successfully identify mentally retarded children in the Paris school system. Based on his work, Binet characterized intelligence as a single attribute that was demonstrated by *inventiveness* dependent on *comprehension* and marked by *purposefulness* and corrective *judgment* (Binet, 1911).

Since Binet, others have characterized intelligence as consisting of multiple factors or components. Spearman (1927), from his observation that performance on a variety of different tasks tended to be substantially correlated, hypothesized the existence of a general factor (*g* factor) that would account for the related performance on seemingly different tasks. Besides the *g* factor, there were some specific factors that determined the performance on specific tasks. Spearman's two-factor theory (general factor and specific factors) of intelligence has been very influential in research on intelligence and continues to receive a lot of attention.

Thurstone (1938) argued that intelligence consisted of several major groups of mental abilities (primary mental abilities), such as verbal comprehension, visual or perceptual ability, inductive reasoning, and numerical ability. He argued that a person could have high scores in one area such as spatial relations and low scores in

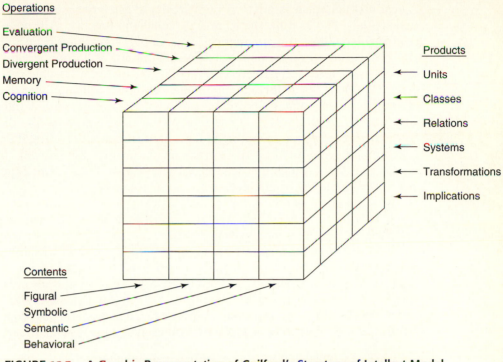

Operations
Evaluation
Convergent Production
Divergent Production
Memory
Cognition

Products
Units
Classes
Relations
Systems
Transformations
Implications

Contents
Figural
Symbolic
Semantic
Behavioral

FIGURE 16.3 **A Graphic Representation of Guilford's Structure of Intellect Model**

another area such as verbal reasoning. Guilford (1969) extended this reasoning in proposing his "structure of intellect" model, in which intelligence comprises 120 different factors described on 3 dimensions: the *operation* performed, the *product* involved, and the material or *content* involved (see Figure 16.3).

Cattell (1941, 1971) and Horn (1968, 1985), based on their empirical work, proposed another influential explanation for intelligence. They proposed that intelligence consisted of two main components: *fluid* intelligence and *crystallized* intelligence. *Fluid* intelligence tended to be nonverbal in nature, and be more related to inherent capacity, minimally dependent on specific cultural settings, such as abstract reasoning and adaptation to new situations. On the other hand, *crystallized* intelligence tended to be culturally dependent, and was usually used for tasks requiring learned and habitual responses (Gregory, 1992). Based on this theory and in an effort to minimize cultural bias in intelligence testing, Cattell developed his famous *Culture-Fair Intelligence Test;* which was designed to tap *fluid* intelligence rather *crystallized* intelligence. Distinctions between *fluid* and *crystallized* intelligence can still be seen in current intelligence testing. For example, the development of the current version of Stanford–Binet Intelligence Test is heavily influenced by this theory.

Some recent theorists of intelligence have proposed new definitions of intelligence and, as a result, some very different approaches to measuring it. Gardner (1983) proposed a theory of multiple intelligence that consists of six major and relatively independent human intelligences: linguistic (similar to verbal), musical, logical-mathematical (similar to numerical and analytical), spatial (visual-perceptual-spatial), bodily kinesthetic, and personal intelligence. Although three of the six (linguistic, logical-mathematical, and spatial) have long been under intensive study, the other three are new concepts that are not well understood. From a much broader perspective, Sternberg (1985, 1986) proposed a triachic theory of intelligence that consists of three components: componential intelligence (components of internal mechanisms for intelligent behaviors), experiential intelligence (the ability to deal with novel tasks based on previous experience with other tasks), and contextual intelligence (adapting to new environments, selecting the most suitable environment, and shaping the environment to one's advantage). Based on this model, Sternberg claims that traditional intelligence tests fail to capture some important components of intelligence.

Disagreement over the nature of intelligence will likely continue. As early as 1921, the editor of the *Journal of Educational Psychology* asked 14 prominent psychologists to define the nature of intelligence. Fourteen clearly different conceptions of intelligence were presented. Some stressed acquired learning, some the ability to think abstractly; whereas others focused on the adaptive nature of intelligence or the ability to learn. In response to the confusion produced by these articles, Peak and Boring (1926) suggested that one should define intelligence as "that which an intelligence test measures." That suggestion, as naively simplistic as it appears, still has proponents among some prominent researchers, as shown by Jensen's (1969) comment many years later.

> Intelligence, like electricity, is easier to measure than to define. . . . There is no point in arguing the question to which there is really no answer, the question of what intelligence *really* is. The best we can do is to obtain measurements of certain kinds of behavior and look at their relationships to other phenomena and see if these relationships make any kind of sense and order. (p. 6)

Definitions of intelligence in the early 1900s tended to regard it as some innate and unchangeable capacity. Later definitions, such as that given by Cleary, Humphreys, Kendrick, and Westman (1975, p. 19), emphasized acquired behaviors rather than innate capacity. This definition states that intelligence is "the entire repertoire of acquired skills, knowledge, learning sets, and generalization tendencies considered intellectual in nature that are available at any one period in time." As Mehrens and Lehman (1984, p. 362) point out, "Intelligence is not something people have, like brains and nervous systems. Rather it is a description of how people behave." More recently, Sternberg (1998) has argued that abilities which are measured by IQ tests "are forms of developing expertise" (p. 11), and these abilities should not be regarded as some largely inborn and fixed constructs.

Despite the obvious lack of consensus on the definition of intelligence, *learning* from experience and *adaptation* to new environments are now generally considered core functions of intelligence (Gregory, 1996). Also, based on voluminous data, it is clear that the current intelligence tests have considerable degree of predictive value about many meaningful and important academic behaviors. There are, however, different types of intelligence tests based on different theoretical perspectives; therefore, in selecting and interpreting the results of any intelligence test, it is important to understand clearly the test developer's definition of intelligence.

Further, it is important to note that not everyone agrees that intelligence can or should be measured (see, for example, Garcia, 1981; Gould, 1981; Houts, 1975). Even the legal system has become involved with contradictory rulings as summarized in Chapter 2. For the time being, however, it is clear that intelligence tests continue to be widely used in our educational system. It is therefore important for educators to have a basic understanding of what intelligence tests measure and how they can be used most appropriately.

Is Intelligence Acquired or Inherited?

The argument over whether intelligence is inherited or acquired (often referred to as the nature–nurture controversy) has raged for years. Until the early twentieth century, most experts believed that intelligence was mostly, if not totally, inherited. Today, most agree that it is a combination of inheritance and acquisition. Believing that intelligence is partly acquired does not rule out an important genetic influence. For example, a great basketball player has many *acquired* skills even though inherited abilities are likely to have influenced the speed of development and the maximum level of skill achieved.

Hundreds of research studies have examined the issue of heredity versus environment with respect to intelligence, at least as it has been traditionally measured. Erlenmeyer-Kimling and Jarvik (1963) reviewed 52 studies examining the correlation of intelligence test scores between identical twins, fraternal twins, siblings, relatives, and genetically unrelated children who had been raised together or apart. Based on more than 30,000 correlational pairings, they produced average correlations, some of which are shown in Table 16.2.

These data provide strong evidence that both environment and heredity contribute to a person's score on intelligence tests. For example, if heredity did not contribute, the correlation for identical twins reared apart would be expected to be substantially lower than .75. If environment did not contribute, the correlation between genetically unrelated children reared together would be close to 0, but it is .23.

The furious nature–nurture controversy in intelligence testing has centered on the issue of how to explain the consistent performance difference on a variety of different intelligence tests between some ethnic or racial groups. Other than test bias hypothesis we alluded to in previous chapters, two other explanations have been fiercely debated over the years: genetic explanation and environmental explanation.

Table 16.2 **Correlations of IQ Scores for Pairs of Children of Differing Genetic and Environmental Circumstances**

Correlation Between	r
Genetically unrelated children, reared apart	−.01
Genetically unrelated children, reared together	.23
Siblings, reared together	.49
Identical twins, reared apart	.75
Identical twins, reared together	.87

Although intelligence as a trait with strong genetic inheritance has been largely accepted by most people familiar with the research literature, the question remains whether the observed differences in measured IQ between blacks and whites is primarily a function of genetic factors or environmental factors. The genetic explanation for such difference was first implied in an article by Arthur Jensen (1969), in which such explanation was formulated as a hypothesis. That article immediately led to the fierce debate nationwide about the issue, which has lasted up to now (for example, Herrnstein & Murray, 1994). The major evidence used for the genetic explanation has come from a large body of research that has shown a strong genetic component in intelligence. The problem with such hypothesis for *between* group difference is that it is largely based on *extrapolation* from *within* group research results. Scarr (1981) insisted that it was entirely inappropriate to infer about the cause for *between* group difference based on what we knew about *within* group differences. Even if we acknowledge that a strong genetic component exists in measured intelligence, an environmental hypothesis is entirely tenable for the observed *between* group difference. Scarr-Salapatek's (1971, p. 1226) simple example explains this point well: you plant two randomly drawn samples of seeds from a genetically heterogeneous population in two types of soil, good conditions and poor conditions. The heights of the fully grown plants from these two soil conditions could be compared. Although *within* each type of soil, individual variations in the heights are primarily genetically determined, the average difference in height *between* the two samples is mainly a function of environment. Indeed, some important research (Scarr, Pakstis, Katz, & Barker, 1977) that has *directly* examined this issue has not supported the strong hypothesis of genetic racial differences in intelligence.

The nature–nurture issue aside, the more important question in which educators should be interested is how much can environment affect a person's intelligence as measured by current tests. Although performance on intelligence tests tends to show remarkable stability over a long period, that stability may partially be the result of stable environment, whether good or bad (Anastasi, 1988). So by itself, the observed stability in intelligence may not be so informative about how intelligence may change under drastically *different* environmental conditions. One study (Scarr & Weinberg, 1976, 1983) provides some important insight into this question. In this study, black and interracial children were located who had been adopted early in life by middle- or upper-middle-class white families. These children were tested using the most popular intelligence tests, and their average performance was above the national norm, and substantially above other black children in the same geographical areas (20 points, or $1\frac{1}{3}$ standard deviations). It was also shown that the earlier the adoption had occurred for the children, the higher their IQ scores. The results of this study indicate that *early* environment is very important in shaping a person's intellectual development as measured by typical IQ tests.

Based on many different research studies, there is little doubt that both heredity and environment are important contributors to a child's score on intelligence tests. Obviously, educators cannot change the inherited component that contributes to intelligence test scores. We can, however, structure the environment so that it facilitates learning. Of course, individual differences in how children learn will not be eliminated by changes in the environment. Finally, even though the influence of inherited components cannot be eliminated, it is important to recognize that intelligence is not unchangeable.

Measuring Aptitudes for Culturally Different Children

Because aptitude tests are often used to make important decisions, many people worry about the influence of cultural differences on such test scores. Differences in language usage and mastery is one of the most obvious concerns. But other cultural differences may also affect performance on aptitude tests—differences in motivation and competitiveness, attitudes toward schooling, familiarity with test-taking procedures, and opportunities to learn the skills measured by the test.

Concerns about cultural bias in aptitude tests have led to the development of what are often referred to as *culture-free* or *culture-fair* tests. The goal of such tests is to minimize to eliminate the effects of extraneous cultural influences so that resulting scores are a pure measure of aptitude. Many different tests purport to be culture fair, and most of them share a number of characteristics.

1. Test materials are mostly nonverbal and include diagrams or pictures appropriate for the cultures with which the test will be used.
2. Additional time is provided beyond that thought to be necessary so that speed of completion will not be an important factor.
3. Individualized testing or other motivational techniques are used to encourage participants to do as well as possible.
4. Simplified test procedures are used to eliminate the effects of test-taking experience.

While all the preceding are consistent with good test construction and administration practices, research results show that culture-free testing is more an ideal than a reality, and the typical instruments developed for the purpose generally have not lived up to the expectations (Anastasi, 1988; Hopkins, Stanley, & Hopkins, 1990; Linn & Gronlund, 1995).

The concern about having culture-free tests was a response to the recognition that African-American, Latin-American, and some other minority groups consistently received lower scores than white children. Because it is often socially accepted that there are no genetic differences in intelligence among subcultures, such differences in scores are often accepted as *prima facia* evidence that the tests must be biased. Efforts were consequently initiated to develop general aptitude measures that were predictive of later school success, but on which members of different ethnic groups did not score differently.

Unfortunately, the premise behind such test development efforts may be flawed. As noted by some, it is as incorrect to condemn tests for revealing inequalities between different ethnic groups as it is for the residents of Bismarck, North Dakota, to condemn the use of thermometers because it was minus 11 degrees in Bismarck when it was 73 degrees in Miami, Florida (Clifford & Fishman, 1963, p. 87). The important point is that if inequalities *do* exist, the measuring device should not be blamed. If, on the other hand, the measuring device is creating the appearance of inequalities when none exist, the measuring device should be blamed—and changed.

Obviously, tests can be biased in a variety of ways, and some are. Consider a hypothetical item on a *geography* test where Latin-Americans score lower than whites.

Which city is in the closest proximity to Los Angeles?

a. San Francisco   c. Chicago
b. New York   d. Atlanta

If the lower average scores of Latin-Americans occurred because fewer Latin-Americans knew that San Francisco was closest to Los Angeles, then the test is still a "culture-fair" test for those two groups. If the difference in average scores occurred because fewer Latin-Americans knew the meaning of the word *proximity,* then the test is linguistically biased against Latin-Americans.

In the same sense, consider the time it takes to run the 100-yard dash. If an electronically controlled stopwatch reveals that the average time for 10 African-American athletes is 2/10 of a second faster than the average time for 10 white athletes, is the measurement device biased against whites? Of course not. The question in culture-fair testing is whether the vocabulary, procedures, or tasks in any given test are biased against one subculture, not whether people in two groups score differently.

One of the best known efforts to develop culture-free tests is the *Culture–Fair Intelligence Test* (CFIT) developed by R. B. Cattell. The final version of the test was exclusively reviewed by experts from different cultures to eliminate those items that might be biased against one particular culture. Tasks are simplified, and extensive verbal directions are given to make sure that the tasks are understood. Emphasis is on nonverbal tasks. In spite of this, there is no empirical evidence that the CFIT is a better measure of intelligence than other widely used intelligence tests (Anastasi, 1988).

A somewhat different approach to developing a culturally fair measure of aptitude has resulted in the *System of Multi-Cultural Pluralistic Assessment* (SOMPA) developed by Mercer (1977). This approach uses two different sets of norms—a national norm group and a norm group that is similar to the examinee in social and cultural background. The assessment of aptitude is made by collecting information from two sources.

■ A test session in which the child is given the *Wechsler Intelligence Scale for Children-Revised* (WISC-R), physical dexterity tasks, and the Bender Gestalt test

■ Information from the child's primary caretaker, which is designed to measure the differences between the child's culture at home and the culture at the school

Using this additional information, statistical "corrections" are made to the WISC-R score as the best estimate of the child's intellectual aptitude.

Uncorrected scores are used to determine the child's immediate educational needs, whereas corrected scores are used to determine the child's "latent scholastic potential." So far, there is no evidence that this relatively elaborate procedure results in any better information than traditional measures of aptitude. In fact, Hilliard has concluded that the SOMPA had all the weaknesses of the old tests *and* a whole host of new weaknesses all its own, especially its absence of construct validity (National Institute of Education, 1979). Reynolds (1985) notes that "the SOMPA cannot be recommended for use at this time. Its conceptual, technical, and practical problems are simply too great. Nevertheless, it was an innovative, gallant effort. . . . Current evidence would point to failure; however, it may serve as a springboard in some ways for future assessment systems" (p. 1521).

Although culture-fair testing has largely failed to demonstrate any advantage over traditional methods, the rationale behind the development of such tests is good. Children should be given an opportunity to demonstrate their skills and aptitude in a way that is free from extraneous influences. To the degree that tests are influenced by extraneous variables, we will be measuring something different from what we want to measure, and the test will be less valid for that particular purpose. But there is no such thing as an aptitude test that is totally independent of previous experience. The focus of any aptitude testing should be to make sure that every child who takes the test has an opportunity to do as well as possible, and that the influence of extraneous variables is minimized.

The results from the research on *culture-free* or *culture-fair* testing indicate that current intelligence and aptitude tests themselves may not be systematically biased against minority groups as they were previously perceived since, typically, racial or ethnic group differences of similar magnitudes appeared on *culture-fair* tests as they did on more traditional intelligence and aptitude tests (Koch, 1984). This indicates that the explanation for group differences on the traditional intelligence tests may probably lie elsewhere, such as environmental factors and influences.

How Useful Are Intelligence Test Scores?

The main purpose of aptitude tests, of which intelligence tests are one example, is to predict future performance. How well do intelligence test scores do that? Although a complete answer would fill a book, we can give you a number of examples to provide the basic understanding needed for appropriate use of intelligence test results in educational settings.

Intelligence test scores and age.   Hundreds of research studies show that intelligence test scores become more stable as children grow older. Kubiszyn and Borich (1987) estimated that the correlation among IQ tests given at ages 10 and 14 would be about .90; the same tests given at ages 6 and 14 would correlate .70; and at ages 2 and 14, only .20.

It is now generally accepted that results from infant "intelligence" tests have little predictive validity. By the time children reach age 6, however, measures of intelligence are relatively stable. The stability of group-administered intelligence tests is somewhat lower than that of individually administered tests although the gradual increase in stability as children grow older is the same. Dozens of studies demonstrate that for school-aged children, results of individualized or group intelligence tests are highly correlated with scores on academic achievement tests. Most of those studies demonstrate correlation coefficients of .70 to .80 (see Hopkins, Stanley & Hopkins, 1990).

Based on work reported by Wechsler (1955), it was first believed that measured intelligence tends to increase until about age 30 and then begins to diminish gradually. However, Wechsler's data were based on a *cross-sectional* sample in which many variables were not controlled, especially the confounding of educational disparities among different age groups: younger subjects or generations were generally better educated than their elder counterparts. Many subsequent research studies using more appropriate designs, however, have shown that intellectual functioning as measured by intelligence tests is much more resilient to aging than previously thought, especially such aspects of intelligence as verbal, spatial visualization, and reasoning (Baltes, 1968; Bayley, 1955; Botwinick, 1984; Hopkins, et al., 1990; Jarvik, Eisdorfer, & Blum, 1973; Shaie, 1980, 1984; Shaie & Willis, 1984). The environment in which a person lives may contribute to increases or decreases in intellectual performance, but unless there are health problems or other disrupting circumstances, a 50-year-old will have as much or more intellectual ability as she had at age 25.

Intelligence tests as meaningful indicators.   Some interesting evidence about the validity of intelligence test scores is found in the results of a study conducted during World War II, in which more than 90,000 recruits were tested on the *Army General Classification Test* (see Stewart, 1947). Intelligence test scores of these people, averaged for each occupation, are partially summarized in Figure 16.4. These data indicate clearly that in the 1940s intelligence test scores were clearly related to occupational level. For example, the median IQ for accountants is more than 30 points higher than that for miners. These differences are consistent with what one would logically expect. However, there is wide variability within groups. For example, even though the average IQ of barbers was 94, 25 percent of the barbers had IQs over 106. Similarly, even though the average IQ for accountants was 123, many had IQs less than 115, and some less than 100. The average intelligence score for different occupations can be somewhat misleading. As pointed out by White (1982) and ETS (1980), the correlation between occupational level and IQ is only about .30— much lower than most people assume. Furthermore, there are people with very high IQ scores in every occupation. Nonetheless, the fact that average IQ varies by occupation lends strength to the position that intelligence tests are measuring something important.

Research studies show that intelligence tests generally show similar meaningful relationships with other independent criteria, especially academic criteria. For example, substantial relationships (.40–.70) were reported between *Wechsler Adult Intelligence Scale-Revised* (WAIS-R) scores and achievement tests scores, especially for WAIS-R verbal score. Also, strong relationships were found between WAIS (earlier version of WAIS-R) scores and high school rank and college grades (Conry & Plant, 1965). Educational attainment (as measured by years of education completed) was also found to be strongly related to performance on WAIS-R

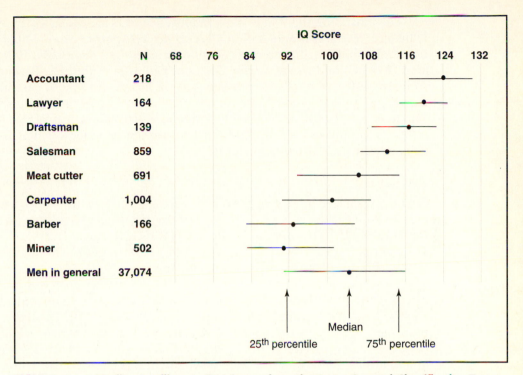

FIGURE 16.4   Median Intelligence Test Scores from the Army General Classification Test for Men Having Different Occupations

Source: Hopkins & Stanley, 1981, and Stewart, 1947; all data converted to deviation IQ equivalents.

(Matarazzo & Herman, 1984). Similar evidence abounds for other popular intelligence tests. Although, as we discussed previously, there may not be a consensus on what intelligence tests are measuring, based on all these empirical results, we can at least conclude that intelligence tests are most probably measuring something *meaningful* that is *valued* in this society.

Individually Administered Intelligence Tests

Most intelligence tests used in educational settings are group-administered tests. Individually administered intelligence tests are used primarily for clinical applications such as deciding whether children need special education services. Individual tests require more training to administer, provide greater flexibility in testing, can be used with younger children, and depend less on the child's ability to read. Although they are more costly and time consuming to use, individually administered tests provide a number of benefits. The examiner is able to observe the respondent's approach to problem solving and is better able to control extraneous influences that might affect performance. Thus individualized administrations generally result in more reliable measurement and a better understanding of what factors contribute to the child's score.

The most prominent individual intelligence tests are probably the Wechsler intelligence test series and the *Stanford–Binet Intelligence Scale.* Other frequently used individual intelligence tests include the *Kaufman Assessment Battery for Children* (K-ABC) and the McCarthy Scales of Children's Abilities. Because there are so many different intelligence scales, it is important for you to carefully consider the reliability and validity data for a particular test before using it. One excellent source is the *Mental Measurements Yearbook,* which offers critical reviews of many tests. As examples, we'll give you a brief overview of several widely used individually administered intelligence tests.

Wechsler Tests

Current Wechsler intelligence test series consist of three tests designed for different age groups: *Wechsler Adult Intelligence Scale-Revised* (WAIS-R; ages 16 and up), *Wechsler Intelligence Scale for Children-III* (WISC-III; ages 6 years to 16 years and 11 months), and *Wechsler Preschool and Primary Scale of Intelligence-Revised* (WPPSI-R; ages 3 years to 7 years and 3 months). The three tests share similar structure and consist of similar subscales. For illustrative purposes, we will briefly discuss only the WISC-III since it is used most often for school population.

Wechsler Intelligence Scale for Children-III (WISC-III) is the revised and renormed version of the popular *Wechsler Intelligence Scale for Children-Revised* (WISC-R), and it shares substantially with WISC-R in content and other features and qualities. Since it is relatively new, much of our discussion will be related to its early version of WISC-R because a substantial body of research literature has accumulated for it.

WISC-R is the most widely uesd intelligence test for 6- to 16-year-old children. As is the case with all Wechsler tests, besides the full-scale IQ score, the test yields verbal and performance IQs, with each consisting of six subscales.

Verbal	Performance
Information	*Picture Completion*
Similarities	*Picture Arrangement*
Arithmetic	*Block Design*
Vocabulary	*Objective Assembly*
Comprehension	*Coding*
Digit Span (optional)	*Mazes* (optional)

Bortner (1985, p. 1713) noted that the WISC-R was "the best standardized, most objectively administered and scored test of its kind. . . . The manual is a model for other test makers." Norms are based on a sample of 2200 children stratified on the basis of age, sex, race (white-nonwhite), geographic region, occupation of head of household, and urban-rural residence. Reported reliabilities are in the .90s. Although little validity data were reported in the original test manual, subsequent research has shown that WISC-R scores correlated substantially with other intelligence tests, such as Stanford–Binet test, and with measures of academic achievement (Kaufman & Van Hagen, 1977; Brooks, 1977; Sattler, 1988; Sattler &

Ryan, 1981). Since the primary difference between the WISC-III and the WISC-R is the updated norm, there is reason to believe that the WISC-III will exhibit similar technical qualities similar to the WISC-R.

Stanford–Binet Intelligence Scale

The fourth edition of *Stanford–Binet Intelligence Scale* (S-B) (Thorndike, Hagen, & Sattler, 1986) is the latest edition of the intelligence scale first developed by Alfred Binet in 1905 and later revised for use with American children in 1916. The S-B is designed for persons between ages 2 and 23 and yields a single score based on how well the subject performs a variety of tasks requiring responses to concrete pictorial stimuli at younger ages and abstract verbal stimuli at older ages. The current S-B has been heavily influenced by Cattell's theory of intelligence, that is, crystallized abilities (more context-dependent and school-related) and fluid/analytic abilities (more cognitive in nature and less context-dependent). Besides crystallized/fluid distinction, S-B has a more comprehensive short-term memory component than other intelligence tests. Tasks on S-B include

Crystallized abilities

Verbal Reasoning

Vocabulary
Comprehension
Absurdities
Verbal relations

Quantitative Reasoning

Quantitative
Number series
Equation building

Fluid/analytic abilities

Abstract/Visual Reasoning

Pattern analysis
Copying
Matrices
Paper folding and cutting

Short-term memory

Bead memory
Memory for sentences
Memory for digits
Memory for objects

Standardized on about 5000 subjects ranging in age from 2 to 23 years, the normative sample was considered representative of the target population. The test appears to have excellent psychometric properties, with impressive reliability data, both for internal consistency and stability over time. Research studies show that there is a great deal of support for its predictive and concurrent validity.

Kaufman Assessment Battery for Children (K-ABC)

K-ABC is the newest addition to the collection of widely used intelligence tests. Several characteristics of K-ABC distinguish it from other intelligence tests. As its title indicates, K-ABC was designed only for children ranging from age of 2-6 (two years and six months) to 12-5 (twelve years and five months). The K-ABC was developed based on the theory that intelligence is defined by how efficiently people process information, which can be divided into sequential processing and simultaneous processing. The Sequential Processing subtests on K-ABC measure performance related to serial or temporal arrangement of verbal, numerical, or visual-perceptual information. The Simultaneous Processing subtests, on the other hand, require synthesis and organization of visual-perceptual or spatial information in an immediate or wholistic fashion. These two scales are designed to provide information about what type of learner—sequential or simultaneous—a student is so that optimal instructional approach may be designed to match the learning style. Children who score high on sequential processing "are presumed to learn best by encountering small amounts of information in consecutive, step-by-step order, such as a series of clear-cut verbal instructions." Children who score high on simultaneous processing "are presumed to learn best by integrating and synthesizing many related pieces of information at the same time, such as found in visual media (pictures, maps, or charts)" (Gregory, 1996, p.182). The K-ABC also includes an Achievement scale that is supposed to measure content areas more directly related to schooling.

The K-ABC includes the following subtests:

Mental Processing Composite

Sequential Processing Scale	Simultaneous Processing Scale
Hand movement	Magic windows
Number recall	Face recognition
Word order	Gestalt closure
	Triangles
	Matrix analogies
	Spatial memory
	Photo series

Achievement Scale

Expressive vocabulary
Arithmetic
Riddles
Reading/decoding
Reading/understanding

Standardized on a nationally representative sample of two thousand children, K-ABC has good reliability results for both internal consistency and score stability. Empirical evidence for the validity of K-ABC is generally good although not as clear-cut as for reliability. Also, K-ABC tends to show smaller racial or ethnic group differences than those typically observed on other intelligence tests. Although K-ABC is regarded as innovative in its approach and interesting in its design, some questions remain concerning the meaningfulness of the distinction between the two mental processing scales, and the appropriateness of the Achievement scale (Conoley, 1990; Goetz & Hall, 1984; Keith, 1985, 1986; Strommen, 1988).

Examples of Group-Administered Aptitude Tests

Although the data they yield is not as precise, group-administered aptitude tests are used more extensively in educational settings because they cost substantially less to administer, and teachers, who have received basic inservice training, can give them. Most group aptitude tests provide both verbal and nonverbal scores. Following are brief descriptions of two widely used group administered aptitude tests.

Cognitive Abilities Test (CogAT)

This test was developed as a companion to the *Iowa Tests of Basic Skills* for children in grades K through 13. The test consists of a nonreading test for kindergarten and first grade children and provides verbal, quantitative, and nonverbal scores for older children. The most recent version of this test became available in 1993. CogAT was standardized concurrently with the Iowa Test of Basic Skills so as to facilitate the comparison of aptitude and achievement. According to Ansorge (1985), the test has high reliability and correlates between .65 and .78 with the Stanford-Binet and in the .70s to .80s with the ITBS. Administration requires about 1 hour and 40 minutes although no time limit is imposed. According to the manual, correlations with school grades are about .50.

The Otis–Lennon School Ability Test

This test can be administered in as little as 30 minutes at lower grade levels, and about 50 minutes at the higher grade levels. It is designed for use with children in grades K through 12. Though designed to measure verbal, numerical, and abstract reasoning abilities, it yields a single IQ score. It consists of six levels, with the first three requiring no reading ability. Norms are based on a very large nationwide standardization sample, and were done concurrently with the *Stanford Achievement Test* and the *Metropolitan Achievement Test*. Reliabilities are generally above .90. Evidence for validity is based on correlations with achievement tests mostly in the .70s, correlations with teacher's grades between .50 and .75, and correlations with other aptitude tests between .70 and .90.

Application Problem 1

You are having a conference with the parents of a third grader who has just moved into your district. The parents tell you that the child was given an IQ test at the end of last year in the school district from which they just moved. The results indicated she had an IQ in the lowest 25 percent of all the children tested. The principal of the last school reportedly told the parents they should not ever expect much from their daughter since IQ determines how much a child is able to learn in school and IQ does not change. What advice would you give them?

Multiple Aptitude Batteries

Some experts believe that an adequate representation of aptitude requires a profile of scores that describe relatively independent abilities. Such tests are described as multiple aptitude test batteries. The earliest such battery (the *Chicago Test of Primary Mental Abilities*) was developed by Thurstone (1938) using factor analysis techniques. Mehrens and Lehman (1991) suggest that their development was due to the growth of vocational and educational counseling because such tests provided the kind of information counselors were seeking to guide people into different vocations, professions, and schooling options.

The rationale for multiple aptitude batteries is seductively simple, as described in the administration manual for the Differential Aptitude Tests.

> Let us suppose that two students have taken a . . . test which is comprised equally of verbal and numerical items. John answers only a few of the verbal items correctly, but gets almost every numerical item right. Jim, on the other hand, picks up very few points on the numerical part, but answers almost every verbal item correctly. If John and Jim are the same age, they will be classed, by this test, as having the same IQ—yet they are *not* the same in their abilities. . . . The need for differential measurement—and multiple scores—is self-evident. (p. 2)

Although the rationale for multiple aptitude batteries is appealing, existing research does not provide strong evidence that differential prediction, which is supposedly made possible by multiple aptitude batteries, has been very effective. Generally, the different aptitudes measured by these tests tend to be highly correlated, and very few activities require very high skill in one aptitude and low skill in other aptitudes. However, multiple aptitude batteries are still used frequently. Examples of several multiple aptitude batteries are given next.

Differential Aptitude Tests (DAT)

First published in 1947, the DAT has been revised periodically, most recently in 1982 (Bennett, Seashore, & Westman, 1982). Over the years, DAT has become one of the most widely used multiple aptitude test batteries. The DAT consists of the following eight independent tests for students in grades 8 through 12:

1. Verbal Reasoning
2. Numerical Ability
3. Abstract Reasoning
4. Clerical Speed and Accuracy
5. Mechanical Reasoning
6. Space Relations

7. Spelling
8. Language Usage

Norms for the test are based on more than 60,000 public and private school students in 64 districts from 32 states. Percentile and stanine norms are given in the manual for male and female students in each grade from 8 through 12. Reliabilities for the test are typically in the .90s, and dozens of studies demonstrate that DAT scores are predictive of high school achievement in both academic and vocational programs. According to Anastasi (1988, p. 394), however, the evidence is less encouraging with regard to differential prediction.

The General Aptitude Test Battery (GATB)

The GATB was developed by the U.S. Employment Service. It is used frequently in state employment offices for counseling and job referral and is available to public school programs. Although the original norms are quite old, hundreds of recent studies provide evidence of the test's reliability (high .80s to low .90s) and validity. The 12 tests included in the GATB yield the following 9 factor scores, which can be grouped into 3 areas:

Cognitive

- *General Learning Ability*—the sum of scores for vocabulary, arithmetic reasoning, and three-dimensional space.
- *Verbal Aptitude*—measured by the respondent indicating which two words in each set are either the same or opposite in meaning.
- *Numerical Aptitude*—combines scores from the computation and arithmetic reasoning tests.

Perceptual

- *Spatial Aptitude*—a measure of the ability to comprehend two-dimensional representation of three-dimensional objects and the ability to visualize the effects of movement in three dimensions.
- *Form Perception*—requires the respondent to match identical drawings of tools in one test and of geometric forms in the other.
- *Clerical Perception*—requires the respondent to match names rather than pictures or forms.

Psychomotor

- *Motor Coordination*—requires the respondent to make specified pencil marks in a series of squares.
- *Finger Dexterity*—requires the assembling and disassembling of rivets and washers.
- *Manual Dexterity*—requires the respondent to transfer and reverse pegs in a board.

Hunter (1982, 1994) suggested that the nine specific factors could be combined into three general factors: cognitive, perceptual, and psychomotor. Each of the three general factors would consist of three original specific factors in the order indicated. Empirical results (Hunter, 1982) show that the general factors have more predictive power than the original specific factors.[2]

School Readiness Tests

Readiness tests, used most frequently at kindergarten and first grade levels, are a type of aptitude test designed to determine if children are ready to begin formal instruction. According to Anastasi (1988), "School readiness refers essentially to the attainment of prerequisite skills, knowledge, attitudes, motivations, and other appropriate behavioral traits that enable the learner to profit maximally from school instruction" (pp. 441–442). In most cases, readiness tests emphasize the prerequisites for reading instruction; however, some tests also measure readiness for numerical computation, writing, and behavioral prerequisites for school, such as ability to pay attention for sustained periods.

For many years, people believed that readiness was a maturational characteristic, and tests were designed to determine if children had matured sufficiently to begin school. It is true that some sorts of maturation are essential for academic learning (for example, to learn to write, a child must have developed sufficient motor skills to be able to hold a pencil). However, the notion that school readiness is strictly a function of maturation may lead to the inappropriate conclusion that when a child scores low on a school readiness test, there is nothing that can be done except to wait. In reality, low scores on a school readiness test suggest that the child has not yet acquired the prerequisite skills *and* that the teacher needs to design appropriate instruction to assist the child in developing those skills. As Mehrens (1982) noted, "Aptitude test scores should be used in helping teachers form realistic expectations of students; they should not be used to help teachers develop fatalistic expectations" (p. 140).

Two cautions are in order. First, there may not be sufficient data substantiating the predictive validity of school readiness tests in general. The prerequisites measured may be logical enough, but there is not sufficient evidence to show that children who score low cannot be successful. This is particularly true for those readiness tests that can be administered in a very short time. Thus decisions about individual children based on school readiness test scores should be made carefully and only in conjunction with other information. Second, school readiness tests are sometimes used as measures of current functioning or to document student progress. Because the tests were not designed as achievement measures, such uses are generally inappropriate and should be avoided.

---

[2]Because of space limit, we did not discuss some other types of aptitude tests, such as tests of musical and artistic aptitudes. Interested readers are referred to Worthen, Borg, and White (1993) for information about these aptitude tests.

Since the early 1970s, a large number of school readiness tests have been developed. Excellent discussions of the criteria for selecting readiness tests and analyses of several available tests are presented by Salvia and Ysseldyke (1988) and Meisels (1978). Two of the more widely used readiness tests are described next.

Metropolitan Readiness Tests

MRT is a "group administered test designed to assess a diverse range of prereading skills . . . and more advanced skills that are important in beginning reading and mathematics" (Nurss & McGauvran, 1986, p. 7). Level I (preschool through midkindergarten) assesses immediate recall of words; discrimination of initial sounds; recognition of uppercase and lowercase letters; ability to match a series of letters, words, numbers, and other symbols; and mastery of basic cognitive concepts and complex grammatical structure. Level II (midkindergarten through beginning of first grade) has ten subtests: quantitative language, beginning consonants, sound–letter correspondence, visual matching, finding patterns, school language, listening, quantitative concepts, quantitative operations, and copying. Within Levels I and II, separate norms are provided for fall, midyear, and spring. Reliabilities are generally in the high .80s and low .90s, and the test is an unusually good predictor of achievement on the Stanford Achievement Test (with correlations as high as .83 between the prereading composite score on the MRT and the total SAT scores) and a modest predictor of achievement on the Metropolitan Achievement Test.

Boehm Test of Basic Concepts–Revised (BTBC-R)

The BTBC-R (Boehm, 1986) assesses a child's knowledge of 50 abstract, relational concepts that occur frequently in preschool and early primary curricula. According to Boehm (1986, p. 1), these particular concepts are "both fundamental to understanding verbal instruction and essential for early school achievement." The test was designed to identify those children who do not understand these essential concepts and consequently are at risk for later learning problems. The test requires approximately 40 minutes to administer for a group. In taking the test, the child is required to mark the picture that best answers the question read by the teacher (for example, "Mark the one where the boy is *next* to the horse"). Reliability of the test is somewhat lower than for many readiness tests (.65 to .80), with test–retest coefficients after one year being about .70. BTBC-R scores correlate modestly (about .40) with achievement after one year.

Tests of Creativity

Some experts believe that creativity is a part of intelligent behavior and is adequately measured with existing tests of intelligence. Others believe that creativity is a distinct ability. It is logical that to be creative one must be reasonably intelligent, but it is not necessarily true that one must be creative to score high on an IQ test.

It is easy to think of words that are related to creativity—*ingenuity, originality, inventiveness*—but to operationally define creativity without using such words is a formidable task. For example, when we speak of creativity, are we talking about a creative process or a creative product or both? Is creativity more closely aligned with divergent thinking or inductive logic? Who is more "creative"—the person who comes up with a multitude of unworkable solutions to a problem or the person who comes up with one highly effective solution?

The most widely known and best documented tests of creativity are *Guilford's Aptitudes Research Project Test of Divergent Thinking* (Guilford & Hoepfner, 1971), and the *Torrance Tests of Creative Thinking* (Torrance, 1965). Current tests of creativity should be viewed as experimental efforts and should be used very carefully, if at all, by practitioners. Predictive validity tends to be low (Hoepfner, 1967); the tests are usually too unreliable—about .65—for individual use (Yamamoto, 1962; Cooper, 1991), and the construct validity of these tests is considered weak (Chase, 1985; Cooper, 1991). As an example of the types of tests available, a brief description of one of the most popular is given next.

Torrance Tests of Creative Thinking (TTCT)

This is really a series of tests consisting of Thinking Creatively with Words (a series of seven verbal subtests), Thinking Creatively with Pictures (a series of three pictorial subtests), Thinking Creatively with Sounds and Words (two subtests administered using a record that provides both instructions and stimuli), and Thinking Creatively in Action and Movement (in which all responses are limited to motor responses). As an example of the kinds of items included on the tests, consider the subtests of Thinking Creatively with Words. In this battery, respondents are shown a picture and are asked to write all the questions they would ask to find out what is happening, list the possible causes of the action shown in the picture, and list all possible consequences of the action. Another item asks respondents to list all the unusual uses of a common object he or she can think of. The individual test items are described as activities, and the instructions emphasize that respondents are to have fun with the test.

The tests are designed to be used at kindergarten through adult levels, but below the fourth grade these tests have to be administered individually and orally. Two equivalent forms of each battery are available, and speed is an important component of scores on most activities. Typically reported test-retest reliabilities range from .60 to .80 (Haensly & Torrance, 1990).

There are four possible scores for each activity: fluency (the number of relevant responses), flexibility (the number of different categories of response), originality (whether responses are routine or unique), and elaboration (the amount of detail used in responses). Scoring can be done only by people who have been trained, and tentative norms are available in current editions. In his review of the TTCT, Chase (1985, p. 1632) notes,

> the tests are engaging to take. However, the theory of this trait is loosely formed and is not well equipped to become the basis for generating hypotheses. The TTCT, therefore, does not have a firm base in construct validation. Reliabilities are adequate, especially

for assessing group changes or differences, but the subareas in the test—flexibility, fluency, originality—are clearly overlapping and suggest that a single total score might be appropriate. . . . Torrance originally presented the tests for the purpose of "research and experimentation." It appears that this reservation still is an appropriate one for users and potential users of the TTCT.

Professional and Vocational Aptitude Tests

Many academic, professional, and vocational training programs have a limited number of openings. To make placement as fair as possible, aptitude tests are used to identify those individuals most likely to succeed. Examples of such tests include the *Scholastic Assessment Test* (SAT) for admissions to undergraduate colleges and universities, the Graduate Record Examination (GRE) for admission to graduate school, the *Law School Admission Test* (LSAT) and the *Medical College Admission Test* (MCAT) for admission to training in those respective specialties. All are secure measures that are administered only by licensed centers, and the contents of the test are not available to the public. A brief description of three such tests follows.

Scholastic Assessment Test (SAT)

Formerly known as the *Scholastic Aptitude Test,* SAT recently underwent some major revisions and acquired its new name. Current SAT consists of the SAT-I Reasoning Tests and the SAT-II Subject Tests. SAT-I Reasoning Tests contain both verbal reasoning (SAT-I Verbal Reasoning Test) and quantitative reasoning (SAT-I Math Reasoning Test). One important difference between old SAT and new SAT is that part of the new SAT-I Math Reasoning Test requires test takers to work out problems and provide answers instead of all multiple-choice items as in old SAT.

SAT-I test scores are reported in standard score units ranging from 200 to 800. SAT test norms are historically anchored, with 500 and 100 as the mean and standard deviation of the original SAT anchor group in the early 40s. In other words, current SAT scores indicate test takers' performance relative to that of the original anchor sample who took SAT tests in the 1940s. This point may not be well understood since the misconception persists that the mean (500) and standard deviation (100) are based on the current population of SAT takers.

The psychometric quality of SAT has been shown to be good from many studies, with consistently high reliability estimates. The major validity evidence of SAT is its predictive validity for college success. In this regard, a large number of studies have overwhelmingly shown that SAT has adequate predictive validity, with the correlation between SAT scores and college GPA about .40 to .50 under possible restriction of range condition due to the college admission selection process (Donlon, 1984, Chapter VII). The moderate positive correlation indicates that, by and large, the higher the test scores, the more successful the students tend to be in college.

The American College Test (ACT)

The *American College Test* (ACT) program was started in the late 1950s and was designed for the same purpose as the SAT: to provide predictive information about performance in postsecondary education. ACT contains four major sections: English, Mathematics, Reading, and Science Reasoning. In addition to the four section scores, ACT reports a composite score, which is the average of the four section scores. ACT scores are reported on a 36-point scale, and in 1992, the mean and standard deviation for high school graduates were 20.7 and 5, respectively (Maxey, 1994).

Like the SAT, the ACT has demonstrated high psychometric quality, with consistently high reliability and adequate predictive validity. Similar to SAT, ACT's predictive validity coefficients from a variety of studies generally range from .40 to .50 with college freshmen GPA as the criterion. Also, the correlation between ACT and SAT scores has been shown to be very high, making them almost equivalent for the purpose of making admission decisions. Because of these characteristics, the scores from ACT and SAT are generally considered substitutable, and many colleges and universities accept either SAT or ACT scores for making admission decisions.

Graduate Record Examination (GRE)

Originally developed in 1936, the GRE is available throughout the United States and in many other countries. The test consists of a general test (which reports verbal, quantitative, and analytical scores although most graduate programs use only the first two) and subject area tests in various fields of specialization (biology, computer science, psychology, and so on). The verbal subtest requires verbal reasoning and comprehension of reading passages from several different fields. The quantitative subtest requires mathematical reasoning, and interpretation of graphs, diagrams, and descriptive data. Success on the GRE depends substantially on the student's past achievement. Reliabilities are generally at .90 and above for the various subtests. Predictive validity has been assessed using graduate school grade-point average, performance on departmental comprehensive examinations, overall faculty ratings, and attainment of the Ph.D. degree as criteria (Anastasi, 1988). Scores on the GRE are a better predictor of graduate school performance than undergraduate grade-point average.

Specific Aptitude Tests

Many aptitude tests have been developed to predict success in specific areas. The most widely used are probably clerical and mechanical aptitude tests, but there are many others—such as the Purdue Pegboard Tests, which measure manual dexterity, and the Computer Aptitude, Literacy, and Interest Profile, which is designed to predict success in computer-related activities. The skills measured by these specific aptitude tests often overlap with skills measured by multiple aptitude batteries such as the Differential Aptitude Tests. Specific aptitude tests have advantages: they can be longer, better normed, and better validated for specific applications. Because these tests are not used often in schools, we will not elaborate on them.

Application Problem 2

You are on a committee at your school to select criteria for identifying children to participate in a gifted and talented program. The committee is currently working on the criteria to be used for first- and second-grade children, and has decided that only one standardized test can be used. The following standardized measures have been suggested as one basis for selection. Which one would you recommend? Why?

- Stanford–Binet Intelligence Scale
- Cognitive Abilities Test
- Metropolitan Readiness Tests

SUGGESTED READINGS

Anastasi, A. & Urbina, S. (1997). *Psychological testing* (7th ed.). Upper Saddle River, NJ: Prentice-Hall.

Now in its seventh edition, this is one of the classic textbooks in psychological measurement. The book devotes substantial attention to aptitude tests as well as providing extensive discussion of the psychometric properties of all psychological tests.

Crouse, J. & Trusheim, D. (1988). *The case against the SAT.* Chicago: University of Chicago Press.

Based on existing research literature, this book builds a case for why the SAT should not be used for making admissions decisions to postsecondary educational institutions, and proposes an alternative method using high school course work and grades. The perspective presented in this book demonstrates that assessment issues have a political as well as a scientific dimension and emphasizes the need to carefully consider alternative points of view before making a decision.

Herrnstein, R. J. & Murray, C. (1994). *The bell curve: Intelligence and class structure in American life.* New York, NY: The Free Press.

A widely debated, but nevertheless influential, book about the controversial topics concerning the relationships between performance on aptitude and achievement tests and some important social outcomes, as well as the societal implications of such relationships. Although opinions differ diametrically about the book, the topics covered in the book highlight some of the most important social concerns and controversies related to aptitude testing.

Jensen, A. R. (1980). *Bias in mental testing.* New York: The Free Press.

Although many people disagree with its conclusions, no one can argue that this is not the most comprehensive book ever done of bias in mental testing. Most of the book deals with aptitude tests, and it is "must" reading for anyone who is seriously interested in the issue of bias in aptitude tests.

Reynolds, C. R. & Kamphaus, R. W. (1990). *Handbook of psychological and educational assessment of children: Intelligence and achievement.* New York: The Guilford Press.

This book provides a more in-depth assessment of the issues related to measuring intelligence than was possible in the text. Included are chapters on measuring infant intelligence; the value of nonverbal and psychological measures of intelligence, and extensive discussions of the Wechsler, McCarthy, Kaufman, and Stanford–Binet scales.

SUGGESTION SHEET

If your last name starts with the letter V or W, please complete the Suggestion Sheet at the end of the book while this chapter is still fresh in your mind.

Answers to Chapter 16 Application Problems

1. Before giving any advice, it would be wise to learn more about the situation at the last school. For example, had their daughter been having difficulty in school prior to the time she was given an IQ test? What kind of an IQ test was it—group or individually administered? Has she been checked for vision or hearing loss? Have there been any unusual health or behavior problems? Was this the first IQ test she had been given, and if not, how did it compare to previous tests? The answers to these questions would affect any advice given. Certainly, if the results of the IQ test contradict other information, another test should be given. A second test should be an individually administered IQ test since these are more reliable and valid. Prior to another test, the parents should be sure that there are no other factors which may be inappropriately lowering their daughter's score, (for example, health, vision, or behavior problems).

   You should also inform the parents that although IQ tests are a good predictor of future academic performance, many variables can affect an IQ score at any given time. If it is established that their daughter does score relatively low on a measured IQ at this time, that will affect how instruction is designed and may suggest that consideration be given to having her participate in special programs. However, it is incorrect to assume that she will never be successful in school. It should also be noted that an IQ in the lowest 25th percentile is not dramatically low, and that the school will continue to work with her to enable her to achieve her potential.

2. It is important to emphasize that the standardized test should be only a part of the selection criteria for the gifted and talented program. In considering which one test should be used (we are assuming here that financial or time constraints preclude the use of more than one test), the following issues should be considered:

   ■ As a standardized test of intelligence, the *Stanford–Binet* is one of the best. However, it requires highly trained test administrators and must be administered individually to children. It requires from one to two hours to administer and yields a single IQ score. Thus if the committee is considering a test that can be given to every child in the school, it would probably be prohibitively expensive and logistically difficult.

   ■ The *Cognitive Abilities Test* is a group-administered IQ test that yields verbal, quantitative, and nonverbal scores for children K–13. It can be administered in a group setting in less than an hour and was normed concurrently with the Iowa

Test of Basic Skills so that it would be good for comparing the match between achievement and aptitude. It would be much less expensive and more feasible to administer to all children in the school, and it yields appropriate information.

■ The *Metropolitan Readiness Test* is a good screening measure to assess readiness for first grade and prereading skills. As a measure to select children for a gifted and talented program in first and second grade, however, it would be inappropriate. The test measures basic prerequisites, and children who are gifted would "top out" on the test.

Based on this information, the Cognitive Abilities Test would be the most appropriate choice if only one standardized test can be used.

CHAPTER 17

Understand Your Students' Special Needs

Using Tests for Diagnosis and for Special Populations

OVERVIEW

One of the greatest challenges a teacher faces is to know where a student has learning difficulties and to provide useful remedial instruction. Early diagnosis of student learning problems in reading and mathematics is critical because of the sequential nature of learning in these areas. In other words, failure to master one step will make subsequent learning increasingly difficult. As a result, one of the most important things for teachers is to have good measurement tools to diagnose students' specific learning difficulties in many areas of the curriculum.

Educators are also obligated to provide appropriate education to those who have some special needs due to disabilities of various sorts, or to limited language proficiency. Public laws require that the needs of these special population groups be properly identified, and appropriate education be provided to them. Owing to some constraints often imposed by these special conditions, testing students in these special populations often poses special difficulties.

In this chapter, we discuss the topics related to using tests for understanding the specific needs of students, including those with special needs. We have organized this chapter into two major sections. In the first section, we discuss diagnostic measures for reading and math problems. In the second section, we discuss assessment of students with mental or physical disabilities or limited language proficiency. Admittedly, our discussions related to the topics are brief. Since many of these assessment needs should be handled by specialists instead of ordinary classroom teachers, our intention is to provide educators with some general knowledge rather than expertise. It is our belief that all educators need some knowledge about these special assessment needs to participate actively in the education of these students. For this purpose, the brief discussions in this chapter should suffice.

OBJECTIVES

Upon completing your study of this chapter, you should be able to

1. Explain why diagnostic tests are used and how they differ from other standardized achievement tests.

2. Briefly describe the Stanford Diagnostic Reading Test (SDRT) and the California Diagnostic Mathematics Test (CDMT), and interpret data provided by these tests.

3. Briefly describe the assessment of mental retardation and some instruments that can be used for such assessment.

4. Explain learning disabilities, some major considerations for assessing learning disabilities, and some appropriate measures for assessing learning disabilities.

5. Discuss some common conditions of physical disabilities and assessment issues related to these conditions.

6. Describe some major instruments appropriate for students with different physical disabilities.

7. Briefly describe major assessment issues for students with limited language proficiency.

8. Describe several tests appropriate for assessing aptitudes of students with limited English language proficiency.

Using Tests to Diagnose the Needs of Students

Diagnostic tests are useful to the degree that they help identify ways in which we can teach students more effectively. Before discussing some of the more frequently used diagnostic tests that are currently available, we will discuss how such tests are used and some of the issues to be considered in selecting an appropriate test in various situations. In this section, we will deal primarily with diagnostic tests used with students who have not been identified as having any specific needs related to language deficiencies or disabilities. After that, we will focus on diagnostic tests for students identified with or suspected of having some type of disability.

What Are Diagnostic Tests?

When used with students in regular education (as compared to special education) settings, diagnostic tests are designed to identify specific strengths and weaknesses in a given subject area. Developers of such tests typically analyze a complex task such as reading, divide it into a series of specific skills, then develop items to measure a student's ability to perform each skill. These tests are not diagnostic in the medical sense—that is, they do not identify the underlying *cause* of the student's difficulty. For example, reading difficulties could have many causes, such as poor motivation, low verbal fluency, limited scholastic aptitude, or short attention span, to name just a few. Diagnostic reading tests do not identify such causes. They do, however, identify the *specific nature* of the difficulty so that the teacher can focus remedial work on a student's particular deficiencies.

Most diagnostic tests currently being used in regular education settings measure skills in reading and mathematics. Reading and math are generally regarded as the most basic of school subjects and are primarily process oriented, as compared with such subjects as social studies, which are more content oriented. Furthermore, because reading is essential to learning other school subjects, most educators feel it merits special attention. In process-oriented subjects, such as mathematics and reading, failure to master one step in the process can seriously affect mastery of subsequent steps. Most diagnostic reading and mathematics tests are designed to determine the specific deficiencies of low-achieving children in regular classrooms.

Diagnostic reading and math tests are intended to supplement information provided through standardized achievement tests. In fact, many current achievement test batteries have some characteristics of group-administered diagnostic tests. They divide complex tasks into components and provide test items to measure each component. They also compare each student's scores to criterion-referenced cutoff points to indicate which students have yet to master each specific learning objective. The diagnostic tests we will discuss in this chapter, however, are better diagnostic tools than standardized achievement tests in mathematics and reading in several important ways.

1. They are aimed at low achievers, the group most in need of diagnosis and remediation, and can measure the performance of this group better than an achievement test—which must contain items appropriate for students across a wide achievement range.
2. By focusing on a single subject and a narrow achievement range, good diagnostic tests include more items to measure each component of the process, thus providing more detailed and more reliable information to facilitate the identification of specific difficulties. Standardized achievement tests may identify students achieving below expectations, but typically do not provide enough specific information about students' difficulties to help teachers plan effective instruction.
3. A diagnostic test is often an integral part of a larger system of diagnosis and remediation that provides the teacher with a variety of instructional materials and ideas to help remediate problems revealed by the diagnostic measure.

Many diagnostic tests are administered individually. Individual administration permits the examiner to observe and record many errors, such as mispronunciation, that are difficult to measure in group-administered tests. Listening to a child read or having him "talk through" the solution to an arithmetic problem can provide the trained examiner with a great deal of useful diagnostic information. The examiner can also estimate the student's level of anxiety, attention, and motivation. Thus even though individual diagnostic tests are more expensive to administer, they have substantial advantages over group-administered tests.

On the other hand, administration of many individual diagnostic tests requires skills and experience that the typical teacher has not developed; therefore, these tests must often be administered by a specialist or school psychologist. Further, because of the extensive time required for individual administration, a useful strategy is to identify *areas* of poor performance using a standardized achievement test, and then to administer a diagnostic test to determine specific steps in the learning process that need remediation. This strategy requires that the diagnostic measure be administered only to those students who show significant weaknesses on the standardized achievement measure.

As with other types of tests, a diagnostic test will be useful only to the extent that it is technically sound and suits the specific purpose for which you wish to use it. Therefore, we must consider how to select a diagnostic test that will serve you well.

Selecting Diagnostic Tests

In addition to the test characteristics that need to be considered in selecting any test as discussed in previous chapters, some special considerations are needed in selecting a diagnostic test. More specifically, you should consider the following:

1. *Specific skills.* Does the diagnostic test break down the broad skills of reading or mathematics into *specific subskills?* Are a sufficient number of test items included to measure the student's mastery of each subskill? If not, the test will probably add little to what you can learn from a standardized achievement test.
2. *Subtest reliabilities.* Because these tests are used for individual diagnosis, subtest reliabilities should be high (for example, .85 and higher). Remember, as reliability declines, the standard error of measurement becomes larger, and the chance of your making a faulty diagnosis of an individual student's needs increases.
3. *Administration time.* Many diagnostic tests must be administered individually, and they tend to be long because of the need for multiple items to measure each objective or step in the learning process. Can the necessary time be scheduled?
4. *Resources.* Administering and interpreting some diagnostic tests require special training. Is someone available who is qualified to administer and interpret this measure?
5. *Linking diagnosis to remediation.* Can a student's deficiencies, revealed by the subtest scores, be translated into specific remedial strategies? In other words, can you decide what kind of remediation is needed by reviewing the student's test performance? This link is essential to effective use of diagnostic test results.
6. *Remedial materials.* Does the test developer recommend or provide specific instructional materials or procedures that can be used to remediate student deficiencies revealed by the subtest scores? Although not essential, such material can be very helpful to the teacher. (Of course, you need not restrict yourself to remedial material supplied by the test developer.)

No diagnostic test is perfect, but if you find one that meets these criteria reasonably well, it will probably suit your purposes.

Diagnostic Reading and Mathematics Tests

Diagnostic tests used primarily with regular students who are having difficulties in mathematics and reading are aimed at diagnosing very specific deficiencies. A common weakness of many such diagnostic tests in the past has been their failure to give teachers guidance in designing instruction to help students overcome deficiencies identified by the test. Recently published measures, however, tend to provide teachers with more help—both in interpreting test results and in planning remedial teaching. The measures discussed in this section are designed to be used in conjunction with suggested remedial activities and supplemental teaching materials designed to help remediate each specific learning deficit. These examples are illustrative only of the abundance of alternative diagnostic tests currently available.

Stanford Diagnostic Reading Test (SDRT)

The SDRT is based upon the view that reading is a developmental process that can be divided into four major components: decoding, vocabulary, comprehension, and rate. At different grade levels, the relative importance of these components and the specific skills related to each changes. The test is available at four levels (called Red, Green, Brown, and Blue) that collectively cover grades 1 through 12.

The SDRT Red Level (for grades one and two and low achievers in succeeding grades) consists of five different tests measuring *Auditory Discrimination, Phonetic Analysis, Auditory Vocabulary, Word Reading,* and *Reading Comprehension.* For illustrative purposes, let's look at one of these SDRT tests, *Phonetic Analysis,* in some depth to show how the test is constructed and how it can be used in diagnosing individual performance.

Phonetic Analysis. This test measures the child's ability to relate sounds and letters, a skill essential to sounding out unfamiliar words. Two major objectives for this subtest, called *skill domain objectives,* relate consonant and vowel sounds to their most common spellings. Five *item cluster* objectives deal with specific aspects of the skill domain objectives. In Part A of this subtest, the pupil is asked to identify the letter or letter combination that matches the initial sound of a given word. For example, after administering the practice item, the examiner says, "Look at box number 1. You see a picture of a coat. Mark the space next to the letter that stands for the beginning sound of *coat.*"

Part B is similar, except the pupil is asked to give the *ending* sound of each word. A total of 24 items in this subtest cover consonant sounds, and 16 items cover vowel sounds. In turn, the 24 consonant sound items are divided into 3 item clusters, which include 8 items for single-letter consonant sounds, 8 items for sounds represented by consonant clusters, and 8 items for consonant sounds represented by digraphs.[1] The 16 items on vowel sounds are divided into 2 item clusters: short vowel sounds and long vowel sounds. The specific sound measured by

---

[1] A digraph is a group of two letters whose phonetic value is a single sound.

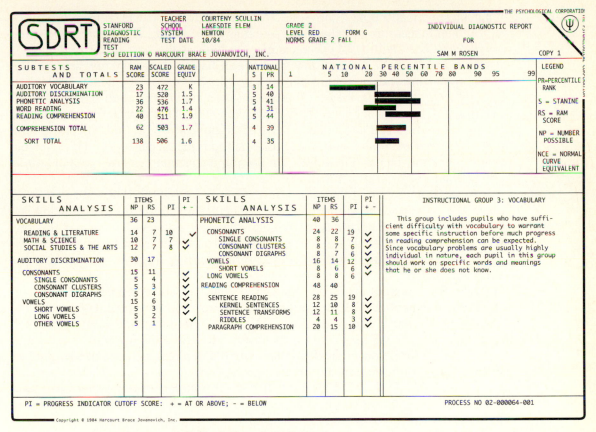

FIGURE 17.1   Individual Diagnostic Report

Source: Bjorn Karlsen and Eric Gardner (1986), *Stanford Diagnostic Reading Test, 3rd Edition Manual for Interpreting,* by permission.

each item is given in the *Manual for Interpreting* (Karlsen & Gardner, 1986). The other subtests are similarly divided into skill domain objectives and item clusters.

SDRT information provided to teachers.   Widespread use of computers has made it possible for test publishers to provide teachers with a great deal of information useful in interpreting test results. For example, eight kinds of scores are available for the SDRT: content-referenced scores, raw scores, progress indicators, norm-referenced scores, percentile ranks, stanines, grade equivalents, and scaled scores. These can be used both for individual and class diagnosis.

In addition to a variety of scores, the SDRT supplies the teacher with various reports containing profiles and summary sheets that can aid in diagnosis and interpretation. Here we examine only the *Individual Diagnostic Report* (IDR) in some detail to see what types of information are available from this and similar types of tests.

This report provides up to five different scores on each subtest for the pupil, indicates which of several reading groups is most appropriate for him, and gives *progress indicators,* telling whether he is above or below a critical cutoff score in the skill domains measured by the SDRT, such as *vowel sounds, consonant sounds,* and *vocabulary* (see Figure 17.1). For example, a look at the first entry under *Skills Analysis* in Figure 17.1 shows that Sam Rosen has a vocabulary raw score of 23, meaning he gave the correct answer on 23 of the 36 vocabulary items. Looking at the *Subtotals* and *Totals,* we see this student has a grade equivalent score[2] of K, indicating that his auditory vocabulary level is lower than the typical first grade pupil tested in October. The next columns give his stanine score (3) and percentile rank (14) compared with the national norms. The top right corner of the IDR gives national percentile bands. These indicate the pupil's percentile rank, plus or minus one standard error of measurement.

You will note that all the scores on the upper half of the IDR tell the teacher essentially the same thing: that Sam's performance on all the subtests is below average while the vocabulary subtest is much below average. Except for the raw score, these are all *norm-referenced* scores—that is, they tell Sam's performance *relative* to other students. For most uses, the raw score, percentile, and stanine are sufficient.

Like most current diagnostic measures, the SDRT also reports criterion-referenced information. The progress indicators refer to a criterion—that is, the level of performance the student should attain to demonstrate mastery of each test objective. The skill analysis on the lower left side of the form gives criterion-referenced information, indicating the student's performance on specific subtest skills. Scores at or above the cutoff are checked in the plus (+) column, those below the cutoff are checked in the minus (–) column. For example, Sam correctly answered 11 of 15 items on consonant sounds, and 6 of 15 items on vowel sounds. Both of these scores are checked in the plus (+) column, and we can conclude that Sam reached the criterion or cutoff score in these areas, and remediation is not needed. Note in the lower right corner of the IDR, it is recommended that Sam be placed in Instructional Group 3: vocabulary. Students with low scores on the vocabulary subtest would be placed in Group 3, those with low comprehension scores in Group 4, and so on. Students may be classified into as many as eight groups.

Application Problem 1

Study the report data in Figure 17.1 for Sam Rosen and answer the following questions:

a. Under which instructional group is he classified?

b. On what subtest did this student earn his highest score relative to the test norms?

c. On what skill domains was this student below the progress indicator cutoff score?

---

[2]You will recall our caution in Chapter 3 concerning problems with grade equivalent scores. Our statements did not rid the world of grade equivalents, however, so we discuss them here in relation to their actual use by others.

Using the SDRT to prescribe learning. The SDRT comes with *Handbooks of Instructional Techniques and Materials* for each of the four test levels. The handbook for the Red Level (grades one and two) describes skill areas covered at that level—such as consonant sounds, vowel sounds, word division, and blending. Instructional techniques appropriate for these groups are briefly described. In addition to the suggested instructional techniques, a selected bibliography and list of commercially available instructional materials are provided. Although such materials are not designed to be detailed lesson plans, they do provide a great many ideas and resources that teachers can adapt to their own needs.

The California Diagnostic Mathematics Tests (CDMT)

Here is another example of a complete system for diagnosis, prescription, and instruction. Although the CDMT was designed as a diagnostic test, it contains enough information to be used as an objective-based system to provide an integrated program for mathematics assessment and instruction for students with below average performance on regular standardized math achievement tests. The system contains materials designed to assist in (1) placing students for assessment at their correct instructional levels, (2) diagnosing each student's mathematics strengths and instructional needs, (3) prescribing appropriate materials and activities, (4) teaching specific mathematics skills, (5) monitoring student's progress in the skills taught, and (6) reinforcing and enriching mastered skills.

The CDMT is available in 6 levels (A through F), ranging from grades 1 to 12. Combined, the 6 levels of the CDMT cover 70 instructional objectives in mathematics in 4 broad areas of math: number concepts, computation, applications, and life skills (CTB/McGraw-Hill, 1989, 1991). Different levels of the CDMT cover different numbers of instructional objectives. For example, Level A (grades 1–2) of the CDMT assesses 20 instructional objectives, and Level C (grades 3–4) includes 27 instructional objectives. These two levels (A and C) of the CDMT share 8 common objectives although the items for the common objectives at the two levels are different in terms of their difficulty levels. The CDMT is not a timed test, and a higher level of the CDMT requires more time to complete than a lower level. The publisher suggests that test administrators should allow at least 90 percent of the students to complete a given section of the test before instructing students to proceed to the next section.

Several report forms available from the publisher summarize and organize score data on the CDMT. The most important form, the *Objectives Performance Report* (OPR), lists for each student the specific instructional objectives the student has mastered (+) or not mastered (−), and those for which he or she needs to continue to practice (P). For example, four objectives are related to whole number addition and subtraction. As Figure 17.2 shows, Patrick Milton reached mastery on one of these, needs practice on two, and has yet to learn one. Summary data are also given for each objective, indicating the percentage of children in the class who have mastered that objective, as well as the number who have yet to master the objective or who need further practice.

average objective performance of class

average objective performance category for class

average objective performance for school

student objective performance category

instructional strand

objective

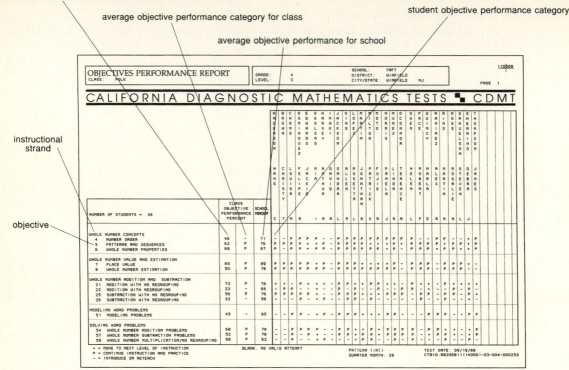

FIGURE 17.2   Objectives Performance Report

Source: California Diagnostic Mathematics Tests: Teachers Guide, Levels E and F. CTB/McGraw-Hill (1989), Monterey, CA. Used with permission of the publisher.

Application Problem 2

Study Figure 17.2 and answer the following questions:

a. In this class, how many students have not mastered Objective 21, *Addition with No Regrouping?* How many need practice?

b. On what objective did the students have the lowest average objective performance?

c. Which students are weakest in the Instructional Strand *Whole Number Value and Estimation* (Objectives 7 and 8)?

In addition to the OPR in Figure 17.2, the CDMT provides a variety of other report forms, including the Parent's Report, the Individual Test Record, and the Class Grouping Record (CTB/McGraw-Hill, 1989). In both the Individual Test Record and the Class Grouping Record, instructional priorities, materials, and activities are sug-

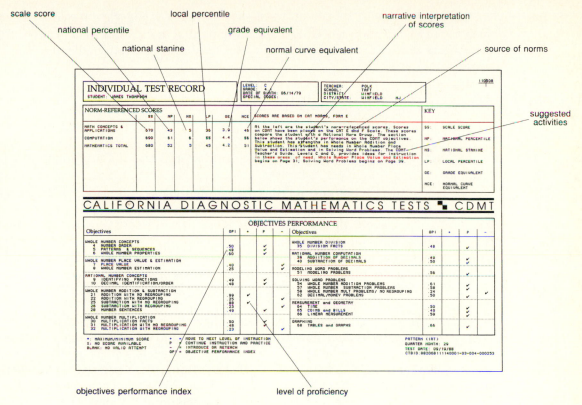

FIGURE 17.3 Individual Test Record

Source: California Diagnostic Mathematics Tests: Teachers Guide, Levels E and F. CTB/McGraw-Hill (1989), Monterey, CA. Used with permission of the publisher.

gested so that remedial instruction can be more easily implemented to strengthen the weak areas of either individuals or a group of students. An example of the Individual Test Record is presented in Figure 17.3. The narrative interpretation in this report indicates that the student in this report (James Thompson) has some remedial needs in the areas of *Whole Number Place Value and Estimation* and of *Solving Word Problems.* The sources for instructional ideas are also suggested in this narrative interpretation.

The Utility of Diagnostic Math and Reading Systems

In summary, diagnostic tests like the CDMT and SDRT are extensive systems designed to assist the teacher in dealing with all aspects of math or reading diagnosis, prescription, and instruction. Considerable study and knowledge is necessary if a teacher is to make effective use of such diagnostic systems. However, when a teacher's knowledge of the children in his or her classroom is combined with conscientious use of one of these diagnostic-prescriptive systems, the teacher can probably do as good a job of diagnosis and remediation as the average clinician or content specialist. Teachers have the advantage of observing their students every day. The use of adequately developed and field-tested systems such as the SDRT and the CDMT has great potential to enhance the effectiveness of teachers who already have a general sense of students' strengths and weaknesses.

Standardized Achievement Versus Diagnostic Tests

Now that you have learned something about diagnostic tests, let's review in greater depth some of the important differences between diagnostic tests and standardized achievement tests that we briefly outlined at the beginning of this chapter.

1. Standardized achievement tests cover content areas, but usually not specific processes for the content areas. For example, the teacher may determine from a standardized achievement test that Jose is weak in word decoding, but he or she usually cannot determine from that test score the specific steps in the decoding process where Jose is making his mistakes. In contrast, diagnostic tests divide broad content areas into specific learning objectives or processes in considerable detail. Such detail gives the teacher a better understanding of each student's specific needs.

2. Standardized achievement tests usually have a smaller number of items for a comparable objective than a diagnostic test. In relation to specific content areas covered, the additional items make the results of the diagnostic test about that specific content area more reliable than what is available from a standardized achievement test. Because of the length of many diagnostic tests, it is often a good alternative to identify a student's area of deficiency, using a standardized achievement measure, and then administer only that part of the diagnostic test that explores that deficiency.

3. Diagnostic tests are aimed primarily at the low achiever, whereas standardized achievement tests are designed to measure achievement over the entire range of pertinent instruction at a given grade level. Thus the diagnostic test contains a greater proportion of easy items. This not only provides more accurate assessment for low-achieving students, but also makes it possible for most of them to obtain *some* correct answers.

4. Diagnostic tests are primarily related to criteria although most report some normative data. This means that specific learning objectives are spelled out, and cutoff points are established to determine whether the student has reached the criterion on test items designed to measure each objective. In contrast, achievement batteries are primarily designed to provide a measure of general competence in the subject being tested, in relation to national (or local) norms. As a result, standardized achievement tests often report individual scores as *below average, average,* or *above average* instead of being weighed against a criterion or progress indicator.

Using Tests for Special Populations

During the last 25 years, more students with disabilities are being educated in regular education classes. Although this has many advantages, it requires regular classroom teachers to acquire some additional skills, including skills in the areas of

Table 17.1   Classification Guidelines by Category of Exceptionality

Category of Disability	Types of Assessment Data That Should Be Collected
Mentally retarded	Intellectual functioning, adaptive behavior, academic achievement, medical/developmental, language
Hard of hearing/deaf	Audiological, intellectual, language, speech, academic achievement, social/emotional, psychomotor
Speech impaired	Audiological, articulation, fluency, voice, language, academic achievement, social/emotional
Visually handicapped	Ophthalmological, academic achievement, intellectual, social/emotional
Seriously emotionally disturbed	Intellectual, social/emotional, adaptive behavior, academic achievement, medical/developmental
Orthopedically impaired and other health impaired	Medical, motor, adaptive behavior, intellectual, academic achievement, social/emotional
Deaf-blind	Audiological, ophthalmological, language, medical, adaptive behavior
Multiply handicapped	Medical, intellectual, motor, adaptive behavior, social/emotional, academic achievement, language speech, audiological and ophthalmological (if appropriate)
Specific learning disabilities	Intellectual, academic achievement, language, social/emotional, classroom behavior
Gifted	Intellectual, academic achievement, social/emotional, creativity

diagnosis and assessment. In some cases, regular education teachers participate directly in these procedures. In others, they need to be aware of what happens so that they can appropriately use the resulting information.

Legal Considerations in Identifying Students with Special Needs

Federal legislation has mandated that there be appropriate mechanisms for identifying students with special needs and that appropriate education be provided to these students. Testing and assessment is an integral part of these federal mandates for education of students with special needs. Testing is involved in either identification of special needs or evaluating the effectiveness of special education programs specifically designed for these special groups. Table 17.1 lists the various categories of children with disabilities and the assessment data that must be collected for each category. Note that a variety of assessment data is needed to identify a child's disabilities and determine whether special education or related services are required.

The most influential federal law that has direct implications for testing and measurement in public schools is the *Public Law 94-142* (PL 94-142), the *Education For All Handicapped Children Act*. PL 94-142 stipulates that, among other things, schools are required to (1) identify these children using reliable and valid procedures, (2) implement assessment using multidisciplinary approaches, and (3) develop individualized education programs for these children. Later, PL 99-457 expanded the coverage down to children at age three. Another federal law, *Public Law*

95-561 (PL 95-561), The *Gifted and Talented Children's Educational Act* (Heward & Orlansky, 1988), provides financial incentives for programs designed specifically for identifying and educating academically talented students although this law does not *require* schools to set up special programs for these students of higher ability levels.

Testing students with special needs often poses problems not typically encountered in testing regular students. In this section, we discuss some issues related to such testing. Our discussion will not be comprehensive owing to space limitations, but it will provide a starting point for those who need more information.

Different Types of Special Needs and Related Assessment

Since different groups of students have different special needs, which in turn require different assessment approaches and different tests, our discussion will separately cover several major categories of special needs and relevant assessment instruments in each situation.

Mental Retardation

Mental retardation is used to indicate a *considerable degree* of deficit in *intellectual* development and functioning. Children with such intellectual functioning deficit normally require substantial individualized assistance to benefit from a regular classroom curriculum. To provide appropriate education for this special group of children, some type of special educational program needs to be set up so that relevant materials and activities can be implemented.

In addition to other sources of information, although it should never be used alone in diagnosing mental retardation, performance on relevant tests is an important source of information for making such diagnostic decisions. The American Association of Mental Retardation (AAMR) defines mental retardation as (1) significant subaverage intellectual functioning and (2) impairment in adaptive behavior (Gregory, 1996). The major measurement instruments used for measuring intellectual functioning are standardized intelligence tests, some of which have been discussed in the previous chapter. Although there does not seem to be any rigid cutoff scores on standardized intelligence tests for identifying mental retardation, some approximate ranges are frequently used. For example, an approximate IQ score range of 50–55 to 70–75 has been used to classify a respondent as mildly mentally retarded, and the range of 35–40 to 50–55 (assuming 100 as population mean, and 15 as standard deviation) has been used to define moderate mental retardation (AAMR, 1992; Grossman, 1983; Patton, Payne, & Beirne-Smith, 1986). As can be seen from these suggested IQ score ranges, mental retardation is associated with a *very low* intellectual functioning level. Furthermore, IQ score is only one component needed in this identification process, and other sources of information, such as adaptive behavior, are also needed in this process.

Tests of adaptive behavior.   In addition to a low level of intellectual functioning, impairment in adaptive behavior is another defining characteristic of mental retardation (AAMR, 1992). Limitations in adaptive skills are often considered more difficult to assess than the intellectual functioning level. A variety of adaptive behavior measures are available, and here we examine two of them.

1. *Vineland Adaptive Behavior Scales* (VABS) (Sparrow, Balla, & Cicchetti, 1984). As the descendent of the first standardized measure for assessing adaptive behaviors (Vineland Social Maturity Scale, Doll, 1935), VABS is a well-respected and widely used measure for adaptive behaviors. The measure is suitable for subjects from young infants to age 18 and low-functioning adults. This measure is sometimes considered the standard in the area of adaptive behaviors because it is so widely used.

2. The VABS has three forms: two forms of the Interview Edition (regular and expanded structured interviews) to be used with a parent or a person very familiar with the examinee, and the Classroom Edition focusing on behavior in academic context, which is to be completed by a teacher. All forms of the VABS focus on the areas of daily living, socialization, motor function, and communication. The Interview Editions also have items assessing maladaptive behavior. Reports about the psychometric characteristics of VABS have been somewhat mixed, with good reliability and validity evidence in some situations, and disappointing evidence in others (Cohen, Swerdlik, & Phillips, 1996).

3. *Scales of Independent Behavior* (SIB) (Bruininks, Woodcock, Weatherman, & Hill, 1984). Designed for subjects ranging from infants to adults, SIB provides a multidimensional measure of adaptive behavior. The SIB consists of 14 subscales grouped into 4 clusters of skills: motor skills, social and communication skills, personal-living skills, and community-living skills. The examiner needs minimum training to complete the SIB, but the examiner must be someone very familiar with the examinee's daily behavior (for example, parent, caregiver, teacher who spends a lot of time with the examinee).

Like VABS, the SIB has a separate Problem Behavior Scale that assesses maladaptive behaviors in several major areas (Disruptive Behavior, Socially Offensive Behavior, Uncooperative Behavior, and so on). The reported psychometric quality of the SIB is respectable, with good reliability and promising validity evidence (Bruininks, Woodcock, Weatherman, & Hill, 1985). In short, the SIB is considered a good measure for adaptive behaviors, and it provides information about the examinee's social functioning level in different settings.

Learning Disabilities

Many different definitions have been proposed for learning disability (Bennett & Ragosta, 1984). One defining characteristic, however, for all these definitions is that the low academic performance is *not* the result of mental retardation, or physical disabilities, or some type of environmental, cultural, or economic disadvantage. Instead, a learning disability is considered to be present when a child has normal levels of intellectual functioning, but lower than expected achievement due to problems with psychological processing or the use of language. For this reason, scholastic aptitude tests (for example, intelligence tests) are often used to measure intellectual functioning, whereas achievement tests, especially those related to language skills, are often used to measure academic performance. If the achievement level is significantly lower than would be predicted from the child's performance on the aptitude test, the child may have a learning disability.

If a student is suspected of having a learning disability based on the aptitude/achievement discrepancy, the nature of the learning problem needs to be identified. Establishing that there is an aptitude/achievement discrepancy is usually relatively easy, and many tests discussed in the previous two chapters can be readily used. But pinpointing the cause of the discrepancy is often a challenging task for which diagnostic tests can be quite helpful.

Because diagnostic tests such as those we have discussed in the first section of this chapter are primarily concerned with diagnosis of students' remedial needs, and thus tend to focus on the low achiever, they may also be used for diagnosis of students with mild mental handicaps or learning disabilities. For example, the CDMT, although designed primarily for use with regular students, can also be used to diagnose the mathematics learning needs of students with mild disabilities. With some adaptation, such as use of a lower level of the test, most current diagnostic tests in reading and mathematics will provide useful information to the teacher who has children with disabilities in his class.

In addition, a number of tests have been developed specifically to diagnose various aspects of the performance of students with disabilities. Before we say more about such tests, however, we must provide an important caution. Assessing students with learning disabilities is very complex, and although the regular classroom teacher often assists in the process, the main responsibility usually falls to specialists. For example, if such a student needs help with prevocational or daily living skills, usually a special education teacher or consultant will develop an individualized education plan (IEP) for the child and assist the classroom teacher in implementing that plan within the regular classroom. Consequently, it is the special educator who must learn a wide variety of specialized techniques for assessing these children. It is beyond the scope of this chapter, and this book, to attempt to deal with these specialized diagnostic techniques in any detail. Yet we are reluctant to omit entirely any mention of them since most regular classroom teachers will be team members in working with special educators to meet the needs of students with disabilities who are mainstreamed into their classes.

We wish to make clear that our use of some existing instruments as examples is not an endorsement of them. Tests for assessing students with disabilities are not nearly as well established as are diagnostic measures like the SDRT or CDMT, and some we mention here are promising, but have not yet been adequately validated. Also, there are other equally useful measures we do not have space to describe.

In addition to the widely used aptitude tests described in Chapter 16, some more specialized measures are often used to identify students with learning disabilities. Most of these measures used with children with disabilities can be grouped into two major categories: (1) tests that assess skill or process deficits and (2) measures that assess students' adaptive behaviors. In addition, some comprehensive measures are concerned with performance in all relevant areas.

Tests assessing skill or process deficits. A variety of tests are available in this category, and here we discuss only a few of them. Since learning disabilities are conceptualized as being caused by factors other than mental retardation, physical disabilities, cultural or socioeconomic disadvantages, it is often reasoned that some type of skill or process deficits may be causing the student to achieve at a lower level than would be expected based on his intellectual ability. To check out such possibilities, special tests are often used. The following are a few examples:

1. *Woodcock Reading Mastery Tests—Revised* (WRMT-R). Published by American Guidance Service, this is a series of tests for diagnosing reading problems suitable for students ranging in age from kindergarten to college (Woodcock, 1987). The test includes measures of reading skills such as letter identification, word identification, word comprehension, and passage comprehension. The WRMT-R is both norm-referenced and criterion-referenced in relation to mastery of objectives. The purpose of the test is to aid educators in identifying the precise nature of reading problems.

2. *Test of Language Development* (TOLD). Although reading tests such as WRMT-R or SDRT assess reading problems, they do not focus on *process* problems that may have caused the reading problems. TOLD (Newcomer & Hammill, 1988) focuses on identifying process deficits that underlie the reading problems. As a general rule, tests of language development are designed for young children (Newcomer & Hammill, 1988).

3. *Bender Visual Motor Gestalt Test* (Bender). This test is designed to assess process deficits associated with visual-perceptual functioning (Koppitz, 1975). Suitable for children to adults, the *Bender* is used to investigate the ability to organize visual components into a whole pattern so as to reveal any visual-perceptual functioning deficits.

Assessment of academic performance. In addition to the diagnostic measures for regular students, such as the SDRT and the CDMT, a few diagnostic measures and systems of diagnosis and instruction have been developed specifically to appraise the academic performance of special populations. One example here should suffice.

Criterion-Referenced Curriculum (CRC) The CRC is a comprehensive system of criterion-referenced tests and teaching materials in mathematics and reading designed for K–6 students with mild disabilities. It can be used for individual tutoring or small-group instruction. It can be used either as a core curriculum or as a supplemental curriculum in which the teacher selects only those skills that students are having difficulty learning. The system includes components designed to assist the teacher in diagnosis, teaching, evaluation, and development of teaching plans for IEPs (Stephens, 1982).

Physical Disabilities

Obviously, *physical disabilities* can mean many different physical conditions that may hinder students' efforts in the process of learning. Other than obvious handicapping physical conditions such as loss of limb, severe cerebral palsy, or other physical birth defects, there are other physical conditions that may not be so obvious, such as speech impaired, visually impaired, or hearing impaired (not total loss of vision, speech, or hearing). Assessment of scholastic aptitude or academic achievement for these students usually poses special problems we have not discussed before. The assessment of these special students normally requires specialists' expertise, such as school psychologists and special education teachers. However, educators in general can benefit from knowledge about the assessment issues related to these special students. Our discussion here is brief and is by no means complete. We present a few tests: motor-reduced tests for the physically handicapped, tests for the visually impaired, and nonreading tests for the speech impaired.

Peabody Picture Vocabulary Test–Revised (PPVT-R). Published by American Guidance Service, this test is probably the best known nonreading and motor-reduced test (Dunn & Dunn, 1981). PPVT-R is especially suitable for assessing vocabulary for persons who have difficulty verbalizing and for persons who have some motor-impairing conditions. In test administration, the administrator says a word orally, and the respondent points to which one of several pictures matches the stated word. Raw scores are converted to standardized scores with 100 as mean and 15 as standard deviation. Because the respondent is required only to point, this test is suitable for many people with physical disability conditions.

Although the relationship between PPVT-R and some other general measures of intelligence is reasonably high, especially with Verbal IQ (Davis & Kramer, 1985; Haddad, 1986), the PPVT-R is intended to be a test of vocabulary, and not a substitute for general measure of intelligence (Gregory, 1992). The PPVT-R is well standardized on a representative national sample of 4200 subjects, and it is quick and relatively simple to administer. For students with speech or motor impairing conditions, it is a good measure of receptive vocabulary.

Columbia Mental Maturity Scale (CMMS). Published by the Psychological Corporation, CMMS is designed to measure reasoning ability for young children (ages 3–11). Intended for children with sensory, motor, or speech deficits (Burgemeister et al., 1972), the requirements for respondents are simple: from a group of objects presented in a picture, the child is required to point out one object that does not belong to the group because of its unique characteristic(s) (size, color, shape, or difference on some other dimensions). Essentially, perceptual discrimination and reasoning are required to complete the tasks, and no reading skills are involved. Similar to PPVT-R, CMMS is quick to administer, and its raw scores are converted to standardized scores with mean of 100 and standard deviation of 16. As a nonverbal measure of reasoning ability, CMMS has been used for children in many situations where some physical disability conditions are involved. The correlations between CMMS and other standardized intelligence tests, such as Stanford-Binet, are moderately high (Gregory, 1996).

Tests for the visually impaired. Obviously, most aptitude tests are not applicable for people who have severe visual impairments. To assess the intellectual functioning of this special group, special tests are needed. Most attempts of constructing such tests involve adaptation of existing general aptitude tests (for example, Stanford-Binet, Wechsler tests, Cattell Culture-Free Test) by presenting test items in a form suitable for the visually impaired. Here we briefly discuss Perkins-Binet, one of these general aptitude tests, as an example.

Perkins-Binet (Davis, 1980) is the most recent intelligence test for the visually impaired. Like some other similar tests designed for the visually impaired, Perkins-Binet is adapted from a standardized intelligence test, in this case, from Stanford-

Binet: Fourth Edition. Most verbal items and many other items from Stanford-Binet: Fourth Edition were retained but presented in an appropriate mode. The psychometric properties of Perkins-Binet have been shown to be good, with good reliability estimates, and good criterion-related validity evidence. Since visual impairment has different degrees, Perkins-Binet attempts to accommodate such differences by providing different forms and separate norms for different degrees of visual impairment.

Testing Students with Limited English Proficiency

Any discussion about assessing special populations would not be complete without some information about non-English-speakers, or students with very limited English proficiency. Although non-English-speaking students generally are normal students in every sense other than the fact that they speak another language as their native tongue, the fact that these students have no or very limited English language proficiency obviously makes it very difficult to use many of the assessment instruments we have discussed. As more public schools provide education to students with limited English proficiency, the need for appropriate assessment of these students increases. Since assessing aptitude or achievement depends heavily on verbal stimuli (oral or written), special problems exist in the assessment of these students.

As a rule of thumb, it is usually inappropriate to use those well-established *standardized* tests for students with limited English proficiency because these standardized tests are, for the most part, tests of second language proficiency for these students rather than tests of the original constructs for which they are designed. The *Standards for Educational and Psychological Testing* (AERA et al., 1985) provides some specific standards for testing students with limited English proficiency, and these guidelines should be carefully consulted and followed.

Different approaches have been suggested and used in dealing with such situations. One intuitively appealing solution is to translate the tests into another language, and to administer the tests in the students' primary language. Although this approach may be workable for local and classroom testing where other sources of information are readily available in addition to test scores, extreme caution is warranted for this approach in situations where *standardized* tests are used. This is because this process may cause some problems that may not be obvious at first. For example, language translation is deceptively difficult, and the quality of translation is often quite uncertain. In addition, some content and vocabulary may not be meaningful or at the same level of difficulty in another language, thus making the translated version inappropriate for the students being tested. Third, after translation, we often simply do not know if the original norms and psychometric properties of the test are still applicable for the new group. For these and other reasons, we do not believe that translation should be done locally for *standardized* tests. If it is necessary to administer these tests to students with limited English proficiency, professional help will be needed (for example, use a version in another language provided by the test developer if such a version is available, administer the test in another language or bilingually by a specially trained test administrator).

For achievement tests that are intended to assess *language* use, there is no alternative except to administer the tests as they are. For assessing other school subjects such as math, if conditions permit, school teachers may try to administer the tests in students' primary language or bilingually with the help of a specially trained test administrator. In either case, caution is warranted in interpreting the test scores for these students, and other sources of information become more important in supplementing the test scores than they are for regular students. For assessing students' learning aptitudes or general intellectual functioning, some measures depend less on language proficiency. We briefly discuss two of them here.

Several well-established general aptitude measures are nonlanguage tests, thus making them suitable for testing linguistic minorities when language proficiency is our major concern.

1. *Test of Nonverbal Intelligence* (TONI). This is often referred to as a language-free measure of cognitive abilities intended for linguistic minority populations (Brown, Sherbenou, & Dollar, 1982). Pantomime is used for instruction, and students respond by pointing to one of several options. Like some other measures, TONI requires students to identify relationships among abstract figures. Psychometric properties of TONI appear to be reasonable, with good reliability data but somewhat scant validity data (Gregory, 1992). The standardization of TONI appears to be carefully implemented. For non-English-speaking examinees, this may be a good choice.

2. *Cattell's Cultural-Fair Test.* We mentioned this test in our previous discussion. Although this test focuses on *fluid intelligence* in Cattell's intelligence model, and was originally designed to offer culture-free or culture-fair assessment of intellectual functioning, its nonlanguage feature makes it suitable for non-English-speaking students. Abstract figures are used, and the respondent is required to show understanding of the relationships among different abstract figures.

As mentioned repeatedly in this chapter, testing special populations poses some unique problems, some of which are quite difficult to handle. For this reason, it is usually the school psychologist's or special education specialist's responsibility to conduct this kind of assessment. More important, performance on tests is only one source of information, which *must* be combined with other sources of information in order to minimize errors in the identification of special needs of the students.

Application Problem 3

Why should we not blindly use our conventional aptitude tests for some special populations? For example, why is it usually inappropriate to use the WISC-III for children with motor-impairing conditions or for nonnative children with limited English language proficiency? What would be the major measurement consequences of such a practice?

SUGGESTED READINGS

Beattie, J. & Algozzine, B. (1982). Testing for teaching. *Arithmetic Teacher, 30*(1), 47–51.

Teachers are encouraged to use test results to plan specific educational programs. Information is provided about the nature of diagnostic testing, with both content and process error analysis discussed. Prescriptive teaching is described to show how to devise remedial activities after student problems have been identified.

Fry, E. B. (1981). *Reading diagnosis: Informal reading inventories.* Providence, RI: Jamestown Publishers.

The reading diagnosis tests and observations in this book provide a systematic way of gathering information about a student. The first ten chapters provide measures to test a variety of abilities in language arts and handwriting, as well as vision and student interests. The final three chapters explain how a teacher can obtain information through a structured parent–guardian interview, can summarize school records for maximum effectiveness, and can summarize the entire reading diagnosis process.

Lerner, J. (1993). *Learning disabilities: Theories, diagnosis & teaching strategies.* Boston, MA: Houghton Mifflin.

This book provides comprehensive discussion related to all relevant topics about learning disabilities, from various theoretical definitions of learning disabilities to different instructional strategies to tackle the different sorts of problems associated with learning disabilities. Both regular education and special education teachers will benefit from the discussion in the book.

Salvia, J. & Ysseldyke, J. E. (1995). *Assessment* (6th ed.). Boston, MA: Houghton Mifflin Company.

Written primarily for educators involved with remedial and special education, this book is an excellent reference for obtaining a brief critical review about frequently used aptitude tests as well as other tests. Each chapter contains a brief section on issues and problems with using that particular type of test.

Venn, J. (1994). *Assessment of students with special needs.* New York: Merrill/Macmillan.

This text helps teachers and other professionals acquire the knowledge base associated with assessment of students with special needs. It provides comprehensive coverage of the process of assessing students at all age levels. It also includes material appropriate for assessing students across a broad range of performance levels that include mild, moderate, and severe disabilities.

SUGGESTION SHEET

If your last name starts with the letter X, Y, or Z, please complete the Suggestion Sheet at the end of the book while this chapter is still fresh in your mind.

Answers to Chapter 17 Application Problems

1. a. Instructional Group 3
   b. Phonetic analysis, PR 41
   c. Reading and literature, vocabulary. Other vowels, auditory discrimination
2. a. Four students failed to master Objective 21, and seven needed more practice.
   b. Objective 22, Addition with Regrouping.
   c. David Inoki, Terence O'Connor, Alex Ramirez, and James Thompson are all at nonmastery level for both objectives.
3. Conventional tests for intellectual functioning are designed for a normal population of native speakers of English. If they are blindly used for some special populations, the inferences we make based on the scores will often be erroneous, and consequently, the validity of such measurement will be seriously compromised. For example, if WISC-III is used for children with motor-impairing conditions, the children may fail to complete some tasks that require hand–finger coordination, *even if* the children understand what is required and know how to do it. Such failure is not a reflection of their intellectual functioning, but rather is caused by their unique physical conditions. Because the test scores are interpreted as indicators of *intellectual functioning,* not of *motor coordination,* the validity of such test score interpretation for this special group is questionable. Similar reasoning applies to the situation when WISC-III is used for children with limited English language proficiency.

Statistical Formulas and Computation Examples

1. Formula for the Mean

$$\overline{X} = \frac{\Sigma X_i}{N}$$

(Formula 1)

where, the symbol $\overline{X}$ represents the mean, and X_i represents each individual score. The uppercase Greek letter Σ (sigma) means to "sum up" or "add together," and N represents the total number of scores used for calculation. For example, for the data in Table 3.2, the mean is obtained by

$$\overline{X} = \frac{\Sigma X_i}{N}$$

$$= \frac{(24 + 27 + 18 + 40 + 27 + 15 + 33 + 17 + 25)}{9}$$

$$= \frac{226}{9} = 25.11$$

2. Formulas for Variance and Standard Deviation

To understand *standard deviation* (*SD*), it is often unavoidable to encounter another closely related measure of dispersion, *variance* (s^2). As is shown here, the two are so closely related statistically that it does not require any special effort to understand variance. Here are the statistical formulas for variance and standard deviation:[1]

---

[1] In our presentation, we use N rather than $N - 1$ as the denominator in the formulas because statistical inference is not our major concern for this book, so we simply use *variance* or *standard deviation* as population descriptors.

$$Variance\ (s^2) = \frac{\Sigma(X_i - \overline{X})^2}{N} = \frac{\Sigma x_i^2}{N} \qquad \text{(Formula 2)}$$

$$Standard\ Deviation\ (SD) = \sqrt{variance} = \sqrt{\frac{\Sigma x_i^2}{N}} \qquad \text{(Formula 3)}$$

In the preceding two formulas, N represents the number of test scores in a distribution, $\overline{X}$ represents the mean of the score distribution, X_i represents each individual score, and the lower case x_i represents the deviation score, that is, how far an individual score deviates from the mean. Put verbally, *variance* is the average of squared deviation scores, and *standard deviation* is the square root of variance.

A simple calculation example is shown next for interested readers.

Raw Score	Deviation Score	Squared Deviation	Variance and Standard Deviation
X_i	$x_i = X_i - \text{Mean}$	x^2	
65	33	1089	Variance = $\Sigma x^2/N$
40	8	64	= 2030/5
30	−2	4	= 406
20	−12	144	
5	−27	729	SD = $\sqrt{406}$ = 20.15
Mean$(\overline{X})$ = 32	$\Sigma x_i = 0$	$\Sigma x^2 = 2030$	

Though small data set such as this allows for hand calculation of standard deviation, the calculation can be very tedious and time consuming when the number of scores increases. Most of us prefer to leave such calculation to calculators or computer programs.

3. Formula for computing z scores:

$$z_i = \frac{X_i - \overline{X}}{SD} \qquad \text{(Formula 4)}$$

where X_i represents an individual score, $\overline{X}$ is the mean of the score distribution, SD is the standard deviation of the distribution, and z_i is the z score for X_i. For example, for Jessica and Linda discussed in Chapter 3, who have scores of 62 and 51, respectively, with a mean of 65 and SD of 8, their z scores are

$$z_{Jessica} = \frac{Xi - \overline{X}}{SD}$$
$$= \frac{(62 - 65)}{8}$$
$$= \frac{-3}{8} = -0.375$$

$$z_{Linda} = \frac{X_i - \overline{X}}{SD}$$
$$= \frac{(51 - 65)}{8}$$
$$= \frac{-14}{8} = -1.75$$

4. Formulas for Correlation Coefficient

The correlation coefficient used here is formally known as the *Pearson product-moment correlation coefficient,* symbolized by *r*. Originally, Karl Pearson, an English statistician, defined this correlation coefficient by using standard *z* scores, rather than raw scores, as follows:

$$r_{xy} = \frac{\Sigma z_x z_y}{n - 1} \qquad \text{(Formula 5)}$$

where n is the sample size, z_x and z_y are the *z* scores on *X* and *Y* variables for each sample member in the sample, and r_{xy} is the correlation coefficient between *X* and *Y* variables. For hand calculation, it is often simpler to use raw scores instead of standard scores. The equivalent raw score formula for Formula 5 is

$$r_{xy} = \frac{n\Sigma XY - \Sigma X \Sigma Y}{\sqrt{[n\Sigma X^2 - (\Sigma X)^2][n\Sigma Y^2 - (\Sigma Y)^2]}} \qquad \text{(Formula 6)}$$

A small computation example ($N = 10$) is illustrated next for interested readers.

ID	X	Y	XY	X²	Y²
1	3	5	15	9	25
2	3	8	24	9	64
3	5	8	40	25	64
4	2	7	14	4	49
5	9	12	108	81	144
6	4	10	40	16	100
7	9	11	99	81	121
8	4	8	32	16	64
9	8	10	80	64	100
10	7	11	77	49	121
Σ	54	90	529	354	852

$$
\begin{aligned}
r_{xy} &= \frac{n\Sigma XY - \Sigma X \Sigma Y}{\sqrt{[n\Sigma X^2 - (\Sigma X)^2][n\Sigma Y^2 - (\Sigma Y)^2]}} \\[2mm]
&= \frac{10 \times 529 - 54 \times 90}{\sqrt{[10 \times 354 - (54)^2][10 \times 852 - (90)^2]}} \\[2mm]
&= \frac{5290 - 4860}{\sqrt{(3540 - 2916)(8520 - 8100)}} \\[2mm]
&= \frac{430}{\sqrt{624 \times 420}} \\[2mm]
&= \frac{430}{511.937496} \\[2mm]
&= .83995
\end{aligned}
$$

As you can see, even for a small problem like this, the computation becomes tedious. So whenever possible, it is better to leave the task to calculators or computer programs.

5. A Hypothetical Example for Calculating the Cronbach's Coefficient Alpha

Illustration of Coefficient Alpha Calculation

			Items				
Persons	**1**	**2**	**3**	**4**	**5**	**6**	**Total Score**
1	1	0	1	0	2	1	5
2	3	2	3	3	5	3	19
3	4	5	5	4	3	3	24
4	2	2	3	1	3	3	14
5	0	0	1	1	1	0	3
6	3	5	4	4	4	3	23
7	1	1	0	0	1	0	3
8	4	5	4	5	5	5	28
9	2	1	1	0	2	1	7
10	3	3	4	4	5	5	24
Variance	1.61	3.64	2.64	3.56	2.29	3.04	86.4

$$\alpha = \left(\frac{K}{K-1}\right)\left(1 - \frac{\Sigma \sigma_i^2}{\sigma^2}\right) = \left(\frac{6}{6-1}\right)\left(1 - \frac{1.61 + 3.64 + 2.64 + 3.56 + 2.29 + 3.04}{86.4}\right)$$

$$= \left(\frac{6}{5}\right)\left(1 - \frac{16.78}{86.4}\right) = .97$$

Coefficient alpha ranges from 0 to 1, with a higher value indicating higher internal consistency reliability. For the small example, an alpha of 0.97 would generally be regarded as indicating a very high degree of internal consistency among the test items.

6. A Hypothetical Example for Calculating KR−20

Illustration of KR−20 Calculation (1 represents a correct response to an item, and 0 represents an incorrect response to an item)

Items

Persons	1	2	3	4	5	6	Total Score
1	1	1	1	1	1	1	6
2	1	0	0	1	1	1	4
3	0	0	1	0	1	1	3
4	0	1	0	0	0	0	1
5	1	1	1	1	1	1	6
6	0	1	1	1	1	1	5
7	0	1	1	1	1	0	4
8	1	1	1	1	1	1	5
9	0	0	0	0	1	1	2
10	0	1	1	1	1	1	5
p	.4	.7	.7	.7	.9	.8	
q	.6	.3	.3	.3	.1	.2	
pq	.24	.21	.21	.21	.09	.16	$\sigma^2 = 2.49$

$$KR\text{--}20 = \left(\frac{K}{K-1}\right)\left(1 - \frac{\Sigma pq}{\sigma 2}\right) = \left(\frac{K}{K-1}\right)\left(1 - \frac{.24 + .21 + .21 + .21 + .09 + .16}{2.49}\right)$$

$$= \left(\frac{6}{5}\right)\left(1 - \frac{1.12}{2.49}\right) = .66$$

Fortunately, this is not a reliability estimate for an important test because .66 would usually be regarded as indicating a low degree of internal consistency reliability. Again, although the calculation may not look too complicated conceptually, it can be very tedious for hand calculation when you have more items and more students taking the test in a real classroom situation.

References

Abramson, T. (1969). The influence of examiner race on first-grade and kindergarten subjects' Peabody Picture Vocabulary Test scores. *Journal of Educational Measurement, 6*, 241–246.

Ace, M. C., & Dawis, R. V. (1973). Item structure as a determinant of item difficulty in verbal analogies. *Educational and Psychological Measurement, 6*, 241–246.

Aiken, L. R. (1991). Detecting, understanding, and controlling for cheating on tests. *Research in Higher Education, 32*, 725–736.

Aiken, L. R. (1996). *Assessment of intellectual functioning* (2nd ed.). New York: Plenum Press.

Aiken, L. R. (1997). *Psychological testing and assessment* (9th ed.). Boston, MA: Allyn and Bacon.

Aiken, L. W. (1980). Attitude measurement and research. *New Directions for Testing and Measurement, 7*, 1–24.

Airasian, P. W. (1979). A perspective on the uses and misuses of standardized achievement tests. *Measurement in Education, 10*(3), 1–12. (ERIC Document Reproduction Service No. ED 187 730).

Airasian, P. W. (1996). *Assessment in the classroom*. New York: McGraw-Hill.

Airasian, P. W., & Madaus, G. F. (1983). Linking testing and instruction: Policy issues. *Journal of Educational Measurement, 20*(2), 103–118.

Alderman, D. L., & Powers, D. E. (1980). The effects of special preparation on SAT-Verbal Scores. *American Educational Research Journal, 17*, 239–251.

Allport, G. W. (1935). Attitudes. In C. Murchison (Ed.), *Handbook of social psychology*, (pp. 798–844). Worchester: Clark University Press.

American Association for Mental Retardation. (1992). *Mental retardation: Definition, classification, and systems of supports*. Washington, DC: Author.

American Educational Research Association, American Psychological Association, and National Council on Measurement in Education (1985). *Standards for educational and psychological testing.* Washington, DC: American Psychological Association.

American Federation of Teachers, National Council on Measurement in Education, and National Education Association (Winter, 1990). Standards for teacher competence in educational assessment of students, *Educational Measurement: Issues and Practice, 9*(4), 30–32.

American Psychological Association, American Educational Research Association, & National Council on Measurement in Education. (1966). *Standards for educational and psychological tests and manuals.* Washington, DC: American Psychological Association.

American Psychological Association, American Educational Research Association, & National Council on Measurement in Education. (1974). *Standards for educational and psychological tests.* Washington, DC: American Psychological Association.

Anastasi, A. (1958). Heredity, environment, and the question "How?" *Psychological Review, 65,* 197–208.

Anastasi, A. (1988). *Psychological testing* (6th ed). New York: Macmillan.

Anastasi, A., & Urbina, S. (1997). *Psychological testing,* Upper Saddle River, NJ: Prentice-Hall.

Anderson, L. W. (1981). *Assessing affective characteristics in the schools.* Boston: Allyn & Bacon.

Anderson, B., & Pipho, C. (1984). State-mandated testing and the fate of local control. *Phi Delta Kappa, 66*(3), 209–212.

Anderson, L. W. (1988). Attitude measurement. In J. P. Keeves (Ed.), *Educational Research, Methodology, and Measurement: An International Handbook* (pp. 421–426). Oxford, England: Pergamon Press.

Anderson, L. W. (1994). Attitudes, measurement of. In T. Husen & T. N. Postlethwaite (Eds.), *The International Encyclopedia of Education* (2nd ed.) (pp. 380–390). Oxford, England: Pergamon Press.

Anderson, R. C., Kulhary, R. M., Andre, T. (1971). Feedback procedures in programmed instruction. *Journal of Educational Psychology, 62,* 148–156.

Anderson, B. L., Stiggins, R. J., & Gordon, D. W. (1980). *Educational testing facts and issues: A layperson's guide to testing in the schools.* Portland, OR: Northwest Regional Educational Laboratory and California State Department of Education (contract #400-79-0059).

Anderson, L. W. & Sosniak, L. A. (1994). *Bloom's taxonomy: A forty-year retrospective.* Ninety-third yearbook of the National Society for the Study of Education, Part II. Chicago: University of Chicago Press.

Anderson v. Banks, 520 F. Supp. 472, 509–11 (S.D. Ca. 1981).

Angoff, W. H. (1982). Norms and scales. In H. E. Mitzel (Ed.), *Encyclopedia of educational research* (5th ed.) (pp. 1342–1355). New York: The Free Press.

Angoff, W. H. (1992). Norms and scales. In M. C. Alkin (Ed.), *Encyclopedia of educational research* (6th ed., pp. 909–921). New York: Macmillan.

Ansorge, C. J. (1985). Review of cognitive abilities test, form 3. In J. V. Mitchell, Jr. (Ed.), *The ninth mental measurements handbook,* (pp. 351–352). Lincoln: Buros Institute of Mental Measures, University of Nebraska.

Arter, J. A. & Spandel, V. (1992). Using portfolios of student work in instruction and assessment. *Educational Measurement: Issues and Practice, 11*(1), 36–44.

Aschbacher, P. R. (1994). Helping educators to develop and use alternative assessments: Barriers and facilitators. *Educational Policy, 8,* 202–223.

Austin, G. R., & Garbar, H. (1982). *The rise and fall of national test scores.* New York, NY: Academic Press, Inc.

Baglin, R. F. (1981, Summer). Does "nationally" normed really mean nationally? *Journal of Educational Measurement, 18*(2), 97–107.

Baird, L. L., & Feister, W. J. (1972). Grading standards: The relation of changes in average student ability to the average grades awarded. *American Educational Research Journal, 9,* 431–42.

Bajtelsmit, J. W. (1977). Test-wiseness and systematic desensitization programs for increasing adult test-taking skills. *Journal of Educational Measurement, 14,* 335–341.

Baker, E. L. (1994). Making performance assessment work: The road ahead. *Educational Leadership, 51*(6), 58–62.

Baker, F. B. (1982). Item analysis. In H. E. Mitzel (Ed.), *Encyclopedia of Educational Research* (5th ed.) (pp. 959–967). New York: The Free Press.

Baker, F. B. (1989). Computer technology in test construction and processing. In R. L. Linn (Ed.), Educational measurement (3rd ed.) (pp. 409–428). New York: Macmillan.

Baker, E. L., O'Neil, H. F., Jr., & Linn, R. L. (1993). Policy and validity prospects for performance-based assessment. *American Psychologist, 48,* 1210–1218.

Baltes, P. B. (1968). Cross-sectional and longitudinal sequences in the study of age and generation effects. *Human Development, 11,* 145–171.

Baron, J. B., & Wolf, D. P. (1996). *Performance-based student assessment: Challenges and possibilities.* Ninety-fifth yearbook of the National Society for the Study of Education, Part I. Chicago: University of Chicago Press.

Bateson, D. (1994). Psychometric and philosophic problems in 'authentic' assessment: Performance tasks and portfolios. *Alberta Journal of Educational Research, 40,* 233–245.

Baxter, G. P., Elder, A. & Glaser, R. (1995). Cognitive analysis of a science performance assessment (CSE Technical Report 398). Los Angeles: University of California National Center for Research on Evaluation, Standards, and Student Testing.

Baxter, G. P., Glaser, R. & Raghavan, K. (1993). Analysis of cognitive demand in selected alternative science assessments (CSE Technical Report 382). Los Angeles: University of California National Center for Research on Evaluation, Standards, and Student Testing.

Bayley, N. (1955). on the growth of intelligence. *American Psychologist, 10,* 805–817.

Beattie, J., & Algozzine, B. (1982). Testing for teaching. *Arithmetic Teacher, 30*(1), 47–51.

Beckham, J. C. (1986). Objective testing to assess teacher competency: Emerging legal issues. In T. N. Jones & D. P. Semler (Eds.), *School law update.* Topeka, KS: National Organization on Legal Problems in Education.

Bellanca, J. A., & Kirschenbaum, H. (1976). An overview of grading alternatives. In S. B. Simon & J. A. Bellanca (Eds.), *Degrading the grading myths: A primer of alternatives to grades and marks* (pp. 51–62). Washington, DC: Association for Supervision and Curriculum Development.

Belson, W. A. (1981). *The design and understanding of survey questions.* Aldershot, England: Gower.

Ben-Shakhar, G., & Sinai, Y. (1991). Gender differences in multiple-choice tests: The role of differential guessing tendencies. *Journal of Educational Measurement, 28*(1), 23–35.

Bennett, R. E. & Ragosta, M. (1984). *A research context for studying admission tests and handicapped populations.* Princeton, NJ: Educational Testing Service.

Bennett, G. K., Seashore, H. G., & Westman, A. G. (1982). *Differential aptitude tests: Administrator's handbook.* San Antonio, TX: Psychological Corporation.

Berdie, D. R., & Anderson, J. F. (1974). *Questionnaires: Design and use.* Metuchen, NJ: Scarecrow Press.

Berk, R. A. (Ed.). (1982). *Handbook of methods for detecting test bias.* Baltimore, Maryland: The Johns Hopkins University Press.

Berk, R. A. (1984). Selecting the index of reliability. In R. A. Berk (Ed.), *A guide to criterion-referenced test construction* (pp. 231–266). Baltimore, MD: Johns Hopkins University Press.

Berk, R. A. (1986). Minimum competency testing: status and potential. In B. S. Plake & J. C. Witt (Eds.), *The future of testing,* (pp. 89–144). Hillsdale, NJ: Lawrence Erlbaum Associates.

Berk, R. A. (1988). Criterion-referenced tests. In J. P. Keeves (Ed.). *Educational research methodology, and measurement: An international handbook,* (pp. 365–370). Oxford, England: Pergamon Press.

Bersoff, D. N. (1981). Test bias: The judicial report card. *New York University Education Quarterly 3,* 2–8.

Bersoff, D. N. (1981). Testing and the law. *American Psychologist, 36*(10), 1047–1056.

Bester v. Tuscaloosa City Board of Education, 722 F.2d 1514 (11th Cir. 1984).

Binet, A. (1911). *Les idees modernes sur les enfants.* Paris: Flammarion.

Binet, A., & Simon, T. (1905). Methodes nouvelles pour le diagnostic du niveau intellectuel des anormaux. *Annee Psychologique, 11,* 191–244.

Birenbaum, M. (1994). On the relationship between test anxiety and test performance. *Measurement and Evaluation in Couseling and Development, 27,* 293–301.

Black, H. (1962). *They shall not pass.* New York: Random House.

Blessum, W. T. (1969). *Annual report 1968–1969, Medical Computer Facility.* Irvine, University of California, Irvine, California College of Medicine.

Bloom, B. S., Engelhart, M. D., Furst, G. J., Hill, W. H., & Krathwohl, D. R. (1956). *Taxonomy of educational objectives: Handbook I, The cognitive domain.* New York: David McKay Company Inc.

Board, C., & Whitney, D. R. (1977). *The effect of selected poor item-writing practices on test difficulty, reliability, and validity* (Research Report 55). Iowa City: University of Iowa, University Evaluation and Examination Service.

Boehm, A. E. (1986). *Boehm test of basic concepts—Revised.* San Antonio, TX: Psychological Corporation.

Boersma, W. C. (1967). *The effectiveness of the evaluative criteria as a stimulus for school improvement in eleven Michigan high schools.* Unpublished doctoral dissertation, University of Michigan.

Bond, L. (1995). Unintended consequences of performance assessment: Issues of bias and fairness. *Educational Measurement: Issues and Practice, 14*(4), 21–24.

Bortner, M. (1985). Review of Wechsler Intelligence Scale for Children—Revised. In J. V. Mitchell, Jr. (Ed.), *The ninth mental measurements handbook,* (pp. 1713–1714). Lincoln: Buros Institute of Mental Measures, University of Nebraska.

Botwinick, J. (1984). *Aging and behavior* (3rd ed.). New York: Springer.

Bowman, C. M., & Peng, S. S. (1972). *A preliminary investigation of recent advanced psychology tests in the FRE program—an application of cognitive classification system.* Unpublished ETS report, Princeton, NJ.

Bradburn, N. M., Sudman, S., & Associates (1981). *Improving interview method and questionnaire design.* San Francisco: Jossey-Bass.

Bracey, G. W. (1989). The $150 million redundancy. *Phi Delta Kappan, 70*(9), 698–702.

Brennan, R. L. (1983). *Elements of generalizability theory.* Iowa City, American College Testing Program.

Brennan, R. L., & Johnson, E. G. (1995). Generalizability of performance assessments. *Educational Measurement: Issues and Practice, 14,* (4), 9–12, 27.

Brewer, W. R. (1992, April 15). Can performance assessment survive success? *Education Week.*

Brickell, H. M. (1978). Seven key notes on minimal competency testing. *Educational Leadership, 35*(7), 551–552, 554–557.

Bright, E. L. (1992). *Teachers' views of ethical standardized test use.* Paper presented at the Annual Meeting of the National Council on Measurement in Education. San Francisco, CA, April 21–23, 1992. (ERIC Documentation Reproduction Service No. ED 347 168).

Brookhart v. Illinois State Board of Education, 697 2d. 179, 187 (7th Cir. 1983).

Brooks, C. R. (1977). WISC WISC-R S-B, L & M WRAT: Relationships and trends among children ages six to ten referred for psychological evaluation. *Psychology in the Schools, 14,* 30–33.

Brown, F. G. (1976). *Principles of educational and psychological testing* (2nd ed.) New York: Holt, Rinehart and Winston.

Brown, F. G. (1992). Review of the Stanford Achievement Test, Eighth Edition. *The eleventh mental measurements yearbook.* Lincoln, NE: The Buros Institute of Mental Measurements.

Brown, J. S., Collins, A. & Duguid, P. (1989). Situated cognition and the culture of learning. *Educational Researcher, 18*(1), 32–42

Brown, L., Sherbenou, R. J., & Dollars, S. J. (1982). *Test of Nonverbal Intelligence.* Austin, TX: Pro-Ed.

Brown v. Board of Education, 347 U.S. 483 (1954).

Bruininks, R. H., Woodcock, R. W., Weatherman, R. F., & Hill, B. K. (1984). *Scales of Independent Behavior, Interviewer's Manual.* Allen, TX: DLM Teaching Resources.

Bruininks, R. H., Woodcock, R. W., Weatherman, R. F., & Hill, B. K. (1985). *Technical summary for the Scales of Independent behavior.* Allen, TX: DLM Teaching Resources

Burba, K. V. (1976). A computerized alternative to grading. In S. B. Simon & J. A. Bellanca (Eds.), *Degrading the grading myths: A primer of alternatives to grades and marks* (pp. 64–69). Washington, DC: Association for Supervision and Curriculum Development.

Burgemeister, B. B., Blum, L. H., & Lorge, I. (1972). *Columbia Mental Maturity Scale* (3rd ed.). New York: Harcourt Brace Jovanovich.

Buros, O. K. (1938). *The 1938 mental measurement yearbook.* New Brunswick, NJ: Rutgers University Press.

Burstein, L. (1983). A word about this issue. *Journal of Educational Measurement, 20,* 99–101.

Butler, R. & Nissan, M. (1986). Effects of no feedback, task-related comments, and grades on intrinsic motivation and performance. *Journal of Educational Psychology, 78,* 210–216.

Calsyn, R. J. (1992). Acquiescence in needs assessment studies of the elderly. *Gerontologist, 32,* 246–252.

Cangelosi, J. C. (1982). *Measurement and evaluation: An inductive approach for teachers.* Dubuque, IA: Wm. C. Brown Company Publishers.

Cannell, J. J. (1988). *Nationally normed elementary achievement testing in America's public schools: How all 50 states are above the national average.* Daniels, WV: Friends for Education.

Cannell, J. J. (1989). *How public educators cheat on standardized achievement tests.* Albuquerque, NM: Friends for Education.

Carey, L. M. (1994). *Measuring and evaluating school learning* (2nd ed.). Boston: Allyn and Bacon.

Carlson, R. E. (1990). An alternative methodology for appraising the job relatedness of NTE Program tests. *Applied Measurement in Education, 2* (3), 243–253.

Carlson, S. B. (1985). *Creative classroom testing: Ten designs for assessment and instruction.* Princeton: Educational Testing Service.

Carter, R. S. (1952). How invalid are marks assigned by teachers? *Journal of Educational Psychology, 43,* 218–228.

Cashen V. M., & Ramseyer, G. C. (1969). The use of separate answer sheets by primary school children. *Journal of Educational Measurement, 6,* 155–158.

Cattell, R. B. (1941). Some theoretical issues in adult intelligence testing. *Psychological Bulletin, 38,* 592 (Abstract).

Cattell, R. B. (1971). *Abilities: Their structure, growth, and action.* Boston: Houghton Mifflin.

Cattell, J. McK. (1890). Mental tests and measurements. *Mind, 15,* 373–381.

Chadwick, E. (1864). Statistics of educational results. *The Museum, 3,* 480–484.

Chase, C. I. (1985). Review of the Torrance Test of Creative Thinking. In J. V. Mitchell, Jr. (Ed.), *The ninth mental measurements yearbook* (p. 1637). Lincoln: Institute of Mental Measures, University of Nebraska.

Childs, R. A. (1990). *Legal issues in testing.* (ERIC Documentation Reproduction Service No. ED 320 964.)

Christen, W. (1976). Contracting for student learning. *Educational Technology, 16,* 27.

Cizek, G. J. & O'Day, D. M. (1994). Further investigation of nonfunctioning options in multiple-choice test items. *Educational and Psychological Measurement, 54,* 861–872.

Cizek, G. J. (1991a). Confusion effusion: A rejoinder to Wiggins. *Phi Delta Kappan, 72*(2), 150–153.

Cizek, G. J. (1991b). Innovation or enervation? Performance assessment in perspective. *Phi Delta Kappan, 72*(9), 695–699.

Clark, D. C. (1969). Competition for grades and graduate student performance. *Journal of Educational Research, 62,* 351–354.

Cleary, T. A., Humphreys, L. G., Kendrick, A. S., & Wesman, A. (1975). Educational uses of tests with disadvantaged students. *American Psychologist, 30,* 15–41.

Clifford, P. I., & Fishman, J. A. (1963). the impact of testing programs on college preparation and attendance. *The impact and improvement of school testing programs.* Sixty-second yearbook of the National Society for the Study of Education, Part II. Chicago: University of Chicago Press.

Cohen, S. A., & Hyman, J. S. (1991). Can fantasies become facts? *Educational Measurement: Issues and Practice, 10*(1), 20–23.

Cohen, R. J., Swerdlik, M. E., & Phillips, S. M. (1996). *Psychological testing and assessment: An introduction to tests and measurement* (3rd ed.). Mountain View, CA: Mayfield Publishing Company.

Cole, N. S. (1981). Bias in testing. *American Psychologist, 36,* 1067–1077.

Cole, N. S., & Moss, P. A. (1989). Bias in test use. In R. L. Linn (Ed.), *Educational Measurement* (3rd ed.) (pp. 201–219). London: Collier Macmillan.

Coleman, J. S., et al. (1966). *Equality of educational opportunity.* Washington, DC: Government Printing Office.

Conklin, R. C. (1985). Teacher competency testing. *Education Canada, 25*(1), 12–15.

Conklin, J. E., Burstein, L., & Keesling, J. W. (1979). The effects of date of testing and method of interpretation on the use of standardized test scores in the validation of large-scale educational programs. *Journal of Educational Measurement, 16,* 239–246.

Conoley, J. C. (1990). Review of the K-ABC: Reflecting the unobservable. *Journal of Psychoeducational Assessment, 8,* 369–375.

Conoley, J. C., & Impara, J. C. (Eds.). (1995). *The twelfth mental measurements yearbook.* Lincoln, NE: The Buros Institute of Mental Measurements, the University of Nebraska-Lincoln.

Conroy, M. (1987, November). Coaching for SAT tests: Could it help your child get into college? *Better Homes and Gardens,* 105–106.

Conry, R., & Plant, W. T. (1965). WAIS and group test predictions of an academic success criterion: High school and college. *Educational and Psychological Measurement, 25,* 493–500.

Cooper, E. (1991). A critique of six measures for assessing creativity. *Journal of Creative Behavior, 25,* 194–204.

Cooper, W. H. (1981). Ubiquitous halo. *Psychological Bulletin, 90,* 218–244.

Cox, J. B. (1996). *Your opinion, please!: How to build the best questionnaires in the field of education.* Thousand Oaks, CA: Sage Publications.

Corbett, H. D., & Wilson, B. L. (1990). *Unintended and unwelcome: The local impact of state testing.* Paper presented at the Annual Meeting of the American Educational Research Association. Boston, MA, April 16-20, 1990. (ERIC Documentation Reproduction Service No. ED 377 234.

Cornehlsen, V. H. (1965). Cheating attitudes and practices in a suburban high school. *Journal of the National Association of Women Deans and Counselors, 28,* 106–109.

Cortina, J. M. (1993). What is coefficient alpha? An explanation of theory and applications. *Journal of Applied Psychology, 78,* 98–104.

Costa, A. L. (1989). Re-assessing assessment, *Educational Leadership, 46*(7), 2.

Covington, M. V. (1992). *Making the grade.* Cambridge, England: Cambridge University Press.

Crocker, L., & Algina, J. (1986). *Introduction to classical and modern test theory.* New York: Holt, Rinehart & Winston.

Crocker, L., & Benson, J. (1976). Achievement, guessing, and risk-taking under norm referenced and criterion referenced testing conditions. *American Educational Research Journal, 13,* 207–215.

Cronbach, L. J. (1946). Response sets and test validity. *Educational and Psychological Measurement, 6,* 475–494.

Cronbach, L. J. (1951). Coefficient alpha and the internal structure of tests. *Psychometrika, 16,* 297–334.

Cronbach, L. J. (1984). *Essentials of psychological testing* (4th ed.) New York: Harper and Row.

Cross, L., & Frary, R. (1977). An empirical test of Lord's theoretical results regarding formula scoring of multiple-choice tests. *Journal of Educational Measurement, 17,* 313–322.

CTB/McGraw-Hill. (1989). *California Diagnostic Mathematics Tests (Levels E and F): Teacher's guide.* Monterey, CA: CTB/McGraw-Hill.

CTB/McGraw-Hill. (1991). *California Diagnostic Mathematics Tests Technical Report.* Monterey, CA: CTB/McGraw-Hill.

CTB/McGraw-Hill. (1997). *Teacher's guide to TerraNova.* Monterey, CA: CTB/McGraw-Hill.

Culler, R. E., & Holahan, C. (1980). Test taking and academic performance: The effects of study-related behaviors. *Journal of Educational Psychology, 72,* 16–20.

Culyer, R. C. (1982). Interpreting achievement test data: Some areas of concern. *Clearing House, 55*(8), 374–380.

Cureton, L. W. (1971). The history of grading practices. *National Council on Measurement in Education: Measurement News, 2,* (Whole No. 4), 1–8.

D'Agostino, R. B., & Cureton, E. E. (1975). The 27 percent rule revisited. *Educational and Psychological Measurement, 25,* 41–50.

Dadourian, H. M. (1925). Are examinations worth the price? *School and Society, 21,* 442–43.

Darling, H. L., & Wise, A. E. (1985). Beyond standardization: State standards and school improvement. *The Elementary School Journal, 85,* 315–336.

Darling-Hammond, L. (1991). The implications of testing policy for quality and equality. *Phi Delta Kappan, 73*(3), 220–225.

Darling-Hammond, L. Ancess, J. & Falk, B. (1995). *Authentic assessment in action: Studies of schools and students at work.* New York: Teachers College Press.

Darling-Hammond, L., & Lieberman, A. (January 29, 1992). The shortcomings of standardized tests. *Chronicle of Higher Education,* pp. B1–2.

Davis, C. (1980). *Perkins-Binet Tests of Intelligence for the blind.* Watertown, MA: Perkins School for the Blind.

Davis, R. V. (1980). Measuring interests. In David A. Payne (Ed.), *Recent development in affective measurement.* San Francisco: Jossey-Bass.

Davis, S. E. & Kramer, J. J. (1985). Comparison of the PPVT-R and WISC-R: A validation study with second-grade students. *Psychology in the Schools, 22,* 265–268.

Debra, P. v. Turlington, 474 F. Supp. 244, 265 (M. D. Fla. 1979).

DeCecco, J. P. (1968). *The psychology of learning and instruction: Educational psychology.* Englewood Cliffs, NJ: Prentice-Hall.

DeLandsheere, V. (1991). In A. Lewy (Ed.), *The international encyclopedia of curriculum* (pp. 317–327). Oxford, England: Pergammon Press.

Diana v. California State Board of Education, No. C-70 37 RFP, District Court of Northern California, 1970.

Dobbin, J. E. (1984). *How to take a test.* Princeton, NJ: Educational Testing Service.

Doll, E. A. (1935). The Vineland Social Maturity Scale. *Training School Bulletin, 32,* 1–7, 25–32, 48–55, 68–74.

Dolly, J. P., & Williams, K. S. (1983). *Teaching testwiseness.* Paper presented at the annual meeting of the Northern Rocky Mountain Educational Research Association, Jackson, WY.

Donlon, T. F. (1984). *The College Board technical handbook for the Scholastic Aptitude Test and achievement tests.* New York: College Entrance Examination Board.

DuBois, P. H. (1970). *A history of psychological testing.* Boston: Allyn and Bacon.

Dunbar, S. B., Koretz, D. M. & Hoover, H. D. (1991). Quality control in the development and use of performance assessments. *Applied Measurement in Education, 4,* 289–303.

Dunn, L. M. & Dunn, L. M. (1981). *Peabody Picture Vocabulary Test-Revised.* Circle Pine, MN: American Guidance Service.

Dwyer, C. A. (1982). Achievement Testing. In H. E. Mitzel, (Ed.), *Encyclopedia of Educational Research,* (5th ed.) (pp. 13–21), New York, NY: The Free Press.

D'Costa, A. G. (1993). The impact of courts on teacher competence testing. *Theory into Practice, 32,* 104–112.

Eagly, A. H. & Chaiken, S. (1993). *The psychology of attitudes.* Ft. Worth, TX: Harcourt Brace Jovanovich.

Ebel, R. L. (1965). *Measuring educational achievement.* Englewood Cliffs, NJ: Prentice-Hall.

Ebel, R. L. (1979). *Essentials of educational measurement* (3rd ed.) Englewood Cliffs, NJ: Prentice-Hall.

Echternacht, G. J. (1976). Reliability and validity of item option weighting schemes. *Educational and Psychological Measurement, 36,* 3-1-309.

Educational Measurement: Issue and Practice. (1982). How other organizations view testing, *1*(1), 17–19.

Educational Measurement: Issues and Practice. (1988), 7(4).

Educational Testing Service (1963). *Multiple choice questions: A close look.* Princeton, NJ. (Reprinted in G. H. Bracht, K. D. Hopkins, & J. C. Stanley, (Eds.), 1972. *Perspectives in educational and psychological measurement.* Englewood Cliffs, NJ: Prentice-Hall.)

Educational Testing Service (1980). *Test scores and family income: A response to changes in the Nader/Nairn report on ETS.* Princeton, NJ: Educational Testing Service.

Educational Testing Service (1987). *ETS standards for quality and fairness.* Princeton, NJ: Educational Testing Service.

Edwards, A. L. (1957a). *The social desirability variability in personality assessment and research.* New York: Dryden Press.

Edwards, A. L. (1957b). *Techniques of attitude scale construction.* NY: Appleton-Century-Crofts.

Eells, W. C. (1930). Reliability of repeated essay grading of essay type questions. *Journal of Educational Psychology, 31,* 48-52.

Enright, B. (1992). Helping mainstreamed students develop successful test-taking skills. *Diagnostic, 17* (2), 128–136.

Epstein, J. L. (Ed.). (1981). *The quality of school life.* Lexington, MA: Lexington Books.

Epstein, J. L., & McPartland, J. M. (1976). The concept and measurement of the quality of school life. *American Educational Research Journal, 13*(1), 15–30.

Erlenmeyer-Kimling, L., & Jarvik, L. F. (1963). Genetics and intelligence: A review. *Science, 142,* 1477–1479.

Esposito, D. (1973). Homogeneous and heterogeneous ability grouping: Principal findings and implications for evaluating and designing more effective educational environments. *Review of Educational Research, 43,* 163–179.

Evans, W. (1984). Test wiseness: An examination of cue-using strategies. *Journal of Experimental Education, 52,* 141–144.

Everson, H. T. (1992). *Exploring the relationship of test anxiety and metacognition on reading test performance: A cognitive analysis.* Paper presented at the Annual Meeting of the American Psychological Association. Washington, DC, August 14–18. ERIC Documentation Reproduction Services No. ED 363 624.

Fan, X., Willson, V. L., & Kapes, J. T. (1996). Ethnic group's representation in test construction samples and test bias: The standardization fallacy revisited. *Educational and Psychological Measurement, 56,* 365–381.

Fazio, R. H. (1989). On the power and functionality of attitudes: the role of attitude accessibility. In A. R. Pratkanis, S. J. Breckler, & A. G. Greenwald (Eds.). *Attitude structure and function* (pp. 153–179). Hillsdale, NJ: Erlbaum.

Feldmesser, R. A. (1971). *The Positive Function of Grades.* Paper presented at the Annual Meeting of the American Educational Research Association, New York.

Ferrara, S. & McTighe, J. (1992). Assessment: A thoughtful process. In A. L. Costa, J. Bellanca, & R. Fogarty (Eds.), *Id minds matter* (pp. 337–348). Palantine, IL: Skylight Publishing.

Findley, W. G. (1963). Purpose of school testing programs and their efficient development. In W. G. Findley (Ed.), *The impact and improvement of school testing programs.* Sixty-second yearbook of the National Society for the Study of Education, Part II. Chicago, IL: University of Chicago Press.

Findley, W. G., & Bryan, M. M. (1971). *Ability grouping: 1970 status, impact, and alternatives.* Athens, GA: University of Georgia, Center for Educational Improvement. (ERIC Document Reproduction Service No. ED 060 595).

Flanders, N. A. (1970). *Analyzing teaching behavior.* Reading, MA: Addison-Wesley.

Fleming, M. & Chambers, B. (1983). Teacher-made tests: Windows on the classroom. In W. E. Hathaway (Ed.), *Testing in the schools: New directions for testing and measurement,* (Vol. 19, pp. 29–38). San Francisco, CA: Jossey-Bass.

Floden, R. E., Porter, A. C., Schmidt, W. H., & Freeman, D. J. (1978). *Don't they all measure the same thing? Consequences of selecting standardized tests.* East Lansing, MI: Michigan State University, National Institute for Research on Teaching (ERIC Document Reproduction Service No. ED 167632).

Foddy, W. (1993). *Constructing questions for interviews and questionnaires.* Cambridge, England: Cambridge University Press.

Frary, R. B., Cross, L. H., & Weber, L. J. (1993). Testing and grading practices and opinions of secondary teachers of academic subjects: Implications for instruction in measurement. *Educational Measurement: Issues and Practice, 12*(3), 23–30.

Frederiksen, N. (1984). The real test bias: Influences of testing on teaching and learning. *American Psychologist, 39,* 193–202.

Freeman, D., Kuhs, T., Knappen, L., & Porter, A. (1979). *A closer look at standardized tests* (Research Series No. 53). East Lansing, MI: Michigan State University, Institute for Research on Teaching (ERIC Document Reproduction Service No. ED 179581).

Fricke, B. G. (1975). *Report to the faculty: Grading, testing, standards, and all that.* Ann Arbor: University of Michigan, Evaluation and Examination Office.

Frisbie, D. A. & Becker, D. F. (1990). An analysis of textbook advice about true-false tests. *Applied Measurement in Education, 4,* 67–83.

Frisbie, D. A. & Waltman, K. K. (1992). Developing a personal grading plan. *Educational Measurement: Issues and Practice, 11*(3), 35–42.

Fry, E. B. (1981). *Reading diagnosis: Informal reading inventories.* Providence, RI: Jamestown Publishers.

Fuchs, D., & Fuchs, L. S. (1986). Test procedure bias: A meta-analysis of examiner familiarity effects. *Review of Educational Research, 56,* 243–262.

Furst, E. J. (1958). *Constructing evaluation instruments.* New York: David McKay, Inc.

Gaffney, R. F., & Maguire, T. O. (1971). Use of optically scored test answer sheets with young children. *Journal of Educational Measurement, 8,* 103–106.

Gafni, N., & Estela, M. (1990). *Differential tendencies to guess as a function of gender and lingual-cultural reference group.* ERIC Documentation Reproduction Services No. ED 322 181.

Gagné, R. M. (1985). The conditions of learning (4th ed.). New York: Holt, Rinehart and Winston.

Gao, X., Shavelson, R. J., & Baxter, G. P. (1994). Generalizability of large-scale performance assessments in science: Promises and problems. *Applied Measurement in Education, 7,* 323–342.

Garcia, J. (1981). The logic and limits of mental aptitude testing. *American Psychologist, 36*(10), 1172–1180.

Gardner, H. (1983). Frames of mind: The theory of multiple intelligence. New York: Basic Books.

Gardner, H. (1992). Assessment in context: The alternative to standardized testing. In B. R. Gifford & M. C. O'Connor (Eds.), *Changing assessments: Alternative views of aptitude, achievement and instruction* (pp. 77–119). Boston: Kluwer.

Gardner, P. L. (1975). Attitude measurement: A critique of some recent research. *Educational Research, 17,* 101–109.

Gay, L. R. (1980). The comparative effects of multiple-choice versus short-answer tests on retention. *Journal of Educational Measurement, 17,* 45–50.

Geisinger, K. F. (1979). A note on grading policies and grade inflation. *Improving College and University Teaching, 27,* 113–115.

Geisinger, K. F. (1980). Who are giving all those A's? *Journal of Teacher Education, 31,* 11–15.

Geisinger, K. F. (1982). Marking systems. In H. E. Mitzel (Ed.), *Encyclopedia of Educational Research (5th ed.),* (Vol. 3, pp. 1139–1149). New York: The Free Press.

Geisinger, K. F., & Rabinowitz, W. (1979). Grading attitudes and practices among college faculty members. In H. Dahl, A. Lysne, & P. Rand (Eds.), *A Spotlight on Educational Problems* (pp. 145–172). New York: Columbia University Press.

Geisinger, K. F., Wilson, A. N., & Naumann, J. J. (1980). A construct validation of faculty orientations toward grading: Comparative data from three institutions. *Educational and Psychological Measurement, 40,* 413–417.

Georgia Association of Educators v. Nix, 407 F. Supp. 1102 (N.D. Ga. 1976).

Ghiselli, E. E. (1966). *The validity of occupational aptitude tests.* New York: Wiley.

Glaser, R. (1963). Instructional technology and the measurement of learning outcomes: Some questions. *American Psychologist, 18,* 519–521.

Glaser, R. & Silver, E. (1994). Assessment, testing, and instruction: Retrospect and prospect. In L. Darling-Hammond (Ed.), *Review of Research in Education, 20,* 393–419.

Glasser, W. (1969). *Schools without failure.* New York: Harper & Row.

Glazer, N. (1970). Are academic standards obsolete? *Change in Higher Education, 2,* 38–44.

Goetz, E. T. & Hall, R. J. (1984). Evaluation of the Kaufman Assessment Battery for Children from an information-processing perspective. *Journal of Special Education, 18,* 281–396.

Gold, R. M., Reilly, A., Silberman, R., & Lehr, R. (1971). Academic achievement declines under pass-fail grading. *Journal of Experimental Education, 39,* 17–21.

Gonzalez, M. (1985). Cheating on standardized tests: What is it? In P. Wolmut & G. Iverson (Eds.), *National association of test directors 1985 symposia* (pp. 4–16). Portland, OR: Multnomah ESD.

Goodwin, W. L. (1966). Effect of selected methodological conditions on dependent measures taken after classroom experimentation. *Journal of Educational Psychology, 57,* 350–358.

Gould, S. J. (1981). *The Mismeasure of Man.* New York: Norton.

Graziano, W. G., Varca, P. E., & Levy, J. C. (1982). Race of examiner effects and the validity of intelligence tests. *Review of Educational Research, 52,* 469–497.

Green, B. F. (1981). A primer of testing. *American Psychologist, 36,* 1001–1011.

Green, D. R. (1983). *Content validity of Standardized Achievement Tests and test curriculum overlap.* Symposium conducted at the annual meeting of the National Council on Measurement in Education, Montreal.

Green, L. T. (1990). Test anxiety, mathematics anxiety, and teacher comments: Relationships to achievement in remedial mathematics classes. *Journal of Negro Education, 59,* 320–335.

Green, D. R. & Draper, J. F. (1972, September). *Exploratory studies of bias in achievement tests.* Paper presented at the Annual Meeting of the American Psychological Association. Honolulu, Hawaii. (ERIC Document Reproduction Service No. ED 070 794).

Greenwald, A. G. (1989). Why attitudes are important? In A. R. Pratkanis, S. J. Breckler, & A. G. Greenwald (Eds.). *Attitude Structure and Function* (pp. 1–10). Hillsdale, NJ: Erlbaum.

Gregory, R. J. (1992). *Psychological Testing: History, principles, and applications.* Needham Heights, MA: Allyn & Bacon.

Gregory, R. J. (1996). *Psychological Testing: History, principles, and applications (2nd ed.).* Needham Heights, MA: Allyn & Bacon.

Grier, J. B. (1975). The number of alternatives for optimum test reliability. *Journal of Educational Measurement, 12,* 109–113.

Griffith, J. (1996). Relation of parental involvement, empowerment, and school traits to student academic performance. *Journal of Educational Research, 90,* 33–41.

Gronlund, N. E. (1985). *Measurement and Evaluation in Teaching* (5th ed.). New York: Macmillan.

Gronlund, N. E. (1991). *How to write and use instructional objectives* (4th ed.). New York: Macmillan.

Gronlund, N. E. (1993). *How to make achievement tests and assessments* (5th ed.). Boston: Allyn & Bacon.

Gross, M. (1962). *The Brain Watchers.* New York: Random House.

Grossman, H. J. (1983). *Classification in Mental Retardation.* Washington, DC: American Association of Mental Deficiency.

Guilford, J. P. (1969). *Intelligence, creativity and their educational implications.* San Diego: Educational and Industrial Testing Service.

Guilford, J. P., & Hoepfner, R. (1971). *The analysis of intelligence.* New York: McGraw-Hill.

Gulliksen, G. (1986). Perspective on educational measurement. *Applied Psychological Measurement, 10,* 109–13.

Gullickson, A. R., & Ellwein, M. (1985). Post hoc analysis of teacher-made tests: The goodness-of-fit between prescription and practice. *Educational Measurement: Issues and Practice, 4,* 15–18.

Guskey, T. R. (Ed.) (1996). *Communicating student learning.* Washington, D.C.: Association for Supervision and Curriculum Development.

Guskey, T. R. (Ed.) (1994). *High stakes performance assessment: Perspectives on Kentucky's educational reform.* Thousand Oaks, CA: Corwin Press.

Gustav, A. (1963). Response set in objective achievement tests. *Journal of Psychology, 56,* 421–427.

Gutbezahl, J. (1995). How negative expectancies and attitudes undermine females' math confidence and performance: A review of the literature. (ERIC Documentation Reproduction Service No. ED 380 279).

Haas, N. S., Haladyna, T. M., & Nolen, S. B. (1989). *Standardized testing in Arizona: Interviews and written comments from teachers and administrators* (Tech. Rep. No. 89-3). Phoenix, AZ: Arizona State University West Campus.

Haddad, F. A. (1986). Comparison of the WISC-R, PPVT-R, and PPVT for learning disabled children. *Psychological Reports, 58,* 659–662.

Hadley, S. T. (1954). A school mark—Fact or fancy? *Educational Administration and Supervision, 40,* 305–12.

Haensly, P. A., & Torrance, E. P. (1990). Assessment of creativity in children and adolescents. In C. R. Reynolds & R. W. Kamphaus (Eds.), *Handbook of psychological and educational assessment of children: Intelligence and achievement.* New York: The Guilford Press.

Hakstian, A. R., & Kansup, W. (1975). A comparison of several methods of assessing partial knowledge in multiple-choice tests: II. Testing procedures. *Journal of Educational Measurement, 12,* 231–240.

Haladyna, T. M. (1994). *Developing and Validating Multiple-Choice Test Items.* Hillsdale, NJ: Lawrence Erlbaum.

Haladyna, T. M. (1997). *Writing Test Items to Evaluate Higher Order Thinking.* Boston: Allyn and Bacon.

Haladyna, T. M., & Downing, S. M. (1989a). A taxonomy of multiple-choice item-writing rules. *Applied Measurement in Education, 2*(1), 37–50.

Haladyna, T. M., & Downing, S. M. (1989b). Validity of a taxonomy of multiple-choice item-writing rules. *Applied Measurement in Education, 2*(1), 51–78.

Haladyna T. M. & Downing, S. M. (1993). How many options is enough for a multiple-choice test item? *Educational and Psychological Measurement, 53,* 999–1010.

Haladyna, T. M., Nolen, S. B., & Haas, N. S. (1991). Raising standardized achievement test scores and the origins of test score pollution. *Educational Researcher, 20*(5), 2–7.

Haladyna, T. M., & Roid, G. (1981). The role of instructional sensitivity in the empirical review of criterion-referenced test items. *Journal of Educational Measurement, 18,* 39–53.

Haladyna, T. M., & Roid, G. H. (Fall, 1983). A comparison of two approaches to criterion-referenced test construction. *Journal of Educational Measurement, 20*(3), 271–282.

Haladyna, T., & Thomas, G. (1979a). The affective reporting system. *Journal of Educational Measurement, 16*(1), 49–54.

Haladyna, T., & Thomas, G. (1979b). The attitudes of elementary school children towards school and subject matters. *Journal of Educational Measurement, 48*(1), 18–23.

Hambleton, R. K. (1989). Principles and selected applications of item response theory. In R. L. Linn (Ed.), *Educational Measurement* (3rd ed., pp. 147–200). New York: Macmillan.

Hambleton, R. K. & Jones, R. W. (1993). Comparison of classical test theory and item response theory and their applications to test development. *Educational Measurement: Issues and Practice, 12*(3), 38–47.

Hambleton, R. K., Swaminathan, H., & Rogers, H. J. (1991). *Fundamentals of Item Response Theory.* Newbury Park, CA: Sage.

Hambleton, R. K., & Traub, R. E. (1974). The effects of item order on test performance and stress. *Journal of Experimental Education, 43,* 40–46.

Haney, W. (1981). Validity, vaudeville, and values: A short history of social concerns over standardized testing. *American Psychologist, 36*(10), 1021–1034.

Haney, W. (1984). Testing reasoning and reasoning about testing. *Review of Educational Research, 54*(4), 597–654.

Haney, W., & Madaus, G. (1989). Searching for alternatives to standardized tests: Whys, whats, and whithers. *Phi Delta Kappan, 70*(9), 683–687.

Haney, W., Madaus, G. F., & Lyon, R. (1993). *The fractured marketplace for standardized testing.* Boston: Kluwer.

Hardy, R. (1996). Performance assessment: Examining the costs. In M. B. Kane & R. Mitchell (Eds.). *Implementing performance assessment: Promises, problems, and challenges* (pp. 107–117). Mahwah, NJ: Elrbaum.

Harmon, L. W. (1992). Interest measurement. In M. C. Alkin (Ed.), *Encyclopedia of educational research* (pp. 636–642). New York: MacMillan.

Harmon, M. G., Morse, D. T, & Morse, L. W. (1996). Confirmatory factor analysis of the Gibb Experimental Test of Testwiseness. *Educational and Psychological Measurement, 56,* 276–286.

Harrington, G. M. (1984). An experimental model of bias in mental testing. In C. R. Reynolds & R. T. Brown (Eds.), *Perspectives on bias in mental testing* (pp. 101–138). New York: Plenum.

Hassencahl, F. (1979). Contract grading in the classroom. *Improving College and University Teaching, 27,* 30–33.

Hatch, J. A., & Freeman, E. B. (1988). Who's pushing whom? Stress and kindergarten. *Phi Delta Kappan, 69,* 145–147.

Haynes, L. T., & Cole, N. S. (1982, March). *Testing some assumptions about on-level versus out-of-level achievement testing.* Paper presented at the annual meeting of the National Council on Measurement on Education, New York, NY.

Heberlein, T. A., & Baumgartner, R. (1978). Factors affecting response rates to mailed questionnaires: A quantitative analysis of the published literature. *American Sociological Review, 43,* 82–101.

Henrysson, S. (1971). Gathering, analyzing, and using data on test items. In R. L. Thorndike (Ed.), *Educational measurement* (pp. 130–159). Washington, DC: American Council on Education.

Herman, J. L., & Dorr-Bremme, D. W. (1984, April). *Teachers and testing: Implications from a national study.* Paper presented at the annual meeting of the American Educational Research Association, New Orleans, LA.

Herrnstein, R. J. & Murray, C. (1994). *The bell curve: Intelligence and class structure in American life.* New York, NY: The Free Press.

Hicklin, N. J. (1962). *A study of long-range techniques for predicting patterns of scholastic behavior.* Unpublished Ph.D. thesis, University of Chicago.

Hickman, J. A., & Reynolds, C. R. (1986–87). Are race differences in mental test scores an artifact of psychometric methods? A test of Harrington's experimental model. *The Journal of Special Education, 20,* 409–430.

Hieronymous, A. N., & Hoover, H. D. (1985). *Iowa Test of Basic Skills—Forms G and H.* Chicago: Riverside Publishing Co.

Hill, K. T. (1984). Debilitating motivation and testing: A major educational problem, possible solutions, and policy applications. In R. Ames & C. Ames (Eds.), *Research on motivation in education: Student motivation.* New York: Academic Press.

Hill, K. T., & Wigfield, A. (1984). Test anxiety: A major educational problem and what can be done about it. *The Elementary School Journal, 85*(1), 105–126.

Hills, J. R. (1986). *All of Hills' handy hints.* Washington, DC: National Council on Measurement in Education.

Hobson v. Hansen, 269 F. Supp. 401 (D.D.C. 1967), *off'd sub nom.* Smuck v. Holson, 408 F. 2d 175 (D.C. Cir. 1969).

Hoepfner, R. (1967). Review of the Torrance tests of creative thinking. *Journal of Educational Measurement, 4,* 191–192.

Hoffmann, B. (1962). *The tyranny of testing.* NY: Crowell-Collier Press.

Hogan, T. P. (1975). *Survey of school attitudes, manual for administering and interpreting.* New York: Harcourt Brace Jovanovich.

Honig, B., Alexander, F., & Wolf, D. P. (1996). Rewriting the tests: Lessons from the California State Assessment System. In J. B. Baron and D. P. Wolf (Eds.). *Performance-based student assessment: challenges and possibilities* (pp. 143–165). Ninety-fifth yearbook of the National Society for the Study of Education, Part I. Chicago: University of Chicago Press.

Hopkins, K. D. (1998). *Educational and psychological measurement and evaluation.* Boston: Allyn & Bacon.

Hopkins, K. D., & Stanley, J. C. (1981). *Educational and Psychological Measurement and Evaluation* (6th ed.). England Cliffs, NJ: Prentice-Hall.

Hopkins, K. D., Stanley, J. C., & Hopkins, B. R. (1990). *Educational and psychological measurement and evaluation.* Boston: Allyn & Bacon.

Horn, J. L. (1968). Organization of abilities and the development of intelligence. *Psychological Review, 75,* 242–259.

Horn, J. L. (1985). Remodeling old models of intelligence. In B. B. Wolman (Ed.), *Handbook of Intelligence: Theories, Measurements, and Applications.* New York, Wiley.

Houston, J. P. (1976). Amount and loci of classroom answer copying, spaced seating, and alternate test forms. *Journal of Educational Psychology, 68,* 729–735.

Houts, P. L. (1975). Standardized testing in America, II. *The National Elementary Principal, 54,* 2–3.

Hoyt, D. P. (1970). Rationality and the grading process. *Educational Record, 41,* 105–109.

Hu, C. T. (1984). The historical background: Examinations and control in pre-modern China. *Comparative Education, 20*(1), 7–26.

Huang, S. Y. L., & Waxman, H. C. (1995). Motivation and learning environment differences between Asian-American and white middle school students in mathematics. *Journal of Research and Development in Education, 28,* 208–219.

Hunter, J. E. (1982). *The dimensionality of the General Aptitude Test Battery and the dominance of general factors over specific factors in the prediction of job performance.* Washington, DC: US Employment Service, U.S. Department of Labor.

Hunter, J. E. (1994). General Aptitude Test Battery. In R. J. Sternberg (Ed.), *Encyclopedia of human intelligence.* New York: Macmillan.

Jaeger, R. M. (1982). The final hurdle: Minimum competency achievement testing. In G. R. Austin & H. Garber (Eds.), *The rise and fall of national test scores* (pp. 223–246). New York: Academic Press.

Jaeger, R. M. (1989). Certification of student competence. In R. L. Linn (Ed.), *Educational measurement* (3rd ed., pp. 485–514). London: Collier Macmillan.

Jaeger, R. M. (Winter, 1990). Establishing standards for teacher certification tests. *Educational Measurement: Issues and Practices, 9*(4), 15–20.

Jarvik, L. F., Eisdorfer, C., & Blum, J. E. (Eds.) (1973). *Intellectual functioning in adults: Psychological and biological influences.* New York: Springer.

Jencks, C., & Riesman, D. (1968). *The academic revolution.* New York: Doubleday.

Jenkins, J. R., & Pany, D. (1978). Standardized achievement tests: How useful for special education? *Exceptional Children, 44*(6), 448–453.

Jensen, A. (1969). How much can we boost IQ and scholastic achievement? *Harvard Educational Review, 39,* 5–28.

Jensen, A. (Ed.) (1980). *Bias in Mental Testing.* New York: The Free Press.

Jessell, J. C., & Sullins, W. L. (1975). The effect of keyed response sequencing of multiple choice items on performance and reliability. *Journal of Educational Measurement, 12,* 45–48.

Johnson, F. W. (1911). A study of high school grades. *School Review, 19,* 130–124.

Johnson, Orval G. (1976). *Tests and Measurements in Child Development—Handbooks I and II.* San Francisco: Jossey-Bass.

Jolly, S. J., & Gramenz, G. W. (1984). Customizing a norm-referenced achievement test to achieve curricula validity: A case study. *Educational Measurement: Issues and Practice, 3*(3), 16–18.

Jongsma, K. S. (1989). Portfolio assessment. *The Reading Teacher, 43*(3), 264–265.

Kane, M. B., & Mitchell, R. (1996). *Implementing performance assessment: Promises, problems, and challenges.* Mahwah, NJ: Lawrence Erlbaum.

Kaplan, R. M., & Saccuzzo, D. P. (1997). *Psychological testing: Principles, applications, and issues* (4th ed.). Pacific Grove, CA: Brooks/Cole Publishing Company.

Karlson, B., & Gardner, E. F. (1986). *Stanford Diagnostic Reading Test, 3rd ed., red level, manual for interpreting.* New York: Harcourt Brace Jovanovich.

Kaufman, A. S., and Van Hagen, J. (1977). Investigation of the WISC-R for use with retarded children: Correlation with the 1972 Stanford-Binet and comparison of WISC- and WISC-R profiles. *Psychology in the Schools, 14,* 10–14.

Keith, T. Z. (1985). Questioning the K-ABC: What does it measure? *School Psychology Review, 14,* 9–20.

Keith, T. Z. (1986). Factor structure of the K-ABC for referred school children. *Psychology in the Schools, 23,* 241–246.

Kellaghan, T., Madaus, G. F., & Airasian, P. W. (1982). *The Effects of Standardized Testing.* Boston, MA: Kluwer-Nijhoff.

Kelley, T. L. (1939). The selection of upper and lower groups for the validation of test items. *Journal of Educational Psychology, 30,* 17–24.

Keyser, D. J., & Sweetland, R. C. (1984–1994). *Test critiques* (Vols. 1–10). Austin, TX: Pro-Ed.

Keyser, D. J., and Sweetland, R. C. (1984–88). *Test critiques,* Kansas City, MO: Test Corporation of America. A total of six volumes have been publisher as of November, 1989.

Khattri, N. & Sweet, D. (1996). Assessment reform: Promises and challenges. In M. B. Kane & R. Mitchell (eds.), *Implementing performance assessment: Promises, problems, and challenges* (pp. 1–21). Mahwah, NJ: Elrbaum.

Kirkland, K., & Hollandsworth, J. (1979). Test anxiety, study skills, and academic performance. *Journal of College Personnel,* 431–435.

Kirschenbaum, H., Simon, S. B., & Napier, R. W. (1971). *Wad-ja-get? The grading game in American education.* New York: Hart.

Kirst, M. S. & Mazzeo, C. (1996). The rise, fall, and rise of state assessment in California: 1993–1996. *Phi Delta Kappan, 78*(4), 319–323.

Klosner, N. C., & Gellman, E. K. (1973). The effect of item arrangement on classroom test performance. *Educational and Psychological Measurement, 33,* 413–418.

Koch, W. R. (1984). Culture Fair Intelligence Test. In: D. J. Keyser and R. C. Sweetland (Eds.). *Test Critiques* (Vol. I). Kansas City, MO: Test Corporation of America.

Kohn, A. (1993). *Punished by rewards: The trouble with gold stars, incentive plans, A's, praise, and other bribes.* Boston: Allyn & Bacon.

Kohn, A. (1994). Grading: The issue is not how, but why. *Educational Leadership, 52*(2), 38–41.

Koppitz, E. M. (1975). *The Bender-Gestalt Test for Young Children: Vol. II. Research and Application, 1963–1975.* New York: Grune & Stratton.

Koretz, D. (1988). Educational practices, trends in achievement, and the potential of the reform movement. *Educational Administration Quarterly, 24*(3), 350–359.

Krathwohl, D. R. (1994). Reflections on the taxonomy: Its past, present, and future. In L. W. Anderson & L. A. Sosniak (Eds.), *Bloom's taxonomy: A forty year retrospective.* Ninety-third yearbook of the National Society for the Study of Education, Part II (pp. 181–202). Chicago: University of Chicago Press.

Krenz, C., & Sax, G. (1987). Acquiescence as a function of test type and subject uncertainty. *Educational and Psychological Measurement, 47,* 575–581.

Kubiszyn, T., & Borich, G. (1987). *Educational testing and measurement: Classroom application and practice* (2nd ed.). Glenview, IL: Scott, Foresman and Company.

Kuder, G. F., & Richardson, M. W. (1937). The theory of the estimation of test reliability. *Psychometrika, 2,* 151–160.

Kuehn, P. A., Stallings, W. M., & Holland, C. L. (Winter, 1990). Court-defined job analysis requirements for validation of teacher certification tests. *Educational Measurement: Issues and Practices, 9*(4), 21–24.

Kulik, J. A., Kulik, C-L. C., & Bangert, R. L. (1984). Effects of practice on aptitude and achievement test scores. *American Educational Research Journal, 21,* 435–447.

Kunder, L. H., & Porwoll, P. J. (1977). *Reporting pupil progress: Policies, procedures, and systems.* Arlington, VA: Educational Research Service, Inc.

Kurland, D. M. (1991). *Text browser: A computer-based tool for managing, analyzing, and assessing student writing portfolios.* Paper presented at the annual meeting of the American Educational Research Association, Chicago, IL.

LaBenne, W. D., & Greene, B. I. (1969). *Educational implications of self-concept theory.* Pacific Palisades, CA: Goodyear.

Lambert, N. M. (1981). Psychological evidence in Larry P. v. Wilson Riles: An evaluation by a witness for the defense. *American Psychologist, 36*(9), 937–952.

Larry P. v. Riles, 343 F. Supp. 1306 (N.D. Cal. 1972) (preliminary injunction), affirmed, 502 F.2d. 963 (9th Cir. 1974), opinion issued No. C-71-2270 RFP (N.D. Cal. October 16, 1979).

Lasden, M. (1985). The trouble with testing. *Training, 22*(5), 79–86.

Lavin, D. E. (1965). *The prediction of academic performance.* New York: Wiley.

Levine, E. M. (1987). Grade inflation in higher education: Its causes and consequences. *Free Inquiry in Creative Sociology, 15*(2), 113–121.

Learner, B. (1981). Representative democracy, "men of zeal", and testing legislation. *American Psychologist, 36,* 270–275.

Lehman, R. S. (1995). *Statistics in the behavioral sciences: A conceptual introduction.* Pacific Grove, CA: Brooks/Cole Publishing Company.

Leinhardt, G. (1992). What research on learning tells us about teaching. *Educational Leadership, 49*(7), 20–25.

Lenke, J. M., & Keene, J. M. (1988). A response to John J. Cannell. *Educational Measurement: Issues and Practice, 7,* 16–18.

Lerner, B. (1980). *Minimum competency, maximum choice: second chance legislation.* New York: Irvington.

Lerner, B. (1981). The minimum competency testing movement: Social, scientific, and legal implications. *American Psychologist, 36,* 1056–1066.

Lerner, J. (1993). *Learning disabilities: Theories, diagnoses & teaching strategies.* Boston, MA: Houghton Mifflin.

Lessinger, L. M. (1970). Engineering accountability for results in public education. *Phi Delta Kappan, 52,* 217–225.

Lessinger, L. M., & Tyler, R. W. (Eds.) (1971). *Accountability in Education.* Worthington, OH: Charles A. Jones.

Lewy, A. & Bathory, Z. (1994). The Taxonomy of Educational Objectives in Continental Europe, the Mediterranean, and the Middle East. In L. W. Anderson & L. A. Sosniak (Eds.), *Bloom's taxonomy: A forty year retrospective.* Ninety-third yearbook of the national society for the study of education, Part II (pp. 146–163). Chicago: University of Chicago Press.

Light, R. J., & Smith, P. V. (1969). Social allocation models of intelligence: A methodological inquiry. *Harvard Educational Review, 39*(3), 484–510.

Likert, R. (1932). A technique for the measurement of attitudes, *Archives of Psychology,* #140.

Linn, R. L. (1979). Issues of reliability in measurement for competency-based programs. In M. A. Bunda & J. R. Sanders (Eds.), *Practices and problems in competency-based measurement.* Washington, DC: National Council on Measurement in Education.

Linn, R. L. (1982). Admissions testing on trial. *American Psychologist, 37*(3), 279–291.

Linn, R. L. (1993). Educational assessment: Expanded expectations and challenges. *Educational Evaluation and Policy Analysis, 15,* 1–16.

Linn, R. L. (1997). Evaluating the validity of assessments: The consequences of use. *Educational Measurement: Issues and Practice, 16*(2), 14–16.

Linn, R. L. & Baker, E. L. (1996). Can performance-based student assessments be psychometrically sound? In J. B. Baron & D. P. Wolf (Eds.), *Performance-based student assessment: Challenges and possibilities.* Ninety-fifth yearbook of the national society for the study of education: Part I (pp. 84–103). Chicago: University of Chicago Press.

Linn, R. L., Baker, E. L. & Dunbar, (1991). Complex, performance-based assessment: Expectations and validation criteria. *Educational Researcher, 20*(8), 15–21.

Linn, R. L., & Burton, E. (1994). Performance-based assessment: Implications of task specificity. *Educational Measurement: Issues and Practice, 13*(1), 5–8, 15.

Linn, R. L., & Drasgow, F. (1987). Implications of the Golden Rule Settlement for Test Construction. *Educational Measurement: Issues and Practice, 6*(2), 13–17.

Linn, R. L., Graue, M. E., & Sanders, N. M. (1990). Comparing state and district test results to national norms: The validity of claims that everyone is above average. *Educational Measurement: Issues and Practice, 9*(3), 5–14.

Linn, R. L. & Gronlund, N. E. (1995). *Measurement and Assessment in Teaching* (7th ed.). Upper Saddle River, New Jersey: Prentice-Hall.

Lippman, W. (1922). The mental age of Americans. *New Republic, 32,* 213–215.

Livingston, S. A. (1988). Reliability of test results. In J. P. Keeves (Ed.). *Educational research methodology, and measurement: An international handbook,* (pp. 386–392). Oxford, England: Pergamon Press.

Lloyd, B. H. (1988). Implications of item response theory for the measurement practitioner. *Applied Measurement in Education, 1,* 135–143.

Longstreth, L. E. (1979). Pressures to reduce academic standards. In K. F. Geisinger (Chair), *University grade inflation: Documentation, causes, and consequences.* Symposium presented at the annual meeting of the American Psychological Association, New York.

Lord, F. M. (1977). Optimal number of choices per item: A comparison of four approaches. *Journal of Educational Measurement, 14,* 33–38.

Luckner, J. L. (1991). Mainstreaming hearing-impaired students: Perceptions of regular educators. *Language, Speech, and Hearing Services in Schools, 22,* 302–307.

Lyon, H. C., Jr. (1974). The other minority. *Learning: The Magazine for Creative Teaching, 2*(5), 65.

MacDonald, K. (1985, April 3). Students flunk test to score a point. *The Washington Post,* p. D4.

Mac Iver, D. J., & Reuman, D. A. (1994). Giving their best: Grading and recognition practices that motivate students to work hard. *American Educator, 17*(4), 24–31.

Mac Iver, D. J., Reuman, D. A., & Main, S. R. (1995). Social structuring of the school: Studying what is, illuminating what could be. *Annual Review of Psychology, 46,* 375–400.

McCown, R., Driscoll, M., & Ropp, P. G. (1996). *Educational psychology,* Boston: Allyn & Bacon.

Madaus, G. F. (Ed.). (1983). *The courts, validity, and minimum competency testing.* Boston, MA: Kluwer-Nijhoff.

Madaus, G. F. (1985a). Public policy and the testing profession: You've never had it so good? *Educational Measurement: Issues and Practice, 4*(4), 5–11.

Madaus, G. F. (1985b). Test scores as administrative mechanisms in educational policy. *Phi Delta Kappan, 66,* 611–617.

Madaus, G. F. (1994). A technological and historical consideration of equity issues associated with proposals to change the nation's testing policy. *Harvard Educational Review, 64* (1), 76–95.

Madaus, G. F., Airasian, P., & Kellaghan, T. (1980). *School Effectiveness.* New York: McGraw-Hill.

Madaus, G. F., & Pullin, D. (1987). Teacher certification tests: Do they really measure what we need to know? *Phi Delta Kappan, 69*(1).

Maeroff, G. I. (1991). Assessing alternative assessment. *Phi Delta Kappan, 73*(4), 272–281.

Maguire, T. (1994). Construct Validity and Achievement Assessment. *Alberta Journal of Educational Research, 40*(2), 109–126.

Mann, H. (1845). Report of the annual examining committee of the Boston grammar and writing schools. *Common School Journal, 7,* 326–336.

Marso, R. N. (1985). Testing practices and test item preferences of classroom teachers. (ERIC Document Reproduction Service No. ED 268 145).

Martin, D. V. (1986). Teacher testing: I'm O.K., You're O.K., But Somebody's Not! (ERIC Document Reproduction Service No. ED 169 130).

Martineau, J. A. (1997). Exchangeability of two modes of performance assessment. Unpublished masters project, Brigham Young University, Provo, Utah.

Marzano, R. J., Pickering, D., & McTighe, J. (1993). Assessing student outcomes: Performance assessment using the dimensions of learning model. Alexandria, VA: Association for Supervision and Curriculum Development.

Matarazzo, J. D., & Herman, D. O. (1984). Relationship of education and IQ in the WAIS-R standardization sample. *Journal of Consulting and Clinical Psychology, 52,* 631–634.

Maxey, J. (1994). American College Test. In R. J. Sternberg (Ed.), *Encyclopedia of Human Intelligence.* New York: Macmillan.

McBride, J. R. (1985). Computerized adaptive testing. *Educational Leadership, 43*(2), 25.

McCabe, D. L., & Trevino, L. K. (1996). What we know about cheating in college: Longitudinal trends and recent developments. *Change, 28*(1), 28–33.

McCall, W. A. (1936, December). *The Test Newsletter.* Teacher's College, Columbia University.

McCown, R., Driscoll, M., & Roop, P. G. (1996). *Educational Psychology* (2nd ed.). Boston: Allyn and Bacon.

McKellar, N. A. (1986). Behaviors used in peer tutoring. *Journal of Experimental Education, 54*(3), 163–167.

McKinley, R. L. (1989). An introduction to item response theory. *Measurement and Evaluation in Counseling and Development, 22,* 37–57.

McMorris, R. F., Brown, J. A., Snyder, G. W., & Pruzek, R. M. (1972). Effects of violating item construction principles. *Journal of Educational Measurement, 9,* 287–295.

McNeal, R. B., Jr. (1995). Extracurricular activities and high school dropouts. *Sociology of Education, 68,* 62–81.

McShane, D. A., & Plas, J. M. (1984). The cognitive functioning of American Indian children: Moving from the WISC to the WISC-R. *School Psychology Review, 13*(1), 61–73.

McTighe, J. (1997). What happens between assessments? *Educational Leadership, 54*(4), 6–12.

Mehrens, W. A. (1982). Aptitude measurement. *Encyclopedia of educational research* (5th edition, Vol. 1, pp. 137–144). New York, Macmillan.

Mehrens, W. A. (1997). The consequences of consequential validity. *Educational Measurement: Issues and Practice, 16*(2), 16–18.

Mehrens, W. A., & Kaminski, J. (1989). Methods for improving standardized test scores: Fruitful, fruitless, or fraudulent. *Educational Measurement: Issues and Practice, 8*(3), 14–22.

Mehrens, W. A., & Lehmann, I. J. (1989). *Measurement and evaluation in education and psychology* (3rd ed.). New York: Holt, Rinehart and Winston.

Mehrens, W. A., & Lehmann, I. J. (1991a). *Measurement and evaluation in education and psychology* (4th ed.). Fort Worth, TX: Holt, Rinehart and Winston.

Mehrens, W. A., & Lehmann, I. J. (1991b). *Using standardized tests in education.* New York: Holt, Rinehart & Winston.

Mehrens, W. A., & Popham, W. J. (1992). How to evaluate the legal defensibility of high-stakes tests. *Applied Measurement in Education, 5,* 265–283.

Meisels, S. (1978). *Developmental screening in early childhood.* Washington, DC: National Association for the Education of Young Children.

Menacker, J., & Morris, V. C. (1985). Intelligence testing, civil rights, and the federal courts. *The Educational Forum, 49*(3), 285–296.

Mercer, J. (1977). *SOMPA, System of Multicultural Pluralistic Assessment.* New York: Psychological Corporation.

Merwin, J. C., & Gardner, E. F. (1962). Development and application of tests of educational achievement. *Review of Educational Research, 32,* 40–50.

Messick, S. (1980). *The effectiveness of coaching for the SAT: Review and reanalysis of research from the fifties to FTC.* Princeton, N.J.: Educational Testing Service.

Messick, S. (1981). Evidence and ethics in the evaluation of tests. *Educational Researcher, 10*(9), 9–20.

Messick, S. (1982). Issues of effectiveness and equity in the coaching controversy: Implications for educational and testing practice. *Educational Psychologist, 17,* 67–91.

Messick, S. (1988). The once and future issues of validity: Assessing the meaning and consequences of measurement. In H. Wainer & H. I. Braun (Eds.), *Test Validity.* Hillsdale, New Jersey: Erlbaum.

Messick, S. (1989). Validity. In R. L. Linn (Ed.). *Educational Measurement* (3rd ed.), pp. 13–103. New York: American Council on Education and Macmillan Publishing Company.

Messick, S. (1994). The interplay of evidence and consequences in the validation of performance assessments. *Educational Researcher, 23*(2), 13–23.

Messick, S. (1995b). Standards of validity and the validity of standards in performance assessment. *Educational Measurement: Issues and Practice, 14*(4), 5–8.

Messick, S. (1995a). Validity of psychological assessment: Validation of inferences from persons' responses and performances as scientific inquiry into scoring meaning. *American Psychologist, 50,* 741–749.

Messick, S., & Jungeblut, A. (1981). Time and method in coaching for the SAT. *Psychological Bulletin, 89,* 191–216.

Metfessel, N. S., & Sax, G. (1958). Systematic biases in the keying of correct responses on certain standardized tests. *Educational and Psychological Measurement, 18,* 787–790.

Meyer, M. (1908). The grading of students. *Science, 27,* 243–50.

Michael, W. B., Michael J. J., & Zimmerman, H. S. (1980). *Study attitudes and methods survey, Manual of instructions and interpretation.* San Diego: Educational and Industrial Testing Service.

Millman, J., & Harrington, P. J. (1982). Standards for tests and ethical test use. In H. E. Mitzel, J. H. Best, & W. Rabinowitz (Eds.), *Encyclopedia of Educational Research: Vol. 4* (pp. 1767–1769). New York: Macmillan.

Milman, J., Bishop, C. H., & Ebel, R. (1965). An analysis of test-wiseness. *Educational and Psychological Measurement, 25,* 707–727.

Milton, O., Pollio, H. R., & Eison, J. A. (1986). *Making sense of college grades.* San Francisco: Jossey-Bass.

Monk, D. (1996). Conceptualizing the costs of large-scale pupil performance assessment. In M. B. Kane & R. Mitchell (eds.). *Implementing Performance Assessment: Promises, Problems, and Challenges* (pp. 119–137). Mahwah, NJ: Elrbaum.

Moore, J. C., Schutz, R. E., & Baker, R. L. (1966). The application of a self-instructional technique to develop a test-taking strategy. *American Educational Research Journal, 3,* 13–17.

Moss, P. A. (1992). Shifting conceptions of validity in educational measurement: Implications for performance assessment. *Review of Educational Research, 62,* 229–258.

Moss, P. A. (1994). Can there be validity without reliability? *Educational Researcher, 23*(2), 5–12.

Moynihan, P. (1971). Seek parity of educational achievement, Moynihan urges. *Report on Educational Research, 3,* 4.

Mueller, D. J. (1986). *Measuring Social Attitudes.* New York: Teachers College Press.

Mullis, I. V. S., Dossey, J. A., Owen, E. H., & Phillips, G. W. (1991). The state of mathematics achievement: NAEP's 1990 assessment of the nation and the trial assessment of the states (Executive Summary). Princeton, NJ: Educational Testing Service (20-ST-04); Washington, DC: National Center for Education Statistics (91-1259).

Naccarato, R. W. (1988). *A Guide to Item Banking in Education.* Portland, OR: Northwest Regional Educational Laboratory.

Nairn A. (1980). *The Reign of ETS: The Corporation that Makes up Minds.* Washington, DC: Ralph Nader.

National Commission on Excellence in Education (1983). *A national at risk: The imperative for educational reform.* Washington, DC: U.S. Government Printing Office.

National Institute of Education (1979). *Testing, teaching and learning.* Washington, DC: Author.

Natriello, G. (1987). The impact of evaluation processes on students. *Educational Psychologist, 22,* 155–175.

Natriello, G. (1992). Marking systems. In M. C. Alkin (Ed.), *Encyclopedia of Educational Research* (pp. 772–776). New York: MacMillan.

Natriello, G. (1996). Evaluation processes and student disengagement from high school. In A. M. Pallas (Ed.), *Research in sociology of education and socialization* (Vol. 11, pp. 147–172). Greenwich, CT: JAI Press.

Neill, D. M., & Medina, N. J. (1989). Standardized testing: Harmful to educational health. *Phi Delta Kappan, 70*(9), 688–697.

Nell, W. (1963). A comparative investigation of teacher assigned grades and academic achievement in the Aztec Junior High, New Mexico. In Society for the Study of Education. *Educational Research Bulletin,* 15–16.

Nevo, B. (1985). Face validity revisited. *Journal of Educational Measurement, 22*(4), 287–293.

Newcomer, P. L. & Hammill, D. D. (1988). *Test of Language Development-2 Primary.* Austin, TX: PRO-ED.

Newmann, F. M. & Archbald, D. A. (1992). In B. Berlak, F. M. Newmann, E. Adams, D. A. Archbald, T. Burgess, J. Raven & T. A. Romberg (Eds.), *Toward a New Science of Educational Testing and Assessment* (pp. 71–83). Albany: State University of New York Press.

Nickell, P. (1993). *Alternative assessment: Implications for social studies.* ERIC Clearinghouse for Social Studies/Social Science Education. (Sponsored by the Office of Educational Research and Improvement, Department of Education, Washington, DC. EDO-SO-93-1). ERIC Documentation Reproduction Service No. ED 360 219.

Nitko, A. J. (1984). Book review of Roid and Haladyna's *A Technology for Item Writing. Journal of Educational Measurement, 21,* 201–204.

Nitko, A. J. (1989a). Designing tests that are integrated with instruction. In Linn, R. L. (Ed.), *Educational measurement* (3rd ed., pp. 447–474). London: Collier Macmillan Publishers.

Nitko, A. J. (1989b). Review of Metropolitan Achievement Test (6th ed.) *Tenth mental measurements yearbook.* Lincoln, NE: University of Nebraska Press.

Nitko, A. J. (1996). *Educational assessment of students* (2nd ed.). Englewood cliffs, NJ: Merrill.

Nolen, S. B., Haladyna, T. M., & Haas, N. S. (1989). *A survey of Arizona teachers and administrators on the uses and effects of state-mandated standardized achivement testing* (Tech. Rep. No. 89-2). Phoenix, AZ: Arizona State University West Campus.

Noll, V. H., Scannel, D. P., & Craig, R. C. (1979). *Introduction to educational measurement* (4th ed.). Boston, MA: Houghton Mifflin.

Nungester, R. J., & Duchastel, P. C. (1982). Testing vs. review: Effects on retention. *Journal of Educational Psychology, 74,* 18–22.

Nurss, J. R., & McGauvran, M. E. (1986). *Metropolitan readiness tests.* San Antonio, TX: Psychological Corporation.

O'Leary, B. S. (1980). *College grade point average as an indicator of occupational success: An update* (PRR-80-23). Washington, DC: U.S. Office of Personnel Management, Personnel Research and Development Center.

Oakland, T., & Laousa, L. M. (1977). Professional, legislative, and judicial influences on psychoeducational assessment practices in schools. In T. Oakland (Ed.), *Psychological and educational assessment of minority children.* New York: Brunner/Mazel.

Oakland, T., & Parmelee, R. (1985). Mental measurement of minority-group children. In. B. B. Wolman (Ed.), *Handbook of intelligence: Theories, measurements, and applications,* (pp. 699–736). New York: Wiley & Sons.

Olsen, J. (1989). *Applying computerized adaptive testing in schools.* Unpublished manuscript.

Olson, J. M. & Zanna, M. P. (1993). Attitudes and attitude change. In L. W. Porter & M. Rosenzweig (Eds.). *Annual Review of Psychology, 44,* 117–154.

Oosterhof, A. (1994). *Classroom applications of educational measurement* (2nd ed.). New York: Macmillan.

Oosterhof, A. (1996). *Developing and using classroom assessments.* Englewood Cliffs, NJ: Merrill.

Osgood, C. E., Suci, G. J., & Tannenbaum, P. H. (1957). *The Measurement of Meaning.* Urbana, IL: University of Illinois Press.

Osterlind, S. J. (1989). *Constructing test items.* Boston: Kluwer Academic.

Owen, S. V. & Froman, R. D. (1987). What's wrong with three-option multiple-choice items? *Educational and Psychological Measurement, 47,* 513–522.

Palmer, O. (1962). Seven classic ways of grading dishonestly. *English Journal, 51,* 464–467.

PASE v. Hannon. 506 F. Supp. 831 (N.D. Ill. 1980).

Pashler, H. (1989). Dissociations and dependence between speed and accuracy: Evidence for a two–component theory of divided attention in simple tasks. *Cognitive Psychology, 21,* 469–514.

Patton, J. R., Payne, J. S., & Beirne-Smith, M. (1986). *Mental retardation* (2nd ed.). Columbus, OH: Merrill.

Paulman, R. G., & Kennelly, K. J. (1984). Test anxiety and ineffective test-taking: Different names, same construct? *Journal of Educational Psychology, 76,* 279–288.

Payne, D. A. (1982). Measurement in Education. In H. E. Mitzel (Ed.), *Encyclopedia of educational research* (5th ed.), Vol. 3, pp. 1182–1190). New York: The Free Press.

Payne, O. L. (1993). *A comparison of majority and minority studetns on variables of an educational productivity model.* Paper presented at the Annual Meeting of the American Educational Research Association. Atlanta, GA, April 12–16.

Peak, H., & Boring, E. G. (1926). The factor of speed in intelligence. *Journal of Expeirmental Psychology, 9,* 71.

Perkins, M. R. (1982). Minimum competency testing: What? Why? Why not? *Educational Measurement: Issues and Practice, 1*(4), 5–9, 26.

Peterson, N. S., Kolen, M. J., & Hoover, H. D. (1989). Scaling, norming, and equating. In R. L. Linn (Ed.), *Educational Measurement* (pp. 221–262). New York: MacMillan.

Phillips, L. H., & Rabbitt, P. M. A. (1995). Impulsivity and speed-accuracy strategies in intelligence test performance. *Intelligence, 21*(1), 13–29.

Phillips, S. E. (1993). Legal issues in performance assessment. *Education Law Reporter, 79,* 709–738.

Phillips, B. N., & Weathers, G. (1958). Analysis of errors in scoring standardized tests. *Educational and Psychological Measurement, 18,* 563–567.

Phillips, G. W., & Finn, C. E. (1988). The Lake Wobegon effect: A skeleton in the testing closet? *Educational Measurement: Issues and Practice, 7,* 10–12.

Piacentini, J. (1993). Checklists and rating scales. In T. H. Ollendick & M. Hersen (Eds.), *Handbook of child and adolescent assessment* (pp. 82–97). Boston: Allyn and Bacon.

Pike, L. W. (1978). *Short-term instruction, test-wiseness, and the Scholastic Aptitude Test: A literature review with research recommendations* (Research Bulletin RB-78-2). Princeton, NJ: Educational Testing Service.

Popham, W. J. (1978). The case for criterion-referenced measurement. *Educational Researcher, 7,* 6–10.

Popham, W. J. (1984, April). Action implications of the Debra P. decision. Symposium presented at the annual meeting of the American Educational Research Association, New Orleans, LA.

Popham, W. J. (1987). The merits of measurement-driven instruction. *Phi Delta Kappan, 68,* 679–682.

Popham, W. J. (1990). *Modern educational measurement* (2nd ed.). Englewood Cliffs, NJ: Prentice-Hall.

Popham, W. J. (1991, June). *Circumventing the high costs of authentic assessment.* Paper presented at the Annual Education Commission of the States/Colorado Department of Education Assessment Conference, Breckenridge, CO.

Popham, W. J. (1995). *Classroom assessment: What teachers need to know.* Needham Heights, MA: Allyn & Bacon.

Popham, W. J. (1997). Consequential validity: Right concern—wrong concept. *Educational Measurement: Issues and Practice, 16*(2), 9–13.

Popham, W. J., & Husek, T. (1969). Implications of criterion referenced measurement. *Journal of Educational Measurement, 6,* 1–9.

Popham, W. J., & Kerby, W. N. (1987). Recertification tests for teachers: A defensible safeguard for society. *Phi Delta Kappan, 69*(1), 45–48.

Powers, D. (1993). *Coaching for the SAT: A summary of the summaries and an update.* Educational Testing Service Report: ETS-RR-93-32. (Education Document Reproduction Service No.: ED 385 593).

Pullin, D. (1982). *Minimum competency testing, the denied diploma and the pursuit of educational opportunity and educational adequacy.* (ERIC Document Reproduction Service No. ED 228 279)

Pyrczak, F. (1973). Validity of the discrimination index as a measure of item quality. *Journal of Educational Measurement. 10,* 227–231.

Quellmalz, E. S. (1991). Developing criteria for performance assessments: The missing link. *Applied Measurement in Education, 4,* 319–331.

Raffeld, P. (1975). The effects of Guttman weights. *Journal of Educational Measurement, 12,* 179–185.

Raju, N. S. (1992). Review of Iowa Test of Basic Skills. *Eleventh mental measurements yearbook.* Lincoln, NE: University of Nebraska Press.

Ralph, E. (1994). Teaching to the test: Principles of authentic assessment for second-language education. *Mosaic, 1*(4), 9–13.

Ramos, C. (1996). The computation, interpretation, and limits of grade equivalent scores. Paper presented at the Annual Meeting of the Southwest Educational Research Association. New Orleans, LA, January 1996. (ERIC Documentation Reproduction Services No. ED 395 009.).

Ramseyer, G. C., & Cashen, V. M. (1971). The effect of practice sessions on the use of separate answer sheets by first and second graders. *Journal of Educational Measurement, 8,* 177–182.

Raven, J. (1992). A model of competence, motivation, and behavior, and a paradigm for assessment. In B. Berlak, F. M. Newmann, E. Adams, D. A. Archbald, T. Burgess, J. Raven & T. A. Romberg (Eds.), *Toward a new science of educational testing and assessment* (pp. 85–116). Albany: State University of New York Press.

Ravitch, D. (1984). The uses and misuses of tests. *The College Board Review, 130,* 23–26.

Remmers, H. H. (1963). Rating methods in research on teaching. In N. L. Gage (Ed.). *Handbook of Research on Teaching* (pp. 329–378). Chicago: Rand McNally.

Renninger, K. A., Hidi, S., & Krapp, A. (Eds.) (1992). *The role of interest in learning and development.* Hillsdale, NJ: Lawrence Erlbaum.

Report on Education Research (April 29, 1992a). NAEP study casts doubt on national portfolio assessment. *Report on Education Research,* 1–2.

Reschly, D. J. (1980). *Nonbiased assessment.* Des Moines, IA: Iowa State Department of Public Instruction; Iowa State University of Science and Technology, Department of Psychology. (ERIC Document Reproduction Service No. 140 324).

Reschly, D. J. (1981). Psychological testing in educational classification and placement. *American Psychologist, 36*(10), 1094–1102.

Resnick, D. P. & Resnick, L. B. (1992). Assessing the thinking curriculum: Now tools for educational reform. In B. R. Gifford & M. C. O'Connor (Eds.), *Changing assessments: Alternative views of aptitude, achievement and instruction* (pp. 37–75). Boston: Kluwer.

Resnick, D. P. & Resnick, L. B. (1996). Performance assessment and the multiple functions of educational measurement. In M. B. Kane & R. Mitchell (Eds.), *Implementing performance assessment: Promises, problems, and challenges* (pp. 23–38). Mahwah, NJ: Elrbaum.

Reynolds, C. R. (1981). *In God we trust, all others must have data* (Report No. TM8 10684). Paper presented at the Annual Meeting of the American Psychological Association, Los Angeles, CA. (ERIC Document Reproduction Services No. ED 209 252)

Reynolds, C. R. (1985). Review of system of multicultural pluralistic assessment. In J. V. Mitchell, Jr. (Ed.), *The ninth mental measurements yearbook* (Vol 2, pp. 1519–1521). Lincoln: Buros Institute of Mental Measurement of The University of Nebraska-Lincoln.

Reynolds, C. R. (1994). Bias in testing. In R. J. Sternberg (Ed.), *Encyclopedia of human intelligence* (pp. 175–178). New York: Macmillan.

Rice, J. M. (1897a). The futility of the spelling grind: I. *Forum, 23,* 163–172.

Rice, J. M. (1897b). The futility of the spelling grind: II. *Forum, 23,* 409–419.

Richards, J. M., & Lutz, S. W. (1968). Predicting student accomplishment in college from the ACT assessment. *Journal of Educational Measurement, 5,* 17–29.

Roberts, D. M. (1993). An empirical study on the nature of trick test questions. *Journal of Educational Measurement, 30,* 331–344.

Robinson, G. E. & Craver, J. M. (1989). Assessing and grading student achievement. Arlington, VA: Educational Report Service.

Rogers, B. (1989). Review of Metropolitan Achievement Test (6th ed.) *Tenth mental measurements yearbook.* Lincoln, NE: University of Nebraska Press.

Rogers, T. B. (1995). *The psychological testing enterprise: An introduction.* Pacific Grove, California: Brooks/Cole Publishing Company.

Rogers, W. T. & Bateson, D. J. (1991). Verification of a model of test-taking behavior of high school seniors. *Journal of Experimental Education, 59,* 331–350.

Roid, G. H. (1986). Computer technology in testing. In B. S. Plake & J. C. Witt (Eds.), *The future of testing,* (pp. 29–69). Hillsdale, NJ: Lawrence Erlbaum.

Rosenbaum, P. R. (1988). A note on item bundles. *Psychometrika, 53,* 349–360.

Rossman, H. E. (1970). Graduate school attitudes to S-U grades. *Educational Record, 41,* 310–313.

Rothman, R. (1995). *Measuring up: Standards, assessment, and school reform.* San Francisco: Jossey-Bass.

Rudman, H. C. (1977). The standardized test flap: An effort to sort out fact from fiction, truth from deliberate hyperbole. *Phi Delta Kappan, 59,* 179–185.

Ruiz-Primo, M. A. & Shavelson, R. J. (1996). Rhetoric and reality in science performance assessments: An update. *Journal of Research in Science Teaching, 33,* 1045–1063.

Sabot, R., & Wakeman-Linn, J. (1991). Grade inflation and course choice. *Journal of Economic Perspectives, 5,* 159–170.

Salmon-Cox, L. (1981). Teachers and standardized achievement tests: What's really happening? *Phi Delta Kappan, 62,* 631–634.

Salvia, J., & Hughes, C. (1990). *Curriculum-based assessment: Testing what is taught.* New York: MacMillan.

Salvia, J., & Ysseldyke, J. E. (1988). *Assessment* (4th edition). Boston, MA: Houghton Mifflin.

Salvia, J., & Ysseldyke, J. E. (1995). *Assessment* (6th edition). Boston, MA: Houghton Mifflin.

Sandefur, J. T. (1985). Competency assessment of teachers. *Action in Teacher Education, 7*(1–2), 1–6.

Sanders, J. R. & Sachse, T. (1975). Problems and Potentials of Applied Performance Testing. *Proceedings of the National Conference on the Future of Applied Performance Testing.* Portland, OR: Northwest Regional Educational Laboratory.

Sansome, C., & Morgan, C. (1992). Intrinsic motivation and education: Competence in context. *Motivation and Emotion, 16,* 249–270.

Sarason, I. G. (1980). *Test anxiety, theory, research, and applications.* Hillsdale, NJ: Erlbaum.

Sattler, J. M. (1988). *Assessment of children* (3rd ed.). San Diego, CA: Jerome M. Sattler.

Sattler, J. M. & Ryan, J. J. (1981). Relationship between WISC-R and WRAT in children referred for learning difficulties. *Psychology in the Schools, 15,* 486–489.

Sax, G. (1980). Principles of test construction: True-false, multiple-choice, and matching items. In G. Sax (Ed.), *Principles of educational and psychological measurement and evaluation* (pp. 91–122). Belmont, CA: Wadsworth.

Sax, G. (1989). *Principles of educational and psychological measurement and evaluation* (3rd ed.). Belmont, CA: Wadsworth.

Sax, L. J. (1994). Mathematical self-concept: How college reinforces the gender gap. *Research in Higher Education, 35,* 141–166.

Sax, G., & Cromack, T. R. (1966). The effects of various forms of item arrangements on test performance. *Journal of Educational Measurement, 3,* 309–311.

Scarr, S. (1981). Genetics and the development of intelligence. In S. Scarr (Ed.), *Race, social class, and individual differences in I. Q..* Hillsdale, New Jersey: Erlbaum.

Scarr, S., Pakstis, A. J., Katz, S. H., & Barker, W. B. (1977). Absense of a relationship between degree of white ancestry and intellectual skills within a black population. *Human Genetics, 39*, 69–86.

Scarr, S. & Weinberg, R. A. (1976). IQ test performance of black children adopted by white families. *American Psychologist, 31*, 726–739.

Scarr-Salapatek, S. (1971). Unknowns in the IQ equation. *Science, 174,* 1223–1228.

Scarr, S. & Weinberg, R. A. (1983). The Minnesota Adoption Studies: Genetic differences and malleability. *Child Development, 54,* 260–267.

Schiefele, U. (1991). Interest, learning, and motivation. *Educational Psychologist, 26,* 299–323.

Schriesheim, C. A., & Hill, K. D. (1981). Controlling acquiescence response bias by item reversals: The effect of questionnaire validity. *Educational and Psychological Measurement, 41,* 1101–1114.

Schroeder, D. H. (1989). *Is Cognitive Style Bipolar?* Paper presented at the 97th Annual Meeting of the American Psychological Association. New Orleans, LA, August 11–15, 1989. (ERIC Documentation Reproduction Services No. ED 341 716).

Scriven, M. (1970). Discussion. *Proceedings of the 1969 Invitational Conference on Testing Problems* (pp. 112–117). Princeton, NJ: Educational Testing Service.

Scruggs, T. E., White, K. R., & Bennion, K. (1986). Teaching test-taking skills to elementary-grade students: A meta-analysis. *The Elementary School Journal, 87,* 69–82.

Selden, R. W. (1985). Measuring excellence: The dual role of testing in reforming education. *Curriculum Review, 25*(1), 14–32.

Sesnowitz, M., Bernhardt, K. L., & Knain, D. M. (1982). An analysis of the impact of commercial test preparation courses on SAT Scores. *American Educational Research Journal, 19,* 429–441.

Shaie, K. W. (1980). Cognitive development in aging. In L. K. Obler & M. Alpert (Eds.), *Language and communication in the elderly.* Lexington, MA: Heath.

Shaie, K. W. (1984). Midlife influences upon intellectual functioning in old age. *International Journal of Behavioral Development, 7,* 463–478.

Shaie, K. W. & Willis, S. L. (1984). *Adult development and aging.* Boston: Little Brown.

Shanker, A. (1985). A national teacher examination. *Educational Measurement: Issues and Practice, 4*(3), 28–31.

Shaugnessy, A. (1994). Teaching to the test: Sometimes a good practice. *English Journal, 83*(4), 54–56.

Shavelson, R. J., Baxter, G. P., Copeland, W., Ruiz-Primo, M. A., Brown, J., Decker, L. & Druker, S. L. (1994). Performance assessments in science: A teacher enhancement workshop. University of California, Santa Barbara, CA.

Shavelson, R. J., Baxter, G. P. & Gao, X. (1993). Sampling variability of performance assessments. *Journal of Educational Measurement, 30,* 215–232.

Shavelson, R. J. & Webb, N. M. (1991). *Generalizability theory: A primer.* Newbury Park, California: Sage Publications, Inc.

Shepard, L. A. (1980). Definition of bias. *Test item bias methodology: The state of state of the art.* Washington, DC: The Johns Hopkins University National Symposium on Educational Research.

Shepard, L. A. (1990, Fall). Inflated test score gains: Is the problem old norms or teaching the test? *Educational Measurement: Issues and Practice, 9*(3), 15–22.

Shepard, L. (1991). Interview on assessment issues with Lorrie Shepard. *Educational Researcher, 20*(2), 21–27

Shepard, L. A. (1992). What policy makers who mandate tests should know about the new psychology of intellectual ability and learning. In B. R. Gifford & M. C. O'Connor (eds.), Changing assessments: *Alternative views of aptitude, achievement and instruction* (pp. 301–328). Boston: Kluwer.

Shepard, L. A. (1997). The centrality of test use and consequences for test validity. *Educational Measurement: Issues and Practice, 16*(2), 5–8, 13, 24.

Shepard, L. A., Flexer, R. J., Hiebert, E. H., Marion, S. F., Mayfield, V. & Weston, T. J. (1996). Effects of introducing classroom performance assessments on student learning. *Educational Measurement: Issues and Practice, 15*(3), 7–18.

Shepard, L. A., & Kreitzer, A. E. (1987). The Texas teacher test. *Educational Researcher, 16*(6), 22–31.

Shimberg, B. (Winter, 1990). Social considerations in the validation of licensing and certification exams. *Educational Measurement: Issues and Practices, 9*(4), 11–14.

Shulman, L. S. (1987). Assessment for teaching: An initiative for the profession. *Phi Delta Kappan, 69*(1), 38–44.

Simpson, R. H. (1944). The specific meanings of certain terms indicating different degrees of frequency. *Quarterly Journal of Speech, 30,* 328–330.

Slack, W. V., & Porter, D. (1980). The Scholastic Aptitude Test: A critical appraisal. *Harvard Educational Review, 50,* 154–175.

Slakter, M. J. (1969). Generality of risk taking on objective examinations. *Educational and Psychological Measurement, 29,* 115–128.

Smith, A. Z., & Dobbin, J. E. (1960). Marks and marking systems. In C. W. Harris (Ed.), *Encyclopedia of educational research* (3rd ed., pp. 783–792). New York: Macmillan.

Smith, M. L. (1991a). Put to the test: The effects of external testing on teachers. *Educational Researcher, 20*(5), 8–11.

Smith, M. L. (1991b). Meaning of test preparation. *American Educational Research Journal, 28*(3), 521–542.

Smith, I. L., & Hambleton, R. K. (1990). Content validity studies of licensing examinations. *Educational Measurement: Issues and Practice, 9*(4), 7–10.

Smith, E. R., & Tyler, R. W. (1942). *Appraising and Recording Student Progress.* New York: Harper & Row.

Snow, R. E., Corno, L., & Jackson, D., III (1996). Individual differences in affective and cognitive functions. In D. C. Berliner & R. C. Calfee (Eds.). *Handbook of educational psychology* (pp. 243–310). New York: MacMillan.

Sparrow, S. S., Balla, D. A., & Cicchetti, D. V. (1984). *Vineland Adaptive Behavior Scales.* Circle Pines, MN: American Guidance Service.

Spearman, C. (1927). *The abilities of man.* New York: Macmillan.

Spector, P. E. (1992). *Summated rating scale construction: An introduction.* Newbury Park, CA: Sage Publications.

Starch, D. (1913). Reliability and distribution of grades. *Science, 38,* 630–636.

Starch, D., & Elliot, E. C. (1912). Reliability of grading high school work in English. *Scholastic Review, 20,* 442–457.

Starch, D., & Elliot, E. C. (1913a). Reliability of grading high school work in history studies. *School Review, 21,* 676–681.

Starch, D., & Elliot, E. C. (1913b). Reliability of grading high school work in mathematics. *Scholastic Review, 21,* 254–259.

Steinkamp, M. W., & Maehr, M. L. (1984). Affect, ability, and science achievement: A quantitative synthesis of correlational research. *Review of Educational Research, 53*(3), 369–396.

Stephens, T. M. (1982). *Criterion-referenced curriculum guide.* Columbus, Ohio: Charles E. Merrill.

Sternberg, R. J. (1985). *Beyond IQ: A triarchic theory of human intelligence.* Cambridge: Cambridge University Press.

Sternberg, R. J. (1986). *Intelligence applied: Understanding and increasing your intellectual skills.* San Diego, CA: Harcourt Brace Jovanovich.

Sternberg, R. J. (1998). Abilities are forms of developing expertise. *Educational Researcher, 27*(3), 11–20.

Stewart, N. (1947). AGCT scores of army personnel grouped by occupation. *Occupations, 26,* 5–41.

Stiggins, R. J. (1991a). Assessment literacy. *Phi Delta Kappan, 72*(7), 534–539.

Stiggins, R. J. (1991b). Trainer's guide: Developing assessments based on observation and judgment. Portland, OR: Northwest Regional Educational Laboratory.

Stiggins, R. J. (1994). *Student-centered classroom assessment.* Upper Saddle River, NJ: Merrill.

Stiggins, R. J., & Bridgeford, N. J. (1985). The ecology of classroom assessment. *Journal of Educational Measurement, 22,* 271–286.

Stiggins, R. J., Conklin, N. F., & Bridgeford, N. J. (1986). Classroom assessment: A key to effective education. *Educational Measurement: Issues & Practice, 5*(2), 5–17.

Stoker, H. (1992). Review of the Stanford Achievement Test, Eighth Edition. *The eleventh mental measurements yearbook.* Lincoln, NE: The Buros Institute of Mental Measurements.

Strickland, G. P. (1970). *Development of a school attitude questionnaire for young children.* (CSE Report #59). Los Angeles: University of California, Center for the Study of Evaluation.

Strickland, G. P., Hoepfner, R., & Klein, S. P. (1976). *Attitude towards school questionnaire manual.* Hollywood, CA: Monitor.

Strommen, E. (1988). Confirmatory factor analysis of the Kaufman Assessment Battery for Children: A reevaluation. *Journal of School Psychology, 26,* 13–23.

Subkoviak, M. J. (1988). A practitioner's guide to computation and interpretation of reliability indices for mastery tests. *Journal of Educational Measurement, 25,* 47–55.

Sudman, S., & Bradburn, N. M. (1982). *Asking questions: A practical guide to questionnaire design.* San Francisco, CA: Jossey-Bass.

Sudweeks, R. R & Clay, S. (1995, April). Two alternative approaches to performance assessment. Paper presented at the annual meeting of the National Association for Research in Science Teaching, San Francisco.

Suen, H. K. (1990). *Principles of test theories.* Hillsdale, NJ: Lawrence Erlbaum.

Suhor, C. (1985). Objective tests and writing samples: How do they affect instruction in composition? *Phi Delta Kappan, 66*(9), 635–639.

Summerville, R. M., Ridley, D. R., & Maris, T. L. (1990). Grade inflation: The case of urban colleges and universities. *College Teaching, 38,* 33–38.

Sweetland, R. C. & Keyser, D. J. (1991). *Tests* (3rd ed.). Austin, TX: Pro-Ed.

Tanner, D. E. (1995). The competency test's impact on teachers' abilities. *Urban Review, 27,* 347–351.

Tartre, L. A. & Fennema, E. (1979). Mathematics achievement and gender: A longitudinal study of selected cognitive and affective variables in Grades 6-12. *Educational Studies in Mathematics, 28,* 199–217.

Taylor, C. (1981). *The effect of reinforcement and training on group standardized test behavior.* Unpublished doctoral dissertation, Utah State University, Logan.

Taylor, C., & White, K. R. (1982). The effect of reinforcement and training on group standardized test behavior. *Journal of Educational Measurement, 19,* 198–209.

Taylor, C., White, K. R., Bush, D., & Friedman, S. (1982). *Training teachers in test administration.* Logan: Exceptional Child Center, Utah State University.

Terwilliger, J. S. (1966). Self-reported marking practices and policies in public secondary schools. *National Association of Secondary School Principals Bulletin, 50,* 5–37.

Terwilliger, J. S. (1989). Classroom standard setting and grading practices. Educational Measurement: Issues and Practice, 8(2), 15–19.

Tesser, A. & Shaffer, D. R. (1990). Attitudes and attitude change. In M. Rosenzweig & L. W. Porter (Eds.). *Annual Review of Psychology, 41,* 479–523.

Thissen, D., Steinberg, L. & Mooney, J. (1989). Trace lines for testlets: A use of multiple-categorical response models. *Journal of Educational Measurement, 12,* 241–249.

Thorndike, E. L. (1904). *Introduction to the theory of mental and social measurements.* New York: Teachers College, Columbia University.

Thorndike, R. L. (1951). Reliability. In E. F. Lindquist (Ed.), *Educational measurement.* Washington, DC: American Council on Education.

Thorndike, R. L. (1969). Marks and marking systems in R. L. Ebel (Ed.) *Encyclopedia of Educational Research* (4th ed). New York: Macmillan.

Thorndike, R., & Hagen, E. (1977). *Measurement and evaluation in psychology and education.* New York: Wiley.

Thorndike, R. L., Hagen, E. P., & Sattler, J. M. (1986). *Stanford-Binet Intelligence Scale* (4th ed.). Chicago, IL: Riverside Publishing.

Thorndike, R. M., Cunningham, G. K., Thorndike, R. L., & Hagen, E. P. (1991). *Measurement and evaluation in psychology and education* (5th ed.). New York: Macmillan.

Thurstone, L. L. (1938). Primary mental abilities. *Psychometric Monographs, 1.*

Tittle, C. K. (1978). Sex bias in testing: A review with policy recommendations. (ERIC Document Reproduction Service No. ED 164 623).

Tittle, C. K., & Zytowski, D. G. (Eds.) (1978). *Sex-fair interest measurement: Research and implications.* Washington, DC: National Institute of Education.

Tobias, S. (1984). *Test anxiety: Cognitive interference or inadequate preparation?* Paper presented at the American Educational Research Association, New Orleans, LA.

Torrance, E. P. (1965). *Reward creative behavior.* Englewood Cliffs, NJ: Prentice Hall.

Towle, N. J., & Merrill, P. F. (1975). Effects of anxiety type and item-difficulty sequencing on mathematics test performance. *Journal of Educational Measurement, 12,* 241–250.

Traub, R. E. (1994). *Reliability for the social sciences: Theory and applications.* Thousands Oaks, CA: Sage Publications.

Travers, R. M. W. (1983). *How research has changed American schools.* Kalamazoo, MI: Mythos Press.

Trevisan, M. S., Sax, G., & Michael, W. B. (1991). The effects of the number of options per item and student ability on test validity and reliability. *Educational and Psychological Measurement, 51,* 829–837.

Triandis, H. C. (1971). *Attitude and attitude change.* New York: Wiley.

Tufte, E. R. (1983). *The visual display of quantitative information.* Cheshire, CT: Graphics Press.

Turnbull, W. W. (1985). *Student change, program change: Why SAT scores kept falling.* (ERIC Document Reproduction Service No. ED 266 189)

USA Today. (1996, July 27). 50-year peak for GED diplomas. *USA Today,* p. 5B.

U.S. Congress, Office of Technology Assessment (1992). *Testing in American schools: Asking the right questions* (OTA-SET-519). Washington, DC: U.S. Government Printing Office.

United States v. South Carolina 445 Supp. 1094 (S.C. 1977).

Valencia, S. (1990). The portfolio approach to classroom assessment: The whys, whats, and hows. *The Reading Teacher, 43*(4), 338–340.

van der Vleuten, C. P. M. & Swanson, D. B. (1990). Assessment of clinical skills with standardized patients: The state of the art. *Teaching and Learning in Medicine, 2,* 58–76.

Vasta, R., & Sarmiento, R. F. (1979). Liberal grading improves evaluations but not performance. *Journal of Educational Psychiatry, 71,* 207–221.

Vavrus, L. (1990). Put portfolios to the test. *Instructor, 100*(1), 48–53.

Venn, J. (1994). *Assessment of students with special needs.* New York: Merrill/ Macmillan.

Voeckel, E. L. & Fiore, D. J. (1993, July/August). Electronic test generators: What current programs can do for teachers. *Clearing House, 65,* 356–362.

Waetjen, W. B. (1977, September). *Sex differences in learning: Some open questions.* Paper presented at the fourth annual meeting of the International Society for the Study of Behavioral Development, Pavia, Italy.

Wainer, J. & Kiely, G. L. (1987). Item clusters and computerized adaptive testing: A case for testlets. *Journal of Educational Measurement, 24,* 185–201.

Wallace, B. & Graves, W. (1995). *Poisoned apple: The bell-curve crisis and how our schools create mediocrity and failure.* New York: St. Martin's Press.

Walsh, W. B. & Betz, N. E. (1995). *Tests and assessment* (3rd ed.). Englewood Cliffs, New Jersey: Prentice Hall.

Waltman, K. K. & Frisbie, D. A. (1994). Parents' understanding of their children's report card grades. *Applied Measurement in Education, 7,* 223–240.

Ward, A. W. & Murray-Ward, M. (1994). Guidelines for the development of item banks. *Educational Measurement: Issues and Practice, 13*(1), 34–39.

Warren, J. R. (1971). *College grading practices: An overview* (Report No. 9). Washington, DC: ERIC Clearinghouse on Tests, Measurement, and Evaluation. (ERIC Document Reproduction Service No. ED 117 193.)

Warren, J. R. (1979). The prevalence and consequence of grade inflation. In K. F. Geisinger (Chair), *University grade inflation: Documentation, causes, and consequences.* Symposium presented at the annual convention of the American Psychological Association, New York.

Waters, B. K. (1981). *The test score decline: A review and annotated bibliography.* (ERIC Document Reproduction Service No. ED 207 995)

Webb, M. W. (1995). *Policy considerations in developing standards and assessments for large, diverse school districts.* Paper presented at the Annual Meeting of the National council on Measurement in Education. San Francisco, CA, April 20, 1995. (ERIC Documentation Reproduction Service No. ED 387 938).

Wechsler, D. (1955). *Wechsler Adult Intelligence Scale, Manual.* New York: Psychological Corporation.

Weiss, D. J. (1985). Adaptive testing by computer. *Journal of Consulting and Clinical Psychology, 53*(6), 774–789.

Werts, C., Linn, R. L., & Joreskog, K. G. (1978). Reliability of college grades from longitudinal data. *Educational and Psychological Measurement, 38,* 89–96.

Wesman, A. G. (1971). Writing the test item. In R. L. Thorndike (Ed.), Educational Measurement (2nd ed., pp. 81–129). Washington, DC: American Council on Education.

Wexley, K. N., & Thornton, C. L. (1972). Effect of verbal feedback of test results upon learning. *Journal of Educational Research, 66,* 119–121.

Wheeler, P. H. (1995). *Functional-level testing: A "must" for valid and accurate assessment results.* EREAPA Publication Series No. 95-2. Livermore, CA: EREAPA Associates. (ERIC Document Reproduction Service No. ED 393 915.)

White, E. E. (1886). *The elements of pedagogy.* New York: American Book Company.

White, K. R. (1976). *The relationship between socioeconomic status and academic achievement.* Unpublished doctoral dissertation, University of Colorado at Boulder.

White, K. R., & Carcelli, L. (1982, March). *The effect of item format on computation subtest scores of standardized achievement tests.* Paper presented at the annual meeting of the American Educational Research Association, New York.

Whitney, D. R., Malizio, A. G., & Patience, W. M. (1985). The reliability and validity of the GED tests. *American Council on Education GED Research Brief,* May, 1985, No. 6.

Wiggins, G. (1989). Teaching to the (authentic) test. *Educational Leadership, 46*(7), 41–49.

Wiggins, G. (1990). A conversation with Grant Wiggins. *Instructor, 100*(1), 51.

Wiggins, G. (1991). Standards, not standardization: Evoking quality student work. *Educational Leadership, 48*(5), 18–25.

Wiggins, G. (1992). Creating tests worth taking. *Educational Leadership, 49*(8), 26–33.

Wiggins, G. (1993). Assessment: Authenticity, context, and validity. *Phi Delta Kappan, 75,* 200–214.

Wiggins, G. (1994). Toward better report cards. *Educational Leadership, 52*(2), 28–37.

Wiggins, G. (1997). Practicing what we preach in designing authentic assessments. *Educational Leadership, 54*(4), 18–25.

Wiley, D. E. & Haertel, E. H. (1996). Extended assessment tasks: Purposes, definitions, scoring, and accuracy. In M. B. Kane & R. Mitchell (Eds.), *Implementing performance assessment: Promises, problems, and challenges.* Mahwah, NJ: Lawrence Erlbaum.

Williams, P. L. (1988). The time-bound nature of norms: Understandings and misunderstandings. *Educational Measurement: Issues and Practice, 7*(2), 18–21.

Williams, R. H., & Zimmerman, D. W. (1984). On the virtues and vices of the standard errors of measurement. *Journal of Experimental Education, 52,* 231–233.

Willingham, W. W. (1974). Predicting success in graduate education. *Science, 183,* 273–278.

Wilson, R. (1980). *Early childhood screening under Public Law 94-142.* New York: The Psychological Corporation.

Willson, V. L. (1989). Review of Iowa Tests of Basic Skills. *Tenth mental measurements yearbook.* Lincoln, NE: Buros Institute.

Wilson, S. M., & Hiscox, M. D. (1984). Using standardized tests for assessing local learning objectives. *Educational Measurement: Issues and Practice, 3*(3), 19–22.

Wine, J. (1971). Test anxiety and direction of attention. *Psychological Bulletin, 76,* 92–104.

Witt, J. C., Heffer, R. W., & Pfeiffer, J. (1990). Structured rating scales: A review of self-report and informant rating processes, procedures, and issues. In C. R. Reynolds & R. W. Kamphaus (Eds.), *Handbook of psychological and educational assessment of children* (vol. 2, pp. 364–394). New York: Guilford Press.

Wolf, L. F. (1995). Consequence of performance, test motivation, and mentally taxing items. *Applied Measurement in Education, 8,* 341–351.

Wolf, R. M. (1994). Rating scales. In T. Husen and T. N. Postlethwaite (Eds.). *The International Encyclopedia of Education* (2nd ed., pp. 4923–4930). Oxford, England: Pergamon.

Wolf, D., Bixby, J., Glenn, J., & Gardner, H. (1991). To use their minds well: Investigating new forms of student assessment. In G. Grant (Ed.), *Review of Research in Education* (Vol. 17, pp. 31–65). Washington, D.C.: American Educational Research Associates.

Wolf, D. P. & Reardon, S. F. (1996). Access to excellence through new forms of student assessment. In J. B. Baron & D. P. Wolf (Eds.), *Performance-based student assessment: Challenges and possibilities.* Ninety-fifth yearbook of the National Society for the Study of Education: Part I (pp. 1–31). Chicago: University of Chicago Press.

Wolf, L. F., & Smith, J. K. (1995). The consequence of consequence: Motivation, anxiety, and test performance. *Applied Measurement in Education, 8,* 227–242.

Wolfe, E. W. & Miller, T. R. (1997). Barriers to the implementation of portfolio assessment in secondary education. *Applied Measurement in Education, 10,* 235–251.

Woodcock, R. W. (1987). *Woodcock Reading Mastery Tests-Revised.* Circle Pines, MN: American Guidance Service.

Worthen, B. R. (1993a). Critical issues that will determine the future of alternative assessment. *Phi Delta Kappan, 74,* 444–454.

Worthen, B. R. (1993b). Is your school ready for alternative assessment? *Phi Delta Kappan, 74,* 455–456.

Worthen, B. R., Borg, W. R., & White, K. (1993). *Measurement and evaluation in the schools.* New York, NY: Longman.

Yamamoto, K. (1962). *A study of the relationships between creative thinking abilities of fifth-grade teachers and academic achievement.* Unpublished doctoral dissertation, University of Minnesota, Minneapolis.

Yeh, J. (1978). *Test use in the schools.* Los Angeles: University of California at Los Angeles, Center for the Study of Evaluation.

Yen, W. M. (1992). Item response theory. In M. C. Alkin (Ed.), *Encyclopedia of Educational Research* (6th ed., pp. 657–667). New York: Macmillan.

Young, J. H. (1993). Collaborative curriculum development: Is it happening at the local school level? *Journal of Curriculum and Supervision, 8,* 239–254.

Zangenehzadch, H. (1988). Grade inflation: A way out. *Journal of Economic Education, 19,* 217–230.

Zanna, M. P. & Rempel, J. K. (1988). Attitudes: A new look at an old concept. In D. Bar-Tal and A. W. Kruglanski (eds.), *The social psychology of knowledge* (pp. 315–334). New York: Cambridge University Press.

Zastrow, C. H. (1970). Cheating among college graduate students. *Journal of Educational Research, 64,* 157–160.

Zeller, R. A. (1988). Validity. In J. P. Keeves (Ed.). *Educational research methodology, and measurement: An international handbook,* (pp. 322–330). Oxford, England: Pergamon Press.

Zelniker, T. (1977). Speed versus accuracy as a measure of cognitive style: Internal consistency and factor analysis. *Child Development, 48,* 301–304.

Index

Instructions: The purpose of this suggestion sheet is to get student feedback that can be used to improve the next edition of this book. We have asked for your comments on only one chapter in order to minimize the time needed for you to respond. All comments and suggestions will be greatly appreciated.

Items 1–3: The first four questions are aimed at learning more about the students who use this book. Please circle appropriate alternatives.

Items 4: Be sure to indicate the chapter you are evaluating.

Items 5–9: These are the most important questions. Please be a specific as possible.

When you complete the suggestion sheet, cut along the dashed line, fold and place in a stamped envelope, and mail. Thanks very much for your help.

Blaine R. Worthen, Karl R. White, Xitao Fan, and Richard R Sudweeks

SUGGESTION SHEET

1. Degree you are seeking (circle one): **BA, BS, MA, MS, other:** _____.
   (specify)

2. Graduate major (circle one): **elem educ, sec educ, spec educ, educ adm, other:**
   _____.
   (specify)

3. Have you taken elementary statistics: (circle): **yes, no;** any other educational measurement or psychometries courses: **yes, no;** computer science? **yes, no**

4. Chapter commented on _____.

5. What specific ideas, definitions, descriptions, or examples in this chapter are not clear? (Please give page number and brief description.)

   _____

   _____

6. Should the book include more information on any of the sections in this chapter? (Please give page number and subheading.)

   _____

   _____

7. What sections should be shortened or omitted? (Give page number and subheading.)

   _____

   _____

8. Other comments about this chapter:

   _____

   _____

9. Any other general comments about this book:

   _____

   _____

   _____

9 8 7 6 5 4 3 3 2 1

AddisonWesleyLongman
Attn: Art Pompanio, Education Editor
1185 Avenue of the Americas
New York, NY 10036